Consumer Behavior, Organizational Development, and Electronic Commerce:
Emerging Issues for Advancing Modern Socioeconomies

Mehdi Khosrow-Pour
Information Resources Management Association, USA

Information Science REFERENCE

INFORMATION SCIENCE REFERENCE
Hershey · New York

Director of Editorial Content: Kristin Klinger
Director of Production: Jennifer Neidig
Managing Editor: Jamie Snavely
Assistant Managing Editor: Carole Coulson
Typesetter: Lindsay Bergman
Cover Design: Lisa Tosheff
Printed at: Yurchak Printing Inc.

Published in the United States of America by
Information Science Reference (an imprint of IGI Global)
701 E. Chocolate Avenue, Suite 200
Hershey PA 17033
Tel: 717-533-8845
Fax: 717-533-8661
E-mail: cust@igi-global.com
Web site: http://www.igi-global.com

and in the United Kingdom by
Information Science Reference (an imprint of IGI Global)
3 Henrietta Street
Covent Garden
London WC2E 8LU
Tel: 44 20 7240 0856
Fax: 44 20 7379 0609
Web site: http://www.eurospanbookstore.com

Consumer behavior, organizational development and electronic commerce : emerging issues for advancing modern socioeconomies / Mehdi Khowrow-Pour, editor.

p. cm.

Includes bibliographical references and index.

Summary: "This book offers readers a one-stop resource for contemporary issues, developments, and influences in e-commerce"--Provided by publisher.

ISBN 978-1-60566-126-1 (hardcover) -- ISBN 978-1-60566-127-8 (ebook)

1. Electronic commerce. 2. Consumer behavior. 3. Organizational change. I. Khosrowpour, Mehdi, 1951-

HF5548.32.C664 2009

658.8'72--dc22

2008022539

British Cataloguing in Publication Data
A Cataloguing in Publication record for this book is available from the British Library.

Consumer Behavior, Organizational Development, and Electronic Commerce: Emerging Issues for Advacing Modern Socioeconomies is part of the IGI Global series named *Advances in Electronic Commerce (AEC)* Series, ISBN: 1935-2921

Associate Editors

Editorial Review Board

Table of Contents

Detailed Table of Contents

Consumer-to-consumer (C2C) electronic commerce (e-commerce) is a growing area of e-commerce. However, according to a meta-analysis of critical themes of e-commerce, C2C e-commerce was only represented in the area of online auctions (Wareham, Zheng, & Straub, 2005). C2C e-commerce can encompass much more than just auctions. This study adapts constructs from a B2C e-commerce study of satisfaction (Devaraj, Fan, & Kohli, 2002) to determine what, if any, the differences are in the C2C e-commerce arena. The constructs include elements of the technology acceptance model (TAM), which includes perceived ease of use and usefulness; transaction cost analysis (TCA), which includes uncertainty, asset specificity, and time; and service quality (SERVQUAL), which includes reliability, responsiveness, assurance, and empathy. Participants in the study answered questions regarding these various constructs in relation to their experiences with C2C e-commerce. The findings indicate that TAM, TCA, and SERVQUAL all impact satisfaction in C2C e-commerce. Reliability and responsiveness (areas of service quality) were found to influence C2C e-commerce satisfaction, where as they were not found to be an influence in the B2C study. These findings warrant further research in the C2C e-commerce arena. The study provides implications for future research and practice.

Limited studies have investigated online consumer loyalty and retention from a relationship orientation in electronic commerce research. It is important to understand the differences in relationship orientations between people who have the propensity to stick to particular Web sites ("stayers") and people who have the propensity to switch to alternative Web sites ("switchers"). This study proposes a relationship-based classification schema consisting of five dimensions: that is, commitment, trust, satisfaction, comparison level of the alternatives, and nonretrievable investment. Data were collected from 299 college students

A Web site that wants to increase its number of visitors can pay for search engine ads or attempt to improve its natural search engine ranking. Nobody really knows, which, if either, of these methods provides a positive return on investment. A search engine optimization (SEO) project was undertaken at a new e-commerce site. The site's search engine rankings and traffic were measured after each phase in the project. The results indicate that SEO is an effective method for improving search engine rankings and site traffic. In addition, the costs and benefits of the SEO project are compared with a pay-per-click (PPC) search marketing campaign. The SEO project proved more cost effective than the PPC campaign.

This chapter develops a new model of web IS success that takes into account both intrinsic and extrinsic motivating factors. The proposed model begins with the Garrity and Sanders model of technologic acceptance and develops an extended nomological network of success factors that draws on motivation and flow theory.

The world is witnessing a continuous expansion of electronic commerce into the global digital economy. As an enabler of new businesses, Web-based shopping systems (WBSS) are at the heart of the major issues surrounding electronic commerce growth. Their wide use has profoundly altered the ways in which businesses and customers, and businesses and businesses interact on the basis of digital transactions. Despite the importance of WBSS, the theoretical study of their strategies has been sparse. This article offers a theoretical analysis of evolutionary processes in WBSS strategies. For that purpose, we propose a classification model of WBSS. Based upon the model, WBSS are classified into four types: (1) general-direct-sales (GDS); (2) general-intermediary-sales (GIS); (3) specialized-direct-sales (SDS); and (4) specialized-intermediary-sales (SIS). On the basis of these four categories of WBSS, we analyze the characteristics of WBSS and suggest five evolution strategies for WBSS, which have implications for both theory and practice. Amazon.com's strategic movements, such as product line expansion through alliance and acquisition, provide an exemplary case of the evolution of WBSS strategy. We expect that this article will serve as a guide for Internet businesses and as a catalyst for new research agendas relevant to web-based shopping and electronic commerce.

Internet auctions have received a considerable amount of attention from researchers. We review recent empirical literature pertaining to single-item Internet auctions and observe that existing work has examined the roles of the auctioneer, bidder, and seller in Internet auctions. As this stream of research matures, research will necessarily move from concept discovery and process explanation to theory deepening. As a first step towards synthesis of findings in Internet auctions, we compile a comprehensive list of the various factors that have been examined in empirical studies and note their general impact upon auction outcome. Based upon this extant research, we propose a conceptual model of Internet auctions as a framework for structuring future work into Internet auctions. We then note the existing economic, psychological, sociological, and cognitive theoretical bases for work on Internet auctions. We conclude by highlighting the potential for behavioral economics to bring unity to Internet auction research and by calling researchers to engage in the work of forging a comprehensive theory of Internet auctions.

The increasingly global sourcing of IT work and other socio-economic trends are prompting fundamental changes in the availability of IT skills needed in both client and vendor organizations. This article analyzes the results of a survey conducted in 2005, in which IT executives were asked to describe the skills they felt were critical to keep in house now and in 2008. The top ten current skills included three in project management, five in business domain and three in technical. In 2008, the top five emerging skills are almost all business domain while the top five exiting skills are all technical. Our findings indicate that the critical skills to keep in-house are primarily client-facing skills, even when they are technical. Respondents are moving away from traditional IT skills except when their business model continues to value them. However, traditional technical skills are still important for all new hires while project management skills are the most often cited for mid level hires. The projected number of full time employees is expected to remain approximately the same by 2008 but there will be an increase in sourcing to third party providers (3PP) and a shift from domestic to offshore 3PP staff. The patterns in the data indicate that technical skills that are not client facing and can be done anywhere are the most likely to be sourced. Findings indicate that IT professionals need to have a balance that demonstrates a foundation in the traditional "hard skills" and experience with "softer" business-oriented skills.

This article has investigated the insurance industry and provided insights into the relationships of organizational size and age with outsourcing and organizational structure. Also, this study investigated the relationship between Web site age, outsourcing, and organizational structure. The main findings are that firm size and maturity is related to the decision of Web-based development approach and the best organizational structure to support online activity. The insights obtained by a new variable: Web site age suggests that insurance companies are trying to develop their Web-based activities within their existing organizational structures, rather than creating new e-commerce divisions.

Organizations in the new millennium face relentless pressure to perform better, faster and cheaper, while maintaining high level of guaranteed results. To remain competitive, enterprises have to integrate their business processes with those of their customers, suppliers and business partners. Increasing collaboration is not only relevant within a global multi-national enterprise, but also considering the organization and its relationship to and business processes with its business partners. While standards and technologies make it possible for business partners to exchange information, collaborate and carry out business transaction in a pervasive Web environment, there is however very limited research activity on modeling business process outsourcing underlying semantics. In this chapter, we demonstrate that an in-house business process that has been gradually outsourced to third-parties and analyze how task delegations cause commitments between multiple business parties. Finally we provide process semantics for modeling multi-party business process outsourcing.

Internet technology has impelled us to develop faith in the modern practices of business, commerce, and trade. Offshoring has been viewed as a global phenomenon on the economic frontier. While new technologies need to be framed, stopgap arrangements in the form of transient solutions to upgrade the current systems are also desired. Newer regulations and multi-jurisdictional compliance have profound impacts on the growth of outsourcing projects. The development of new technological solutions must challenge the myth that legislation and statutory practices are the only possible mechanisms to counter the unscrupulous activities in the context of outsourcing. A change in the outlook toward such methodologies is essential to shed away the technological inertia and latency. This article opens up discussion issues in the perspective of hardware and software requirements for efficient offshoring. The aim is to achieve higher precision, protection, and throughput by applying core-computing techniques to the existing practices of outsourcing.

This study surveys the perceptions and experiences of Australian small- and medium-sized enterprises (SMEs) in the implementation of Internet-based Electronic Commerce (EC) as seen from the perspective of the extent of deployment. With a sample of 115 small businesses in Australia, this article uses regression modelling to explore and establish the factors that are related to the extent of deployment in EC. A multiple regression analysis shows that seven factors: perceived relative advantage, trialability, observability, variety of information sources, communication amount, competitive pressure, and non-trading institutional influences, significantly influence the extent of EC deployment by SMEs in Australia. The managerial implications are discussed.

It has long been known that small businesses have realised enhanced profits through the adoption of e-commerce. However, a number of recent studies have suggested that it is the larger businesses that are reaping the rewards of e-commerce rather than the smaller businesses. This slow growth of e-commerce adoption in SMEs has been attributed to various adoption barriers that are faced by small business owners/managers. These barriers have been well documented in numerous research studies. However, the relationship between these barriers has not been fully examined, particularly in developing countries. Of particular concern is the fact that the conclusions concerning the nature and role of barriers to e-commerce adoption have simply been transferred from studies in developed economies to those in developing ones. 96 non-adopting SMEs in Indonesia are compared to 129 in Sweden to determine whether the perception of importance of barriers differs between the two locations. The data is also analysed to determine whether the underlying factors of these barriers differs across the two locations.

Recently, new standards for business-to-business (B2B) e-commerce transactions, to reduce extended record locking, relaxed standard database transaction properties. In this chapter, we provide a parallel methodology employing a mobile/intelligent agent framework to alleviate extended record locking, while adhering to standard database transaction properties. Our methodology provides a minimum 30% reduction of record locking compared to new B2B standards.

E-business is key to export development for developing economy firms. There are however key barriers and facilitators to e-business adoption for small and large internationalizing firms the world over. This chapter sets to find out, by means of the testing of key hypothesis, the main barriers and facilitators of e-business adoption by Ghanaian export firms. We adopt a quantitative approach to this study and draw our study sample from a directory of active non-traditional exporters (NTEs) in Ghana. We find that an export firm's international orientation, owner/management idiosyncrasies, e-sophistication of partners, export firm's characteristics (age, number of employees and location) and weak government regulation have no significant influence on e-business adoption by Ghanaian NTE firms. On the other hand, competitive pressure (as measured by competition from Ghanaian export firms and growth in size of export operations) significantly facilitates e-business adoption. Internal resource constraints (measured by technological and financial resources for e-business adoption and business culture) and environmental bottlenecks (measured by lack of support from export sector regulators and export associations and high internet access fees carged by ISPs) also reduce the likelihood of e-business adoption by Ghanaian NTE firms. We find interestingly that Export facilitation (measured by pressures from GEPC and FAGE) and digitalization (measured by perceived importance of e-business in digitalizing export operations and improving export competitiveness) perceived to facilitate e-business adoption however exhibit significant negative relationships with adoption. We proffer some explanations for this unusual finding and provide general management implications for improving e-business practices amongst the various players in Ghana's non-traditional export sector.

Interorganizational systems (IOS) play a critical role in today's e-commerce environment. These systems are introduced by different organizations following different adoption processes. Existing literature on IOS adoption, however, does not explain the variations in the IOS adoption processes initiated by different organizations. A theory of IOS adoption known as IOS Motivation Model (IMM) has recently been developed by the authors that explains the differences in IOS adoption processes in terms of differences in organizations' adoption motivations for any given IOS project. This chapter reports an application of the model in the Australian automotive industry. The findings provide support for the model and are useful for IT managers.

Preface

Electronic commerce has seen extraordinary growth in the past decade, as businesses, educators, and practitioners have begun to buy, sell, and trade on the Internet. In order to provide a comprehensive and current assessment of the latest developments in the e-commerce revolution, a source containing the latest research on the innumerable discoveries, advancements, and implementations of e-commerce has emerged. *Consumer Behavior, Organizational Development, and Electronic Commerce: Emerging Issues for Advancing Modern Socioeconomies*, part of the *Advances in Electronic Commerce Book Series*, uncovers the rewarding prospects associated with the adaptation of e-commerce for business, academic, and global organizations, while identifying the most effective strategies for employing them worldwide. This book includes many valuable contributions from researchers discussing important social, managerial and organizational issues of e-commerce applications and management in society.

Chapter I, *Consumer-to-Consumer Electronic Commerce: An Emerging Stream of Research* by Kiku Jones and Lori N. K. Leonard, University of Tulsa (USA), presents a study which adapts constructs from a B2C e-commerce study of satisfaction to determine what, if any, the differences are in the C2C e-commerce arena. The constructs include elements of the technology acceptance model (TAM). Participants in the study answered questions regarding these constructs in relation to their experiences with C2C e-commerce. The findings indicate that TAM, TCA, and SERVQUAL all impact satisfaction in C2C e-commerce. Reliability and responsiveness (areas of service quality) were found to influence C2C e-commerce satisfaction, though they were not found to be an influence in the B2C study. These findings warrant further research in the C2C e-commerce arena.

Chapter II, *Online Consumers' Switching Behavior: A Buyer-Seller Relationship Perspective* by Dahui Li, University of Minnesota Duluth (USA), Glenn J. Browne, Texas Tech University (USA), and James C. Wetherbe, Texas Tech University (USA) investigates online consumer loyalty and retention from a relationship orientation, seeking to understand the differences in relationship orientations between people who have the propensity to stick to particular web sites ("stayers") and people who have the propensity to switch to alternative web sites ("switchers"). This study proposes a relationship-based classification schema consisting of five dimensions, i.e., commitment, trust, satisfaction, comparison level of the alternatives, and non-retrievable investment. Using discriminant analysis, the authors found that stayers and switchers were significantly different along the five research dimensions. Satisfaction with the current website was the most important discriminant factor, followed by trust, commitment, comparison level of alternative websites, and non-retrievable investment in the current website. Implications of the findings for researchers and practitioners are discussed.

Chapter III, *From High Tech to High Touch: The Effects of Perceived Touch on Online Customers' Intention to Return* by Hong-Mei Chen, Qimei Chen, and Rick Kazman, University of Hawaii (USA) defines a new construct, Perceived Touch, and provides theoretical underpinnings for the "high touch" assumption of eCRM systems. An empirical study was conducted to examine both the cognitive and affective effects of Perceived Touch on online customers' intention to return after their initial visit in the eCRM context. While past studies of traditional information systems paid more attention to cognition than affect, the affective effect is critical to examine, so that eCRM strategy and system design can be better informed. The current research results validate the antecedent role of Perceived Touch to Perceived Ease of Use (of the Technology Acceptance Model—TAM) and further argue for the renewed importance of Attitude for user acceptance in the eCRM context. This study illuminates the significance of the affective impact of Perceived Touch on online customers' Behavioral Intention to Return through both the Affective Route and the Alternative Cognitive Route where affective effect precedes cognitive effect.

Chapter IV, *A Movie E-Shop Recommendation Model Based on Web Usage and Ontological Data* by Andreas Aresti, University of Patras (Greece), Penelope Markellou, University of Patras (Greece), Ioanna Mousourouli, University of Patras (Greece), Spiros Sirmakessis, Technological Education Institute of Messolonghi (Greece), Athanasios Tsakalidis, University of Patras (Greece) offers a perspective on recommendation systems—special personalization tools that help users to find interesting information and services in complex online shops. The authors contend that by monitoring, analyzing and understanding the behavior of customers, their demographics, opinions, preferences and history, as well as taking into consideration the specific e-shop ontology and by applying web mining techniques, the effectiveness of produced recommendations can be significantly improved. In this way, the e-shop may upgrade users' interaction, increase its usability, convert users to buyers, retain current customers, and establish long-term and loyal one-to-one relationships.

Chapter V, *Search Engine Optimization of an Action Research Project: Initial Results and Two Year Follow-Up,* by Ross A. Malaga, Montclair State University (USA) discusses the results of a search engine optimization (SEO) project that was undertaken at a new e-commerce site. The site's search engine rankings and traffic were measured after each phase in the project. The results indicate that SEO is an effective method for improving search engine rankings and site traffic. In addition, the costs and benefits of the SEO project are compared with a pay-per-click (PPC) search marketing campaign. The SEO project proved more cost effective than the PPC campaign.

Chapter VI, *A Flow Theory-Driven Integrated Model of Web IS Success* by Edward J. Garrity, Canisius College (USA), Yong Jin Kim, Sogang University (Korea), Joseph B. O'Donnell, Canisius College (USA), and Cheul Rhee, State University of New York at Buffalo, (USA) offers a theoretical analysis of evolutionary processes in Web-based shopping systems (WBSS) strategies. For that purpose, the authors propose a classification model of WBSS. Based upon the model, WBSS are classified into four types: (1) general-direct-sales (GDS); (2) general-intermediary-sales (GIS); (3) specialized-direct-sales (SDS); and (4) specialized-intermediary-sales (SIS). On the basis of these four categories of WBSS, the characteristics of WBSS are analyzed and five evolution strategies for WBSS are suggested, which have implications for both theory and practice.

Chapter VII, *Evolving a Strategy for Web-Based Shopping Systems* by Changsu Kim, Yeungnam University (Korea), Robert D. Galliers, Bentley College (USA), Kyung Hoon Yang, University of Wisconsin-La Crosse (USA), and Jaekyung Kim, University of Nebraska-Lincoln (USA) develops a new model of web IS success that takes into account both intrinsic and extrinsic motivating factors. The proposed model begins with the Garrity and Sanders model of technologic acceptance and develops an extended nomological network of success factors that draws on motivation and flow theory.

Chapter VIII, *A Review of Single-Item Internet Auction Literature and a Model for Future Research* by Jeff Baker and Jaeki Song, Texas Tech University (USA) reviews recent empirical literature pertaining to single-item Internet auctions and observes that existing work has examined the roles of the auctioneer, bidder, and seller in Internet auctions. As this stream of research matures, research will necessarily move from concept discovery and process explanation to theory deepening. As a first step towards synthesis of findings in Internet auctions, the authors compile a comprehensive list of the various factors that have been examined in empirical studies and note their general impact upon auction outcome. Based upon this extant research, a conceptual model of Internet auctions as a framework for structuring future work into Internet auctions is proposed. The existing economic, psychological, sociological, and cognitive theoretical bases for work on Internet auctions are noted.

Chapter IX, *Changing IT Skills: The Impact of Sourcing Strategies on In-House Capability Requirements* by Christine V. Bullen, Stevens Institute of Technology (USA), Thomas Abraham, Kean University (USA),Kevin Gallagher, Northern Kentucky University (USA), Kate M. Kaiser, Marquette University (USA), and Judith C. Simon, University of Memphis (USA) analyzes the results of a survey conducted in 2005, in which IT executives were asked to describe the skills they felt were critical to keep in-house now and in 2008. The top ten current skills included three in project management, five in business domain and three in technical. In 2008, the top five emerging skills are almost all business domain, while the top five exiting skills are all technical. Findings indicate that the critical skills to keep in-house are primarily client-facing skills, even when they are technical. Respondents are moving away from traditional IT skills except when their business model continues to value them. However, traditional technical skills are still important for all new hires while project management skills are the most often cited for mid level hires. The projected number of full time employees is expected to remain approximately the same by 2008 but there will be an increase in sourcing to third party providers (3PP) and a shift from domestic to offshore 3PP staff. The patterns in the data indicate that technical skills that are not client facing and can be done anywhere are the most likely to be sourced. Findings indicate that IT professionals need to have a balance that demonstrates a foundation in the traditional "hard skills" and experience with "softer" business-oriented skills.

Chapter X, *Understanding Outsourcing of Web-Based Applications in Organizations: The Case of e-Insurance* by Teuta Cata, Northern Kentucky University (USA) investigates the insurance industry and provides insights into the relationships of organizational size and age with outsourcing and organizational structure. Also, this study contained within this chapter investigates the relationship between web site age, outsourcing, and organizational structure. The main findings are that firm size and maturity are related to the decision of Web-based development approach and the best organizational structure to support online activity. The insights obtained by a new variable—Web site Age—suggests that insurance companies are trying to develop their Web-based activities within their existing organizational structures, rather than creating new e-commerce divisions.

Chapter XI, *Business Process Outsourcing Modeling* by Lai Xu and Paul de Vrieze, SAP Research, (Switzerland) demonstrates an in-house business process that has been gradually outsourced to third-parties and analyzes how task delegations cause commitments between multiple business parties. Since organizations in the new millennium face relentless pressure to perform better, faster and cheaper, while maintaining a high level of guaranteed results, enterprises have to integrate their business processes with those of their customers, suppliers and business partners. While standards and technologies make it possible for business partners to exchange information, collaborate and carry out business transaction in a pervasive Web environment, there is very limited research activity on modeling business process outsourcing underlying semantics.

Chapter XII, *Innovative Technological Paradigms for Corporate Offshoring* by Tapasya Patki, GGSIP University (New Delhi) and A. B. Patki, Government of India, (New Delhi) presents a discussion of hardware and software requirements for efficient offshoring. The aim is to achieve higher precision, protection and throughput by applying core-computing techniques to the existing practices of outsourcing. Internet technology has impelled us to develop faith in the modern practices of business, commerce, and trade. Offshoring has been viewed as a global phenomenon on the economic frontier. While new technologies need to be framed, stopgap arrangements in the form of transient solutions to upgrade the current systems are also desired. Newer regulations and multi-jurisdictional compliance have profound impact on the growth of outsourcing projects. The development of new technological solutions must challenge the myth that legislation and statutory practices are the only possible mechanisms to counter the unscrupulous activities in the context of outsourcing.

Chapter XIII, *Factors Influencing the Extent of Deployment of Electronic Commerce for Small- and Medium-sized Enterprises* by Sandy Chong and Graham Pervan, Curtin University of Technology (Australia) surveys the perceptions and experiences of Australian small- and medium-sized enterprises (SMEs) in the implementation of Internet-based electronic commerce (EC) as seen from the perspective of the extent of deployment. With a sample of 115 small businesses in Australia, this chapter uses regression modelling to explore and establish the factors that are related to the extent of deployment in EC. A multiple regression analysis shows that seven factors: perceived relative advantage, trialability, observability, variety of information sources, communication amount, competitive pressure, and non-trading institutional influences, significantly influence the extent of EC deployment by SMEs in Australia. The managerial implications are discussed.

Chapter XIV, *Barriers to E-Commerce Adoption in SMEs: A Comparison of the Perception of Barriers in a Developed and a Developing Country* by Robert C. MacGregor and Mira Kartiwi, University of Wollongong (Australia) examines the various adoption barriers that are faced by small business owners/managers. These barriers have been well documented in numerous research studies. However, the relationship between these barriers has not been fully examined, particularly in developing countries. Of particular concern is the fact that the conclusions concerning the nature and role of barriers to e-commerce adoption have simply been transferred from studies in developed economies to those in developing ones. In this chapter, 96 non-adopting SMEs in Indonesia are compared to 129 in Sweden to determine whether the perception of importance of barriers differs between the two locations. The data is also analysed to determine whether the underlying factors of these barriers differs across the two locations.

Chapter XV, *A Parallel Methodology for Reduction of Coupling in Distributed Business-to-Business E-Commerce Transactions* by Anthony Mark Orme, Athens State University (USA) and Letha H. Etzkorn, University of Alabama (USA) reflects upon the recent, new standards for Business-to-Business (B2B) e-commerce transactions intended to reduce extended record locking that have relaxed standard database transaction properties. This chapter provides a parallel methodology employing a mobile/intelligent agent framework to alleviate extended record locking, while adhering to standard database transaction properties. The authors' methodology provides a minimum thirty percent reduction of record locking compared to new B2B standards.

Chapter XVI, *E-Business Triggers: Further Insights into Barriers and Facilitators Amongst Ghanaian Non-traditional Exporters (NTEs)* by Olav Sorensen and Robert Hinson, Aalborg University (Denmark) assesses the main barriers and facilitators of e-business adoption by Ghanaian export firms. The authors adopt a quantitative approach to this study and draw their study sample from a directory of active non-traditional exporters (NTEs) in Ghana. They find that an export firm's international orientation, owner/management idiosyncrasies, e-sophistication of partners, export firm's characteristics (age, number of employees and location) and weak government regulation have no significant influence on e-business adoption by Ghanaian NTE firms. On the other hand, competitive pressure significantly facilitates e-business adoption. Internal resource constraints and environmental bottlenecks also reduce the likelihood of e-business adoption by Ghanaian NTE firms. Interestingly, the authors find that Export facilitation and digitalization, perceived to facilitate e-business adoption, instead exhibit significant negative relationships with adoption. Explanations for this unusual finding are offered and general management implications for improving e-business practices amongst the various players in Ghana's non-traditional export sector are provided.

Chapter XVII, *Organizational Motivation and Inter-Organizational Systems Adoption Process: Empirical Evaluation in the Australian Automotive Industry* by Md. Mahbubur Rahim, Monash University (Australia), Graeme Shanks, Monash University (Australia), Robert Johnston, The University of Melbourne (Australia) and Pradip Sarker, RMIT University (Australia) reflects on the critical role that interorganizational systems (IOS) play in today's e-commerce environment and develops a theory of IOS adoption known as IOS Motivation Model (IMM) that explains the differences in IOS adoption processes in terms of differences in organizations' adoption motivations for any given IOS project. This chapter reports an application of the model in the Australian automotive industry. The findings provide support for the model and are useful for IT managers.

Chapter XVIII, *Inter-Organizational E-Commerce in Healthcare Services: The Case of Global Teleradiology* by Arjun Kalyanpur, Teleradiology Solutions (India), Firoz Latif, Teleradiology Solutions (India), Sanjay Saini, Harvard Medical School (USA), and Surendra Sarnikar, University of Arizona (USA) presents the case of electronic delivery of radiological services and describes the market-based and technological factors that have led to the development of internet-based service models for flexible delivery of radiological services. Specifically, the authors describe the technical, regulatory and security issues that affect teleradiology, and propose a service delivery model for providing cost-effective and flexible radiological services.

As e-commerce continues to be an expanding force in modern-day society, its importance in the information age intensifies. The adoption and implementation of e-technologies have become essential to the face of modern business and all competitive modern organizations, researchers, and educators are learning and sharing best practices for their effective utilization. Researchers and practitioners in information technology will find that the *Advances in Electronic Commerce Book Series* provides not only an overview of how far the field has come, but also an insight into the latest developments and technologies that will soon be implemented in society. As a comprehensive compilation of the latest research, most current technologies, and forthcoming tools associated within the latest developments in electronic commerce, *Consumer Behavior, Organizational Development, and Electronic Commerce: Emerging Issues for Advancing Modern Socioeconomies* serves as a pertinent resource for the most up-to-date examination of e-commerce and the pivotal role in plays in reshaping the global landscape.

Mehdi Khosrow-Pour, D.B.A.
Editor-in-Chief
Advances in Electronic Commerce Series

Chapter I
Consumer-to-Consumer Electronic Commerce: An Emerging Stream of Research

Kiku Jones
University of Tulsa, USA

Lori N. K. Leonard
University of Tulsa, USA

ABSTRACT

Consumer-to-consumer (C2C) electronic commerce (e-commerce) is a growing area of e-commerce. However, according to a meta-analysis of critical themes of e-commerce, C2C e-commerce was only represented in the area of online auctions (Wareham, Zheng, & Straub, 2005). C2C e-commerce can encompass much more than just auctions. This study adapts constructs from a B2C e-commerce study of satisfaction (Devaraj, Fan, & Kohli, 2002) to determine what, if any, the differences are in the C2C e-commerce arena. The constructs include elements of the technology acceptance model (TAM), which includes perceived ease of use and usefulness; transaction cost analysis (TCA), which includes uncertainty, asset specificity, and time; and service quality (SERVQUAL), which includes reliability, responsiveness, assurance, and empathy. Participants in the study answered questions regarding these various constructs in relation to their experiences with C2C e-commerce. The findings indicate that TAM, TCA, and SERVQUAL all impact satisfaction in C2C e-commerce. Reliability and responsiveness (areas of service quality) were found to influence C2C e-commerce satisfaction, where as they were not found to be an influence in the B2C study. These findings warrant further research in the C2C e-commerce arena. The study provides implications for future research and practice.

INTRODUCTION

Electronic commerce (e-commerce) is a continuously evolving phenomenon. While media attention of e-commerce has declined in focus, academic research of e-commerce appears to have increased. This can be seen in the amount of e-commerce specific journals as well as the number of e-commerce related articles published in the information systems' main stream journals (Wareham et al., 2005).

In a meta-analysis of the critical themes of e-commerce research, Wareham, Zheng, & Straub (2005) performed a meta-analysis of the critical themes of e-commerce research. The analysis included a review of abstracts from "mainstream IS journals", both academic and professional (a full list of the journals used in the analysis can be found in the referenced article), between the years of 1997 and 2003 (65% of which fell between the years 2001 and 2003). At a top level, there are four main areas: business-to-business (B2B), business-to-consumer (B2C), strategy, and technology adoption. They further refined these broad areas into 17 different themes found in e-commerce research. Of the 17, consumer-to-consumer (C2C) research was not listed. Some may argue that "Auctions" (one of the 17 themes) covers the full realm of C2C e-commerce. However, C2C e-commerce can encompass much more than just auctions.

C2C e-commerce can also take place in online communities, chat rooms, third-party consumer listing services, and web-based discussion forums. For example, one consumer recalled a recent C2C e-commerce transaction conducted in a web-based discussion forum. He indicated to the other participants that he had a car part to sell. Another participant indicated a need for that part. They exchanged address information through the forum. Once the seller received the check from the buyer, he sent the part to him. While the payment and product were sent via postal mail, all interaction regarding the transaction was completed within the web-based forum. Similar to how third-party consumer listing services (such as Half.com) or online auctions (such as eBay) facilitate the transaction between sellers and buyers, so did the web-based forum in this anecdote. The difference comes in the intent of the forum versus the third-party consumer listing service and online auction. However, regardless of the intent of the venue, C2C e-commerce is indeed being conducted in many areas in addition to online auctions. And as such, should be included in the stream of research surrounding C2C e-commerce.

In a quick search for C2C e-commerce, only a few articles could be found which did not solely focus on online auctions and reputation systems. For example, Lin, Li, & Huang (2007), Lin, Li, Janamanchi, & Huang (2006), Livingston (2005), and Melnik & Alm (2002) studied C2C online auctions and reputation systems, and Yamamoto, Ishida, & Ohta (2004) studied C2C reputation management systems. Strader & Ramaswami (2002) examined consumer trust in C2C online markets, Jones & Leonard (2008) studied trust in C2C e-commerce, and Armstrong & Hagel (1996) and Orman (2006) described the value of online communities. Even with the online auction and reputation system articles, Wareham, Zheng, & Straub (2005) found that only 3% of the articles they reviewed dealt with this area. This lack of research leads one to wonder whether or not C2C e-commerce is a different enough research area to have its own stream of research. Anecdotal evidence suggests that there are enough differences to build a new area of research. This research is an exploratory study to empirically determine if there are indeed differences found in C2C e-commerce and B2C e-commerce research which indicate a need for C2C e-commerce to have its own research stream. To do this, a previous study by Devaraj, Fan & Kohli (2002) that focused on the satisfaction of B2C e-commerce over other commerce methods is modified to reflect C2C e-commerce, utilizing three well-known frameworks: technology acceptance model (TAM), transaction cost analysis (TCA), and service quality (SERVQUAL).

The next section of the chapter discusses the research model, followed by the method and sample of the study in the third section. The fourth section provides a discussion of the data analysis and results, and the final section of the chapter provides a discussion, limitations, implications for future research, implications for practice, and conclusions based on the study results.

RESEARCH MODEL

New methods for consumers to facilitate their transactions are increasing. C2C e-commerce is one such method. C2C e-commerce is defined in this study as consumers transacting (buying and selling) electronically. The success of this commerce method depends heavily on the consumers' satisfaction. Satisfaction has long been a central measure of information system success. It is "an important means of measuring customers' opinions of an e-commerce system and should cover the entire customer experience cycle from information retrieval through purchase, payment, receipt, and service" (DeLone & McLean, 2004, p. 34). This definition indicates that components of service quality, ease of use, usefulness, reliability, etc. (DeLone & McLean, 1992, 2003) can have an impact on satisfaction.

Since the C2C area does not have foundation studies at this point, this study builds on the work of Devaraj, Fan, & Kohli (2002), who empirically researched consumers' preferences for the B2C e-commerce channel over the traditional brick-and-mortar channel (i.e., physical building where face-to-face commerce is conducted). Their study measured consumer satisfaction utilizing three different frameworks: TAM, TCA, and SERVQUAL. The results of the study indicate that the TAM components have a significant impact on the consumer's satisfaction with the e-commerce channel. In addition, Devaraj, Fan, & Kohli (2002) found significant support regarding the TCA components. However, only partial support for the SERVQUAL components was found.

The Devaraj, Fan, & Kohli (2002) study focuses on the B2C e-commerce area without making a distinction between B2C and C2C e-commerce. They make reference to B2B e-commerce in the future research section and they encourage researchers to explore their model in this area. However, C2C e-commerce is never mentioned. With the increase in C2C business, it is worth exploring whether or not their model will still hold the same results. That is the focus of our study. Utilizing the same three frameworks, we alter their model to reflect satisfaction of the C2C e-commerce channel. Below is a discussion of the three frameworks to be used in the model.

Technology Acceptance Model (TAM)

TAM is one of the most utilized and referenced models for predicting an individual's use and acceptance of information technology (Venkatesh, 1999). In particular, TAM has been used in several empirical studies regarding B2C e-commerce (e.g., Devaraj et al., 2002; Gefen, Karahanna, & Straub, 2003; Gefen & Straub, 2000; Pavlou, 2003; Pei, Zhenxiang, & Chunping, 2007), and has been found to be valid in explaining user behaviors in a B2C e-commerce context (Chen, Gillenson, & Sherrell, 2002). TAM indicates that there are two determinants of computer acceptance behaviors: perceived usefulness (PU) and perceived ease of use (PEOU) (Davis, 1989; Davis, Bagozzi, & Warshaw, 1989). PU is described as "the degree to which a person believes that using a particular system would enhance his or her job performance" (Davis, 1989 p. 320). In other words, PU reflects the user's belief that the IT will help him/her achieve specific task-related objectives (Gefen & Straub, 2000). PEOU is described as "the degree to which a person believes that using a particular system would be free of effort" (Davis, 1989 p. 320).

Devaraj, Fan, & Kohli (2002) solicited potential respondents from online shoppers, undergraduate and graduate students. Of this mix, 171 agreed to participate in the study. Participants were asked to purchase a product through a traditional brick-and-mortar vendor and then complete an online survey regarding their experience with the channel (not the vendor). They also purchased the same or similar product from an online vendor and answered an online survey regarding their experience with that channel. Only the responses regarding the online channel were analyzed, however the respondents were unaware of this. The study results indicated that both PU and PEOU were significantly related to satisfaction with the e-commerce channel.

Gefen, Karahanna, & Straub (2003) performed a free-simulation experiment with MBA and senior undergraduate students. The students logged into the Internet and searched for the course's textbook on www.amazon.com. The students went through the process of buying their textbook without the final step of completing the transaction. The students then were given an instrument to fill out regarding their experience. The researchers found that the PU of a given website played an important role in determining a repeat customer's intention to purchase on that website. Conversely, it was not significant for potential customers. This supports prior research findings that indicate social factors initially affect intention to use.

Davis, Bagozzi, & Warshaw (1992) explain that intrinsic motivation refers to performing an activity for no other reason than the process of performing that activity (e.g., enjoyment of performing the activity). While extrinsic motivation refers to performing an activity in order to reach a goal separate from the activity itself (e.g., PU). Davis, Bargozzi, & Warshaw (1992) indicate that extrinsic motivation will have a stronger impact on IT adoption than intrinsic motivation. Gefen and Straub (2000) state that PEOU is related to the assessment of intrinsic characteristics of IT (e.g., "ease of use, ease of learning, flexibility, and clarity"). Their study also utilized a free-simulation experiment method and MBA students. The procedure was the same as the Gefen, Karahanna, & Straub (2003) study. They found that PEOU did not affect a consumer's intention to use a website for purchasing; however, PU did have a significant affect on intention. They found for inquiry based tasks, however, that both PEOU and PU were significant predictors. These studies support the original conclusion that extrinsic motivation is more important than intrinsic motivation.

Pavlou (2003) conducted an exploratory study and then a confirmatory study regarding the TAM components and an individual's intention to transact on a web site. The exploratory study utilized 103 students in experimental scenarios. Three possible scenarios were used: using Amazon.com (36 students), selecting a web retailer of their choice (41 students), and discussing web retailers in general (25 students). Regardless of the scenario, the students were asked to search an item of their choice on the web retailer's site and discover the process of purchasing that item without actually purchasing the item. The subjects were then asked to complete a questionnaire regarding their experience. This study found that PU was a significant predictor of intention to transact; while PEOU was not found to be a significant predictor. The confirmatory study utilized 155 on-line consumers. Invitation e-mails were sent to consumers with a URL link to an on-line survey instrument. The confirmatory study found that both PU and PEOU were significant predictors of a consumer's intention to transact. Pavlou felt the difference in finding was due to the real situation vs. the experimental scenario.

Additionally, Chen, Gillenson, & Sherrell (2002) used TAM and the innovation diffusion theory (IDT) to examine consumer behavior in a virtual store context. Surveying online consumers, they found PU and PEOU to determine consumer attitudes towards virtual stores. Vijayasarathy (2004) used TAM, among other constructs, to examine consumer intention to use online shopping. Using a mail survey, 281 consumers were assessed. Both PU and PEOU were found to predict attitude towards online shopping. Based on the theory of reasoned action (TRA) and TAM, Shih (2004) developed an extended model to predict consumer acceptance of electronic shopping. Data was collected from 212 participants using questionnaires. The participants were employees of eight small and medium-sized organizations in Taiwan. He found PU and PEOU to affect an individual's electronic shopping attitude. Grandon & Pearson (2004) examined small and medium-sized organizations in the U.S. to determine factors affecting the adoption of e-commerce. Using an electronic survey, they found PU and PEOU to be determinants of e-commerce adoption. Finally, McCloskey (2006) studied the attitudes and e-commerce participation of older Americans. TAM was used in the study to examine the impact of their attitudes (of PEOU, PU, and trust) on e-commerce usage. She found PU and trust to have a direct effect on usage.

These studies were based on B2C e-commerce. There are no studies utilizing the TAM constructs in a C2C e-commerce setting. It is important to determine if the TAM findings are consistent in this environment.

Transaction Cost Analysis (TCA)

TCA is a framework belonging to the New Institutional Economics paradigm. The framework is based on two main assumptions of human behavior (i.e., bounded rationality and opportunism) and the interplay of the two key dimensions of transactions (i.e., asset specificity and uncertainty) (Rindfleisch & Heide, 1997). Bounded rationality refers to the constraints and limitations of individuals on their cognitive capabilities and rationality. Simon (1977) states that individuals' limited information processing and communication abilities may impede their ability to act rationally. In uncertain environments, these constraints and limitations can become problematic (Rindfleisch & Heide, 1997). Opportunism refers to an individual's quest to serve his/her own self-interests. In uncertain environments, opportunism can increase transaction costs in the form of incomplete or inaccurate information (Devaraj et al., 2002). For example, the seller of a transaction may indicate to the buyer that the product in question is in working condition. However, the seller neglects to tell the consumer that it has been repaired several times. The reason for the seller's incomplete account of the product may be explained by opportunism. Asset specificity refers to any additional investments that have been made to support a relationship. These investments can make it difficult for the buyer and/or seller to switch. However, opportunism may cause the buyer/seller to exploit the relationship in his/her favor (Rindfleisch & Heide, 1997).

Devaraj, Fan, & Kohli (2002) (study described in the TAM section) found that both uncertainty and asset specificity are significantly related to time. This indicates that the online channels provided good information regarding the product and price. In addition, the wider choice among online channels provided a positive contribution to time savings that, in turn, resulted in a significantly positive relationship between time and satisfaction with the e-commerce channel. Devaraj, Fan, & Kohli (2006) also found uncertainty and asset specificity of an electronic marketplace to be associated with time responsiveness, personalization, reliability, security, and design.

Liang & Huang (1998) did an empirical study utilizing 86 Internet users to determine their purchasing intentions of different products in a B2C e-commerce environment. They found support for their hypothesis that the higher the perceived transaction costs (determined by uncertainty and asset specificity), the less likely a product would be purchased electronically.

Once again, TCA has only been tested in a B2C e-commerce environment. It needs to be tested in a C2C e-commerce environment to determine if the B2C findings hold true.

Service Quality (SERVQUAL)

SERVQUAL was developed to assess general service quality. It measures the difference between the individual's expected level of service and the perceived level of service. This difference is referred to as the gap score. A gap score is calculated on five different dimensions: tangibles (appearance of facilities or Web site; equipment; and personnel), reliability (ability to perform the promised service dependably and accurately), responsiveness (willingness to help customers and provide prompt service), assurance (knowledge and courtesy of employees and their ability to inspire trust and confidence), and empathy (providing caring and individualized attention to customers) (Jiang, Klein, & Carr, 2002).

The use of SERVQUAL in the IS field has been the topic of debate (Alzola & Robaina, 2005; Jiang et al., 2002; Kettinger & Lee, 1997; Van Dyke, Kappelman, & Prybutok, 1997; Watson, Pitt, & Kavan, 1998). Van Dyke, Kappelman, & Prybutok (1997) found there were both conceptual and empirical obscurities. Conceptual obscurities included using the gap score as the operationalized perceived service quality, using the ambiguous expectations construct, and using a single measure of service quality across industries. Empirical obscurities included reduced reliability, poor convergent validity, and unstable dimensionality. Other researchers surveyed various populations of users to address pieces of these problems such as the reduced reliability (Pitt, Watson, & Kavan, 1997) and dimensionality (Kettinger & Lee, 1997). Jiang, Klein, & Carr (2002) used data from a total of 168 matched sets (IS professionals and IS users) to determine whether or not the problems indicated in the SERVQUAL method were big enough to discredit its use in IS. Their research agreed with previous research that the indicated problems are not substantial enough to lose the capabilities found within the measure.

Kettinger & Lee (2005) tested a new set of scales for SERVQUAL. They posed two levels of IS service quality – desired service and adequate service – and defined the two levels in a zone of tolerance (ZOT). The ZOT represented the satisfactory range of IS service performance. Their research findings indicated validity for a four-dimension IS ZOT SERVQUAL instrument for desired, adequate, and perceived service quality levels. Additionally, Wang & Tang (2003) proposed EC-SERVQUAL (e-commerce service quality) to measure customer perceived service quality of websites that market digital products/services, and Bauer, Falk, & Hammerschmidt (2006) proposed eTransQual, a transaction process-based scale for measuring service quality.

Devaraj, Fan, & Kohli (2002) (study described in the TAM section) found that only the empathy and assurance components of SERVQUAL were significantly related to the satisfaction of the e-commerce channel. Devaraj, Fan, & Kohli (2002) offer a possible explanation for this finding. It could be that the respondents weren't presented with an opportunity to examine the responsiveness and reliability components. These components tend to be established over time and multiple transactions which was not represented in the study.

Some additional research has been done in the area of service quality and B2C e-commerce (Cao, Zhang, & Seydel, 2005; Gounaris & Dimitriadis, 2003; Lee & Lin, 2005). Varying results indicate that future research is needed to determine additional mediating factors that may be present. It is also easily seen that the issue of how to measure service quality in IS continues to be debated. Since this research is based on the Devaraj, Fan, & Kohli (2002) study, the use of a single survey that operationalizes perceived service quality through reliability, responsiveness, empathy, and assurance is used. SERVQUAL has

Figure 1. Predictors of satisfaction of C2C electronic commerce

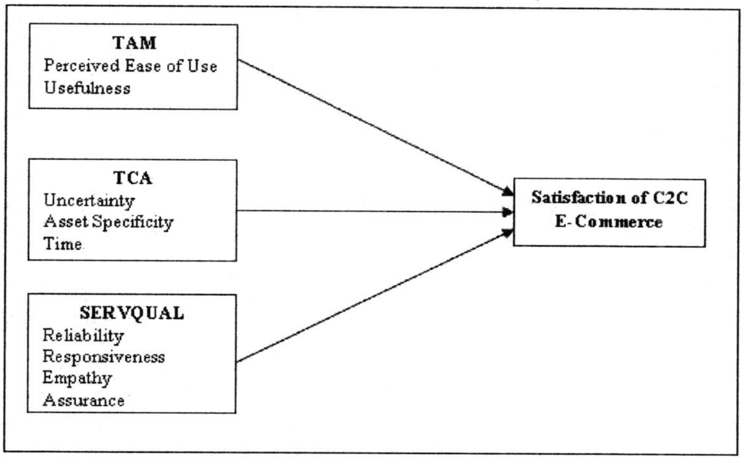

not been tested in the C2C e-commerce environment; therefore, it needs to be tested to determine where, if any, the differences lie between the two areas of e-commerce.

Figure 1 provides the research model of this chapter, which incorporates the three aforementioned constructs. In this model, TAM, TCA, and SERVQUAL are theorized to impact a consumer's satisfaction with C2C e-commerce.

METHODOLOGY

Undergraduate students located in a Southwestern university in the United States of America were used for this study. They were solicited based on their enrollment in an introduction to management information systems course. Drennan, Mort, & Previte (2006) argue that University students are "representative of a dominant cohort of online users" (p.6). College students represent the most connected (online) segment of the U.S. population, shopping online and spending online. Therefore, they are experienced and frequent users of the Internet.

Participants were given a modified version of the instruments created by Devaraj, Fan, & Kohli (2002) used to collect data regarding the TAM, TCA, and SERVQUAL components (see individual statements listed in Tables 1, 2, 3 and 4). Participants were asked to indicate on a seven-point Likert scale the degree to which they agreed with the C2C e-commerce statements. The participants were informed that the survey was completely voluntary and their responses would be kept anonymous and only reported in the aggregate. They were asked to answer the questions regarding their experiences with C2C e-commerce. In addition to these questions, participants were asked to fill out a brief demographics survey. Out of a total of 104 potential respondents, 83 chose to participate (80%).

A majority of the respondents (70%) had participated in C2C e-commerce (such as online auctions, email groups, web-based discussion forums, and/or chat rooms) as either the buyer or seller. However, seventy-two percent had never been the seller of a C2C e-commerce transaction. A majority of the respondents (63%) have purchased an item using this channel more than once; sixty-nine percent of them have done so in the past 12 months. Online auctions were the method of choice for 76% of those who have participated in C2C e-commerce. The respondents' ages ranged from 19 to 41 with the largest majority (59%) between the ages of 20 and 30. A survey of American adults by Pew Internet & American Life Project (2006) found that 67% of Internet users surveyed had made a purchase online (either B2C or C2C), and that the largest age group of Internet users is between the ages of 18 and 29. They also found a larger percentage of Internet users to have some college education versus only a high school education. Therefore, our sample's demographics are consistent with the demographics of Internet users.

DATA ANALYSIS AND RESULTS

Validity and Reliability of Measures

Self-reported data on two or more variables collected from the same source has the potential to lead to common method variance. Therefore, Harman's single-factor test was used in this study to test for this bias (Harman, 1967). This test assumes that if a high level of common method variance is present, then when all of the variables are entered together, all will load on one factor accounting for all of the variance or one factor will account for a majority of the variance. In this study, an exploratory factor analysis (EFA) was performed and seven factors with an Eigenvalue greater than one emerged. The variance explained ranged from 3% to 44% of the total variance. This result provides evidence that common method variance should not be a concern in this study.

The multi-item constructs used in the model were tested for construct validity and reliability. Factors were extracted using principal component analysis (PCA). Each of the TAM constructs' items loaded on one factor. The perceived ease of use construct yielded a Cronbach's alpha score

Table 1. TAM constructs factor analysis

PERCEIVED EASE OF USE (PEOU)	LOADING
Overall, I believe that C2C e-commerce is easier than other forms of commerce.	.50
It is easy for me to buy/sell using C2C e-commerce.	.83
My interactions during C2C e-commerce were clear and understandable.	.89
I believe that it is easy to do what I want to do while conducting C2C e-commerce.	.84
Cronbach's alpha	.77
Eigenvalue	2.43
Variance Explained	60.66%
PERCEIVED USEFULNESS (PU)	
C2C e-commerce gives me greater control over my buying/selling experience.	.78
C2C e-commerce improves the quality of my decision making.	.92
C2C e-commerce is a more effective way to buy/sell products and services.	.87
Overall, I find C2C e-commerce very useful.	.62
Cronbach's alpha	.81
Eigenvalue	2.60
Variance Explained	64.78%

of .77 and the percent of variation explained was 60.66%. The usefulness construct generated a Cronbach's alpha score of .81 with 64.78% of the variation explained. Table 1 shows the results of the factor analysis for the TAM constructs. Variables for each of the TAM constructs (PEOU and PU) were calculated for each subject as the average of those items.

The TCA construct items also loaded on one factor for each construct. The Cronbach's alpha scores for these constructs were calculated as .83, .74, and .75 for uncertainty, asset specificity, and time, respectively. The percent of variation explained was 67.18%, 57.15%, and 69.09%, respectively. Table 2 shows the results of the factor analysis for the TCA constructs. Variables for each of the TCA constructs (UNC, ASSE, and TIME) were calculated for each subject as the average of those items.

The SERVQUAL construct items had similar results to the TAM and TCA constructs. The Cronbach's alpha scores for these constructs were found to be .83, .88, .60, and .84 for reliability, responsiveness, empathy, and assurance, respectively. The percent of variation explained was 66.01%, 81.14%, 56.27%, and 75.95%, respectively.

Table 2. TCA constructs factor analysis

UNCERTAINTY (UNC)	LOADING
It was easy for me to get/provide relevant quantitative (price, taxes, etc.) information using C2C e-commerce.	.83
I believe that it was possible for me to evaluate the various alternative products using C2C e-commerce.	.72
The C2C e-commerce environment provided adequate information.	.90
The C2C e-commerce environment provided sufficient information about the buyer/seller.	.82
Cronbach's alpha	.83
Eigenvalue	2.69
Variance Explained	67.18%
ASSET SPECIFICITY (ASSE)	
There are many Web sites for which the products I have bought/sold are available.	.72
I was satisfied with the number of environments where I could buy/sell products.	.77
C2C e-commerce gives me a wider choice of different sellers/buyers compared to traditional commerce methods.	.79
C2C e-commerce gives me more opportunities compared to traditional commerce methods.	.75
Cronbach's alpha	.74
Eigenvalue	2.29
Variance Explained	57.15%
TIME (TIME)	
C2C e-commerce helps me accomplish tasks more quickly.	.69
I did not have to spend too much time to complete the transaction using C2C e-commerce.	.86
I did not have to spend too much effort to complete the transaction using C2C e-commerce.	.93
Cronbach's alpha	.75
Eigenvalue	2.07
Variance Explained	69.09%

Table 3. SERVQUAL constructs factor analysis

RELIABILITY (REL)	LOADING
I believe that C2C e-commerce is reliable.	.84
I believe that what I ask for is what I get in C2C e-commerce.	.82
I think that the C2C e-commerce seller/buyer with whom I transacted acted in accordance to our agreement.	.74
I trust the C2C e-commerce seller/buyer to complete the transaction on time.	.85
Cronbach's alpha	.83
Eigenvalue	2.64
Variance Explained	66.01%
RESPONSIVENESS (RESP)	
I believe that the C2C e-commerce seller/buyer is responsive to my needs.	.90
In the case of any problem, I think the C2C e-commerce seller/buyer will respond promptly.	.90
The C2C e-commerce seller/buyer will address any concerns that I have.	.91
Cronbach's alpha	.88
Eigenvalue	2.43
Variance Explained	81.14%
EMPATHY (EMP)	
The C2C e-commerce seller/buyer remembers or recognizes me as a repeat customer/seller (after the first time).	.78
I think C2C e-commerce can address the specific needs of each buyer/seller.	.81
I was satisfied with the payment options (e.g., money order, different credit cards) available with C2C e-commerce.	.65
Cronbach's alpha	.60
Eigenvalue	1.69
Variance Explained	56.27%
ASSURANCE (ASSU)	
I felt confident about the C2C e-commerce transaction decision.	.89
I feel safe in my transactions with the C2C e-commerce environment.	.84
The C2C e-commerce seller/buyer had answers to all my questions regarding the transaction.	.88
Cronbach's alpha	.84
Eigenvalue	2.28
Variance Explained	75.95%

Table 3 shows the results of the factor analysis for the SERVQUAL constructs. Variables for each of the SERVQUAL constructs (REL, RESP, EMP, and ASSU) were calculated for each subject as the average of those items.

The multi-item construct for satisfaction was also tested. A Cronbach's alpha score was found to be .85 with 77.64% of the variation explained. Table 4 shows the results of the factor analysis for the satisfaction construct. A variable for the satisfaction construct (SAT) was calculated as the average of the items. Each of the constructs in the model exceeded the recommended Cronbach's alpha threshold score of .50 (Nunnally, 1967), but one did not exceed the mostly commonly used threshold in the literature, .70 (Nunnally & Bernstein, 1994). However, it should be noted that lower (.60) and higher (.80) thresholds are used in the literature (Santos, 1999).

Model Testing

Regression analysis was performed to test the relationships between the construct variables and satisfaction. Residual plots were reviewed for non-random scatter about the zero line. No heteroscedasticity was found in the data. Variance inflation factors (VIF) were examined for each of the independent variables in the model. All values were small (below 10) suggesting there is no problem with multicollinearity in the data.

Table 5 shows the regression results using the TAM variables. Both perceived ease of use and usefulness are positively significant at the .001 level. This indicates respondents are more satisfied with C2C e-commerce when they find the process easy to complete and effective.

Table 6 shows the regression results using the TCA variables. Uncertainty is shown to be posi-

Table 4. Satisfaction construct factor analysis

SATISFACTION (SAT)	LOADING
Overall, I was satisfied with my C2C e-commerce experience.	.87
The C2C e-commerce environment provided information content which met my needs.	.89
It was possible for me to buy the product of my choice easily using C2C e-commerce.	.88
Cronbach's alpha	.85
Eigenvalue	2.33
Variance Explained	77.64%

Table 5. Regression on satisfaction: TAM variables

Dependent Variable: SAT					
Independent Variable	Parameter Estimate	Standard Error	t	p	VIF
PEOU	.56	.10	5.60	.000***	2.47
PU	.42	.10	4.03	.000***	2.47
Overall model fit: p = .000*** R^2 = .37 ***p<.001					

Table 6. Regression on satisfaction: TCA variables

Dependent Variable: SAT					
Independent Variable	Parameter Estimate	Standard Error	t	p	VIF
UNC	.54	.11	4.73	.000***	1.43
ASSE	.26	.13	2.02	.048*	1.33
TIME	.40	.11	3.73	.000***	1.36
Overall model fit: p = .000*** R^2 = .33 ***p<.001; *p<.05					

Table 7. Regression on satisfaction: SERVQUAL variables

Dependent Variable: SAT					
Independent Variable	Parameter Estimate	Standard Error	t	p	VIF
REL	.45	.13	3.39	.002**	3.73
RESP	.36	.11	3.35	.001**	3.59
EMP	.48	.15	3.21	.002**	1.97
ASSU	.42	.11	3.90	.000***	2.54
Overall model fit: p = .022* R^2 = .26 ***p<.001; **p<.01; *p<.05					

tive and significantly associated with satisfaction at the .001 level. Both asset specificity and time are positively significant at the .05 level. This indicates that a respondent is satisfied with C2C e-commerce when information is readily available, there are a variety of choices (both with places to buy/sell and products to buy/sell), and the process can be done quickly.

Table 7 shows the regression results using the SERVQUAL variables. Reliability, responsiveness, and empathy are all positively significant at the .01 level. Assurance was shown to be positively significant at the .001 level. This indicates that respondents are more satisfied with C2C e-commerce when the process is reliable (including receiving the correct products/payment in the agreed upon timeframe), the buyer/seller is responsive to the needs, questions, and concerns of the buyer/seller, the buyer/seller recognizes each buyer's/seller's specific needs (including possible payment options), and the buyer/seller provides assurances that the online purchase is correct.

Discussion

The study findings indicate that many individuals are choosing to participate in C2C e-commerce, both as buyers and sellers. With the increase in this type of e-commerce, a look into the factors affecting this area is appropriate. The findings confirm anecdotal evidence that C2C e-commerce is different from B2C e-commerce and deserves its own research theme. Within this new research theme, models specifically dealing with the C2C e-commerce area need to be developed and tested. The satisfaction model of C2C e-commerce presented and tested here can be a stepping stone for further research.

All model variables from the three constructs, TAM, TCA, and SERVQUAL, were found to be significant influencers on satisfaction. More specifically, the ease of use and usefulness of the C2C online environment (TAM); the amount of information provided to eliminate uncertainty, the additional avenues provided for buying and selling (asset specificity), and the time saved when accomplishing buying/selling (TCA); and the buyers/sellers being reliable, responsive, assuring and empathetic (SERVQUAL) were found to predict satisfaction. It appears that C2C e-commerce relationships can be quite complex, with many factors affecting a consumer's satisfaction with this type of e-commerce.

When comparing these findings to those completed by Devaraj Fan, & Kohli (2002) for B2C e-commerce, there are distinct differences. Devaraj, Fan, & Kohli (2002) found the same variables to be significant in the B2C online arena except reliability and responsiveness (two components of service quality). With C2C e-commerce, this study found an individual's satisfaction to depend on all four aspects of service quality. The reliability the consumer felt toward another consumer predicted his/her satisfaction. The difference found in C2C e-commerce vs. B2C e-commerce may have to do with the feeling of some guarantee of the transaction when a business is involved. This feeling may not be present when dealing directly with other consumers. Therefore, one would expect reliability to influence satisfaction in C2C e-commerce but not in B2C e-commerce. The responsiveness of one consumer to another predicted his/her satisfaction in C2C e-commerce. Again, in a B2C online environment, responsiveness would not be as large of a concern; consumers expect businesses to respond to their needs while they may not hold the same expectation of individual consumers. Therefore, a display of responsiveness from consumers would increase the satisfaction of C2C e-commerce.

LIMITATIONS AND IMPLICATIONS FOR FUTURE RESEARCH

This research provides evidence that differences do exist in the C2C and B2C online realms. Therefore, further investigation is warranted in the broad area of C2C e-commerce, which has been given little attention up to this point. While there are many articles on online auctions, the other methods for conducting C2C e-commerce, for example, web based discussion forums, have yet to make a dent in the potential research opportunities.

One limitation of this study is that it gathered data regarding all forms of C2C e-commerce, but it did not test for differences between the methods. Differences should be investigated between C2C online auctions and the other forms of C2C e-commerce such as web forums and chat rooms.

Another limitation of the study is that mediating factors and interactions between model constructs were not investigated. Researchers may want to consider adding mediating factors to the present research model, as well as any interactions between the constructs. For example, a person's age or gender could mediate the factors provided in this model.

This study provided evidence of differences between C2C and B2C based on variables used in a B2C study. There may be additional variables that are worth investigating. For example, trust in C2C e-commerce may be an avenue worth pursuing. The uncertainty found in C2C e-commerce logically seems to be higher than in B2C e-commerce. This may affect how consumers trust one another and their satisfaction level of C2C e-commerce. Another potential future research study could involve product complexity. Product complexity has been proposed as an important factor in the study of buyer/seller behaviors (Zhang & Reichgelt, 2006). Therefore, a modification of the TCA could be pursued in future C2C e-commerce studies. Also, it appears that additional research is needed in the area of service quality in IS research to determine if a universal measure can be obtained.

IMPLICATIONS FOR PRACTICE

Consumers wishing to practice C2C e-commerce may find this study useful in their preparations to conduct e-commerce with other consumers. The findings of this study indicate that there are many aspects of C2C e-commerce that influence their satisfaction. Consumers would be wise to note that simply having a good website and/or needed products may not be enough for another consumer to be satisfied with the experience. For example, the study indicates that responsiveness to the needs, questions, and concerns of the buyer/seller impact a consumer's satisfaction. In addition, consumers' satisfaction of C2C e-commerce is impacted by the reliable and complete information provided by the buyer/seller in a transaction. Consumers should keep this in mind when preparing information for potential buyers/sellers.

CONCLUSION

C2C e-commerce is a growing area of e-commerce. As such, the field of research in this area should reflect that growth. This study adapted constructs (TAM, TCA, and SERVQUAL) from a B2C e-commerce study of satisfaction and found different results in the constructs that affect satisfaction in the given area. Namely, reliability and responsiveness (components of the SERVQUAL construct) were found to be predictors of satisfaction in the C2C e-commerce environment but not in the B2C e-commerce environment. This evidence provides support that C2C e-commerce is deserving of its own research stream. Future research possibilities for this area of e-commerce include overall C2C e-commerce themes (such as trust) and differences between venues (such as between online auctions and online communities). Focusing research in these areas will provide consumers the needed information to conduct C2C e-commerce in the most effective and efficient way.

REFERENCES

Alzola, L. M., & Robaina, V. P. (2005). SERVQUAL: its applicability in electronic commerce B2C. *The Quality Management Journal, 12*(4), 46-57.

Armstrong, A., & Hagel, J. (1996). The real value of on-line communities. *Harvard Business Review, 74*(3), 134-141.

Bauer, H. H., Falk, T., & Hammerschmidt, M. (2006). eTransQual: a transaction process-based approach for capturing service quality in online shopping. *Journal of Business Research, 59*, 866-875.

Cao, M., Zhang, Q., & Seydel, J. (2005). B2C e-commerce web site quality: an empirical examination. *Industrial Management & Data Systems, 105*(5), 645-661.

Chen, L., Gillenson, M. L., & Sherrell, D. L. (2002). Enticing online consumers: an extended technology acceptance perspective. *Information & Management, 39*(8), 705-719.

Davis, F. D. (1989). Perceived usefulness, perceived ease of use, and user acceptance of information technology. *MIS Quarterly, 13*(3), 319-340.

Davis, F. D., Bagozzi, R. P., & Warshaw, P. R. (1989). User acceptance of computer technology: a comparison of two theoretical models. *Management Science, 35*(8), 982-1003.

Davis, F. D., Bagozzi, R. P., & Warshaw, P. R. (1992). Extrinsic and intrinsic motivation to use computers in the workplace. *Journal of Applied Social Psychology, 22*(14), 1111-1132.

DeLone, W. H., & McLean, E. R. (1992). Information systems success: the quest for the dependent variable. *Information Systems Research, 3*(1), 60-95.

DeLone, W. H., & McLean, E. R. (2003). The DeLone and McLean model of information systems success: a ten-year update. *Journal of Management Information Systems, 19*(4), 9-30.

DeLone, W. H., & McLean, E. R. (2004). Measuring e-commerce success: applying the DeLone & McLean information systems success model. *International Journal of Electronic Commerce, 9*(1), 31-47.

Devaraj, S., Fan, M., & Kohli, R. (2002). Antecedents of B2C channel satisfaction and preference: validating e-commerce metrics. *Information Systems Research, 12*(3), 316-333.

Devaraj, S., Fan, M., & Kohli, R. (2006). Examination of online channel preference: using the structure-conduct-outcome framework. *Decision Support Systems, 42*(2), 1089-1103.

Drennan, J., Mort, G. S., & Previte, J. (2006). Privacy, risk perception, and expert online behavior: an exploratory study of household end users. *Journal of Organizational and End User Computing, 18*(1), 1-22.

Gefen, D., Karahanna, E., & Straub, D. (2003). Inexperience and experience with online stores: the importance of TAM and trust. *IEEE Transactions on Engineering Management, 50*(3), 307-321.

Gefen, D., & Straub, D. (2000). The relative importance of perceived ease of use in IS adoption: a study of e-commerce adoption. *Journal of the Association for Information Systems, 1*(Article 8), 1-28.

Gounaris, S., & Dimitriadis, S. (2003). Assessing service quality on the Web: evidence from business-to-consumer portals. *Journal of Services Marketing, 17*(5), 529-548.

Grandon, E. E., & Pearson, J. M. (2004). Electronic commerce adoption: an empirical study of small and medium US businesses. *Information & Management, 42*(1), 197-216.

Harman, H. H. (1967). *Modern Factor Analysis.* Chicago: University of Chicago Press.

Jiang, J. J., Klein, G., & Carr, C. L. (2002). Measuring information systems service quality: SERVQUAL from the other side. *MIS Quarterly, 26*(2), 145-166.

Jones, K., & Leonard, L. N. K. (2008). Trust in consumer-to-consumer electronic commerce. *Information & Management, in press.*

Kettinger, W. J., & Lee, C. C. (1997). Pragmatic perspectives on the measurement of information systems service quality. *MIS Quarterly, 21*(2), 223-240.

Kettinger, W. J., & Lee, C. C. (2005). Zones of tolerance: alternative scales for measuring information systems service quality. *MIS Quarterly, 29*(4), 607-623.

Lee, G.-G., & Lin, H.-F. (2005). Customer perceptions of e-service quality in online shopping. *International Journal of Retail & Distribution Management, 33*(2), 161-176.

Liang, T.-P., & Huang, J.-S. (1998). An empirical study on consumer acceptance of products in electronic markets: a transaction cost model. *Decision Support Systems, 24*, 29-43.

Lin, Z., Li, D., & Huang, W. (2007). Traders beware: an examination of the distribution of eBay sellers' online reputation. *International Journal of Electronic Business, 5*(5), 499-517.

Lin, Z., Li, D., Janamanchi, B., & Huang, W. (2006). Reputation distribution and consumer-to-consumer online auction market structure: an exploratory study. *Decision Support Systems, 41*(2), 435-448.

Livingston, J. A. (2005). How valuable is a good reputation? A sample selection model of internet auction. *The Review of Economics and Statistics, 87*(3), 453-465.

McCloskey, D. W. (2006). The importance of ease of use, usefulness, and trust in online consumers: an examination of the technology acceptance model with older consumers. *Journal of Organizational and End User Computing, 18*(3), 47-65.

Melnik, M. I., & Alm, J. (2002). Does a seller's ecommerce reputation matter? Evidence from Ebay auctions. *The Journal of Industrial Economics, 50*(3), 337-349.

Nunnally, J. C. (1967). *Psychometric Theory*. New York: McGraw-Hill.

Nunnally, J. C., & Bernstein, I. H. (1994). *Psychometric Theory* (3rd ed.). New York: McGraw-Hill Inc.

Orman, L. V. (2006). Optimum design of electronic communities as economic entities. *Information Systems Frontiers, 8*, 179-194.

Pavlou, P. A. (2003). Consumer acceptance of electronic commerce: integrating trust and risk with the technology acceptance model. *International Journal of Electronic Commerce, 7*(3), 101-134.

Pei, Z., Zhenxiang, Z., & Chunping, H. (2007). An extended TAM modelor Chinese B2C websites design. *Journal of Global Information Technology, 10*(1), 51-66.

Pew.Internet.&.American.Life.Project. (2006). Demographics of internet users. Retrieved January 8, 2007, from http://www.pewinternet.org/trends/User_Demo_4.26.06.htm

Pitt, L. F., Watson, R. T., & Kavan, C. B. (1997). Measuring information systems service quality: concerns for a complete canvas. *MIS Quarterly, June*, 209-221.

Rindfleisch, A., & Heide, J. B. (1997). Transaction cost analysis: past, present, and future applications. *Journal of Marketing, 61*(October), 30-54.

Santos, J. R. A. (1999). Cronbach's alpha: a tool for assessing the reliability of scales. *Journal of Extension, 37*(2), 1-5.

Shih, H.-P. (2004). An empirical study on predicting user acceptance of e-shopping on the web. *Information & Management, 41*(3), 351-368.

Simon, H. A. (1977). *The New Science of Management Decision*. Englewood Cliffs, NJ: Prentice-Hall.

Strader, T. J., & Ramaswami, S. N. (2002). The value of seller trustworthiness in C2C online markets. *Communications of the ACM, 45*(12), 45-49.

Van Dyke, T. P., Kappelman, L. A., & Prybutok, V. R. (1997). Measuring information systems service quality: concerns on the use of the SERVQUAL questionnaire. *MIS Quarterly, June*, 195-208.

Venkatesh, V. (1999). Creation of favorable user perceptions: exploring the role of intrinsic motivation. *MIS Quarterly, 23*(2), 239-260.

Vijayasarathy, L. R. (2004). Predicting consumer intentions to use on-line shopping: the case for an augmented technology acceptance model. *Information & Management, 41*(6), 747-762.

Wang, Y.-S., & Tang, T.-I. (2003). Assessing customer perceptions of website service quality in digital marketing environments. *Journal of End User Computing, 15*(3), 14-31.

Wareham, J., Zheng, J. G., & Straub, D. (2005). Critical themes in electronic commerce research: a meta-analysis. *Journal of Information Technology, 20*, 1-19.

Watson, R. T., Pitt, L. F., & Kavan, C. B. (1998). Measuring information systems service quality: lessons from two longitudinal case studies. *MIS Quarterly, March*, 61-79.

Yamamoto, H., Ishida, K., & Ohta, T. (2004). Modeling reputation management system on online C2C market. *Computational & Mathematical Organization Theory, 10*, 165-178.

Zhang, A., & Reichgelt, H. (2006). Product complexity as a determinant of transaction governance structure: an empirical comparison of web-only and traditional banks. *Journal of Electronic Commerce in Organizations, 4*(3), 1-17.

Chapter II
Online Consumers' Switching Behavior: A Buyer–Seller Relationship Perspective

Dahui Li
University of Minnesota Duluth, USA

Glenn J. Browne
Texas Tech University, USA

James C. Wetherbe
Texas Tech University, USA

ABSTRACT

Limited studies have investigated online consumer loyalty and retention from a relationship orientation in electronic commerce research. It is important to understand the differences in relationship orientations between people who have the propensity to stick to particular Web sites ("stayers") and people who have the propensity to switch to alternative Web sites ("switchers"). This study proposes a relationship-based classification schema consisting of five dimensions: that is, commitment, trust, satisfaction, comparison level of the alternatives, and nonretrievable investment. Data were collected from 299 college students who had experience with e-commerce Web sites. Using discriminating analysis, we found that stayers and switchers were significantly different along the five research dimensions. Satisfaction with the current Web site was the most important discriminant factor, followed by trust, commitment, comparison level of alternative Web sites, and nonretrievable investment in the current Web site. Implications of the findings for researchers and practitioners are discussed.

INTRODUCTION

With the development of electronic commerce, more and more companies have conducted online business transactions with their customers. Why consumers consistently stick to a Web site ("stayers") or switch to an alternative Web site ("switchers") has drawn considerable attention from the research community (e.g., Chen & Hitt, 2002; *Park & Kim, 2006;* Pavlou & Gefen, 2004) due to the ease of jumping from one Web site to many alternative Web sites that offer similar products or services with the mere click of a mouse.

This article conducts a study to compare stayers and switchers in online consumer markets based on relationship marketing theories. We define stayers as those consumers who have the propensity to stay with a particular Web site in the future. Switchers, on the other hand, are those consumers who have no propensity to use the Web site in the future. The abundant literature in relationship marketing has provided sufficient theoretical foundations for the present study. Guided by an integrated model of buyer-seller relationships in the conventional marketplace (Wilson, 1995), this study investigates how online consumers' switching behavior varies along five salient relationship factors drawn from the model (commitment, trust, satisfaction, comparison level of the alternatives, and nonretrievable investment). We believe that these factors will influence the quality of buyer-seller relationships in the online environment.

An investigation of switching behavior will contribute to our understanding of the differences between technology adoption/acceptance and continuous use of the technology. Information systems researchers have found that users' beliefs and attitudes in pre-adoption and post-adoption are different (e.g., Parthasarathy & Bhattacherjee, 1998). The present study will extend these previous findings by providing understanding as to why some adopters stay with a Web site (post-adoption retention) and others switch (post-adoption attrition) in the online environment.

Studying online consumers' switching behavior is also important for marketing research and practice. From the business side, acquiring a customer is much more difficult and more inefficient than keeping a customer. Costs associated with acquiring new customers are five times the costs of retaining customers (Keaveney, 1995). In the context of e-commerce, a high quality buyer-seller relationship is important because keeping existing customers and attracting new customers are so expensive and it is so easy to switch online (Reichheld & Schefter, 2000).

With these motivations in mind, this article reports the results of an empirical study. In the next section, we discuss the conceptual background and develop the research hypotheses. The research method for the empirical study is then explained, followed by a discussion of the data analysis and results. Finally, we discuss the findings and draw implications for researchers and practitioners.

THEORETICAL BACKGROUND

Several studies have investigated online switching behaviors. Keaveney and Parthasarathy (2001) found that online consumers' previous behavioral patterns (e.g., service usage), attitudes (e.g., risk-taking, satisfaction, and involvement), and demographic characteristics (e.g., income and education) were significant discriminating factors between stayers and switchers. In an investigation of the online brokerage industry, Chen and Hitt (2002) found that online consumers' system usage and the breadth and quality of alternative online service providers were significant in predicting switching behavior. Gupta, Su, and Walter (2004) found that consumers switching from off-line to online transactions paid attention to channel risk, search effort, and learning effort.

In addition to these exploratory empirical studies, other researchers have started to apply well-established models and theories to examine online consumer behaviors and customer loyalty (e.g., Gefen, Karahanna & Straub, 2003; Pavlou, 2003; Park & Kim, 2006). The first stream of such literature is based on conventional consumer behavior theories, which suggest that satisfaction and switching barriers are significant antecedents of customer loyalty and retention (e.g., Bhattacherjee, 2001; Flavian, Guinaliu & Gurrea., 2006; Park & Kim, 2006). This stream is also called the "transactional" view of online buyer-seller relationships (Benbasat & DeSanctis, 2001), and emphasizes the importance of providing economic benefit, profit, efficiency, and effectiveness to attract and satisfy consumers.

The second stream of research examines relationship marketing theories, which predict that a customer's commitment to and trust in a business relationship are the main reasons for him or her to stay with a business (Morgan & Hunt, 1994). This "relational" view considers online buyer-seller relationships as personalized, interpersonal social and psychological exchanges and emphasizes the effects of social and psychological factors (such as commitment and trust) on customer retention (Benbasat & DeSanctis, 2001). Most previous e-commerce literature has investigated the significant role of trust (e.g., Pavlou, 2003; Pavlou & Gefen, 2004). Recently, some studies have started to examine commitment (e.g., Park & Kim, 2006).

The current study continues to investigate the differences between switchers and stayers from this relational view of online buyer-seller relationships. The theoretical framework of this study is Wilson's integrated model of buyer-seller relationships for conventional marketing research (Wilson, 1995). The model consists of 13 important factors that are believed to predict the development and success of marketing relationships. We posit that Wilson's model provides an important framework for examining online

Table 1. Research variables and supporting literature

Variables in Wilson's Model	Definition and Similar Terms Used in Other Studies	Selected Supporting Literature
Commitment	Stayers have higher levels of commitment to current Web sites than consumers who switch Web sites. Similar terms: bonding mechanism	Garbarino & Johnson, 1999; Ganesh, Arnold & Reynolds, 2000; Morgan & Hunt, 1994; Park & Kim, 2006
Trust	Stayers trust current Web sites more than switchers trust current Web sites.	Gefen, Karahanna & Straub, 2003; Morgan & Hunt, 1994; Pavlou, 2003; Pavlou & Gefen, 2004
Satisfaction	Long-term judgment based on past interactions with an online Web site over time, rather than single transaction-based satisfaction that is usually an immediate post-buying judgment	Bhattacherjee, 2001; Flavian, Guinaliu & Gurrea., 2006; Ganesh, Arnold & Reynolds, 2000; Keaveney & Parthasarathy, 2001
Comparison Level of the Alternatives	Perceived desirability of alternative Web site to the present relationship with the current Web site Similar terms: quality of alternatives; relational benefit; use of multiple suppliers, pool size of suppliers	Anderson & Narus, 1990; Chen & Hitt, 2002; Hart & Saunders, 1997; Park & Kim, 2006; Rusbult, Martz & Agnew, 1998
Nonretrievable Investment	The extent and importance of resources attached to the relationship with the current Web site. Similar terms: sunk cost, switching cost, investment size, asset specific investment	Anderson & Narus, 1990; Chen & Hitt, 2002; Hart & Saunders, 1997; Rusbult, Martz & Agnew, 1998

buyer-seller relationships. Following Wilson's suggestion, we limit our focus to how consumers view buyer-seller relationships in the consumer market. We emphasize five factors from Wilson's model, which are commitment, trust, satisfaction, comparison level of the alternatives, and nonretrievable investment. In the following sections, we review the literature concerning these five variables and develop research hypotheses. A summary of the research variables and our review of supporting literature are shown in Table 1.

RESEARCH HYPOTHESES

Commitment. Commitment is the most important relationship factor and is central to the success of many buyer-seller relationships (Ganesh, Arnold & Reynolds, 2000; Morgan & Hunt, 1994). People usually realize the importance of keeping a relationship because the benefits for them are inseparable from the benefits for their partners. Highly committed individuals generally believe that the relationship will continue in the future, so they try to maximize their efforts to stay in the relationship (Garbarino & Johnson, 1999; Morgan & Hunt, 1994).

Studying the effect of commitment in online buyer-seller relationships is important because commitment may be difficult to develop. However, we posit that it is possible for an individual to develop commitment to a particular Web site. A consumer's consistent interactions with the Web site may be attributed to his or her commitment level toward the business. If a consumer stays with a Web site, this may result from the commitment level toward maintaining his relationship with the Web site (Park & Kim, 2006). Thus, we hypothesize:

H1: Stayers have higher levels of commitment to current Web sites than switchers.

Trust. Trust is the basic mechanism used to build and maintain a relationship and fosters a long-term orientation in marketing relationships (Morgan & Hunt, 1994). In business-to-consumer relationships, trust is a predictor of Internet buyers' positive attitudes toward online shopping (Gefen, Karahanna & Straub, 2003). Many different positive outcomes may be generated from trusting the vendor's Web site (Pavlou, 2003; Pavlou & Gefen, 2004). If a consumer does not receive positive results, his trust belief toward the Web site will be reduced or destroyed, and the consumer may terminate further interactions and switch to other vendors. Thus we hypothesize:

H2: Stayers trust current Web sites more than switchers trust current Web sites.

Satisfaction. We define satisfaction as a long-term judgment based on past interactions with an online Web site over time, rather than single transaction-based satisfaction that is usually an immediate post-buying judgment. Satisfaction is an important predictor of the intention to use an information system continuously (Bhattacherjee, 2001). Consumers' future buying intentions and behavior can be predicted by their satisfaction with a product or service (e.g., Burnham, Frels & Mahajan, 2003; Ganesh, Arnold & Reynolds, 2000). Using data collected from the customers of a national online service provider, Keaveney and Parthasarathy (2001) found that people who continued to use the online service could be significantly discriminated from switchers in terms of their level of satisfaction with the service. The significant effect of satisfaction on online customer loyalty has also been reported in several studies of online buyer-seller relationships (e.g., Bhattacherjee, 2001; Park & Kim, 2006). Thus, we hypothesize:

H3: Stayers are more satisfied with their current Web sites than are switchers.

Comparison Level of the Alternatives. Comparison level of the alternatives refers to the perceived desirability of alternative Web sites to the present relationship with the current Web site (Anderson & Narus, 1990). It measures how much an individual's needs could be fulfilled by other relationships. In the IS literature, Hart and Saunders (1997) have suggested that the smaller the "supplier pool size," the greater the buyer's dependence on the supplier in an EDI relationship. Marketing research has also shown that dependence on a current supplier will be low if there are many good alternative suppliers available in the marketplace (e.g., Anderson & Narus, 1990). In online consumer markets, comparison level of the best alternative Web site also influences the dependence of online consumers on the present Web site (Chen & Hitt, 2002). If there is a group of high quality Web sites available, dependence on the present Web site will be affected and online consumers are more likely to switch to an alternative Web site. Thus, we hypothesize:

H4: Switchers are more aware of the comparison level of alternative Web sites than are stayers.

Nonretrievable Investment. Nonretrievable investment refers to the extent and importance of resources attached to the relationship with the current Web site (Anderson & Narus, 1990; Burnham, Frels & Mahajan, 2003; Chen & Hitt, 2002). The value of such resources will be lowered or lost if the relationship is ended. Thus, nonretrievable investment acts as a powerful psychological incentive to persist in a relationship. According to Burnham, Frels, and Mahajan (2003), switching costs can be classified further as extra expenditure of time and effort (procedural cost), loss of financial resources (financial cost), and psychological discomfort (relational cost). In the online environment, a consumer could feel tied to the present Web site whenever he recalls the time, money, and effort invested. Further, the anticipation of switching costs such as searching for alternative sites and then learning how to use one may discourage consumers from abandoning the current Web site for another. Thus, we hypothesize:

H5: Stayers value nonretrievable investment more than do switchers.

RESEARCH METHOD

All the scales were adapted from Morgan and Hunt (1994) and Rusbult, Martz, and Agnew (1998) (we have omitted the scales for space purposes). Seven-point Likert scales were utilized. Preliminary investigations were conducted to test the validity of these scales.

The survey method was used to collect data. Student subjects at a large public university were the respondents of the survey. To ensure appropriate motivation, students were given course credit for completing the questionnaire. One of the major advantages of collecting data from university students is that they typically have considerable experience with different types of e-commerce Web sites. Students are very active users of Internet applications and participants in e-commerce activities. In fact, 18-34 year-olds are the heaviest users of the Internet (comScore, 2004; Forrester Research, 2005) compared with other groups in the population. Further, consumers around age 20 have been found to be savvy about online shopping (Forrester Research, 2005). Therefore, student samples have been found feasible for research concerning online behavior and have been used in several recent studies (e.g., Agarwal & Karahanna, 2000; Gefen, Karahanna & Straub, 2003; Meinert, Peterson, Criswell & Crossland, 2006). In our study, the sample statistics indicate that our college student sample is representative of 18-34 year-old users.

The questionnaires were formatted into two versions. One version asked the student to name an e-commerce Web site (defined as a Web site that conducts business transactions) that the student would continue using in the near future, while the other version asked the student to name an e-commerce Web site with which the student did not intend to continue. Asking respondents to subjectively report switching behaviors among a group of service providers has been utilized in previous literature (e.g., Chakravarty, Feinberg & Rhee, 2004; Ganesh, Arnold & Reynolds, 2000; Keaveney & Parthasarathy, 2001). In our study, each student randomly received one version of the questionnaire. Two screening questions were asked to check whether the respondent had enough experience with the e-commerce Web site to be evaluated. The first question was: How long have you used this Web site? The second was: During the time period you checked in question (1), how often did you visit this Web site? Following the screening questions, the respondents were asked to respond to survey questions. Finally, demographic information was collected.

We adopted a two-step approach to classify a respondent as a stayer or a switcher. The first step was based on the version of the questionnaire. If a questionnaire asked a respondent to report a Web site that the individual did not plan to use in the future, the respondent was classified as a "switcher"; otherwise, the respondent was classified as a "stayer." In the second step, we examined the respondent's answers to three survey questions about his intention to stay with the Web site. Using intention to measure actual behavior is consistent with the Theory of Reasoned Action (Fishbein & Ajzen, 1975). The scale used was from Agarwal and Karahanna (2000). If a respondent was classified as a "switcher" in the first step, but the intention to stay was high (above the median score), the response was removed. If a respondent was classified as a "stayer," but the intention was below the median score, the response was also removed.

365 questionnaires were distributed in eight business courses. Juniors, seniors, and graduate students were surveyed, representing all majors in the college. 54 respondents who had used the reported Web site for less than three months and no more than ten times were excluded from the study. In the classification step, noted above, 12 responses were excluded. In the end, 299 responses were kept in the sample, of which 158 were staying responses and 141 were switching responses.

DATA ANALYSIS AND RESULTS

We examined the reliability and validity of the scales using LISREL 8.3 (Tables 2 and 3). While the overall chi-square for the measurement model was significant ($\chi_{(142)} = 223.02$, $p < 0.001$), other fit indices showed that the model had a good fit with the data (RMSEA = 0.046, SRMR = 0.042, GFI = 0.92, AGFI = 0.90, NFI = 0.96, NNFI = 0.98, CFI = 0.98). To evaluate scale reliability and convergent and discriminant validity, we followed the guidelines from Fornell and Larcker (1981). All item loadings were significant and exceeded 0.7. Composite reliabilities of research constructs ranged from 0.88 to 0.95. Average variance extracted (AVE) ranged from 0.64 to 0.78 and all the square roots of AVEs exceeded their respective inter-construct correlations. Thus, the validity and reliability of the scales were acceptable.

After the scales were validated, we tested the research hypotheses using multiple discriminant analysis (Hair, Anderson, Tatham & Black, 1995). The independent variables were commitment, trust, satisfaction, comparison level of the alternatives, and nonretrievable investment.

Results of the analyses are shown in Table 4. The overall canonical discriminant function was significant, with Wilks' Lambda = 0.278 and $\chi_{(5)} = 377.44$ ($p < 0.001$). This indicated that stayers can be discriminated from switchers. As for the predictability of the discriminant function, the percentages correctly classified (or hit ratios) for the analysis sample (93.3%) and the holdout sample (93%) were above the proportional chance criterion (50%) and the maximum chance criterion

Table 2. Measurement model

Item	Mean	Standard Deviation	Standard Loading
COMMT1	3.41	1.94	0.86
COMMT2	2.90	1.67	0.82
COMMT	3.42	1.85	0.83
TRUST1	4.77	1.63	0.82
TRUST2	4.65	1.73	0.95
TRUST3	4.79	1.64	0.88
SATIS1	4.42	2.09	0.96
SATIS2	4.33	2.08	0.97
SATIS3	4.27	2.03	0.81
SATIS4	3.95	1.74	0.84
SATIS5	4.56	1.82	0.83
COMPA1	4.33	1.84	0.85
COMPA2	4.01	1.87	0.84
COMPA3	4.21	1.83	0.93
COMPA4	4.48	1.86	0.84
INVES1	2.78	1.68	0.75
INVES2	2.96	1.68	0.81
INVES3	3.47	1.79	0.84
INVES4	3.38	1.81	0.80

Fit Indices: $\chi(142) = 223.02$ ($p < 0.001$), RMSEA = 0.046, SRMR = 0.042, GFI = 0.92, AGFI = 0.90, NFI = 0.96, NNFI = 0.98, CFI = 0.98

Table 3. Reliability and interconstruct correlations

CONSTRUCT	AVE	RELI	COMMT	TRUST	SATIS	COMPA	INVES
COMMT	0.70	0.88	0.84				
TRUST	0.78	0.92	0.66	0.88			
SATIS	0.78	0.95	0.77	0.84	0.88		
COMPA	0.75	0.92	-0.59	-0.54	-0.65	0.87	
INVES	0.64	0.88	0.61	0.28	0.35	-0.32	0.80

AVE is Average Variance Extracted, computed as $[(\Gamma(8^2)]/[(\Gamma(8^2) + \Gamma(\gamma))]$

RELI is Composite Reliability, computed as $[(\Gamma(8))^2]/[(\Gamma(8))^2 + \Gamma(\gamma))]$

Square roots of AVE are shown on the diagonals of the correlation matrix

(53%). This indicates that the classification was highly accurate.

As shown in Table 4, all tests of the group-mean differences were significant at the χ = 0.001 level. The directions of the mean differences between switchers and stayers show that all the hypotheses were supported. Compared with switchers, stayers were more committed to maintaining the relationship with the current Web site (H1) (mean difference = 2.00, $F_{(1,297)} = 178.83$, $p < 0.001$), consistent with studies in conventional buyer-seller relationships (e.g., Garbarino & Johnson, 1999). Stayers showed a higher level of trust in the current Web site than did switchers (H2) (mean difference = 2.09, $F_{(1,297)} = 250.31$, $p < 0.001$). Stayers were more satisfied with the interactive experience with the current Web site (H3) (mean difference = 2.99, $F_{(1,297)} = 740.13$, $p < 0.001$), and less aware of the comparison level of the alternative Web sites (H4) (mean difference = 2.07, $F_{(1,297)} = 174.82$, $p < 0.001$), consistent with previous studies (e.g., Anderson & Narus, 1990; Keaveney & Parthasarathy, 2001). Finally, stayers were more aware of the size of the nonretrievable investment (H5) (mean difference = 0.81, $F_{(1,297)} = 24.37$, $p < 0.001$).

DISCUSSION

This study has investigated the differences between switchers and stayers in the context of online buyer-seller relationships, based on an integrated buyer-seller relationship model (Wilson, 1995). Our empirical study has shown that stayers are more committed to online businesses than switchers. However, the mean value of commitment for stayers (4.20) in this study is relatively low compared with the commitment levels reported in other types of relationships (e.g., Morgan & Hunt, 1994; Garbarino & Johnson, 1999). This suggests that due to the limited capacity of the Internet as a transmission medium between consumers and Web sites, commitment is not easily developed in the online consumer market.

Stayers were also found to trust online businesses more than switchers, consistent with other studies (e.g., Gefen, Karahanna, & Straub, 2003). Unlike commitment, trust was quite high on a relative basis for consumers in the present study (mean values: 5.73 for stayers, 3.64 for switchers). It is reasonable to speculate that consumers are well aware of the potential risk inherent in online transactions. If a consumer decides to

Table 4. Overall discriminant analysis

	Research Variable	Group Means			Wilks' Lambda	F
		Switchers (n=141)	Stayers (n=158)	Difference		
H1	COMMITMENT	2.20	4.20	2.00	0.62	178.83*
H2	TRUST	3.64	5.73	2.09	0.54	250.31*
H3	SATISFACTION	2.73	5.72	2.99	0.29	740.13*
H4	COM. LEVEL	5.25	3.18	-2.07	0.63	174.82*
H5	NONRETR. INVES.	2.87	3.68	0.81	0.92	24.37*

* $p < 0.001$; Canonical Discriminant Function: Eigenvalue = 2.6, Canonical correlation = 0.85, Wilks' Lambda = 0.278, $\chi_{(5)} = 377.44$ ($p < 0.001$)

Classification Results: Percentage correctly classified (hit ratio): Analysis Sample: 93.3%; Holdout Sample: 93%; Proportional chance criterion = 50%; Maximum chance criterion = 53%.

participate in a transaction, he or she must have a strong perception of the trustworthiness of the online business to minimize the perception of the risks.

This study has also found that stayers are more satisfied with the current online business and less aware of the comparison level of alternative online businesses, consistent with previous research (e.g., Anderson & Narus, 1990; Ganesh, Arnold & Reynolds, 2000; Keaveney & Parthasarathy, 2001). If a consumer is more satisfied with the current business, he or she may be reluctant to look for alternative Web sites. On the other hand, switchers usually are not satisfied with the current online business and thus look for alternative Web sites (and are also therefore able to evaluate the quality of alternatives). Based on the coefficient of satisfaction (Wilks' Lambda = 0.29) in the discriminant function, we conclude that satisfaction is the most important factor in discriminating switchers from stayers in online consumer markets.

Although stayers put more weight on the size of the nonretrievable investments than do switchers, the mean values of investment size (stayers = 3.68; switchers = 2.87) on a 7-point Likert scale are relatively low, suggesting that neither switchers nor stayers put a great deal of weight on their investments in Web sites. It is possible that the effect of investment size varies for different types of B2C Web sites. For example, the effect might be very high for banking or other financial sites. The fact that we pooled different types of Web sites in our empirical study may have led to a low effect for investment. However, Chen and Hitt (2002) found that when multiple factors (such as customer characteristics and firm characteristics) were modeled together with switching costs, the effect of switching costs was not significant in explaining customer switching. Thus, questions concerning the issue of investment size by online users remain.

CONCLUSION

Limitations

There are several limitations in the present study. First, this study may have omitted some important factors, such as product price, incentives, rebates, business reputation, and customer referrals, in the online business environment because the research variables were selected from an established model (Wilson, 1995). Second, we did not investigate whether there is an interaction effect between the business-to-consumer relationship and the Web site-to-consumer relationship. It is not clear whether these two types of relationships are separate or intertwined. Third, because of the specially defined sample in the current study, the generalizability of the findings may be limited. Although college students are in many ways prototypical Internet users, their behavior may be different from that of other consumers among the Internet population (e.g., Agarwal & Karahanna, 2000; Forrester Research, 2005; Gefen, Karahanna & Straub, 2003). Finally, this research utilized only respondents' subjective data rather than objective measures.

Implications for Research

The first contribution of the present study is applying the integrated buyer-seller relationship model (Wilson, 1995) to online consumer markets. The empirical results provide support for the external validity of the model in online business-to-consumer relationships. Second, the five relationship factors we investigated may be used as a classification schema of online consumers, providing a useful starting point for additional research.

An online consumer's continuous patronage of a particular Web site is arguably analogous to an IS user's continuous use of an IS. We speculate that relationship variables such as commitment and trust might be applied to IS implementation research. After adopting, adapting, accepting, and using an IS, a user may have developed a relationship orientation toward using the IS in the latter stages of IS implementation. Future studies could conduct empirical tests of the relational variables in the context of conventional IS. Future studies may also investigate whether and how an IS user develops a relationship with an IS during the IS-user interaction process.

Implications for Practice

For online companies such as Dell Computers, eBay.com, and Amazon.com, consumer retention is especially vital to their success. The results of this study, as well as some previous research, show that there is reason for considerable optimism in making Web sites sticky. Online consumers have a clear inclination toward loyalty and their behaviors are not very different from people in conventional markets. The five factor classification schema can serve as an alternative for businesses to capture the profiles of online consumers. Adopting such an approach will improve the effectiveness of businesses in retaining customers.

Consumers' commitment to online businesses is difficult to develop and is not as strong as commitment in other contexts. This suggests that it is not practical for online businesses to expect persistent and long-term relationship orientations from online consumers. However, various incentive mechanisms other than those focused on relationship building and maintenance may need to be initiated. An online business may adopt different methods to enhance its customer satisfaction level. For example, a company may use its Web site to retain, or "lock," a consumer, by keeping personal data. When people enter a significant amount of personal data at a Web site, they are typically reluctant to change vendors and enter the data again (White, 2004).

In summary, the present research has examined online consumers' switching behavior among different Web sites. Whether a consumer intends to stay with a Web site or switch to another was shown to depend on commitment, trust, satisfaction, comparison level of the alternatives, and nonretrievable investment. Future research can add additional insights into this important area of electronic commerce research.

REFERENCES

Agarwal, R., & Karahanna, E. (2000). Time flies when you're having fun: Cognitive absorption and beliefs about information technology usage. *MIS Quarterly, 24*(4), 665-694.

Anderson, J. C., & Narus, J. A. (1990). A model of distributor firm and manufacturer firm working partnerships. *Journal of Marketing, 54*(1), 42-58.

Benbasat, I., & DeSanctis, G. (2001). Communication challenges: A value network perspective. In G. W. Dickson & G. DeSanctis (Eds.), *Information technology and the future enterprise: New models for managers* (pp. 144-162). Upper Saddle River, NJ: Prentice-Hall.

Bhattacherjee, A. (2001). Understanding information systems continuance: An expectation confirmation model. *MIS Quarterly, 25*(3), 351-370.

Burnham, T. A., Frels, J. K., & Mahajan, V. (2003). Consumer switching costs: A topology, antecedents, and consequences. *Journal of the Academy of Marketing Science, 31*(2), 109-126.

Chakravarty, S., Feinberg, R., & Rhee, E. (2004). Relationships and individuals' bank switching behavior. *Journal of Economic Psychology, 25*(4), 507-527.

Chen, P. Y., & Hitt, L. M. (2002). Measuring switching costs and the determinants of customer retention in Internet-enabled businesses: A study of the online brokerage industry. *Information Systems Research, 13*(3), 255-274.

comScore. (2004). Marketers take note: The elusive 18-34 year-old is habitually online. Retrieved September 10, 2006, from http://www.comscore.com/press/release.asp?press=445

Fishbein, M., & Ajzen, I. (1975). *Belief, attitude, intention, and behavior: An introduction to theory and research.* Reading, MA: Addison-Wesley.

Flavian, C., Guinaliu, M., & Gurrea, R. (2006). The role played by perceived usability, satisfaction and consumer trust on Website loyalty. *Information & Management, 43*(1), 1-14.

Fornell, C., & Larcker, D. F. (1981). Evaluating structural equations with unobservable variables and measurement error. *Journal of Marketing Research, 18*(1), 39-50.

Forrester Research. (2005). Young consumers are the first "technology everywhere" generation. Retrieved September 10, 2006, from http://www.forrester.com/ER/Press/Release/0,1769,1051,00.html

Ganesh, J., Arnold, M. J., & Reynolds, K. E. (2000). Understanding the customer base of service providers: An examination of the differences between switchers and stayers. *Journal of Marketing, 64*(3), 65-87.

Garbarino, E., & Johnson, M. S. (1999). The different roles of satisfaction, trust, and commitment in customer relationships. *Journal of Marketing, 63*(2), 70-87.

Gefen, D., Karahanna, E., & Straub, D. (2003). Trust and TAM in online shopping: An integrated model. *MIS Quarterly, 27*(1), 51-90.

Gupta, A., Su, B., & Walter, Z. (2004). An empirical study of consumer switching from traditional to electronic channels: A purchase-decision process perspective. *International Journal of Electronic Commerce, 8*(3), 131-161.

Hair, J. F., Jr., Anderson, R. E., Tatham, R. L., & Black, W. C. (1995). *Multivariate data analysis* (4th ed.). Upper Saddle River, NJ: Prentice-Hall.

Hart, P., & Saunders, C. (1997). Power and trust: Critical factors in the adoption and use of electronic data interchange. *Organization Science, 8*(1), 23-42.

Keaveney, S. M. (1995). Customer switching behavior in service industries: An exploratory study. *Journal of Marketing, 59*, 71-82.

Keaveney, S. M., & Parthasarathy, M. (2001). Customer switching behavior in online services: An exploratory study of the role of selected attitudinal, behavioral, and demographic factors. *Journal of the Academy of Marketing Science, 29*(4), 374-390.

Meinert, D. B., Peterson, D. K., Criswell, J. R., & Crossland, M. D. (2006). Privacy policy statements and consumer willingness to provide personal information. *Journal of Electronic Commerce in Organizations, 4*(1), 1-17.

Morgan, R. M., & Hunt, S. D. (1994). The commitment-trust theory of relationship marketing. *Journal of Marketing, 58*(3), 20-38.

Park, C., & Kim, Y. (2006). The effect of information satisfaction and relational benefit on consumers' online shopping site commitments. *Journal of Electronic Commerce in Organizations, 4*(1), 70-90.

Parthasarathy, M., & Bhattacherjee, A. (1998). Understanding post-adoption behavior in the context of online services. *Information Systems Research, 9*(4), 362-379.

Pavlou, P. A. (2003). Consumer acceptance of electronic commerce: Integrating trust and risk with the technology acceptance model. *International Journal of Electronic Commerce, 7*(3), 101-134.

Pavlou, P. A., & Gefen, D. (2004). Building effective online marketplaces with institution-based trust. *Information Systems Research, 15*(1), 37-59.

Reichheld, F. F., & Schefter, P. (2000). E-loyalty: Your secret weapon on the Web. *Harvard Business Review, 78*(4), 105-113.

Rusbult, C. E., Martz, J. M., & Agnew, C. R. (1998). The investment model scale: Measuring commitment level, satisfaction level, quality of alternatives, and investment size. *Personal Relationships, 5*(4), 357-391.

White, T. B. (2004). Consumer disclosure and disclosure avoidance: A motivational framework. *Journal of Consumer Psychology, 14*(1-2), 41-52.

Wilson, D.T. (1995). An integrated model of buyer-seller relationships. *Journal of the Academy of Marketing Science, 23*(4), 335-345.

This work was previously published in Journal of Electronic Commerce in Organizations, Vol. 5, Issue 1, edited by M. Khosrow-Pour, pp. 30-42, copyright 2007 by IGI Publishing, formerly known as Idea Group Publishing (an imprint of IGI Global).

Chapter III
From High Tech to High Touch: The Effects of Perceived Touch on Online Customers' Intention to Return

Hong-Mei Chen
University of Hawaii, USA

Qimei Chen
University of Hawaii, USA

Rick Kazman
University of Hawaii, USA

ABSTRACT

Companies are competing intensively using 'high tech' systems such as electronic customer relationship management (eCRM or CRM) to interact with customers online over the Web, aiming to profit from retaining customers through "high touch." This chapter defines a new construct, Perceived Touch, and provides theoretical underpinnings for the "high touch" assumption of eCRM systems. An empirical study was conducted to examine both the cognitive and affective effects of Perceived Touch on online customers' intention to return after their initial visit in the eCRM context. While past studies of traditional information systems paid more attention to cognition than affect, the affective effect is critical to examine so that eCRM strategy and system design can be better informed. Our research results validate the antecedent role of Perceived Touch to Perceived Ease of Use (of the technology acceptance model—TAM) and further argue for the renewed importance of Attitude for user acceptance in the eCRM context. This study illuminates the significance of the affective impact of Perceived Touch on online customers' Behavioral Intention to Return through both the Affective Route and the Alternative Cognitive Route where affective effect precedes cognitive effect. Practical implications of this study are discussed.

INTRODUCTION

In the face of recent dramatic changes in the business landscape because of technology, "relationships continue to maintain their value in determining customer behavior... A business can't control the pace of technology, it can't control the economy, it certainly can't control its competitors, but it can control the way it manages interactions with its customers." (Greensburgh 2001). Electronic Customer Relationship Management (ECRM) systems are tools businesses use to maintain this control. ECRM systems are currently proliferating and being rapidly adopted by many businesses to manage customer interactions in the e- business world (Turban et al, 2006) and have become a strategic imperative for organizations to unlock customer profitability (Chen & Chen, 2004). eCRM (with a small "e") refers to ECRM primarily built for web-site interaction with customers. The important characteristics of the World Wide Web, such as its interactive structure and constant availability of information, have been shown to be central to variables of relationship marketing, such as commitment, satisfaction and trust (Peppers & Rogers, 2004; Park & Kim, 2006; Gefen, Karahanana, & Straub, 2003). Technological advances in databases, data warehousing, data mining, personalization, networking, multimedia communications, and computer-telephone integration have spurred an array of new eCRM tools that offer many new options and opportunities for direct interactive marketing, sales, and personalized customer services. Many "touch" options are available in the new generation of eCRM systems and the level of touch can vary by manipulating communication media, humanization, and interactivity aspects of the system. Touch options range from relatively "low" touch technologies such as simple 1-800 numbers, FAQs, and email, to live chat (connecting with an online agent), to relatively "high" touch technologies like desktop sharing or video conferencing with an online agent. The agent could be an embedded software agent (i.e., intelligent system agent) or a human. The goal of these eCRM systems is to achieve positive affective and cognitive impacts (e.g., toward building a relationship) with their customers to influence their behavioral intention. By being interactive, one-to-one, and personal via the high tech touch option, eCRM aims to appeal to customers' affective response in the hope that customers will have favorable attitudes toward the system. By providing information and decision aids to support customers' tasks, eCRM strives for customers' cognitive satisfaction based on their task performance.

Despite the critical strategic and operational role of eCRM systems for modern organizations, there exists little theoretical examination of eCRM touch deployment in influencing online customers' behavioral intention. The purpose of the present study is to model the distinctive routes of the affective and cognitive influence intended by eCRM systems, to empirically test whether an eCRM system's intended "touch,' as perceived by online customers, influences the customers' intention to return, and finally to provide design guidelines for manipulating such a perception to gain competitive advantage.

Although many eCRM systems are equipped to provide high touch options, it is arguable whether these options are perceived by online customers as the same level of touch *intended* by the system. In this chapter, we focus on *perceived touch*, rather than the actual level of touch deployed by the system, as we believe that the *perception* of touch received by online customers is the key determinant in their behavior intention. We therefore defined a new construct, *Perceived Touch,* as the degree to which an online customer believes they can communicate well (in a natural, real-time, bilateral, immediate, and synchronized fashion) with a web-based system when performing online tasks and how well the system can aid them in their tasks (by being responsive, understanding, affective, helpful, interactive, and flexible).

Whether an online customer's Behavioral Intention to Return is positively influenced by Perceived Touch in the eCRM context is our central research question. Behavioral intention has been extensively studied in the field of technology acceptance (Venkatesh et al., 2003) and consumer behavior (Cheung et al, 2005). Previous research in these areas has provided a basis for our investigation in the new eCRM context. In the past, technology acceptance was broadly studied in an organizational context and a vast body of literature has shown that Perceived Usefulness and Perceived Ease of Use conceptualized in the technology acceptance model (TAM) (Davis 1989) are two strong predictor of a consumer's behavior intention and actual usage of a system. Perceived Usefulness is defined as the degree to which a user believes that using a particular system would enhance his or her job performance while Perceived Ease of Use is a user's assessment that technology interaction will be relatively free of cognitive burden (Davis, 1989, p. 320). In a comprehensive review of the past five years of research on the behavior of online consumers, *attitude* which is a positive or negative feeling (evaluative affect) about performing a target behavior, was widely studied as a determinant of consumers' online purchase intention (Cheung, 2005). Decision Satisfaction—the cognitive evaluation of decision support received from the system—has been shown to influence Behavioral Intention in both Marketing and Information Systems (IS) studies (Garrity et al. 2005; Bharati & Chaudhury, 2004).

These important variables are synthesized in our research model (depicted in Figure 1). Behavioral Intention to Return is the same as Behavioral Intention to Use (Fishbein & Ajzen 1975; Ajzen 1985; Ajzen 1988) due to the duality of on-line customers as system users in the new context of eCRM. Furthermore, the model provides a distinction between cognitive and affective routes from Perceived Touch to Behavioral Intention to Return. We use *affect*—as McLeod (1987, 1991) has suggested—as an umbrella term to include emotions, feelings, preferences, beliefs, and attitudes. By contrast, cognition involves a structured reasoning process emphasizing on information transformations (Zajonc 1980, Zajonc and Markus 1982, 1984). The affective system is judgmental, assigning positive and negative valence to the environment rapidly and efficiently while the cognitive system interprets and makes sense of the world (Norman, 2002). Previous research results have primarily focused on the cognitive impact on behavioral intention, even though affective effects happens before cognitive effects and are often intertwined (Norman, 2002; Russell, 2003). Recently, Bagozzi (2007) stresses the need to strengthen the theories of the role of affect in TAM research. The design intention of eCRM systems is to build toward old-fashioned one-to-one relationships and to be a decision aid at a customer's "pleasure" to support their task. The purpose of communication, hence, is to cause an affective reaction as well as a cognitive one. The neuroimaging literature has already shown that consumer decision-making involves the orbitofrontal (cognitive area) and the amygdala (emotional area) of a consumer (Hsu, et al., 2005). Therefore, it is posited that the Behavioral Intention is jointly impacted by both affective and cognitive effects of Perceived Touch. We argue that it is particularly important to study affective impact in the present context due to the emphasis of the interactive customer "touching" aspect or affective quality embedded in eCRM systems.

The remainder of this chapter is structured as follows: Section 2 describes the conceptual foundations and hypothesis development in our research model. Section 3 details the experimental survey research method used to test this research model. Section 4 presents the results of hypothesis testing using a structured equation modeling (SEM) technique. Section 5 includes the discussion, limitations and possible explanation of the results and directions for future research.

Section 6 concludes with the study's theoretical contributions and the practical implications of the findings.

CONCEPTUAL FOUNDATION AND HYPOTHESIS DEVELOPMENT

In this section, we first provide theoretical background for eCRM applications emphasizing its affective aspect. We then define the focal construct, Perceived Touch. We further provide rationale for including four established constructs in the IS and Marketing literature: Perceived Ease of Use, Attitude Toward the System, Usefulness, and Decision Satisfaction. Finally, we present the hypotheses for the relationships in the research model.

eCRM Conceptual Background

eCRM systems strive under assertions approximating those of relationship marketing theories, even though the meaning of "relationship" may be arguable in a Web-based e-business context. "...Interactive means relationships and relationships often translate to brand loyalty" (Upshaw 1995). *Relationship generalization theory* (Crosby & Stephens 1987) posits that a relationship is a quality surrogate and that buyers generalize positive feelings about the provider to core aspects of the service which is different from *rational evaluation*. For instance, Gronoroos (1986) finds that buyers will become enamored with the interactive aspects of the service and fail to analyze price "rationally" in relation to an objective standard of core service (technical) quality.

This assertion from relationship generalization theory underlies the importance of the affective quality of an eCRM system. Schlosberg (1952) has mapped affect according to two dimensions: attention-rejection and pleasantness-unpleasantness. Essentially, pleasant things work better and are easier to use (Russell 2003). As users aren't always rational beings, affect plays an important, yet often overlooked role in user acceptance of technology (Zhang & Li, 2005). The neuroimaging literature has shown that consumer decision-making involves the orbitofrontal (cognitive area) and the amygdala (emotional area) of a consumer (Hsu, et al., 2005). The importance of affect is re-emphasized by findings from a recent study, where researchers observed that affect increases customers' tolerance of functional (i.e., techni-

Figure 1. Research model

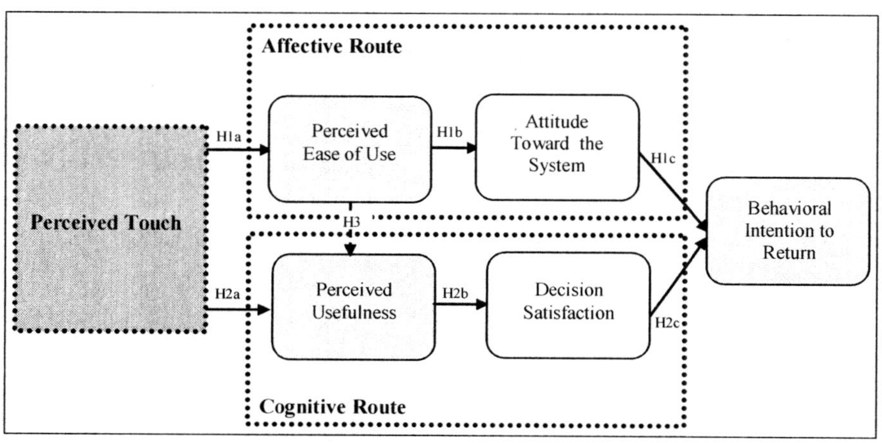

cal) problems (Barnes, Hinton & Mieczkowska, 2005).

Perceived Touch

The word "touch," although not formally defined in the Marketing or IS literature, is commonly used by businesses, practitioners in business, and academicians in textbooks (e.g. Laudon & Traver, 2004, p. 416). Perceived Touch is a customer's belief or subjective assessment of touch rendered by the eCRM system. Touch is a multi-dimensional concept which encompasses three aspects: (1) communication media characteristics (e.g., media richness), (2) the affective quality of touch options (e.g., humanization) and (3) interactivity between the online customers and the system. A rich literature exists in defining media richness in that each medium or communication channel varies in its ability to improve communication. Media can be characterized as high or low in "richness" depending on their ability to facilitate shared meaning based on four criteria: (1) the ability to give immediate feedback which generates and reinforces understanding; (2) the ability to provide multiple cues such as body gesture, voice tone, and graphical symbol; (3) the ability to provide language variety such as natural language, numbers and language symbols for precisely conveying concepts and ideas; and)4) the ability to tailor-make or personalize the communication medium (Daft et al, 1987). As to the affective quality of the touch options, the eCRM system strives to provide system stimuli or human-like touch aspects that will evoke a positive emotional response via the interaction with the online customers. The affective quality refers to the ability to cause a change in affect: feeling good/bad, like/dislike, pleasant/unpleasant, etc. This is separate from the media richness aspect which is to facilitate communication. In the eCRM context, the live or intelligent system agents (in high touch deployment) are devised as servants or assistants for online customers rather than as partners in general computer-mediated communication (CMC). Finally, interactivity distinguishes differences between the older one-to-many static model of CRM and the current one-to-one dynamic customer interaction model of eCRM. Although interactivity is viewed as a technical characteristic of the medium by some researchers (Zack, 1995), in the eCRM context what we are interested in is the perception and actual usage of interactivity functions (e.g., touch options) rather than the normative presence or absence of interactivity in the media. As mentioned, the *intended* touch level by the system is not the focus of this chapter. Our focus is on Perceived Touch which is the customers' perception of belief of touch from both affective and cognition evaluation. In general, beliefs are important not only because they influence subsequent behavior, but also because they are amenable to strategic managerial manipulation through appropriate interventions such as system design (Agarwal 2002). The purpose of our study is to offer insight for such manipulation.

Perceived Ease of Use and Perceived Usefulness (Davis, 1989)

Several theoretical models have been proposed to better understand and explain individual attitudes and behaviors of IT usage: innovation diffusion theory (Rogers 1995), the technology acceptance model (Davis 1989; Davis et al. 1989), the theory of reasoned action (Fishbein & Ajzen 1975), and the theory of planned behavior (Ajzen 1985; 1988). Despite differences among these models regarding the specific constructs and relationships posited, there is some convergence among them that individual's *beliefs* about or perceptions of IT have a significant influence on usage. Perceived Ease of Use and Perceived Usefulness are two widely studied beliefs that have a significant influence on usage behavior (Lee, Kozar, & Larsen 2003; Venkatesh, et al. 2003).

Attitude Toward the System

Attitude is defined as predisposition to respond in a particular way toward a specified class of objects (Rosenberg, 1960). It is a positive or negative feeling (evaluative affect) about performing the target behavior (Fishbein & Ajzen 1975, p. 216). This construct reflects core affect (or feelings) of favorableness or unfavorableness, toward using the system or the web-site in the eCRM context. User attitude is important because it contributes to a user's intention to use a system (Ajzen, 1988) and the user's intention is believed to be the best predictor of actual system use (Davis et al, 1989). This prediction has been validated by many technology acceptance related studies (e.g., Lee, Kozar, & Larsen, 2003; Venkatesh, 2003).

In our model, the major affective impact of Perceived Touch is posited to be mediated by Attitude Toward the System. Although the original formulation of the TAM included attitude as a construct mediating the effects of beliefs on intentions (Davis, 1989), it was subsequently dropped from the specification of the TAM due to the absence of mediation effects (Davis et al, 1989). The present study is conducted to re-examine the mediation effect of attitude in the eCRM context, given its importance today as evidenced by recent studies (e.g., Vehovar et al., 2001;Teo et al., 2003). Online customers' attitude is especially important to commercial web sites because purchase intentions resulting from online visits are found to improve as attitude toward the web site improves (Stevenson et al., 2000).

Some researchers posit that attitude is comprised of both affective and cognitive components (Perloff, 1993). However, the affective component is found to be a crucial element of Attitude. It is believed that one cannot have an attitude until she/he has some feelings about the object in question (Teo, 2003). Attitude can be based entirely on affective feelings (Oskamp, 1991). Rosenberg (1960) demonstrated that changes in the affective component can create continuing parallel changes in the cognitive component. For this reason, we model Attitude Toward the System in the Affective Route.

Decision Satisfaction

Decision Satisfaction is a cognitive evaluation of how satisfied the customer is with the decision support received from the system, including the system's ability to deliver relevant information for decision making and to improve the customer's decisions (Garrity et al. 2005). It characterizes the ability of the system to support decision-making and cognitive tasks (Bharati & Chaudhury, 2003). In the IS field, due to interest in system usage, user (decision) satisfaction has been identified as a critical IS success factor (Delone & McLean, 2003) while in the Marketing field, customer satisfaction has been identified as the key for retaining customers (Crosby, 1987; Krishnan, 1999; Haubl, 2000). Traditionally user satisfaction and customer satisfaction are two different subjective measures and are found in different domains of investigation. However, these two concepts are converging in the eCRM context because online customers *are* the system users (O'Keefe & McEachern, 1998). Specifically, eCRM tools are provided specifically to serve as decision aids (Haubl & Trifts, 2000) for online customers to meet their task goals, for example, to choose products, configure products, plan travel, etc. In this context, the assessment of online customer satisfaction is closely tied to assessing system users' Decision Satisfaction. Hence, this study focuses on the measure of customers' decision satisfaction that results from completion of a task, using the system as a decision aid.

HYPOTHESES

The hypotheses in our study are developed in three paths in our research model: Affective Route, Cognitive Route and Alternative Route. As shown in our research model, Perceived Touch is posited to influence Behavioral Intention to Return through both affective and cognitive routes, mediated through Perceived Ease of Use and Attitude Toward the System in the Affective Route and through Perceived Usefulness and Decision Satisfaction in the Cognitive Route. An Alternative Cognitive Route (Perceived Touch → Perceived Ease of Use → Perceived Usefulness → Decision Satisfaction → Behavioral Intention) is established based on the previously widely validated relationship that Perceived Ease of Use is a determinant of Perceived Usefulness (Teo 2003).

1. Affective Route Hypothesis: Perceived Touch → Perceived Ease of Use → Attitude → Behavioral Intention

H1a: *Perceived Touch has a positive effect on Perceived Ease of Use of the eCRM system.*

One practical implication of the TAM model stems from the fact that a system designer has some degree of control over Perceived Ease of Use and Perceived Usefulness (Taylor, 1995) by altering their antecedent. Although there is limited prior work examining the determinants of ease of use and usefulness, we argue that Perceived Touch has a salient influence on Perceived Ease of Use. We postulate that richer media will allow users to communicate more effectively with the system while higher humanization will enable users to perceive a more personal focus as well as immediate assistance, which will reduce their cognitive burden. A higher level of interactivity with the system indicates that users can seek consultation and assistance in performing their tasks. This is hypothesized to also reduce their cognitive effort and thus increase the perception of ease of use.

H1b: *Perceived Ease of Use has a positive effect on Attitude Toward the System*

Stemming from the theory of reasoned action (Fishbein & Ajzen 1975), Perceived Ease of Use is the determinant of Attitude in the original TAM model (Davis 1989). This study will test this relationship in the new eCRM context. It is hypothesized that the belief that the system is easy to use will evoke favorable feelings from online customers. Ease of use means that customers should require less cognitive effort and thus will have more attention to "socialize" or enjoy the interactivity with the system, particularly with a friendly and personable on-line agent.

H1c: *Attitude Toward the System has a positive effect on online customer's Behavioral Intention to Return*

As mentioned above, many studies have validated that attitude is important because it contributes to a user's intention to use a system (Ajzen, 1988) and the user's intention is believed to be the best predictor of actual system use (Davis et al, 1989). This prediction has been validated by many TAM-related studies (e.g. Lee, Kozar, & Larsen, 2003 and Venkatesh, 2003) and will be tested in the eCRM context in the present study.

2. Cognitive Route Hypothesis: Perceived Touch → Perceived Usefulness → Decision Satisfaction → Behavioral Intention

H2a: *Perceived Touch has a positive effect on Perceived Usefulness*

Perceived Usefulness is a cognitive evaluation and belief indicating whether an eCRM system actually helps in task performance. Since an eCRM system is designed to be a decision aid for the online customer, Perceived Touch is therefore hypothesized to enhance an online customer's task performance and hence has a positive effect on Perceived Usefulness. Online customers may have certain task goals that are complex and they are consciously looking for system functions to reduce their cognitive burden. When online customers have a perception of a high level of touch from the system or have a higher level of interaction with the system, they must have recognized some useful system functions that may increase their task performance.

H2b: *Perceived Usefulness has a positive effect on Decision Satisfaction*

We further hypothesize that the relationship between Perceived Touch and Decision Satisfaction is mediated through Perceived Usefulness. Humans tend to adapt their decision making strategies to specific situations and environments (Payn, 1982). Individuals can be described as cognitive misers who strive to reduce the amount of cognitive effort associated with decision making (Shugan, 1980). When online customers perceive that the system has been useful, by reducing their cognitive effort, helping them make better decisions and improving the quality of their decisions, they feel more satisfied. This requires a cognitive evaluation of touch options supporting task goals: whether they get enough information for making a decision and whether the tools were "useful" for their purpose. This is why this relationship is placed in the Cognitive Route.

H2c: *Decision Satisfaction has a positive effect on an online customer's Behavioral Intention to Return.*

The positive relationship between Decision Satisfaction and Behavioral Intention has been reported in the IS literature and the marketing literature (Anderson, Sullivan, 1993; Mittal, Kumar, Tsiros, 1999; Varki, Colgate, 2001).

Better Decision Satisfaction generated from interacting with an eCRM system that meets customers' "service expectations" (Bhattacherjee, 2001) is likely to positively impact on their Intention to Return. TAM-related studies have shown that Perceived Usefulness is the determinant of Behavioral Intention and we posit that it could be mediated through Decision Satisfaction, for the reasons stated in H2b.

3. Alternative Cognitive Route: Perceived Touch → Perceived Ease of Use → Perceived Usefulness → Decision Satisfaction → Behavioral Intention

H3: *Perceived Ease of Use has a positive effect on Perceived Usefulness*

This Alternative Cognitive Route is developed due to the "Golden Triangle Relationship" among Perceived Ease of Use, Perceived Usefulness, and Behavioral Intention (Teo et al., 2003): (1) Perceived Ease of Use → Perceived Usefulness → Behavioral Intention and (2) Perceived Ease of Use → Behavioral Intention. A number of empirical studies have affirmed the hypothesized influence of Perceived Ease of Use on Perceived Usefulness (Lee, Kozar & Larson, 2003). These relationships are supported by the notion that the lower cognitive burden imposed by a technology frees up attentional resources to focus on other matters, serving the ends of a user (Davis et al, 1989). This link establishes an Alternative Cognitive Route.

METHODOLOGY

Study Context and Sample

To empirically test the relationships implied by our research model and hypotheses we adopted an experimental survey methodology. Four tasks were designed to include a broad range of eCRM services, from routine transactional tasks for financial/tax sectors to information search for pre-purchase decision making. The tasks were: (1) a mortgage application, (2) an IRS tax withholding calculation, (3) a date movie recommendation, and (4) a mobile PC selection.[1] For each task we created a descriptive booklet that included scenarios and decision criteria. Experimental web pages were set up such that all the tasks had the same startup screen. The tasks, booklets, and the experimental systems were iteratively refined and tested in a pilot study. To increase the variance of the perceived touch, subjects in each task randomly received either low or high touch eCRM services: the low touch treatment was equipped with product information, a search engine, a FAQ, chat, and an email address for Q&A; the high touch treatment was additionally equipped with professional human agents via a commercial collaborative eCRM system (WebArrow, 2006).

These four different tasks were then randomly assigned to the subjects. These subjects were recruited, promised a cash compensation of $10 upon completion, scheduled for an one-hour session, and directed to go to one of the experimental rooms (either connected to a live agent using the eCRM system or not), and to use the computer equipment there to access and complete a randomly assigned task. They were also instructed to fill out the survey as completely as possible. 256 business school undergraduate students at a major state university participated in the study; 2 were dropped due to incompletion, leaving a total sample size of 254. Among them, 58% were females and 42% were males. The majority of them (91%) were in the age range 20-35. All of the subjects used computers regularly, and they spent an average of 11.64 hours on the Internet every week. Among all the subjects, 18% identified themselves as having used online customer services (live agents with VoIP and screen sharing) before. These subjects seem to have had "so so" experiences with these eCRM systems (n=46; M=4.83). The subjects, on average, however were very confident about their comfort level (n=252; M=6.15), knowledge (n=252; M=5.31), and familiarity (n=252; M=5.58) with the Internet.

The agents in the experimental system (most of them Business School graduate students) were all extensively trained and well-versed in the task-related eCRM services, so they could help subjects navigate and point them to the right information while talking to them. All agents were trained in the four tasks and in the use of the commercial collaborative eCRM system. The agents were given a script for answering the most frequently asked questions. Via the collaborative system, the agents were able to interact with subjects via VoIP or text chat. In addition, desktop sharing technology allowed the agents to see the customers' screens. An agent could also take direct control of the customer's mouse or keyboard to indicate where to find information or to show search results requested by the customer. Being decision *aids*, the agents were not allowed to tell the subjects "answers" or to correct wrong answers (which the agents could plainly see) unless the subjects specifically asked for help.

For example, Figure 2 shows a typical display that an agent would see. The commercial collaborative eCRM system is running (as indicated by the meeting control window in the upper right-hand corner of the display) and this shows that there are three active services: VoIP (as indicated by the icon), desktop sharing/viewing (as indicated by the and icons), and chat (as indicated by the icon). In the desktop viewer window, the agent is able to see exactly what the subject is seeing (and doing). In the example shown in Figure 2, the subject is working through a withholding calculation on the IRS's web-site.

The agents were thus able to talk with the subjects freely and saw what they were doing in real time as though they were sitting side by side. In addition, via the desktop viewer window the agent was also able to take direct control of the subject's mouse or keyboard, if requested. The agents would do this to show the subjects where to find information or to indicate new information, such as search results requested by the subjects.

Figure 2. An example agent view

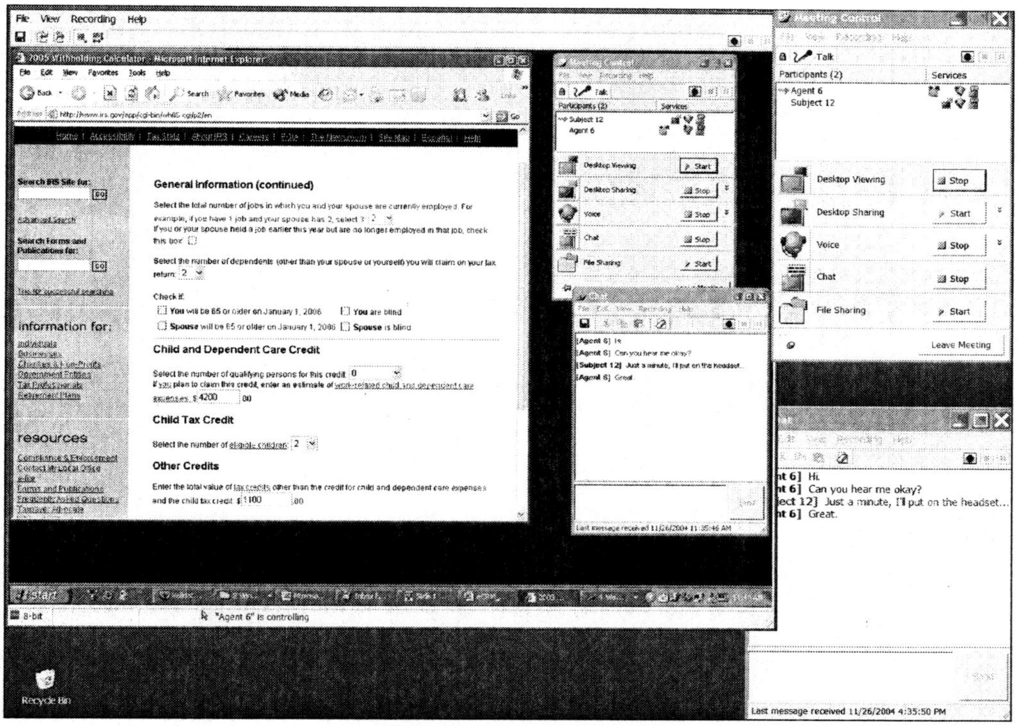

Operationalization of Variables

The major exogenous variable is Perceived Touch. As Perceived Touch is conceptualized as encompassing aspects such as media richness, humanization and interactivity between the online customers and the system, a revised media richness scale (Dennis and Kinney, 1998) was used to emphasize humanization and interactivity (Jee and Lee, 2002; Li, Kuo and Russell, 1999). Hence, different levels of touch in the experiment survey were designed to increase variance of these two constructs in the users' perception. The focal set of variables of interest in this study is not the manipulated treatment, but Perceived Touch. We hence adopted the perceived touch scale as a continuous perception construct in our analysis which is preferred over dichotomizing them into treatment levels when dealing with predictor variables (Irwin and McClelland, 2003). Perceived Touch was then captured with 5 media richness items asking whether the user "could easily explain things using the system," whether "the communication conditions helped [him/her] communicate quickly," whether he/she "couldn't easily communicate some ideas because of the communication conditions," whether "the communication condition helped [him/her] effectively with [his/her] task"; and whether "the system slowed down communication" (Dennis and Kinney, 1998); and 5 humanization/interactivity items asking whether "interacting with this system like having a conversation with a sociable, knowledgeable and warm representative from the company," whether the user "felt as if this system talked back to [him/her] while [he/she] was navigating," whether "[he/she] perceived the system to be sensitive to [his/her] needs for information," whether "[his/her] interaction level with the system was high," and whether "[he/she] doesn't interact with the system much" (Jee and Lee, 2002; Li, Kuo and Russell, 1999).

Five endogenous constructs were included in the causal model: perceived ease of use, perceived usefulness, decision satisfaction, attitude toward the system, and behavioral intention to return.

Perceived Ease of Use was captured, based on a measure used by (Taylor and Todd, 1995), on a two-item, seven point Likert-type scale. The scales ask respondents whether it was difficult to learn how to use this system and whether it was easy to operate the equipment in this system.

Perceived Usefulness was measured by a four-item seven-point scale similar to (Taylor and Todd, 1995). The scale asked respondents whether the system would be of no benefit to them; whether using the system would improve their performance; whether the advantages of this system would outweigh the disadvantages; and whether overall using the system would be advantageous.

Decision Satisfaction was measured by a three-item, seven-point scale anchored by "definitely disagree" and "definitely agree" similar to Sanders (1984). The scales ask respondents whether the utilization of the system has: enabled them to make better decisions; made more relevant information

Table 1. Means, standard deviations, and standardized loadings for the exogenous and endogenous measures

Construct	Item		M	SD	Loadings
Perceived Touch (α=.88)	1.	I could easily explain things using the system	4.85	1.52	.53
	2.	The communication conditions helped me communicate quickly	4.76	1.60	.65
	3.	The communication condition helped me effectively with my task	4.59	1.50	.64
	4.	Interacting with this system is like having a conversation with a sociable, knowledgeable and warm representative from the company	4.21	1.75	.82
	5.	I felt as if this system talked back to me while I was navigating	3.91	1.74	.73
	6.	I perceive the system to be sensitive to my needs for information	4.47	1.59	.86
	7.	My interaction level with the system was high	4.45	1.67	.73
Ease of Use (r=.63)	1.	It was difficult to learn how to use this system.	2.82	1.59	-.47
	2.	It was easy to operate the equipment in this system.	5.30	1.60	.41
Usefulness (α=.87)	1.	The system will be of no benefit to me.	2.81	1.54	-.59
	2.	Using the system will improve my performance.	4.92	1.37	.78
	3.	The advantages of the system will outweigh the disadvantages.	5.23	1.30	.92
	4.	Overall, using the system will be advantageous.	5.35	1.36	.94
Attitude Toward the System (α=.92)	1.	Using the eCRM system is a good idea	5.72	1.30	.90
	2.	Using the eCRM system is a wise idea	5.51	1.33	.79
	3.	I like the idea of using the eCRM system.	5.44	1.33	.91
	4.	Using eCRM would be (pleasant, unpleasant)	5.30	1.42	.84
Decision Making Satisfaction (α=.94)	1.	Utilization of the system has enabled me to make better decision.	4.98	1.48	.93
	2.	The system has improved the quality of decisions I made.	4.84	1.49	.94
	3.	As a result of the system, the speed at which I analyze decisions has increased.	4.81	1.54	.84
	4.	As a result of the system, more relevant information has been available to me for decision making.	5.00	1.43	.89
Behavioral Intention (α=.91)	1.	I intend to use the system to fulfill similar task.	4.84	1.58	.94
	2.	I intend to use the system in the future.	4.90	1.59	.96
	3.	I intend to use the system frequently.	4.04	1.61	.74

Note: All constructs were measured on a 7-point scale where 7 represents greatest agreement with the statement.

available to them for decision making; and improved the quality of decisions they made.

Attitude Toward the System Usage was captured using a four-item, seven-point Likert scale similar to (Taylor & Todd, 1995). The first three items state: (1) Using the eCRM system is a good idea, (2) Using the eCRM system is a wise idea, (3) I like the idea of using the eCRM system. Responses were recorded on a one-to-seven scale, with the endpoints labeled "definitely disagree" and "definitely agree". The last item asks the respondent "Using the eCRM system would be unpleasant (1) or pleasant (7).

Behavioral Intention to Return was captured by a three-item, seven point scale anchored by "definitely disagree" and "definitely agree" similar to (Taylor & Todd, 1995). This scale measures respondents' future intentions to use the system: (1) to fulfill similar tasks; (2) in the future; and (3) frequently.

The means, standard deviations, reliability alpha and standardized loadings for the exogenous and endogenous variable measures are provided in Table 1. Convergent validity and reliability tests were then conducted for the instrument. Based on the steps proposed by Straub (1989), convergent validity is fathomed by the item-to-total correlation. Items with item-to-total correlation score lower than .40 were dropped from further analysis (Park & Kim, 2006) thus reducing Perceived Touch from a ten to a seven item scale. Further, as measures of all six constructs are derived from existing IS literature, as a result of our extensive literature review, content validity was thus achieved. Next, we conducted the confirmatory factor analysis to investigate the distinctions among the four constructs. As shown in Table 1, all but four factor loadings for six constructs were greater than 0.60. However, all estimates are significant at $p<.001$. Discriminate validity was hence supported. Finally, the internal consistency reliability was captured by the Cronbach alpha coefficient (Straub, 1989). As shown in Table 1, reliability alphas were acceptable for all constructs, ranging from .92 for attitude toward system usage to .63 for ease of use—all were higher than 0.6, the lowest acceptable limit for Cronbach's alpha suggested by (Hair et al., 1998).

RESULTS

The hypothesized paths in the research model described earlier (Figure 1) were tested using Amos 5.0 with maximum likelihood estimation. Overall the fit index suggest a good fit between our proposed research model and the data (χ^2=435.823; df=234; p=0.000; χ^2/df=1.862; GFI=.877 AGFI=.877; NFI=.922, TLI=.955, CFI=.962, RMSEA=.059). Although the χ^2 statistic is significant, it is not always the best indication of model fit (e.g., Bagozzi and Yi, 1988; Mulaik et al., 1989) since it has the drawback of being sensitive to sample size and the number of parameters in the model (Bentler & Bonett, 1980). The alternative fit indices—(a) the goodness-of-fit index (GFI), which outperformed other alternative indices in a study by Marsh et al. (1988), (b) the adjusted goodness-of-fit index (AGFI), which adjusts the GFI for degrees of freedom, (c) (Steiger, 1990) root mean square error of approximation (RMSEA), which is recommended by (Browne & Cudeck, 1993)—are all within the ranges suggestive of a reasonably good fit. The regression estimate for each hypothesized path is detailed in Table 2. Specifically, H1a, b and c are supported; H2a is not supported while H2b and c are supported. Finally, H3 is supported. Figure 3 displays the final analytical model showing the paths found to be significant.

Hence, the results demonstrate that the effect of Perceived Touch is completely mediated by Perceived Ease of Use and ultimately impacts on the eCRM users' Behavior Intention to Return through both the affective route as well as the cognitive route. The *direct* path from Attitude to Behavioral Intention to Return suggests the important roles that affect might play in predict-

Table 2. Structural equation model results[a]

Structural Path			Estimate	Standardized Estimate	S.E.	C.R.	P	Conclusion
Perceived Touch	→	Perceived Ease of Use	.515	.857	.083	6.179	.000	H1a supported.
Perceived Ease of Use	→	Attitude toward Usage	1.564	.921	.214	7.299	.000	H1b supported.
Attitude Toward System	→	Behavioral Intention	.552	.442	.083	6.660	.000	H1c supported.
Perceived Touch	→	Perceived Usefulness	.031	.040	.131	.239	.811	H2a not supported.
Perceived Usefulness	→	Decision Satisfaction	1.294	.865	.142	9.116	.000	H2b supported.
Decision Satisfaction	→	Behavioral Intention	.492	.451	.072	6.825	.000	H2c supported.
Perceived Ease of Use	→	Perceived Usefulness	1.202	.924	.297	4.043	.000	H3 supported.

[a] *Fit index are as follows: (GFI=.877 AGFI=.877; NFI=.922, TLI=.955, CFI=.962, RMSEA=.059, χ^2=435.823; df=234; p=0.000; χ^2/df=1.862)*

Figure 3. Significant estimates in final model

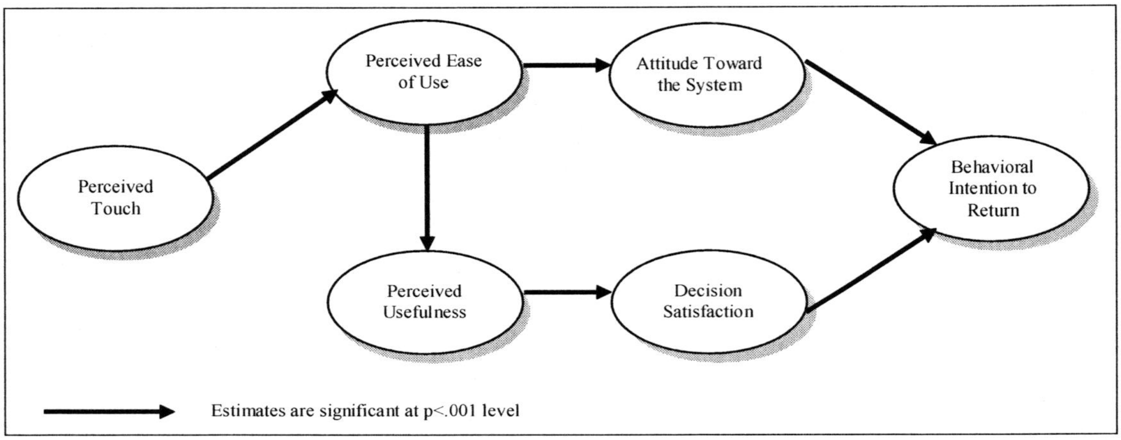

ing behavioral outcomes. Identification of this significant path argues for the future inclusion of the Attitude construct to the TAM in the eCRM context.

DISCUSSION

Our model illuminates the importance of the affective impact of Perceived Touch. In our results, Perceived Touch is found to be a significant antecedent to Perceived Ease of Use as hypothesized but *not* to Perceived Usefulness. The cognitive effect is through the Alternative Cognitive Route in which the effect is mediated through Perceived Ease of Use from Perceived Touch to Perceived Usefulness. Although no amount of ease of use will compensate for low usefulness, in the current e-business world online customers will not use a system if it is not perceived as easy to use. This indicates that the affective effect may have to take place first, before the cognitive effect. This finding is consistent with previous results (Norman 2002, Russell 2003). Further, according to our results, the system should be appealing to the customers' affect for online customers to perceive it as easy to use. We conjecture that this result may be influenced by the fact that going online is a way of life for most people in the last five years[2] and online customers generally have a high expectation of system ease of use which must be met as a gateway for cognitive elaboration (of usefulness of the system) to incur.

This study supports previous TAM work but takes it in a new direction. That Perceived Ease of Use acts as a significant antecedent to Perceived Usefulness in the eCRM context is in line with what the TAM predicts. One explanation is that there may be an inherent expectation (by online customers) of ease of use that is separate from the utilitarian aspect of the system (e.g., usefulness) and must be achieved by the eCRM system. In fact, 69 of 101 previous TAM studies found a significant link between Perceived Ease of Use and Perceived Usefulness, depending on the context (Lee, Kozar, & Larsen, 2003). Our study adds to the previous studies (and also adds data from a new generation of users in the age range of 20 to 35) and shows that in the context of eCRM the mediating effect of Perceived Ease of Use between Perceived Touch and Perceived Usefulness is critical. Our finding also showed that Perceived Touch's affective impact on Behavioral Intention is mediated by Attitude Toward the System. The significant mediating effect of Attitude found in our study is contrary to most of the prior TAM related studies where the mediating effect was found not significant. Our finding resonates a recent study revisiting the important role of attitude in TAM (Yang & Yoo, 2004) and validates the increasing importance of attitude in Electronic Commerce (Vehovar et al, 2001, Teo et al. 2003).

Furthermore, the importance of perceived affective quality was previously established as the determinant of Perceived Ease of Use and Perceived Usefulness (Zhang and Li, 2005). Our results establish the antecedent effect of Perceived Touch to Perceived Ease of Use. We conjecture that the difference in findings regarding Perceived Usefulness lies in the context: eCRM tasks demand actual decision support from the system and thus the cognitive evaluation of touch options are not as simple as, for instance, evaluating the appearance of a web page. More investigations are needed to understand the multi-dimensional complexity (e.g., media richness, affective quality or humanization, and interactivity) of Perceived Touch and whether these underlying dimensions can be separated and whether they influence variables in the affective and cognitive routes differently or independently.

Limitations

Several limitations in this study need to be pointed out. First, our study is limited due to the inherent nature of the experimental survey where internal validity is high but the results cannot be easily generalized to other contexts beyond the eCRM experimental set up. Our study is also limited by the laboratory setup for the experimental system and the fact that our subjects are college students. Even though we strongly believe the age group of subjects, 20 to 35, is the group that is currently most immersed in the e-business world, the generalization of our findings is nonetheless limited. We also found this group of subjects may not be representative regarding their limited experience with real-world eCRM tasks and technology. As the eCRM touch technologies used—desktop sharing, VoIP, etc.—were quite new at the time of the study, the results may not generalize to more experienced eCRM customers. Second, ideally, one would measure actual customer return by observing customers over time. Such a longitudinal study is difficult to realize and to control. Our study, therefore, used customer *intention* to return, not actual return visits, to measure this outcome. Future research may want to use both longitudinal and objective measures to validate the findings from the present study. Third, as one of the endogenous constructs, ease of use (r=.63) has reliabilities lower than 0.8 (Nunnally, 1978), further refinement of this construct is warranted in future research. Finally, this research only offers one plausible network of relationships for Perceived Touch in three different paths. While others might propose alternative causal pathways, we present theoretical arguments supporting the proposed paths and subsequently present data from our experimental survey in support of these relationships. Thus, our goal is not theory testing *per se* to establish whether one model is more powerful than another; rather, we seek to examine the possible consequences of Perceived Touch, integrating and extending the understanding of existing theories in IS and Marketing to the eCRM context.

Future Research

This study serves as a starting point for further research. While emphasizing the affective impact of Perceive Touch, which has been lacking in previous research, the labeling of the affective and cognitive route is more for conceptual distinction than scientific differentiation. When discussing affect and cognition, the complexity lies in the individual's traits or personality or preferences, demographics, gender, ethnicity or cultural background. This is a topic we are currently researching, exploring a Person-Touch fit model that matches different persons with different touch options. Furthermore, different eCRM applications can be used to attract, interact with, or retain customers. This study focused on providing understanding only in customer interaction applications. The customer relationship building issue for retaining customers is not addressed in this study as we only tested a one-time encounter. There are important variables such as commitment (Park & Kim, 2006) and trust (Gefen, Karahanana, & Straub, 2003) that will need to be explored to fully understand relationship building and customer retention in the eCRM context. Companies, however, have started to realize that, in the digital economy, competitors are just a click away. Initial adoption by consumers is a critical first step toward overall success (Cheung, 2005). Although this study contributes to understanding the effect of Perceived Touch on online customers' intention to return at the first encounter, further longitudinal study may provide insights as to how customers are retained over time and can test the loyalty effect (Smith, 2000) or the effect on the continuance behavior (Bhattacherjee, 2001) of Perceived Touch.

Finally, this study did not investigate *why* online customers came to the site or how they were attracted to the site. Our model cannot distinguish a planned or unplanned first visit. Perhaps the visitors were brought to the site by eCRM target marketing effort via a segmentation technology (Albert, Goes & Gupta, 2004) or by the brand image, or by referral, or by search engine results. This is an interesting research question calling for future investigation.

CONCLUSION

Drawing on theories in technology acceptance and online consumer behavior, the present study distinguishes the affective and cognitive paths where Perceived Touch impacts on online customers' intention to return in the eCRM context. It provides a theoretical underpinning for the central proposition underlying eCRM system design rationale where touch options with rich media, humanized features, and interactivity can be manipulated to increase affective and cognitive impacts on customers' intention to return. This study hence contributes theoretically in several ways: first, it defines an important new construct, Perceived Touch, for studying online customers' behavioral intention in the eCRM context; second, it provides empirical evidence that Perceived Touch positively influences online customers' Behavior Intention to Return via the Affective Route (Perceived Touch → Perceived Ease of Use → Attitude → Behavioral Intention) and the Alternative Cognitive Route (Perceived Touch → Perceived Ease of Use → Perceived Usefulness → Decision Satisfaction → Behavioral Intention); third, it establishes Perceived Touch as a salient antecedent to Perceived Ease of Use, but not directly to Perceived Usefulness, in the eCRM context, indicating the importance of affective impact; forth, this study demonstrates that the behavioral outcome of customer return is determined jointly by affective and cognitive determinants; finally, the results renewed the importance of an affective construct, *Attitude Toward the System,* as a mediating variable for Perceived Touch to predict Behavioral Intention in the eCRM context.

This new predictor, Perceived Touch, is more fundamental as it has a positive impact on well-known predictors for behavior intention, such as perceived ease of use, attitude, perceived usefulness, and decision satisfaction. Our results suggest a strong practical consideration for eCRM system designers or e-business managers: to deploy customer touch applications with increased Perceived Touch that would particularly influence perceived ease of use as it is the key determinant for attitude and decision satisfaction and in turn directly impacts on an e-customer's intention to return. It is essential to provide media rich touch options with affective quality that can provoke positive affective responses to influence attitude and behavioral intention, as our research results suggest. These touch options could include intelligent system agents or a human agents who can get "personal" and "social" with customers and can provide synchronized, immediate, natural feedback for task-specific decision support. Appealing to the customers' positive affective response can make online customers see the system as easy to use through both the Affective Route (Perceived Touch → Perceived Ease of Use → Attitude → Behavioral Intention) or the Alternative Cognitive route (Perceived Touch → Perceived Ease of Use → Perceived Usefulness → Decision Satisfaction → Behavioral Intention). Our results hence caution eCRM system designers against putting too much emphasis on technically sophisticated system functions which may not be pleasing to customers in their first encounter with the web site. This suggests that e-business managers should invest in the design and evaluation of the users' perception of touch options to be deployed and pay special attention to affective quality manipulation. The positive feelings toward the system are likely to be generalized to other aspects of the core service, as theorized by Relationship Marketing researchers and validated by the present study.

REFERENCES

Adams, D.A., Nelson, R.R., & Todd, P.A. (1992). Perceived Usefulness, Ease of Use, and Usage of Information Technology: A Replication. *MIS Quarterly*, 16(2), 227-247.

Agarwal, R., & Venkatesh, V. (2002). Assessing a firm's web presence: a heuristic evaluation procedure for the measurement of usability. Information Systems Research 13, 168–186.

Ajzen, I. (1985). From Intentions to Actions: A Theory of Planned Behavior. in *Action Control: From Cognition to Behavior*, Kuhl, J., & Beckmann, J., Editors. Springer Verlag, New York, 11-39.

Ajzen, I. (1988). *Attitudes, Personality, and Behavior.* Chicago, IL: The Dorsey Press.

Albert, T.C., Goes, P.B., & Gupta, A. (2004). GIST: A Model for Design and Management of Content and Interactivity of Customer-Centric Web Sites. *MIS Quarterly*, 28(2), 161-182.

Anderson, E.W., & Sullivan, M.W. (1993). The antecedents and consequences of customer satisfaction for firms, *Marketing Science* 12(2), 125--143.

Arbuckle, J.L. (1999). *Amos* [Computer Software]. Small Waters: Chicago.

Arbuckle, J.L., & Wothke, W. (1999). *Amos 4.0 User's Guide*. Small Waters: Chicago.

Barnes D., Hinton, M, Mieczkowska. (2005). Enhancing Customer Service Operations in E-business: The Emotional Dimension. *Journal of Electronic Commerce in Organizations*. 3(2), 17-33.

Bagozzi, R.P. (2007). "The Legacy of the Technology Acceptance Model and a Proposal for a Paradigm Shift," *Journal of the Association of Information Systems*), 8, 244-254.

Bagozzi, R.P., & Yi, Y. (1988). On the Evaluation of Structural Equation Models. *Journal of the Academy of Marketing Science*, 16, 74-94.

Bentler, P.M., & Bonnet, D.G. (1980). Significance tests and goodness of fit in analysis of covariance structures. *Psychological Bulletin*, 88, 588-606.

Bharati, P. and A. Chaudhury (2004). An Empirical Investigation of Decision-Making Satisfaction in Web-Based Decision Support Systems, *Decision Support Systems*, 37(2), 187-197.

Bhattacherjee A. (2001), Understanding Information Systems Continuance: An Expectation-Confirmation Model, MIS Quarterly, 25(3), 351- 370.

Browne, M. W. & Cudeck, R. (1993). Alternative ways of assessing model fit. In: Bollen, K. A. & Long, J. S. (Eds.) *Testing Structural Equation Models*, Beverly Hills, CA: Sage, 136-162.

Byrne, B.M. (1989). *A Primer of LISREL*. New York: Springer-Verlag.

Chen, Q., & Chen, H.M. (2004). Exploring the Success Factors of eCRM Strategies in Practice. *Journal of Database Marketing & Customer Strategy Management*, 11(4), 333-343.

Cheung, C., Chan, G., & Limayem, M. (2005). A Critical Review of Online Consumer Behavior: Empirical Research. *Journal of Electronic Commerce in Organizations*, 3(4), 1-19.

Crosby, L.A., & Stephens, N. (1987). Effects of Relationship Marketing on Satisfaction, Retention and Prices in the Life Insurance Industry. *Journal of Marketing Research*. 24, 404-411.

Daft, R.L., Lengel, R. H., & Trevino L. K. (1987). Message Equivocality, Media Selection and Manager Performance. *MIS Quarterly*, 11, 355-364.

Davis, F.D. (1989). Perceived Usefulness, Perceived Ease of Use, and User Acceptance of Information Technology. *MIS Quarterly*, 13(3), 319-340.

Davis, F.D., Bagozzi, R.P., & Warshaw, P.R. (1989). User Acceptance of Computer Technology: A Comparison of Two Theoretical Models. *Management Science*, 35(8), 982-1003.

DeLone, W.H., McLean, E. R (2003). The Delone and McLean Model of Information Systems Success: A ten-year Update. *Journal of Management Information Systems*. 19, 4, 9-30.

Dennis, A.R., & Kinney, S. T. (1998). Testing Media Richness Theory in the New Media: The Effects of Cues, Feedback, and Task Equivocality. *Information Systems Research*, 9(3), 256-274.

Douglas, S.P., Morrin, M.A., & Craig, C.S. (1994). Cross-national consumer research traditions. In G. Laurent, G. Lilien, & B. Bras (Eds.), *Research traditions in marketing*. Boston: Kluwer.

El-Shinnawy, M., & Markus, M. (1997). The poverty of media richness theory: explaining people's choice of electronic mail vs voice mail. *International Journal of Human-Computer Studies*, 46(4), 443-467.

Fishbein, M., & Ajzen, I. (1975). *Belief, Attitude, Intention and Behavior: An Introduction to Theory and Research*. Reading, MA: Addison-Wesley.

Garrity, E. J., Glassberg, B., Kim, Y. J., Sanders, G. L., & Shin, S. (2005). An experimental investigation of web-based information systems success in the context of electronic commerce. *Decision Support Systems,* 39(3), 485-503.

Gerbing, D.W., & Anderson, J.C. (1988). An Updated Paradigm for Scale Development Incorporating Unidimensionality and Its Assessment. *Journal of Marketing Research*, 25, 186-92.

Greenberg, P. *CRM at the speeed of light: capturing & keeping customers in Internet Real Time.* New York, NY: Osborne/McGraw-Hill, 2001.

Gefen, D., Karahanana, E. and Straub D (2003). "Trust and TAM in Online Shopping: An Integrated Model. *MIS Quarterly 27*(1), pp. 51-90.

Hair Jr., J. F., Anderson, R. F., Tatham, R. L., & Black, W. C. (1998). *Multivariate data analysis* (5th ed.). Upper Saddle River, NJ: Prentice-Hall.

Haubl, G., & Trifts, V. (2000). Consumer Decision Making in Online Shopping Environments: The Effects of Interactive Decision Aids. *Marketing Science*, 19(1), 4-21.

Hsu, M., Bhatt, M., Adolphs, R., Tranel, D., and Camerer, C.F. (2005) "Neural Systems Responding to Degrees of Uncertainty in Human Decision-Making.," *Science* (310:5754),, pp. 1680-1683.

Irwin, JR, & McClelland, GH (2003). Negative consequences of dichotomizing continuous predictor variables. Journal of Marketing Research, 40(3), 366-371

Jee, J., & Lee, W-N. (2002). Antecedents and Consequences of Perceived Interactivity: An Exploratory Study. *Journal of Interactive Advertising,* 3(1), Retrieved from http://jiad.org/vol3/no1/jee/index.htm.

Joreskog, K. (1971). Statistical Analysis of Sets of Congeneric Tests. *Psychometrika*, 36, 109-133.

Joreskog, K., & Sorbom, D. (1988). *LISREL 1: A Guide to the Program and Applications.* SPSS: Chicago.

Karahanna, E., & Straub, D.W. (1999). The Psychological Origins of Perceived Usefulness and Ease of Use. *Information and Management*, 35(4), 237-250.

Koufaris, M. (2002). Applying the Technology Acceptance Model and Flow Theory to Online Customer Behavior. *Information Systems Research*, 13(2), 205-223.

Krishnan, M.S., Ramaswamy, V., Meyer, M. C., & Damien, P. (1999). Customer Satisfaction for Financial Services: The Role of Products, Services, and Information Technology. *Management Science*, 45(9), 1194-1209.

Lee, Y., Kozar, K.A., & Larsen, K.R.T. (2003). The Technology Acceptance Model: Past, Present, and Future. *Communications of the Association for Information Systems*, 12(5), 752-780.

Li, H., Kuo, C., & Russell, M. G. (1999). The Impact of Perceived Channel Utilities, Shopping Orientations, and Demographics on the Consumer's Online Buying Behavior. *Journal of Computer Mediated Communication*, 5(2), 1-20.

McLeod, S. (1991). The Affective Domain and the Writing Process: Working Definitions. *Journal of Advanced Composition* 11, 95-105.

McLeod, S. (1987). Some Thoughts about Feelings The Affective Domain and the Writing Process. *College Composition and Communication* 38, 426-35.

Markus, M.L., Tora, K.B., Shinnawy, M., & Louise, L.S. (1993). Fragments of your communication: email, vmail, and fax. *Information Society*, 8, 207-226.

Marsh, H.W., Balla, J.R., & McDonald, R.P. (1988). Goodness-of-fit-indexes in confirmatory factor analysis: The effect of sample size. *Psychological Bulletin*, 103(March), 391-411.

Matsumoto, D. (1989). Cultural Influences on the Perception of Emotion. *Journal of Cross-Cultural Psychology*, 20(March), 92-105.

Mittal, V., Kumar, P., & Tsiros, M. (1999). Attribute-level performance satisfaction, and behavioral intentions over time: a consumption-system approach, *Journal of Marketing* 63 (2), 88– 101.

Morris, M., & Peng, K. (1994). Culture and Cause: American and Chinese Attributions for Social and Physical Events. *Journal of Personality and Social Psychology*. 67(December), 971.

Mulaik, S.A., James, L.R., Van Alstine, J., Bennett, N., Lind, S., & Stilwell, C.D. (1989). Evaluation of Goodness-of-Fit Indices for Structural Equation Models. *Psychological Bulletin*, 105, 430-445.

Norman, D.A. (2002). Emotion and design: Attractive things work better. *Interactions: New Visions of Human-Computer Interaction IX*, 4, 36–42.

Nunnally, J.C. (1978). *Psychometric Theory*. New York: McGraw-Hill Inc.

O'Keefe, R.M., McEachern T. (1998). Web-based customer Decision Support Systems, *Communications of the ACM*, 41(3), 71– 78.

Oskamp, S. (1991). Attitudes and Opinions. 2nd ed. Englewood Cliffs, NJ: Prentice-Hall.

Park, CH., & Kim, YG. (2006). The Effect of Information Satisfaction and Relational Benefit on Consumers' Online Shopping Site Commitments, *Journal of Electronic Commerce in Organizations*. 4(1), 70-91.

Payne, J.W. (1982). Contingent decision behavior, Psychological Bulletin 92(2), 382– 402.

Perloff, R.M. (1993). *The Dynamics of Persuasion*. Hillsdale, NJ: Lawrence Erlbaum and Associates.

Peppers, D. & Rogers, M. (2004), *Managing Customer Relationship: A Strategic Framework*. Hoboken, New Jersey: John Wiley & Sons, Inc.,

Pew Internet Project. (2005). http://www.pewinternet.org/pdfs/PIP_Future_of_Internet.pdf

Rafaeli, S. (1988). Interactivity: from new media to communication. in *Advancing communication science: merging mass and interpersonal processes*, R.P. Hawkins, Wieman, J.M., Pingree, S., Editor. Sage Perceived Usefulnessblications: Newbury Park, CA. pp. 110-134.

Rafaeli, S., & Sudweeks, F. (1997). Networked Interactivity. *Journal of Computer Mediated Communication*, 2(4).

Rice, R.E., & Shook, D.E. (1988). Access to, usage of and outcomes from electronic messaging. *ACM Transactions on Office Information Systems*, 6, 255-276.

Rogers, E. M. (1995). *Diffusion of Innovations* (4th ed.), The Free Press, New York.

Rosenberg, M.J. (1960). An analysis of affective-cognitive consistency. in *Attitude Organization and Change*, C.I. Hovland, Rosenberg, M.J., Editor. Yale University Press: New Haven, CT. pp. 15-64.

Russell, J.A. (2003). Core affect and the psychological construction of emotion. *Psychological Review* 110, 1, 145–172.

Sanders, G.L. (1984). MIS/DSS Success Measure. *Systems, Objectives, Solutions*, 4, 29-34.

Short, J., Williams, E., & Christie, B. (1976). *The Social Psychology of Telecommunications*. London: Wiley.

Singelis, T.M. (1994). The Measurement of Independent and Interdependent Self-Construals. *Personality and Social Psychology Bulletin*, 20(October), 580-591.

Singelis, T.M., Bond, M.H., Sharkey, W.F., & Lai, C. (1999). Unpacking Culture's Influence on Self-Esteem and Embarrassability. *Journal of Cross-Cultural Psychology*, 30(3), 315-341.

Schlosberg, H. (1952). The Description of Facial Expressions in Terms of Two Dimensions. *Journal of Experimental Psychology* (44), 229-237.

Shugan, S.M. (1980). The cost of thinking, *Journal of Consumer Research* 7(2), 99–111.

Smith, E. R (2000). e-Loyalty: How to keep Customers coming back to your website. NY, NY: HarperCollins Publishers Inc.

Soe, L.L., & Markus, M.L. (1993). Technological or social utility? Unraveling explanations of email, vmail, and fax use. *Information Society*, 9(3), 213-236.

Sproull, L., Subramani, M., Kiesler S., Walker J., & Waters, K. (1997). When the Interface Is a Face. in *Human Values and the Design of Computer Technology*, CSLI Lecture Notes, No. 72, B. Friedman, Editor. Cambridge University Press: Stanford, CA. pp. 163-190.

Straub, D. W. (1989). Validating instruments in MIS research. *MIS Quarterly*, 13(2), 147-169.

Steiger, J.H. (1990). Structural model evaluation and modification: An interval estimation approach. *Multivariate Behavioral Research*, 25(April), 173-180.

Stevenson, J.S., Bruner, G.C., Kumar, A. (2000). Webpage background and viewer attitudes. *Journal of Advertising Research* 40, 29–34.

Vehovar, V., Manfreda, K.L., Batagelj, Z. (2001). Sensitivity of Electronic Commerce Measurement to the Survey Instrument. *International Journal of Electronic Commerce* 6, 31–51.

Taylor, S., & Todd, P. A. (1995). Understanding Information Technology Usage: A Test of Competing Models. *Information Systems Research*, 6(23), 144-176.

Teeni, D. (2001). Review: A Cognitive-Affective Model of Organizational Communication For Designing IT. *MIS Quarterly*, 25(2), 251-312.

Teo, H.-H., Oha, L-B, Liua, C., & Wei, K-K. (2003). An empirical study of the effects of interactivity on web user attitude. *International Journal of Human-Computer Studies*, 58, 281-305.

Turban, E., King, D., Lee, J., & Viehland, D. (2006). *Electronic Commerce 2006: A Managerial Perspective*. Upper Saddle River, NJ: Prentice-Hall.

Upshaw, L. (1995). "The Keys to Building Cyberbrands," *Advertising Age*, May 29,

Varki, S., & Colgate, M. (2001). The role of price perceptions in an integrated model of behavioral intentions, *Journal of Service Research* 3(3), 232– 240.

Vehovar, V., Manfreda, K.L., & Batagelj, Z. (2001). Sensitivity of electronic commerce measurement to the survey instrument. *International Journal of Electronic Commerce*, 6, 31-51.

Venkatesh, V., Morris, M., Davis G., & Davis F. (2003). User Acceptance of Information Technology: Toward a Unified View. *MIS Quarterly*, 27(2), 425-478.

Walther, J.B. (1996). Computer-mediated communication: impersonal, interpersonal and hyperpersonal interaction. *Communication Research*, 23, 3-43.

WebArrow (2006), http://www.webarrow.com.

Yang, H., & Yoo, Y. (2004). It's all about attitude: revisiting the technology acceptance model. *Decision Support Systems*, 38(1), 19-31.

Zack, M.H. (1993). Interactivity and Communication Mode Choices in Ongoing Management Groups. *Information System Research*, 4(3), 207-239.

Zeithaml, V.A. (1981). How Consumer Evaluation Processes Differ Between Goods and Services. in

Marketing of Services, Donnelly, J.H. & George, W. R., Editors. American Marketing Association: Chicago, IL. pp. 186-190.

Zeithaml, V.A., Berry, L.L., & Parasuraman, A. (1981). The Behavioral Consequences of Service Quality. *Journal of Marketing*, 60, 31-46.

Zeithaml, V.A. *Parasuraman*, A. & *Malhotra*, A. (2002). Service quality delivery through Web sites: A critical review of extant knowledge. *Academy of Marketing Science Journal*, 30(4), 362-76.

Zanjonc, R. (1980). Feeling and Thinking: Preferences Need No Inference. *American Psychologist*, 35(February), 152-171.

Zajonc, R., & Markus, H. (1982). Affective and Cognitive Factors in Preferences. *Journal of Consumer Research*, 9, 123-31.

Zajonc, R., & Markus, H. (1984). Affect and Cognition: The Hard Interface. *Emotions, Cognition, and Behavior.* Izard, C., Kagan, J. & Zajonc, R. Editors. Cambridge: Cambridge University Press, 73-102.

Zhang, P., & Li, N. (2005). The importance of affective quality. *Communications of the ACM*, 48(9), 105-108.

ENDNOTES

1. Detailed task descriptions are available upon request.
2. 88% of online Americans say that the internet plays a role in their daily routines and 64% say that their daily lives would be affected if they did not have Internet access (Pew, 05).

Chapter IV
A Movie E-Shop Recommendation Model Based on Web Usage and Ontological Data

Andreas Aresti
University of Patras, Greece

Penelope Markellou
University of Patras, Greece

Ioanna Mousourouli
University of Patras, Greece

Spiros Sirmakessis
Technological Education Institute of Messolonghi, Greece

Athanasios Tsakalidis
University of Patras, Greece

ABSTRACT

Recommendation systems are special personalization tools that help users to find interesting information and services in complex online shops. Even though today's e-commerce environments have drastically evolved and now incorporate techniques from other domains and application areas such as Web mining, semantics, artificial intelligence, user modeling, and profiling setting up a successful recommendation system is not a trivial or straightforward task. This chapter argues that by monitoring, analyzing, and understanding the behavior of customers, their demographics, opinions, preferences, and history, as well as taking into consideration the specific e-shop ontology and by applying Web mining techniques, the effectiveness of produced recommendations can be significantly improved. In this way, the e-shop may upgrade users' interaction, increase its usability, convert users to buyers, retain current customers, and establish long-term and loyal one-to-one relationships.

INTRODUCTION

Nowadays, e-commerce is seen as an extremely dynamic economic sector and at the same time, as one of the most appealing ways of beginning or expanding a business activity. Statistics for its future are quite optimistic indicating that the business-to-consumer (B2C) e-commerce will grow rapidly in the years to come (Browne, Higgins, & Hunt, 2003). In fact, despite the recent talking about businesses cases that went online but did not manage to profit, looking at the big picture reveals that such cases comprise just a small portion of the market and most "inhabitants" of the e-commerce world are not only surviving, but also doing very good business. This is a strong indication for assuming that there are certain distinctive features that make the difference and which result in either success or failure. Moreover, surveys and studies have shown that consumers are increasingly giving online commerce a chance (E-commerce Alert, 2006). Taking also into account the rapidly growing number of those that have access to the Internet and those that gain familiarity with the medium, we have a quite promising picture (Internet World Stats, 2006).

In this article we argue that one of the factors that may block or urge online sales concerns the *individuality* of Internet shoppers. There is no dispute about whether or not e-commerce has a future; it is a new philosophy in conducting business and it is here to stay. The question is how easily Internet users become e-consumers and which are the internal "mechanisms" and external factors that participate in an e-purchase. The problem arises from the fact that shoppers with varying needs, preferences, and background navigate through large and complex Web structures and are confronted with too many options, missing in many cases the goal of their inquiry. Generally, search engines are used for filtering pages according to explicit users' queries. However, their results are often poor since the produced lists are long, unmanageable, and contain irrelevant pages (Middleton, De Roure, & Shadbolt, 2004).

Web personalization is one of the most promising approaches to alleviate this information overload problem and to provide users with tailored experiences. Eirinaki and Vazirgiannis (2003, p. 1) define personalization as "any action that adapts the information or services provided by a web site to the knowledge gained from the users' navigational behavior and individual interests, in combination with the content and the structure of the site." In this direction, recent Web technological advances help online companies to acquire individual customer's information in real time and with low cost. Based on this information, they construct detailed profiles and provide personalized services. Thus, e-shops now have the opportunity to improve their performance by addressing individual user preferences and needs, increasing satisfaction, promoting loyalty, and establishing one-to-one relationships.

Recommendations systems or *recommender systems (RSs)* that comprise the most popular forms of personalization are becoming significant business tools. They emerged in the middle of 1990s (Resnick & Varian, 1997) and from novelties used by a few Web sites have changed to important tools incorporated to many e-commerce applications (e.g., Amazon.com, eBay.com, CDNow.com). Specifically, these systems take advantage of users' and/or communities' opinions in order to help individuals identify information or products of interest (i.e., relevant to their needs and/or preferences). The recommendations may have various forms, for example, personalized offers, prices, products, or services; inserting or removing paragraphs, sections, or units; sorting, hiding, adding, removing, or highlighting links, explanations, or detailed information, and so forth. (Brusilovsky, 2001).

Early efforts were limited to *check-box personalization*, where portals allowed users to select the links they would like on their "personal" pages. This was very restrictive since it relied on users being able to know and specify their preferences in advance. Moving towards more intelligent approaches, *collaborative filtering (CF) or social filtering* (Goldberg, Nichols, Oki, & Terry, 1992; Jung, Na, & Lee, 2003) was deployed for implementing personalization based on knowledge about likes/dislikes of past users that are considered "similar" to the current one (using a certain similarity measure). These techniques required users to input personal information about their interests, needs, and/or preferences but this posed in many cases a big obstacle, since Web users are not usually cooperative in revealing this type of data. In contrast, *observational personalization* is based on the assumption that we can find "clues" about how to personalize information, services or products in records of users' previous navigational behavior (Mulvenna, Anand, & Bchner, 2000).

Web mining is defined as the use of data mining techniques for discovering and extracting information from Web documents and services and is distinguished as *Web content, structure,* or *usage mining* depending on which part of the Web is mined (Kosala & Blockeel, 2000). In the majority of cases, Web applications base personalization on Web usage mining. This process involves the tasks of gathering and extracting all required data for constructing and maintaining user profiles. These structures can be either *individual* or *aggregate* (when working with groups of users) and include information for users' behavior as recorded in server logs (Markellou, Rigou, & Sirmakessis, 2005a).

A relatively recent development that is foreseen to greatly affect personalization (and more specifically the Web mining subtasks) is the creation of the *semantic Web* (Berners-Lee, Hendler, & Lassila, 2001). Semantic web mining (Berendt, Hotho, & Stumme, 2002) combines the two fast-developing research areas of semantic Web and Web mining with the purpose of improving Web mining by exploiting the new semantic structures. The Web will reach its full potential when it becomes an environment where data can be shared and processed by automated tools, as well as by people. The notion of being able to semantically link various resources (e.g., documents, images, people, concepts, etc.) is essential for the personalization domain. With this we can begin to move from the current Web of simple hyperlinks to a more expressive, semantically rich Web, where we can incrementally add meaning and express a new set of relationships (e.g., isAuthorOf, dependsOn, worksFor, hasSubjectOf, hasLocation, etc.) among resources and making explicit the particular contextual relationships that are implicit in the current Web. The semantic Web will allow the application of sophisticated mining techniques, which require more structured input (Markellou, Rigou, Sirmakessis, & Tsakalidis, 2004). This will open new doors for effective information integration, management, and automated e-services. Especially e-shops will become smarter and more comprehensive; will enhance searching and information retrieval; and will provide intelligent recommendations (Ding, Fensel, Klein, Omelayenko, & Schulten, 2004).

This article introduces an approach for generating personalized e-commerce recommendations. We focus on the movie domain and extract the knowledge about customers and products from usage mining and ontological data in conjunction with customer-product ratings and matching techniques between similar customers. The underneath ontology consists of movie attributes and the relationships among movies. This representation can enrich the semantics of movies, as well as various relationships that may exist among them in order to increase recommendation effectiveness. This integration provides additional knowledge about customers' preferences and may contribute significantly to the search of related movies in recommendation process by utilizing information inherently embedded within ontology such as semantics of attributes. Even in the case of *cold-start problem, new-user problem,* and *new-item problem* where no initial behavioral information is available, it can offer logical and relevant recommendations to the customers. The provided recommendations are expected to have higher accuracy in matching customers' requirements and thus higher acceptance by them.

The remainder of this chapter is structured as follows. The related work section reviews and compares our approach to other efforts from various domains. The next section describes the e-shop ontological schema. The fourth and fifth sections present data acquisition and analysis tasks correspondingly. The sixth section introduces the approach for finding recommendations based on Web usage mining and ontological data. The seventh section summarizes the most interesting conclusions of the article and presents open issues and thoughts for future research.

RELATED WORK

The need to provide personalized services over the Web has been a strong driving force behind numerous research efforts. Most of movie e-shops combine CF and *content-based filtering* techniques; CF (Basilico & Hofmann, 2004; Goldberg et al., 1992; Jung et al., 2003; Resnick, Iacovou, Suchak, Bergstrom, & Riedl, 1994; Sarwar, Karypis, Konstan, & Riedl, 2001; Shardanand & Maes, 1995) typically based on product ratings explicitly defined by the users. The system recommends which products have been evaluated positively by similar user(s) whose ratings are in the strongest correlation with the current user. In a general perspective, it tries to model the way people take recommendations from friends, which would be the ideal situation. Content-based filtering (Balabanovic & Shoham, 1997; Mooney & Roy, 2000; Pazzani, 1999) on the other hand, uses product features and recommends products to users that have similar features with those they rated highly during the past.

Grant and McCalla (2001) propose the MovieMagician system that combines collaborative and content-based filtering by creating relativistic cliques (cliques of users having similar interest about movies of a certain kind). Movies' features are organized in a granularity hierarchy, having broader terms at the top, like "genre" and narrower terms at the bottom levels, like "action." This way, each movie can be realized as an instantiation of this hierarchy and the similarity of two movies can be determined by how much their hierarchies overlap. Each time a movie is instantiated a similarity list is created, that is, a list of all similar movies to that movie. User preference is acquired through an overall rating on a 7-point scale about the movie or through individual feature rating (i.e., actors, plot, etc.). In order to predict a rating for an unseen movie, the system calculates cliques of users having similar interest with the active user about the specific movie and its similarity list and then ranks users with regard to how similar they are with the active user. The recommended rating will be the rating of the most similar user in the clique. A very important feature that MovieMagician incorporates is the explanation of movie recommendations by means of personalized reviews.

Melville, Mooney, and Nagarajan's (2002) approach called *content-boosted collaborative filtering* uses a content-based predictor to create a full pseudo user-ratings matrix based on the sparse user-ratings matrix provided by the EachMovie dataset. Then, CF is used by applying the Pearson correlation formula on the full pseudo user-ratings matrix. The content-based predictor uses a naïve Bayesian text classifier on the movie content having a vector of bag-of-words like title or cast as input and producing the predicted rating to the unseen movies as output. The CF algorithm used is a neighborhood-based algorithm that firstly computes with the Pearson correlation the similarity of all users with the active user, it selects the N top highest similarities, and then it computes the prediction with the weighting combination of the top-N most similar users.

Garden (2004) proposes a cross-domain system called Recommendz that uses both collaborative and content-based filtering to generate recommendations and the final recommendation is created with a weighted combination. It provides users with the ability, just like MovieMagician, to rate individual features of a movie. Moreover, the system encourages the provision of different types of feedback: overall rating of movie, selection of a relevant movie's feature, specification of quantity of that feature in the item, and of the degree to which the presence of this feature is positive or negative. Also, users can add their own features that they think best characterize a movie, although such ability can import many redundant features. The hybrid filtering algorithm incorporates three similarity metrics to measure the similarity between two users: (1) Pearson correlation of the overall ratings of the items, (2) Pearson correlation of particular features, and (3) Pearson correlation of the common features rated. These three similarities are combined into a weighted average to produce the recommended rating of the active user towards a movie.

Salter & Antonopoulos (2006) propose Cinemascreen (2006), a system that provides movie recommendations. Firstly, it uses collaborative filtering to produce an initial recommendation list and then it passes that list as input to a content-based algorithm. This way the system bypasses the new item problem, as the final recommendation list may contain movies that it has not rated, but it has features similar to movies that other people have rated. The system uses a Web robot to collect information about movies and show times from multiple sources on the Internet. The CF algorithm is a typical neighborhood-based one, that is, it calculates the users having similar rating history with the active user using the Pearson correlation. However, the system uses a threshold to distinguish significantly similar users, that is, users showing high similarity with the active user. The rating of the active user is acquired by the weighted mean of the neighborhood users' ratings. Afterwards the CF recommendation list is fed to the content-based filtering algorithm. Here, each movie's rating is added to the score of each of the movie's features (actors, directors, genre, etc.) and then the mean is calculated for each feature. The three scores calculated express the degree of user's preference towards each feature. Then, for each actor, the system searches the movies they have appeared in and adds up the actor's score to each movie's score. The same procedure is followed for the directors and genres. Finally, the average of the scores is calculated for each movie and so the final predicted ratings for the movies are acquired.

Schafer, Konstan, and Reidl (2004) propose a slightly different kind of recommendation model, a meta-recommender system. A meta-recommender system accesses many different information sources and/or recommender systems and returns results related to a user query that reflects an ephemeral need. An instance of this model for the movie domain, Metalens, has an initial preference screen where the active user can select the features that the recommended movies like to have and the weight of each feature. The system forms the user demands as a query and forwards it to the sources of information, specifically Yahoo Movies, Rotten Tomatoes, and Movielens. Yahoo Movies provides movie information; Rotten Tomatoes provides movie reviews; and Movielens provides personalized recommendations based on CF. The results returned from all sources are united and ranked according to the extended Boolean model and then are displayed to the active user. The strengths of such recommender systems are the capability for both ephemeral and persistent recommendations and the combination of multiple recommendation techniques. A recent optimisation on Metalens' interface had resulted to DynamicLens (Schafer, 2005), which uses Metalens inner engine as is and additionally unites the preference and recommendation screens into one. The user can select the features he/she likes and see dynamically the recommendations they induce, making it easier for the user to select the correct features and weights.

Beyond the movie domain, a variety of applications that combine algorithms and techniques from Web usage mining, semantic Web, and ontologies can be reported. The variety of these applications is a solid indication of the area maturity. In the next paragraphs some characteristic applications are presented.

Berendt (2001) proposes concept hierarchies for analyzing complex Web usage data of visitors. These hierarchies are used as a basic method for aggregating Web pages. Moreover, interval-based coarsening and its inverse zooming are described as a technique to mine Web usage at different levels of abstraction. Basic and coarsened stratograms have been exploited to visualize Web usage at different degrees of detail. Using a case study of online shopping with an anthropomorphic agent has been demonstrated that this kind of abstraction offers new possibilities of understanding complex paths through a semi-structured, interaction-rich environment.

Eirinaki, Lampos, Paulakis, and Vazirgiannis (2004) propose a recommendation method that integrates content semantics and navigational data. Their technique uses the terms of a domain ontology in order to uniformly characterize both the content and the users' navigational patterns and thus produce a set of recommendations that are semantically related to the user's current visit. The work deals with the important problem of multilingualism, which arises when the content of a Web site appears in more than one language and is integrated in the personalization system SEWeP (Eirinaki, Vazirgiannis, & Varlamis, 2003).

Middleton, Shadbolt, and De Roure (2004) describe an ontological approach to user profiling within recommender systems, working on the problem of recommending online academic research papers. The papers are classified using ontological classes. Collaborative and content-based recommendation algorithms are used to recommend papers seen by similar people on their current topics of interest. They use the ontological relationships between topics of interest to infer other topics not yet browsed and recommend them to the users.

Mobasher, Jin, and Zhou (2004) introduce an approach for semantically enhanced CF. In this work, structured semantic knowledge about items, extracted automatically from the Web based on domain-specific reference ontologies, is used in conjunction with user-item ratings (or weights) to create a similarity measure for item comparisons. Provided experimental results on two different data sets demonstrate that their approach yields significant advantages both in terms of improving accuracy, as well as in dealing with very sparse data sets or new items.

Choa and Kimb (2004) propose a recommendation methodology based on Web usage mining and product taxonomy to enhance the recommendation quality and the system performance of current CF-based systems. Web usage mining populates the rating database by tracking customers' shopping behaviors on the Web, thereby leading to better quality recommendations. The product taxonomy is used to improve the performance of searching for nearest neighbors through dimensionality reduction of the rating database.

Our intention was to construct a new recommendation model based on Web usage mining and ontological data. Most movie RSs do not take into consideration semantic characteristics resulting in poor prediction accuracy. Without the deeper semantic knowledge about the underlying domain, the RS cannot handle heterogeneous and complex objects based on their properties and relationships. Our approach combines usage and ontological data in the off-line phase in order to generate the user navigational model. It distinguishes between new and known user and further incorporates ratings and similarities with other users in the online phase to sort the recommendations. By combining different available information channels, we succeed to better meet users' needs and preferences. The advantages of our approach include the capability of application in cross-domain recommenders and the simplicity compared to other recommendation techniques. Moreover, it overcomes the drawbacks of CF: new-item problem where a new item is not recommended unless a notable number of users rate it and new-user problem, where a new user is registered and has not rated enough items so that the recommender can make accurate recommendations. The integration of ontological data provides additional knowledge about customers' preferences and allows the production of logical and relevant recommendations. In the next section, we introduce a movie RS approach that tries to overcome the shortcomings of most RSs and produce full personalization. In this way, we can offer every user different recommendations that change during their navigation.

E-SHOP ONTOLOGICAL SCHEMA

In many online shops a basic classification schema for the provided items is available. This schema can be depicted as a tree, where the root represents the most general class, the internal nodes all intermediate classes, and the leaves the specific items. Its role is important, especially in the knowledge discovery process, since it represents e-shop's dependent knowledge and may affect the results. In this framework, the proposed recommendation approach is based on an ontological schema and has been incorporated in a pilot e-shop that rents movies to customers. Specifically, the Web site consists of a collection of pages containing information about movies' attributes such as title, category, studio, actor, director, producer, awards, year, duration, audience, story, and so forth. The initial data has been retrieved from the Internet Movie Database (http://www.imdb.com), organized in the ontological schema and enhanced in order to comprise a rich superset covering all needed concepts and relations.

The underneath ontological schema formulates a representation of the e-shop domain by specifying all of its concepts, the relations between them, and other properties, conditions, and "regulations." It allows semantic annotation and has the ability to perform semantic querying and ontology-based browsing. The ontology

Figure 1. Part of the e-shop ontology (Extended version of Mobasher et al., 2004)

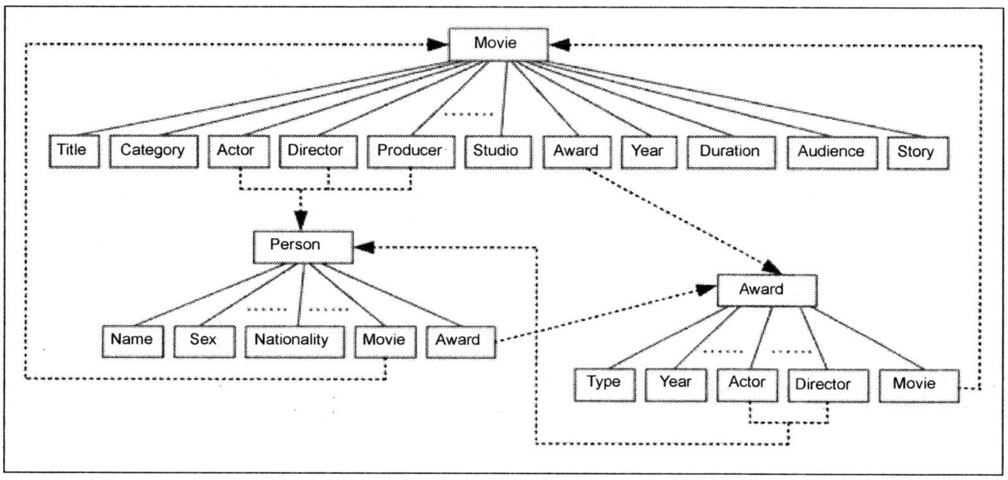

"building" was a complex and time-consuming task and was based on our intuition in order to depict all e-shop notions, organize their taxonomic hierarchies, and represent their relationships. The development was akin to the definition of a set of data and their structure. In this way, the ontology can be considered as a knowledge base that is used further for extracting useful knowledge. Specifically, its role is to be used as an input for the mining phase in order to extract, combine, and transform the existing implicit and explicit knowledge (user class, history profile, e-shop content, and structure) into new forms. The output of this task is a list of possible recommendations.

A part of the e-shop ontology is depicted in Figure 1. In particular, the ontology creates connections between movies according to different attributes that characterize them. Using now the specific customer's history file, his/her preferences can be figured out. For example, it can be found if the customer likes or dislikes watching movies:

- From a certain category, for example, action, drama, comedy, westerns, musicals, and so forth.
- By a certain director, for example, Steven Spielberg, Francis Ford Copolla, Sydney Pollack, and so forth.
- With a certain actor, for example, Sean Penn, Nicole Kidman, Brad Pitt, Julia Roberts, and so forth.
- Other attribute combinations.

When one or more matching criteria are met, then other movies can be discovered according to the ontological schema that have similar attributes with those that the customer has already rented. In the case of a new customer (history file=∅), the information from his/her registration form is analyzed and the recommendations are based on the ontology.

DATA ACQUISITION, PRE-PROCESSING, AND TRANSFORMATION

Data acquisition refers to the construction of customer models that hold information about the *user* (demographics, user knowledge, skills, capabilities, interests, preferences, goals, etc.), the *usage* (selective actions, ratings, usage frequency, action correlations or sequences, etc.), and the *usage environment*, hardware, software, and physical (browser version, available plug-ins, bandwidth, display/input devices). These data can be collected either *explicitly* (the user is asked to provide them using questionnaires, fill-in preference forms, etc.) or *implicitly* (the data are derived without initiating any interaction with the users using acquisition rules, plan recognition, and stereotype reasoning).

However, in both approaches, we have to deal with different but equally serious problems. In the case of explicit profiling, users are often negative about filling in questionnaires and revealing personal information online, they comply only when required and even then the submitted data may be poor or false. On the other hand, in implicit profiling, even though the source of information is not biased by the users' negative attitude, the problems encountered derive once again from the invaded privacy concern and the loss of anonymity. Personalization is striving to identify users, record their online behavior in as much detail as possible, and extract needs and preferences in a way they do not notice, understand, or control (Kramer, Noronha, & Vergo, 2000; Mesquita, Barbosa, & Lucena, 2002).

Collecting accurate and sufficient data comprises a crucial task of every RS. For our approach we use the model introduced in Markellou, Rigou, and Sirmakessis (2005b, 2006), which helps us to better understand the interactions between consumers and e-businesses. This model represents the *overall consumer purchase decision cycle* and investigates the issues that affect Web users, from selecting a specific e-shop to the delivery of the product and the overall assessment of the shopping experience. This process has been divided into 13 states under three successive stages: (1) outside the e-shop, (2) inside the e-shop, and (3) after sales, with each stage analyzed on the basis of customer states and transition conditions. Special focus is set on identifying the data that the Web site gathers from customers' interactions and that can be used for mining purposes. The most important data sources that our model uses are: registration, log-in/password, history file, navigation, search keywords, support, and product/service evaluation.

DATA ANALYSIS

The step following the data acquisition (a task that is in continuous execution) and the building of user profiles is data analysis. Initially, some preparation activities take place in order to clean the data and facilitate their manipulation. Data cleaning removes all irrelevant entries from the Web server logs in order to facilitate their manipulation. For instance, entries that do not reveal actual usage information are removed and missing data are completed. Moreover, data compression algorithms are used in this stage in order to reduce the size and dimension of the data and achieve efficient mining of the data. The problems that we face during this phase include: *user identification, session identification, path completion,* and *transaction identification.*

- **User identification:** Registration and log-in/password procedures, as well as the combination of other heuristics are used for assuring the identification of unique users.
- **Session identification:** Session is a set of user clicks across one or more Web servers and session identification aims to group the page accesses of each individual user into sessions. Time windows are used to identify the different sessions of a user.
- **Path completion:** This problem is caused from local caching and proxy server activities creating gaps in the users' access paths. Referrer log for identifying the page that the request came from and also the site topology are used to fully cover this issue.
- **Transaction identification:** This problem (grouping the references of each user) is solved by using time windows that partitions a user session based on time intervals (specified thresholds).

Figure 2. Proposed recommendation approach

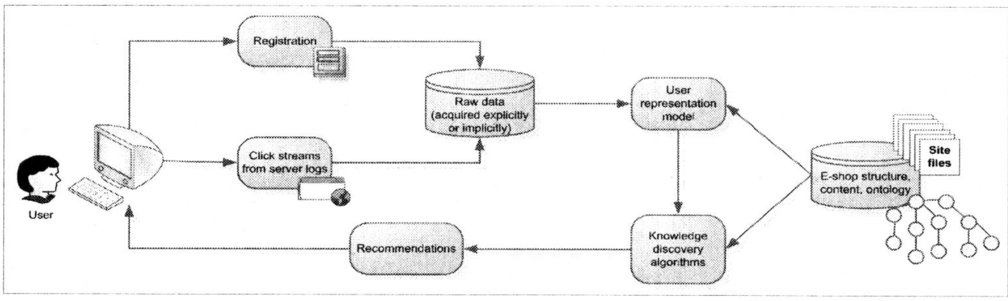

Then follows the application of statistical and data mining techniques in order to detect interesting patterns in the pre-processed data. The most well-known techniques used for data analysis include clustering (Hand, Mannila, & Smyth, 2001), classification (Chakrabarti, 2003), and association rules mining (Agrawal & Srikant, 1994).

Our recommendation approach is depicted in Figure 2. As we have mentioned before, the pilot e-shop rents movies to the customers. The production of recommendations is based on Web usage mining techniques and semantic metadata, as well as customer-product ratings and matching techniques between customers. The operation of the e-shop is straightforward. In the case of a new customer the e-shop motivates the user to become a member by filling in the registration form. In this way the e-shop collects the necessary initial information about the customer in order to support him/her in their navigation. In the case of an old customer, the e-shop identifies them via a log-in/password procedure and provides a personalized greeting. Then the customer can navigate the e-shop; select movies from the online cataloge or use the search facility; be informed about their features, for example, story, cast, and so forth; add them to his/her basket and pay for the renting total. Moreover, the user can rate a specific movie using a range from 1 to 10, where 1 means a very bad movie and 10, a very good one. So "excellent" movies have ratings from 8 to 10, "good" movies have ratings 6 to 7, "indifferent" movies have ratings 4 to 5 and "poor" movies have ratings 1 to 3. But other than that, the model recommends to the user the movies with the upper ratings from a specific list of movies. This list is created according to the algorithm presented in next sections. The approach incorporates classification and association rules mining. In the following sections, the way that recommendations are produced is described.

Table 1. Part of a user profile

age	"30"
sex	"Male"
occupation	"seller"
education	"higher"

Table 2. A snapshot of the database

userID	age	sex	occupation	education	class:rent comedies
1	30	F	engineer	higher	yes
2	25	M	student	medium	no
3	34	F	salesman	lower	yes
4	18	M	student	lower	yes
5	45	F	director	higher	no
...	...	...	...	...	...
100	28	F	artist	higher	yes

Customers Classification

The main objective of the classification step is to assign customers to a set of predefined classes. These classes represent different user profiles, and classification is performed by using selected features with high discriminative ability as refers to the set of classes describing each profile. The features that determine a specific class can be tuned and typically include age, sex, nationality, occupation, as well as education, and preferences (Registration Form's Data). For example, from the class "rent comedies," customers that like to rent comedies and customers that do not can be extracted. Table 1 depicts the profile of an active buyer. Consider the attributes and the values presented in Table 2 and suppose we want to decide if the next unknown user X rents or not comedies: X={age=22, sex=F, occupation=student, education=medium}.

Classification requires a training data set with pre-assigned class labels, since it is categorized as a supervised machine learning technique. Then the classifier (by observing the class assignment in the training set) learns to assign new data items in one of the classes. It is often the case that clustering is applied before classification to determine the set of classes.

We have based our categorization model on a Naïve Bayes classifier (Hand et al., 2001), where each snapshot X consists of a set of attributes x_1, x_2, ... x_n. We have defined m classes C_1, C_2, ... C_m. Given an unknown snapshot X for which we do not know its class, the classifier predicts that X belongs to the class with the higher probability. The classifier assigns X in class C_i if $P(C_i|X) > P(C_j|X)$ for $1 \leq j \leq m, j \neq i$. According to Bayes theorem $P(C_i|X)=P(X|C_i)*P(C_i)/P(X)$. P(X) is constant for all snapshots, so we need to maximize the expression $P(X|C_i)*P(C_i)$. For categorizing X, we compute the probability $P(X|C_i)*P(C_i)$ for each class C_i. X will be assigned in class C_i if $P(X|C_i)*P(C_i) > P(X|C_j)*P(C_j)$ for $1 \leq j \leq m$, $j \neq i$. This means that X is assigned in the class with the maximum probability.

This classification model may be revised as time passes and updated based on collected transactions data. User assignment to classes might also be used for provoking interactions among users and enhancing, this way, collaboration and communication, as well as for allowing e-shop to perceive a useful insight of the "virtual communities." For each class a set of recommendations is attached. These recommendations are lists with, for example, the best and worst movies that other users "close" to the current have contributed.

Association Rules Mining on Clickstreams

Association' rules connect one or more events. Their aim is to discover associations and correlations between different types of information without obvious semantic dependence. Moreover, correlations between pages not directly connected and previously unknown associations between groups of users with specific interests may be revealed.

The model tracks all user actions as successive page requests recorded in server logs. Log files are then cleaned from all redundant information (such as secondary, automatically generated requests for page images, etc.). Combining the remaining requests with information about the way the Web site content is structured, the system distills user accesses to movies pages. The set of movies that have been accessed by a certain user during all past visits to the e-shop are stored in the user profile, and this is where the generator seeks for discovering association rules.

An association rule example is {$movie_i$, $movie_j$} -> {$movie_x$}, with support=0.02 and confidence=0.68. This rule conveys the relationship that users who accessed $movie_i$ and $movie_j$ also tend (with a confidence of 68%) to be interested in $movie_x$. Support represents the fact that the set {$movie_i$, $movie_j$, $movie_x$} is observed in 2% the sets of movies accessed. Other examples of association rules are the following:

- Sixty percent of users that rent the movie *Lord of the Rings—The Fellowship of the Ring* in sequence select *Lord of the Rings—The Two Towers* and *Lord of the Rings—The Return of the King.*
- Seventy-five percent of users who visited the *Shrek* movie belong to the 15-20 age group.
- Twenty-five percent of users who rent the movie Harry Potter and the Philosopher's Stone, were in the 20-30 age group and lived in Athens.

The discovered association rules may use as input, either the sets of movies accessed by all users, or just the ones accessed by users that belong to the same class as the current one. Another option is to use both approaches and suggest the union of discovered topics. This scenario is very useful when association rules inside classes fail to produce reliable recommendations due to lack of adequate input.

PRODUCTION OF MOVIE RECOMMENDATIONS

This section describes in detail the algorithm used for the production of movie recommendations. These recommendations are suggested to the customer in the form of "customers who liked/rented this movie also rented…". The filtering procedure is based on different kinds of data. More precisely it depends on the cluster in which the user was classified; his/her click-streams; transaction history and ratings; and the Web site ontology metadata. The main idea is to generate an initial set of recommendations combining all the aforementioned data and then prune (using a pre-defined threshold $-\alpha$) this set and sort the remaining items in an ascending order (first the movie with the higher predicted rate).

We separate between two cases according to the existence of user's history data:

- **Case 1:** When the user is an existing one and system has kept track of his history.

We define as $M_{History}$ the set of movies that the user has seen and rated. In this case, the system according to $M_{History}$ finds the users "close" to him/her with similar history and ratings. We define this set of users as U_L. Every user U_i that belongs to U_L is associated with a number s_i, which depicts the similarity of U_i with the current user. Also, we define as U_M the set of users that belong to U_L and have seen movie M. Moreover, according to $M_{History}$ the model uses the ontology to discover the associations between the items that the user has rated. Therefore, we define as $R_{ontology}$ the list of recommendations that derive from the ontology based on user's history file.

- **Case 2:** When the user is a new one.

In this case, the system uses information from the user's registration and consequently the initial class in which he/she has been assigned to. We define as U_K the set of users in the class that have similar attributes with the current one. These attributes are the information that the user gave to the system after filling the registration form. For example age, sex, occupation, education, preferences, and so forth. Every user U_i that belongs to U_K is associated with a number s_i that depicts the similarity of U_i with the current user according to the aforementioned attributes. We define as U_M the set of users that belong to U_K and have seen movie M. Every class is attached with a set of movies. We define as $R_{cluster}$ the recommended movies according to the user's class.

Continuing, we define as $W_{current}$ the current session window, which contains the movies that the user has accessed in the current transaction. We can produce recommendations in accordance to the user's current clickstream by using association rules and the site ontology. So $R_{rules\text{-}current}$ are the recommendations that derive from the current session window and association rules mining and $R_{ontology\text{-}current}$ are those that derive from the current session window and the ontology.

We use two methods for processing the information of current sessions because by their combination we achieve better predictions. Each method uses different ways to predict user's preferences, that is, association rules encapsulate the navigational behavior of users, while the ontology reflects the connections between items' attributes and discovers patterns that explain user's preferences. In sequence, we name $R_{initial}$ the initial recommendation set that will be filtered by the algorithm and ordered in ascending form. It is computed by the union of $R_{ontology\text{-}current}$, $R_{rules\text{-}current}$, and in the first case (when the user has historical data) we use the $R_{ontology}$, while in the second case (when the user is a new one) we use the $R_{cluster}$. Consequently, we compute $R_{initial}$ for each case as follows:

- **Case 1:** $R_{initial} = R_{ontology\text{-}current} \cup R_{rules\text{-}current} \cup R_{ontology}$

Table 3. The algorithm used for producing recommendations

Input
$M_{i,j}$: movie i that the user j has seen and rated
s_j: the similarity of U_j with the current user
$R_{Mi,Uj}$: the rating of movie i from the user j
U: all users
U_i: user with ID i
M: all movies
M_j: movie j
$M_{History}$: movies that the customer has rated
$R_{initial}$: initial recommendations
Algorithm

<pre>**if** M_History = Ø **then**
    Find U_M in U_K
else Find U_M in U_L
for each M_i in R_initial
    r_Mi = Ø
    for each U_j in U_M
        if M_i,j ≠ Ø **then**
            if s_j >1 **then**
                r_Mi = r_Mi + R_Mi,Uj * 1/s_j
            else
                r_Mi = r_Mi + R_Mi,Uj
    end
    if r_Mi > α **then**
        R = R ∪ {M_i:r_Mi}
end</pre>

Output
A list R of movies recommendations in ascending order (first the movie with the biggest r_{Mi}) that user U_i has not seen and probably would like to see

- **Case 2:** $R_{initial} = R_{ontology\text{-}current} \cup R_{rules\text{-}current} \cup R_{cluster}$

The algorithm used for producing recommendations to the e-shop customers is presented in Table 3. As far as similarity among users is concerned, we consider that every user has a vector with the movies he/she has rated (i.e., a history vector). For example, let X and Y be two users. We define as X_R and Y_R their history vectors respectively and R_X and R_Y the sets with the rated movies. Then C is the set with the rated movies that they have in common, so $C = R_X \cap R_Y$. If the users do not have any movie in common then $C=\emptyset$. Additionally, we define X_C and Y_C the vectors with the movies that both users have rated (movies that belong to C). A limitation that arises in this step concerns the percentage of common rated movies in relation to all rated movies. For example, if the user X has rated 60 movies, $R_X=60$, and the user Y has rated 40 movies, $R_Y=40$, and their common movies are only 5, C=5, then these users are not similar. For considering two users as similar they should have in common more than 50% of the one with the fewer rated movies.

Another limitation of our approach is that the algorithm uses users' ratings. If users do not take the time to evaluate the movies that they saw then the system will record only what movies the users saw but will not understand which of them were liked most. Also, this raises some problems with the computation of similarity between users. On the other hand the algorithm could extract users' preferences from their choices according to e-shop's ontology schema and association rules mining.

Then the similarity between users X and Y is the distance between vectors X_C and Y_C and can be computed from the following type:

$$s = sim(X_C, Y_C) = \sqrt{\sum_{i=1}^{N} (R(X_C, M_i) - R(Y_C, M_i))^2}$$

Note that $sim(X_C, Y_C)$ is a heuristic artifact that is introduced in order to be able to differentiate between levels of user similarity (e.g., to be able to find a set of "closest peers" or "nearest neighbors" for each user) and at the same time simplify the rating estimation procedure. Different recommendation approaches can use their own user similarity measure, as long as the calculations are normalized. The most commonly used similarity measures are Euclidean Distance, Pearson Correlation, Cosine, and so forth (Adomavicius & Tuzhilin, 2005; Papagelis, 2005).

When the user is a new one, we compute the similarity among users in the same class. In this case we use the attributes that derived from the registration form. These attributes have a certain position in the vector that describes the user's profile. For example, if the attributes are sex, age, occupation, and education an instance of this vector for user X could be {0, 22, 3, 2}. This means: {sex=Male, age=22, occupation=student, education=medium}. In other words, every attribute takes values that correspond to certain information, for example, occupation=3 denotes a student.

To sum up, we have used the explicit data that the user provides during registration in order to categorize him/her into a class of predefined groups. These groups (classes) are static and generated according to the system's characteristics. A user can belong in many different classes. This classification cannot be altered in accordance to user's navigational activity. It is static and it can only be modified if the user changes his/her preferences, that is, his/her registration data. On the other hand, we have used the association rules and the ontology of the site. This information derives dynamically from user's navigational activity. Rules' extraction is performed during the off-line process, while the discovery of the proper ones (according to the current session window) is performed during the online process. Association rules are created by Apriori Algorithm (Agrawal, Imielinski, & Swami, 1993) and the algorithm is implemented in C++.

For the evaluation of our approach we use two data sets. The first set includes 100 snapshots of the ontological scheme of the pilot movie e-shop. A spider is used to mine the information from HTML pages and store them in the database. The second set includes data for the navigation users' behaviors that was collected from the log files. This set includes now 25 users and 218 separate visits. Then, we follow the next steps:

- We collect samples of users' ratings for the movies that they have seen.
- For each user u we calculate the rating r_{um} that the model predicts the user will give to the movie m that he/she has not see.
- We present to the user the Web page that includes all information about the movie m that has the biggest r_{um}.
- We ask the user to rate the movie m without seeing the movie based on the Web page data.
- We ask the user to see the movie and re-rate it.

We define as estimated rating er_{um} the rating that the user u gives without seeing the movie m and as actual rating er_{um} the rating after the user has seen the movie. We use the mean absolute error (MAE) to calculate the mean deviation between the prediction and the actual ratings of a user. First, we calculate the absolute error (AE) of every prediction and then we compute the MAE as the sum of all AE divided by the number of predictions. The smaller the MAE the better technique efficiency is. Specifically, we calculate the MAE for evaluating the RS model in conjunction with the estimated rating ($|E_{er}|$) and actual rating ($|E_{ar}|$) and between them ($|E_{ear}|$):

- $|E_{er}| = \dfrac{\sum_{u \in U'} \sum_{m \in M'} |er_{um} - r_{um}|}{\#\ predictions},$
- $|E_{ar}| = \dfrac{\sum_{u \in U'} \sum_{m \in M'} |ar_{um} - r_{um}|}{\#\ predictions},$
- $|E_{ear}| = \dfrac{\sum_{u \in U'} \sum_{m \in M'} |er_{um} - ar_{um}|}{\#\ predictions}.$

for measuring the accuracy of recommendations where U' is the set of users for which the RS made predictions and M' is the set of movies that they have not seen yet. The experiments showed firstly that estimated ratings from the actual ratings of user differ by 8.99%. The RS predicted ratings r_{um} deviates from the estimated ratings by 9.68%, while from the actual ratings by 10.38%. These percentages indicate that the whole process is strengthened by the combination of ontology, history files, registration data, usage data, and association rules that incorporate essential knowledge for the navigational behavior of users. Screenshots of the RS are depicted in Figure 3.

CONCLUSION AND FUTURE WORK

In this article we introduce a recommendation approach for e-shops that extends Web usage-based techniques by incorporating semantic annotations, in order to better meet the customers' preferences. The preliminary evaluation experiments show that the whole process has been enhanced by the combination of site's ontology, user's history files, user's registration data, and association rules, which encompasses all necessary knowledge about users' navigational attitudes. Currently we are working on collecting further data in order to extensively evaluate the approach using more metrics such as *coverage* that measure the ability of the system to produce all pages that are likely users to visit.

Figure 3. The pilot movie e-shop

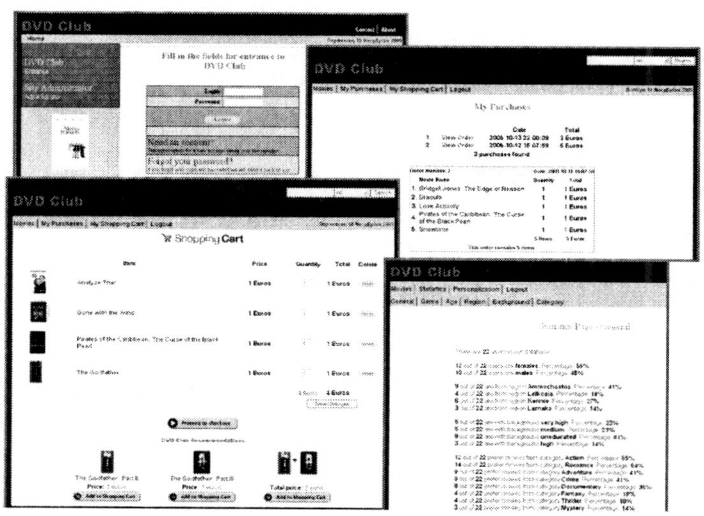

An important point of future consideration relates to the close dependence of the algorithm from the e-shop ontological schema, which can be overbalanced by the association rules mining. Rules catch all users' navigational activity and their relative behavior in relation on products. Another interesting area of work concerns the improvement of algorithm performance by decreasing its complexity, which is augmented analogically with the number of products, of users, and their history files. Finally, it will be interesting to investigate different approaches to combine various information channels in order to generate more accurate recommendations.

REFERENCES

Adomavicius, G., & Tuzhilin, A. (2005). Toward the next generation of recommender systems: A survey of the state-of-the-art and possible extensions. *IEEE Transactions on Knowledge and Data Engineering, 17*(6), 734-749.

Agrawal, R., Imielinski, & T., Swami, A. (1993). Mining association rules between sets of items in large databases. In *Proceedings of the ACM SIGMOD International Conference on Management of Data* (pp. 207-216).

Agrawal, R., & Srikant, R. (1994). Fast algorithms for mining association rules. In J. Bocca, M. Jarke, & C., Zaniolo (Eds.), *Proceedings of the 20th VLDB* (pp. 487-499). Morgan Kaufmann.

Balabanovic, M., & Shoham, Y. (1997). Fab: Content-based, collaborative recommendation. *Communications of the ACM, 40*(3), 66-72.

Basilico, J., & Hofmann, Th. (2004). Unifying collaborative and content-based filtering. In *Proceedings of the 21st International Conference on Machine learning* (69: 9). New York: ACM Press.

Berendt, B. (2001). Understanding Web usage at different levels of abstraction: Coarsening and visualizing sequences. In *Proceeding of the Mining Log Data Across All Customer TouchPoints*, San Francisco.

Berendt, B., Hotho, A., & Stumme, G. (2002). Towards semantic Web mining. In I. Horrocks & J. Hendler (Eds.), *Proceedings of the ISWC 2002* (pp. 264-278). Springer-Verlag.

Berners-Lee, T., Hendler, J., & Lassila, O. (2001). Semantic Web. *Scientific American, 284*(5), 34-43.

Browne, J., Higgins, P., & Hunt, I. (2003). E-business principles, trends, visions. In J. Gasos & K. D. Thoben (Eds.), *E-business Applications, Technologies for Tomorrow's Solutions* (pp. 3-16). Springer-Verlag.

Brusilovsky, P. (2001). Adaptive hypermedia [Ten Year Anniversary Issue]. In A. Kobsa (Ed.), *User Modeling and User Adapted Interaction*, 11(1/2), 87-110.

Chakrabarti, S. (2003). *Mining Web: Discovering knowledge from hypertext data.* Morgan Kaufmann.

Choa, Y. H., & Kimb, J. K. (2004). Application of Web usage mining and product taxonomy to collaborative recommendations in e-commerce. *Expert Systems with Applications, 26,* 233-246.

Cinemascreen. (2006). Retrieved December 20, 2006, from http://www.cinemacreen.co.uk

Ding, Y., Fensel, D., Klein, M., Omelayenko, B., & Schulten, E. (2004). The role of ontologies in ecommerce. In S. Staab & R. Studer (Eds.), *Handbook on Ontologies* (pp. 593-615). Springer-Verlag.

E-commerce Alert. (2006). *Surveys and reports.* Retrieved December 20, 2006, from http://blogs.library.ualberta.ca/ecommerce

Eirinaki, M., Lampos, C., Paulakis, S., & Vazirgiannis, M. (2004, November, 12-13). Web personalization integrating content semantics and navigational patterns. In *Proceedings of 6th ACM International Workshop on Web Information and Data Management* (pp. 72-79).Washington.

Eirinaki, M., & Vazirgiannis, M. (2003). Web mining for Web personalization. *ACM Transactions on Internet Technology, 3*(1), 1-27.

Eirinaki, M., Vazirgiannis, M., & Varlamis, I. (2003). SEWeP: Using site semantics and a taxonomy to enhance the Web personalization process. In *Proceedings of 9th ACM Conference on Knowledge Discovery and Data Mining* (pp. 99-108). Washington.

Garden, M. (2004). *On the use of semantic feedback in recommender systems.* Unpublished master's thesis, McGill University, Montreal, Canada.

Goldberg, D., Nichols, D., Oki, B. M., & Terry, D. (1992). Using collaborative filtering to weave an information tapestry. *Communication of ACM, 35*(12), 61-70.

Grant, S., & McCalla, G. (2001). A hybrid approach to making recommendations and its application to the movie domain. In *Proceedings of the 14th Biennial Conference of the Canadian Society on Computational Studies of Intelligence: Advances in Artificial Intelligence* (LNCS 2056, pp. 257-266). London, UK: Springer-Verlag.

Hand, D., Mannila, H., & Smyth, P. (2001). *Principles of data mining.* Cambridge, MA: MIT Press.

Internet World Stats. (2006). *Internet usage statistics, the big picture, world Internet users and population stats.* Retrieved December 20, 2006, from http://www.internetworldstats.com/stats.htm

Jung, K., Na, Y., & Lee, J. (2003). *Creating user-adapted design recommender system through collaborative filtering and content based filtering,* (LNCS 2902, pp. 204-208).

Kosala, R., & Blockeel, H. (2000). Web mining research: Survey. *SIGKDD Explorations, 2*(1), 1-15.

Kramer, J., Noronha, S., & Vergo, J. (2000). A user-centered design approach to personalization. *Communications of the ACM,* 8, 45-48.

Markellou, P., Rigou, M., & Sirmakessis, S. (2005a). Web personalization for e-marketing intelligence. In S. Krishnamurthy (Ed.), *Contemporary research in e-marketing: Volume 1* (pp. 48-68). Hershey, PA: Idea Group Publishing.

Markellou, P., Rigou, M., & Sirmakessis, S. (2005b). An online consumer purchase decision cycle. In I. Clarke III & Th. Flaherty (Eds.), *Advances in electronic marketing: Volume 1* (pp. 287-299). Hershey, PA: Idea Group Publishing.

Markellou, P., Rigou, M., & Sirmakessis, S. (2006). A closer look to the online consumer behavior. In M. Khosrow-Pour (Ed.), *Encyclopedia of e-commerce, e-government and mobile commerce* (pp. 106-111). Hershey, PA: Idea Group Reference.

Markellou, P., Rigou, M., Sirmakessis, S., & Tsakalidis, A. (2004, September, 3-11). Personalization in the semantic Web era: A glance ahead. In *Proceedings of the 5th International Conference on Data Mining, Text Mining and their Business Applications, Data Mining 2004* (pp. 15-17). Malaga, Spain. Wessex Institute of Technology (UK)

Melville, P., Mooney, R., & Nagarajan, R. (2002). Content-boosted collaborative filtering for improved recommendations. In *Proceedings of the Eighteenth National Conference on Artificial Intelligence (AAAI-02)* (pp. 187-192).

Mesquita, C., Barbosa, S. D., & Lucena, C. J. (2002). Towards the identification of concerns in personalization mechanisms via scenarios. In *Proceedings of 1st International Conference on Aspect-Oriented Software Development.* Retrieved December 20, 2006, from http://trese.cs.utwente.nl/AOSD-EarlyAspectsWS/Papers/Mesquita.pdf

Middleton, S. E., De Roure, D. C., & Shadbolt, N. R. (2004). Ontology-based recommender systems. In S. Staab & R. Studer (Eds.), *Handbook on ontologies* (pp. 477-498). Springer-Verlag.

Middleton, S. E., Shadbolt, N. R., & De Roure, D. C. (2004). Ontological user profiling in recommender systems. *ACM Transactions on Information Systems, 22*(1), 54-88.

Mobasher, B., Jin, X., & Zhou, Y. (2004). Semantically enhanced collaborative filtering on the Web. In B. Berendt et al. (Eds.), *Proceedings of the European Web Mining Forum*(LNAI). Springer-Verlag.

Mooney, R., & Roy, L. (2000, June 2-7). Content-based book recommending using learning for text categorization. In *Proceedings of the 5th ACM Conference on Digital Libraries*, San Antonio, Texas (pp. 195-204).

Mulvenna, M., Anand, S., & Bchner, A. (2000). Personalization on the net using Web mining. *Communications of ACM, 43*(8), 122-125.

Papagelis, M. (2005). *Crawling the algorithmic foundations of recommendation technologies.* Unpublished master's thesis, University of Crete, Heraklion, Greece.

Pazzani, M. (1999). A framework for collaborative, content-based and demographic filtering. *Artificial Intelligence Review, 13*(5-6), 393-408.

Resnick, P., Iacovou, N., Suchak, M., Bergstrom, P., & Riedl, J. (1994). GroupLens: An open architecture for collaborative filtering of netnews. In *Proceedings of the ACM Conference on Computer Supported Cooperative Work*, (pp. 175-186).

Resnick, P., & Varian, H. (1997). Recommender systems. *Communications of the ACM, 40*(3), 56-58.

Salter, J., & Antonopoulos, N. (2006). CinemaScreen recommender agent: Combining collaborative and content-based filtering. *IEEE Intelligent Systems, 21*(1), 35-41.

Sarwar, B., Karypis, G., Konstan, J., & Riedl, J. (2001). Item-based collaborative filtering recommendation algorithms. In *Proceeding of the 10th World Wide Web Conference*, (pp. 285-295).

Schafer, J. B. (2005, January 9). DynamicLens: A dynamic user-interface for a meta-recommendation system. *Beyond Personalization: A Workshop on the Next Stage of Recommender Systems Research*, in conjunction with the 2005 International Conference on Intelligent User Interfaces (IUI'05), San Diego, California, (pp. 72-76).

Schafer, J. B., Konstan, J. A., & Reidl, J. (2004). The view through MetaLens: Usage patterns for a meta-recommendation system. *IEE Proceedings Software, 151*(6), 267-279.

Shardanand, U., & Maes, P. (1995). Social information filtering: Algorithms for automating "Word of Mouth." *Human Factors in Computing Systems ACM CHI*, (pp. 210-217).

This work was previously published in Journal of Electronic Commerce in Organizations, Vol. 5, Issue 3, edited by M. Khosrow-Pour, pp. 17-34, copyright 2007 by IGI Publishing, formerly known as Idea Group Publishing (an imprint of IGI Global).

Chapter V
Search Engine Optimization an Action Research Project: Initial Results and Two Year Follow-Up

Ross A. Malaga
Montclair State University, USA

ABSTRACT

A Web site that wants to increase its number of visitors can pay for search engine ads or attempt to improve its natural search engine ranking. Nobody really knows, which, if either, of these methods provides a positive return on investment. A search engine optimization (SEO) project was undertaken at a new e-commerce site. The site's search engine rankings and traffic were measured after each phase in the project. The results indicate that SEO is an effective method for improving search engine rankings and site traffic. In addition, the costs and benefits of the SEO project are compared with a pay-per-click (PPC) search marketing campaign. The SEO project proved more cost effective than the PPC campaign.

INTRODUCTION

A recent report from DoubleClick.com (2005) reveals that about half of all purchases in the business-to-consumer (B2C) e-commerce category are preceded by a Web search. A business that wants its Web site to be "found" by a potential customer using a search engine has two choices. The first is to pay for advertisements based on the key words or phrases used as search criteria. This type of advertising is typically sold on a pay-per-click basis (PPC). That is, the site owner only pays when a user clicks on the ad and visits the target site. Certain key words might cost only pennies per click, while highly competitive key words cost up to $50 per click (CyberWyre 2006).

The other option is for the site to appear toward the top of the search engine results page (SERP). This is the page, or more often series of pages, that list the results of a specific search.

A recent report from iProspect (2006) revealed that 62% of search engine users click on results appearing on the first results page and 90% click on results on the first three pages. In addition, MarketingSherpa's study (2005) of the search engine marketing industry shows that Web sites that are optimized to appear higher in search engine results pages (SERPs) have a higher conversion rate (sales per visit) (4.2%) than PPC ads (3.6%). Clearly, it is important for a site to rank well on the SERPs—within the first three pages and preferably on the first page. Therefore, some Web site owners attempt to manipulate where their sites appear on the SERPs through a process called search engine optimization (SEO).

According to a report by Sherman (2005), 45% search marketers cannot determine whether SEO or pay-per-click advertising provides a higher return on investment. Sherman (2005) specifically found that, "35% [of search marketers] said that algorithmic search engine optimization produces higher ROI than search ads. Just 11% said that search engine optimization produces lower ROI than search advertising. Fully 45% said they cannot determine whether SEO or pay-per-click provides a higher ROI." (para. 10).

The goal of this chapter is to ascertain the impact of a search engine optimization (SEO) project on Web site traffic and determine if such a project provides monetary value to the business. The goal was achieved by implementing an SEO project at a new e-commerce Web site, called MyBestiPodStuff.com (this name has been changed to protect the identity of the actual site) that sells iPods and iPod accessories. At the time of the study, the site has little traffic and no profits. The goal of the SEO project was to increase the site's ranking on the search engines and drive more traffic (and eventually profits) to the site.

Since the goals of the research were aligned with the company's goals and an intervention (in the form of a search engine optimization project) was required in order to gather data, an action research approach was chosen. Action research was appropriate in this instance since the company wanted the authors to apply their knowledge of search engine optimization to their problem. In addition, both the authors and the company believed that action must be taken in order to solve the problem of low site traffic. The action research methodology has been used successfully in a number of information systems studies (Kohli & Kettinger 2004; Street & Meister 2004) and is discussed in more detail below.

This research makes the following three specific contributions to knowledge in the fields of search engine optimization and search engine marketing: (1) it examines SEO in the context of a working e-commerce site, (2) unlike previous research it uses an integrative approach to SEO, incorporating three main concepts—indexing, use of links, and on-site factors, and (3) since it uses an e-commerce site, the monetary value of the SEO effort can be determined and compared to other search engine marketing approaches—namely pay-per-click advertisements.

The next section of the chapter provides a review of the literature on search engine optimization. The research approach and actions taken are then described. Conclusions are then detailed, along with an analysis of the value of search engine optimization as compared to pay-per-click advertising. Finally, the chapter concludes with a discussion that examines the limitation of this study, contributions for academic and practitioner research, and future directions.

LITERATURE REVIEW

A search engine is simply a database of Web pages (called an index), a method for finding Web pages and indexing them, and a way to search the database. Search engines rely on spiders—software that follows hyperlinks—to find new Web pages to index and insure that pages that have already been indexed are kept up to date.

There are currently dozens, perhaps hundreds, of search engines available on the World Wide Web (WWW). However, the majority of searches are conducted on just three sites—Google (www.google.com), Yahoo (www.yahoo.com), and MSN (search.msn.com). Figure 1 shows the relative share of searches conducted by each of these sites. Since these three sites account for almost 84% of all searches, this study focused exclusively on them.

Although more complex searches are possible, most Web users conduct simple searches on a key word or key phrase. Search engines return the results of a search based on a number of factors. All of the major search engines consider the relevance of the search term to sites in its index when returning search results. So a search for the word "car" would return Web pages that have something to do with automobiles. The exact algorithms used to determine relevance are constantly changed and often kept secret. For example, Google's algorithm considers over 60 factors to determine relevance ("Google's Patent," n.d.).

Search Engine Optimization

Curran (2004) states, "search engine optimization is the process of improving a website's position so that the webpage comes up higher in the search results of major search engines" (p. 202). This process includes manipulation of dozens or even hundreds of Web site elements. For example, some of the elements used by the major search engines to determine relevance include, but are not limited to: age of the site, how often new content is added, the ratio of key words or terms to the total amount of content on the site, and the quality and number of external sites linking to the site (Sullivan 2003).

Review of Academic Literature

Zing and Lin (2006) state, "As a new phenomenon, while SEO is drawing much of the attention in online advertising industry, there has been very few published academic research in this area" (p.519). However, the academic community is beginning to turn its attention to SEO. Sen (2005), for example, developed a purely theoretical model to compare search engine optimization with paid placement. While he found that SEO is never an optimal search marketing strategy, his model assumes that SEO always costs more than paid placement and it does not consider that paid advertisements usually produce lower conversion rates (MarketingSherpa 2005).

Raisinghani (2005) and Curran (2004) point out there are a number of steps a Webmaster can

Figure 1. Search market share —March 2006 (Adapted from http://searchenginewatch.com/reports/article.php/2156431)

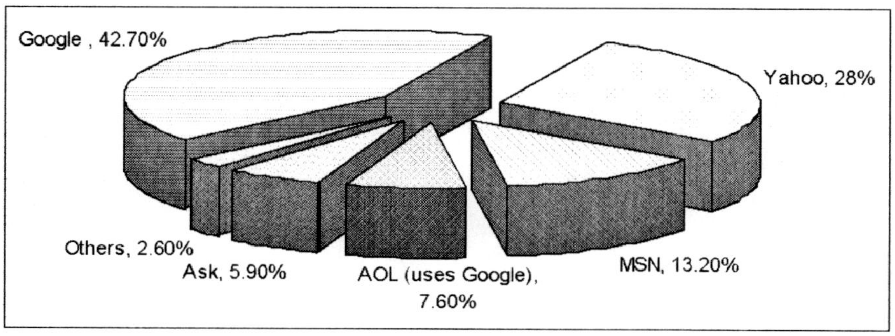

take to raise a Web site's search engine ranking. Some of these steps include—fine tuning the site's title tag and ensuring that the search engines can easily index the site. Curran (2004) also suggests conducting extensive key word or key term research to determine what people are searching for. In addition, he stresses the importance of choosing a good site title, as well, as proper use of Meta tags and site content.

Raisinghani's and Curran's recommendations are further supported by the work of Zhang and Dimitroff (2005b) who examined a large number of SEO components in controlled experiments. Their results show that sites that make proper use of Meta tags achieve better search engine results. Zhang and Dimitroff (2005a) also found that sites with key words that appear in both the site title and throughout the site's text have better search engine results than sites that only optimize the title.

The academic community has contributed to the development of links-based ranking algorithms. Links-based algorithms use the number of incoming links, their anchor text, and the linking site to determine, in part or whole, where a target Web site should rank. The most successful implementation of a links-based ranking algorithm is Google (see Brin and Page (1998). However, very little research has been done on how links can be manipulated in order to improve a site's ranking in the search engines.

Curran (2004) points out the importance of a site's inclusion in the various search engines as a part of SEO. However, Curran only makes some general recommendations concerning paying for inclusion in certain directories. Rapidly attracting search engine spiders has been largely overlooked in the academic literature.

Review of Practitioner Literature

Since an action research approach was used, relying solely on the academic literature was not appropriate. We therefore conducted an extensive review of practitioner best practices. This review revealed two major gaps in the academic literature. First, practitioners point out the importance of attracting the search engine spiders in order to have them quickly index a site (Morgan and Hunt 2006). Second, all of the major search engines consider the number of back links (incoming links) to a Web page (Sullivan 2003). Back links are links coming into a Web page from external sites. The precise manner in which search engines use back links varies considerably. Google, for instance, places a considerable amount of weight on back links (Google 2004). Each page indexed by Google is given a Page Rank (PR) based on the number and quality of back links to the page. Page Rank is measured from 0 to 10 and higher numbers are better. A site with a high PR will usually rank higher in Google's SERPs than a lower PR site. Web sites can increase their own PR by having high PR pages link to them.

Comprehensive SEO Approach

We combined the academic and practitioner literature to develop the following three phase approach to search engine optimization: (1) indexing, (2) back links, and (3) on-site optimization. Indexing refers to the process of getting a site included in a search engine. Therefore, this is an obvious first step. Back links are one of the major factors used by the three main search engines to determine relevance. They also play a potential role in indexing, since search engine spiders will follow links in order to find new sites. Thus, this was a natural second phase. Finally, many of the recommendations made by Zhang and Dimitroff (2005a; 2005b), Raisinghani (2005), and Curran (2004), such as use of Meta tags, good site title, key words in content can be grouped into a category called on-site optimization. On-site optimization includes any Web site element that can be directly manipulated by the Webmaster.

Conceptual Framework

The conceptual framework for this research is detailed in Figure 2.

As the figure shows, site profit is dependent, in part, on site traffic. As traffic increases, revenue should increase as well. Search engines are a major traffic driver for many sites. Search engine traffic may be increased through the use of pay-per-click advertising or search engine optimization. Finally, search engine optimization is influenced by indexing, back links, and on-site optimization.

A number of factors, such as hosting costs and general overhead, may have a negative impact on site profit. However, in this research we are interested only in those factors that are involved with increasing traffic. Thus pay-per-click advertising and the purchase of back links are shown as negative factors (dashed lines).

METHODOLOGY

A widely cited definition of action research comes from Rapoport (1970), who states, "action research aims to contribute both to the practical concerns of people in an immediate problematic situation and to the goals of social science by joint collaboration within a mutually acceptable ethical framework" (p. 499). According to Baskerville and Wood-Harper (1996), "action research methods are highly clinical in nature, and place IS researchers in a 'helping-role' within the organizations that are being studied" (p. 1). In this case the researchers were the search engine optimization consultants. In addition, the goal of the project and the research goals were closely aligned.

This study uses the five step action research cycle (ARC) put forward by Susman and Evered (1978). The five ARC steps are: (1) diagnosing, (2) action planning, (3) action taking, (4)

Figure 2. Conceptual framework

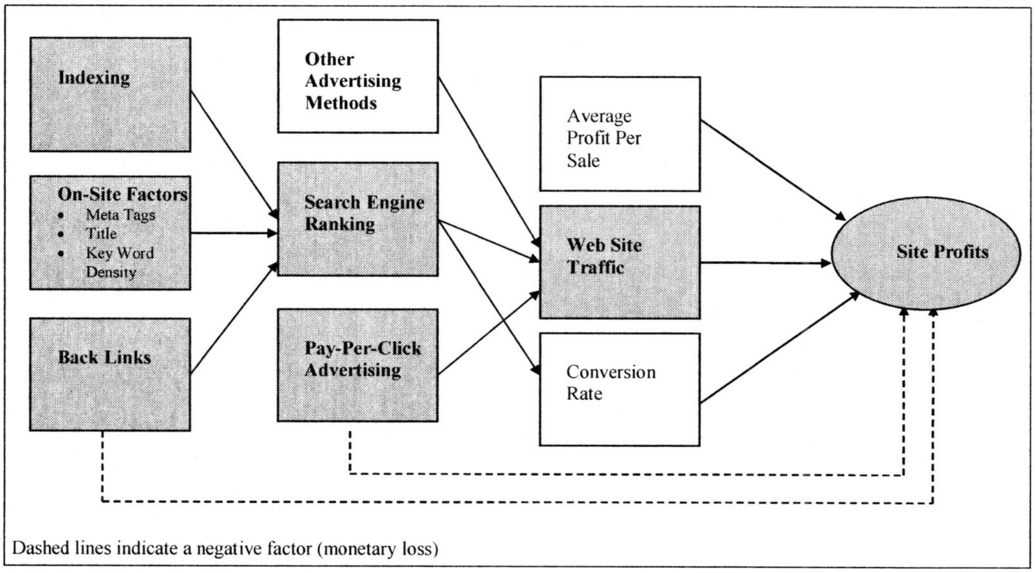

evaluating, and (5) specifying learning. Each intervention entails working through each phase of the ARC.

Measures

The ultimate goal of this project was to increase MyBestiPodStuff.com's profits. Thus, we consider the increase in revenue generated from the SEO project and the costs involved. Data was gathered prior to and at the completion of the project. In addition, two intervening metrics were of interest—search engine rank and Web site traffic. Data for each of these measures were gathered prior to project initiation and after each intervention. Search engine rank was determined by entering the target search term in each of the major search engines on a daily basis and examining the SERPs for the site. Web site traffic data came from the site's log file, which recorded the number of daily visitors.

Baseline Analysis

MyBestiPodStuff.com was founded in June 2005 to sell iPods and iPod accessories online. The owner ran the business and all products were drop shipped to customers. The company's owner spent a considerable amount of time developing the Web site, which came online in July 2005. After a month the site had not been indexed by any of the three major search engines (Google, Yahoo, and MSN). Thus, the site was not ranked for any key word or term. At this point traffic to the site was virtually non-existent and the business was running at a net monetary loss.

The site's owner had considered the use of pay-per-click (PPC) advertising. However, the iPod area was highly competitive and the owner determined he would need to pay about $0.40 for each click. The small amount of traffic to the site had a conversion rate of 1.2%. That is, 1.2% of the sites' visitors actually made a purchase. The

Table 1. Optimization level and rank improvement

Intervention	Date Range	Optimization Level	Search Engine Rank	Visitors (during time period)	Page Views (during time period)
Baseline	8/1/05—8/8/05	None	None	16	901
Intervention One	8/8/05—8/15/05	RSS Feed	None	31	2381
	8/15/05—8/22/05	RSS Feed	None	93	3353
	8/22/05—8/29/05	N/A	Yahoo—15 MSN—34 Google—N/A	543	1908
Intervention Two	8/29/05—9/5/05	High PR Backlink	Yahoo—13 MSN—28 Google—N/A	884	2536
	9/5/05—9/12/05	Google Sitemap	Yahoo—13 MSN—28 Google—N/A	996	3063
	9/12/05—9/19/05	Site indexing for Yahoo and MSN completed	Yahoo—9 MSN—14 Google—N/A	1109	3654
Intervention Three	9/19/05—9/26/05	On Page Optimization	Yahoo—3 MSN—2 Google—N/A	1866	5423

site also had an average profit per sale of $18.25. Thus, for every 100 visitors the site would expect a profit of about $21.90 ($18.25 x 1.2). A PPC advertising campaign would cost about $40 for every 100 visitors—resulting in an expected loss of $18.10. Clearly, a PPC campaign would not be a profitable endeavor.

In August 2005 the site's owner decided to implement a search engine optimization initiative. The authors were brought in to oversee the SEO project. The goal of the project was to have the major search engines to index the site and rank it well for chosen keywords and phrases. Based on an analysis of the competition it was determined that the site should be optimized for the key phrase "discount iPod accessories." As a baseline the site's search engine rankings and traffic statistics were recorded at the beginning of the project (see Table 1).

Intervention One: Indexing (Yahoo and MSN)

Diagnosing

Indexing is concerned with quickly getting the search engines to index the site. It is the obvious first step in any search engine optimization project. Morgan and Hunt (2006) point out the importance of attracting the search engine spiders—usually the first step in the indexing process. In addition, Raisinghani (2005) points out that the ability of search engine spiders to easily index a site is a vital characteristic of good search engine optimization.

Action Planning

There are a number of methods that can be used to have a site indexed by the search engines. First, all of the major search engines have a page that allows users to suggest a new site that should be included in the index. However, using this process is typically very slow. In addition, certain search engines, like Yahoo, charge for expedited review of submitted sites, but do not guarantee the site will be included in the search engine's index.

Second, the Webmaster can attempt to have a site that is already indexed include a link to the target site. As the search engine spiders revisit the indexed site, they will follow the link to the new site.

Third, there are a number of SEO tricks that have been reported as successfully having new sites indexed very quickly. These include using multiple Blogs with a link to the target site (AbayomiPaul 2005) and using really simple syndication (RSS) feeds (Wall 2005). The RSS feed approach is further detailed in the next section

Action Taking

RSS is a method for syndicating Web based content by creating an extensible markup language (XML) formatted file. Each RSS XML file contains title, link, description, and other optional information.

According to Wall (2005) adding an RSS feed from a Web site to either MyYahoo or MyMSN (both of these allow users to develop a custom Web portal) will make their associated spiders aware of the site and thus index it quickly. Since Google did not have a customized portal at the time of this study, this technique was only used with Yahoo and MSN.

An RSS feed of the site's featured products was created using Tristiana (a RSS creation tool). Accounts were established on MyYahoo and MyMSN and the site's feed was added to both.

Evaluating

Search engine spiders have known Internet Protocol (IP) addresses, so determining which spiders were visiting the site was easy. The site's log files show that Yahoo's spider began indexed the site within three days of adding the RSS feed. MSN's spider took eight days to begin indexing the

Figure 3. Weekly site rankings

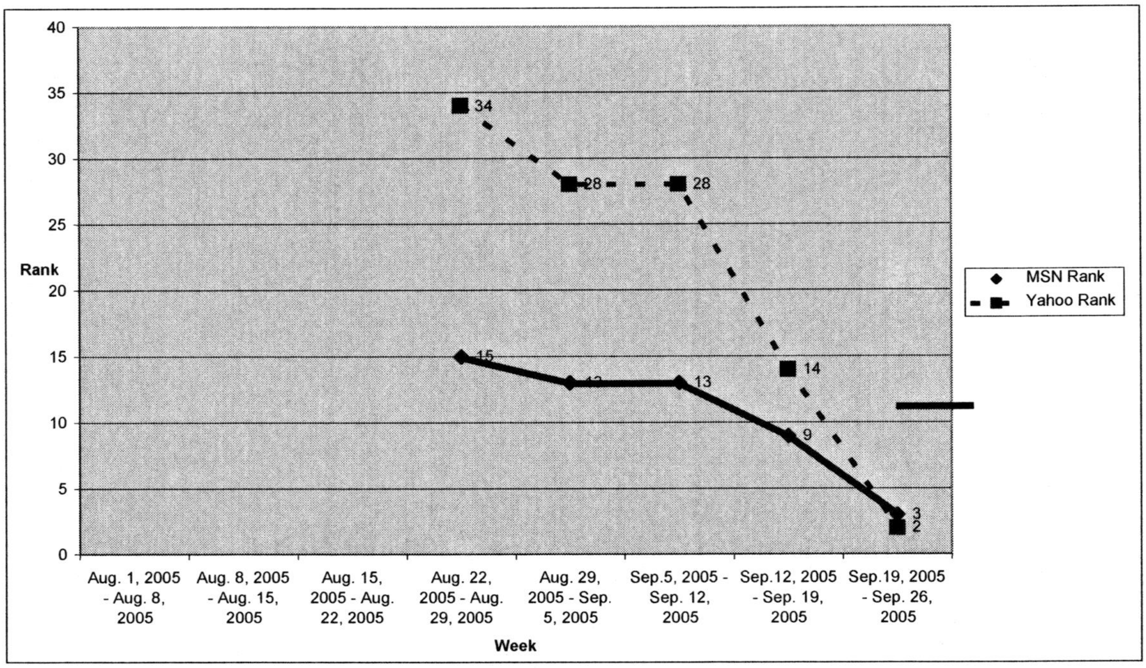

Figure 4. Site visitors and page views

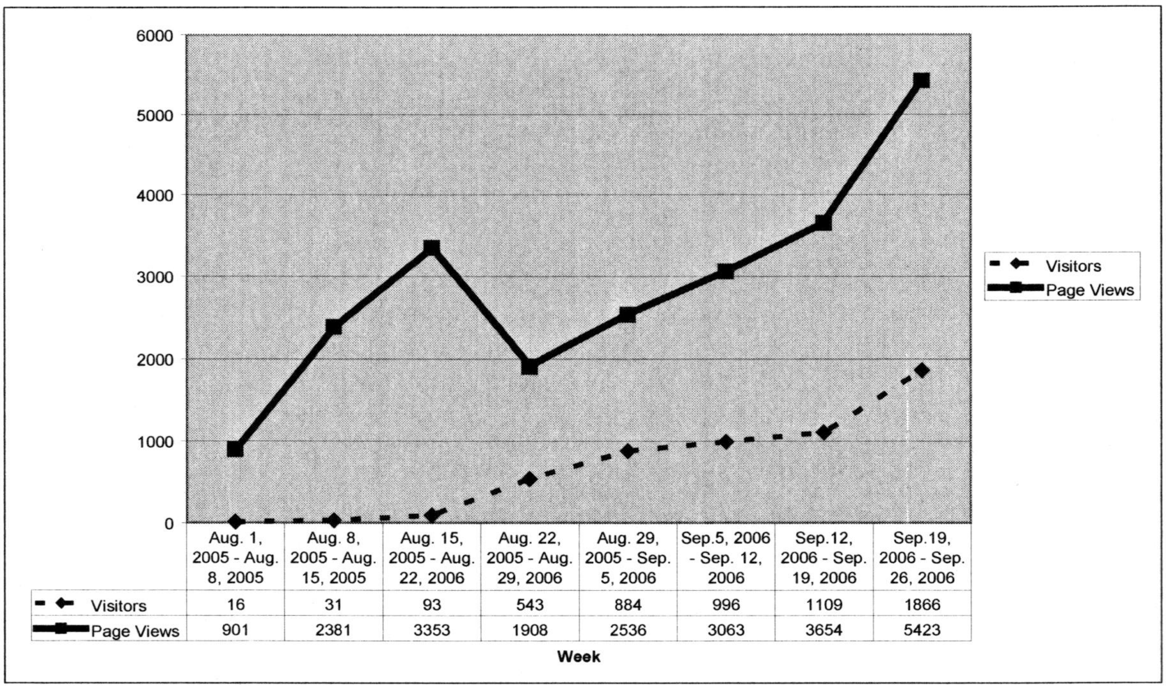

	Aug. 1, 2005 - Aug. 8, 2005	Aug. 8, 2005 - Aug. 15, 2005	Aug. 15, 2005 - Aug. 22, 2006	Aug. 22, 2005 - Aug. 29, 2006	Aug. 29, 2005 - Sep. 5, 2006	Sep.5, 2006 - Sep. 12, 2006	Sep.12, 2006 - Sep. 19, 2006	Sep.19, 2006 - Sep. 26, 2006
Visitors	16	31	93	543	884	996	1109	1866
Page Views	901	2381	3353	1908	2536	3063	3654	5423

Week

site. Indexing by Yahoo and MSN, of the site's main page and first level sub-pages, was largely complete by August 22, 2005. After the site was indexed we checked its rank for the chosen key phrase. At this point the site ranked 15th on Yahoo and 34th on MSN (see Figure 3). In addition, the number of weekly visitors increased 580% over the preceding week (see Table 1 and Figure 4).

Specifying Learning

Based on the results detailed above we conclude that using RSS is an effective means of attracting Yahoo's and MSN's spiders to a new site. In addition, simply having the site indexed for a moderately competitive key term led to fairly good rankings and a huge increase in site traffic.

Intervention Two: Google Indexing

Diagnosing

At this point the site had not been indexed by Google. As the most widely used search engine, a listing in Google was seen as an important part of the project.

Action Planning

Google does have a page that allows site owner's to submit their site for consideration by Google. However, submission does not guarantee that Google will include the site and there is anecdotal evidence to suggest that it might consider submitted site as less important than those the Google spider finds on its own.

One of the main methods SEO consultants use to attract Google's spider is to include a link to the target site on another site with a high Google PageRank (PR). Sites with a high PR are visited more often by the Google spider. When the spider visits it should see and follow the link to the target site.

Another approach that may be used to attract the Google spider is submitting a sitemap to Google. A sitemap is a file that specifies each of the pages in a Web site. Search engines use sitemaps to help them index a site more quickly. Google's sitemap program was still in a beta period at this point.

Action Taking

The site's owner decided to spend $100 to purchase a link to his site from a well known site with a Google page rank of eight. The link was purchased on August 29, 2005 and remained in place for one month.

In addition, the SEO team downloaded and modified an active server page (ASP) script that automatically generated an XML file that complied with the Google Sitemap Protocol (GSP). This file was uploaded to MyBestiPodStuff.com's server and the URL for the file was submitted to Google. The sitemap was submitted on September 8, 2005.

Evaluating

Logs from MyBestiPodStuff show that the Google spider visited the site within three days of purchasing the link. However, the spider only visited 20 times and was responsible for only 30 page views. This is fairly low for a site with over 100 pages and indicates that the Google spider did not visit every page. The sitemap file was retrieved by Google within 24 hours of submitting it. The sitemap system indicated that the Google spider encountered no errors in attempting to crawl the site.

The Google spider continued to visit the site periodically. However, by the end of this study, the site still had not been included in Google's index. A final check of Google on October 1, 2005 revealed that MyBestiPodStuff.com had still not been included in Google's index.

Specifying Learning

While the link from the well known site did not achieve the goal of causing Google to include the site in its index, it did slightly improve rankings on both Yahoo and MSN (see Table 1). Based on our results, we conclude that acquiring a link from a high page rank site will cause the Google spider to find a site. However, Google's spider seems to take an inordinately long time to index sites. Furthermore, it appears that links from well-known sites lead to a modest improvement in search engine ranking on both Yahoo and MSN.

In addition to the link from the well known site, the shopping cart system used for the site created links back to the homepage from every page on the site (this resulted in over 100 back links to the homepage). While Google puts little weight on these internal links, both Yahoo and MSN consider them when determining ranking on their SERPs. Table 1 and Figure 3 show that as Yahoo and MSN continued to index the site (find more of the site's internal pages) its ranking increased.

Intervention Three: Improve Rankings

Diagnosing

Based on the fact that the site had already achieved a good ranking in both Yahoo and MSN, it was determined that the next phase of the project should focus on improving those rankings by changing the site's content and underlying Meta tags.

Action Planning

The project proceeded by analyzing those sites that ranked well for the chosen key phrase. The key phrase was used on all three major search engines and the top ten results on each were analyzed. Comparing the features of the high-ranking sites with MyBestiPodStuff.com revealed four areas that required significant improvement—site title, header tags, Meta tags, and keyword density.

Action Taking

First, the original site title was "Your source for discount iPod accessories, including FM transmitters, cases, skins, chargers, and much more." A comparison with the well ranking sites revealed that this title was way too long and unfocused. The site title was changed to "Discount iPod Accessories" which is the targeted key phrase.

Second, the site did not use any H1 headers. The major search engines consider text in an H1 HTML header to be of increased importance (K'necht 2004). Therefore the phrase "Discount iPod accessories—we carry the latest iPod cases, chargers, FM transmitters, skins, and much more" was added at the top of the main page within an H1 tag.

Third, the title, description, and keyword Meta tags were analyzed and compared with the high-ranking sites. Zhang and Dimitroff (2005b) specifically examined the use of Meta tags in a controlled experiment. They found that including the key phrase in certain Meta tags—title, description, and subject—led to higher search engine rankings. The shopping cart system used to create MyBestiPodStuff.com did not allow for inclusion of the subject Meta tag.

The title Meta tag was changed to match the new Web site title, "Discount iPod Accessories." Like the site title, the description Meta tag was too long and not focused on the main key phrase. It originally read "MyBestiPodStuff.com offers iPod and iPod accessories. We're your one stop source for iPod FM transmitters, cases, skins, chargers, and much more." In this version of the Meta tag, the main key phrase does not appear at all. Therefore, the description Meta tag was changed to "Discount iPod accessories. MyBestiPodStuff offers a large selection of accessories for iPod,

iPod mini, iPod shuffle, and iPod Photo. We carry iPod FM transmitters, iPod cases, iPod chargers, iPod skins, iPod batteries, iPod speakers, and other cool iPod gear all at discount prices."

The final phase of the analysis compared the keyword density of each high-ranking site versus the keyword density of MyBestiPodStuff.com. This analysis was performed using the Keyword Density tool from SEOchat.com (http://www.seo-chat.com/seo-tools/keyword-density/). Keyword density is a measure of how often a key word or phrase appears on a page. It is shown as a percentage, so a page containing ten words total, one of which is a key word, would have a key word density of ten percent. The analysis indicated that the high ranking sites had a key word density of 1.2—1.6% for the phrase "discount iPod accessories." However, MyBestiPodStuff.com had a density of only 0.3% for the key phrase. Zhang and Dimitroff (2005a) specifically conclude that increasing the keyword density increases search engine rank.

There are two ways to increase the keyword density of a Web page. The first, obviously, is to add more of the keyword to the page. However, this must be done in a natural way. Simply adding line after line of the keyword or adding it out of context will cause the search engines to penalize the site and in the worst case scenario actually ban the site from the search engine index. Therefore, the key phrase was added cautiously and in a natural manner. This resulted in a key word density of 0.65%, which was still too low. The second way to increase key word density is to reduce the overall number of non-key words on the page. The main page for MyBestiPodStuff.com contained a number of featured products, each with a detailed description. The main page was redesigned to eliminate the detailed descriptions and only show the products' names. After this was completed the key word density rose to 0.91%. While this is still lower than competing sites, it was felt that it would be difficult to increase the key word density further without making major changes to the site.

Evaluating

At the conclusion of this intervention the site's ranking in both Yahoo and MSN improved dramatically and quickly. Within two days of making the changes the site ranked 3rd on Yahoo and 2nd on MSN for the key phrase (see Figure 3). In addition, site traffic increased 60% over the preceding week.

Specifying Learning

The main conclusion from this intervention is that small, easily made, changes to a Web site can lead to dramatic improvements in search engine rankings. In addition, Web developers would be well served to check on the competition prior to the development process. High ranking sites in the same industry should be analyzed to generate a list of Meta tags and determine an appropriate key word density.

Six Month Follow-Up

We rechecked the site in each of the three major search engines in March 2006—after about six months. The site ranked first for the key phrase on Yahoo and second on MSN. However, while the site was included in Google's index, the site still did not appear within the first 500 results returned for the key phrase on Google. The poor results on Google are most likely a result of an aborted link building campaign on the part of the site's owner. A check of the number of links at this time showed that the site only had 36 incoming links from other sites. This resulted in a Google Page Rank of zero. By comparison, the top ranked site on Google for the key phrase had almost 300 links and a Page Rank of five.

Long Term Follow-up

After the initial SEO project no further changes were made to the site. In fact, the site was sold, but the new owner abandoned it (did not update or maintain it). Approximately 8 months after the project concluded the site was ranked #1 on Google for "discount Ipod accessories." A follow-up at 1year showed that the site maintained the top rankings on both Google and Yahoo. However, during that time MSN had undergone a major change to its algorithm and the site appeared on the second page of the results.

An additional follow-up was conducted in December 2007, more than two years after the project. No changes had been made to the site and no backlinks had been added since the initial project. At this follow-up the site was ranked second on Yahoo, 14 on Google, and 11 on MSN.

CONCLUSION

This research has two main goals: (1) determine the impact of search engine optimization on a site's ranking and traffic and (2) determine if a search engine optimization project provides a positive return on investment.

Site Ranking and Traffic

Clearly, the search engine optimization project led to a dramatic improvement in the site's rankings on both Yahoo and MSN. Merely having the search engines index the site led to an increase in traffic of over 500%. During the project's two month time frame site traffic increased over 125 times.

We were not successful in our attempts to have Google index and rank the site. While we were able to attract the Google spider, indexing proceeded at a very slow pace. The main reason for this failure may be due to the so called Google "sandbox." The "sandbox" refers to the fact that Google applies an aging filter to its index (SEOmoz 2005). Basically, it prefers older sites to newer sites. In addition, Google wants to be sure a site is going to be around for a while before it adds it to the index. Therefore, new sites are "sandboxed"—excluded from Google for a period of about 6-8 months.

Return on Investment

The cost of this SEO effort was $1200 ($1100 for consultant time and $100 for the high page rank link). It should be noted that the consultant fees were relatively low for a complete SEO project. Many SEO consultants charge $5000 or more for a project like that described above. As mentioned above the site has had a conversion rate of 1.2%, which is in line with most other online retailers in this sector. The average profit per sale is $18.25.

Before the SEO project the site had about 60 unique visitors and perhaps 1 sale per month. Due to hosting fees of $57 per month, the site was actually losing about $40 per month. At the conclusion of the SEO project the site had about 7,500 unique visitors per month and about 90 sales per month. This leads to an average monthly profit of about $1,585 per month and a return on investment of over 30%. In addition, the SEO project was expected to continue to produce positive returns, with little or no additional cost, into the future.

Comparison with Pay-Per-Click

The real value of an SEO project is increased site traffic. Online marketing is another method for increasing site traffic. Therefore, the value of the SEO project was compared with the potential value of a search marketing campaign. Search marketing measures cost per click (CPC). The cost per click for the SEO project was $0.16 ($1200/7500). In addition, the CPC for the SEO project will continue to decrease over time. This is due to the fact that monthly traffic should continue with little additional cost.

Due to the competitive nature of the iPod accessories market, MyBestiPodStuff.com would need to pay about $0.40 per click to run pay-per-click ads on Google and $0.30 to run Overture (Yahoo) search ads. These figures are in line with those charged by product search sites, such as Shopping.com ($0.50/click), Bizrate.com ($0.30/click), and Nextag.com ($0.30/click). We therefore conclude that a successful SEO project is a cost effective means of driving traffic to a new Web site.

DISCUSSION

Academic Contributions

This chapter contributes to academic literature in the area of search engine optimization and search engine marketing in three specific ways. First, this research examined SEO in the context of a working e-commerce site. While previous researchers, notably Raisinghani (2005) and Curran (2004), make useful suggestions for SEO, their work is based on a review of the practitioner literature and not empirical data. Zhang and Dimitroff (2005a, b) do manipulate a Web site in their experiments, but the site was informational (not e-commerce), was developed specifically for their study and was not revenue generating.

Second, most previous research has focused on only one aspect of SEO. For instance, Zhang and Dimitroff's (2005a; 2005b) primary focus is on-site factors (those that can be manipulated by the Webmaster). This study combines both academic and practitioner knowledge to develop an integrated approach to SEO based on indexing, on-site optimization, and the use of back links.

Third, since this chapter uses an e-commerce site, the monetary value of the SEO effort was determined and compared to other search engine marketing approaches—namely pay-per-click advertisements. The result of this analysis is that SEO is a more cost effective search engine marketing mechanism, in this particular case. This finding contrasts directly with the economic model developed by Sen (2005). In his model Sen found that SEO is never an optimal search engine marketing strategy. The Sen Model is somewhat supported by a recent study from the Search Engine Marketing Professional Organization (SEMPO). In its annual survey of search engine marketers the organization found that 81.8% used pay-per-click advertising, but only 12% used search engine optimization (SEMPRO 2004). However, the Sen Model assumes that a site has a fixed probability of becoming listed on the first page of the SERPs. As this research shows, it is possible to manipulate that probability.

Contributions for Practice

The research presented above has a number of practical applications for those involved in SEO and search engine marketing. First, rapid indexing is a vital element in any search engine optimization project. Simply getting the site indexed, in this case, led to a rapid increase in site visitors and eventually profits.

Second, Web developers and site owners should include SEO as part of the Web development process. Specifically, they should review competing, well ranking sites, to determine the best site title, Meta tags, and key word density.

Third, due to the rise in popularity of Google, obtaining back links has become a primary focus of many optimizers. This phenomenon has led to two new industries—brokering the purchase and sale of links (see www.textlinkbrokers.com), and systems that help Webmasters manage link exchange (such as www.linkmetro.com and www.gotlinks.com). However, this study shows that even a single link from a highly regarded source can lead to large improvements in a site's ranking. It should be noted that this might not hold true for a more established site that already has a substantial number of back links. In addition, link building campaigns are time consuming and often expensive. On page optimization techniques can usually be accomplished quickly and with minimal expense.

Fourth, focus on Yahoo and MSN first. Based on the fact that Google has a dominate amount of market share in the search arena, this advice might seem counter intuitive, . However, Google's "sandbox" means that a new site is unlikely to be included in Google's search engine results for at least a few months. Therefore, the best search engine marketing strategy may be to optimize initially for Yahoo and MSN, and purchase ads from Google. As the site emerges from the Google "sandbox" the optimizer can focus more on building links and improving the sites PageRank. Further investigation into this approach is an interesting area for future research.

Fifth, the follow-up after two years is revealing. While the search engines have changed their algorithms and other sites have emerged to compete with MyBestIpodStuff.com, the site has maintained strong positions in the SERPs. This was achieved without any additional changes to the site or backlinks. In fact, the site had not been updated in two years. This result flies in the face of SEO practitioner wisdom that the search engines like fresh content and will penalize static sites. For practitioners and site owners it may mean that SEO does not require constant updates and tweaking. This is another ripe area for future research.

Limitations

The one obvious limitation of this study is the fact that it uses only one Web site. The fact that the site sells iPod accessories, which is a very competitive market, may have skewed the conclusions away from pay-per-click advertising. Therefore, future research should extend this chapter by observing the results of SEO on other sites and for a variety of products.

The SEO project described also reveals the difficultly involved in having a site added to the Google index. Therefore, the impact of on site optimization and outside links on Google ranking could not be determined. As Google is the most widely used search engine, this is a serious limitation of this research.

Future Directions

The conceptual framework detailed in Figure 2, can act as a guide for future research. The academic and practitioner communities require a better understanding of the impact and correlations of the elements specified in the framework. Such research would require extensive data from a number of e-commerce sites, in multiple industries.

Future research should specifically focus on the interaction between position in the SERPs and e-commerce conversion. Obviously, converting Web site traffic to buyers is essential for e-commerce success. A recent study (WebSideStory 2006) found that while Google is responsible for a majority of Web searches; however, its traffic also has the lowest conversion rate of the major search engines—only 3.83 percent, as compared with 4.07 percent for Yahoo and 6.03 percent for MSN.

Most previous research on SEO (including this chapter) has used fairly simple scenarios—optimizing for one or a few key words. However, many e-commerce sites contain hundreds, thousands, and even tens of thousands of products. Each of these is a potential target for search engine optimization efforts. How should practitioners manage an SEO effort that contains hundreds or thousands of key words and terms? This question can be combined with the previous suggestion to develop a very complex SEO situation where there are thousands of key words that need to be optimized for the best search engine (in terms of conversion potential).

The search engines constantly change their ranking algorithms. This leads to situations in which a site might rank well one day and completely disappear from the search engine the next. How should site owners plan and manage in such a volatile situation? Are there any methods or techniques that are more likely to provide long term results?

One new approach that practitioners have begun to use is to incorporate Web 2.0 techniques into their SEO strategy. This approach involves creating Web 2.0 content sites and using social bookmarking in order to have a number of sites ranking at the top of the search engines. Web 2.0 content sites are Web sites where users can easily create and/or upload content. Some examples include blogs, wikis, YouTube, Squidoo, and Hubpages. Social bookmarking is a way for Web users to store, organize, share and search bookmarks of web pages. These bookmarks are typically public, meaning anyone can see them. Bookmarks are usually categorized and also tagged. Tagging allows the user to associate a bookmark with any chosen words or phrases. Tags are completely created by the user, not the social bookmarking site. Some of the more popular social bookmarking sites include Del.icio.us, Digg, and StumbleUpon. Using the Web 2.0 SEO approach multiple content sites are created with links back to the target site. Social bookmarking is used to bookmark and tag all of the content sites and the original site. The overall result is an increase in backlinks to the target site and the potential to have some of the content and social bookmarks rank for the chosen terms. Using this approach some practitioners have been able to claim all of the top ten spots on the major search engines.

REFERENCES

AbayomiPaul, T. (2005). Can a Ping Really Help Your Blog Get Top Search Engine Rankings?. *Search Engine Journal*, January 19, 2005. Retrieved July 17, 2006, from http://www.searchenginejournal.com/?p=1243

Baskerville, R. L. & Wood-Harper, A. T. (1996). A Critical Perspective on Action Research as a Method for Information Systems Research, *Journal of Information Technology* (11:3), 1996, pp. 235-246.

Brin, S. & Page, L. (1998). The anatomy of a large-scale hypertextual Web search engine. *Proceedings of the 7th International World Wide Web Conference*, April 1998, Computer Networks and ISDN Systems, 30 (1998), 107 - 117. Available from http://www-db.stanford.edu/pub/papers/google.pdf

CyberWyre. (2006) Updated: Highest Paying AdSense Keywords. Retrieved July 17, 2006, from *http://www.cwire.org/2006/03/23/updated-highest-paying-adsense-keywords/*

Curran, Kevin. (2004). Tips for Achieving High Positioning in the Results Pages of the Major Search Engines, *Information Technology Journal* 3 (2): 202-205

DoubleClick.com (2005). Search Before the Purchase - Understanding Buyer Search Activity as it Builds to Online Purchase. Retrieved July 17, 2006, from *http://www.doubleclick.com/us/knowledge_central/documents/RESEARCH/searchpurchase_0502.pdf*

Google (2004). Google searches more sites more quickly, delivering the most relevant results. Retrieved July 17, 2006, from *http://www.google.com/technology/index.html*

iProspect (2006). iProspect Search Engine User Behavior Study. Retrieved July 17, 2006, from h*ttp://www.iprospect.com/premiumPDFs/WhitePaper_2006_SearchEngineUserBehavior.pdf*

K'necht, A. (2004). SEO and Your Web Site. *Digital Web Magazine*, August 4, 2004. Retrieved July 17, 2006, from *http://www.digital-web.com/articles/seo_and_your_web_site/*

Kohli, R. & Kettinger, W.J. (2004). Informating The Clan: Controlling Physicians' Costs And Outcomes, *MIS Quarterly* (28:3), September 2004, pp. 363-394.

MarketingSherpa.com. (Sept. 20, 2005). MarketingSherpa Study Results: 3,271 Marketers Reveal Search Marketing Costs, Clicks, & Conversions. Retrieved October 3, 2005, from *http://www.marketingsherpa.com/sample.cfm?contentID=3078*

Morgan, M. & Hunt, B. (2005). Search engine optimization basics, Part 3: Get your Web pages into search indexes - A search engine can't find what it doesn't see. March 21, 2006. Retrieved July 17, 2006, from *http://www-28.ibm.com/developerworks/web/library/wa-seo3.html*

Rapoport, R. (1970). Three dilemmas of action research, *Human Relations*, Vol. 23 No. 6, pp. 499-513.

Raisinghani, Mahesh S. (2005). Future Trends in Search Engines, *Journal of Electronic Commerce in Organizations*; Jul-Sep 2005; 3, 3

SEMPRO (2004). The State of Search Engine Marketing 2004 - Survey of Advertisers and Agencies Search Engine Marketing Professional Organization (SEMPO). Retrieved July 17, 2006, from *http://www.sempo.org/learning_center/research/sempo_trends/SEMPO-Market-Sizing-2004-SUMMARY-v1.pdf*

SEMPRO (2005). Press Release - Search Engine Marketers Spent $5.75 Billion in 2005, According to the Search Engine Marketing Professional Organization (SEMPO). Retrieved July 17, 2006, from *http://www.sempo.org/news/releases/Search_Engine_Marketers*

Sen, R. (2005). Optimal Search Engine Marketing Strategy, *International Journal of Electronic Commerce* (10:1), Fall 2005, pp. 9-25.

SEOmoz. Google's Patent: Information Retrieval Based on Historical Data. Retrieved July 17, 2006, from *http://www.seomoz.org/articles/google-historical-data-patent.php*

SEOmoz (2005). 2005 Analysis of Google's Sandbox. Retrieved July 17, 2006, from *http://www.seomoz.org/articles/google-sandbox-analysis.php*

Sherman, Chris. (Sept. 28, 2005). How are Search Marketers Performing?. Retrieved October 3, 2005, from *http://searchenginewatch.com/searchday/article.php/3551921*

Street, C.T. & Meister, D.B. (2004). Small Business Growth and Internal Transparency: The role of information systems, *MIS Quarterly* (28:3), September 2004, pp. 473-506.

Sullivan, D. (2006). The mixed message of paid inclusion. Search Engine Report, May 6, 2002. Retrieved July 17, 2006, from *http://searchenginewatch.com/sereport/02/05-inclusion.html*

Sullivan, D. (2003). How Search Engines Rank Web Pages July 31, 2003. SearchEngineWatch. Retrieved July 17, 2006, from *http://searchenginewatch.com/webmasters/article.php/2167961*

Susman, G. I., and Evered, R. D. (1978). An Assessment of the Scientific Merits of Action Research, *Administrative Science Quarterly* (23:4), 1978, pp. 582-603.

Wall, Danny. (Feb. 22, 2005). An Insider's Secret To Seriously High Rankings With Yahoo. Retrieved October 3, 2005, from *http://www.seochat.com/c/a/Yahoo-Optimization-Help/An-Insiders-Secret-To-Seriously-High-Rankings-With-Yahoo*

WebSideStory (2006). Press Release - New WebSideStory Study Reveals Conversion Rate for Each Major Search Engine. February 15, 2006. Retrieved July 17, 2006, from *http://www.websidestory.com/company/news-events/press-releases/view-release.html?id=319*

Zhang, J. and Dimitroff, A. (2005a). The impact of webpage content characteristics on webpage visibility in search engine results (Part I), *Information Processing and Management* 41: 665-690.

Zhang, J. and Dimitroff, A. (2005b). The impact of metadata implementation on webpage visibility in search engine results (Part II), *Information Processing and Management* 41: 691-715.

Zing, B. and Lin, Z. (2006). The Impact of Search Engine Optimization on Online Advertising Market, *Proceedings of the 8th international conference on Electronic commerce: The new e-commerce: innovations for conquering current barriers, obstacles and limitations to conducting successful business on the internet*, Fredericton, New Brunswick, Canada, pp. 519—529.

Chapter VI
A Flow Theory Integrated Model of Web IS Success

Edward J. Garrity
Canisius College, USA

Yong Jin Kim
Sogang University, South Korea
State University of New York at Binghamton, USA

Joseph B. O'Donnell
Canisius College, USA

Cheul Rhee
State University of New York at Buffalo, USA

G. Lawrence Sanders
State University of New York at Buffalo, USA

ABSTRACT

This chapter develops a new model of web IS success that takes into account both intrinsic and extrinsic motivating factors. The proposed model begins with the Garrity and Sanders model of technologic acceptance and develops an extended nomological network of success factors that draws on motivation and flow theory.

INTRODUCTION

The technology acceptance model (TAM) has been the dominant framework for explaining the acceptance and use of information technology for nearly twenty years (Keil, Beranek, & Konsynski, 1995). In particular, research has found that perceived usefulness and perceived ease of use are important predictors of the acceptance of information systems technologies (Adam, Nelson,

& Todd, 1992; Davis, 1989; Doll, Hendrickson, & Deng, 1998).

The difficulty comes in applying the TAM model to the Web shopping experience. Unlike traditional organizational information systems, web systems are used for a variety of activities including both work and pleasure. This leads to a disconnect in terms of applying the perceived usefulness and perceived ease of use constructs to the shopping experience because they are typically not the only driving forces behind web use (Moon & Kim, 2001).

Recent research has extended the TAM model to the Web environment by including intrinsic motivating factors to take into account a wider and more realistic assessment of users' goals (Hackbarth, Grover, & Yi, 2003; Koufaris, 2002; Moon & Kim, 2001; Venkatesh, 2000).

For example, Koufaris (2002) examined the dual role of the consumer in using a web-based system environment, where an individual can be viewed as both a computer user and a consumer. When viewed as a consumer, Koufaris (2002) argues that perceived shopping enjoyment (an intrinsic motivator) is important for on-line shopping since it can have an impact on attitudes and usage intentions. His rationale was based on the findings of Jarvenpaa & Todd (1997a; 1997b).

However, their studies did not adequately explain perceived usefulness and ease of use and their nomological net did not integrate TAM with their intrinsic motivation factor, perceived shopping enjoyment.

This chapter uses the Garrity and Sanders (1998) model as a vehicle to integrate the individual as a consumer perspective, wherein shopping enjoyment is used as an intrinsic motivator, and the individual is also viewed as a computer user, wherein an extrinsic motivator is implemented using task support satisfaction. Our approach treats shopping enjoyment as a state variable that emerges from the interaction between the user and the information system. This perspective is consistent with flow theory (Ghani & Deshpande, 1994; Trevino & Webster, 1992), motivation theory (Deci, 1971; Scott et al., 1988) as well as environmental psychology (Mehrabian & Russel, 1974).

This chapter contributes to the literature in three ways. Firstly, the proposed model provides a nomological network of success factors that provides a better understanding of how intrinsic and extrinsic motivation factors impact the use of systems in general and websites in particular. Secondly, this chapter incorporates two dimensions, decision support satisfaction and interface satisfaction, as antecedent variables to expand our understanding of perceived usefulness (implemented as task support satisfaction). Thirdly, decision support satisfaction not only provides for enhanced explanatory power in the model, but it can also offer important insights into the decision support provided by consumer shopping-oriented web information systems (Garrity et al., 2005). This is especially important because consumer shopping-oriented web information systems differ from conventional DSS in a number of ways, including and most notably that consumers have an extensive and different decision making process from managers (O'Keefe & McEachern, 1988).

LITERATURE REVIEW

Research in IS success has tended to concentrate on user satisfaction and technology acceptance (Wixom & Todd, 2005). Research on the IS success focuses on user attitudes toward information and systems (DeLone & McLean, 1992) while research on technology acceptance focuses on how individuals perceive ease of use to predict their behavioral attitudes and actions (Venkatesh et al. 2003).

Wixom's & Todd's (2005) research builds a conceptual bridge between evaluating system success and predicting system use. They contend that information-related attitudes and system-related attitudes can converge through behavioral beliefs about such factors as ease-of-use.

The goal satisfaction-based IS success model (Kim et al. 2004) also integrates two research approaches. Instead of dividing information-based beliefs and systems-based beliefs, this model combines decision-support satisfaction and task-support satisfaction. This model is especially useful when the evaluative function of a model is stressed. In a rigorous sense, information quality such as completeness, accuracy, format, and currency cannot be easily measured. Thus, researchers have instead measured users' perceptions about information, but this is not ideal, either, because perceived information quality is in fact the information within the system. Information quality in its purest sense could be measured if a text-based set of information were given to survey participants.

Rather than perceived information quality, in the goal satisfaction-based IS success model,

Figure 1. Garrity and Sanders (1998) model of IS success

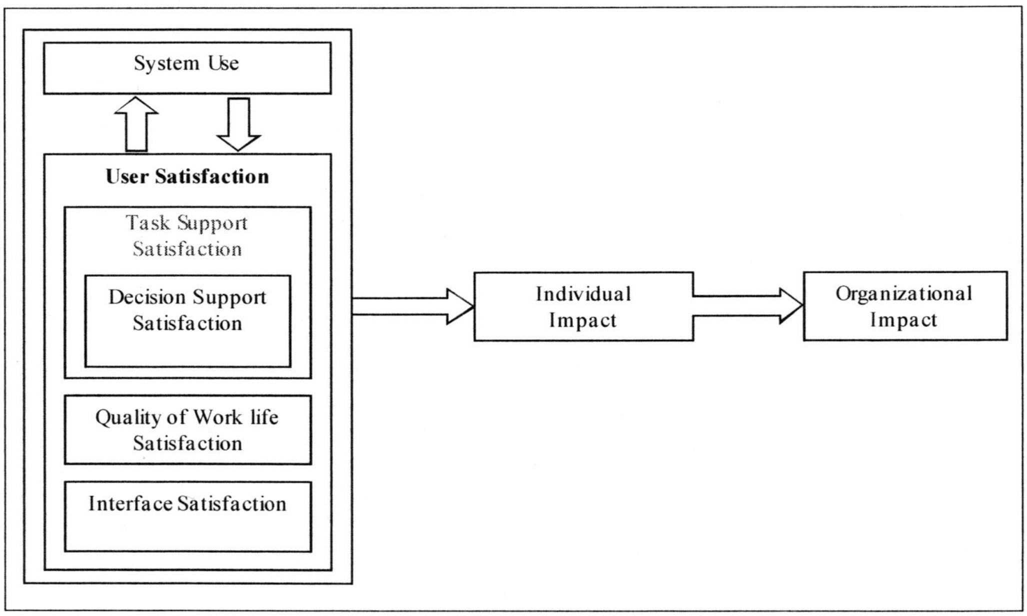

Figure 2. GSISS model: Goal satisfaction-based IS success model

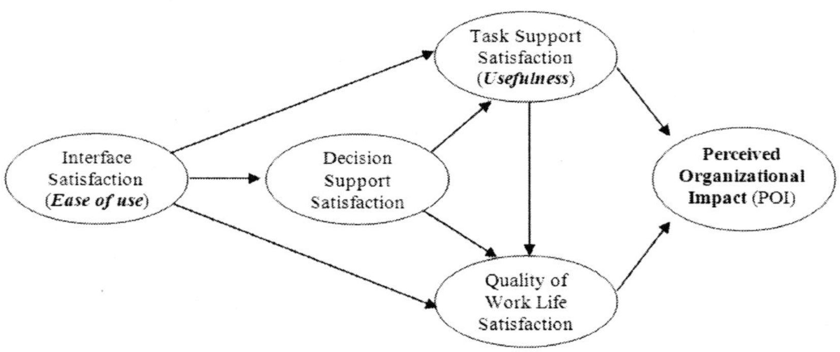

decision support satisfaction and task support satisfaction with information systems are both measured because users' ultimate behaviors may be affected by complete information systems, not by information alone.

Garrity and Sanders Model of IS Success and the GSISS Model

Garrity and Sanders (1998) adapted the DeLone & McLean (1992) model and proposed an alternative model in the context of organizational systems and socio-technical systems. They developed a user satisfaction inventory comprised of questions from six well-developed instruments. Garrity and Sanders expand on the DeLone and McLean model by identifying four major factors they assert are the basic underlying constructs that make up existing success measures in the IS field (Figure 1). They validate these constructs using a modified Delphi technique whereby IS research experts mapped existing measurement items into one of four factors.

The four factors they identify are task support satisfaction, decision support satisfaction, interface satisfaction, and quality of work life satisfaction.

In order to better understand the underlying dimensions, Kim et al. (2004) developed and tested a revised model, which arranges the IS success dimensions into a nomological net in order to further understand IS success and to test the construct validity of their dimensions. The revised or detailed model, called Goal Satisfaction-based IS Success Model (GSISS Model) is presented in Figure 2.

Although the origins of the GSISS model are derived from general systems theory and TAM is derived from the Theory of Reasoned Action (Ajzen & Fishbein, 1980; Fishbein & Ajzen, 1975), the GSISS model is related to TAM. Essentially, interface satisfaction is equivalent to perceived ease of use; and task support satisfaction is equivalent to perceived usefulness. In essence, usefulness is expanded in the GSISS model into two components: usefulness toward task accomplishment or overall job support (task support satisfaction) and usefulness toward decision making (decision support satisfaction). Since most jobs are composed of both decision making and clerical or processing tasks, the GSISS model provides additional precision and usefulness above and beyond TAM.

Extrinsic and Intrinsic Motivation: Flow Theory and Shopping Enjoyment

Extrinsic motivation is defined as the motivation to perform an activity because it is perceived to produce valued outcomes that are distinct from the activity itself (Webster & Martocchio, 1992). For example, one may be motivated to use information technology because it helps one to achieve better job performance. Thus, Perceived usefulness or task support satisfaction would be regarded as extrinsic motivators. In contrast to this, intrinsic motivation is the motivation to perform the activity due to the direct reinforcement of performing the activity per se´. An example of this is Enjoyment towards the system (Davis, Bagozzi, & Warshaw, 1992).

TAM was first modified and extended to include intrinsic motivation using the variable Enjoyment (Davis, Bagozzi, & Warshaw, 1992). An intrinsic motivating variable or construct that has recently received a great deal of attention in web-based technology utilization studies is "computer playfulness" or "playfulness" (Hoffman & Novak 1996; Novak, Hoffman, & Yung, 2000; Moon & Kim, 2001; Novak, Hoffman, & Duhachek, 2003; Pace, 2004). Playfulness has been operationalized in a number of ways however, most researchers start with the definition based on the pioneering work on flow theory by Csikszentimihalyi (1975).

Flow theory focuses on the *state of playfulness* which emphasizes the interaction of the individual in a *specific context*, whereas a strict interpretation of the original TAM model, which is based on the theory of reasoned action (TRA), requires that individual beliefs impact attitudes through perceived usefulness and perceived ease of use (Davis, et al., 1989). Thus, TAM forces researchers to treat all variables as antecedents to ease of use and perceived usefulness. Therefore, intrinsic motivation factors such as playfulness or enjoyment cannot be easily incorporated into TAM unless these variables are treated as traits of individuals (as done by Moon & Kim, 2001), but this is in direct contradiction to flow theory.

According to flow theory, people feel enjoyment when perceived action opportunities are in balance with action capabilities (Nakamura & Csikszentmihalyi, 2002). In the context of internet shopping experience, consumers may be motivated to use an e-commerce Web site unless they are bored or anxious, which are the results of imbalance between perceived action opportunities and action capabilities. Unlike walk-in shopping, consumers will leave an e-commerce Web site before they get bored. On the other hand, consumers may be less anxious when the Web site is easy to use and useful. Thus, interface satisfaction and task support satisfaction will affect shopping enjoyment. And also, consumers are more likely to use the Web site when they feel the enjoyment.

RESEARCH MODEL AND HYPOTHESES

Integrating intrinsic motivation into a model of IS success requires decisions on two major issues: (1) the selection of a variable or construct to operationalized intrinsic motivation, and (2) the decision to model intrinsic motivation as either a state variable or as a trait variable.

First, we prefer the use of shopping enjoyment as a measure of intrinsic motivation since intrinsic motivation is concerned with, and defined as

Figure 3. An integrated model of Web information system success (IWISSM)

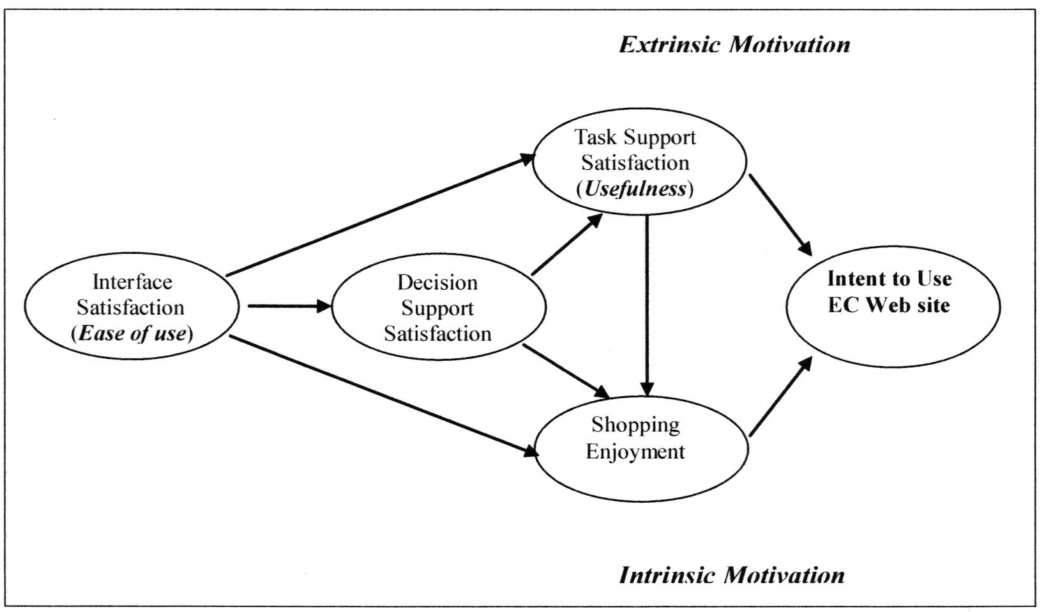

the performance of an activity for the inherent reward of doing the activity itself; Enjoyment has the advantage of simplicity and also has a great deal of face validity. Finally, shopping enjoyment is a more specific measure that is applicable in the consumer-oriented, web-based application domain.

Second, we view intrinsic motivation and specifically, shopping enjoyment, as a function of the interaction of the individual within a *specific context* (with the computer-based artifact or interface). Such an interpretation is consistent with flow theory and the perspective of environmental psychology. According to Mehrabian and Russel (1974), emotional responses to the environment mediate the relationship between the environment and one's behavior. Figure 3 displays the research model and hypotheses, now termed the Integrated Web Information System Success Model (IWISSM).

Consumer Trust in the Web Retail Environment

Consumer trust in the web retail environment is critical for B2C ecommerce where the possibility exists that a web retailer can take advantage of online consumers. Trust in the web retail environment is the "willingness of the consumer to rely on the [web retailer] when there is vulnerability for the consumer" (Jarvenpaa et al., 1999, p. 2). Consumer vulnerability relates to the risk that customers encounter when visiting a problematic site during a purchase. In this context, web retailers may use personal information to the detriment of the consumer, purchased products may not meet consumer specifications, and or the delivery of purchased products may be late or may not occur at all (O'Donnell, Ferrin, Glassberg, & Sanders, 2004).

Consumers' trust in the web retailer has been empirically shown to influence their intention to use the merchant site for Ecommerce purposes (Gefen, Karahanna, Straub, 2003; Jarvenpaa, Tractinsky, Saarinen, & Vitale, 1999; Jarvenpaa, Tractinsky & Vitale, 2000). Gefen, Karahanna & Straub (2003) suggest that trust increases the perceived usefulness of the site by improving the perceived likelihood that consumers will gain expected benefits of product purchases from the site.

Individual Characteristics

One can expect certain individual characteristics (or traits) to be related to computer shopping

Table 1. Hypotheses

Hypothesis	
H1a	Interface satisfaction positively influences decision support satisfaction.
H1b	Interface satisfaction positively influences task support satisfaction.
H1c	Interface satisfaction positively influences shopping enjoyment.
H2	Decision support satisfaction is positively associated with task support satisfaction.
H3	Task support satisfaction positively affects intention to use EC Website.
H4a	Decision support satisfaction positively affects shopping enjoyment.
H4b	Task support satisfaction positively affects shopping enjoyment.
H4c	Shopping enjoyment positively affects intention to use EC Website.
H5a	Product involvement positively affects shopping enjoyment.
H5b	Web skills positively affects shopping enjoyment.
H5c	Trust positively affects intention to use EC Website.

enjoyment. Webster and Martocchio (1992) and Hackbarth et al. (2003) found strong associations between computer experience and playfulness (which has a component of shopping enjoyment). Koufaris (2002) also found strong correlations between a consumer/computer user's product involvement and shopping enjoyment. Product involvement is defined as the degree to which a consumer is involved with or finds a particular product to be interesting, fascinating, or enjoyable to use. Since a user of a web-based consumer purchasing website is both a consumer and a computer user, one's experience level (or Self-Efficacy) and one's degree of product involvement should influence one's degree of shopping enjoyment in a particular web information system context. Table 1 summarizes the study hypotheses.

METHODOLOGY

Data Collection and Experimental Procedure

In order to examine the proposed model in this study, we identified three diverse, commercial web sites for selecting a digital camera: myCamera.com, Active Buyers Guide, and Amazon.com. "myCamera.com" is a digital camera comparison guide that lists products and their corresponding critical attributes in a table or list format. "Active Buyers Guide," is a sophisticated decision guide for the purchase of digital cameras. This website provides a number of features and functions to guide a user to "narrow down" the large potential list of products. "Amazon.com" was selected because it represents a very successful commercial website that includes a feature not present in the other two experimental sites – "the average customer rating." The average customer rating features gives users the opportunity to see how other consumers rate the various products.

The data collection was conducted in two steps. First, a pilot test was performed involving 52 subjects and 104 observations. It was used to test the experimental procedure and to refine the items and constructs used in the study. It also enabled the researchers to clarify the wording, content and general layout of the survey instrument.

Next, the actual experiment was conducted. Students in an introductory computer course at a large research university were given a questionnaire set consisting of two identical sets of survey items for each of the two websites assigned. Student subjects were assigned at random to one of 6 possible website combinations. Subjects were given an overview of the task and told that they had a budget of $200 and were asked to select the best camera from the website. This budget restriction was used to ensure a moderately involved cognitive task. Specifically, subjects were instructed to visit the website listed on their questionnaire packet, select a digital camera from the website, and then to fill-out the questionnaire. Each questionnaire included a section requiring subjects to list the price, make and model of the camera selected from the website. Subjects were then told to repeat this procedure for the second website listed on their packet. Subjects were given one week to complete the experiment and were given extra credit in the course for their participation. In addition, as extra incentive subjects were informed that completed questionnaires would be placed in a raffle drawing for gift certificates to Circuit City. A total of 300 sets of questionnaires were distributed. One-hundred and ninety (190) questionnaire sets were returned for a response rate of 63% (190/300).

Demographics

Tables 2 and 3 show the demographic and web access information and the web use and web skills for the subjects of this study. Microsoft Internet Explorer was the major Web browser used and over 90% of the subjects had some prior experience with Internet shopping. Interestingly, the majority (over 60%) of the subjects accessed the

Internet through their home office to perform the assignment given for this study.

Operationalization of Research Variables

Measures for product involvement and Web skills were adapted from Koufaris (2002). Product involvement was described on the questionnaire as – "We would like to know how interested you are in digital cameras. Please use the series of descriptive words listed below to indicate your level of interest." The instrument then listed two 7-point semantic differential scales ranging from Un-Exciting to Exciting and from Boring to Interesting. Web skills was implemented using a 7-point Likert scale, anchored by Strongly Disagree to Strongly Agree:

1. I am very skilled at using the Web,
2. I know how to find what I want on the Web, and

Table 2. Descriptive statistics on demographics and Web access

Demographic Information	N	Minimum	Maximum	Mean	Std. Deviation
Age (in years)	189	18	48	**22.21**	4.308
Gender	188	Male 79 (42%), **Female 109 (58%)**			
Browser used for this survey	187	**Microsoft Internet Explorer 169 (90.4%)** AOL Browser 10 (5.3%) Netscape Navigator 7 (3.7%)			
Location where the Internet was accessed	151	**Home using network 74 (49.0%)** School 48 (31.8%) Home using modem 20 (13.2%) Work place using network 5 (3.3%) Work place using modem 4 (2.6%)			

Table 3. Descriptive statistics on Web use and Web skills

Web Use/Skills Information	N	Minimum	Maximum	Mean	Std. Deviation
G6. I am very skilled at using the Web	188	1	7	**5.74**	1.333
G7. I know how to find what I want on the web	188	1	7	**5.88**	1.309
G8. I know more about using the web than most users	188	1	7	**5.26**	1.336
How would you rate your experience with Web technology?	188	1	7	**5.28**	1.089
How many **hours** per week do you use the Internet?	187	0	100	**16.21**	13.584
How many **hours** per week do you spend overall on a computer?	188	0	100	**25.59**	20.039
How long have you been using the Internet?	175	**Between 1 and 1.5 years 170 (97.1%)** More than 3 years 2 (1.1%) Less than 6 months 2 (1.1%) Between 6 months and 1 years 1 (0.6%)			
Number of purchases you have made through the Internet in the last year	189	**1-5 times 91 (48.1%)** 11 or more 53 (28.0%) 6-10 times 32 (16.9%) Never 13 (6.9%)			

3. I know more about using the Web than most users (See items G6-G8 in Table 3).

The other major questionnaire items are shown in Appendices 1-3. The variables in the study were operationalized based on a variety of sources and existing instruments.

Order Effects and Treatment Effects

The survey questionnaires were designed in six different formats with identical measures (Each set of the questionnaires includes two web sites for assessment out of three with the order of web sites reversed for each of the website pairs). Order effects during the experiments were investigated. The results of two-way ANOVA (Table 4) showed that there was no statistically significant difference in behavioral intention to use (the website) caused by the order of the presentation of the Web sites on the questionnaire.

The order of site presentation (or evaluation) did not appear to affect respondents' decisions about which site they preferred to buy a digital camera. As shown in Table 5, there was no significant interaction effect between the selected site to buy from and the order of evaluation of e-commerce sites.

Table 4. Tests of between-subjects effects

Source	Sum of Squares	Df	Mean Square	F	Sig.
SITE	12.432	2	6.216	2.945	.054
SITE * SORD	.987	2	.493	.234	.792
Error	785.264	372	2.111		
Total	7206.778	378			
Corrected Total	798.912	377			

Note: Dependent Variable: behavioral intention to use an EC Web site
SITE: Target e-commerce sites (Amazon, Decision Guide, and MyCamera.com)
SORD: Site evaluation Order by respondents

*Table 5. Selected site to buy from * Site Evaluation Order Cross-tabulation*

	Site Evaluation Order		Total
	1	2	
Buy from Amazon	63	65	128
Buy from Decision Guide	68	60	128
Buy from MyCamera.com	58	64	122
Total	189	189	378

Note: Pearson Chi Square value =.826 and p=.662.

ANALYSIS AND RESULTS

We employed the Partial Least Squares (PLS) approach to analyze the data. The emphasis of PLS is on predicting the responses as well as in understanding the underlying relationship between the variables (Tobias, 1999). PLS is a powerful approach for analyzing models and theory building because of the minimal demands on measurement scales, sample size, and residual distributions (Fornell, 1982). In addition, the component-based PLS avoids two serious problems, inadmissible solutions, and factor indeterminancy (Fornell & Bookstein, 1982). SEM approaches, such as LISREL and AMOS, are not able to deal with non-standardized distributions (Fornell, 1982), and they can yield non-unique or otherwise improper solutions in some cases (Fornell & Bookstein, 1982). PLS is not as susceptible to these limitations (Wold, 1974; Wold, 1985).

Assessment of the Measurement Model

PLS analysis involves two stages: (1) the assessment of the measurement model, including the reliability and discriminant validity of the measures, and (2) the assessment of the structural model. For the assessment of the measurement model, individual item loadings and internal consistency were examined as a test of reliability (See Table 6). Individual item loadings, and internal consistencies greater than 0.7 are considered adequate (Fornell & Larker, 1981).

As shown in Table 6, loadings for all measurement items are above 0.8 (except for I1 in interface satisfaction), which indicates there is sound internal reliability. The almost uniformly distributed weights show each item contributes to each construct equivalently. We used PLS-Graph Version 2.91.03.04 to perform the analysis.

Table 6. Measures, loadings, and weights

Decision Support Satisfaction			Task Support Satisfaction			Interface Satisfaction			BI to use EC Web site		
Item	Loadings	Weight	Item	Loadings	Weight	Item	Loadings	Weight	*Item*	Loadings	Weight
D7	0.8984	0.2818	T7	0.8510	0.3550	I1	0.7904	0.1749	U2	0.8953	0.3563
D8	0.9246	0.2819	T9	0.9020	0.3674	I5	0.8392	0.1784	U5	0.9432	0.3724
D9	0.9096	0.2965	T10	0.9228	0.3973	I8	0.8622	0.2174	U6	0.9254	0.3568
D10	0.8686	0.2534				I92	0.8965	0.2050			
						I13	0.8774	0.1997			
						I16	0.8645	0.1936			
Shopping Enjoyment			Web Skills			Product Involvement			Trust		
P4	0.8828	0.2778	G6	0.9568	0.3736	PI3	0.8920	0.4707	TR1	0.8709	0.1717
P5	0.9274	0.2800	G7	0.9382	0.3929	PI4	0.9389	0.6179	TR2	0.8584	0.1929
P6	0.9214	0.2637	G8	0.8753	0.3130				TR3	0.9230	0.1859
P7	0.9294	0.2722							TR4	0.8772	0.1526
									TR5	0.9134	0.2104
									TR6	0.9161	0.2054

Note: Items were not included if either: (1) loadings are less than 0.7 and (2) bivariate correlations are higher than .60.

Table 7. Composite reliability (CR) and average variance extracted (AVE)

Constructs	CR	AVE	Formula
Decision Support Satisfaction	0.9449	0.8109	$CR = (\sum\lambda_i)^2 / [(\sum\lambda_i)^2 + \sum_i var(\epsilon_i)]$
Task Support Satisfaction	0.9214	0.7965	$AVE = \sum\lambda_i^2 / [\sum\lambda_i^2 + \sum_i var(\epsilon_i)]$
Interface Satisfaction	0.9425	0.7322	
Shopping Enjoyment	0.9539	0.8377	
Web Skills	0.9460	0.8539	
Product Involvement	0.9121	0.8384	
Trust	0.9596	0.7984	
Behavioral Intention to Use EC Web site	0.9441	0.8492	

*Note: λ_i is the component loading to an indicator and $var(\epsilon_i) = 1 - \lambda_i^2$

Reliability and Validity Tests

In assessing the internal consistency for a given block of indicators, the composite reliability (CR), also referred to as convergent validity (see Werts, Linn, & Joreskog, 1974), was calculated. All the CR values are over 0.9, which suggests that the parameter estimates are sound (Table 7).

The Average Variance Extracted (AVE) was also calculated. AVE measures the amount of variance that a construct captures from its indicators relative to the variance contained in measurement error. This statistic can be interpreted as a measure of reliability for the construct and as a means of evaluating discriminant validity (Fornell & Larker, 1981). AVE values should be greater than 0.50. All AVEs for the constructs used in this study are greater than 0.70. This indicates that more than 70% of the variance of the indicators can be accounted for by the latent variables.

The AVE can also be used to assess discriminant validity. The AVEs should be greater than the square of the correlations among the constructs. That is, the amount of variance shared between a latent variable and its block of indicators should be greater than shared variance between the latent variables. In this study, the square-roots of each AVE value are greater than the off-diagonal elements (Table 8). This indicates that there exists reasonable discriminant validity among all of the constructs. The correlation between decision support satisfaction and task support satisfaction

Table 8. Correlations of latent variables

	DSS	IFS	TSS	SE	WSKL	PI	TR	BI
Decision Support Satisfaction	(0.901)							
Interface Satisfaction	0.628	(0.856)						
Task Support Satisfaction	0.699	0.604	(0.892)					
Shopping Enjoyment	0.522	0.458	0.613	(0.915)				
Web Skills	0.107	0.226	0.057	0.119	(0.924)			
Product Involvement	-0.039	-0.075	-0.029	-0.074	-0.123	(0.915)		
Trust	0.421	0.459	0.400	0.429	0.217	-0.129	(0.894)	
Behavioral Intention to use	0.532	0.422	0.680	0.668	0.007	-0.031	0.402	(0.922)

*Note: the number in parenthesis is the square root of AVE .

appears to be a little high although valid in terms of discriminant validity criteria. Such a close but distinctive relationship between decision support satisfaction and task support satisfaction was expected (see Garrity & Sanders, 1998)). Hence, decision support satisfaction together with task support satisfaction can be used to provide more insight into the features of the Web site.

Assessment of the Structural Model

The path coefficients in the PLS model represent standardized regression coefficients. The suggested lower limit of substantive significance for regression coefficients is 0.05 (Pedhazur, 1997). In a more conservative position, path coefficients of 0.10 and above are preferable. As shown in Figure 4, all path coefficients except product involvement to shopping enjoyment, Web skills to shopping enjoyment, and trust to behavioral Intention are over 0.10 thus satisfying both conservative criteria and the suggested lower limit. They are also statistically significant at $p = 0.001$. Overall, the IWISSM model explains a significant amount of variation in the dependent variable, intention to use the EC Website ($R^2 = 0.57$). Both task support satisfaction as a measure of extrinsic motivation and shopping enjoyment as a measure of intrinsic motivation are significant predictors of intention to use the EC Website.

The IWISSM model is also a nomological network and can be used to test the construct validity of the success dimensions. Constructs in a nomological network are considered valid if they predict or are predicted by the other constructs consistent with theoretical models and past research (Bagozzi, 1980; Straub, Limayem, & Karahanna-Evaristo, 1995). As shown in Figure 4, a high R^2 for each endogenous variable in the structural model demonstrates that this model can

Figure 4. Path coefficients: Integrated model of Web information system success

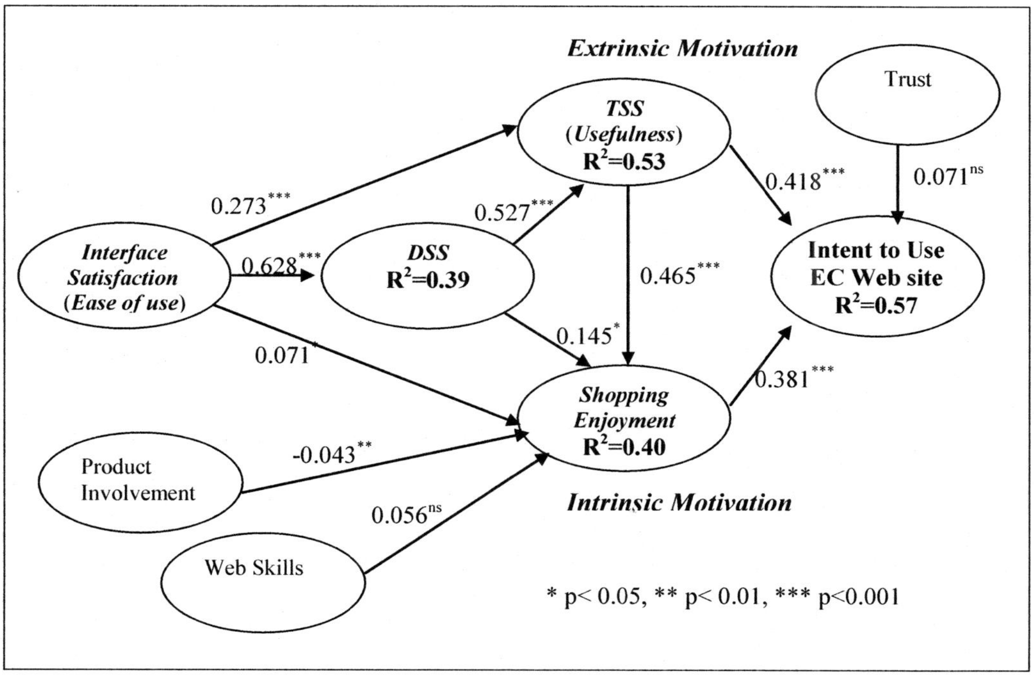

be used to predict each of the success dimensions within the nomological net.

Specifically, over 50% of the variance in task support satisfaction is explained via interface satisfaction and decision support satisfaction, and by the indirect effects of interface satisfaction through decision support satisfaction. In addition, close to 40% of the variation in decision support satisfaction is explained by interface satisfaction. Over 40% of the variance in shopping enjoyment is explained by interface satisfaction, decision support satisfaction, and task support satisfaction and the indirect effects of interface satisfaction through decision support and task support satisfaction. However, product involvement, Web skills and trust do not provide for significant paths in the model. Table 9 summarizes the results of the hypothesis testing.

DISCUSSION

Interestingly, the major IS success dimensions from the Garrity and Sanders model all yielded significant path coefficients in the structural model test of the IWISS model (Figure 4). Both the extrinsic motivating factor, task support satisfaction, and the intrinsic motivating factor, shopping enjoyment, yielded significant paths to the dependent variable, intention to use the EC Web site and helped to explain over 56% of the variance ($R^2 = 0.57$). The model lends support to the IWISS model.

In the web-based, consumer shopping environment, the primary intrinsic motivating factor is shopping enjoyment. That is, users are motivated by the holistic experience of interacting with computer technology in a manner that promotes enjoyment, (and perhaps also captivates their attention, and maintains their curiosity).

Interface satisfaction is shown as a significant factor in determining decision support, task support satisfaction and indirectly through those dimensions to shopping enjoyment (intrinsic motivation). This is consistent with the proposed model, since computer tools that are easy to use with well-designed interfaces should be enjoyable and captivating (shopping enjoyment), aid in the support of decision making (decision support satisfaction), and support the entire task process (task support satisfaction).

It is interesting to note that the additional variables from previous web use studies were not statistically significant. That is, hypotheses H5a,

Table 9. Summary of hypothesis testing

Hypothesis		Support	Significance Level
H1a	Interface satisfaction positively influences decision support satisfaction.	Yes	$p < 0.001$
H1b	Interface satisfaction positively influences task support satisfaction.	Yes	$p < 0.001$
H1c	Interface satisfaction positively influences shopping enjoyment.	Yes	$p < 0.001$
H2	Decision support satisfaction is positively associated with task support satisfaction.	Yes	$p < 0.001$
H3	Task support satisfaction positively affects intention to use EC Website.	Yes	$p < 0.001$
H4a	Decision support satisfaction positively affects shopping enjoyment.	Yes	$p < 0.001$
H4b	Task support satisfaction positively affects shopping enjoyment.	Yes	$p < 0.001$
H4c	Shopping enjoyment positively affects intention to use EC Website.	Yes	$p < 0.001$
H5a	Product involvement positively affects shopping enjoyment.	No	
H5b	Web skills positively affects shopping enjoyment.	No	
H5c	Trust positively affects intention to use EC Website.	No	

H5b, and H5c are not supported. Although trust has a 0.40 correlation with Intent to Use the EC Website, its path is not significant in the model. In other words, the IWISS model accounts for most of the variation in Intent to Use the EC Website ($R^2 = 0.57$) but trust does not add significant explanation of Intent to Use the EC Website above and beyond what is already explained by the main IS success factors. The high correlations between trust and the main dimensions of the IWISS model can also be observed in Table 8 and indicate the likelihood of shared variance within the model.

Study results suggest that trust does not directly influence intention to use the web site *which appears contradictory to prior studies* involving TAM constructs (Gefen, Karahanna, & Straub, 2003; O'Donnell, Ferrin, Glassberg, & Sanders, 2004). However, in the development of the IWISS model we were not specifically interested in modeling trust as an additional, endogenous variable or dimension of IS success. In our view, the level of trust of a website by a user is best modeled as an independent variable or predictor but not as a component of IS success.

Upon closer examination, *trust is significantly related to the major dimensions of the model, including task support (perceived usefulness) and intention to use, which is consistent with prior studies of trust* (Table 8). The major difference in this study is that the IWISS model already accounts for significant variation in intention to use and trust (modeled only as a direct effect on intention to use) does not explain significant variation above what is already predicted[3].

A further explanation of trust in this study relates to study participants' perceived level of vulnerability (Risk) in using the sites. In the absence of risk, trust is not important in choosing one's actions (Lewis & Weigert, 1985; Rousseau et al., 1998). It may be inferred that the level of perceived risk could have lessened the importance of trust in our study.

In order to test for moderating influences of perceived risk on trust's direct impact on intention to use, we divided the study sample into a high risk group and a low risk Group based on respondents' answers to the following questionnaire item: "I would use my credit card to purchase from this Web site." Subjects that felt their use of the website was a high risk undertaking would be reluctant to use their credit card for purchases, whereas subjects in the low risk group are those that are willing to use their credit card.

The correlation between trust and intention to use was 0.13 for the low risk group. This was not statistically significant at the 0.05 level. However, the correlation between trust and intention to use for the high risk group was 0.33, which was significant at the 0.01 level. In addition, the difference in the correlations between the two samples is significant[2] ($p<0.01$, t-statistic = 3.5). The results lend support to the notion that trust directly impacts behavioral intention to use, but only when the level of perceived risk is relatively high. Further research should investigate the influence of varying levels of perceived risk on the relative importance of trust on intention to use a web site.

Finally, the shopping enjoyment factor (Intrinsic Motivation) was modeled as a function of Interface, decision support, and task support satisfaction, as well as product involvement, and Web Skills. Although this model explained over 40% of the variation in shopping enjoyment ($R^2 = 0.40$) both product involvement and Web Skills did not have significant path coefficients to shopping enjoyment. This suggests that shopping enjoyment, as implemented in our study, is correctly modeled as a "state variable," meaning that it is a situational characteristic of the interaction between an individual and the situation. Since interface satisfaction, decision support and task support satisfaction were the primary determinants of shopping enjoyment, this implies that the human computer interaction environment exerts a stronger influence on shopping enjoyment than these individual trait variables.

The nomological network presented in this chapter along with the results regarding shopping enjoyment differ from other researchers findings on intrinsic motivation, such as Venkatesh (2000). Venkatesh (2000) and Moon & Kim (2001) view intrinsic motivation via playfulness as an individual difference variable (trait) that is system-independent. Our results offer an alternative explanation of how intrinsic motivation (viewed as shopping enjoyment) fits within the realm of web-based IS success and Use. Future research will have to explore playfulness or Enjoyment as a component of the IS success model, especially in web-based environments.

CONCLUSION

The IWISS model extends the work of Koufaris (2000) and others by providing and validating a nomological network of factors based on motivation and flow theory and the Garrity and Sanders (1998) model. One of the objectives of this research project was to compare the IWISS model to TAM. In the IWISS model, Perceived usefulnessis expanded into two closely related but separate dimensions – task support satisfaction and decision support satisfaction. The two dimensions provide additional precision and explanatory power that is helpful to both system designers, who want to design specific support features, and for researchers, who wish to evaluate the system's impact on Task Support or decision support satisfaction (Figure 5).

An important goal of our research was to understand why users find web systems acceptable and useful, and indeed this is important for both researchers and practitioners involved in web-based systems development. From a practical standpoint, systems that are judged successful become a part of the organizational decision making framework and or part of the organization's system structure and processes. Additionally, IS success models are used by researchers who wish to build models and enhance our understanding of the factors that generate successful systems. A by-product of this empirical research is the development of normative guidelines that will then be used by practitioners. It is thus imperative for IS success models to be both valid and precise enough to be useful for developing practical guidelines.

The IWISS model provides for additional explanatory power and provides for a greater understanding of the complex factors that may be used to predict web site use. As Table 10 illustrates, this has received significant research attention over the past decade.

From a researchers perspective, the IWISS model is both a nomological network that can be used to test the construct validity of the variables involved in technology acceptance and IS success measurement as well as a path for conducting future research. Future research can apply an empiri-

Figure 5. Path coefficients: A comparison of TAM and IWISSM

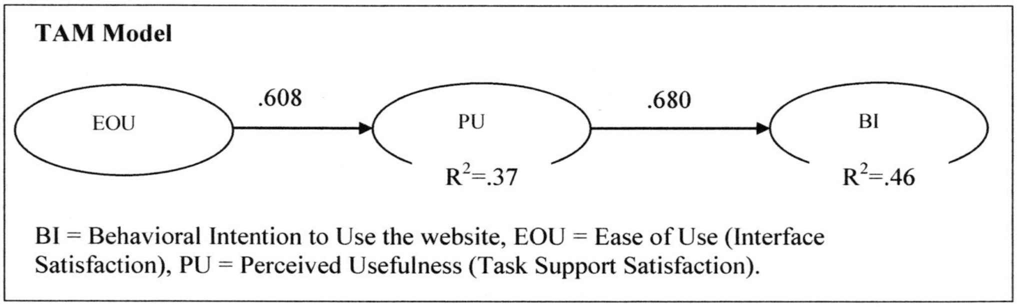

Table 10. Summary of selected studies of Web site usage and explained variance

Literature	Dependent	Independent	Explained Variance (R^2)
This Paper, IWISSM Model	Intention to Use EC Website	Task support, decision support, interface satisfaction, shopping enjoyment, (trust, product involvement, Web skills)	0.57
Koufaris (2002)	Intention to return	Perceived usefulness, shopping enjoyment, (perceived control, concentration, perceived ease of use)	0.55
Moon and Kim (2001)	Behavioral intent to use Web	Perceived usefulness, ease of use, attitude toward using	0.38
Venkatesh (2000)	Behavioral intention to use	Perceived usefulness, computer self-efficacy, perceptions of external control, computer anxiety, objective usability (playfulness, perceived enjoyment, ease of use)	0.35
Lederer et al., (2000)	Web site usage	Ease of use, usefulness	0.15

(Variables in parentheses are insignificant within the model tested).

cal test of the model for the further enhancement and understanding of IS success measurement and prediction.

REFERENCES

Adams, D.A.; Nelson, R.R.; & Todd, P.A. (1992). Perceived usefulness, ease of use, and usage of information technology: A replication. *MIS Quarterly*, 16(2), 227-247.

Agarwal, R. & Prasad, J. (1999). Are individual differences germane to the acceptance of new information technologies? *Decision Sciences*, 30(2), 361-391.

Ajzen, I. & Fishbein, M. (1980). *Understanding attitudes and predicting social behavior*. Englewood Cliffs: Prentice Hall.

Bagozzi, R.P. (1980). *Causal methods in marketing*. New York: John Wiley and Sons.

Csikszentimihalyi, M. (1975). *Beyond boredom and anxiety*. San Francisco: Jossey-Bass.

Davis, F.D. Bagozzi, R.P., & Warshaw, P.R. (1992). Extrinsic and intrinsic motivation to use computers in the workplace. *Journal of Applied Social Psychology*, 22(14), 1111-1132.

Davis, F.D. (1989). Perceived usefulness, perceived ease of use, and user acceptance of information technology. *MIS Quarterly*, 13(3), 319-340.

Davis, F.D.; Bagozzi, R.P.; & Warshaw, P.R. (1989). User acceptance of computer technology: a comparison of two theoretical models. *Management Science*, 35(8), 982-1003.

Deci, E.L. (1971). Effects of externally mediated rewards on intrinsic motivation. *Journal of Personality and Social Psychology*, 18, 105-115.

DeLone W.H. & McLean, E.R. (1992). Information systems success: The quest for the dependent variable. *Information Systems Research*, 3(1), 61-95.

Doll, W.J.; Hendrickson, A.; & Deng, X. (1998). Using Davis's perceived usefulness and ease of use instruments for decision making: A confirmatory and multi-group invariance analysis. *Decision Sciences*, 29(4), 839-869.

Doll, W.J. & Torkzadeh, G. (1988). The measurement of end-user computing satisfaction. *MIS Quarterly*, 12(2), 259-274.

Fishbein, M. & Ajzen, I. (1975).*Belief, attitude, intentions and behavior: An introduction to theory and research*. Boston: Addison-Wesley.

Fornell, C., & Larcker, D. (1981). Evaluating structural equation models with unobservable variables and measurement error. *Journal of Marketing Research*, 18, 39-50.

Fornell, C. (1982). *A second generation of multivariate analysis*. New York, NY: Praeger.

Fornell, C. & Bookstein, F.L. (1982). Two structural equation models: LISREL and PLS applied to consumer exit-voice theory, *Journal of Marketing Research*, 19(4), 440-452.

Franz, C.R. & Robey, D. (1986). Organizational context, user involvement and the usefulness of information systems. *Decision Sciences*, 17(3), 329-356.

Garrity, E.J.; Glassberg, B.; Kim, Y.J.; Sanders, G.L.; & Shin, S.K. (2005). An experimental investigation of web-based information systems success in the context of electronic commerce. *Decision Support Systems*, 39(3), 485-503.

Garrity, E.J. & Sanders, G.L. (1998). Dimensions of information systems success measurement, in *Information Systems Success Measurement*. Garrity, E.J. & Sanders G.L (eds.), Hershey: Idea Group Publishing, 13-45.

Gefen, D.; Karahanna, E.; & Straub, D. (2003). Trust and TAM in online shopping: An integrated model. *MIS Quarterly* 27(1), 51-90.

Ghani, J.A. & Deshpande, S.P. (1994). Task characteristics and the experience of optimal flow in human-computer interaction. *The Journal of Psychology*. 128(4), 381-391.

Ghani, J.A., Supnick, R., & Rooney, P. (1991). The experience of flow in computer-mediated and in face-to-face groups. J.I. DeGross, I. Benbasat, G. DeSanctis, & C.M. Beath, (eds.) *Proceedings of the 12th International Conference on Information Systems*, New York, 229-237.

Goodhue, D.L. (1990). Developing a theory-based measure of user satisfaction: The task systems fit questionnaire. *Working Paper, Information and Decision Sciences, University of Minnesota*.

Hackbarth, G.; Grover, V.; & Yi, M.Y. (2003). Computer playfulness and anxiety: positive and negative mediators of the system experience effect on perceived ease of use. *Information and Management*, 40, 221-232.

Hoffman, D.L. & Novak, T.P. (1996). Marketing in hypermedia computer-mediated environments: Conceptual foundations. *Journal of Marketing*, 60, 50-68.

Jarvenpaa, S.L.; Tractinsky, N.; Saarinen, L.; & Vitale, M. (1999). Consumer trust in an Internet store: A cross-cultural validation. *Journal of Computer Mediated Communications*. 5(2) 1-35.

Jarvenpaa, S.L.; Tractinsky, N.; & Vitale, M. (2000). Consumer trust in an Internet store. *Information and Technology Management*, 1(1), 45-71.

Jarvenpaa, S.L.; & Todd, P.A. (1997a). Is there a future for retailing on the Internet? R.A. Peterson, (ed.) *Electronic Marketing and the Consumer*. Thousand Oaks, CA: Sage.

Jarvenpaa, S.L.; & Todd, P.A. (1997b). Consumer reactions to electronic shopping on the World Wide Web. *International Journal of Electronic Commerce*, 1(2), 59-88.

Keil, M.; Beranek, P.M.; & Konsynski, B.R. (1995). Usefulness and ease of use: Field study evidence regarding task considerations. *Decision Support Systems*, 13(1), 75-91.

Kim, Y.J., E.J. Garrity, G.L. Sanders, and B.A. Sherman. (2004). A means-end model of IS success: Toward understanding the cognitive structure of IS users. *Working Paper State University of New York at Buffalo.*

Koufaris, M. (2002). Applying the technology acceptance model and flow theory to online consumer behavior. *Information Systems Research*, 13(2), 205-223.

Lederer, A.L., Maupin, D.J., Sena, M.P., & Zhuang, Y. (2000). The technology acceptance model and the World Wide Web. *Decision Support Systems*, 29(3), 269-282.

Lewis, D., & Weigert, A. (1985). Trust as a social reality. *Social Forces*, 63, 967-985.

Mathieson, K. (1991). Predicting use intentions: Comparing the technology acceptance model with the theory of planned behavior. *Information Systems Research*, 2(3), 173-191.

Mayer, R.C. & Davis, J.H. (1999). The effect of the performance appraisal system on trust for management: A field quasi-experiment. *Journal of Applied Psychology*, 84(1), 123-136.

Mehrabian, A. & Russel. (1974). *An approach to environmental psychology*. Cambridge, MA.: MIT Press.

Moon, J. & Kim, Y. (2001). Extending the TAM for a world wide web context. *Information and Management,* 38, 217-230.

Nakamura, J., & Csikszentmihalyi, M. (2002). The concept of flow. In C. R. Snyder & S. J. Lopez (Eds.), *Handbook of Positive Psychology*: Oxford University Press US.

Novak, T.P., Hoffman, D.L., & Yung, Y.F. (2000). Measuring the customer experience in online environments: A structural modeling approach. *Marketing Science*, 19(1), 19-42.

Novak, T.P., Hoffman, D.L., & Duhachek, A. (2003). The influence of goal-directed and experiential activities on online flow experiences. *Journal of Consumer Psychology*, 13(1-2), 3-16.

O'Donnell, J.B.; Ferrin, D.L.; Glassberg, B.; & Sanders, G.L. (2004). The influence of web site characteristics on consumer trust and the purchase decision. *Working Paper, Canisius College.*

O'Keefe, R.M. & McEachern, T. (1998). Web-based customer decision support systems. *Communications of the ACM*, 41(3), 71-78.

Pace, S. A grounded theory of the flow experiences of web users. (2004). *International Journal of Human-Computer Studies*, 60(3), 327-363.

Pedhazur, E.J. (1997). *Multiple regression in behavioral research: Explanation and prediction.* Fort Worth: Harcourt Brace College Publishers.

Rousseau, D.M.; Sitkin, S.B.; Burt, R.S.; & Camerer, C. (1998), Not so different after all: A cross-disciplined view of trust. *Academy of Management Review*, 23(3), 393-404.

Sanders, G.L. (1984). MIS/DSS success measure. *Systems, Objectives, Solutions*, 4, 29-34.

Scott, W.E., Farh, J., & Podaskoff, P.M. (1988). The effects of intrinsic and extrinsic reinforcement contingencies on task behavior. *Organizational Behavior and Human Decision Processes*, 41, 405-425.

Straub, D.; Limayem, M.; & Karahanna-Evaristo, E. (1995). Measuring system usage: Implications for IS theory and testing. *Management Science.* 41(8), 1328-1342.

Tobias, R.D. (1999). *An introduction to partial least squares regression.* SAS Institute, Inc., 1-8.

Trevino, L.K. & Webster, J. (1992). Flow in computer-mediated communication: Electronic mail and voice mail evaluation and impacts. *Communication Research*, 19(5), 539-573.

Venkatesh, V. (2000). Determinants of perceived ease of use: Integrating control, intrinsic motivation, and emotion into the technology acceptance model. *Information Systems Research*, 11(4), 342-365.

Venkatesh, V; Morris M.G.; Davis G.B.; & Davis F.D. (2003). User acceptance of information technology: toward a unified view. *MIS Quarterly,* 27(3), 425-478.

Webster, J., & Martocchio, J.J. (1992). Microcomputer playfulness: Development of a measure with workplace implications. *MIS Quarterly,* 16(2), 201-226.

Wixom, B.H. & Todd, P.A. (2005). A theoretical integration of user satisfaction and technology acceptance. *Information System Research,* 16(1), 85-102.

Werts, C.E.; Linn, R.L.; & Joreskog, K.G. (1974). Interclass reliability estimates: Testing structural assumptions. *Educational and Psychological Measurement*, 34(1), 25-33.

Wold, H. (1974). Causal flows with latent variables, *European Economic Review*, 5, 67-86.

Wold, H. (1985). Partial least squares, in *Encyclopedia of Statistical Sciences*, Kotz, S. & Johnson, N.L. (eds.), 6, New York: Wiley, 581-591.

ENDNOTES

1. Some items from frequently used instruments were classified by the expert panel as "out of place," and were later identified as independent variables.
2. The correlations were first converted to z-scores and a two-tailed test of significance was performed to determine if the correlations were drawn from the same population.
3. Our main concern was to test the validity of the integrated Web information system success Model. Alternatively, trust could also be modeled as an antecedent to task support satisfaction.

APPENDIX 1. OPERATIONALIZATION OF LATENT VARIABLES: DECISION SUPPORT, TASK SUPPORT, INTERFACE SATISFACTION

Decision Support Satisfaction		
D7	This Web site improves the quality of my purchasing decision. making.	Sanders (1984)
D8	Use of this Web site enables me to make better purchasing decisions.	Sanders (1984)
D9	This Web site assists me in making a decision more effectively.	Davis (1989)
D10	Use of this Web site enables me to set my priorities in making the purchase decision.	Sanders (1984)
Task Support Satisfaction		
T7	I could come to rely on this Web site in performing my task.	Sanders (1984)
T9	Using this Web site enables me to accomplish tasks more quickly.	Davis (1989)
T10	This Web site makes it easier to do my task.	Davis (1989)
Interface Satisfaction		
I1	This Web site contains understandable graphics.	Adapted from Lederer et al (2000)
I5	Learning to use this Web site was easy for me.	Davis (1989)
I8	This Web site is user-friendly.	Davis (1989), Doll & Torkzadeh (1988), Goodhue (1990; 1998), Goodhue & Thompson (1995)
I9	This Web site is easy to use.	Davis (1989), Doll & Torkzadeh (1988), Goodhue (1990; 1998), Goodhue & Thompson (1995)
I13	It would be easy for me to become skillful at using this Web site.	Davis (1989)
I16	This Web site is easy to navigate.	Lederer et al (2000)

APPENDIX 2. OPERATIONALIZATION OF LATENT VARIABLES: BEHAVIORAL INTENTION TO USE, SHOPPING ENJOYMENT

Behavioral Intent to Use		
U2	The use of this Web site would be critical in my future decisions.	Adapted from Franz & Robey (1986)
U5	I intend to increase my use of this Web site in the future.	Agarwal & Prasad (1999)
U6	In the future, I plan to use this Web site often.	Adapted from Moon & Kim (2001)
Shopping Enjoyment		
P4	I found this Web site interesting.	Ghani, et al. (1991)
P5	I found my Web site visit enjoyable.	Ghani, et al. (1991)
P6	I found my Web site visit exciting.	Ghani, et al. (1991)
P7	I found my Web site visit fun.	Ghani, et al. (1991)(Franz & Robey, 1986)

APPENDIX 3. OPERATIONALIZATION OF LATENT VARIABLE: TRUST

Trust		
TR1	I would be comfortable dealing with this retailer having responsibility for the delivery of the product.	Adapted from Mayer & Davis (1999)
TR2	I would be comfortable dealing with this retailer, even if I could not monitor its actions.	Adapted from Mayer & Davis (1999)
TR3	This retailer is trustworthy.	Jarvenpaa et al. (2000)
TR4	This retailer wants to be known as one who keeps promises and commitments.	Jarvenpaa et al. (2000)
TR5	I trust that this retailer keeps my interests in mind.	Jarvenpaa et al. (2000)
TR6	This retailer's behavior meets my expectations.	Jarvenpaa et al. (2000)

* Note: All questionnaire items in Appendices use a 7-point Likert scale, varying from *Strongly disagree* to *Strongly agree*.

Chapter VII
Evolving a Strategy for Web-Based Shopping Systems

Changsu Kim
Yeungnam University, Korea

Robert D. Galliers
Bentley College, USA
London School of Economics, UK

Kyung Hoon Yang
University of Wisconsin-La Crosse, USA

Jaekyung Kim
University of Nebraska-Lincoln, USA

ABSTRACT

The world is witnessing a continuous expansion of electronic commerce into the global digital economy. As an enabler of new businesses, Web-based shopping systems (WBSS) are at the heart of the major issues surrounding electronic commerce growth. Their wide use has profoundly altered the ways in which businesses and customers, and businesses and businesses interact on the basis of digital transactions. Despite the importance of WBSS, the theoretical study of their strategies has been sparse. This article offers a theoretical analysis of evolutionary processes in WBSS strategies. For that purpose, we propose a classification model of WBSS. Based upon the model, WBSS are classified into four types: (1) general-direct-sales (GDS); (2) general-intermediary-sales (GIS); (3) specialized-direct-sales (SDS); and (4) specialized-intermediary-sales (SIS). On the basis of these four categories of WBSS, we analyze the characteristics of WBSS and suggest five evolution strategies for WBSS, which have implications for both theory and practice. Amazon.com's strategic movements, such as product line expansion through alliance and acquisition, provide an exemplary case of the evolution of WBSS strategy. We expect that this article will serve as a guide for Internet businesses and as a catalyst for new research agendas relevant to web-based shopping and electronic commerce.

INTRODUCTION

Electronic commerce has been actively diffused on the basis of advanced Internet technologies, enlarging its sphere of utilization and the scale of the global electronic market radically (Feeny, 2001; Looney & Chatterjee, 2002; Kraemer & Wigand, 2004). The most well-known Internet business models are the so-called dot.coms, which have adopted several types of Web-based shopping system (WBSS) applications (Porter, 2001; Kim & Galliers, 2006; Kim et al., 2007). Dot.coms are located around the world and are pursuing a variety of opportunities as global marketers, interacting with global customers and businesses through the Internet (Howcroft, 2001; Worthington & Boyes, 2001; Rifkin & Kurtzman, 2002; Thomas et al., 2005).

However, early in 2000, many dot.com companies collapsed. The lesson learned is that making money on the Internet is still not easy, which makes it necessary to create new ways of doing business (Gulati & Garino, 2000; Paper et al., 2003; Thomas et al., 2005 Holzwarth et al., 2006). Even though many dot.com companies have disappeared and competition is getting severe, the diffusion of Web-based shopping businesses is continuous, increasing in both the number of customers and the volume of business (Kim & Galliers, 2006; Kim et al., 2007).

The aim of this chapter is to address what WBSS must do to survive and prosper continuously. We insist that the appropriate evolution strategy can be one of the most critical factors. To verify our premise, we classify four types of WBSS models, analyze the characteristics of each WBSS model and attempt to address the evolutionary path of each WBSS strategy. We show the case of Amazon.com's evolutionary path as an example to demonstrate our theory. Thus, we expect this study to serve as a useful guide for researchers to build theoretical e-commerce models and for practitioners to make plans for their Internet businesses.

WEB-BASED SHOPPING SYSTEMS

Web-Based Shopping in E-Commerce

According to Arlitt et al. (2001), web-based shopping aims to personalize online shopping to provide global interactive business, customer convenience and global market efficiency, which implies that Web-based shopping belongs to the B2C e-commerce business model. As of yet, there is no agreed upon terminology for Web -based shopping (Van Slyke et al., 2002). There are, however, many terms in use, which include Internet mall, virtual mall, cyber mall, electronic mall, virtual storefront, online storefront, online store, online shopping mall, electronic shopping mall, Internet shopping mall, electronic shopping systems, cyber mall systems and WBSS. Generally, WBSS are described as Internet-based shopping systems for selling and buying products, information and services. They are classified by transactions patterns (Arlitt et al., 2001), which include e-tailers such as the virtual merchant, clicks and bricks, manufacturer direct, and the market creator. Therefore, we limit the scope of research to part of the business to consumer (B2C).

Web-Based Shopping Systems

WBSS have been researched from two viewpoints: business and technical. Studies focusing on the business aspects explored the phenomenon of Internet business through websites, online stores, and virtual markets as a limited concept of WBSS (Nour & Fadlalla, 2000; Heijden, 2003). Spiller and Lohse (1998) identified five different types of Internet retail stores: Super Stores, Promotional Store Fronts, Plain Sales Stores, One Page Stores, and Product Listings. These are classified by size, type of services, and interface quality. However, this classification system does not consider the technical aspects of the Internet.

Nour and Fadlalla (2000) also classified Internet-based virtual markets according to two principal categories: product type and delivery mode. They identified four distinct Internet-based virtual markets: electronic publishing and software, electronic tele-services, digitally-enabled merchandising and digitally-enabled services. However, this is a broad conceptual model for virtual markets rather than a model of WBSS. This research, therefore, seems somewhat limited in explaining the taxonomy and the evolution of WBSS. Torkzadeh and Dhillon (2002) measured factors that influence the success of Internet commerce. They suggested that the relative strength of shopping convenience and ecological issues are fundamental objectives. Heijden (2003) investigated an extension of the Technology Acceptance Model (TAM) to explain the individual acceptance and usage of a Dutch generic portal Website. Recently, Kim et al. (2007) dealt with a theoretical analysis of evolutionary patterns on Web-based shopping systems strategy. The WBSS evolution model would provide an academic background for further study and a practical implication.

Several studies explored the technical aspects of WBSS, including scalability, network traffic, architecture, and virtual reality. Baty and Lee (1995) proposed a functional architecture of electronic shopping systems to promote comparison and contrast between product differentiations. Choi et al. (1998) examined the issue of reducing the volume of network traffic in the cyber mall system. They also suggested that the basic architecture of the cyber mall system consists of four major technical components: the cyber mall creator, the cyber mall server, the cyber mall player, and the WWW server. They argued that the increasing demands for virtual reality are placing excessive strain on the current network volume. Arlitt et al. (2001) investigated the issues affecting the performance and scalability of WBSS. They found that personalization and robots can have a significant impact on scalability. Their study was one of the first to adopt the terminology of WBSS. Recently, Kim and Galliers (2006) addressed the development and application of a configuration model of Web-based shopping systems. They highlighted the significance of a balanced view concerning the electronic commerce applications.

In sum, most studies focused on a limited view of WBSS and considered WBSS only as a static system, ignoring WBSS as an evolving system in dealing with environmental and organizational change. To understand the general characteristics of WBSS, it is necessary to consider them as dynamic systems that evolve corresponding to changes encountered. The strategic and evolutionary paths of WBSS can provide information that has been neglected in previous WBSS studies. Therefore, this study attempts to develop a WBSS classification model and provide strategic planning for each type of WBSS.

A CLASSIFICATION MODEL OF WBSS

According to Piercy and Cravens (1995), marketing planning should integrate the type of product and the approach to generating sales as the key enterprise process. As a global business medium, it would appear helpful to classify various types of WBSS applications, therefore, by product type and sales type.

As a business channel, WBSS supports two sales types between the seller and the customer. One is direct sales, in which the WBSS is directly responsible for the guarantee of quality and delivery of products or services (Ranchhod & Gurau, 1999). In the other type, indirect sales, the WBSS relays business transactions between the manufacturer, merchant, distributor and consumer (Kim et al. 2005).

Many dot.com companies such as Amazon.com and Dell are directly responsible for the products sold on their WBSS, while eBay.com, in the role of intermediary, is indirectly responsible for sales products. On the basis of this observation, the sales types of WBSS are classified into two types: direct sales and indirect sales, as seen in Figure 1.

Another distinguishing factor of a WBSS is the type of product being sold. There are vertical products and horizontal products. Vertical industry product and unified group image products are two types of vertical products. Vertical industry products are defined as the products that have a vertical relationship in an industry, such as auto parts, tires, and automobile accessories. Unified group image products are defined as products that can create synergy effects even though they belong to different industries.[1] Examples of unified group image products are movies and movie-related toys, beer and baby diapers, and ski and golf equipment.[2] In contrast to these vertical products, horizontal products are defined as two or more industrial products that are not unified into a group. This type of sales attracts customers by the variety of products.

In order to gain meaningful insight into classifying different product types sold by WBSS, this study explores the products sold by some well-known dot.com companies. For example, Dell.com and Amazon.com sell products directly to global customers without any intermediaries. Dell.com handles only a vertically-related product line of computers and computer accessories, and Amazon.com carries unified group image products that have synergy effects with books, such as CDs and software. In this chapter, these kinds of product lines will be referred to as vertical products. On the other hand, Walmart.com carries a variety of products that do not have any related synergy effects. Therefore, these are referred to horizontal products. Based on this observation, the product types sold on WBSS are divided into two groups: vertical product and horizontal product, as outlined in Table 1.

On the basis of the product and the sales type of WBSS, a classification model of WBSS can be developed (Table 2). In the model, the vertical axis displays the product type and the horizon-

Figure 1. The sales type of WBSS

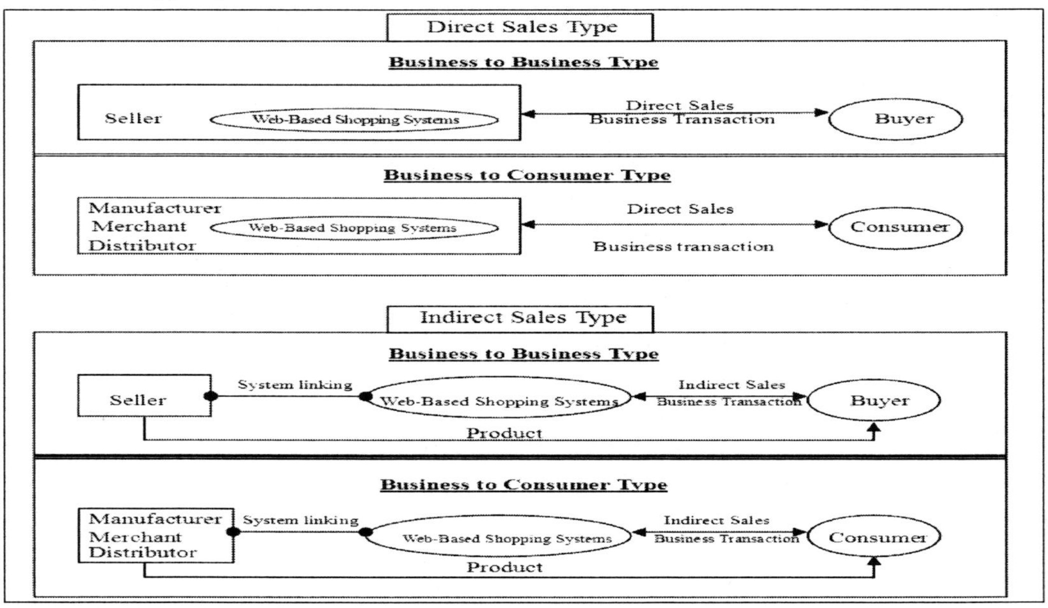

Table 1. Product type of WBSS

Type	Definition	Examples
Vertical Product	Vertical industry product	Computer, computer accessories and computer software.
	Unified group image product	Beer and baby diapers in convenience stores, and ski and golf equipment
Horizontal Product	More than two industrial products and products that are not unified into a group	Department store products

Table 2. Classification model of WBSS

Classification Model of WBSS		Sales Type of WBSS	
		Direct sales	Indirect sales
Product Type	Vertical	SDS	SIS
	Horizontal	GDS	GIS

tal axis displays the sales type. This research thereby proposes a model that classifies WBSS into the following types: 1) Specialized-Direct-Sales (SDS); 2) General-Direct-Sales (GDS); 3) Specialized-Intermediary-Sales (SIS); and 4) General-Intermediary-Sales (GIS). However, not all WBSS conform to these four types: Hybrids are possible, for example. Nonetheless, this model serves primarily as a basic model of WBSS for analytical purposes. Characteristics of each type of WBSS, with exemplary cases and their strategic evolutionary paths, are introduced in detail in sections 4 and 5, respectively.

CHARACTERISTICS OF THE FOUR TYPES OF WBSS

We analyzed the characteristics of the four categories of WBSS based on eight analysis domains: seller/WBSS relationship, number of sellers in WBSS, product type, responsibility of guarantee for the product sold, comparable firms, e-commerce strength, and recommended strategy (Piercy & Cravens, 1995; Looney & Chatterjee, 2002; Molenaar, 2002; Thomas et al., 2005). These domains are well aligned with the logic of classifications of WBSS.

First, the relationship between the seller and the WBSS is examined. For example, some sellers are owners of the WBSS, while others are a lessee or brokerage within the WBSS (Looney & Chatterjee, 2002). Our second focus is on the number of sellers (Piercy & Cravens, 1995), the third on product type, and the fourth on responsibility of guarantee for the product sold (Molenaar, 2002). Based on these four analyses, a comparable WBSS is suggested. Next, we illustrate the strength of the four types of WBSS (Looney & Chatterjee, 2002). Finally, an attempt is made to analyze the strategic paths each WBSS follows, in accordance with the strategic options suggested by Rackoff et al. (1985). In their theory of strategic thrusts, five major competitive moves (defensive or offensive) are introduced: differentiation, low cost, innovation, growth and alliance.

While this theory is based on Porter's competitive strategy model (1980), Rackoff et al. (1985) expanded the original generic strategies with two additional strategies. They also addressed the strategic use of information systems to uncover opportunities related to supplier, customer and competitor. Since a WBSS is an information system that can be strategically utilized to deliver more value to customers and suppliers, and to achieve a competitive advantage over competitors, we believe the theory of strategic thrusts can explain the strategic paths of WBSS properly. According to the analysis domains defined above, detailed characteristics of the four types of WBSS with four dot.com company cases are investigated.

General-Direct-Sales (GDS)

The general-direct-sales type is applicable to direct sales and horizontal products. This type uses the WBSS to sell many products that are identical to those of an actual department store. Examples of GDS are Buy.com and Overstock.com. In this type, the owner of the WBSS is the only seller, selling several kinds of products to multiple buyers in the world. The GDS type is therefore directly responsible for the guarantee of the product sold. The strength of the GDS type is that it provides a cyber warehouse that needs less initial investment expense and fewer staffing requirements in comparison to actual department stores. Therefore, the GDS type cannot only make high profits due to a reduction in maintenance and other costs. However, it can also solve traffic and parking problems, because customers do not need to leave home to go shopping. Furthermore, there are claims that this cyber department store reduces traffic congestion and avoids parking difficulties because it does not have physical stores or parking lots.

WBSS of this type are in keen competition with each other. Therefore, a differentiation strategy would be well-matched with a GDS type to gain a competitive advantage through differentiation of service or products, in comparison to other competitor WBSS. Detailed explanations follow.

Example 1: Overstock.com

Overstock.com is an online closeout store selling excess inventory through the Internet, including bed-and-bath goods, home decor, kitchenware, watches, jewelry, electronics and computers, sporting goods, apparel and designer accessories, among other products. Overstock.com offers manufacturers, distributors and other retailers an alternative sales channel for liquidating their inventory. Overstock.com is a GDS WBSS because it sells general merchandise to the customers.

Example 2: Buy.com

Buy.com is a cyber department store, which means that it does not have any physical shops and it sells several kinds of products that are identical to those of an actual department store. The product prices in this category are cheap because goods can be sold directly to the customer without a salesperson, and intermediaries such as suppliers can be cut out. In doing so, Buy.com can reduce the transaction costs of selling products. In addition, Buy.com provides one-to-one marketing based on customer management databases that store information to analyze customers' needs and preferences. Moreover, it carries out differentiation strategies such as a "Bill Me Later" payment option, quick delivery, membership management and a variety of other services such as BuyMagazine. "Bill Me Later" is a payment option that provides customers with the flexibility to purchase without using their credit card.

General-Intermediary-Sales (GIS)

The general-intermediary type of WBSS is suitable for indirect sales and horizontal products. This type includes many shops such as book stores, computer shops, gift shops, wine stores, and sports stores. There are many sellers dealing in several types of products for a variety of customers in the GIS type of WBSS. These sellers are lessees within the GIS. Thus, the GIS itself has an indirect responsibility for products sold because individual sellers within the GIS are directly responsible for the products. This type of WBSS provides a strategic opportunity to small and medium-sized enterprises, which are faced with a shortage of funds, human resources and technical expertise in comparison to larger companies. This is because this type of WBSS allows relatively easy and low-cost entry of small and medium-sized enterprises into web-based shopping business areas. The strength of the GIS type of WBSS is that it provides various cyber malls that customers can choose from according to their needs and preferences. This kind of selective buying can serve as a major attraction to customers, as compared to other types of WBSS. Other types of WBSS cannot establish the variety of shops nor provide the range of products that the GIS type can, due to limited capability such as systems management, operating costs and human resources. Therefore, GIS has a competitive advantage over other types of WBSS, through its ability to provide a diversity of products, high quality service and many kinds of shops. Thus, the most suitable strategy for the GIS would appear to be a growth strategy. WBSS in these categories include Yahoo! Shopping, Amazon.com and Pricegrabber.com. Yahoo! Shopping and Amazon.com lease cyber store space under the WBSS to many individual stores. Therefore, these WBSS have multiple sellers who directly sell a variety of products. It can be regarded as an online marketplace provider, which creates a place and gathers sellers and buyers. Pricegrabber.com is explained below as a type of GIS WBSS.

Example 1: PriceGrabber.com (http://www.pricegrabber.com/about.php)

PriceGrabber.com is a leading electronic commerce company that helps businesses participate in WBSS. Based on its full suite of e-commerce solutions, PriceGrabber.com claims that it helps customers and merchants safely and easily compare prices and allows them to buy and sell merchandise online. The PriceGrabber.com WBSS provides millions of products and services from more than 40,000 merchants. Customers can rapidly and efficiently search the variety of products by comparative shopping functions on the PriceGrabber.com WBSS. It not only supports technology and outsourcing services to retailers, manufacturers and other businesses, but also launches and manages the WBSS on their behalf. Shoppers can purchase desired products and services from merchants located around the world. The major strategic option of PriceGrabber.com focuses on the global community. By pursuing strategic alliances and partnerships in other regions of the world, PriceGrabber.com is hoping to accelerate its goal of becoming a pre-eminent Internet business service provider worldwide.

Example 2: Yahoo! Shopping (http://shopping.yahoo.com)

Yahoo! Shopping is another example of a GIS WBSS. It is a cyber mall with many lessees that handle a variety of products. Products offered by individual stores are tied to the Yahoo search engine and reviews compiled by its massive user base are also listed. Consumers on Yahoo! Shopping can visit a retailer's store site directly or through the search result of the Yahoo search engine. The Yahoo! Shopping WBSS takes care of billings and charges commissions on the purchases made through the retailers, who then ship the goods to the consumers.

Specialized-Direct-Sales (SDS)

The specialized-direct-sales type is a specialized WBSS dealing with direct sales and vertical products. The seller is identical to the owner of the SDS WBSS. Thus, the seller is a single seller as well as an owner of the SDS type of WBSS. As a result, the SDS itself bears direct responsibility for the product sold. This type of WBSS provides opportunities for global business to manufacturing companies and smaller shops, which have limited capital and business resources. For example, manufacturing companies can sell products directly to the customer without any intermediary. Also, this WBSS type can help smaller shops compete with giant corporations because physical size is not an important factor in determining market strength. The strength of the SDS type lies in its ability to provide a specialized cyber shop. Organizations that have limited resources can efficiently focus their capabilities in selling a specialized vertical product. The initial stage of Dell.com is a major example of this type of application. The SDS type needs to concentrate on a cost strategy since it is necessary to maintain lower prices for specialized products in comparison to prices listed on WBSS that sell various kinds of products. Through the lowered cost of selling products, this kind of WBSS will have a competitive advantage against general types of WBSS. Other examples in this category are online financial institutions. Online financial institutions such as PayPal.com, esurance.com and Egg-online.co.uk provide specialized products in direct sale mode through the Internet. They can provide financing at a lower cost. This is a strength of these WBSS. Detailed examples of SDS are represented below.

Example 1: Dell.com

Dell.com is one of the best examples of the specialized direct sales type of WBSS. Dell.com sells computer equipment directly to its customers on the WBSS. Dell.com currently sells more than $14 million in PC products over WBSS each day. Its web-based shopping business has over 25 million visits per quarter (Hollander, 1999). The company expects to handle half of all its business, ranging from customer inquiries to orders and follow-up services, through the SDS type of WBSS. The advantages of the Dell.com model are claimed to include near-zero inventory; less risk of obsolescence; more customized state-of-the-art products; and a favorable cash flow (Kraemer et al., 2000; Bharati & Chaudhury, 2004).

Example 2: PayPal.com

PayPal provides an online money transaction service to individuals and businesses. Buyers can tie any of their existing banking services (e.g., credit card, debit card, or bank account) into their PayPal account and pay for their purchases from online stores. On the other hand, PayPal allows sellers to accept credit cards, debit cards, and bank account payments from buyers in exchange for the transaction fee. PayPal also provides about 5% average yield rate for their account balances, which is higher than the usual bank deposit. As characteristics of SDS WBSS, this unique middleman service for individual or business online transactions is the specialization of PayPal, which has direct control of its service.

Specialized-Intermediary-Sales (SIS)

This type of WBSS sells vertical products indirectly. The SIS type of WBSS can be thought of as a basic level of a virtual organization that links people, assets and ideas to create and distribute products and service (Sadeh & Lee, 2003). This is because buyers and sellers can negotiate and trade products, services and information in real-time, based on a specialized-intermediary-sales shopping architecture. As seen in the case of Fastparts.com, there are many sellers selling vertical products, within SIS. These sellers take on the role of a broker. Thus, the SIS type itself has an indirect responsibility for the product sold, because individual sellers within the SIS type of WBSS are directly responsible for the product guarantee. The SIS architecture offers a significant opportunity for auction markets, in particular, and acts as an intermediary between seller and buyer. Therefore, the SIS type needs to be kept up-to-date to provide the most recent data on products and services because companies may want to access the latest information related to their market. The strength of the SIS type of WBSS is that it plays the role of a cyber agent that is able to support business-to-business electronic commerce. Its role as cyber agent between businesses is a basic form of virtual organization because the key attribute of a virtual organization is strategic alliances or partnering (Introna, 2001). The successful evolution of this type of WBSS will depend on alliances and tight coordination with various WBSS. Therefore, an alliance strategy is well matched with this type of WBSS in order to gain a competitive advantage because firms can negotiate directly with each other and trade products and services with other types of WBSS. Examples in these categories include online travel agency websites such as Orbitz.com, Expedia.com, and Travelocity.com. These WBSS mediate airline and hotel reservation sales. Multiple sellers are involved, and products and services are sold indirectly. Since many sellers are involved in the WBSS, auction is the more suitable form, and it is usually aligned with airline and hotel companies. Fastparts.com is another example of a SIS WBSS. Detailed explanations follow.

Example 1: Expedia.com

Through its WBSS, Expedia.com provides direct access to a broad selection leading of travel industry companies offering products and services that include airline tickets, hotel reservations, car rental, and cruises. Working with a number of internationally recognized airline, hotel, cruise and rental car brands, Expedia.com provides reservation service. This makes Expedia a specialized intermediary in the WBSS travel industry.

Example 2: Fastparts.com

Fastparts.com provides an Internet-based trading exchange and marketplace for the electronics manufacturing and assembly industry. Fastparts.com has sold $140 billion in electronic parts and hundreds of millions of dollars in manufacturing equipment. In addition, FastParts.com periodically offers various inventories to sell its members' products on Internet auctions. Auctions are pre-announced to all members, and bidding is generally open for two or three days. Though anyone can use the FastParts.com to access information on parts, price and availability, the actual bidding, buying or selling of parts requires membership. There is no charge to become a member. All members must agree to abide by the FastParts.com operating rules and protocols.

In this section, we have analyzed the major characteristics of the four types of WBSS, utilizing appropriate examples from practice. As a result of this analysis, specific characteristics are synthesized in Table 3. As shown in Table 3, the four kinds of WBSS have different characteristics, each having its own strengths and weaknesses as an enabler of new business. As such, the development of new business processes, strategic planning, and system architectures should be necessary for success. The characteristics of the four categories of WBSS provide insight for researchers investigating web-based shopping

Table 3. A taxonomy of WBSS

Analysis Domain	Types of WBSS			
	GDS	GIS	SDS	SIS
Seller	Owner	Lessee	Host	Brokerage
Seller Number	Single	Multiple	Single	Multiple
Product Type	Horizontal	Horizontal	Vertical	Vertical
Guarantee of Product Sold	Direct	Indirect	Direct	Indirect
Comparable Firm	Department Store	Small & Medium Enterprise	Shop Manufacture	Auction
Strength	Cyber Warehouse	Cyber Malls	Cyber Shop	Cyber Agent
Strategy Type	Differentiation	Growth	Cost	Alliance
Similar Business Model	Catalog- Merchant	Portal, Virtual- merchant	Merchant-direct	Service- provider, Community- provider

business and potentially helpful guidelines for practitioners seeking ways to gain sustainable advantages over their e-business competitors.

STRATEGIC EVOLUTION PATHS OF WBSS

Review of Evolutionary Path

Organizations such as dot.com companies need to continuously improve the functionality of their WBSS in order to survive and progress in the web-based shopping business world (Pinker et al., 2002; Rifkin & Kurtzman, 2002; Thomas et al., 2005). Therefore, these organizations must consider multiple strategies to find the best ways to expand.

Based on our observations of evolutionary paths of WBSS, we can suggest a model of strategic planning for WBSS to provide useful guidelines for practitioners and for academic research. While it appears unprofitable to shift from horizontal to vertical products or from indirect to direct sales type, a shift from vertical to horizontal products or from direct to indirect sales type can be a successful evolutionary path for WBSS.

The theory of strategic thrusts (Rackoff et al. 1985) provides an explanation for the success of these evolutionary paths. There are five strategic thrusts proposed in this theory: differentiation, low cost, innovation, growth, and alliance. Among the five strategic thrusts, growth and alliance are the most useful in explaining evolutionary paths of WBSS. When a WBSS evolves from dealing with vertical product types to horizontal product types (SDS → GDS or SIS → GIS), the evolutionary path can be seen as a growth strategy through which the WBSS achieves a competitive advantage by volume or geographical expansion, backward or forward integration, or product-line or entry diversification. On the other hand, when a WBSS evolves from selling products directly to selling products indirectly (SDS → SIS or GDS → GIS), this path can be seen as an alliance strategy through which a WBSS achieves competitive advantage by forging marketing agreements, forming joint ventures, or making acquisitions of other WBSS.

While growth and alliance strategies can be viewed as the major thrusts, differentiation, cost and innovation strategies can be achieved in the context of the growth and alliance strategy thrusts. For example, a WBSS may expand its product type to differentiate itself from other WBSS. Amazon.com started as bookstore WBSS and expanded its product lines to toys and other goods (SDS→GDS) sold directly and indirectly through alliances. Amazon.com achieved cost leadership because it utilized an existing infrastructure to handle additional product types (Cost). It also allows a customer to buy many types of products without leaving the WBSS, making it a one-stop shopping place. This convenience of broad selection differentiates Amazon.com from Barnsandnoble.com, an SDS WBSS (Differentiation). When both product and sales types change (SDS → GIS), we need an innovation strategy to support rapid change of the WBSS structure caused by product and sale type expansions (Innovation).

As seen in Figure 2, we suggest five evolutionary paths of WBSS: (1) from SDS to GDS, (2) from SDS to SIS, (3) from SDS to GIS, (4) from GDS to GIS, and (5) from SIS to GIS. A detailed explanation of each path follows.

Evolutionary Paths

Evolutionary Path from SDS to GDS

This evolutionary path implies that the organization expands its vertical product type into horizontal products. The case of Amazon.com is one of the best examples. Initially Amazon.com sold vertical products—books. Subsequently, it has diversified its range to include products such as CDs, software and the like. This strategy option can reduce the initial risk of WBSS investment. This is because organizations can initially build the SDS type of WBSS based on a vertical product type and then easily expand the product type into a horizontal product type. Therefore, this may be an effective strategy for small to medium sized firms.

Evolutionary Path from SDS to SIS

This strategic option is suitable for special businesses of small to medium size. For example, in the case of flower selling, no one shop can cover an entire country. In a situation like this, the owner of the WBSS constructs a countrywide chain for flower selling, and entrusts a district flower

Figure 2. Strategic evolution of WBSS

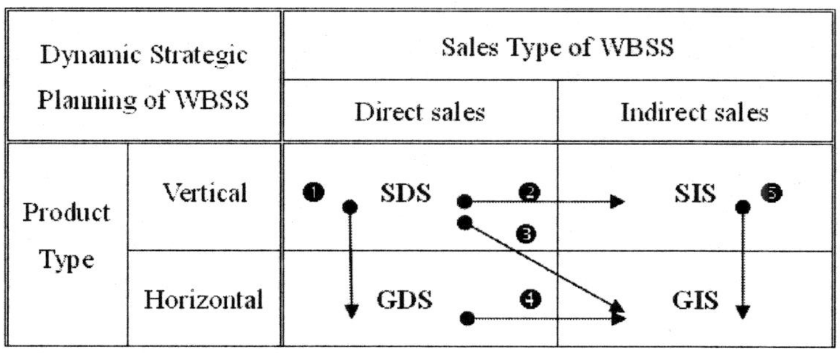

shop with the delivery and guarantee of quality for the sales product. However, before shops can be admitted into the partnership, they must be carefully reviewed by the company managing the WBSS. This process can directly affect the reliance of the customer on this type of WBSS. Major businesses suitable for this type of strategic planning are furniture, clothes, real estate, books, tourist bureaus, stationary, computers, and software. Through this strategic planning, businesses of small to medium size can strengthen national or global business power. However, this strategic option might need considerable investment and time for advertising and publicizing to establish a critical mass-scale WBSS.

Evolutionary Path from SDS to GIS

Though the starting point is the same as the above strategy, the strategic direction is different. SDS shifts from a vertical cyber shop to a horizontal cyber mall, as well as from vertical to horizontal product types. In the final stage of this shift, an organization rents out shops in the cyber mall to businesses that want to provide products or services via a WBSS. Throughout this process, organizations can shift from the SDS type to the GIS type of WBSS. This approach can be well matched with venture businesses (e.g., finding new business models related to electronic commerce). This is because venture businesses initially implement the SDS type of WBSS, consisting of a vertical product such as software or CDs. After this, they increase the number of cyber shops and products for sale. However, not all venture businesses can adopt this strategy because of the risk associated with the heavy investment required.

Evolutionary Path from GDS to GIS

The GDS type of WBSS is similar to an actual department store. Similarly, it is difficult to supply all the products a customer may wish to purchase. Therefore, it is an effective strategy to entrust the selling of certain products to other specialized sellers. Based on this strategy, organizations can concentrate their core competence on best-selling products, carrying out the sales of other products through other vendors within its WBSS. Through this process, a GDS type can shift to a GIS type, which has various cyber shops and sells horizontal products. It is essential, however, that the quality of products or services supplied by these other sellers is strictly maintained by this kind of GIS.

Evolutionary Path from SIS to GIS

Organizations can carry out the SIS to GIS evolutionary path more easily than others because they can simply add product types for sale within the same WBSS. At this time, it is a better approach to add a product type that is closely related to the current product type of SIS. Based on this strategy, organizations can aim at arriving at a similar level as Amazon.com which is one example of the GIS type. With regards to its responsibility for products sold, an IT/telecommunication company carrying out web-based shopping business on its WBSS seems to be best suited for this strategic approach. This is because this sort of company can easily switch from vertical to horizontal product types.

EXEMPLARY CASE OF STRATEGY: AMAZON.COM

Founded as an online bookstore in July 1995, Amazon.com is one of the most prominent Internet retailers. Amazon.com has expanded its product lines to include music, electronics, health and beauty products, kitchen and housewares, tools, toys, videos, and services such as auctions, 1-Click ordering, and zShops (Filson & Willimson, 2001).

There are two reasons for focusing on Amazon.com in this study. One is that Amazon.com is an excellent example of a WBSS starting as a SDS type and expanding to other types of WBSS in our taxonomy. The other is that Amazon.com has announced its major strategic movements (e.g., strategic alliances and acquisitions) publicly on its web page. Thus, it is possible to follow its strategic planning clearly, as shown in Figure 2.

Amazon.com has expanded its product line through a series of alliances, which exemplifies the alliance strategic thrust (Rackoff et al., 1985), and through the acquisitions of providers of a variety of products, which exemplifies the growth strategic thrust (Rackoff et al., 1985). Acquisitions usually require the removal of redundant operations and functionalities, while alliances usually keep the partners' business operations and entities. Examining Amazon.com's strategic movements, we analyze its strategic planning of WBSS in this section.[3]

Evolutionary Path from SDS to GDS

This evolutionary path implies that the WBSS expands its sales of vertical products type to sales of horizontal products. The case of Amazon.com is one of the best examples. Initially Amazon.com sold vertical products—books. Subsequently, it has diversified its range to include products such as CDs, and software. This strategy option can reduce the initial risk of WBSS investment. This is because organizations can initially build the SDS type of WBSS based on a vertical product type, and then can easily expand the product type into a horizontal group. Therefore, this may be an effective strategy for small and medium-sized firms.

Evolutionary Path from SDS to SIS

In April 2001, Amazon.com announced its alliance with Borders Group, one of the largest book superstores, to provide the e-commerce platform needed to re-launch Borders.com as a co-branded website. This is one of the most significant strategic movements of Amazon.com for the evolution from SDS to SIS because Borders.com deals with the same product types as Amazon.com and the products of Borders.com are not sold directly through Amazon.com.

Other examples for this strategic path include Amazon.com's expansion to similar products such as audio books and electronic books.[4] Through the alliance with Audible.com on May, 2000, Amazon.com, expanded its spoken audio content and had more than 4,700 audio books and speeches, lectures, and other audible materials (e.g. audio files for newspaper articles). This alliance gives Amazon.com a variety of book- related products while Audible.com has a better platform for audio service.

It also launched an electronic book store through the strategic alliance with Microsoft in August, 2000. Microsoft provides a customized Amazon.com version of Microsoft Reader, giving consumers the ability to purchase and download eBook titles directly from Amazon.com. (www.microsoft.com/presspass/ press/2000/Aug00/AmazonPR.mspx, 2000)

Evolutionary Path from SDS to GIS

This type of strategic movement was achieved through alliances with or acquisition of other WBSS. For Amanzon.com, these alliances brought more variety of product types, which means more potential customers with different buying needs. For other alliance partners, alliances brought powerful and proven marketing channels because the name value and recognition of Amazon.com is strong and people on the Internet visit Amazon.com frequently. These visitors have more chances to find products through Amazon.com than on the individual alliance partner's WBSS.

One of the early efforts on the path from SDS to GIS was the acquisition of Drugstore.com in February, 1999 and Pets.com in March, 1999. This was an effort to provide a one-stop online shopping experience. Amazon.com launched a full-service pharmacy and health and beauty store with content and buying guides. Pets.com, the online category leader for pet products, information and services, was acquired by Amazon.com in 1999.

Other major movements of Amazon.com are its alliance with Toysrus.com in August, 2000, to create a co-branded toy and video games store, its alliance with Ofoto in October, 2000, to provide information, products and service for cameras and photos, and its alliances with AT&T, Sprint PCS, and Voicestream Wireless in November, 2000, for wireless phones and service.

Evolutionary Path from GDS to GIS

After becoming a GDS WBSS with direct sales of horizontal products such as books, pharmaceutical products, and pet products, Amazon.com expanded its product line by allowing other WBSSs to join its platform to sell the same type of products. This is indirect sales of similar horizontal products that Amazon.com already sells. In this case, Amazon.com is now an e-marketplace where many products are sold from many sellers in one single market place. Not only does Amazon.com allow Borders.com to sell books, CDs, and movies, it also allows virtually all categories of products (Table 4) to be sold through numerous WBSS, off-line retailers and even individuals.

Products are sold and shipped through these varying sources. The only part of the transaction that Amazon.com is involved in is information listing and payment on which a commission for each transaction is based.

DISCUSSION AND CONCLUSION

WBSS are spreading very rapidly across national boundaries. From groceries stores to department stores, from small and medium-sized enterprises (SMEs) to large firms, and from young organizations to well-established organizations, a growing number of companies are taking advantage of WBSS by selling products, services and information. WBSS not only increase the ability of organizations to trade with customers, but they also offer firms a new opportunity to reach millions of consumers worldwide. WBSS also have the potential to radically change the way businesses interact with their customers. However, many WBSS are disappearing from the Internet, so organizations are struggling to find new strategies in order to survive in the world of electronic commerce (Arlitt et al., 2001; Lumpkin et. al, 2002; Van Slyke & Belanger, 2004; Thomas et al., 2005). In order to provide meaningful

Table 4. Strategic evolution of Amazon.com (SCCI, 2006)

Amazon.com WBSS Product Line Expansion		Strategic Evolution of Amazon.com WBSS	
Date	Event	Type of WBSS	Strategic Path
1995 July	Amazon.com Sells First Book	SDS	
1999 July	Opens Consumer Electronics, and Toys & Games Stores	SDS, GDS	Expanding to GDS (SDS → GDS)
1999 Sept.	Launches zShops	SDS,GDS, GIS	Expanding to GIS (SDS → GIS, GDS → GIS)
2000 Aug.	Announces Toys "R" Us Alliance	SDS, GDS, GIS, SIS	Expanding to SIS (SDS →SIS)

Table 5. Overall strategic planning of WBSS

Types of Strategic Planning	Strategic Approach	Strength	Suitable Firm	Customer	Supplier	Competitors
SDS ⇨ GDS	• Vertical product ⇨ Horizontal product	• Lower initial investment & risk	• SME • Shop	Extend the scope of core customers' purchase	Diversify the suppliers	Growth, Differentiation, Cost
SDS ⇨ SIS	• Direct sales ⇨ Indirect sales	• Partnership	• Specialized small-medium size business	Focus on existing customers	Focus on existing suppliers or just extend the scope a little	Alliance, Cost, Differentiation
SDS ⇨ GIS	• Direct sales ⇨ Indirect sales • Vertical product ⇨ Horizontal product	• WBSS provider	• Venture business	Resources needed for customers and suppliers strategies.	Need resources both customers and suppliers strategies.	Innovation
GDS ⇨ GIS	• Direct sales ⇨ Indirect sales	• Global intermediary	• IT / Telecommunications Company	Use current customer strategies	Emphasize the supplier and supply chain management	Alliance, Cost, Differentiation
SIS ⇨ GIS	• Vertical product ⇨ Horizontal product	•Strengthening core competence	• Department store	Extend the scope of core customers' purchase	Similar to strategy SDS ⇨ SIS Diversify the suppliers	Growth, Differentiation, Cost

guidelines for such a situation, we have attempted to provide a taxonomy of four types of WBSS. On the basis of four types of WBSS, this study presents five evolutionary paths for strategic planning: (1) from SDS to GDS, (2) from SDS to SIS, (3) from SDS to GIS, (4) from GDS to GIS, and (5) from SIS to GIS. As a consequence of the discussion so far, the accompanying Table 5 presents the characteristics of the five types of strategic planning.

As seen in Table 5, each of the five evolutionary paths has its associated strengths and weaknesses, which require shrewd consideration by potential adopters before practical application. Although we believe that the WBSS strategic planning presented in this chapter is a fundamental concept, evolutionary paths of each taxonomy category could prove useful in advancing WBSS, in providing guidelines into new business opportunities, and in providing academic insights for further WBSS research. Their practical application seems to depend on organizational circumstances, considering the whole organizational capability to determine the most appropriate option. The discussion in this chapter is an on-going study of how we can extend and apply the concept of WBSS strategic planning. The model of WBSS strategic planning suggested in this chapter can be a useful guideline for organizations seeking the best way to advance their WBSS, for achieving continuous competitive advantages, and surviving in a global electronic commerce environment.

The limited number of analyzed cases may be a weakness of this chapter. However we are hopeful that this chapter will provide researchers and practitioners with both a detailed understanding of WBSS and a theoretical base for further research of web-based shopping businesses and electronic commerce.

REFERENCES

Arlitt, M., Krishnamurthy, D. & Rolia, J. (2001). Characterizing the scalability of a large web-based shopping system. ACM Transactions on Internet Technology, 1(1), 44-69.

Baty, J.B. & Lee, R.M. (1995). InterShop: enhancing the vendor/customer dialectic in electronic shopping. Journal of Management Information Systems, (11), 9-31.

Bharati, P. & Chaudhury, A. (2004). Using choiceboards to create business value. Communications of the ACM, 47(12), 77-81.

Choi, J.D., Choi, J.S., Park, C. & Kim, D. (1998). A cell-based shared virtual world management mechanism in the cyber mall system. Computer Networks and ISDN Systems, 30, 1865-1874.

Feeny, D. (2001). Making business sense of the e-opportunity. Sloan Management Review, 42(2), 41-51.

Filson, D. & Willimson, K. (2001). The impact of e-commerce strategies on firm value: lessons from Amazon.com, Working paper.

Gulati, R. & Garino, J. (2000). Get the right mix of bricks & clicks. Harvard Business Review, 78(3), 107-114.

Heijden, H. (2003). Factors influencing the usage of websites: the case of a generic portal in the netherlands. Information & Management, 40, 541-549.

Hollander, J. (1999). Dell and amazon link sites, and possibly fortunes. E-Commerce Times. Retrieved from http://www.ecommercetimes.com/story/281.html/

Howcroft, D. (2001). After the goldrush: deconstructing the myths of the dot.com market. Journal of Information Technology, 16(4), 195-204.

Holzwarth, M., Janiszewski, C. & Neumann, M.M. (2006). The influence of avatars on online consumer shopping behavior. Journal of Marketing, 70(4), 19-36.

Introna, L. (2001). Defining the virtual organization, E-Commerce & V-Business, Barnes, S. & Hunt, B., (Eds.). Oxford: Butterworth-Heinemann, 143-152.

Kim, C., Galliers, R.D. & Yang, K.H. (2005). Comparison of web-based shopping systems in the UK and Korea. International Journal of Global Information Technology Management, 8(4), 49-66.

Kim, C. & Galliers, R.D. (2006). The development and application of a configuration model of web-based shopping systems. International Journal of Electronic Business, 4(1), 1-17.

Kim, C., Galliers, R.D., Yang, K.H. & Kim, J. (2007). Evolution of web-based shopping systems: characteristics and strategies. Journal of Electronic Commerce in Organizations, 5(4), 70-87.

Kraemer, K. & Wigand, R. T. (2004), "Introduction to Globalization and Electronic Commerce Special Issue," Electronic Markets, 14(1), January, 2-3.

Kraemer, K.L., Dedrick, J. & Yamashiro, S. (2000). Refining and extending the business model with information technology: Dell Computer corporation. Information Society, 16(1), 5-21.

Looney, C.A. & Chatterjee, D. (2002). Web-enabled transformation of the brokerage industry. Communication of the ACM, 45(8), 75-81.

Lumpkin, G.T., Droege, S.B. & Dess, G.G. (2002). E-commerce strategies: achieving sustainable competitive advantage and avoiding pitfalls. Organizational Dynamics, 30(4), 325-340.

Molenaar, C. (2002). The Future of Marketing: Practical Strategies for Marketers in the Post-Internet Age. London: Financial Times Prentice Hall.

Nour, M.A. & Fadlalla, A. (2000). A framework for web marketing strategies: the e-commerce revolution. Information Systems Management, 17(22), 41-50.

Paper, D., Pedersen, E. & Mulbery, K. (2003). An e-commerce process model: perspectives from e-commerce entrepreneurs. Journal of Electronic Commerce in Organizations, 1(3), 28-47.

Piercy, N.F. & Cravens, D.W. (1995). The network paradigm and the marketing organization. European Journal of Marketing, 29(3), 1995 7-34.

Pinker, E. J., Seidmann, A. & Foster, R. C. (2002). Strategies for transitioning 'old economy' firms to e-business. Communications of the ACM, 45(5), 77-83.

Porter, M.F. (1980). Competitive Strategy, New York: The Free Press.

Porter, M. E. (2001). Strategy and the Internet. Harvard Business Review, 79(3), 63-76.

Rackoff, N, Wiseman, C. & Ullrich, W. (1985). Information systems for competitive advantage: implementation of a planning process. MIS Quarterly, 9(4), 285-294.

Ranchhod, A. & Gurau, C. (1999). Internet-enabled distribution strategies. Journal of Information Technology, 14(4), 333-346.

Rifkin, G. & Kurtzman, J. (2002). Is your e-business plan radical enough? Sloan Management Review, 43(3), 91-95.

Sadeh, N.M. & Lee, J.K. (2003). advances in b2b e-commerce and e-supply chain management. Journal of Organizational Computing & Electronic Commerce, 13(3/4), 163-165.

SCCI (2006). Amazon timeline and history, Retrieved December 8, 2006, from http://phx.corporate-ir.net/phoenix.zhtml?c=176060&p=irol-corporateTimeline/

Spiller, P. & Lohse, G.L. (1998). A classification of internet retail stores. International Journal of Electronic Commerce, 2(2), 29-56.

Thomas, D., Ranganathan, C. & Desouza, K. C. (2005), "Race to Dot.com ad Back: lessons on E-Business Spin-Offs and Reintegration," Information Systems Management, 22(3), 23-30.

Torkzadeh, G. & Dhillon, G. (2002). Measuring factors that influence the success of internet commerce. Information Systems Research, 13(2), 187-204.

Van Slyke, C., Comunale, C.L. & Belanger, F. (2002). Gender differences in perceptions of web-based shopping. Communications of the ACM, 45(7), 82-86.

Van Slyke, C. & Belanger, F. (2004). Factors influencing the adoption of web-based shopping: the impact of trust. Database for Advances in Information Systems, 35(2), 32- 49

Worthington, S.L.S. & Boyes, W. (2001). E-business in manufacturing: putting the Internet to work in the industrial enterprises, Research Triangle Park, NC: Instrumentation, Systems and Automation Society.

ENDNOTES

1. These can be considered complementary goods
2. These are classical examples of products that have been found to have synergy effects.
3. Since Amazon.com started as SDS, the SIS→ GIS evolutionary path is not applicable.
4. These product expansions might be viewed as SDS to GIS path if we regard audio books or electronic books as separate types of product from different industries. Due to the expansion that occurred through the alliance, this is labeled as an evolutionary path from direct sales to indirect sales.

Chapter VIII
A Review of Single-Item Internet Auction Literature and a Model for Future Research

Jeff Baker
Texas Tech University, USA

Jaeki Song
Texas Tech University, USA

ABSTRACT

Internet auctions have received a considerable amount of attention from researchers. We review recent empirical literature pertaining to single-item Internet auctions and observe that existing work has examined the roles of the auctioneer, bidder, and seller in Internet auctions. As this stream of research matures, research will necessarily move from concept discovery and process explanation to theory deepening. As a first step towards synthesis of findings in Internet auctions, we compile a comprehensive list of the various factors that have been examined in empirical studies and note their general impact upon auction outcome. Based upon this extant research, we propose a conceptual model of Internet auctions as a framework for structuring future work into Internet auctions. We then note the existing economic, psychological, sociological, and cognitive theoretical bases for work on Internet auctions. We conclude by highlighting the potential for behavioral economics to bring unity to Internet auction research and by calling researchers to engage in the work of forging a comprehensive theory of Internet auctions.

INTRODUCTION

The e-commerce revolution is transforming the way goods are bought and sold. Consumers now have access to astounding volumes of information via the Internet and enjoy considerable power within the marketplace. Consumers now have the choice of either making purchases through established fixed-price channels or dictating the price they are willing to pay for an item. The unrivalled dominance of the fixed-price marketing model has diminished somewhat as a new avenue for purchases has gained popularity—the Internet auction. Not only are consumers enjoying the benefits of auction pricing, but Web technologies have allowed businesses to conduct auctions with other businesses to streamline their supply chains and reduce transaction costs (Lucking-Reiley & Spulber, 2001). These auctions, unheard of a scant ten years ago, have transformed vast segments of the marketplace and rank among the most dramatic business developments of the Internet Era.

A host of questions have been asked with regard to Internet auctions. Do bidders in Internet auctions behave in the same manner and according to the same principles as participants in traditional auctions? Do the various auction formats used on the Internet yield equivalent revenues? Researchers have begun to examine the myriad factors sellers should consider when placing items in an Internet auction (e.g., Ba & Pavlou, 2002; Gilkeson & Reynolds, 2003; Standifird, Roelofs & Durham, 2004). For instance, how does the initial bid price, the use of an escrow service, the seller's feedback rating, or the product description impact the revenue generated? Others scholars have begun to examine the impact that consumer characteristics may have upon Internet auction transactions (e.g., Stafford & Stern, 2002; Mollenberg, 2004; Dholakia, 2005b). Are all bidders motivated solely by value-maximization or are some participating in auctions out of a hedonic motivation? Researchers and practitioners alike are interested in the answers to these and other questions. In the following pages, we present a model for investigating Internet auctions that may facilitate the investigation of many of the questions asked in each of these streams of research.

What has not yet emerged from research into Internet auctions is a comprehensive theoretical explanation that encompasses the aforementioned perspectives (Dholakia, 2005a). Theory development often takes many years and builds upon vast numbers of studies. As research streams mature, there are a number of preliminary steps on the road to full-fledged theory (Runkel & Runkel, 1984; Webster & Watson, 2002). For instance, Weick (1995) argues that references, data, lists of variables, diagrams, and hypotheses all fall short of the standard for theory, but are necessary steps in the development of theory. It can be argued that these five items listed by Weick accurately describe the present state of work in Internet auctions. As research into online auctions matures, it too must move from concept discovery and process explanation to theory deepening (Dholakia, 2005a).

We believe this article may be a step towards crafting a comprehensive theoretical explanation of the various phenomena associated with Internet auctions. While our model is not yet full-fledged theory, we believe it incorporates significant findings over the past decade and is a meaningful advance towards cohesion, synthesis, and most importantly, towards explanation of phenomena associated with Internet auctions. This article will proceed as follows. We will first examine existing literature to introduce the topic of auctions and, more specifically, Internet auctions. Second, we will examine the dependent variables that have been most frequently used to quantify the outcome of Internet auctions. Third, we will compile a list of the independent variables that have been examined as determinants of auction outcome and note the general findings regarding each of these variables. Fourth, we will place the aforementioned variables in a conceptual model that may serve as a framework for future inquiry into the various aspects of the Internet auction phenomenon. We will note the role various existing theories may play in explaining phenomena associated with Internet auctions. We will conclude by noting the implications of our findings for both scholars as well as practitioners.

A BRIEF HISTORY OF INTERNET AUCTION RESEARCH

Auction Theory

Auctions have been described as *"a market institution with an explicit set of rules determining resource allocation and prices on the basis of bids from the market participants"* (McAfee & McMillan, 1987, p. 701). Kagel (1995) provides a comprehensive review of experimental literature investigating traditional (off-line) auctions and notes several of the theories that have been applied in auction research. Auction mechanisms are often categorized as (1) English or ascending-price auctions, (2) Dutch or descending-price auctions, (3) first-price sealed-bid auctions, (4) second-price sealed bid or Vickrey auctions, or (5) reverse auctions (McAfee & McMillan, 1987). A thorough description of these mechanisms can be found in the recent work of Lucking-Reiley (2000a). Internet auctions, such as those discussed herein, generally use a variant of the English or ascending-price auction format. Some have noted that many Internet auctions do not use a pure form of any of the mechanisms just described, but have argued that the eBay mechanism is a hybrid of the English and second-price auctions (Lucking-Reiley, 2000a, b; Ward & Clark, 2002; Wilcox, 2000). Those researchers assert that eBay uses a hybrid auction type on the grounds that the presence of a proxy-bidding mechanism ensures that a winning bidder will pay only one increment more than the second-highest bidder's price (Lucking-Reiley, 2000a, b; Ward & Clark, 2002; Wilcox, 2000).

Auction Theory is often centered around or developed in response to the seminal work of William Vickrey, who described the Independent Private Values Model (IPV) (Vickrey, 1961). In this model of auctions, each bidder knows the value of the item they are bidding on with certainty, but does not know the valuation placed on the item by competing bidders. Bidders gain no additional information regarding the valuation of the item by observing the behavior of other bidders (Gilkeson & Reynolds, 2003; Wilcox, 2000). The bidder's own, independent private valuation will not change based upon the behavior of other bidders. This model applies in situations such as an antique auction where a bidder plans to purchase an item to use for himself or herself and not for resale, or in government contract bidding where a bidder knows the exact cost that will be incurred if he or she wins the auction (McAfee & McMillan, 1987).

In contrast, the Common Values Model (CV) posits that in many cases, the bidder's valuation of the item is unknown prior to the conclusion of the auction (Rothkopf, 1969; Wilson, 1969). For example, in a government auction for drilling rights, it is impossible for the bidder to know the exact value of the rights for sale until extraction has taken place and the oil has been sold on the market. Because the true value of the item is determined by resale, its value at the time of the auction can only be estimated by each bidder (Wilcox, 2000). Therefore, uncertainty about the exact value causes bidders to observe the behavior of competing bidders in the auction. A bidder gains information about the value of the item by observing the behavior of other bidders who may have different information about how much the item is objectively worth (Gilkeson & Reynolds, 2003; McAfee & McMillan, 1987). Because the auction winner is the bidder with the highest estimated value of the auctioned item, the CV model introduces the concept of the "winner's curse," where the winner's estimated value of the item often exceeds the true value of the item (Wilcox, 2000).

An integrative approach, referred to as the Affiliated Values Model (AV), has been presented as being more representative of real-world bidder behavior (Milgrom & Weber, 1982). Here, bidding depends upon the bidder's personal preferences, the preferences of others, and the intrinsic qualities of the item being sold. This theory best describes real world auctions, including Internet auctions, where bidders may be influenced not only by their own valuation of the item, but also by the behavior of other bidders.

Recent empirical work noting the potential of competing bidders' preferences to influence a given bidder's behavior supports the view that the AV model is the most descriptive of Internet auctions. For instance, Gilkeson and Reynolds (2003) find that the number of bids in an auction influenced auction success and Dholakia and Soltysinski (2001) observe a "herd behavior bias" in which bidders are inclined to bid on items with more bids, ignoring comparable or superior items with fewer bids. Other studies have also noted the influence of bidder behavior upon other bidders by noting that factors such as number of unique bidders, total number of bids submitted (Wilcox, 2000), bidder arrival rate, and number of bidders in an auction (Segev, Beam & Shanthikumar, 2001) influence auction outcome. The aforementioned Internet auction studies all explicitly mention the merit of the AV model and demonstrate that auction bidders are clearly influenced by the preferences of other bidders.

Internet Auctions

Online auctions are a relatively recent development in the history of auction research. The earliest such auctions took place in the early 1990s with the auction of pigs in Singapore (Neo, 1992) and flowers in Holland (van Heck & van Damme, 1997). As the World Wide Web gained popularity, auctions began to be conducted via newsgroups or e-mail message discussion lists (Lucking-Reiley, 2000a). The most well-known examples of Internet auctions, however, are those conducted by international market leader eBay, a company started in 1995 that has since grown to include over 180 million registered users and generated US$4.552billion in sales in 2005 (eBay, 2006). Following Möllenberg (2004), we will define Internet auctions to mean *virtual marketplaces relying on Internet services (such as the World Wide Web) and Internet protocols to conduct auctions.*[1]

Researchers have classified Internet auctions as business-to-business (B2B), business-to-consumer (B2C), and consumer-to-consumer (C2C) (Bapna, Goes & Gupta, 2001). While all are fruitful areas for research, this review will be confined to an examination of consumer-oriented auctions, both B2C and C2C. We circumscribe the scope of our study in this manner because of our interest in the behavior of individual bidders rather than that of firms. Within the chosen domain of B2C and C2C auctions, both single-item and multiple-item auctions exist. Single-item auctions may include sales of electronics, collectibles, autos, or a host of other items. Such auctions seem to have received the lion's share of researchers' interest. Multiple-item auctions have also received a fair amount of attention in literature (Bapna, Goes & Gupta, 2000, 2003a; Bapna, Goes, Gupta & Karuga, 2002; Easley & Tenorio, 2004; Oh, 2002) and include a number of interesting issues such as the development of algorithms for revenue optimization in iterative combinatorial auctions (Bapna, Goes & Gupta, 2003b). Multiple-item auctions often involve B2B or government-to-business (G2B) transactions, such as raw materials allotment or telecommunications spectrum auctions. We will place multi-item auctions outside the scope of our present review due to the additional theoretical complexities of understanding revenue maximization and bidder behavior when dealing with multiple items that may be auctioned in a lot.

At this point, we will turn to a more detailed explanation of findings in Internet auction research. We will describe the various independent and dependent variables that have been examined in previous studies. After cataloguing these variables, we will note general findings regarding the impact of particular variables upon auction outcome and build a conceptual model of factors impacting auction outcome.

Outcomes of Internet Auctions

The most commonly used measures of auction outcome are (1) auction success, (2) final closing price, (3) seller revenue, (4) price premiums, and (5) number of bids. These outcomes are listed in Table 1. Auction success is defined as whether a given auction results in a completed sale (Gilkeson & Reynolds, 2003). Several situations can lead to an "unsuccessful" auction. For instance, if a reserve price is not met or if no bids are placed on an item, the auction will be unsuccessful. Final closing price is simply defined as the value of the winning bid placed in a successful auction (e.g., Gilkeson et al., 2003). Seller revenue is another dependent variable that has been studied. It is generally defined as the gross amount of the sale (Lucking-Reiley, 1999; Subramaniam, Mittal & Inman, 2004; Ward & Clark, 2002). The ability to generate price premiums, which are defined as the monetary amount above the average price received by sellers of identical products, are yet another dependent variable (Ba & Pavlou, 2002; Pavlou, 2002a). Finally, the number of bids placed for an item has been measured as a dependent variable in some studies. While number of bids is more often used as an independent variable, it has also been examined as an outcome in its own right (Ottaway, Bruneau & Evans, 2003; Subramaniam et al., 2004).

Factors Affecting Auction Outcome

Recent findings and their implications cover a vast scope. Before proceeding to introduce the numerous independent variables that have been investigated as determinants of auction outcome, we wish to introduce a taxonomy for these variables that will help give structure to the following discussion. Three parties are involved in single-item B2C and C2C Internet auctions: the seller, the auctioneer, and the bidder (Klein,

Table 1. Dependant variables in extant Internet auction research

Variable	General Description	Source
(1) Auction Success	Whether or not a given auction results in a completed sale	(Dholakia, 2005b; Gilkeson & Reynolds, 2003)
(2) Final Closing Price	The highest bid in a successful auction	(Brint, 2003; Bruce, Haruvy & Rao, 2004; Dholakia & Soltysinski, 2001; Gilkeson & Reynolds, 2003; McDonald & Slawson, 2002; Ottaway, Bruneau & Evans, 2003; Standifird, 2001; Standifird, Roelofs & Durham, 2004; Subramaniam, Mittal & Inman, 2004; Wilcox, 2000)
(3) Seller Revenue	The gross amount of the sale	(Lucking-Reiley, 1999; Subramaniam, Mittal & Inman, 2004; Ward & Clark, 2002)
(4) Price Premiums	The monetary amount above the average price received by sellers of identical products	(Ba & Pavlou, 2002; Pavlou, 2002a)
(5) Number of Bids	The total number of bids placed for a given item	(Bruce, Haruvy & Rao, 2004; McDonald & Slawson, 2002; Ottaway, Bruneau & Evans, 2003; Subramaniam, Mittal & Inman, 2004; Wilcox, 2000)

Figure 1. Conceptual model of Internet auctions

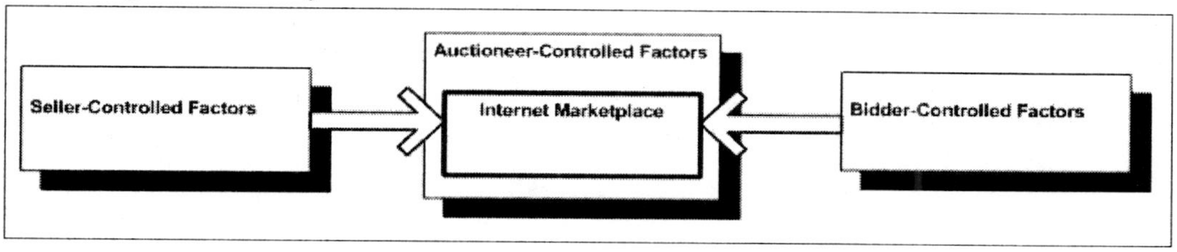

1997; Möllenberg, 2004). In Figure 1, we illustrate these three parties with the three largest rectangles, which are entitled "Seller-Controlled Factors," "Auctioneer-Controlled Factors," and "Bidder-Controlled Factors." Seller-controlled factors are simply variables under the control of the seller that may impact the outcome of the auction. Likewise auctioneer-controlled factors and bidder-controlled factors are variables under the control of the auctioneer and bidder, respectively, which may impact the outcome of the auction.

The two arrows in Figure 1 depict the fact that seller(s) and bidder(s) interact in the Internet marketplace. Echoing Mollenberg's (2004) aforementioned definition of an Internet auction, we define the Internet marketplace as a *virtual marketplace relying on Internet services (such as the World Wide Web) and Internet protocols to conduct auctions.* The Internet marketplace is located within the rectangle entitled "Auctioneer-Controlled Factors" to illustrate that the marketplace is primarily constructed and controlled by the auctioneer. Restated, the Internet marketplace and the rules for transacting business within it are defined by the factors under the control of the auctioneer. For instance, a seller might list an item for sale on the popular eBay Internet auction Web site where it would be viewed by potential bidders. In this example, eBay is the auctioneer who constructs the Internet marketplace using various Internet technologies. We will now turn our attention to recent findings and their significance in the process of using this model to help forge a cohesive theory of Internet auctions. At the conclusion of this discussion, we will return to the Figure presented here to update and enrich it as a conceptual model of Internet auctions.

Seller-Controlled Factors

Variables under the control of the seller are numerous. Sellers are able to influence or control (1) their reputation rating, (2) the initial bid price, (3) the option of setting a reserve price and the level of the reserve price, (4) the option to offer a buy-now price and the level of the buy-now price, (5) the number of payment options offered to bidders, (6) the auction ending time, (7) the duration of the auction, (8) the amount, type, and specificity of the product information, (9) the number and type of delivery options, (10) the shipping cost, (11) the auction mechanism, and (12) whether they (the seller) have a new or recently changed Internet ID. It should be noted here that a few items, such as the number of payment methods and the auction format may be controlled by the seller, the auctioneer, or both. For instance, Internet auctioneer eBay, allows PayPal to be offered as a payment option, although each individual seller may choose whether or not they would like to accept Paypal payments.

Each of these variables has been investigated in previous research for a linkage to one or more of the dependent variables mentioned earlier. Table 2 lists these seller-controlled variables, defines each of them, and notes the empirical studies in which they have been studied. We acknowledge that there are slight variations in the definitions of some

Table 2. Seller-controlled factors in Internet auctions

Factor	General Definition	Source
(1) Reputation Rating	The number of positive feedback responses, negative feedback responses, and neutral feedback responses; or aggregate feedback rating	(Ba & Pavlou, 2002; Brint, 2003; Dholakia, 2005b; Gilkeson & Reynolds, 2003; McDonald & Slawson, 2002; Ottaway, Bruneau & Evans, 2003; Standifird, 2001; Standifird, Roelofs & Durham, 2004)
(2) Initial Bid Price	The price above which the first bidder to enter an auction must bid	(Brint, 2003; Gilkeson & Reynolds, 2003; McDonald & Slawson, 2002; Standifird, 2001; Standifird, Roelofs & Durham, 2004)
(3) Reserve Price	The option for a seller to specify a bid price below which an item will not be sold	(Brint, 2003; Bruce, Haruvy & Rao, 2004; McDonald & Slawson, 2002; Standifird, Roelofs & Durham, 2004; Subramaniam, Mittal & Inman, 2004)
(4) Buy Now Option	The presence or absence of the option for a bidder to end an auction early by purchasing at a seller-determined fixed price (eBay's Buy-it-Now option)	(Budish & Takeyama, 2001; Standifird, Roelofs & Durham, 2004)
(5) Payment Options	The number of various payment methods available to bidders (check, credit card, PayPal, etc.)	(Gilkeson & Reynolds, 2003; McDonald & Slawson, 2002)
(6) Auction End Time	Day and time auction ends	(Brint, 2003; Dholakia & Soltysinski, 2001; Gilkeson & Reynolds, 2003; Lucking-Reiley, 1999; McDonald & Slawson, 2002; Mehta, 2002; Standifird, 2001)
(7) Auction Duration	Length of auction in days, hours, minutes, or some similar measure	(Brint, 2003; Dholakia & Soltysinski, 2001; Gilkeson & Reynolds, 2003; Lucking-Reiley, 1999; McDonald & Slawson, 2002; Mehta, 2002; Standifird, 2001; Standifird, Roelofs & Durham, 2004; Subramaniam, Mittal & Inman, 2004)
(8) Product Information	The number of pictures of an item or the level of detail of an item's description	(Bruce, Haruvy & Rao, 2004; Dholakia & Soltysinski, 2001; Lucking-Reiley, 1999; Ottaway, Bruneau & Evans, 2003; Standifird, Roelofs & Durham, 2004)
(9) Delivery Options	The availability of international or expedited delivery	(Gilkeson & Reynolds, 2003; McDonald & Slawson, 2002)
(10) Shipping Cost	The amount of shipping and handling charges	(Bruce, Haruvy & Rao, 2004; Gilkeson & Reynolds, 2003; McDonald & Slawson, 2002)
(11) Auction Mechanism	The choice of first-price sealed-bid, Dutch, second-price sealed bid, or English auction format	(Lucking-Reiley, 1999; Rafaeli & Noy, 2005)
(12) New ID	The use of a new or recently-changed online identity by the seller	(Standifird, 2001)

variables from one study to the next. Interested readers may consult the individual studies listed to locate the specific definition used. Our goal is not to compare and contrast the various ways each variable has been measured, but instead to highlight the general variables of interest in Internet auction research. We wish to emphasize that there is general agreement on many of these items. For instance, reputation rating is sometimes measured as an overall reputation score, sometimes as the total number of positive feedback responses, or at other times as a ratio of positive to negative feedback responses. In each case, the variable of interest can be generally referred to as "reputation rating" and the number of references cited in Table 2 allows readers to understand that it is one of the most frequently studied factors influencing auction outcome.

As we now turn to a review of findings regarding seller-controlled factors, we will note theoretical explanations of observed relationships where they have been provided. Some studies of Internet auctions, however, are exploratory in nature and do not provide extensive theoretical explanation for their findings. In these cases, we will simply report the studies' findings and reserve possible theoretical explanations for the final section of this article.

Within the realm of seller-controlled factors, seller reputation is one of the most thoroughly examined predictors of auction outcome (Ba & Pavlou, 2002; Brint, 2003; Dholakia, 2005b; Gilkeson & Reynolds, 2003; McDonald & Slawson, 2002; Ottaway, Bruneau & Evans, 2003; Pavlou & Gefen, 2005; Standifird, 2001; Standifird, Roelofs & Durham, 2004; Strader & Ramaswami, 2002). Not surprisingly, these studies indicate that sellers with high reputation scores are more successful by most any measure chosen. These studies explain the linkage between reputation and desirable auction outcomes such as higher closing price, successful sale, or increased number of bids by appealing to general behavioral economics arguments that explain that transacting with reputable parties reduces uncertainty in decision making. Additionally, it has been found that negative feedback is highly influential in predicting auction outcome while positive feedback is only mildly influential (Standifird, 2001). The asymmetric impact of positive and negative feedback scores has been explained by an appeal to Prospect Theory (Kahneman & Tversky, 1979)—a theory that explains that individuals evaluating potential gains and losses weight losses more heavily than wins.

An item's initial bid price has been investigated to ascertain an impact upon the winning bid price. Findings here are mixed. Some have appealed to Signaling Theory (Spence, 1973) to explain that high initial prices may indicate quality items and thereby result in successful sales and higher closing prices (Gilkeson & Reynolds, 2003). Other studies have failed to find a significant relationship between initial price and final sales price (Standifird, 2001). Reserve prices have been shown to positively impact auction success and final closing price (Gilkeson & Reynolds, 2003). The presence of a buy-now option has been found in one study to be relatively insignificant to bidders; Standifird and colleagues (2004) found that bidders at times ignore the buy-now price even when that price is below prevailing market prices. This finding is explained by noting that some bidders may participate in auctions out of a hedonic rather than a purely utilitarian motivation. This study stands in contrast to a theoretical paper that argues for a positive relationship between the availability of a buy-now price and auction success (Budish & Takeyama, 2001). All the findings relating initial bid price, reserve price, and buy-now options to auction outcome generally challenge prevailing notions about bidder rationality. Earlier experimental research into auctions argued that positive outcomes would result from initial prices being set as low as possible to allow as many potential bidders as possible to enter the auction (Kagel, 1995).

The number of payment methods has not been conclusively linked to either auction success or increased revenues. The number of payment methods, however, is frequently used as a control variable, giving a level of informal credence to its status as a possible determinant of auction outcome. If bidders value the ease with which a transaction can be completed, it is plausible that they will patronize a seller who offers a large number of payment options (Gilkeson & Reynolds, 2003). Other variables frequently used as control variables, but that have not been conclusively linked to auction outcome include the time of day or week an auction ends and the duration of an auction (Brint, 2003; Dholakia & Soltysinski, 2001; Gilkeson & Reynolds, 2003; McDonald & Slawson, 2002; Mehta, 2002; Standifird, 2001; Standifird, Roelofs & Durham, 2004; Subramaniam, Mittal & Inman, 2004).

Detailed descriptions of products are significant predictors of a successful sale (Gilkeson & Reynolds, 2003). It has been argued that pictures of an item may affect information processing and thereby influence success of the sale, but perhaps not for commodity-like items (Ottaway, Bruneau & Evans, 2003). Numerous other researchers have included product description as a control variable in their studies, measuring this variable as the number of pictures, the number of lines of text describing a product, or some similar measure (Bruce, Haruvy & Rao, 2004; Dholakia & Soltysinski, 2001; Standifird, Roelofs & Durham, 2004).

Delivery options refers to the shipping options available and their costs. One study argues that high seller reputation and delivery efficiency may be correlated (McDonald & Slawson, 2002), while another includes shipping cost as a control variable (Gilkeson & Reynolds, 2003). Simple economic explanations of rational behavior explain that shipping price will take on greater significance to the bidder as shipping price becomes a greater proportion of the total transaction price.

Whether various auction mechanisms provide revenue equivalence has been a topic of intense interest in traditional auction literature (Kagel, 1995). Auction mechanism, however, has been relatively infrequently investigated in the Internet auction context—perhaps due to the dominance of the English or English-Vickrey hybrid auction mechanism. One study found that Dutch auctions produced revenues thirty percent higher than first-price sealed bid auctions and also found that English and Vickrey auctions produce roughly equivalent revenues (Lucking-Reiley, 1999).

Finally, it has been noted that a new or recently changed seller ID may influence final bid price under certain circumstances (Standifird, 2001). While that study fails to provide an extended explanation of this finding, we observe that, all else equal, a seller with an established ID and numerous high ratings would likely elicit more trust from potential bidders than a seller with a new ID. Trust has been linked to the ability to generate price premiums (Ba & Pavlou, 2002).

Auctioneer-Controlled Factors

After examining recent literature, we conclude that characteristics of the auction under the control of the auctioneer include (1) the auction mechanism, (2) the availability of an option to end an auction early and purchase the item immediately ("BuyNow" on eBay), (3) the number of payment options, (4) the perceived ease of use of the Internet auction Web site, (5) the perceived usefulness of the Internet auction Web site, (6) the presence of a feedback mechanism through which bidders and/or sellers can leave comments about parties to auction transactions, and (7) the availability of an escrow service that helps mediate the transaction between bidder and seller. As with the foregoing list of seller-controlled factors, we provide a table with a general definition of each of these variables as well as the studies that have included these variables (see Table 3).

Table 3. Auctioneer-controlled factors in Internet auctions

Factor	General Description	Source
(1) Auction Mechanism	The choice of first-price sealed-bid, Dutch, second-price sealed bid, and English auction format	(Lucking-Reiley, 1999; Rafaeli & Noy, 2005)
(2) Buy-Now Option	The presence or absence of the option for a bidder to end an auction early by purchasing at a seller-determined fixed price (eBay's Buy-it-Now option)	(Standifird, Roelofs & Durham, 2004)
(3) Payment Options	The number of various payment methods available to bidders (check, credit card, PayPal, etc.)	(Gilkeson & Reynolds, 2003; McDonald & Slawson, 2002)
(4) Perceived Ease of Use	The degree to that an Internet auction site is easy to use	(Pavlou, 2002b; Stafford & Stern, 2002)
(5) Perceived Usefulness	The degree to that use of an Internet auction site is free of effort	(Pavlou, 2002b; Stafford & Stern, 2002)
(6) Feedback Mechanism	The presence or absence of a mechanism that allows bidders and/or sellers to leave comments about other parties to auction transactions	(Pavlou, 2002a)
(7) Escrow Service	The availability of an escrow service to mediate the transaction between the bidder and seller	(Hu, Lin, Whinston & Zhang, 2004)

The reader will recall from the previous section describing seller-controlled factors that auction format has been linked in one study to variation in seller revenue (Lucking-Reiley, 1999). Specifically, the use of a Dutch auction may produce higher revenues than will a first-price sealed-bid auction (a type of auction very similar to the popular eBay and yahoo.com auctions). Also, revenues are essentially equivalent in English and second-price sealed bid (Vickrey) auctions. Another factor that may, in many auctions, be under the control of both seller and auctioneer is the availability of a buy-now option. To restate an earlier point, offering a buy price may increase revenue for sellers, as has been argued by Budish and Takeyama (2001), but this proposed relationship has not yet been borne out by empirical findings (Standifird, Roelofs & Durham, 2004). Still another factor under the control of both seller and auctioneer is the number of payment methods accepted. This variable has been investigated with regard to both auction success and final bid price (Gilkeson & Reynolds, 2003). Similar to the argument advanced in the section on bidder-controlled factors, if bidders value the ease with which a transaction can be completed, it is plausible that they will utilize an auctioneer that has a large number of payment options (Gilkeson & Reynolds, 2003).

The remaining auctioneer-controlled factors are generally understood to be under the exclusive direction of the auctioneer. First, the Technology Acceptance Model (TAM) (Davis, 1989) has been found to have explanatory power when predicting participation in Internet auctions. Bidders who find a Web site useful and easy to use are more likely to participate in an Internet auction (Pavlou, 2002b; Stafford & Stern, 2002). Several researchers have examined the development of trust through feedback mechanisms as a predictor of success in Internet auctions (Ba & Pavlou, 2002; Ba, Whinston & Zhang, 2003; Pavlou, 2002a). The use of escrow services has also been shown to have a key role in developing trust in Internet bidders (Hu, Lin, Whinston & Zhang, 2004). The use of an escrow service has been linked to Internet auction outcome as well. Collectively, these studies indicate that auctioneers

Table 4. Bidder-controlled factors in Internet auctions

Factor	General Description	Source
(1) Bidder Experience	Whether a bidder has participated in or won previous Internet auctions	(McDonald & Slawson, 2002; Ottaway, Bruneau & Evans, 2003; Wilcox, 2000)
(2) Bidder Type	The motivations of a bidder (bargain-hunter, hedonically-motivated bidder, relationally-oriented bidder); or risk propensity of a bidder	(Bapna, Goes & Gupta, 2000; Bapna, Goes, Gupta & Jin, 2004; Dholakia, 2005b; Mehta, 2002; Ward & Clark, 2002)
(3) Intention to Use	Behavioral intention to use an auction Web site	(Pavlou, 2002b; Stafford & Stern, 2002)
(4) Affinity with the Computer	An individual's liking or preference for computer-mediated shopping	(Stafford & Stern, 2002)
(5) Involvement	The individual's inherent cognitive processing activities, including emotions, moods, and feelings, in response to a stimulus	(Stafford & Stern, 2002)
(6) Number of Bidders	The total number of unique bidders on an item or number of bidders utilizing a given Web site	(Dholakia & Soltysinski, 2001; Subramaniam, Mittal & Inman, 2004; Wilcox, 2000)

(or sellers) who are able to induce trust through a variety of mechanisms may be more successful than competitors in Internet auctions.

Bidder-Controlled Factors

Auction outcome can also be influenced by bidders. These factors include (1) bidder experience, (2) bidder type, (3) intention to use an Internet auction Web site, (4) affinity with the computer, (5) involvement in the Internet auction bidding process, and (6) the number of bidders placing bids on a given item or using a given auction Web site. These bidder-controlled factors and their histories in Internet auction literature are detailed in Table 4.

Experienced bidders have been found to make bids that are consistent with the optimal strategies prescribed in auction theory (Wilcox, 2000). Bidder type has been classified in different ways by different researchers. One study finds some bidders have a relational orientation, preferring to interact with one seller multiple times (Dholakia, 2005b). Another study finds some bidders to be "evaluators," that is, early one-time high bidders with a clear idea of their valuation of the item, while other bidders are "opportunists," who are bargain hunters and generally place minimum required bids just before an auction closes, and still others to be "participators," who enjoy participating in the process of the auction itself and often make a low initial bid then monitor the auction progress and make successive bids (Bapna, Goes & Gupta, 2000). Still another study examined the risk propensity of bidders, using the framework of Prospect Theory (Kahneman & Tversky, 1979) to classify them as risk-averse or risk-seeking (Ward & Clark, 2002). Finally, bidders with hedonic motivations for participating in Internet auctions have been contrasted with those who have purely utilitarian motivations (Standifird, Roelofs & Durham, 2004).

Following from the earlier mention of the TAM model as an explanatory model of Internet auction outcome, behavioral intention to use, a TAM construct, has also been linked to the number of bidders participating in an Internet auction (Stafford & Stern, 2002). The same study notes that an individual's preference for computer mediated shopping and a user's emotional state in response to the stimulus of the Internet auction environment increase the likelihood of a potential bidder to participate in an auction. Thus, both affinity with the computer and a bidder's involvement in the Internet auction bidding process may influence auction outcome.

Finally, the circular effect of high seller volume eliciting high bidder interest, that in turn motivates sellers to continue to utilize a highly-trafficked Internet auction Web site has been noted (Wingfield, 2001). It is therefore not surprising that as an independent variable, the number of bids and bidders leads to auction success and increased revenues for sellers (Dholakia & Soltysinski, 2001; Gilkeson & Reynolds, 2003).

TOWARDS A THEORETICAL UNDERSTANDING OF INTERNET AUCTIONS

Based upon our review of literature, this research stream has matured to the point that pure concept discovery is becoming less necessary. As mentioned earlier, scholars have called for additional theory development to help understand Internet auctions (Dholakia, 2005a). We concur and call researchers to bring synthesis to studies of Internet auctions by moving into process explanation and ultimately towards theory development.

It has been argued that a complete theory must contain four elements, including a list of what factors are relevant to the explanation of the phenomenon of interest, a description of how the factors are related, an explanation of the psychological, economic, or other dynamics that justify the selection of factors and their relationships, and finally a description of the limitations of the theory to pertinent places, times, and people (Whetten, 1989). We have endeavored to develop the first element by noting the factors that have been shown to be significant predictors of Internet auction outcome. These factors have been enumerated in previous sections of this article. This section provides the second and third of Whetten's (1989) four elements for a complete theory: descriptions of how factors are related and explanations of their relationships. We will reserve our discussion of limitations to the conclusion section of the article.

At this point, we would like to add information to the conceptual model of Internet auctions (presented earlier in this article as Figure 1) and

Figure 2. Parties to the auction transaction and factors under their control

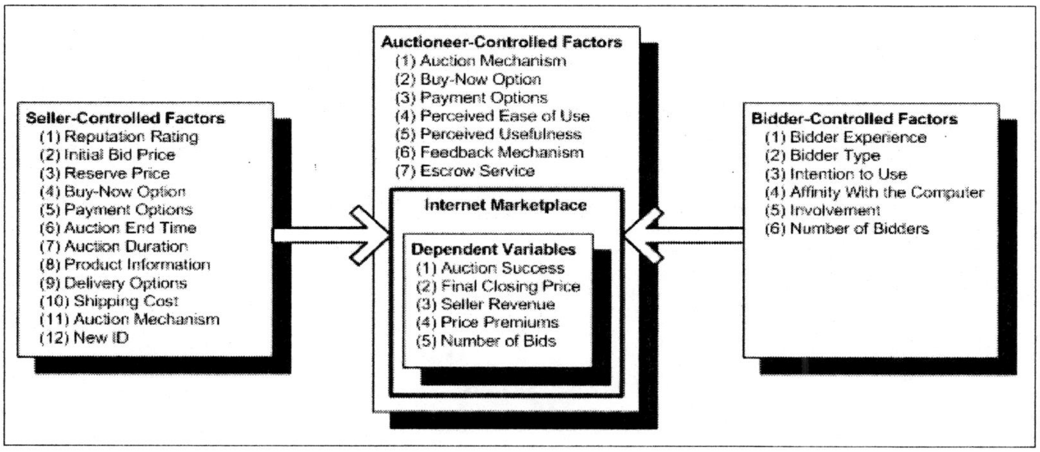

advance a possible explanation of how these factors may be related. We enrich Figure 1 to illustrate the factors that each party to the auction transaction may manipulate to determine auction outcome. In Figure 2, we place the list of seller-controlled factors into the left-most rectangle entitled "Seller-Controlled Factors." Similarly, we populate the remaining rectangles with the "Auctioneer-Controlled Factors," "Bidder-Controlled Factors," and "Dependent Variables" that have been described in the previous section of this article. We place the dependent variables within the "Internet Marketplace," which is itself within the "Auctioneer-Controlled Factors" rectangle. We locate the dependent variables here to illustrate first, that transactions are brokered by the auctioneer, and second, that auctions are conducted in the virtual marketplace maintained by the auctioneer.

To validate our three-way categorization of independent variables, we employed cluster analysis, a statistical technique that identifies homogeneous subgroups of cases within a dataset (Hair, Anderson, Tatham, & Black). We identified 25 empirical studies of single-item Internet auctions and noted the independent variables recorded in each study [see Appendix A, where Table A.1 lists the research studies used in this dataset, and where Table A.2 lists the independent variables recorded in each study]. We adopted the *k*-means method that will product exactly *k* different clusters based on the greatest possible distinction using Euclidean distance (Johnson & Wichern, 1992). The membership of each cluster was fixed using *k*-mean cluster analysis in SPSS software. A three-cluster solution was found to be the most parsimonious grouping of the studies and the solution that best reflected the meaningful patterns of the relationships among the control factors. Table 5 shows the means of the clustering variables for each of the three groups; the values for cluster centers in Table 5 represent the distance among the clusters. Thus, our categorization of independent variables as either seller-controlled, auctioneer-controlled, or bidder-controlled is validated. Table 6 shows the classification results of a one-way ANOVA analysis. ANOVA indicates that the three groups are significantly different and thereby affirms the stability of the three-cluster solution.

We now turn our attention to theories utilized in extant Internet auction research (summarized in Table 7) and note how they may collectively point towards a comprehensive, systematic understanding of Internet auctions. The reader will recall that Image Theory (Beach, 1993) and the TAM model (Davis, 1989) have been applied in the context of Internet auctions. These psychological theories have been provided valuable insight into bidder behavior. Investigation of auctions has, however, long been dominated by economic rather than primarily psychological explanations. Within Internet auction literature, the theory of Information Cascades (Banerjee, 1992; Bikhchandani, Hirshleifer & Welch, 1992), Signaling Theory (Spence, 1973), and Prospect Theory (Kahneman & Tversky, 1979) have been applied to explain bidder behavior. Based upon the review of literature in the previous section of this article, none of these theories seem to be

Table 5. Distance between clusters

Clusters	**Cluster 1**	**Cluster 2**	**Cluster 3**
Cluster 1	-----	1.829	2.445
Cluster 2	1.829	-----	1.340
Cluster 3	2.445	1.340	----

Table 6. One-way ANOVA analysis

	Cluster		Error			
Variable[+]	Mean Square	d.f.	Mean Square	d.f.	F-value	*p*-value
S1	1.330	2	0.159	22	8.360	0.002**
S2	1.291	2	0.130	22	9.944	0.001***
S3	0.351	2	0.175	22	2.004	0.159
S4	0.063	2	0.078	22	0.807	0.459[a]
S5	0.420	2	0.045	22	9.240	0.001***
S6	1.341	2	0.107	22	12.520	0.000***
S7	1.286	2	0.156	22	8.250	0.002**
S8	1.273	2	0.146	22	8.712	0.002**
S9	0.420	2	0.045	22	9.240	0.001***
S10	0.323	2	0.123	22	2.617	0.096*
S11	0.063	2	0.078	22	0.807	0.459[b]
S12	0.105	2	0.034	22	3.080	0.066*
A1	0.063	2	0.078	22	0.807	0.459[b]
A2	0.063	2	0.078	22	0.807	0.459[a]
A3	0.420	2	0.045	22	9.240	0.001***
A4	0.206	2	0.065	22	3.168	0.062*
A5	0.206	2	0.065	22	3.168	0.062*
A6	0.051	2	0.039	22	1.320	0.287
A7	0.051	2	0.039	22	1.320	0.287
B1	0.019	2	0.151	22	0.128	0.881
B2	0.566	2	0.156	22	3.630	0.043*
B3	0.206	2	0.065	22	3.168	0.062*
B4	0.051	2	0.039	22	1.320	0.287
B5	0.051	2	0.039	22	1.320	0.287

[+] here, variable S1 denotes the first variable under the control of the seller—namely reputation rating. Similarly, S2 denotes initial bid price, S3 denotes reserve price, etc. This numbering of variables appears in the body of the paper, in Table 2, and in Figures 2-4.

* significant at .1 level; ** significant at .01 level; *** significant at .001 level

[a] Buy-now option is duplicated. As noted in the body of the text, this factor is under the control of both the seller (S4) and the auctioneer (A2). An insignificant p-value on these two measures should not, therefore be construed as a lack of statistical support for the clustering solution.

[b] Auction mechanism is duplicated. As noted in the body of the text, this factor is under the control of both the seller (S11) and the auctioneer (A1). An insignificant p-value on these two measures should not, therefore be construed as a lack of statistical support for the clustering solution.

comprehensive enough to explain the influence of all independent variables upon auction outcome. Each, however, seems to play a significant role in explaining how some subset of independent variables determines auction outcome.

We argue that the role of these theories is to explain how bidders evaluate the utility of a given item up for auction. For instance, TAM explains that if a Web site is perceived to be useful and easy to use, the bidder experiences a lower cost (in terms of time and effort) to bid on an item than if the site were neither useful nor easy to use. An item auctioned on a Web site that is perceived to be easy to use and useful will have greater utility than an item auctioned on a Web site that does not have these characteristics. In another easily imagined example, Signaling Theory appears to explain that a high reputation rating, a high initial bid price, a high reserve price, and a buy-now option set at a relatively high level will allow bidders to infer that an item is of high quality. Signals of high quality encourage bidders to submit higher and greater numbers of bids and will likely result in a higher final closing price.

We argue that existing psychological theories provide insights into how bidders construct their individual utility functions for a given item being auctioned. Thus, an explanation of how the factors we have identified here are related is:

$$u_i\ (scf_1,\ scf_2,\ \ldots scf_{12},\ acf_1,\ acf_2,\ldots acf_7,\ bcf_1,\ bcf_2,\ldots bcf_6) \qquad (1)$$

Table 7. Theories used in Internet auction research

Theory	Description of Theory	Application to Internet Auctions
Image Theory	When individuals are forced to select one item from a vast, unmanageable set of alternatives, they apply a heuristic to pre-screen items for suitability (Beach, 1993).	An awareness of bidders' pre-screening heuristics (such as, "I will only bid on items with a shipping cost less than $10.") is of great import to merchants who utilize Internet auctions (Dholakia & Soltysinski, 2001).
Technology Acceptance Model (TAM)	Users will form a behavioral intention to use an information system that they perceive to be easy to use and useful (Davis, 1989).	Internet auction Web sites that are perceived to be useful and easy to use have the potential to draw more participants than Web sites that do not have such a perception. (Pavlou, 2002b; Stafford & Stern, 2002).
Information Cascades	Information Cascades occur when individuals observe the behavior of others as a signal about the usefulness of a behavior, even to the point of disregarding their own information about the value of the behavior in question (Banerjee, 1992; Bikhchandani, Hirshleifer & Welch, 1992).	The behavior of competing bidders, such as the number of previous bids, the price paid, or the choice of item, leads a bidder to choose a particular course of action (Dholakia & Soltysinski, 2001).
Signaling Theory	It is not always possible to know with certainty a given object's true value. In such cases, a conditional probability assessment of value may be inferred based upon signals and indices (Spence, 1973).	Because bidders may view price level as a signal of an item's quality (e.g., a high-priced item is of high quality), independent variables such as initial bid price, the presence and level of a reserve price, and the presence and level of a buy-now option may impact final closing price (Gilkeson & Reynolds, 2003).
Prospect Theory	Individuals deviate from expected utility theory when choosing among risky prospects by underweighting probable outcomes and overweighting certain outcomes as well as by discarding components of a risky prospect that are shared by all such prospects. The result is that decision makers view choices in terms of gains and losses rather than final states; decision makers are generally risk-averse for gains and risk-seeking for losses (Kahneman & Tversky, 1979).	Risk-averse bidders pay "insurance" premiums to ensure successful bidding (Ward & Clark, 2002). Thus, in whatever way an auctioneer or a seller can reduce uncertainty for bidders in an auction, bidders may be more likely to participate.

Here, u_i denotes the utility of a given item *i*, and explains that utility is a function of the value of seller-controlled factors (denoted by scf_n), auctioneer-controlled factors (denoted by acf_n), and bidder-controlled factors (denoted by bcf_n). Items with greater utility will have a higher likelihood of successful sale, have a higher final closing price, product greater revenue for the seller, be more likely to generate price premiums, and be more likely to generate a higher number of bids. Thus, we argue that the relationships between the factors we have listed can be partially explained by existing psychological and economic theories. An application of utility theory, however, may provide a comprehensive and parsimonious explanation of Internet auction outcome. Such an application of utility theory subsumes the explanations of how individual independent variables influence the dependent variable(s) of interest.

IMPLICATIONS FOR RESEARCH AND PRACTICE

A comprehensive list of the factors under the control of sellers, auctioneers, and bidders helps bring synthesis to the exploratory phase of Internet auction research. We argue that by cataloguing and categorizing the variables investigated in previous studies, the major determinants of auction outcome have been identified. This represents the first contribution of this article to scholarship. With a comprehensive review of Internet auction literature completed, and with the relevant variables identified, research can now be undertaken to ascertain the relative importance of various factors and the rationale for their effect on auction outcome. By placing these factors into three categories, an additional, related contribution is made to the literature as well. Researchers may now choose to focus their inquiry more tightly on one set of factors or another. Decomposition of a single list of factors into categories of factors may reduce the complexity of elucidating the economic, psychological, and/or sociological forces that give shape to the behavior of each of the parties to the auction transaction.

A number of perspectives can be adopted in these future studies. Many possible studies may choose to hold constant one set of factors (either bidder-, auctioneer-, or seller-controlled) to isolate the contribution of each set of factors to auction outcome. For instance, if bidders in an Internet auction are treated as a "black box," having unknown, unknowable, or unspecified motivations, then the list of seller- and auctioneer-controlled factors listed in the conceptual model presented here is a comprehensive basis from which to understand Internet auctions. Both field studies using real-world data as well as experiments using laboratory data can be conducted to find the impact of seller-controlled factors as well as auctioneer-controlled factors on auction outcome.

Bidder motivation need not be treated as a black box, however. The conceptual model presented here is an attempt to provide an inclusive list of the factors pertinent to a study of bidder behavior. The list of bidder-controlled factors presented here gives guidance to researchers who may wish to design more carefully controlled research studies. Field studies may provide copious data about the impact of seller- and auctioneer-controlled factors, but they provide relatively little information about bidders. Bidders' experience and the number of bidders can usually be observed from a field study, but bidders' type (motivation), intention to use a Web site, affinity with the computer, or involvement generally cannot. Our list of bidder-controlled factors allows researchers to observe that experiments and field studies have been used in the past to investigate bidder behavior. Other research, however, has paired a survey (as was used by Pavlou (2002b) and by Stafford and Stern (2002)) with a field study or experiment to investigate bidder-controlled factors. We note that surveys, a methodology frequently employed in behavioral research, may be underutilized for investigating bidder behavior in Internet auctions.

Similarly, the pairing of a mathematical model to explain Internet auction outcome (such as the simple utility function developed in this article) with an empirical examination using real-world data to validate the model seems to be an appropriate way in which to investigate Internet auctions. Many studies either develop mathematical models of auctions or collect real-world data to investigate variables, but few combine the two methods in a way that can bring the rigor of a pure science such as mathematics to bear on a social science phenomenon like Internet auctions.

The goal of Internet auction research is not only to provide insights for scholars, but also to give practical guidance to practitioners whose firms utilize Internet auctions as a sales channel. While Internet auctions were once dominated by consumer-to-consumer (C2C) transactions, researchers have noted the increasing number of business-to-business (B2B) and business-to-consumer (B2C) auctions (Bapna, Goes & Gupta, 2001; Lucking-Reiley, 2000a). eBay alone boasts 383,000 eBay stores (eBay, 2006). Furthermore, eBay has begun to court companies such as Dell, Disney, Home Depot, IBM, Motorola, Sears, Sun Microsystems, and Sharper Image to sell outdated, returned, or refurbished merchandise on the Internet (Dholakia, 2005b; Gentry, 2003; Grow, 2002; Vogelstein, Boyle, Lewis & Kirkpatrick, 2004) where they can earn greater profit than by using a liquidator (Gentry, 2003; Grow, 2002). Clearly, in light of the burgeoning use of Internet auctions by businesses, the model presented here has value to organizations that use Internet auctions as a sales channel.

An understanding of the factors a firm can control will aid the development of successful sales strategies for firms. For instance, when a firm auctioning items on the Internet notes the 12 factors under their control (previously described in Table 2 and depicted in Figure 2), they may choose to price an item in such a way that the price communicates a signal about quality and thus stimulates bidding interest. Similarly, a firm making an initial decision to utilize Internet auctions as a sales channel might choose to purchase a firm with an excellent reputation rating rather than invest in the time to build a reputation. Thus, practical insights for firms are given by this model as well.

CONCLUSION

We wish to briefly address the limitations of the theoretical development presented here. The vast majority of the studies considered have been conducted at Internet auction Web sites. We acknowledge that some auctions take place through newsgroups or e-mail (Lucking-Reiley, 1999; Lucking-Reiley, 2000a), and different factors may come into play in such situations. For instance, trust is often developed through feedback mechanisms on Internet auction Web sites, and may be developed differently among members of a newsgroup who have established relationships before the commencement of the auction. Obviously, this review has been constrained to include only single-item consumer-oriented auctions. Future work may address multiple-item auctions, reverse auctions, or business-oriented auctions. Additionally, the ideas advanced here may be specific to individuals in Western countries where the majority of data for the empirical studies discussed here was gathered.

While we do not claim to have developed a comprehensive theory explaining Internet auctions, this study contributes to literature by bringing a measure of cohesion and synthesis to existing findings regarding Internet auctions. As Weick (1995) has argued, findings in datasets are closer to theory than mere lists of references, lists of variables are closer to theory than are data, diagrams are closer than variables, and hypotheses are closer still. All are necessary intermediate stages in theory development, and perhaps the model here may guide future investigations. Specifically, we believe this review makes three primary contributions. First, we believe the compendium of variables presented here will assist researchers attempting to ascertain what variables have been previously investigated. Second, the conceptual model presented earlier may represent a step closer to theory. Third, we have highlighted the existing theoretical explanations of bidder, seller, and auctioneer behavior in auctions and pointed to potential avenues for integration. Moving forward from this point, we contend that a comprehensive theory of behavior in Internet auctions will fit descriptions of auctioneer, bidder, and seller behavior together with explanations of the economic, sociological, cognitive and psychological dynamics at work to enable progress towards a parsimonious theory.

REFERENCES

Ba, S., & Pavlou, P. A. (2002). Evidence of the effect of trust building technology in electronic markets: Price premiums and buyer behavior. *MIS Quarterly, 26*(3), 243-269.

Ba, S., Whinston, A. B., & Zhang, H. (2003). Building trust in online auction markets through an economic incentive mechanism. *Decision Support Systems, 35*(3), 273-286.

Banerjee, A. (1992). A simple model of herd behavior. *Quarterly Journal of Economics, 107*, 797–818.

Bapna, R., Goes, P., & Gupta, A. (2000). A theoretical and empirical investigation of multi-item on-line auctions. *Information Technology and Management, 1*(1-2), 1-23.

Bapna, R., Goes, P., & Gupta, A. (2001). Insights and analyses of online auctions. *Association for Computing Machinery. Communications of the ACM, 44*(11), 42-50.

Bapna, R., Goes, P., & Gupta, A. (2003a). Analysis and design of business-to-consumer online auctions. *Management Science, 49*(1), 85-102.

Bapna, R., Goes, P., & Gupta, A. (2003b). Replicating online Yankee auctions to analyze auctioneers' and bidders' strategies. *Information Systems Research, 14*(3), 244-268.

Bapna, R., Goes, P., Gupta, A., & Jin, Y. (2004). User heterogeneity and its impact on electronic auction market design: An empirical exploration. *MIS Quarterly, 28*(1), 21-43.

Bapna, R., Goes, P., Gupta, A., & Karuga, G. (2002). Optimal design of the online auction channel: Analytical, empirical, and computational insights. *Decision Sciences, 33*(4), 557-578.

Beach, L. R. (1993). Broadening the definition of decision making: The role of prechoice screening of options. *Psychological Science, 4*(4), 215-220.

Bikhchandani, S., Hirshleifer, D., & Welch, I. (1992). A theory of fads, fashions, custom and cultural change as information cascades. *Journal of Political Economy, 100*(5), 992-1026.

Brint, A. T. (2003). Investigating buyer and seller strategies in online auctions. *The Journal of the Operational Research Society, 54*(11), 1177-1188.

Bruce, N., Haruvy, E., & Rao, R. (2004). Seller rating, price, and default in online auctions. *Journal of Interactive Marketing, 18*(4), 37-51.

Budish, E., & Takeyama, L. N. (2001). Buy prices in online auctions: Irrationality on the Internet? *Economics Letters, 72*(3), 325-334.

Damas, Phillip. (2001). "E-shippers Kick the Paper Habit", American Shipper, February 2001. available at: http://www.tradecard.com/languages/EN/news/articles/AmericanShipper_022001.pdf

Davis, F. D. (1989). Perceived usefulness, perceived ease of use, and user acceptance of information technology. *MIS Quarterly, 13*(1), 319-340.

Dholakia, U. M. (2005a). Concept discovery, process explanation, and theory deepening in e-marketing research: The case of online auctions. *Marketing Theory, 5*(1), 117-124.

Dholakia, U. M. (2005b). The usefulness of bidders' reputation ratings to sellers in online auctions. *Journal of Interactive Marketing, 19*(1), 31-41.

Dholakia, U. M., & Soltysinski, K. (2001). Coveted or overlooked? The psychology of bidding for comparable listings in digital auctions. *Marketing Letters, 12*(3), 225-237.

Easley, R. F., & Tenorio, R. (2004). Jump bidding strategies in Internet auctions. *Management Science, 50*(10), 1407-1420.

eBay. (2006). eBay Inc. announces fourth quarter and full year 2005 financial results. Retrieved September 11, 2006, from http://www.investor.ebay.com/news/Q105/ebay0420-2932ld.pdf

Gentry, C. R. (2003). Recycled returns. *Chain Store Age, 79*(1), 72-73.

Gilkeson, J. H., & Reynolds, K. (2003). Determinants of Internet auction success and closing price: An exploratory study. *Psychology & Marketing, 20*(6), 537-566.

Grow, B. (September 9, 2002). Exess inventory? Ebay to the rescue. *Business Week, 3798*, 8. Wingfield, N. (June 1, 2001). Ebay watch: Corporate sellers put the online auctioneer on even faster track: Goods from IBM, Disney help dot-com pioneer post a surge in profits: Why mom and pop are mad. Wall Street Journal, p. A.1.

Hair, J. F., Anderson, R. E., Tatham, R. L., & Black, W. C. (1995). *Multivariate data analysis* (4th ed.). Upper Saddle River, NJ: Prentice Hall, Inc.

Hu, X., Lin, Z., Whinston, A. B., & Zhang, H. (2004). Hope or hype: On the viability of escrow services as trusted third parties in online auction environments. *Information Systems Research, 15*(3), 236-250.

Johnson, R. A., & Wichern, D. W. (1992). *Applied multivariate statistical analysis* (3rd ed.). Upper Saddle River, NJ: Prentice Hall.

Kagel, J. H. (1995). A survey of experimental research. In J. H. Kagel & A. E. Roth (Eds.), *The handbook of experimental economics* (pp. 501-586). Princeton, NJ: Princeton University Press.

Kahneman, D., & Tversky, A. (1979). Prospect theory: An analysis of decision under risk. *Econometrica, 47*(2), 263-292.

Klein, S. (1997). Introduction to electronic auctions. *Electronic Markets, 7*(4), 3-6.

Kite, Shane (November, 2004). Trade Services: Banks Refocus On The EX/IM Business. *Bank Technology News*. http://findarticles.com/p/articles/mi_km2919/is_200411/ai_n8616615

Lucking-Reiley, D. (1999). Using field experiments to test equivalence between auction formats: Magic on the Internet. *The American Economic Review, 89*(5), 1063-1081.

Lucking-Reiley, D. (2000a). Auctions on the Internet: What's being auctioned, and how? *The Journal of Industrial Economics, 48*(3), 227-253.

Lucking-Reiley, D. (2000b). Vickrey auctions in practice: From nineteenth-century philately to twenty-first-century e-commerce. *The Journal of Economic Perspectives, 14*(3), 183-193.

Lucking-Reiley, D., & Spulber, D. F. (2001). Business-to-business electronic commerce. *The Journal of Economic Perspectives, 15*(1), 55.

McAfee, R. P., & McMillan, J. (1987). Auctions and bidding. *Journal of Economic Literature, 25*(2), 699-739.

McDonald, C. G., & Slawson, V. C. (2002). Reputation in an Internet auction market. *Economic Inquiry, 40*(4), 633-650.

Mehta, K. (2002). *Understanding revenue drivers of electronic auctions*. Unpublished Doctoral Dissertation, University of Illinois at Chicago, Illinois.

Milgrom, P. R., & Weber, R. J. (1982). A theory of auctions and competitive bidding. *Econometrica, 50*(5), 1089-1122.

Möllenberg, A. (2004). Internet auctions in marketing: The consumer perspective. *Electronic Markets, 14*(4), 360-371.

Neo, B. S. (1992). The implementation of an electronic market for pig trading in Singapore. *Journal of Strategic Management Systems, 1*(5), 278-288.

Oh, W. (2002). C2C versus B2C: A comparison of the winner's curse in two types of electronic auctions. *International Journal of Electronic Commerce, 6*(4), 115-138.

Ottaway, T. A., Bruneau, C. L., & Evans, G. E. (2003). The impact of auction item image and buyer/seller feedback rating on electronic auctions. *The Journal of Computer Information Systems, 43*(3), 56-60.

Park, Y. H., & Bradlow, E. T. (2005). An integrated model for bidder behavior in internet auctions: Whether, who, when, and how much. *Journal of Marketing Research, XLII*, 470-482.

Pavlou, P. A. (2002a). Trustworthiness as a source of competitive advantage in online auction markets. In *Academy of Management Proceedings* (pp. A1-A7).

Pavlou, P. A. (2002b). What drives electronic commerce? A theory of planned behavior perspective. In *Academy of Management Proceedings 2002 OCIS* (pp. A1-A6).

Pavlou, P. A., & Gefen, D. (2005). Psychological contract violation in online marketplaces: Antecedents, consequences, and moderating role. *Information Systems Research, 16*(4), 372-399.

Rafaeli, S., & Noy, A. (2005). Soicial presence: Influence on bidders in Internet auctions. *Electronic Markets, 15*(2), 158-175.

Rothkopf, M. H. (1969). A model of rational competitive bidding. *Management Science, 15*(7), 362-374.

Runkel, P., & Runkel, M. (1984). *A guide to usage for writers and students in the social sciences*. Totawa, NJ: Rowman and Allanheld.

Segev, A., Beam, C., & Shanthikumar, J. G. (2001). Optimal design of Internet-based auctions. *Information Technology and Management, 2*(2), 121-163.

Spence, M. (1973). Job market signaling. *Quarterly Journal of Economics, 87*, 355-374.

Stafford, M. R., & Stern, B. (2002). Consumer bidding behavior on Internet auction sites. *International Journal of Electronic Commerce, 7*(1), 135-150.

Standifird, S. S. (2001). Reputation and e-commerce: eBay auctions and the asymmetrical impact of positive and negative ratings. *Journal of Management, 27*(3), 279-295.

Standifird, S. S., Roelofs, M. R., & Durham, Y. (2004). The impact of eBay's buy-it-now function on bidder behavior. *International Journal of Electronic Commerce, 9*(2), 167-176.

Strader, T. J., & Ramaswami, S. N. (2002). The value of seller trustworthiness in c2c online markets. *Communications of the ACM, 45*(12), 45-49.

Subramaniam, R., Mittal, V., & Inman, J. J. (2004). Revenue equivalence in online auctions: The case of yahoo and eBay. In P. Leszczyc (Ed.), *Advances in consumer research* (Vol. 31, pp. 1-2).

Van Hasselt, Caroline (2004). Dump LC Headaches Overboard. *Treasury & Risk Management*. http://www.treasuryandrisk.com/issues/2004_01/supply_chain_management/256-1.html

van Heck, E., & van Damme, E. (1997). *New entrants and the role of IT: The tele flower auctions in the Netherlands.* Paper presented at the 30th HICSS, Hawaii.

Vickrey, W. (1961). Counterspeculation, auctions, and competitive sealed tenders. *Journal of Finance, 16*(1), 8-37.

Vogelstein, F., Boyle, M., Lewis, P., & Kirkpatrick, D. (2004). 10 tech trends to bet on. *Fortune, 149*(4), 75-81.

Ward, S. G., & Clark, J. M. (2002). Bidding behavior in on-line auctions: An examination of the eBay Pokemon card market. *International Journal of Electronic Commerce, 6*(4), 139-155.

Weick, K. (1995). What theory is not, theorizing is. *Administrative Science Quarterly, 40*(3), 385-390

Webster, J., & Watson, R. (2002). Analyzing the past to prepare for the future: Writing a literature review. *MIS Quarterly, 26*(2), xiii-xxiii.

Whetten, D. (1989). What constitutes a theoretical contribution. *Academy of Management Review, 14*(4), 490-495.

Wilcox, R. T. (2000). Experts and amateurs: The role of experience in Internet auctions. *Marketing Letters, 11*(4), 363-374.

Wilson, R. B. (1969). Communications to the editor: Competitive bidding with disparate information. *Management Science, 15*(7), 446-449.

Wingfield, N. (2001). Ebay watch: Corporate sellers put the online auctioneer on even faster track: Goods from IBM, Disney help dot-com pioneer post a surge in profits: Why mom and pop are mad. *Wall Street Journal,* p. A.1.

ENDNOTE

1 Online auctions, Internet auctions, and electronic auctions are terms that are often used interchangeably in e-commerce research (Lucking-Reiley, 2000a). We acknowledge both that there are technical distinctions that might be highlighted to differentiate between the terms and that some scholars have made such distinctions in the past (e.g., Klein, 1997). Contrasting such differences, however, is not the focus of this article. Additionally, this article focuses on auctioneer-mediated Internet transactions (such as those that occur on eBay), therefore, we will adopt the term "Internet Auctions" throughout the remainder of this chapter.

This work was previously published in Journal of Electronic Commerce in Organizations, Vol. 5, Issue 1, edited by M. Khosrow-Pour, pp. 43-68, copyright 2007 by IGI Publishing, formerly known as Idea Group Publishing (an imprint of IGI Global).

EXHIBIT A. DATASET FOR CLUSTER AND DISCRIMINATE ANALYSES

All studies selected were of single-item Internet auctions This choice is consistent with the scope of this article, which does not examine multiple-item auctions. The studies included peer-reviewed journal articles, Ph.D. dissertations, and conference proceedings. We chose to research from all three of these sources to make our sample more representative of the total population of research studies than a group of only journal articles would be (King & He, 2005) We chose to use 25 studies because our cluster and discriminant analyses require at least as many observations as variables.

In Table A.2, the first two columns identify the research studies used in the cluster analysis (presented above in Table A.1). The columns ranging from S1 to B6 denote the variables measured in each of the research studies. For example, S1 denotes the first variable under the control of the seller—namely reputation rating. S2 denotes initial bid price, S3 denotes reserve price, etc. In a similar way, A1 denotes the first variable under the control of the auctioneer—the auction mechanism and B1 denotes the first variable under the control of the bidder—bidder experience. This numbering of variables appears in the body of the chapter, in Table 2, and in Figures 2-4.

Within each column, we have indicated whether a given study measured a particular variable. When a study did measure a variable, we have coded that fact with a 1. When a study did not measure a variable, we have coded that fact with a 0. For instance, research study 21, Standifird's 2001 *Journal of Management* paper measured S1, S2, S6, S7, and S12 (but not any of the other variables listed on this table).

The final column, C, denotes the group to which the research study was assigned by the cluster analysis.

Table A.1. Research studies used in cluster analysis

No.	Author	Year	Source
1	Ba and Palvou	2002	MIS Quarterly
2	Bajari and Hortacsu	2002	Rand Journal of Economics
3	Bapna, Goes, Gupta	2000	Information Technology and Management
4	Brint	2003	Journal of the Operational Research Society
5	Bruce, Haruvy, and Rao	2004	Journal of Interactive Marketing
6	Dholakia	2005	Journal of Interactive Marketing
7	Dholakia and Soltysinski	2001	Marketing Letters
8	Gilkeson and Reynolds	2003	Psychology and Marketing
9	Hu, Lin, Whinston, Zhang	2004	Information Systems Research
10	Lucking-Reiley	1999	American Economic Review
11	McDonald and Slawson	2002	Economic Inquiry
12	Mehta	2002	dissertation
13	Mehta and Lee	1999	ICIS
14	Mollenberg	2004	Electronic Markets
15	Ottaway, Bruneau, and Evans	2003	Journal of Computer Information Systems
16	Park and Braklow	2005	Journal of Marketing Research
17	Pavlou - Trustworthiness	2002	Academy of Management Proceedings
18	Pavlou - TPB	2002	Academy of Management Proceedings
19	Rafaeli and Noy	2005	Electronic Markets
20	Stafford and Stern	2002	IJEC
21	Standifird	2001	Journal of Management
22	Standifird, Roelofs, and Durham	2004	IJEC
23	Subramaniam, Mittal, and Inman	2004	Advances in Consumer Research
24	Ward and Clark	2002	IJEC
25	Wilcox	2000	Marketing Letters

Table A.2. Independent variables examined in Internet auction studies

No.	Author	S1	S2	S3	S4	S5	S6	S7	S8	S9	S10	S11	S12	A1	A2	A3	A4	A5	A6	A7	B1	B2	B3	**B4**	**B5**	**B6**	**C**
1	Ba and Palvou	1	0	0	0	0	0	0	0	0	0	0	0	0	0	0	0	0	0	0	0	0	0	0	0	0	2
2	Bajari and Hortacsu	1	1	1	0	0	0	0	1	0	1	0	0	0	0	0	0	0	0	0	0	0	0	0	0	1	2
3	Bapna, Goes, Gupta	0	1	0	0	0	0	0	1	0	0	0	0	0	0	0	0	0	0	0	0	1	0	0	0	0	2
4	Brint	1	1	1	0	0	1	1	0	0	0	0	0	0	0	0	0	0	0	0	0	0	0	0	0	0	1
5	Bruce, Haruvy, and Rao	0	0	1	0	0	0	0	1	0	1	0	0	0	0	0	0	0	0	0	0	0	0	0	0	0	2
6	Dholakia	0	0	0	0	0	0	0	0	0	0	0	0	0	0	0	0	0	0	0	0	1	0	0	0	0	2
7	Dholakia and Soltysinski	0	0	0	0	0	1	1	1	0	0	0	0	0	0	0	0	0	0	0	0	0	0	0	0	1	1
8	Gilkeson and Reynolds	1	1	0	0	1	1	1	0	1	1	0	0	0	0	1	0	0	0	0	0	0	0	0	0	0	2
9	Hu, Lin, Whinston, Zhang	0	0	0	0	0	0	0	0	0	0	0	0	0	0	0	0	0	0	1	0	0	0	0	0	0	1
10	Lucking-Reiley	0	0	0	0	0	1	1	1	0	0	1	0	1	0	0	0	0	0	0	0	0	0	0	0	1	2
11	McDonald and Slawson	1	1	1	0	1	1	1	0	1	1	0	0	0	0	1	0	0	0	0	1	0	0	0	0	0	2
12	Mehta	0	0	0	0	0	1	1	1	0	0	0	0	0	0	0	0	0	0	0	0	1	0	0	0	0	2
13	Mehta and Lee	0	0	0	0	0	0	0	0	0	0	0	0	0	0	0	0	0	0	0	0	1	0	0	0	0	2
14	Mollenberg	0	0	0	0	0	0	0	0	0	0	0	0	0	0	0	0	0	0	0	1	1	0	0	0	0	2
15	Ottaway, Bruneau, and Evans	1	0	0	0	0	0	0	1	0	0	0	0	0	0	0	0	0	0	0	1	0	0	0	0	0	1
16	Park and Braklow	1	1	0	1	0	0	1	1	0	0	0	0	0	1	0	0	0	0	0	0	0	0	0	0	0	2
17	Pavlou - Trustworthiness	1	0	0	0	0	0	0	0	0	0	0	0	0	0	0	0	0	0	0	0	0	0	0	0	0	2
18	Pavlou - TPB	0	0	0	0	0	0	0	0	0	0	0	0	0	0	0	1	1	1	0	0	0	1	0	0	0	3
19	Rafaeli and Noy	1	0	0	0	0	0	0	0	0	0	1	0	1	0	0	0	0	0	0	0	0	0	0	0	0	3
20	Stafford and Stern	0	0	0	0	0	0	0	0	0	0	0	0	0	0	0	1	1	0	0	0	0	1	1	1	0	3
21	Standifird	1	1	0	0	0	1	1	0	0	0	0	1	0	0	0	0	0	0	0	0	0	0	0	0	0	3
22	Standifird, Roelofs, and Durham	1	1	1	1	0	0	1	1	0	0	0	0	0	1	0	0	0	0	0	0	0	0	0	0	0	3
23	Subramaniam, Mittal, and Inman	0	0	1	0	0	0	1	0	0	0	0	0	0	0	0	0	0	0	0	0	0	0	0	0	1	3
24	Ward and Clark	0	0	0	0	0	0	0	0	0	0	0	0	0	0	0	0	0	0	0	0	1	0	0	0	0	3
25	Wilcox	0	0	0	0	0	0	0	0	0	0	0	0	0	0	0	0	0	0	0	1	0	0	0	0	1	2

Chapter IX
Changing IT Skills:
The Impact of Sourcing Strategies on In-House Capability Requirements

Christine V. Bullen
Stevens Institute of Technology, USA

Thomas Abraham
Kean University, USA

Kevin Gallagher
Northern Kentucky University, USA

Kate M. Kaiser
Marquette University, USA

Judith C. Simon
University of Memphis, USA

ABSTRACT

The increasingly global sourcing of IT work and other socio-economic trends are prompting fundamental changes in the availability of IT skills needed in both client and vendor organizations. This article analyzes the results of a survey conducted in 2005, in which IT executives were asked to describe the skills they felt were critical to keep in house now and in 2008. The top ten current skills included three in project management, five in business domain and three in technical. In 2008, the top five emerging skills are almost all business domain while the top five exiting skills are all technical. Our findings indicate that the critical skills to keep in-house are primarily client-facing skills, even when they are technical. Respondents are moving away from traditional IT skills except when their business model continues to value them. However, traditional technical skills are still important for all new hires while project management skills are the most often cited for mid level hires. The projected number of full time employees is expected to remain approximately the same by 2008 but there will be an increase in sourcing to third party providers (3PP) and a shift from domestic to offshore 3PP staff. The patterns in the data indicate that technical skills that are not client facing and can be done anywhere are the most likely to be sourced. Findings indicate that IT professionals need to have a balance that demonstrates a foundation in the traditional "hard skills" and experience with "softer" business-oriented skills.

INTRODUCTION

The increasingly global sourcing of IT work, the shift from exclusively IT services to business process services, pending baby-boomer retirements, and a period of declining IT enrollments in universities are prompting fundamental changes in the availability of IT skills and capabilities needed in both client and service provider organizations. The impact of these changes affects employers and employees:

- How can organizations respond to these changes through hiring their workforce or retraining employees?
- How can students learn the needed skills to become marketable for a changing workforce?
- How can mid-level workers insure their marketability?

In order to answer these questions, we will review literature pertaining to information technology skills and capabilities both from an academic and practitioner perspective. Then we will describe the research methods used to understand the changing workforce. The results follow with a discussion of implications for individuals, academics and future research.

Terminology

Here are some working definitions for terms that we use frequently:

- Skill: Proficiency that is acquired or developed through training or experience, e.g. Java or Visual Basic programming. For simplicity, we sometimes use the term "skill" to cover both skill and capability
- Capability: The ability to acquire and apply skills in different settings. For instance, a programming capability is the ability to learn and apply many programming languages in many settings.
- Client facing: "Client" in this phrase is the client of the IT organization, which is usually an internal department or business area within the organization. "Client facing" is an activity that requires intensive interaction with the business client, requiring a common business language and sharing a common business knowledge base with the business users.

LITERATURE REVIEW

The very significance of IT to an organization has been questioned. Carr (2003) argued that as information technology becomes more pervasive it will become more of a commodity and that investing in IT for differentiation or for competitive advantage is futile. This argument would appear to call for greater outsourcing of the IT function and a greatly reduced need for in house IT skills and capabilities. More recently, Gottfredson et al (2005) suggest that sourcing is itself becoming a strategic opportunity and that even strategic functions like engineering, R&D, manufacturing, and marketing can be moved outside. In a report published by the Cutter Consortium, Rottman and Lacity describe the positive effect that sourcing has had in the U.S. on IT jobs, IT productivity, IT costs and IT quality (Rottman and Lacity, 2004). UBS, in a report for their investors, predicts a labor drought in the U.S. that will require some jobs to move offshore (Ryan, Farrell and Doerflinger, 2005).

Tapscott (2004), in a rebuttal of Carr, responded that companies with bad business models tend to fail, regardless of whether they use IT or not. In a recent Deloitte Consulting report, the authors conclude that outsourcing is complex and that results have been mixed (Deloitte, 2005). Their evidence suggests that most (70%) of the participants in the study had significant negative experiences with outsourcing and will be more selective in using it. A McKinsey report (Farrell et al., 2005) finds that a single global labor market exists but that it is small. Offshoring accounts now for only about 1% of the service jobs in developed countries. Even though the report projects that this proportion will gradually increase as the global market becomes more efficient, it does not forecast a sudden discontinuity in employment for developed countries. The report cites a US Bureau of Labor statistic that the growth rates for wages and jobs in computer and data-processing services are higher than those in the economy as a whole. The extent to which organizations subscribe to one or another viewpoint on the importance of IT and sourcing to a business strategy will affect the changes in the IT skill set.

A literature review looking at IT workforce, skills, employment and outsourcing uncovers many articles that were written which focus on the movement of "non-core" IT skills out of the corporate organization and into the realm of 3PPs, both foreign and domestic (Slaughter and Ang, 1996). In addition Ang and Slaughter (2001) have applied social exchange theory to the study of workplace attitudes and behaviors of contract and permanent professionals. They discussed the Internal Labor Market theory where they propose two approaches an organization can take to develop career paths: Industrial and Craft. Under the Industrial strategy, employees enter the organization and progress along clearly marked job ladders. They are selected based on high education requirements, they receive training in skills and knowledge specific to the organization, and they advance due to merit and personality. Under the Craft strategy, employees often are viewed as having more loyalty to the profession than to the organization and that their skills are less organization specific and more mobile. Their work suggests that contractors are typically given tasks with low task identity and low autonomy, often coding narrowly specified programs. Contractors have little business and industry knowledge. Understanding the quality of the skills at 3PPs may be a key to understanding the workforce decisions that client companies will make.

An assessment of workforce globalization found that businesses want to retain certain kinds of IT services and software work in the United States (Anonymous, 2004). The report states that the characteristics of such IT work includes products or processes in which there is uncertainty about customer needs or specifications, projects requiring highly iterative development processes, work that involves a high degree of personal interaction with end-users or clients, work that crosses many disciplines, applications with complex procedures, applications that involve a high degree of integration with other systems developed and maintained on-shore, work involving nuances or deep cultural understanding, work in which much of the knowledge exists only in the minds of the on-shore IT staff, analytical tasks, leading-edge research, non-rule-based decision-making, high levels of creativity, high management interaction requirements, process design, business analysis, technology and systems integration, and fusion of industry knowledge, high level IT skills, and business process expertise. A key aspect of our research is to better understand the skills that organizations deem critical to maintain in house as opposed to those that can be sourced to 3PPs.

Several articles have applied theories from diverse fields to study IT skills and the approach to outsourcing. Gomes and Joglekar (2005) have applied the theory of transaction cost economics to explore the nature of software development tasks that remain in-house. Their analyses show that process asset specificity indicated by task interdependence and task size predicts outsourcing the task. Ang and Slaughter (2004) apply Internal Labor Market strategies to classify the human resource rules used to govern IT workers. - Chief Information Officer (CIO), Applications Manager (AM), Project Leader/Analyst (PLA), Programmer (PGM), Infrastructure Manager (IM), Database Administrator (DBA), Network Specialist (NWS), Systems Programmer (SP). They found that the more managerial jobs – CIO, AM and IM – are usually governed by the Industrial strategy, leading to lower turnover and higher tenure. The other, more technical, jobs were governed by the Craft strategy, leading to higher turnover and shorter tenure. There are factors affecting the individual career decision which must also be considered in trying to understand the trajectory of workforce skill trends.

IT Skills and Capabilities

Reviewing the literature on the skills and capabilities themselves reveals a number of interesting research projects that are related to ours. In a very recent paper, Prabhakar, Litecky and Arnett (2005) reviewed the current IT job market and conclude that the need for development work in web-related applications has changed the demand for these programming skills. They report that these skills are mentioned in 42.6% of job ads. Specifically, Java has remained important and is required in more than one-fifth of all jobs. However, it has not replaced the need for C++ and C programmers. SQL programming is also required in more than one-fifth of the job openings. .Net has grown in importance and now represents 13% of skills required by employers.

The demand for network skills was growing in 1995 as increasing numbers of companies entered the world of the Web (Litecky, Prabhakar and Arnett, 1996). Koong, et al, noted in 2002 that expertise in Java, XML, TCP/IP and other Internet-related skills demanded higher compensation than other IT professional positions (Koong, Liu, Liu, 2002). Research based on systematic reviews of want ads showed that older IT skills tended to disappear from the advertisements, indicating less interest in hiring those skills on the parts of IT managers (Arnett and Litecky, 1994).

The research based on advertised positions may be biased by a tendency to list required technical skills but omit additional skills that are determined in the interview process. Below we discuss a two stage hiring model that is not reflected in the want ads.

Previous studies have shown that managers rate non-technical skills higher than technical skills even for entry-level employees. In addition, managers' expectations with regard to the non-technical abilities of new hires are usually higher than the actual ability the new hires exhibit (Cappel, 2001/2002, Van Slyke, Kittner and Cheney, 1998). An earlier paper looked at the "expectation gap" between what skills and experience industry expects from college graduates in IT versus what they find (Trauth, Farwell and Lee, 1993). A survey of ACM SIGCPR proceedings resulted in the same general conclusion that non-technical skills were equally or more important than technical skills for IT professionals (Nakayama and Sutcliffe 2001). In addition, managers have less of a preference for a specific programming language, but rather value the learning of programming concepts in any language (Cappel, 2001/2002).

ITAA (2004) found that interpersonal skill was the highest rated non-technology skill in the survey. Fifty-two percent of respondents cited this attribute, far more than any other. This preference proved true for IT and non-IT companies as well as companies big, small and in-between. A few variations also appeared when comparing IT and non-IT hiring manager responses in this area. IT companies placed substantially higher importance on project management than non-IT firms. The report suggests that project management may be more of a core competence for IT firms—a critical component of what these companies offer their clients.

An evolution of the relationship between clients and 3PPs proposes that under certain conditions "cosourcing" is an appropriate model that requires the parties to work in a close partnership, which results in an exchange of skills and capabilities (Kaiser and Hawk, 2004).

Ross, Beath and Goodhue (1996) identify three IT assets for competitiveness. One of these is the human asset which they describe as an IT staff that solves business problems and takes advantage of business opportunities through the application of information technology. They conclude that the IT professional needs a blend of current technical skills, a deep understanding of the business and a talent for problem solving. Foote describes the "hybrid" IT job that requires multidimensional skill sets blending technology skills and customer focus (Foote, 2005).

A variety of studies have been done to assess the quality of IT professionals' skills and knowledge. Two of these have established sets of skills/knowledge that should be measured: Technical Specialties, Technical Management, Business Functional, and Interpersonal and Management (Lee, Trauth and Farwell, 1995 and Byrd and Turner, 2001). Generally the results of these studies have indicated that a blend of all of the skills is required for success as an IT professional.

All of these research areas underline the importance of a balance of skills that are both technical and non-technical. This supports our findings.

Inconsistencies between What Is Said and What Is Done

A study of classified advertising for IT positions from 1988 to 2003 found a recruiting gap exists whereby organizations say they want well-rounded individuals with business knowledge and soft skills, however, they advertise for individuals with hard technical skills (Gallivan, Truex and Kvasny, 2004). The paradox is further explored in a study proposing a new model for IS recruiting called Image Theory (Litecky, Arnett and Prabhakar, 2004). This research posits a two-stage hiring process: Selection/Filtration Stage and Choice/Hiring Stage. The Selection/Filtration Stage is what is represented in job postings. It is the necessary technical background required for a position. The Choice/Hiring Stage is where additional skills and experience on the softer side come into play in the hiring decision

Implications for Academic Programs

George et al (2005) examine the recent and rapid rise and fall of university student enrollments in information systems programs and describe how these enrollment fluctuations are tied to the job opportunities of graduates. Drawing on the work of Ives et al (2002), they recommend that programs can influence the number of majors they attract by focusing more on why information technology is valuable to an organization rather than on what the technology is or how it works. Foote reported a 10.3% decline in computer science undergraduate enrollment from 2000 to 2004 and noted that UCLA had calculated a 60% decline in undergraduates declaring computer science as their major from 2000 to 2004 (Foote, 2005). Other universities have indicated similar drops (Trewyn, 2005)

In the Gallivan, Truex and Kvasny paper they also determine a need for life-long learning for IT professionals and the academics who teach them (Gallivan, Truex and Kvasny, 2004). Cappel also addresses the issue of how students can better prepare for the marketplace requirements (Cappel, 2001/2002).

The decreasing enrollments in all IT-related programs, i.e. MIS and Computer Science, is a concern for the industry and is an important factor motivating our research. Most recently the decline appears to be leveling off, and there is an indication of a new growth in enrollments about to begin. However mixed messages persist about the value of a career in IT.

METHOD

The Society for Information Management (SIM) sponsored a study to explore the impact of socio-economic trends on the IT Workforce. Data was gathered from senior IT managers by 20 researchers in the US and Ireland using a structured interview script.

The objectives of the study were to:

- Explore the current and future needs for IT skills and capabilities in U.S. and European organizations, including private and public sector organizations and client and vendor organizations.
- Determine how organizations do/will recruit, develop, and retain in-house IT skills and capabilities to meet current and future needs.
- Understand how organizations do/will access IT skills and capabilities through third party global sourcing.
- Assess what skills and capabilities universities should be providing in their graduates.
- Identify patterns of skills and how capabilities will change over the next three years.

This article analyzes the results of parts of the survey in which IT executives were asked to describe the skills they felt were critical to keep in house now and in 2008. It also analyzes some of the data on employment trends for IT.[a] This article excludes data from 3PPs. There is a follow-up study underway specifically looking at the workforce needs of these service providers.

The interview script was developed by a subset of the research team, all of whom have extensive experience with interview-based research. The research objectives along with appropriate demographic information were the focus of the design. Pre-test interviews were conducted to verify the practical use of the interview script.

The data was collected using the interview script, through structured, one-hour interviews between a researcher and a respondent. All researchers used the same interview script thus providing the same data for the collective data base of interviews. Some of the interviews were conducted face-to-face and others via the telephone.

The sample was initially chosen from organizations that are members of SIM. There was a goal to include companies of all sizes. In much management research there is a focus on the largest, Fortune 500 companies. In fact, the majority of employers are firms in the SME (Small to Medium Size Enterprises) category and these are often overlooked. While we would have liked to have even more firms in this category, we were pleased to have 37% of the sample fall into the SME group. The sample was increased through references from respondents and through personal contacts. A structured interview script with multiple choice answers wherever possible was used by all researchers which mitigated any individual researcher bias. Respondents were asked to discuss what they were actually doing and their formal strategy for the next 3 years. There were checks built into the script. For example, if a respondent said they were not hiring in the current year, then we did not use their answers about what skills they were looking for in new hires. This was to avoid "blue skying" and stay with actual activities.

DEMOGRAPHICS

The initial sample was drawn from senior IT executives solicited through members of the Society for Information Management and expanded through references from those respondents and through researchers' contacts to organizations that recruit from their universities. The design included organizations of varying sizes, both profit and non-profit, in a range of industries and geographies in the United States and Europe. More than 100 interviews were conducted with 96 usable for analysis, representing more than 80 different organizations.

Table I illustrates that the majority of respondents, approximately 82%, were executives in the IT organization. Since we were asking respondents about the hiring strategies of their organizations, we decided that the highest level managers would be able to give us the most accurate picture of the current and future (three years out) plans. While lower level managers, if interviewed, may have focused more on specific technical skills, we were looking at the career paths for IT professionals and were therefore interested in what top IT management judged were the critical skills for someone to have a productive career path within the organization.

The industries represented in the sample are shown in Table 2.

Table I. Respondents by title

Respondent Title	Percent
CIO	38%
Vice President	24%
Executive Director/Director	16%
CTO	4%
CIO Report	3%
HR Related	7%
Top Management	7%

Table 2. Respondents by industry group

Industry Group	Percent
Heavy Industry	22%
Financial Services	18%
Professional Services	18%
Other[b]	28%

Table 3. Respondents by size

Size by Revenue	Percent
Fortune 500+	41%
Large	22%
SME	37%

The sample included a range of organizational sizes based on revenue. For analysis purposes, size categories were created as follows:

- Fortune 500 – greater than USD 3 billion
- Large – between USD 3 billion and USD 500 million
- SME – less than USD 500 million

Table 4 lists the 5 categories and their related skills drawn from previous research (Lee, Trauth and Farwell, 1995; Byrd and Turner, 2001) and adding skills related to sourcing and to IT administration. We reorganized the categories to reflect where we felt they fit in terms of the type of work being done. For example, we did not have a separate category of "interpersonal skills" but rather included such skills in the category where it would be employed. Thus skills and capabilities related to planning, organizing and leading projects appear under Project Management.

We asked subjects the following:

- What skills and capabilities they believed were critical to keep in house in 2005
- Which skills and capabilities they thought would be critical to keep in house by 2008

- To identify skills and capabilities that they planned to source either through independent contractors (ICs) or third party providers (3PPs)
- To identify critical skills and capabilities for both entry-level and mid-level hires.
- Which critical skills and capabilities were usually absent in the new hires.

We coded all responses into the same sets of skills and capabilities. This approach allowed us to better understand the desirability of each as indicated by the respondent. Thus, as opposed to previous studies that determined skills based on what appeared in classified advertising or based on existing in-house talent, we investigated how organizations valued skills and capabilities, measured by what they wanted in house versus what they wanted to source.

The categories covered a variety of aspects of work carried out in IT. We used both specific skills and more generalized capabilities. For example, the first item listed under Technical is Systems Analysis. We viewed this as a broad capability that included any form of systems analysis regardless of platform such as traditional computing, desktop computing or Web development. Using this approach we are able to report on the generalized need for talent in each of the specific areas. This logic carries through to all the items allowing us to look at the broad capability rather than the application of the capability. Therefore the capability is relevant to any and all IT projects regardless of specific technology or specific business application.

RESULTS / ANALYSIS

Overview of Critical Skills and Capabilities

Figure 1 shows the top ten skills (with a tie for tenth) that were cited by respondents as "critical to keep in house in 2005". The top item and two

Table 4. Skills/capabilities by category

TECHNICAL
Systems Analysis
Systems Design
Programming
System Testing
Database Design/Management
Data Warehousing
IT Architecture/Standards
Voice/Data Telecommunications
Operating Systems
Server Hosting
Security
Mainframe/Legacy
Operations
Continuity/Disaster Recovery
Desktop Support/Helpdesk
Other
BUSINESS DOMAIN
Industry Knowledge
Company Specific Knowledge
Functional Area Process Knowledge
Business Process Design/Re-engineering
Change Management/Organizational Readiness
Managing Stakeholder Expectations
Communication
Other
PROJECT MANAGEMENT
Project Planning/Budgeting/Scheduling
Project Risk Management
Negotiation
Project Leadership
User Relationship Management
Project Integration/Program Management
Working with Virtual Teams
Working Globally
Capability Maturity Model Utilization
Other

continued on following page

Table 4. continued

SOURCING
Sourcing strategy
Third party provider selection
Contracting and legal
Managing 3rd party providers
Other
IT ADMINISTRATION
Financial Management
Internal HR management
IT Governance
Other

others are in project management (indicated by the darkest shading), five are in the business domain category (the lightest shading) and three are in technical (the medium shading). It is interesting to note that two of the technical items, Systems Analysis and Systems Design, are technical skills that are client facing. Therefore the top ten shows a strong bias toward skills that require this type of interaction between clients and IT professionals.

Thus our research supports the strategy that IT executives value the skills and capabilities that are client facing and want to keep them in house rather than source them. While this is consistent with previous research, we have been able to demonstrate that this is an explicit choice of IT executives.

We asked our respondents what skills and capabilities they thought would become less critical to keep in house in 2008 - because they would become irrelevant, be automated or be outsourced, for example. Figure 2 shows the top five that are not critical to keep in house. In general, there were very few skills that more than 10% of our respondents thought would disappear by 2008. The top ranked ones in this question were programming, desktop/help and mainframe/legacy items. Note that only technical skills were mentioned by more than 10% of the respondents. No business domain, project management, sourcing or IT administration items were identified as potentially disappearing. In fact the skills that are leaving in house appear to be migrating to 3PPs. This will be discussed further in the section below on the changes in Full Time Equivalent (FTE) data.

We asked our respondents what skills and capabilities they thought would emerge as newly critical to keep in house in 2008. Figure 3 shows the top five in this category. Five emerging items are in the business domain. This reinforces the

Figure 1. Top ten critical skills and capabilities in house in 2005

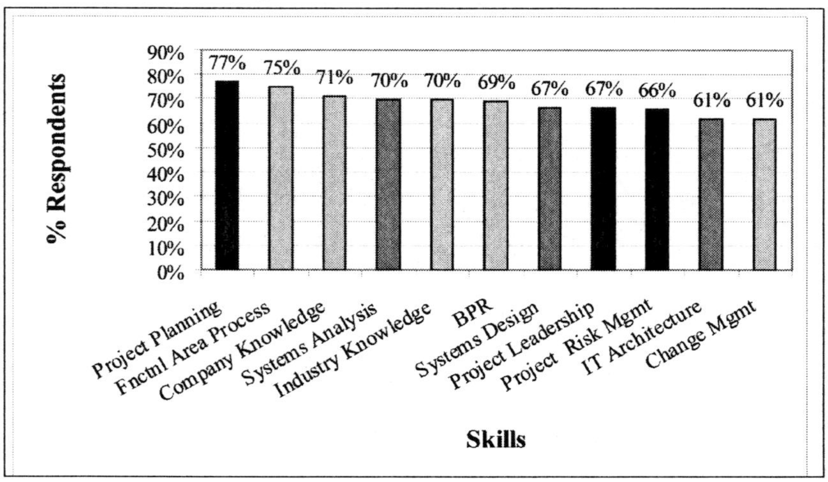

interpretation that client-facing skills are and remain important to keep in house. One technical and one project management skill are tied for fifth place.

Respondents also mentioned items that might be considered "new" programming or operations skills and capabilities, e.g., Java, .Net, Linux, wireless, etc. While these were mentioned by 10% of the respondents, they were specifically named during the interviews. This is consistent with the interpretation that skills related to newer technologies need to be in house while they are being learned and understood. It is also consistent with the pattern that previous researchers have found that the items listed in classified advertising change depending on the technologies that are becoming of interest.

Some respondents pointed out that their mainframe operations were not going away any time soon. While this would, on the surface, appear to be contradictory, we believe that this represents a business-specific need related to an organization's culture and values. That is, when an organization is in a stage in which it is still highly dependent on a technology, e.g., mainframe technology, it will want to maintain some of those skills in

Figure 2. Top five skills and capabilities leaving in house by 2008

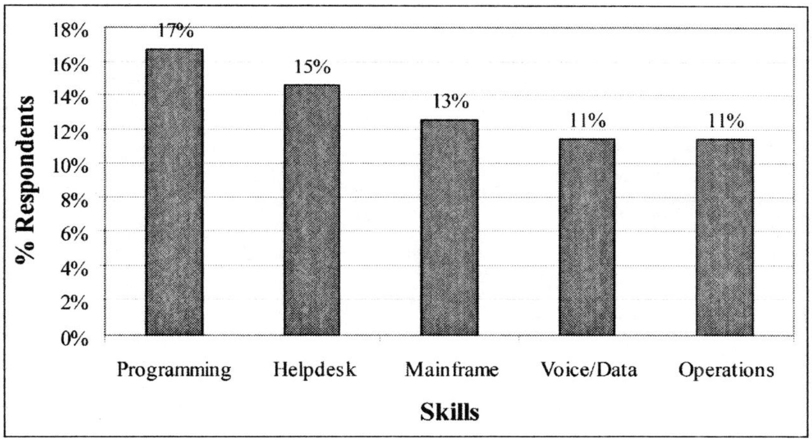

Figure 3. Top five emerging skills and capabilities in house in 2008

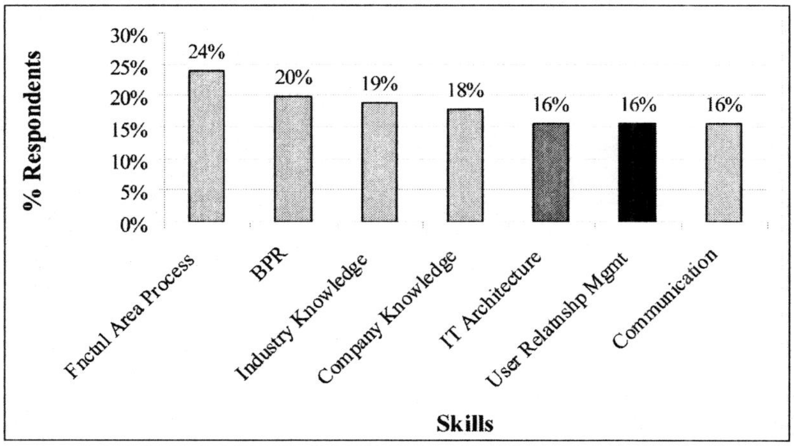

house, and therefore the skills and capabilities would not disappear.

Managing third party providers and IT governance were also becoming more important capabilities to have in house. There were a few items in the technical category that were seen to be increasingly critical to have in house in 2008 – notably security and IT architecture. In addition the one technical item whose criticality increased the most was continuity/disaster recovery.

We asked what skills and capabilities are critical for new hires. Figure 4 shows the top ten entry level items. It is interesting to note that 8 of the top 10 are technical and that programming is at the top. As discussed previously, we used skill categories to describe broad capabilities,

Figure 4. Top ten entry level skills and capabilities

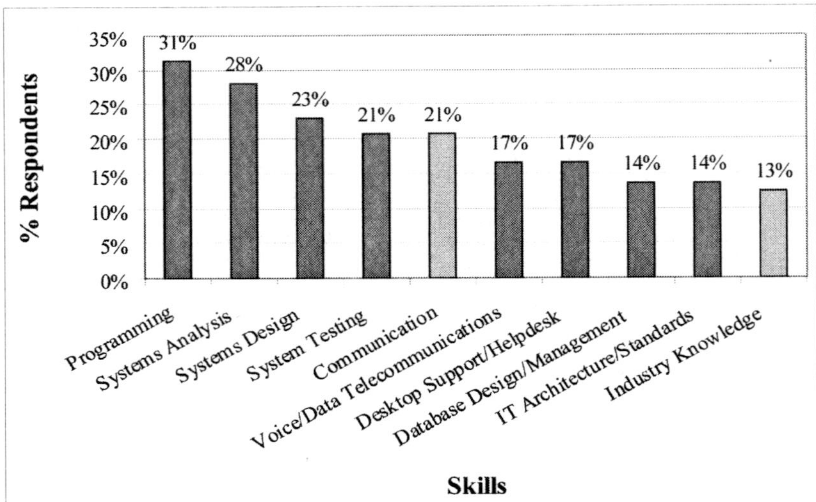

Figure 5. Top ten mid level skills and capabilities

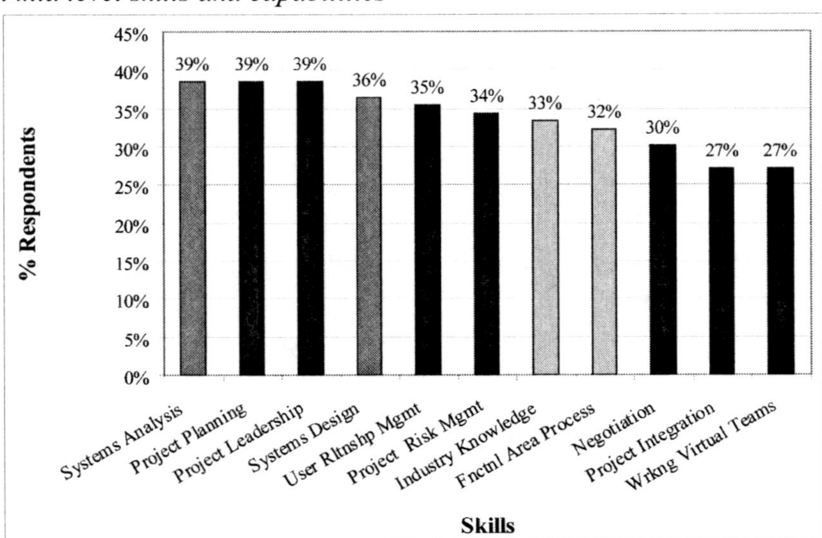

therefore "programming" here includes any form of programming regardless of platform such as traditional computing, desktop computing or Web development.[c] Organizations still value the traditional IT skill set for entry level hires. We investigated the degrees that organizations sought and found that entry-level applicants with undergraduate degrees in Computer Science are desirable.[d] Communication skills and industry knowledge are now also highly valued.

It is important to note that programming represent the generalized capability of programming and not a specific programming language skill. By combining the fact that programming is the highest entry level skill or capability with the generally accepted evolution toward newer technical areas, one can interpret this to mean that organizations are looking for programming skills in the newer technologies, e.g. Java, .Net, Linux along with more traditional programming language skills. This is supported by the respondents who specifically named newer technology skills and capabilities that are critical to have in house in 2008.

This data supports the concept of the two stage model in hiring IT professionals (Litecky, Arnett and Prabhakar, 2004). The technical skill set is necessary to be considered for a position; however, it is not sufficient. The softer skills represented by communication skills and industry knowledge must be present to create the balance that makes a candidate desirable.

We asked respondents what skills and capabilities are critical for hiring employees into mid-level positions. Figure 5 shows the top ten items shown for mid-level positions. At the mid level the set shifts away from the technical skills of the entry level and towards project management skills and capabilities. Gomes & Joglekar (2005) found increased project management expertise is positively correlated with increased outsourcing. Therefore as sourcing has increased in recent years, organizational need for project management skills is also increasing. Most of these mid-level skills can be described as client facing, even the technical ones such as systems analysis and systems design.

Figure 6. Top five technical skills and capabilities in house in 2005

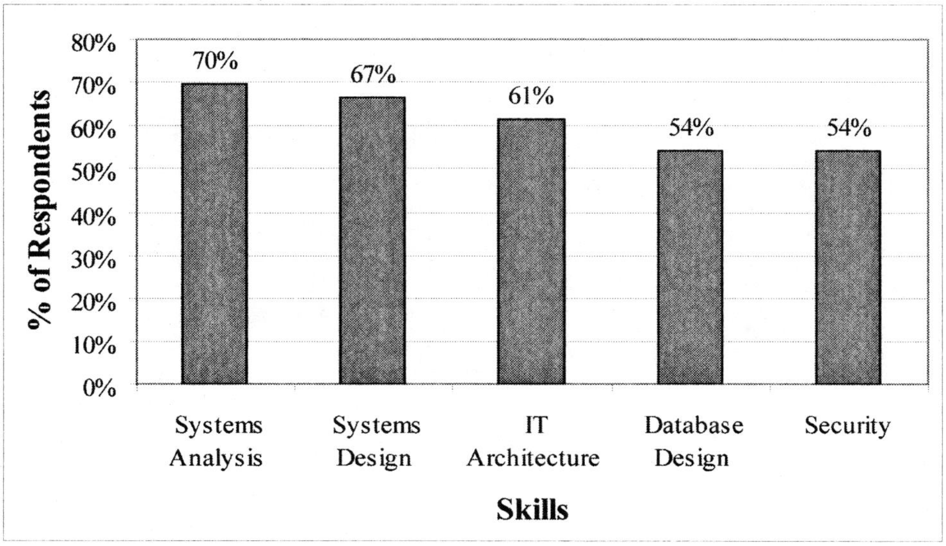

Specific Skill Categories

In order to better understand the specific skill categories, we looked at the top five skills reported in each of the five categories of skills.

Figure 6 shows the top five in-house items in the Technical category. Numbers one, two and four, Systems Analysis, Systems Design and Database Design/Management are client-facing technical skills that require a lot of interaction between IT professionals and clients in the course of their accomplishment. IT Architecture/Standards and Security, numbers three and five, represent technical areas that are critical today in most organizations. One would expect a standard-setting capability such as IT Architecture to be one that is needed in house where the specific nature of the business and the IT required to enable it are well understood. The Security skill encompassed both the management of security and the day-to-day operations of security. Many firms indicated that they are sourcing the day-to-day operations (e.g., issuing security cards and passwords, maintaining a security force); however, it became clear in our interviews that the management-level functions of security strategy and standards are seen as skills best maintained in house at the present time.[e]

Figure 7 illustrates the top five Project Management skills and capabilities kept in house in 2005. The five items shown here are unsurprising as they are core skills in project management. The high percentage of respondents choosing these as critical skills to keep in house indicates the increasingly important role of project management in organizations. Comments made by the respondents indicate that project management is important both for improving the management of in-house projects and for management of projects that have been sourced to 3PPs. The IT organizations appear to be responding to past criticism of IT projects being traditionally late and over budget.

The data in Figure 8 emphasize the importance of specific business knowledge for today's IT professional, with Functional Knowledge, Company Knowledge and Industry Knowledge as the top three in this category. Business Process Design/Reengineering is fourth, indicating the degree to which organizations today are engrossed in implementing ERP systems. Change Management/Organizational Readiness is the last item in this category and represents a clear understanding on the parts of IT executives of their roles as change agents for the organization.

Figure 7. Top five project management skills and capabilities in house in 2005

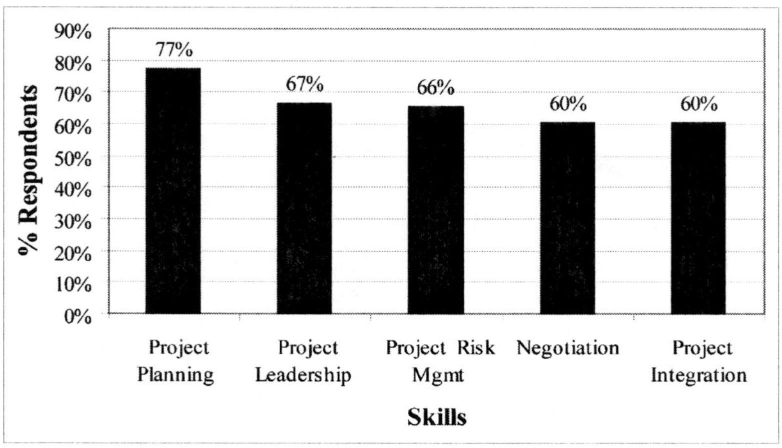

Figure 8. Top five business domain skills and capabilities in house in 2005

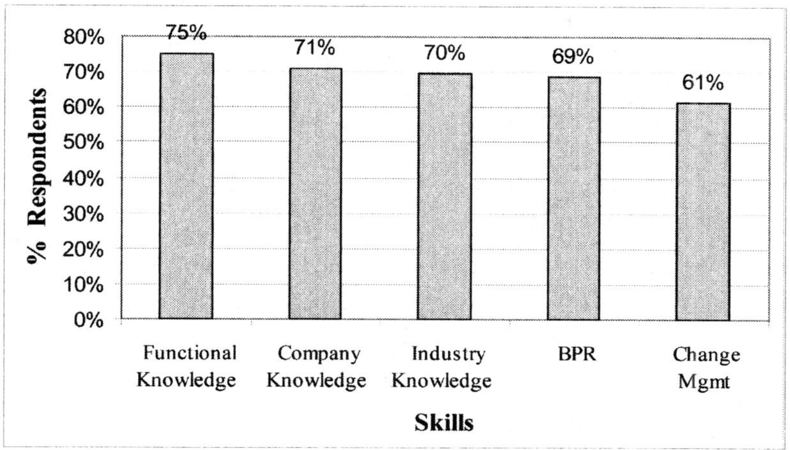

Figure 9. Top five sourcing skills and capabilities in house in 2005

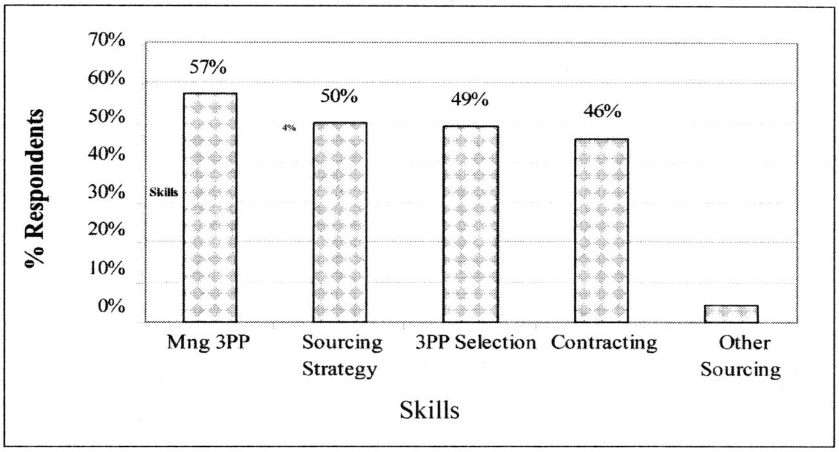

Figure 10. Top IT administration skills and capabilities in house in 2005

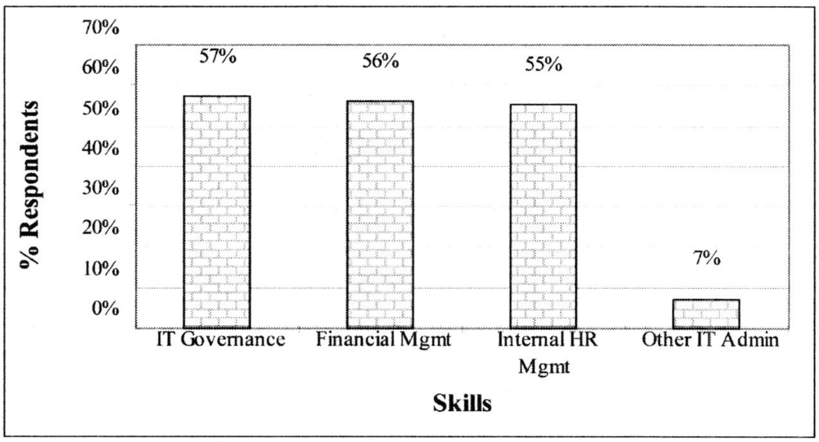

Past research efforts have not focused on sourcing skills for IT professionals. Our investigation of these skills covers new ground in understanding the nature of work within the IT organization and demonstrates that this is becoming part of the job of an IT professional. As sourcing to 3PPs has increased, so has the need to manage these relationships. Thus we find items represented in Figure 9 for the various phases of the sourcing activity. The "Other" category included resource management and PMO (project management office) experience.

Finally, in the skill category of IT Administration, Figure 10 indicates that IT Governance skills are the most critical to maintain in house, along with Financial Management and Human Resource Management skills. In the "Other" category, the most frequent answer was Program Management. This answer most likely represents the increasing complexity that the typical CIO faces in today's organization, necessitating a strong ability to manage multiple high-pressure projects.

Full-Time Equivalent IT Employment Data

Although this study looked primarily at predictions of IT skills and capabilities that would remain in-house versus those that would disappear or be sourced elsewhere, we also asked participants about their expectations for changes in overall full-time equivalent (FTE) IT employment. Using total FTEs provided by the participants, we found a very small decrease (0.2%) expected in overall FTEs. Although the total FTEs will continue to be largest in-house (over 70%), the largest increase in FTEs is expected in the use of third-party providers.

The distribution of FTEs going to third-party providers is currently greatest for domestic third-party providers using domestic staff and will continue to be the largest group in 2008. Projections for 2008 indicate increases in FTEs for all four categories (domestic 3PP with domestic staff, domestic 3PP with offshore staff, foreign 3PP with

Figure 11. Projected full time equivalent (FTE) changes

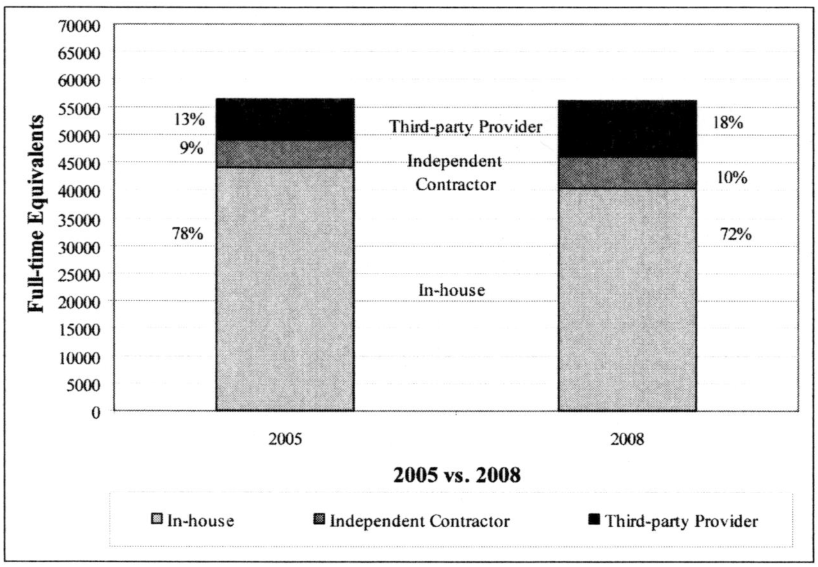

Figure 12. Projected third party provider (3PP)

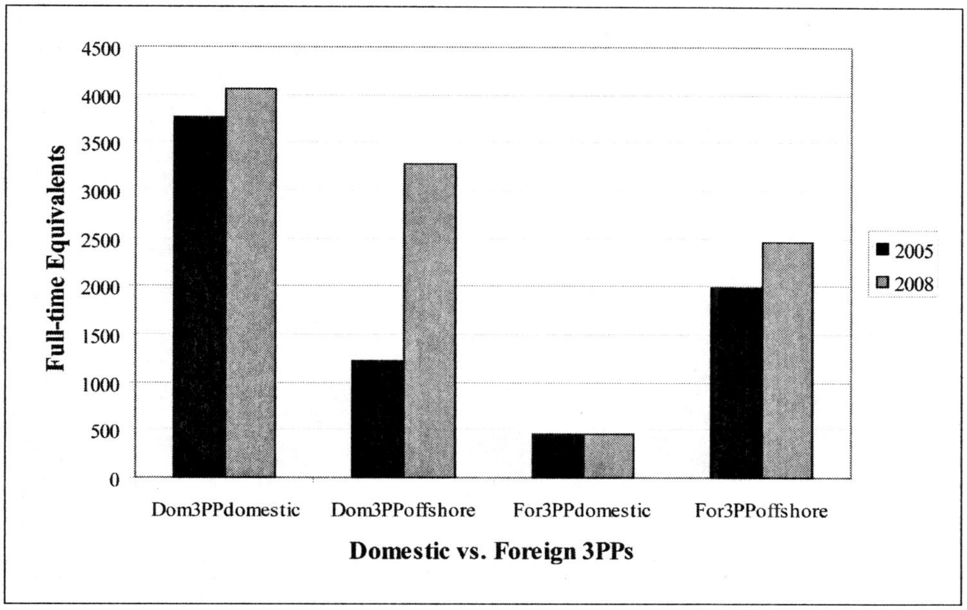

Figure 13. Projected changes in distribution of third party provider (3PP) staff

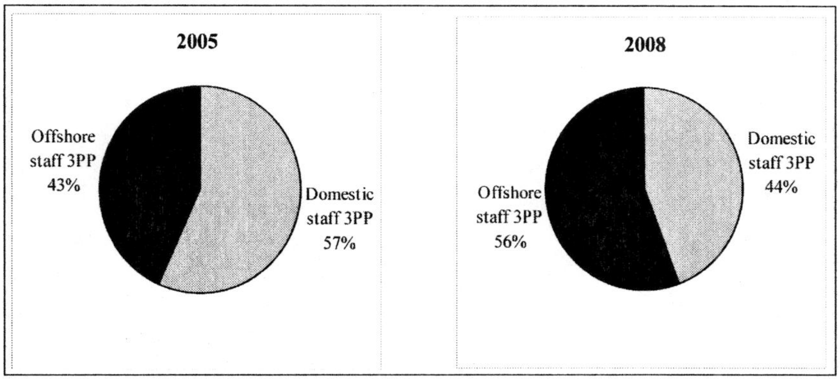

domestic staff, and foreign 3PP with offshore staff), although the increase is negligible for those with a foreign headquarters using domestic staff. The greatest increase will occur in the category of providers with domestic headquarters using offshore staff.

Further analysis (Figure 13) of IT employment was done by counts of individual organization responses rather than by total FTEs, since a change in FTEs of one very large organization could significantly influence the trend picture. A comparison of the expected change in FTEs by size of organization showed that the largest organizations (i.e., Fortune 500 and Large categories) expected a decrease in total FTEs by 2008, while the small and medium enterprises (SMEs) expected an increase in FTEs.

The McKinsey study (Farrell et al. 2005) predicted a gradual increase in overall off-shore FTEs. Figure 11 shows a 5% increase by 2008 in

Figure 14. Projected changes in full time equivalents (FTEs)

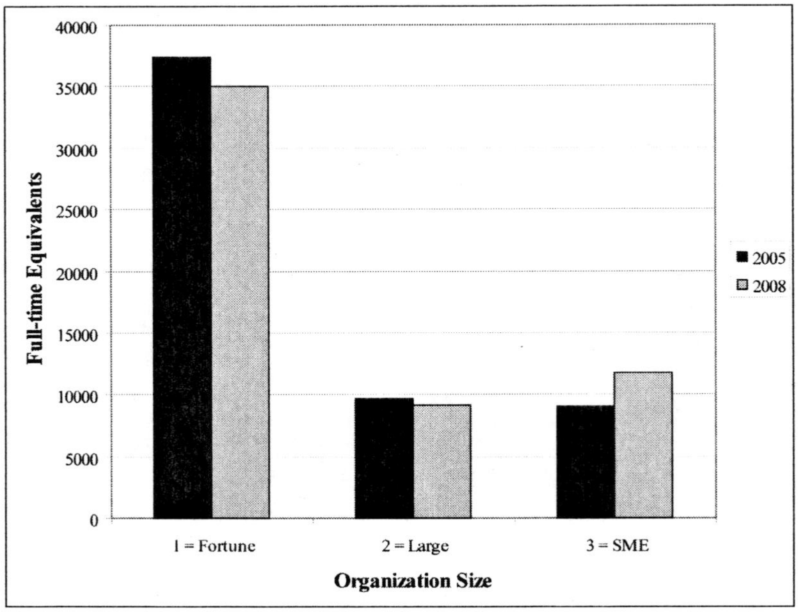

the FTEs based in 3PPs in all locations. In Figure 13, however, we separate the domestic and off-shore FTEs of 3PPs indicating an increase of off-shore staff of 13%. This is the increase reported by client firms, that is, client firms are planning to increase their use of off-shore 3PPs by 2008 in the amount of 13%. In the next figure, Figure 14, it is clear that the largest organizations are those decreasing their in-house FTEs in favor of increasing their use of 3PPs.

Further analysis (Figure 14) by numbers of organizations rather than by total FTEs determined that a majority of firms expect an increase in FTEs by 2008. Less than one-third of the Fortune organizations expect a decrease in FTEs by 2008, with over half expecting an increase. Over half of the Large and SME organizations also expect an increase in FTEs.

Table 5. Expected changes in FTEs by number of firms

Size	Decrease	No Change	Increase
Fortune	29.4%	14.7%	55.9%
Large	38.9%	5.5%	55.6%
SME	15.6%	21.9%	62.5%

The data shown in the FTE figures indicates a rearrangement of IT FTEs. The overall number of FTEs from 2005 to 2008 remains basically stable. However there is a shift away from in-house FTEs and towards 3PPs. This illustrates the migration of skills from in house to service providers. Given the previous data presented on what is happening to specific skills, the migration is very clearly one of traditional technical skills (e.g., programming) to service providers. It is important to understand that what is specifically included in the technical category may be dependent on the culture of the organization. Thus for some, the skills that are migrating are those related to "old" technology (e.g. mainframe, COBOL) while for others they are "newer" technologies (e.g., HTML, web design). However, the client-facing technical skills along with the many in project management, business domain, sourcing and IT administration are not migrating at this time.

DISCUSSION

Our research has implications in a variety of areas:

- Understanding how organizations value skills and capabilities in IT.
- Considerations for career development within organizations.
- Guidelines for universities educating graduates in computer science and information technology.

Understanding How Organizations Value IT Skills and Capabilities

There has been much discussion and concern about the impact of IT outsourcing on IT jobs here in the U.S. People have predicted a serious loss of positions. Vocal detractors such as Lou Dobbs on CNN have been declaring the crisis. This concern added to the depressed state of employment in IT stemming from the dot com bust has filtered to the university community and had the effect of decreasing enrollments in computer science and IT programs. Nicholas Carr's article declaring that IT doesn't matter gained notoriety and added to the confusion (Carr, 2003). Unfortunately much of this discussion has been based on emotions and not on facts.

Our data confirms that some IT jobs are moving to 3PPs in off shore locations; however, more importantly it also confirms the continuing need and value for people trained in technical skills. It is also clear from the data that the technical capabilities should be coupled with soft skills in project management and the business domain. This is evident in that the technical items that top the list of most critical now and continue to be important in the next three years are client-facing technical skills – Systems Analysis and Systems Design. The message here is that whatever technical expertise individuals develop, e.g., programming in Java, designing in .Net, wireless networking, they should also be developing project management and general business/industry knowledge.

The specific technical skills and capabilities that are critical are dependent on the organization's business model, culture and values. Organizations' needs vary depending on what technologies they are working with and whether the culture believes in maintaining in-house talent that might otherwise be sourced, e.g., mainframe technologies. Therefore, while the majority of our respondents were tending to source traditional technical work like programming, mainframe, operations, there were some who did not.

Skills specific to Internet applications inhabit a complex space in the IT skill world. They are not limited to the skills required to create Web pages such as Java, PHP, and HTML, but rather become a critical element of the problems that many organizations face in integrating their many platforms. The focus of this integration task is allowing Web-based applications to draw from and interact with the existing legacy foundation. For example, a legacy customer database developed from the 1970s may be the base of a Web-based customer relationship management (CRM) application. Therefore when we discuss Internet skills we include their interaction with legacy applications as well as the stand-alone Web languages and tools.

Previous research has shown that the specific technical skills appearing in want ads change depending on the technology du jour. With the migration pattern that we are seeing in this research, there will be a similar change in technical talent considered critical to have in house that relates to the ability to source this work adequately. IT sourcing decision research indicates that the decision making is dependent on a variety of factors: demand and supply, transaction cost economics and IT executive choice. Each of these will influence the migration of technical skills to 3PPs.

Respondents tended to focus on the need for basic technical skills in hiring at the entry level. They also named the undergraduate degree in computer science as the one they would look for the most. At the same time, they chose skills in business knowledge and communication as important in an entry-level candidate for this person to have a successful career within the organization.

This apparent inconsistency can be explained by understanding that for most IT organizations in client firms (i.e. not in service providers) technical skills are necessary but not sufficient for career success. The majority of our interviews took place in client firms, therefore this finding relates to the clients and not to the service providers. This is supported by the Image Theory, a two stage model of IS recruiting where the first stage is a filtration stage as an employer screens potential hires for a minimum requirement of technical skills. This is followed by the second stage where the final choice is made and influenced by softer skills and other factors (Litecky, Arnett and Prabhakar, 2004). Such a finding raises the question of whether individuals who have chosen a technical track for their careers will be able to succeed. Our research does not address this directly.

Hiring at the mid-level exhibited a similar inconsistency: while the critical skills were in the project management and business domain categories, the IT executives still wanted their mid-level candidates to have a strong basic technical foundation. The end result is that IT professionals at all levels need to be concerned about developing a balance between the hard technical skills and the soft client-facing skills.

Career Development Programs

The need for a balance in hard and soft skills calls for organizations to create career development programs for their IT professionals that enable them to create the needed balance. The increase in sourcing as an IT strategy underlines the need for strength in both hard and soft skill areas. As sourcing increases, the criticality of IT professionals who can manage sourcing effectively will also increase. IT professionals will need their technical skill foundation in a variety of areas plus skills in project management, business knowledge, team leadership and managing 3PPs.

Ang and Slaughter's (2001) discussion of the two approaches an organization can take to develop career paths: Industrial and Craft, can be used to describe the heyday of the dot com boom, in which most IT professionals appeared to be using the Craft approach – they were like "hired guns" who came into an organization, performed and then moved on to a higher level at the next organization. To a certain extent there is an analogy here with sourcing: the client organizations that are sourcing certain skills are using the Craft approach for those skills. However, for the skills respondents reported as critical to maintain in house, firms need to use the Industrial strategy in order to develop the strength and depth in those particular areas. Thus the technical skills that we see migrating to 3PPs are in the Craft mode, while the project management and business domain skills are in the Industrial mode.

Interestingly the above strategy is only from the point of view of the client organization. Service providers, on the other hand, will need to follow the Industrial strategy for technical skills that they are called upon to provide. The dual project management hierarchy model provides a mechanism for clients and vendors to share career development and learn from each other (Kaiser and Hawk, 2004).

Guidelines for Computer Science and Information Technology Programs

Our research also has implications for universities in developing programs that support the need for a balance of skills in their graduates. This balance has been called for in the past (Lee, Trauth and Farwell, 1995) specifically noting that computer science programs should be restructured to include more breadth and business education. Cappel made the specific recommendation that undergraduate programs include more opportunities for internships to help students gain the necessary business education (Cappel, 2001). We echo this call for diversifying the traditional undergraduate program through internships and relationships with the business community.

We understand that traditional computer science curriculum is fundamental to training the highly-skilled CS graduates that are needed for future generations of hardware and software development. We are not calling for a merger of CS and IT programs. What we are recommending is that even within the traditional CS curriculum it is becoming critical to expose students to real organizations, solving real problems. One approach is through internships and work-study programs.

SUMMARY

We have investigated the impact of sourcing strategies on what skills IT executives prefer to maintain in house versus source to third party providers. IT executives indicate that the critical skills to keep in house today are primarily client facing, including technical items with client facing elements. Looking to 2008, the only skills that are seen as no longer critical to maintain in house are technical skills which do not contain any client-facing activities. There are exceptions to this pattern based on organizational-specific characteristics of business model and culture. This result is also moderated by the position level in the organization. Entry level positions tend to require more technical skills while mid level positions tend to require more project management skills.

We have also looked at how the total number of IT FTEs will change from 2005 to 2008. Our research shows that while the mixture of in-house FTEs versus sourced FTEs is changing, the overall number of IT FTEs will remain stable over the next three years. The changing mix indicates an increase in IT FTEs at 3PPs with off shore locations. Looking at the migration of certain technical skills out of organizations along with the FTE patterns implies that the most likely skills to be sourced to 3PPs are the non-client facing technical skills. Our study is consistent with previous findings that indicated the migration of traditional technical skills (e.g., programming) to 3PP. However many of those were based on the availability of technical talent in 3PPs and on the definition of technical skills as being "non-core." In our research the IT executives explicitly chose which skills they wanted to hire and maintain in house as opposed to those they were willing to source to a 3PP. As a result, some technical skills migrated to 3PPs while others remained in house.

The findings are consistent with the paradox observed by others of a "recruiting gap" where organizations purport to seek well-rounded individuals although they advertise for those with "hard skills" and technical backgrounds. Findings indicate that IT professionals need to have a balance that demonstrates a foundation in the traditional "hard skills" and experience with "softer" business-oriented skills.

FUTURE RESEARCH

This chapter is focused on the changing skills from the viewpoint of the client organizations. We are currently conducting further research into the skills and capabilities desired by the service provider organizations. The client organization choices will cause a migration of some skills to 3PPs. This migration needs further investigation in order to provide a comprehensive picture of how skills and capabilities are evolving in the

IT industry. In our first study the universe of 3PPs was too small to perform any meaningful analysis.

The research raises questions for further exploration about the needs for entry-level professionals and how those candidates are filtered based on their technical skills. Future research should investigate actual job hiring data in specific industries. Young people entering the market and making career decisions will be better served by an increased understanding of these dynamics.

ACKNOWLEDGMENT

The following researchers made up the original team that conducted the SIM research project. All team members contributed to this chapter by collecting data and sharing their thoughts and insights.

- Pamela Abbott
University College Dublin
- Thomas Abraham
Kean University
- Cynthia Beath
University of Texas at Austin
- Christine Bullen
Stevens Institute of Technology
- Erran Carmel
American University
- Roberto Evaristo
University of Illinois Chicago
- Mike Gallivan
Georgia State University
- Kevin Gallagher
Florida State University
- Tim Goles
University of Texas-San Antonio
- Steve Hawk
University of Wisconsin-Parkside
- Joy Howland
Seattle SIM
- Kate Kaiser
Marquette University
- Seamas Kelly
University College Dublin
- Mary Lacity
University of Missouri
- John Mooney
Pepperdine University
- Judith Simon
University of Memphis
- C. Ranganathan
University of Illinois Chicago
- Joe Rottman
University of Missouri
- Terry Ryan
Claremont Graduate School
- Rick Wion
Smith Bucklin Associates

REFERENCES

Ang, S. & Slaughter, S. (2004). Turnover of Information Technology Professionals: The Effects of Internal Labor Market Strategies. The DATA BASE for Advances in Information Systems 35(3), 11-28.

Ang, S. & Slaughter, S.A. (2001). Work Outcomes and Job Design For Contract versus Permanent Information Systems Professionals On Software Development Teams. MIS Quarterly 25(3), 321-350.

Anonymous. ((2004)). Six-Month Assessment of Workforce Globalization in Certain Knowledge-Based Industries. Technology Administration (July). P1-12.

Arnett, K.P. & Litecky, C. R. (1994). Career Path Development for the Most Wanted Skills in the MIS Job Market. Journal of Systems Management, February, 45(2), 6-11.

Byrd, T. A. & Turner, D. E. (2001). An Exploratory Analysis of the Value of the Skills of IT

Personnel: Their Relationship to IS Infrastructure and Competitive Advantage. Decision Sciences, 32(1), 21-54.

Cappel, J. J. (2001). Entry-Level IS Jobs Skills: A Survey of Employers. The Journal of Computer Information Systems 42(2), 76-83.

Carr, N. (2003). IT Doesn't Matter. Harvard Business Review 81(5), 41-49.

Deloitte (2005). Calling a Change in the Outsourcing Market. Deloitte Consulting Report (April).

Farrell, D., Laboisiere & M.A., Rosenfeld, J. (2005). Sizing the Emerging Global Labor Market. The McKinsey Quarterly, 3, 93-103.

Foote, D. (2005). "Managing IT Organizations and Professionals" presentation to The Advisory Council, Foote Partners, LLC.

Gallivan, M. J., Truex Iii D. P. & Kvasny, L. ((2004)). Changing Patterns in IT Skill Sets 1988-2003: A Content Analysis of Classified Advertising. Database for Advances in Information Systems 35(3), 64-88.

George, J.F., Valacich J.S. & Valor J. (2005). Does Information Systems Still Matter? Lessons for a Maturing Discipline. Communications of the Association for Information Systems 16, 219-232.

Gomes P.J., Joglekar N.R. (2005). The Costs of Coordinating Distributed Software Development Tasks. Working Paper.

Gottfredson, M., Puryear, R., Phillips, S. (2005). Strategic Sourcing: From Periphery to the Core. Harvard Business Review, February 2005.

ITAA (2004). Adding Value...Growing Careers - The Employment Outlook In Today's Increasingly Competitive It Job Market. Information Technology Association of America (ITAA) Annual Workforce Development Survey (September).

Ives, B., Valacich, J., Watson, R., Zmud, R., Et Al. (2002). What Every Business Student Needs to Know About Information Systems. Communications of the Association for Information Systems, 9, 467-477.

Kaiser, K.M. & Hawk, S. ((2004)). "Evolution of Offshore Software Development: From Outsourcing to Cosourcing," MIS Quarterly Executive, 3 (2), June (2004), 69-81.

Koong, K. S., Liu, Lai C. & Liu, X. (2002). A Study of the Demand for Information Technology Professionals in Selected Internet Job Portals. Journal of Information Systems Education 13(1), 21-29.

Lee, D.M.S., Trauth, E. M. & Farwell, D. (1995). Critical Skills and Knowledge Requirements of IS Professionals: A Joint Academic/Industry Investigation. MIS Quarterly 19(3), 313-341.

Litecky, C. R., Arnett, K. P. & Prabhakar, B. (2004). The Paradox of Soft Skills Versus Technical Skills in IS Hiring. The Journal of Computer Information Systems, 45(1), 69-77.

Litecky, C.R., Prabhakar, B. & Arnett, K. P. (1996). MIS Job Market: Shaken But Not Stirred. Journal of Systems Management, 47(4), 50-54.

Nakayama, M. & Sutcliffe, N. G. (2001) "IT Skills Portfolio Research in SIGCPR Proceedings: Analysis, Synthesis and Proposals," ACM SIGCPR, 1-58113-361.

Prabhakar, B., Litecky, C.R. & Arnett, K.P., (2005). IT Skills in a Tough Job Market, Communications of the ACM, 8(10), 91-104.

Ross, J. W., Beath, C. M. & Goodhue, D. L. (1996). Develop Long-Term Competitiveness Through IT Assets. Sloan Management Review 3813; 38(1), 31–42.

Rottman, J.W. & Lacity, M.C. (2004). Proven Practices for IT Offshore Outsourcing, Cutter Consortium Executive Report, 5(12), 1-31.

Ryan, M.P., Farrell, M.C. & Doerflinger, T.M. (2005). Where Have All the Workers Gone?, UBS Financial Services Report, UBS Wealth Management, 27 June 2005.

Slaughter, S. & Ang, S. (1996). Employment Outsourcing in Information Systems. Communications of the ACM 39(7), 47-55.

Tapscott, D. (2004). The Engine That Drives Success: The Best Companies Have the Best Business Models Because They Have the Best IT Strategies. CIO Magazine (May) 1-6.

Trauth, E.M., Farwell, D. & Lee, D.M.S.(1993). The I/S Expectation Gap: Industry Expectation vs. Academic Preparations, MIS Quarterly, 17(3), 293-308.

Trewyn, P. (2005). U.S. faces IT worker shortage. Milwaukee Business Journal, http://milwaukee.bizjournals.com/milwaukee/stories/2005/05/23/focus3.html, May 20, last viewed November 13, 2005.

Van Slyke, C., Kittner, M. & Cheney, P. (1998). Skill Requirements for Entry-Level Information Systems Graduates. Journal of Information Systems Education (Fall 1998), 6-10.

ENDNOTES

[a] A white paper describing the full results of the research is available via the SIM website: http://www.simnet.org

[b] The "Other" is large at 28%, however it contains a diverse group of primarily services organizations, e.g., publishing, entertainment, non-profit, etc, Analysis indicated that there were not enough organizations in any one area to merit additional breakdowns.

[c] We found in our interviews that this was how the respondents discussed skills. They were less interested in specific programming skills, for example, than in the programming capability that anyone who learns to program acquires.

[d] Additional analysis on our data focusing on hiring characteristics such as desired degrees will be reported in future publications.

[e] In addition to the information collected using the standard script, each researcher also recorded the anecdotes and explanations supplied by each respondent. These are being compiled into individual case studies for further research.

Chapter X
Understanding Outsourcing of Web-Based Applications in Organizations: The Case of E-Insurance

Teuta Cata
Northern Kentucky University, USA

ABSTRACT

This article has investigated the insurance industry and provided insights into the relationships of organizational size and age with outsourcing and organizational structure. Also, this study investigated the relationship between Web site age, outsourcing, and organizational structure. The main findings are that firm size and maturity is related to the decision of Web-based development approach and the best organizational structure to support online activity. The insights obtained by a new variable: Web site age suggests that insurance companies are trying to develop their Web-based activities within their existing organizational structures, rather than creating new e-commerce divisions.

INTRODUCTION

Electronic commerce (e-commerce) is now considered to be a very important component of a business strategy for sales and customer service. An online presence increases a firm's credibility if the Web site is able to communicate and deliver the message and services that the firm wants to convey to its online audience (D'Angelo & Little, 1998). An interesting and successful approach to creating and maintaining the smooth operation of Web-based applications is outsourcing them to firms that are able to provide professional and reliable Web services. The financial industry is perceived the one which can reap significant benefits from offshore outsourcing of their IT services

(Schaaf, 2004). By outsourcing their IT-based services, banks can save 8-12% of their overall cost and insurance companies 10-15%. Financial companies have begun to consider outsourcing as an alternative, and they are considering Web site maintenance as the most efficient approach to a successful Web-based activity (Minkoff, 2000). Practitioners in the insurance industry consider outsourcing of Web-based applications as a potential to reduce costs and risks in the industry (Ahmed, 2002). Applications such as collaborative claims litigation; niche product development, deployment, and administration; and bringing agents and insured services closer to policy holders are only the start of insurance applications that can be outsourced to application service providers (ASPs).

Outsourcing makes it possible for companies to have an instant Web environment without increasing traffic on the firm's LAN/WAN or putting more pressure on its Information Technology (IT) staff to support the 24x7 Web environment. At the same time, outsourcing allows companies to focus on their core competencies, provide better Web service, and reduce the cost of online activity (Sibley, 2001). While all of this is true, companies may very well have different strategies for outsourcing.

This research will address the issue of developing Web-based applications as one of the most important decisions in e-commerce initiatives. Investigating Web-based applications in the financial industry has a specific importance because this industry is an information-intensive industry, where the adoption of technology has a significant impact not only on the products and services offered, but also on business strategies and the process of business core redesign (Dos Santos & Peffers, 1995). At the same time, the insurance sector is lagging the banking sector in e-commerce (Burger, 2005). As online banking has been growing dramatically in the last 10 years, online sales have just gotten started.

The research problem of our study has focused on two main areas aspects: first, how firm size and age influence the decision to outsource the development of Web-based applications and second, what organizational structures are suitable for supporting Web sites for e-commerce. Reasons to investigate the impact of organization variables in sourcing e-commerce activities come from the need to identify how organizational context influences important decisions related to participate or not in Web-based applications. Organization variables such as organization maturity and size has been under investigated in e-commerce context.

This study has aimed to answering the following questions:

- What approach to Web development do insurance companies tend to apply? Do they develop it in-house? Do they outsource it? Do they use a combination of these two approaches?
- What organizational structure do insurance companies choose to support e-commerce initiative? Do they develop it as part of existing structure or as a separate division?
- How do the insurance company's size and age relate to decisions on how to develop the Web site?
- How do the company's size and age relate to different organizational structures for e-commerce?

The remainder of this chapter is presented in four sections. First, we discuss outsourcing, organizational structure for e-commerce, and organizational variables. Then, we describe the sample and the methodology used to capture data. The third section presents the findings from this study and relates them to the hypotheses of this research. In the final section, we draw conclusions from these data and identify the limitations of the study.

LITERATURE REVIEW

Information Systems Outsourcing

IS outsourcing is the process of contracting out the firm's products or activities to another organization that agrees to provide and manage these products for a set fee over a set period (Kern & Willcocks, 2002). Dibbern, Goles, Hirschheim, and Jayatilaka (2004) suggest two reasons for outsourcing: first, IS functions are considered as non-core functions, which can be better managed by outside vendors; and second, IS functions are considered an overhead cost that has to be minimized.

Research in IS outsourcing has attempted to identify the forces that motivate firms to outsource their IT functions. Loh and Venkatraman (1992) suggest that the degree of IT outsourcing is related to both the structure of the business and the IT cost structure. The IT cost structure is related to expenditures for the purpose of keeping up with the latest developments in IT. Most of the time, companies find difficulties in efficiently controlling this cost and, therefore, try to delegate these expenditures to IT vendors. Ang and Cummings (1997) suggest that the decision to outsource IS functions is related to company size. Large companies consider IT functions more complex and more strategic than in small firms. Small firms use IT functions as "backroom cost machinery" where they are used to reduce cost. Goo, Kishore, and Rao (2000) suggest that there are internal and external drivers. Beyond the business and technology drivers within each company, outside drivers, such as competitors, customers, and technological innovation are the factors that lead companies to negotiate with IS vendors for managing their IS functions.

Interestingly, contradictory results are found in analyzing outsourcing trends in the financial industry. McFarlan and Nolan (1995) suggested that service firms were not interested in outsourcing IS functions. However, recent research shows that even service firms, such as financial firms, are outsourcing their IS functions. The outsourcing trend in financial firms has been focused more on front-and-back office applications in functions such as finance, accounting, human resource management, and customer support (Tas & Sunder, 2004). Trade journals support the potentials of outsourcing Web-based applications in insurance industry. Ahmed (2002) suggests that insurance companies can outsource many of their Web-based applications to ASPs and obtain significant benefits from outsourcing.

Another important issue related to the decision of whether to outsource or not is related to the resources that the firm has. Lee, Huynh, Kwok, and Pi (2003) tried to generalize the patterns of outsourcing by investigating outsourcing of IS services over time. The historical data suggest that, in the past, the small companies with problematic and mismanaged IS departments were the companies which were outsourcing their IS functions. Recently, the IS outsourcing trend has included even large companies with mature IS departments.

Recent research attempted to explain the decision to manage IS resources based on the stage of a firm's technological development. Kishore, Agrawal, and Rao (2004) investigated the sourcing of e-commerce technology for firms in early and late stages of technological maturity. The results of this study suggest that in the early stages, companies try to source by using a hybrid approach: they try to develop the Web-based applications in-house and outsource part of them to vendors. As technology matures, the companies try to increase their relationships with vendors. These results suggest that companies need to develop some expertise in-house and develop tacit knowledge about e-commerce applications. Another study on sourcing of technology applications (Al-Qerim & Bathula, 2002) suggests that the complexity of IT applications and the dependency on the supplier are the main factors which lead companies to the decision to totally outsource, use hybrid sourcing, or in-source their IT applications.

The retail industry is a good example of this sourcing strategy. Retailers such as Marks & Spencer (M&S) (Brooks, 2006) are delegating the e-commerce operation to other companies (Amazon) to operate it more efficiently, after they setup the operation by themselves. The hybrid approach will allow M&S to control the management of the site by itself and reduce cost by allowing a third party to operate it more efficiently.

Organizational Structure for E-commerce

E-Commerce initiatives have raised organizational-structure issues because companies are aware that the online channel is not only a technology solution, but it is a business strategy, or a "moving target." The best solution is to have a flexible integrated platform (Sauer & Willcocks, 2002) and a business model which will address the organization goals, strategies, and objectives for the e-commerce project (Wang, 2000).

Some organizational structures are considered to better support such Web initiatives. Solutions vary from supporting Web activities totally in-house by the organization's IS department, to creating a separate division which will totally integrate all functions related to an online business in a single division, and to the separation of the online business as a totally new independent business (or a spin-off) created by an existing company.

Several attempts have been made to understand what the best approach is to managing e-commerce activity and how companies can best make such decisions. Grant (2003) conducted an exploratory study that tried to investigate how Canadian companies designed the organizational structure of their e-commerce initiative. The results of the study suggest that companies prefer to trust their business applications to their existing IT structures rather than to a specific e-business division.

Barthelemy and Geyer (2005) tried to identify the relationship of internal and external factors that leads companies to the decision of whether they need a separate division to support their e-commerce applications. Results of the study suggest that a company will create a spin-off IS division if its IS activities are highly asset-specific, its IS departments are large and perform as profit centers, and if a high degree of interconnectedness exists between financial companies and manufacturer firms.

Another interesting perspective in this research stream is the investigation of what happens with organizational structure once a company has made its outsourcing decision. Chu and Smithson (2003) conducted a case study of changes that two organizations undertook in order to create an e-commerce solution. The authors observed that neither company under study was satisfied with having new organizational structures created for the e-commerce initiative, and so, these were changed back to the traditional in-house approach, in which the e-commerce was better understood by manufacturing, sales, marketing, and other divisions. A reason for the reversal could be a gap that IT creates between business units if it takes the leading role (Gordon & Gordon, 2000). The e-commerce initiatives are established in order to get more information about the company's customers. If this information is located within a separate division or a new company branch, then companies are not reaping the entire benefit from their online channel.

Organizational Variables

This study investigates the relationship between the decision of outsourcing Web-based applications and e-commerce organizational structures with two of the most important organizational variables: organizational size and age. Research in IS has examined the impact of organizational variables on issues related to technology assimilation, technology adoption, and technology innovation in general. Unfortunately, there is little evidence of investigating how these two organizational variables influence adoption of Web-based technologies in particular. The following discussion of organizational variables is based on findings of technology innovation in general. Hopefully the findings of this research will help to fill the gap in literature and help understanding of the relationship between organizational variables and e-commerce technologies.

Organizational Size

The literature offers contradictory findings about the relationship and direction between organizational size and innovation (Camison-Zornoza, Lapiedra-Alcami, Segarra-Cipres, & Boronat-Navarro, 2004; Lee & Xia, 2006). An organization's size affects not only business structure and processes, but also managerial decisions to apply technology innovation in organizations. There is a stream of research that argues that large organizations are more innovative and better equipped to apply new technology developments. This argument is based on the fact that large organizations have a greater potential for the application of new technology because they have more technical, human, and financial resources to support the adoption of new technologies (Yap, 1990). Small firms lack the managerial resources and technical expertise required to implement and use network technologies (Min & Galle, 2001). Two recent meta-analysis research of 54 and 53 empirical studies focus on the relationship between organization size and IT innovation adoption (Lee & Xia, 2006; Camison-Zornoza et al., 2004) suggest that a positive effect exists between the indicated variables. This positive relationship exists for profit organizations and is stronger if the adoption is considered as IT process innovation, IT mixed innovation, adoption stages, and so forth (Lee & Xia, 2006). On the other hand organization size affects the decision for organizational structures. Harris and Katz (1991) contend that small organizations have simple and flexible structures, which makes them more adoptable to change. As the organization grows larger it becomes more structured, hierarchical, bureaucratic, and less flexible and able to adapt to changes.

Organizational Age

How does a firm's activity change with maturity? This question has been investigated many times and is important to understanding the changes that firms adopt over the course of time. Henderson (1999) advocates that there is a strong relationship between a firm's maturity and the IT strategy it adopts. Mature firms, through in-house R&D, are more likely to develop proprietary solutions, while younger firms show a tendency towards purchasing off-the-shelf solutions. Following this discussion stream, Thornhill and Amit (2003) suggest that young firms possess different resources and suffer different managerial issues than older firms. Less mature firms are at risk due to a lack of valuable resources, while mature firms are at risk because they are not able to adapt themselves to a changing competitive environment.

The relationship between a firm's maturity and the adoption of new technological innovations is very intriguing and interesting. Sorensen and Stuart (2000) meticulously investigate this relationship. They present two scenarios related to the relationship between a firm's age and technological innovation. On the one hand, older firms are more stable and focus on innovation more frequently. Their innovations are more incremental and comply with the firm's existing technologies. Furthermore, technology adoption tends to be self-reinforcing, which puts older firms in a positive situation because they have already perfected their routines, structures, and incentives (Cohen & Levinthal, 1990). Support for this theory lies in the large number of patents held or pursued by older, Fortune 500, firms. On the other hand, young firms are more willing to adopt new technologies, especially if these technologies provide radical technical changes.

Research on IS has not yet addressed the impact of the Web site age on the different strategic decisions that organizations make. Companies have consistently changed their strategies for their Web-based activities as online sales volume increased and as the companies were more confident in applying the latest Web technologies. The Web site age is a new organizational variable which has to be involved as a way to collect information on how business strategies have changed as Web technology matures. Web site age is considered as a positive factor to increase the legitimacy of the business and increase ranking in some search engines, such as Google (Melbourne, 2005) and shows firm's commitment to e-commerce activities (Kowtha & Choon, 2001). Another study (Vaughan & Wu, 2004) made the first effort to explore the relationship between the Web site age and the links that a Web site has. Both those variables were used to test if the Web site age impacts the business performance measures such as profit, R&D, revenue, and so forth. Results of the study show the older Web sites have more links to them, but Web site age is not a confound variable between number of links and the business performance measures.

In summary, literature suggests that IS outsourcing is related to organizational variables (Ang & Cummings, 1997). Small organizations with limited or mismanaged IT departments (Lee et al., 2003) and young companies (Henderson, 1999) are the ones who prefer to buy off-the-shelf or outsource their applications. Large and mature companies are more stable and can better support in-house development of applications. Organizational structure variable is basically discussed from the business perspective, how a new business division is related to organizational goals and strategies (Wang, 2000), and only few attempts are made to investigate this variable in light of organizational variables (size and maturity). A European study (Barthelemy & Geyer, 2005) suggests that companies with large IT departments are more willing to create spin-off IT divisions. Mature organizations possess more managerial resources and are not able to adopt themselves to environmental changes (Thornhill & Amit, 2003), which was very evident in the first wave of e-commerce.

METHODOLOGY

In order to address our research problem and questions discussed previously, given the evidence and gaps identified in the literature, we have tested several hypotheses as follows. Figure 1 shows the hypothesis tested in this study.

- **H1:** Organizational size is positively related to the decision to develop the Web-based applications in-house.

Figure 1. The hypothesis and relation of the variables in the study

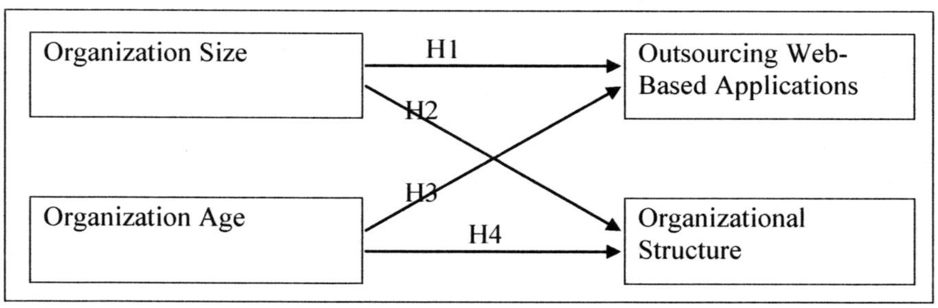

- **H2:** Organizational size is negatively related to the decision of creating new organizational structures for e-commerce activity.
- **H3:** There is a positive relationship between organizational age and the decision to develop Web-based applications in-house.
- **H4:** There is a positive relationship between organizational age and the decision to develop Web-based applications in the existing structures.

Our study used a survey of insurance companies that have Web sites. A preliminary pilot study with four insurance experts helped us better understand the insurance process and ensured that items in the questionnaire were easily understood. The unit of analysis is organization. We did not attempt to perform an in-depth analysis of either the technical implementation of Web-based activities or other technical details and problems.

This study used quantitative methodology. The first step was to identify which insurance services would be the target of this study. The various types of insurance coverage were carefully analyzed and two types—automobile and life—were selected for inclusion in this study. These two types of insurance are considered as the most appropriate products for e-commerce ("Web News," 2003).

Participants in this study were identified from two sources—the Internet (Yahoo.com, Google.com, and Hoover.com) and Best Key Rating Guide (2002) published by AM Best. Companies identified on the Internet were invited to participate in the study by e-mail. Each received an invitation letter with a survey questionnaire attached. The invitation letter stated IT managers or other managers related to Web-based activity should complete the questionnaire. A total of 522 e-mails were sent to companies that provided e-mail ad-

Table 1. Survey characteristics

Type of Distribution	Electronically (e-mail)	Mail
Number of questionnaires distributed	568 (522 + 46)	385
Number of questionnaires undelivered	37 (6.5%)	23 (5.9 %)
Number of companies responding	53 (10 %)	56 (15. 4 %)
Number of responses discarded	2 (0.3%)	0 (0%)
Number of responses included in statistical analysis	51 (9.6)	56 (15.45)
Responses according to insurance types:		
Life	24 (47%)	39 (69.6%)
Auto	15 (29.4%)	0 (0%)
Life and Auto	12 (23.6%)	17 (30.4%)

dresses on their Web sites, and 97 online forms were completed for companies that did not provide e-mail addresses. Thirty-seven e-mails were returned as undelivered. Those companies were invited to participate in the study by traditional mail in the second round of data collection.

Due to the low response rate obtained by the e-mail survey, the data collection phase of the study continued by sending traditional mail to life insurance companies identified in Best's Key Rating Guide (2002). A total of 385 companies were invited to participate in the study by sending a letter of invitation and a printed questionnaire. In this phase, careful consideration was taken to invite companies that were not contacted via e-mail survey, companies whose e-mails were returned, and companies whose service rate was above an F rating (in liquidation). The identified companies operate in almost every state in the United States.

Twenty-three postal questionnaires were returned as undelivered due to either dissolution or simple changes of address. A total of 109 questionnaires were completed and returned, 53 via e-mail, and 56 via traditional mail. Two questionnaires were partially completed and could not be used for statistical analysis and hypothesis testing. Fifteen respondents were engaged in auto insurance, 63 in life insurance, and 29 provided both types of insurance (see Table 1).

Survey respondents hold a variety of positions in their respective organizations. As shown in Table 2, 72% of participants were associated with the IT function in their organization or with the firm's e-commerce/Web site activity. The remaining questionnaires (25%) were completed by managers with other responsibilities for their organizations, mainly marketing managers. Three questionnaires did not provide information about the job title of the respondents.

A survey questionnaire was created in order to obtain information about each company's age; size; insurance types served; Web site characteristics age; the percentage of sales which come from Web-based activity; Web development approaches; and the organizational structure supporting e-commerce operations.

Data analysis has involved several measurement-related issues. The dependent variable outsourcing is measured by three ordinal values: (1) in-house, (2) partly outsourced, and (3) partly in-house, and totally outsourced. The dependent variable related to a new organizational structure related to Web-based activity, named in statistical analysis as "eDepartment," is measured as an ordinal variable with three levels: (1) part-of-or-

Table 2. Profile of job title of survey respondents

Criteria	Job Title	Number of Respondents	% of Respondents
IT-related positions	CIO	3	2.8 %
	IT director	21	19.6%
	Vice Director of IT	19	17.8%
	Web manager	24	22.4%
	E-commerce manager	10	9.3%
	Totals	77	71.9%
Management-related positions	CEO	4	3.7%
	President	1	0.9%
	Vice President	3	2.8%
	Other managers (mainly marketing)	19	17.8%
	No response	3	2.8%
	Totals	30	25.2%

ganization, mixed-approach, and new-division. In the survey questionnaire this variable was broken in two categories: part of organization and new-department. Several respondents reported a mixed approach as well. Therefore, in statistical analysis this variable is included as an ordinal variable with three levels. Moreover, firm age and Web site age are measured in years. Based on the suggestions given by insurance experts who participated in the pilot study, companies are grouped as new companies if they are younger than 20 years old, moderate-age if they are between 21 and 100 years old, and mature if they are more than 100 years old. The Web site age has two groups based on the very limited time insurance companies have been operating online. Companies are considered to have a new Web site if they have been operating online for fewer than 4 years and mature if their activity is 4 or more years. Insurance experts suggested the following classification based on the experience with operating the Web site and other problems related with the adoption of Web-based applications.

It was intended that organizational size be measured by the number of employees and sales. Unfortunately, few companies agreed to share sale figures with us. Therefore, organizational size is operationalized as the number of employees reported. Insurance firms are considered small if they have fewer than 50 employees, medium if they have more than 51, and less than 500 employees, and large if the firm has 500 or more employees. This study uses crosstab analysis as the best method for analyzing the relationship between two ordinal variables and a third as a control variable (Agresti, 1996).

FINDINGS

Table 3 summarizes the mean values and standard deviation of the company's age, Web site age, organizational size, and online sales investigated in this study. As Table 3 shows, the companies participating in this study vary according to the time they have been operating in the insurance industry (from 7 to 293 years old) and the length of time they have been conducting business online (one to 10 years).

Crosstabs analysis is used to identify any relationship between the decision to outsource Web-based functions and create new organizational structure and independent variables related to organizational size, organizational maturity, and Web site age. The three levels of the outsourcing decision (in-house, mixed, and outsourced) and new organizational structures (part-organization, both, new-division) are considered as ordinal variables. The independent variable firm size is controlled by measuring the time-varying variables (firm age and Web site age) and online-sales variable because of a strong positive correlation that exists between the variables (Barron, West, & Hannan, 1994). The strong correlation between

Table 3. Descriptive statistics for firm age, Web site age, firm size

Variables	N	Minimum	Maximum	Mean
Firm age	107	7.00	293.00	75.1028
Web site age	107	1.00	10.00	5.2523
Firm size (employees)	107	11.00	320,000	7,199
Online sales (%)	107	0.00	100.00	16.24

Table 4. Results of crosstab analysis for firm size by controlling firm age

Variables	**Chi-Square**			**Hypotheses**
Firm size * Outsourcing decision * (Control: Firm age) *(Small, Medium, Large)*	*Small* 14.693**	*Medium* 8.839	*Large* 5.871	H1 Supported
Firm size * Org. structure * (Control: Firm age) *(Small, Medium, Large)*	*Small* 6.256*	*Medium* 2.726	*Large* .244	H2 Supported

Table 5. Count table of the relationship between organizational size and decision of outsourcing Web-based activities (Hypothesis H1)

		Firm Age			
Firm size		Young	Med	Mature	Total
Small	in-house	5	19	6	**30**
	both	11	6	1	**18**
	outsource	2	7	5	**14**
Total		**18**	**32**	**12**	**62**
Medium	in-house	3	2	2	**7**
	both	0	1	3	**4**
	outsource	0	6	3	**9**
Total		**3**	**9**	**8**	**20**
Large	in-house		2	9	**11**
	both		8	5	**13**
	outsource		1	0	**1**
Total			**11**	**14**	**25**

Table 6. Count table of the relationship between organizational size and decision of creating new organizational structures (Hypothesis H2)

		Company Age			
Firm Size		Young	Med	Mature	Total
Small	part-organization	18	25	8	**51**
	spin-off	0	7	4	**11**
Total		**18**	**32**	**12**	**62**
Medium	part-organization	3	8	5	**16**
	spin-off	0	1	3	**4**
Total		**3**	**9**	**8**	**20**
Large	part-organization		6	9	**15**
	mixed		3	3	**6**
	spin-off		2	2	**4**
Total			**11**	**14**	**25**

variables can be avoided by using one of them as the control variable in order to identify if any relationship exists between the second variable and the dependent variable.

Crosstab analysis for the firm-size variable has been tested to explore firm size in its relation to both dependent variables: Web site development and organization structure (Table 4, 5, and 6). Firm age is used as the controlling variable in order to get a clear relationship between the independent and the dependent variables.

Results of chi-square value show different approaches of Web development based on the company size. Small size insurance companies develop the Web site applications not only in-house or partly in-house but also outsource them at third parties. Those companies have considered seriously the three approaches, where outsourcing is not determinant but still is considered as a trend by chi-square test (p<.01). The count table shows that in-house development for small size firms has the majority by 30 counts, followed by mixed approach with 18 counts, and outsourcing by 14 counts (Table 5). Medium-size firms overall do not show any trend towards which approach is more favorable. Within this group of firms, the medium size and medium age subgroup shows a clear trend towards outsourcing the Web-based functions (6 counts). Large insurance companies show a clear trend towards in-house or partly in-house development of Web-based applications (11+13 counts).

The other organizational decision tested in this study: to create a new e-commerce division or keep it within the existing organizational structure, shows a positive trend to create spin-off (p<.05) for small insurance companies. The reason that this group, in particular, wants to create spin-off structure may be related to the fact that small size companies are more flexible and less bureaucratic and they were able to follow the hype of e-commerce developments late in 20th century. The counts table (Table 6) clarify the Pearson chi-square results and clearly shows a trend to keep Web-based applications as part of the organization in the two groups of firm size (medium = 16 counts, and large 15= counts).

The variable firm age is tested toward the dependent variables on the three levels of controlling variable (firm size). Chi-square test shows significant trends toward using different approaches for Web-based development (p<.001 and p<.05) for two groups of firm age (medium and mature) (Table 7). To better clarify chi-square results, this study will use the counts tables to pertain detailed information as to which Web-developing alternatives the insurance companies had chosen (Table 8). Counts table shows young firms prefer to develop their application in-house or partly in-house (8+11 counts). Some subgroups hesitate on trusting only one approach of Web-based application development (young-small group and medium-large group). Therefore, those groups have preferred the mixed approach of developing their Web-based applications in-house and outsourcing some functions to third parties. Interestingly, only mid-age mid-size companies have chosen outsourcing as the main approach

Table 7. Results of crosstab analysis for firm age by controlling firm size

Variables	Chi-Square			Hypotheses
Comp. age * Outsourcing decision *(Control: Firm size)	*Young* 5.688	*Medium* 20.670***	*Mature* 9.518*	H3 Rejected
Comp. age * Org. structure * (Control: Firm size) *(Young, Medium, Mature)*	*Young* -	*Medium* 12.500*	*Mature* 5.666	H4 Rejected

Table 8. Count table testing the relationship between firm age and decision of outsourcing Web-based activities (Hypothesis H3)

Firm Age		Firm Size			Total
		Small	Medium	Large	
Young	in-house	5	3		**8**
	both	11	0		**11**
	outsource	2	0		**2**
Total		**18**	**3**		**21**
Med	in-house	19	2	2	**23**
	both	6	1	8	**15**
	outsource	7	6	1	**14**
Total		**32**	**9**	**11**	**52**
Mature	in-house	6	2	9	**17**
	both	1	3	5	**9**
	outsource	5	3	0	**8**
Total		**12**	**8**	**14**	**34**

Table 9. Testing the relationship between organizational age and decision of creating new organizational structures (Hypothesis H4)

Firm Age		Firm Size			Total
		Small	Medium	Large	
Young	part-organization	18	3		**21**
Total		**18**	**3**		**21**
Med	part-organization	25	8	6	**39**
	both	0	0	3	**3**
	new division	7	1	2	**10**
Total		**32**	**9**	**11**	**52**
Mature	part-organization	8	5	9	**22**
	both	0	0	3	**3**
	new division	4	3	2	**9**
Total		**12**	**8**	**14**	**34**

to Web site development (6 counts). The reason of applying a mixed development approach (in-house and outsourcing) may be related to the fact that medium and mature companies have legacy systems which are hard to integrate to new technology developments. For this reason they may need specialized help from vendors.

As far as the decision to develop the Web activities within the company or create new Web division, young and mature insurance companies show a clear trend toward keeping them as part of the organization. Chi-square test shows a trend of medium-age companies to create new divisions ($p<.05$) (Table 7), which indicates an inclination toward trying new organizational forms for managing Web-based activities (Table 9, counts = 10). This trend is evident for mature group as well (count = 9), but chi-square test does not confirm this trend. The reason may be the small sample size for the mature group.

The analysis of this study will continue with another variable: Web site age, which is not previously investigated in IS research. The gap in literature does not allow us to build hypotheses for this new IS variable, but the analysis in this section will allow us to shed some light on how this variable is related to organizational variables: firm size and firm age.

Table 10. Results of crosstab analysis for Web site age by controlling firm size

Variables	Chi-Square	
Web site age * Outsourcing decision * (Control: Firm size) *(Young, Mature)*	*Young* 19.460 ***	*Mature* 10. 068*
Web site age * Org. structure * (Control: Firm size) *(Young, Mature)*	*Young* 3.644	*Mature* 17,731**

Table 11. Testing the relationship between Web site age and decision of outsourcing Web-based activities

Website Age		Firm Size			Total
		Small	Medium	Large	
Young	in-house	12	2	4	**18**
	both	10	0	0	**10**
	outsource	5	8	0	**13**
Total		**27**	**10**	**4**	**41**
Mature	in-house	18	5	7	**30**
	both	8	4	13	**25**
	outsource	9	1	1	**11**
Total		**35**	**10**	**21**	**66**

Table 12. Testing the relationship between Web site age and decision of creating new organizational structures

Website Age		Firm Size			Total
		Small	Medium	Large	
Young	part-organization	21	10	4	**35**
	new division	6	0	0	**6**
Total		**27**	**10**	**4**	**41**
Mature	part-organization	30	6	11	**47**
	both	0	0	6	**6**
	new division	5	4	4	**13**
Total		**35**	**10**	**21**	**66**

The analysis of the variable Web site age is interesting because it tries to investigate the trend of how Web sites are created and managed as the Web-based technology matures. Chi-square test (young $p<.001$ and mature $p<.05$) shows that insurance firms have developed and continue to develop their Web sites based in different approaches (in-house, outsourced, and both). The crosstab table (Table 11) shows that large companies trend more towards in-house or partly in-house applications and do not prefer outsourcing approach (large-young = 0, large-medium= 1). The other two groups (small and medium size) prefer both in-house and outsourcing approach.

Interesting insights are obtained at observing the different organizational structure approach as Web-technology matures. Crosstab analysis shows that the mature Web site shows a clear trend ($p<.01$) toward new e-business organizational structures. With the development and maturity of e-commerce activity, firms are considering bringing or creating the Web-based activities within their existing organizational structures (Table 12). In particular medium and large size firms are integrating their Web-based applications with their existing structures (new-division young-medium counts = 0, new-division young-large counts = 0).

Discussion of Findings

This study reveals many interesting findings related to the decisions of Web site development and organizational structure. The size of firms is related to the decision of what approach will be used when they develop their Web-based activity. Findings in this study suggest that small companies and mid-size mid-age companies are the ones experimenting with external sources for Web development. These groups are not totally depending on their IT department, but they are using the external expertise that outsourcing companies provide. Large and medium size companies depend more on internal resources to develop their Web-based applications. These findings support previous studies (Min & Galle, 2001; Yap, 1990) that suggest that large companies, which have more technical and managerial support, are in advantage to apply technology innovation.

Results of the analysis indicate that as an organization matures it attempts to trust third parties to develop their Web sites totally or partially. Interestingly, this study found that financial companies are considering outsourcing of the front-office applications, where the leaders are medium-age and mid-size companies. The findings support the suggestions by Kishore et al. (2004) who suggest that both companies and outsourcers are maturing and that companies are delegating more responsibilities to the outsourcing companies and reaping more benefits of their expertise developed in the last few years. Other reasons that might have pushed the medium and mature segment of the insurance industry to outsource their Web-based functions might be related with the scarcity of IT resources. Insurance companies are transaction-oriented firms where their IT staff is mainly oriented on supporting and maintaining their legacy systems, and the knowledge and expertise to support the Web environment might be missing.

Interesting findings are to be found even in the trends of organization structures that support e-commerce initiatives. Small size firms were more willing to create new organizational structure for their Web-based activities. The reason is related to the flexibility that small size brings to companies in case they need to rearrange their structure. As Harris and Katz (1991) suggest, large size firms are unable to be flexible and adaptable to structural changes. Interestingly, the findings suggest that as organization matures, it tries new ways to manage its functions. Organizations that have been in business for a considerable time (medium and mature firms) are more willing to create new business divisions, which will manage the Web-based activity. The reason might be that they want to bring the new technology development in the most incremental and visible way to their business partners and customers.

Web site age is an underdeveloped variable in IS research. Therefore, understanding the trends of Web site development as the technology and business approach mature requires a notable consideration. Web site development shows that insurance firms do not have any specific preference for Web-based developments. The three development approaches (in-house, mixed, and outsourced) are applicable. A close-up investigation by crosstabs suggests that large companies have tried to develop all or part of their Web-based functions in-house. Small and medium size insurance companies are still considering IT departments as a major developer for their Web-based application in cooperation with outsourcing companies.

Results of this study suggest that in the first steps of e-commerce activities, companies came up with new organizational structures which divided those operations from existing organizational departments. As the online activity matures, insurance firms understand that online sales are part of the firm and therefore they have to be integrated with the "brick and mortar" operations of the company.

CONCLUSION AND LIMITATIONS

In summary, this research indicates that the insurance industry still hesitates to rely on third parties to develop their Web-based applications and prefers to consider online sales as an enhancement of the current activity rather than to adopt a totally new and different sales approach. Part of the reason is that the insurance sector has, already, a well-developed IS infrastructure and a skilled IT staff, which are able to support Web-based activities.

Data collected on Web site age clarify this issue further. The results suggest that companies that were the pioneers of online sales were more willing to come up with new organizational divisions, which were going to take care of their e-commerce part of the activity. The recent trend shows that insurance companies feel more comfortable with developing the Web-based applications and are trying to keep this expertise in-house. This study identified a very specific group within the insurance industry: mid-size mid-age companies, which are exhibiting new approaches related to Web site development and management.

This study contributes to both practitioner and research community. The findings of this research help practitioners to understand the trends of e-commerce sourcing and realize the best course of action for them based on the maturity and size of their company. These findings will contribute to the academic community as well to increase the body of knowledge on e-commerce and understand patterns of decision making based on organizational variables.

This study did not identify the reasons that push insurance companies to outsource their Web-based functions. Do insurance firms feel comfortable on sharing sensitive data about their customers to the third parties and if so, how do they make sure that those data are not sold to their competitors by the outsourcer? A follow-up research will focus in-depth on these issues and will try to explore the relationship between the nature of information collected and saved via Web-based activities and the decision to outsource those activities.

Certain limitations should be noted when considering these findings. The major limitation of this study is the sample size. As mentioned previously, the population of auto and life insurance firms is limited, and it is difficult to secure a large sample size. Insurance firms were contacted via e-mails and the postal mail to increase the sample size. The number of insurance firms that are conducting a major portion of their businesses online is still quite limited.

Another limitation is generalizability of the results of this study. The data collected for this study are entirely from American insurance firms; thus the findings identified in this study may not apply to other service industries or other regions of the world. Also, this study is snap-shot research rather than a longitudinal study. These results do not indicate the current trends of the e-insurance adoption process, and therefore they do not provide any insights into what their strategies might be in the future.

REFERENCES

Agresti, A. (1996). *An introduction to categorical data analysis.* New York: John Wiley and Sons.

Ahmed, A. (2002). E-outsourcing cuts costs and risks. *National Underwriter/Property & Casualty/Risk & benefit Management Edition, 106*(34), 12-13.

Al-Qerim, N. A., & Bathula, H. (2002). IT and eCommerce outsourcing in small to medium-size enterprises in New Zealand: An exploratory research. In *Proceedings of the 15th Bled Electronic Commerce Conference* (pp. 537-551).

Ang, S., & Cummings, L. L. (1997). Strategic response to institutional influences on information systems outsourcing. *Organization Science, 8*(3), 235-256.

Barron, D. N., West, E., & Hannan, M. T. (1994). A time to grow and a time to die: Growth and mortality of credit unions in New York City, 1914-1990. *American Journal of Sociology, 100,* 196-241.

Barthelemy, J., & Geyer, D. (2005). An empirical investigation of IT outsourcing versus quasi-outsourcing in France and Germany. *Information & Management, 42,* 533-542.

Best's key rating guide, life-health United States. (2002). Oldwick, NJ: AM Best.

Brooks, G. (2006, March 23). In-house or outsource? *New Media Age, Supplement,* 6-8.

Burger, K. (2005). Laggards no more. *Insurance & Technology, 30*(7), 4.

Camison-Zornova, C., Lapiedra-Alcami, R., Segarra-Cipres, S., & Boronat-Navarro, M. (2004). A meta-analysis of innovation and organizational size. *Organization Studies, 25*(3), 331-361.

Chu, C., & Smithson, S. (2003). Organizational structure and e-commerce: A structurational analysis. In *Proceedings of the 5th International Conference on Electronic Commerce* (pp. 205-212).

Cohen, W. M., & Levinthal, D. A. (1990). Absorptive capacity: A new perspective on learning and innovation. *Administrative Science Quarterly, 35,* 128-152.

D'Angelo, J., & Little, S. K. (1998). Successful Web pages: What are they and do they exist? *Information Technology & Libraries, 17*(2), 71-80.

Damanpour, F. (1996). Organizational complexity and innovation: Developing and testing multiple contingency models. *Management Science, 42,* 693-716.

Dibbern, J., Goles, T., Hirschheim, R., & Jayatilaka, B. (2004). Information systems outsourcing: A survey and analysis of the literature. *The Data Base for Advances in Information Systems, 35*(4), 6-102.

Dos Santos, B. L., & Peffers, K. (1995). Rewards to investors in innovative information technology applications: First movers and early followers in ATMs. *Organization Science, 6,* 241-259.

Eder, L. B., & Igbaria, M. (2001). Determinants of intranet diffusion and infusion. *Omega, 29,* 233-242.

Goo, J., Kishore, R., & Rao, H. R. (2000). A content-analytical longitudinal study of the drivers for information technology and systems outsourcing. In *Proceedings of the Twenty First International Conference on Information Systems* (pp. 601-611).

Gordon, J. R., & Gordon, S. R. (2000). Structuring the interaction between IT and business units, Prototypes for service delivery. *Information Systems Management, 17*(1), 7-16.

Grant, R. (2003). Canadian approaches to e-commerce implementation. *Canadian Journal of Administrative Sciences, 20*(1), 3-20.

Harris, S., & Katz, J. (1991). Firm size and the information technology investment intensity of life insurers. *MIS Quarterly, 15,* 333-352.

Henderson, A. D. (1999). Firm strategy and age dependence: A contingent view of the liabilities of newness, adolescence, and obsolescence. *Administrative Science Quarterly, 44,* 281-314.

Kern, T., & Willcocks, L. (2002). Exploring relationships in information technology outsourcing: The interaction approach. *European Journal of Information Systems, 11,* 3-19.

Kishore, R., Agrawal, M., & Rao, H. R. (2004). Determinants of sourcing during technology growth and maturity: An empirical study of e-commerce sourcing. *Journal of Management Information Systems, 21*(3), 47-82.

Kowtha, N. R., & Choon, T. W. I. (2001). Determinants of Website development: A study of electronic commerce in Singapore. *Information & Management, 39*(3), 227-242.

Lee, G., & Xia, W. (2006). Organizational size and IT innovation adoption: A meta-analysis. *Information & Management, 43*(8), 975-985.

Lee, J. N., Huynh, M. Q., Kwok, R. C., & Pi, S. (2003). IT outsourcing evolution-past, present and future. *Communications of the ACM, 46*(5), 84-87.

Loh, L., & Venkatraman, N. (1992). Determinants of information technology outsourcing: A cross sectional analysis. *Journal of Management Information Systems, 9*(1), 7-24.

McFarlan, W., & Nolan, R. (1995). How to manage an IT outsourcing alliance. *Sloan Management Review, 36*(2), 9-23.

Melbourne IT. (2005). *Website age and search engine rankings.* Retrieved January 13, 2007, from http://www.melbourneitcbs.com/news.php?article=9&title=Website%20age%20and%20search%20engine%20rankings&year=2005&month=12

Min, H., & Galle, W. P. (2001). Electronic commerce-based purchasing: A survey on the perceptual differences between large and small organizations. *International Journal of Logistics: Research and Applications, 4,* 79-95.

Minkoff, J. (2000). Outsourcing takes the worry out of the Web sites for financial services companies. *Web Finance, 4*(15), 9-10.

Sauer, C., & Willcocks, L. (2002). The evolution of the organizational architect. *MIT Sloan Management Review, 43*(3), 41-49.

Schaaf, J. (2004). *Offshore outsourcing in financial industry.* Retrieved January 13, 2007, from http://www.dbresearch.com/prod/dbr_internet_en-prod/prod0000000000180100.pdf

Sibley, K. (2001). Outsourcing Web-hosting. *Computing Canada, 27*(9), 7.

Sorensen, J. B., & Stuart, T. E. (2000). Aging, obsolescence, and organizational innovation. *Administrative Science Quarterly, 45,* 81-112.

Tas, J., & Sunder, S. (2004). Financial services business process outsourcing. *Communications of the ACM, 47*(5), 50-52.

Thornhill, S., & Amit, R. (2003). Learning about failure: Bankruptcy, firm age, and the resource-based view. *Organization Science, 14*(5), 497-509.

Vaughan, L., & Wu, G. (2004). Links to commercial Websites as a source of business information. *Scientometrics, 60*(3), 487-496.

Wang, S. (2000). Managing the organizational aspects of electronic commerce. *Human Systems Management, 19,* 49-59.

Web news you can use. (2003, January). *Best's Review, 103*(9), 80.

Yap, C. S. (1990). Distinguishing characteristics of organizations using computers. *Information & Management, 18,* 97-107.

This work was previously published in Journal of Electronic Commerce in Organizations, Vol. 5, Issue 4, edited by M. Khosrow-Pour, pp. 1-17, copyright 2007 by IGI Publishing, formerly known as Idea Group Publishing (an imprint of IGI Global).

Chapter XI
Business Process Outsourcing Modeling

Lai Xu
SAP Research, Switzerland

Paul de Vrieze
SAP Research, Switzerland

ABSTRACT

Organizations in the new millennium face relentless pressure to perform better, faster and cheaper, while maintaining high level of guaranteed results. To remain competitive, enterprises have to integrate their business processes with those of their customers, suppliers and business partners. Increasing collaboration is not only relevant within a global multi-national enterprise, but also considering the organization and its relationship to and business processes with its business partners. While standards and technologies make it possible for business partners to exchange information, collaborate and carry out business transaction in a pervasive Web environment, there is however very limited research activity on modeling business process outsourcing underlying semantics. In this chapter, we demonstrate that an in-house business process that has been gradually outsourced to third-parties and analyze how task delegations cause commitments between multiple business parties. Finally we provide process semantics for modeling multi-party business process outsourcing.

INTRODUCTION

Outsourcing has been a worldwide phenomenon for the past four decades (Gereffi & Sturgeon, 2004). Growth of outsourcing is driven by a number of business forces, such as, competition escalation, organizational reengineering, and new technology trends. Over the past decade, the number and quality of suppliers offering price-competitive and high-quality services has increase significant. It enables the organization to focus on its core competencies.

In addition, large organization sizes are no longer necessarily an advantage in production of products or services, and neither are small sizes. Quality, flexibility, agility and the ability to meet diverse consumer demands count for more (Drucker, 1992). Firms now respond to change by outsourcing when they face heightened competition pushes. Traditionally, after the part of business services is assigned, the initial organization can hardly monitor or get to control of the outsourced services. Even a minor change of service is not easy.

The advent of global digital networks, the Internet, the World Wide Web, and more recently Web services has drastically lowered the cost of coordination between firms and improved the possibilities for organizations and individuals to communicate in an effective and standard manner. New environments, newer technology and rapid technological change provide an avenue for reducing human and equipment resources that do not fit with a company's strategic direction, for meeting latest needs with up-to-date resources at competitive rates by outsourcing those business processes. Furthermore, the current technologies are also allow to get control of outsourced business processes.

Rather than outsourcing an entire business process to a single supplier, multi-souring using more than one supplier is used. A classic example is Alcatel. Alcatel has outsourced supply chain management and R&D functions to Wipro, and its SAP and ERP environment work to Infosys (Pinto & Harms, 2005).

Business process multi-outsourcing causes business collaboration. As business collaboration increases between different enterprises, the need for semantics also increases as a mediator between the structure and content of the different knowledge based. There will be a need, not just for semantics to mediate the structure and content, but also for the services themselves. Semantics of multi-party business collaboration has been recognized as a major problem for a long time, but relatively little fundamental research has been devoted it. From the semantic perspective, we model the way organizations co-operate in a multi-party involved situation. A high-level view of the collaboration is provided, in terms of the parties involved, the roles they perform and the way they're related, also in terms of business functions they fulfill and the interactions between those.

The Benefits of Multi-Party Business Collaboration Modeling

Outsourcing business processes is highly complex. They consist of several organizations interconnected through networks and working together using sophisticated computer applications. When trying to understand, reorganize or develop systems to support multi-party business collaborations one is confronted with that complexity. As in any modeling activity, modeling multi-party business collaboration can help to deal with this (Rechtin & Maier, 1997; Wolstenholme, 1990).

There are many possible reasons to create a model of multi-party business collaboration. The goal of multi-party business collaboration modeling may be:

- To understand the functioning of an existing multi-party business collaboration.
- To provide a starting point for analysis of requirements of design and for the redesign of an outsourced business process.
- To offer a starting point for the implementation of computer applications to support multi-party business collaboration.
- To serve as a basis for analysis, for example, answer ``what-if" question, to evaluate the responsibilities between involved parties, or simulate an inter-organizational business process before implementing it.

The benefits of using models to support these objectives, rather than a textual description, are as follows (Biemans et al., 2001; Booch et al., 1999):

- Models help us to visualize a system as it is or as we want it to be. it create a common frame of reference for those who have to understand a design, and facilitate the communication between clients, business analysts, designers and engineers.
- Models permit us to specify the structure or behavior of multi-party business collaboration by representing only their essentials and abstracting from what we consider irrelevant. Abstraction can be done in two ways: by abstracting from details or by abstracting from aspects.
- Models give us a template that guides us in constructing a system. Properties of models can be thus analyzed. This can be used to assess the expected performance of business collaboration, or check conformance to a set of business rules.
- Models document the decisions we have made, motivate changes or point alternatives.

In modeling it is definitely true that the larger and more complex the system, the more important modeling becomes. A business involving multi-party business collaboration is a complex system. To be able to model this system, we have to understand concepts and issues in multi-party business collaboration which will be discussed in the following sections.

In the rest of this chapter, we provide the definitions of outsourcing, business transactions and business collaborations in Section 2. The following section starts by elaborating how an in-house business process has been gradually outsourced by using a multi-party business collaboration case. Moreover, we explain the issues in multi-party business collaboration modeling. We furthermore define all concepts needed for modeling multi-party business collaborations. We first introduce our meta-model of multi-party business collaboration language, which defines the attributes and relationships of the modeling concepts. Then, multi-party collaboration language is given with a concrete graphical syntax. We also evaluate relate work in this area. The chapter concludes with a summary and directions for further research.

TERMINOLOGY

In this section, we will discuss terms like outsourcing, transaction, transaction properties, business transaction and business collaboration. Finally, we provide our definition of multi-party business collaborations.

Outsourcing is a generic term of farming out certain company activities or processes, often previously performed by company employees, to external contractors specializing in such activities or processes. It is used in most branches of industry and services worldwide.

Transactions are a fundamental concept in building reliable distributed applications. A transaction is a mechanism to insure all the participants in an application achieve a mutually agreed outcome. Traditionally, transactions have held the following properties collectively referred to as ACID (Haerder & Reuter, 1983):

- Atomicity: if successful, then all the operations happen, and if unsuccessful, then none of the operations happen.
- Consistency: the application performs valid state transitions at completion.
- Isolation: the effects of the operations are not shared outside the transaction until it completes successfully.
- Durability: once a transaction successfully completes, the changes survive failure.

According to the International Organization for Standardization (ISO), a *business transaction* is "a predefined set of activities or processes of organization to accomplish an explicitly shared business goal" (ISO/IEC, 1997). A business transaction may involve any number of participants, it may be instant or last for years, and it can have various degrees of complexity.

Following the ebXML Business Process Specification Schema (ebXML, 2001), the concepts of business transaction and business collaboration are defined as follows,

- A *business transaction* involves two parties, and is an atomic unit of work that can result in either a success or a failure.
- A *business collaboration* can involve any number of parties and is a combination of choreographed business transaction, defining the ordering and transition between them.

According above ebXML definitions of business transaction and collaboration. It implicates that collaboration is a number of two-party transactions. This assumption is not reasonable. For example, if there is a broadcast message or an activity benefits to multiple parties, this assumption cannot hold anymore.

In the next section we will analyze *multi-party business collaborations* that involve more than two autonomous parties that are coordinated and lead to the accomplishment of some result. Looking at such collaboration one cannot just see it as a number of two-party transactions.

OUTSOURCING AND MULTI-PARTY BUSINESS COLLABORATIONS

We provide a car insurance case for explaining how a car insurance business is gradually outsourced and in which collaborations are involved afterward. This case is an abstract version of a car insurance scenario involving AGF Irish Life Holdings Plc. It was taken from the CrossFlow project (Browne & Kellett, 1999).

Initially, a car insurance company probably only involves a group of garages to assess car damages and to repair damaged cars for an insurant who has bought car insurance from the car insurance company. The insurance company deals with the rest of the issues. More precisely, after the occurrence of car damage, a process starts, including many interactions among the insurant, a garage and the insurance company (see Figure 1(a)).

After some time, the insurance company decides to outsource its phone service to a call center. The business process is consequently changed (along the line of Figure 1(b)). The call center is responsible for registering the insurant information, suggesting an appropriate garage (most time a close by garage is assigned) and notifying the insurance company about the insurant's claim. Except the phone service, the insurance company still needs to handle the rest of services for the insurant.

Continuing it could be an alternative to outsource the inspection of damaged vehicles to an association of assessors. In this business model (see Figure 1(c)), the assessors conduct the physical inspections of damaged vehicles and agree upon repair figures with the garages. After the call center, the garages and the assessors finish their obligations, the insurance company performs the rest services.

Due to the increasing amount of different insurance businesses, the insurance company might finally decide to outsource the daily service to a day to day handling company. The day to day handling company coordinates and manages the operation on a day-to-day level on behalf of the insurance company (see Figure 1(d)). The detailed obligations of the day to day handling company are provided in Figure 2. After receiving the forward claim from the insurance company, the day to day handling company will agree upon repair costs

Figure 1. Car insurance business processes

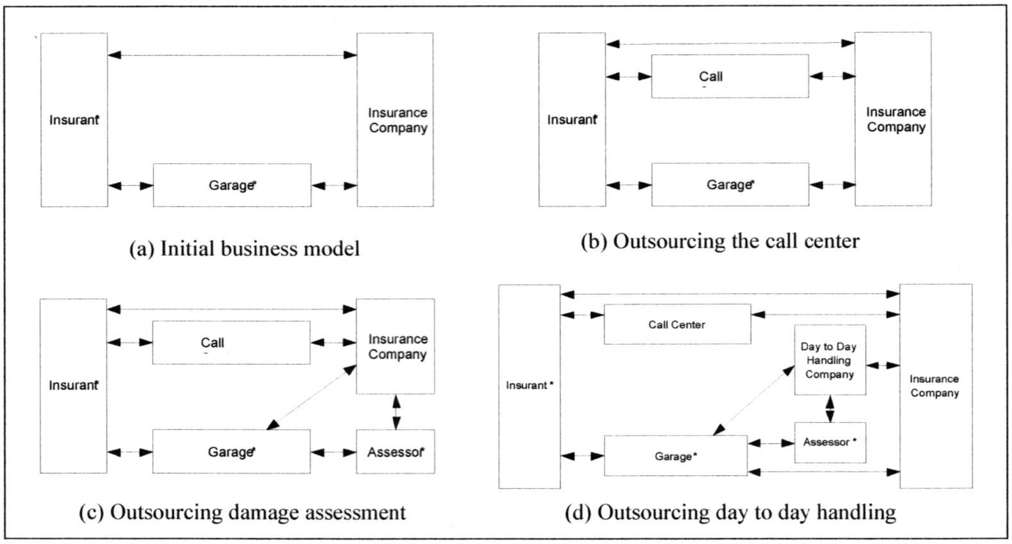

Figure 2. The process diagram of car insurance case

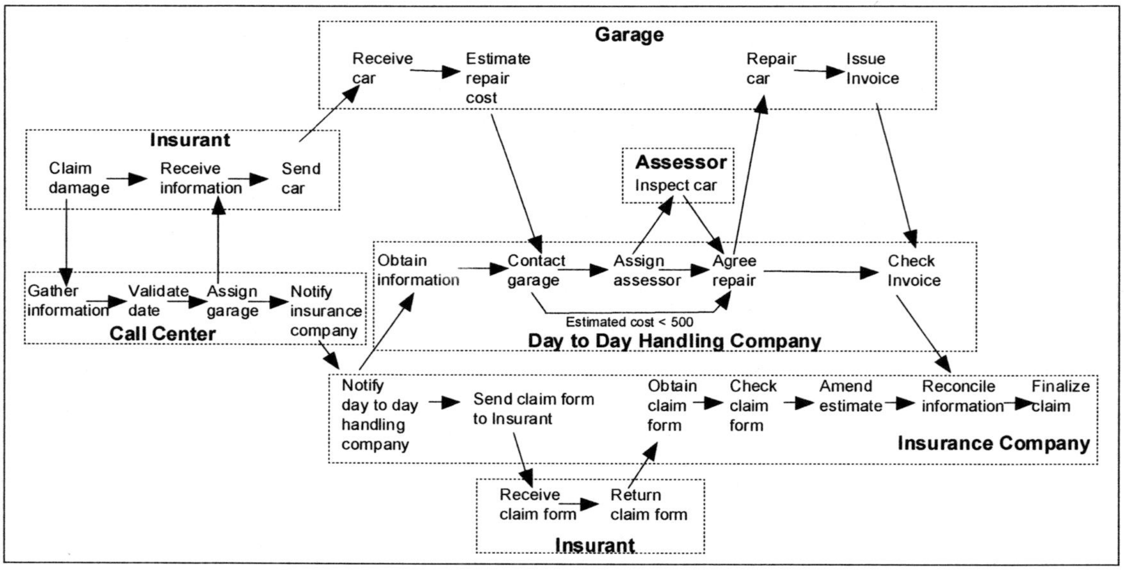

if an assessor is not required for small damages; otherwise, an assessor will be assigned. After finishing repairs, the garage will issue an invoice to the day to day handling company, which in turn will check the invoice against the original estimate. The day to day handling company returns all invoices to the insurance company monthly. As a result the workload of the insurance company is significantly reduced.

Changes of the business models do not necessarily go through from Figure 1 (a) to (b), then from (b) to (c) and finally from (c) to (d). Changes can happen, for example, directly from (a) to (d). Figure 1 demonstrates that how a business process is collaborated by more business parties in different circumstances. It also shows some essential characters of multi-party collaborations. One of them is that it is critical to understand *when* and *who* did, is doing or will do *what* in a multiple parties involved business process.

ISSUES IN MULTI-PARTY BUSINESS COLLABORATION MODELING

A distinction between a bilateral business process and multi-party business collaboration is the way of interactions. In a multi-party collaboration, many business activities which involve different parties can be performed in parallel. The order of interactions is no longer sequential. Therefore to use a full ordering to specify the collaboration (many bilateral collaborations are specified in this way) is not suitable for specifying multi-party collaborations.

In addition, because different parties can operate different activities at the same time, it is difficult to find all violators responsible for even an unsatisfied performance or a mis-performance. Therefore, modeling multi-party business collaborations is different from modeling bilateral collaborations. Because there are in total only two parties involved in a collaboration, in modeling a bilateral collaboration it is not an important issue to identify who does not do what. In a multi-party collaboration, it is however an important concern.

There are many potential violations in the case as outlined in (Xu & Jeusfeld, 2004; Xu et al., 2005). For example, after sending invoices to the day to day handling company; the garage does not get money back from the insurance company. It could be caused by

- The day to day handling company, because the day to day handling company did not forward the invoices to the insurance company (see Figure 3 mark 1).

Figure 3. The violation of car insurance case

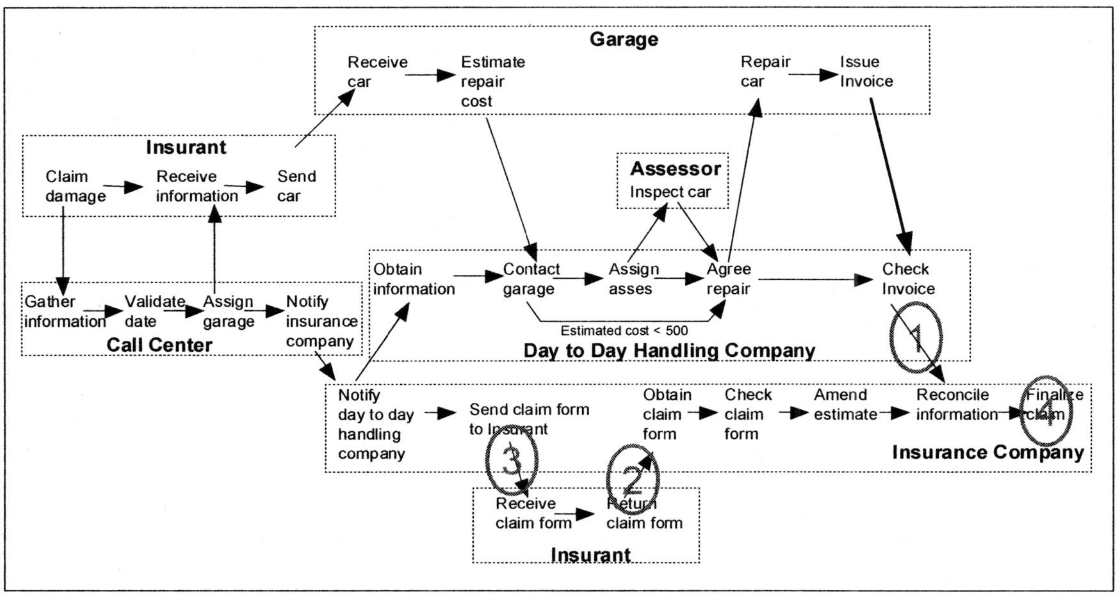

Figure 4. Metamodel for multi-party collaboration

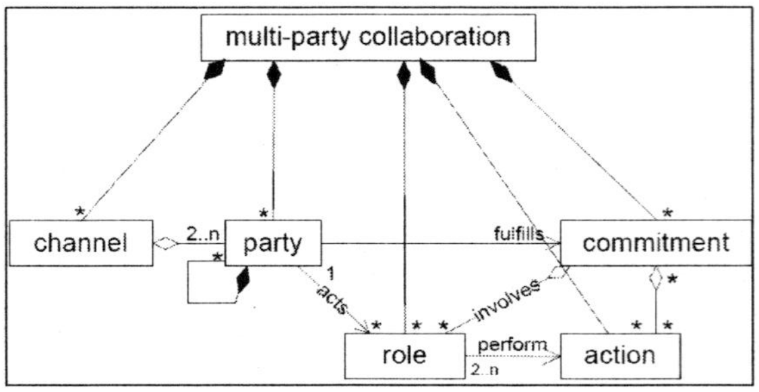

- The insurant, because the insurant did not return the completed claim form to the insurance company (see Figure 3 mark 2).
- The insurance company, because the insurance company forgot to send the claim form to the insurant (see Figure 3 mark 3) or simply because the insurance company did not pay the garage in time (see Figure 3 mark 4).
- Some combinations of the above.

Therefore a model of parties' responsibilities is needed. In multi-party business collaboration, one contract violation can be caused by more than one contractual party, which motivates us to model multi-party business collaboration from different perspectives.

CONCEPTS FOR MODELING MULTI-PARTY BUSINESS COLLABORATION

Many business applications can involve multi-party business collaboration. For example supply chains, electronic markets, online auctions, virtual enterprises and multi-supplier business process outsource. The central concept of modeling multi-party business collaboration is that multi-party business collaboration is not to model a number of bilateral business collaborations. In some simple cases, a chain relationship between multiple parties for example, it is possible to break down multi-party business collaboration into a number of bilateral business transactions. However, in complicated multi-party collaborations, this conversion results in information of relations being lost or hidden. Consequently this option to split the multi-party collaborations up into several bilateral transactions won't work. Especially when something is going wrong during automation of multi-party business collaboration, to find all violators is a big challenge.

During a bilateral collaboration execution process it is easier to discover the responsible party for an existing violation. In multi-party business collaboration, an existing violation can have its cause in a set of directly or indirectly involved parties (some examples are provided from the previous section). This thus raises the issue of finding all responsible parties for an unsatisfied or mis-performance in the execution of multi-party business collaboration. Those concepts should be reflected to our modeling of multi-party business collaborations.

The use of modeling has a rich history in all the engineering disciplines. One of four basic principles of modeling is that no single model is sufficient (Booch et al., 1999). Every nontrivial system is best approached through a small set of nearly independent models. Following this basic principle, we distinguish three aspects that are relevant for modeling multi-party business collaboration.

- In terms of its structure: which are the parties involved and how are they interconnected?
- In terms of the commitments associated with those parties: which responsibility do they commit to each other and which roles may the parties play within a commitment?
- And in terms of its processes: what actions are performed by which parties after

which properties are satisfied according to per-defined rules and which output can be expected, etc.

Parties and Channels

In order to survive, companies are forced to constantly revise their business processes. Due to decision of multi-supplier business process outsourcing, involved parties and their interconnections are modeled as parties and channels. Depending on the chosen scope of the model, *parties* may represent individual people, organizational units, such as departments, or an entire organization. Furthermore, A *party* represents an active organizational entity. Parties can be assigned a name to distinguish them.

Parties may be connected by *channels* through which they interact. For example, parties may be linked by Internet, by telephone or by truck. Usually channels can connect two parties, but multi-access channels can also be envisioned, for example a broadcast channel. Channels can further specified as bi-directional, uni-directional channels. A *channel* thus represents an interconnection between parties for the exchange of objects or information. Channels may be named by the medium (e.g. Internet, Post, EDI, etc.)

Commitments and Roles

To model responsibilities between multi-parties, we use speech act theory and make an extension. Applying those theories we will provide our definition of commitments and roles. To do that we first explain speech act theory and the used extension.

Part of Austin's work on speech act theory (Austin, 1975), is the observation that utterances are not implied propositions that are true or false, but attempts on the part of the speaker that succeed or fail. Perfomatives, acts, or actions are organized as speech acts and non-speech acts. An individual speech act is either a *solicit*, which explains an attempt to achieve mutual belief with the addressee that the sender wants the addressee to perform an act relative to the sender's wanting it done, or an *assert*, which expresses an attempt to achieve mutual belief with the addressee that the asserted statement is true.

The model of speech acts and repartee developed by Longacre recognizes two kinds of relations among successive utterances: replay and resolution in (Longacre, 1976) and another two kinds of relations: resolves and completes by Van Dyke Parunakin in (Van Dyke Parunak, 1996). In the model of speech acts and repartee, every utterance in a conversation except for the first must "respond", "reply", "resolve" or "complete" to another, otherwise there would be no conversation. Analyzing relations between utterances some characters can be split (Dooley, 1976).

In the business process domain physical actions and messages convey information between participants. An initial proposal can be triggered by a certain action and later on be finished by another action. During multi-party business collaboration, several proposals are initiated by different business parties. Each of them is followed and eventually finished by some actions. Actions are thus sorted into different commitments.

A *commitment* is a guarantee by one party towards another party that some action sequences provided that some "trigger", "involve", or "finish" action happens and all involved parties fulfill their side of the transactions (Xu & Jeusfeld, 2003; Xu, 2004; Xu & Jeusfeld, 2004). To finish a commitment, more than one party must finish the relevant actions. A commitment is associated with one particular party. This means that the fulfillment of a single commitment (from the point of view of the receiver) may involve multiple parties.

From this point of view, the concept of our commitment is different from the definition of a commitment in papers (Verdicchio & Colombetti, 2002; Ervin, 2002), where a commitment only refers to two parties, a debtor and a creditor (Verdicchio & Colombetti, 2002), or a vendor and customer (Ervin, 2002). The notion of commitment in this chapter is not related to beliefs, desires, or intentions. In the research of Cohen and Levesque (1995), commitments are related to establishing common beliefs about a certain state of the world.

All parties involving multi-party business collaboration fulfill different roles in different commitments. One role cannot be part of another role. However, it is possible for an actor to fulfill multiple roles in business collaboration. Each role is specified by a unique name. We will provide some examples, such as how to identify commitments, or which party plays which role.

Interaction and Properties of Actions

Multi-party interaction models are composed of actions, commitments, properties of party and connectors. An action is the atomic unit of behavior. The orders between actions are causal, conjunctive "splits", disjunctive "splits", conjunctive "joins" and disjunctive "joins".

Each party has a set of predetermined properties. The party's properties consist of three parts which are inputs, outputs and rules. The inputs and outputs of properties are domain related. The input property specifies a list of the domain elements, which will be formulated as preconditions. The rules property is specified as the set of rules using predicate logic. The rules property provides logic formulas to specify the preconditions of fulfilling actions and also some domain elements as a consequence of performing the actions. The output property specifies those domain objects which are the results of the executing action. When the party attempts to execute an action, it first checks whether the input of the property is satisfied, and subsequently generates the output of the property according the rules.

METAMODEL OF MULTI-PARTY BUSINESS COLLABORATION MODELING LANGUAGE (MBCML)

In this section, we define the metamodel for MBCML. A concrete syntax is proposed in the next section. MBCML is used to define multi-party business collaboration models (MBCMs). An MBCM defines the cooperation of a number of organizations to involve a common business process. In order to capture all relevant aspects of collaboration. A variety of diagrams can be used, each offering a different view on the model. We distinguish three different diagram types, one for each conceptual domain which has been defined. The notation used for representing the metamodel of MBCM is the Unified Modeling Language (UML) (Booch et al., 1999).

An overview of the basic modeling concepts and their relationships is given as a metamodel in Figure 4. A multi-party collaboration consists of role, party, channel, commitment and actions. Parties perform different roles in a commitment and fulfill different commitments. The roles perform actions. A channel connects two or more parties. A commitment aggregates many actions.

Multi-Party Collaboration Structure Metamodel

The parties involved and channels connected of all parties of a business collaboration are interrelated in Figure 5. How the parties are linked

Figure 5. Metamodel for multi-party collaboration structure

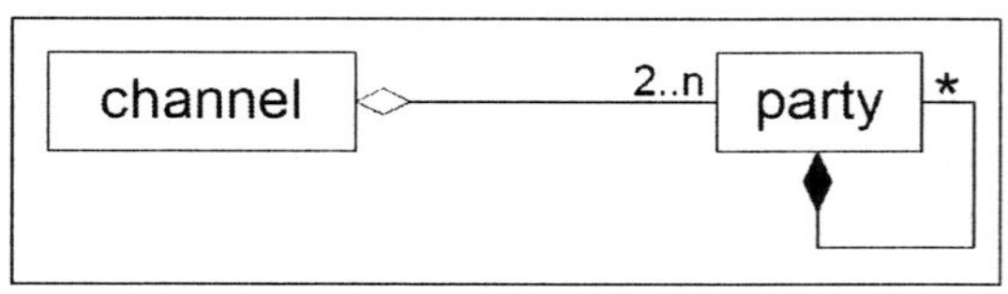

by the channels is presented in a collaboration structure model. A party may contain other parties. A channel connects two or more parties, and as an option, attributes like medium and direction can be indicated.

Multi-Party Collaboration Commitment Metamodel

Commitments and roles construct a commitment model. All concepts involved in the commitment model are roles, actions, commitments, commitment segments and connectors. The relationship between those concepts are provided in Figure 6.

A party guarantees another party to perform a commitment to another party. A party performs different roles in different commitments. A commitment is a set of actions and is made up of one or more commitment segments. An action contains zero or more connectors that interconnect these commitment segments to make up the commitment. A role (roles) performs (perform) an action within a commitment.

The connectors are used to introduce relationships between commitments or commitment segments. There are four notations for specifying the connectors. The connectors can be specialized to "and-join" connector, "or-join" connector, "and-split" connector and "or-split" connector. Commitments can be linked by causality, or-split, and-split, or-join, and and-join as Figure 7. Besides, the connectors may contain other connectors to specify more complex relationships. The causality relation is represented by an *arrow* from one node to another node. The "or-split" relation is

Figure 6. Metamodel for multi-party collaboration commitment

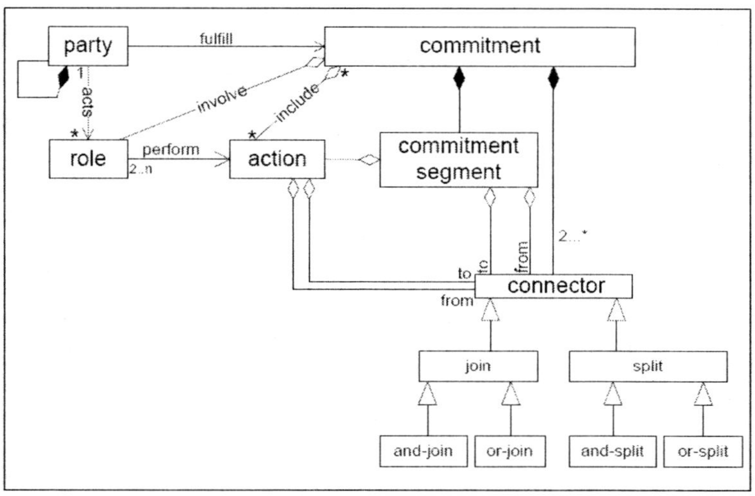

Figure 7. Connector representation

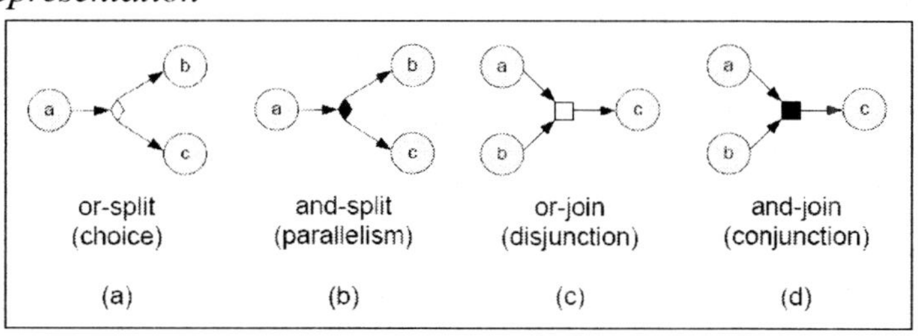

represented by an *empty-diamond*, which means that a commitment from a role triggers exactly one of multiple commitments from other roles (see Figure 7(a)). The ``and-split'' relation is expressed by a *solid-diamond*, which means that a commitment from a role triggers other multiple commitments (see Figure 7 (b)). The "or-join" relation is denoted by an *empty-box*, which means that one of multiple commitments triggers another commitment (see Figure 7(c)). The "and-join" relation is shown by a *solid-box*, which means that multiple commitments together trigger a commitment (see Figure 7(d)).

A multi-party business collaboration consists of a set of commitments. A collaborating party can thus be involved in different commitments playing different roles and an action may be involved in more than one commitment.

Multi-Party Collaboration Interaction Metamodel

The part of the metamodel concerning interactions is refined in Figure 8. Interaction model consists of actions, connectors, parties, properties of parties. The property of a party includes inputs and rules and outputs.

Each party has a set of per-determined properties, namely: inputs, outputs and rules. After the input property of a party is satisfied, the role of the party performs the action(s) and the result of actions will provide some output. Besides, the actions can be also linked by the connectors which are provided in Figure 7. Those connectors represent the occurrence relationship of the actions.

MULTI-PARTY COLLABORATION MODELING LANGUAGE

In the business domain, we need to provide detailed and precise descriptions of multi-party business collaborations. In order to represent construct in the business domain, a language for modeling multi-party collaborations should be sufficiently expressive to represent a multi-party collaboration in terms of its structure, commitments and interactions. We separate views to represent a structural model, a commitment model and a interaction model in the following sections respectively.

Figure 8. Metamodel for multi-party collaboration interaction

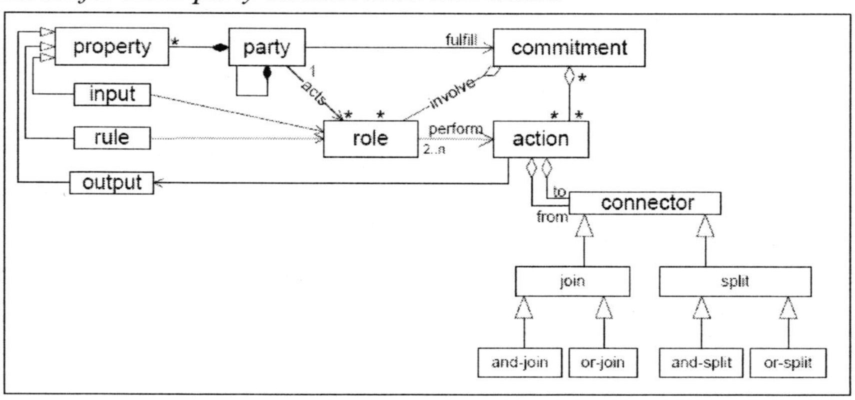

Collaboration Structure Model

Collaborated parties involved and channels in a business process are modeled in collaboration structure model. Figure 9 shows collaboration structure model for the six parties involved care insurance case. It depicts how the insurance company and its co-operators are interconnected. It is an important model for future mapping to a specific implementation suits/toolkit.

For example, the insurance company and its insurant can be connected by internet such as, web and email; by post office so they can send letters to each other; by telephone network like they can use fax or phone calls to contact each other, or by a bank system which means they can transfer money. It is not always necessary to have all communication channels. It is up to the customer requirements. However, for each communication channel, it does require different implementation.

Modeling collaboration structure is useful to identify the parties involved in business collaboration. It also provides a further step to clarify the responsibilities of parties.

Commitment Model

To model commitments between multiple parties, we use concepts of commitments. The approach of how to determine the commitments in business collaboration which have introduced in Section *Commitments and Roles*.

We use the six parties involved in the car insurance case (see Figure 2) to explain how to determine the commitments. For example an insurant phones a call center for a claim. Action A_phoneClaim triggered a conversation between the insurant and the call center to deal with the claim. Actions A_sendInfo and A_assignGarage follow, and action A_notifyClaim finishes the conversation. Actions A_phoneClaim, A_sendInfo, A_assignGarage and A_notifyClaim are sorted within a commitment which records obligations of the call center to deal with the insurant claim. Action A_phoneClaim is a trigger of a conversation; actions A_sendInfo and A_assignGarage are the actions as "involved"; and action A_notifyClaim is an action to "finish" the conversation.

Furthermore, six commitments of the care insurance case are identified according to the

Figure 9. Collaboration structure model

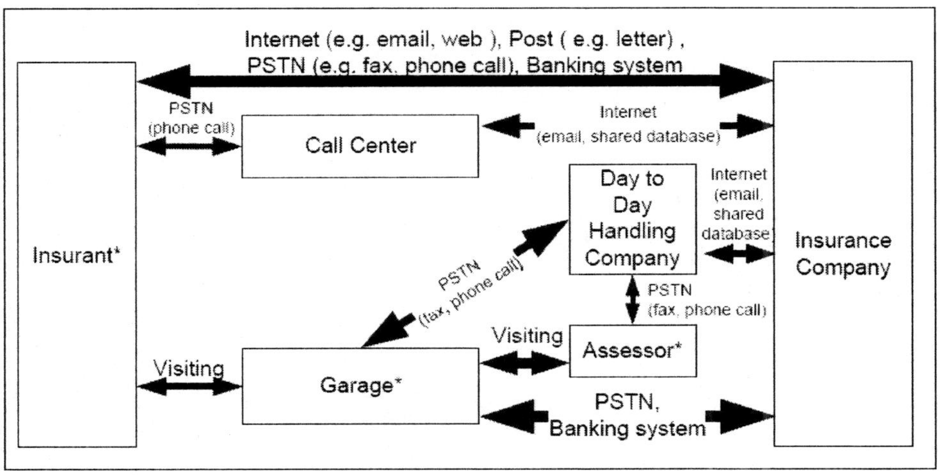

Table 1. Commitments, actions, and action abbreviations

Commitment	Classification of Actions and Commitments			Labels
	Trigger	Involved	Finish	
C_phoneService (PS)	A_phoneClaim			PS.1
		A_sendInfo		PS.2
		A_assignGarage		PS.3
			A_nitifyClaim	PS.4, CF.1, DS.1
C_repairService (RS)	A_sendCar			RS.1
		A_estimateRepairCost		RS.2
	A_agreeRepairCar			RS.3, DS.7
			A_repairCar	RS.4, DS.8
C_claimForm (CF)	A_notifyClaim			CF.1, PS.4
		A_sendClaimForm		CF.2
			A_returnClaimForm	CF.3, PR.2
C_dailyService (DS)	A_notifyClaim			DS.1, PS.4, CF.1
		A_forwardClaim		DS.2
		A_contactGarage		DS.3
		A_sendRepairCost		DS.4
		A_assignAssessor		DS.5, IC.1
		A_sendNewRepairCost		DS.6, IC.3
			A_agreeRepairCar	DS.7, RS.3
	A_repairCar			DS.8, RS.4
		A_sendInvoices		DS.9
			A_forwardInvoice	DS.10, PR.1
C_inspectCar (IC)	A_assignAssessor			IC.1, DS.4
		A_inspectCar		IC.2
			A_sendNewRepariCost	IC.3, DS.5
C_payRepairCost (PR)	A_forwardInvoices			PR.1, DS.10
	A_returnClaimForm			PR.2, CF.3
			A_payRepairCost	PR.3

Box 1. Six commitments of Table 6

C_phoneSercie	=	{(A_phoneClaim, *tr*), (A_sendInfo, *in*), (A_assignGarage, *in*), (A_notifyClaim,*fi*)}
C_repairService	=	{(A_sendCar, *tr*), (A_estimateRepariCost, *in*), (A_agreeRepairCar, *tr*), (A_reparicar, *fi*)}
C_claimForm		{(A_notifyClaim, *tr*), (A_sendClaimForm, *in*), (A_returnClaimForm, *fi*)}
C_dailyService	=	{(A_notifyClaim, *tr*), (A_forwardClaim, *in*), (A_contactGarage, *in*), (A_sendRepairCost, *in*), (A_assignAssessor, *in*), (A_sendNewRepairCost, *in*), (A_agreeRepairCar, *fi*), (A_repairCar, *tr*), (A_ sendInvoices, *in*), (A_forwardInvoices, *fi*)}
C_inspectCar	=	{(A_assignAssessor, *tr*), (A_inspectCar, *in*), (A_sendNewRepairCost, *fi*)}
C_payRepairCost	=	{(A_forwardInvoices, *tr*), (A_returnClaimForm, *tr*), (A_payRepairCost, *fi*)}

Figure 10. Example commitments in a multi-party collaboration model

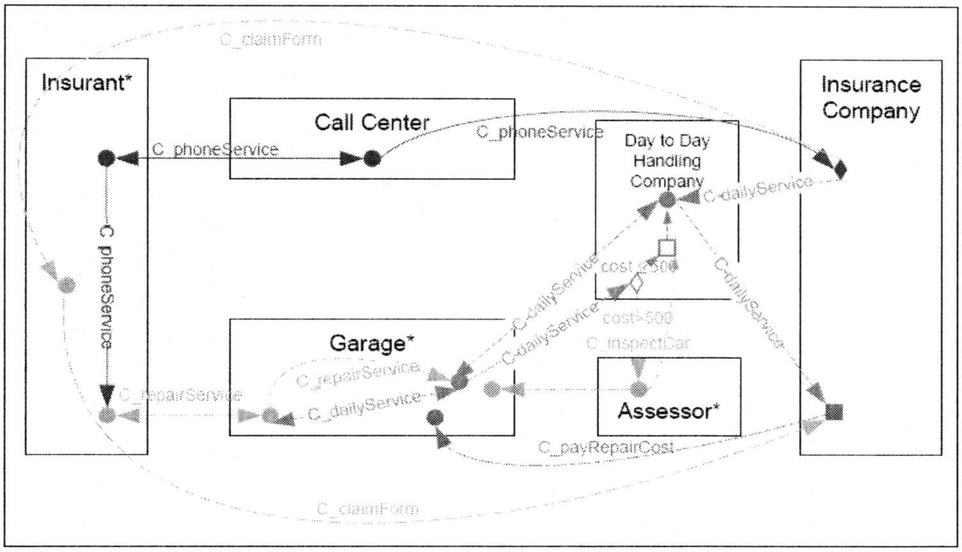

theory introduced in Section *Commitments and Roles*.

According to Table 1. There are six commitments. They are simplified in Box 1.

In commitment C_dailyService, actions A_agreeRepairCar and A_forwardInvoice are both marked as "finished". Action A_agreeRepairCar finishes a proposal by action A_notifyClaim and action A_forwardInvoice finishes a proposal by action A_sendInvoice.

It is difficult to represent commitments graphically. In our commitment model, a party is represented as a rectangle with a name. A node denotes a role which should stay in a rectangle. A commitment is indicated by a set of nodes (or commitment connectors) and a set of arrows.

Figure 10 depicts the six parties and six commitments of the case in Figure 9. For example, in party "insurance company", the solid-diamond connects commitments C_phoneService, C_claimForm and C_dailyService. It means that after commitment C_phoneService is fulfilled, both commitments C_claimForm and C_dailyService are triggered. A solid-box is also in party "insurance company", it connects commitments C_dailyService, C_claimForm and C_payRepairCost. It means that commitment C_payRepairCost will be performed after commitments C_dailyService and C_claimForm.

In the commitment model, we present the position of each commitment in terms of which parties and roles are involved, and which com-

Figure 11. Examples of actions and their parameters

CF2	Input	Records2
	Rule	Records2 → CF2; CF2 → ClaimForm
	Output	ClaimForm
DS2	Input	Records2
	Rule	Records2 → DS2; DS2 → Records3
	Output	Records3

mitments are triggered, chose and paralleled by other commitments. In the commitment model, we provide an overview of each party's responsibilities. This is very important for both the business side and the IT side as it helps creating a common understanding. In the next section, the behavior of the parties is modeled.

Modeling Behaviors of the Parties

In collaboration interaction modeling, behavior is modeled as inter- or intra-organizational business processes. The vertical dimension is the time axis; time proceeds down the page. Each party is represented by a vertical column. An action is the atomic unit of behavior. The causal ordering between actions is modeled by conjunctive and disconjunctive "splits" and "joins".

Each party's behavior is determined by three parameters as found from the business collaboration. The inputs and outputs of a party are domain related. The rules of a party in our model are specified using predicate logic. The input parameter specifies the actions that this party expects to be involved in as object, while the output parameter specifies results of the action. When a party attempts to execute an action, it first checks whether the current input can trigger this action and subsequently generates the output which may be checked against the possible output.

In Figure 12, an action is noted as a table-box (see Figure 11), where the first column shows the

Figure 12. Interactions between parties

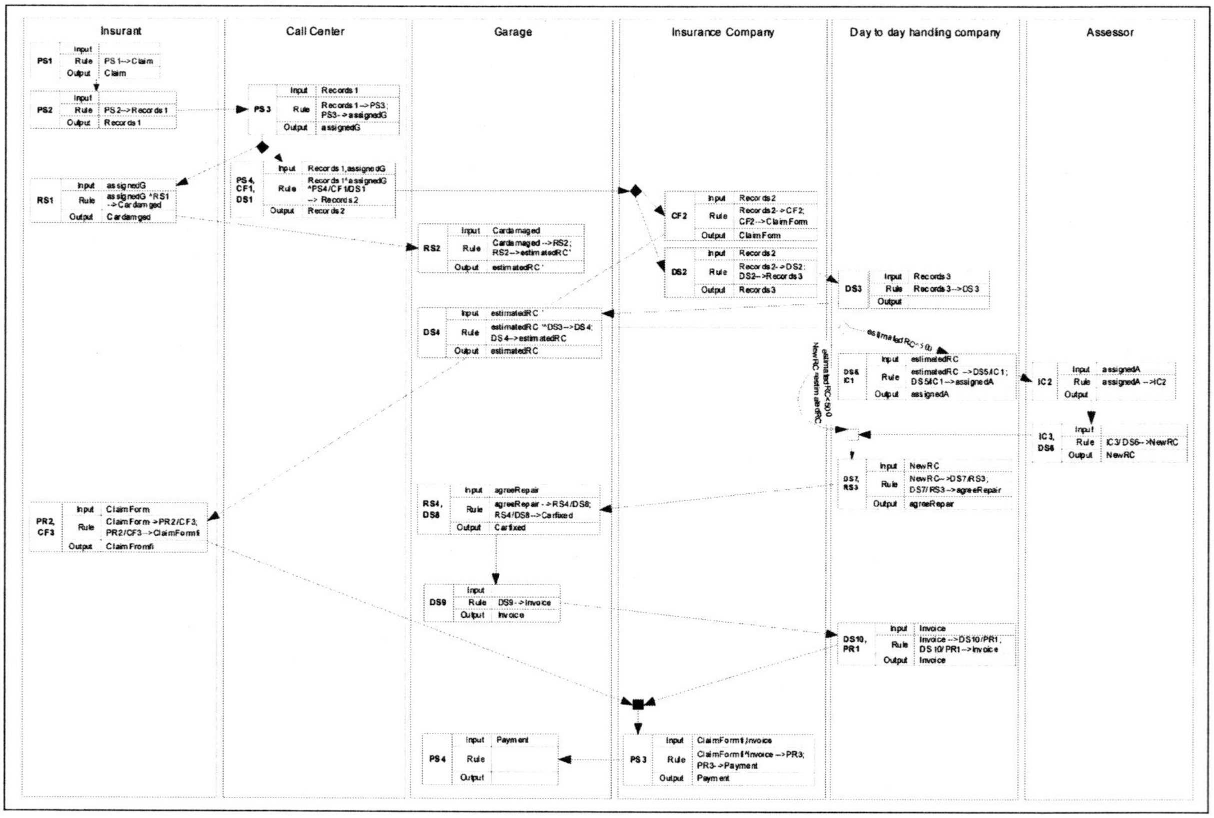

action label which makes it possible to determine the commitment from this action label by looking it up in Table 1; the rest column shows the parameters involved in this action.

The diagram includes a multi-step interaction between participants. It clearly shows which parties will communicate with other parties for which matters. From the insurant's perspective, he only has contact with the call center, the assigned garage and the insurance company. From the insurance company's view, it receives and forwards the claim to the day to day handling company, sends the claim form to the policyholder, and finally pays the repair costs to the garage.

Each party's parameters are also included in the diagram. According to the party properties, each party can determine which actions should or may occur. For example (see Figure 11) after having received an input from the party property "Records2", the insurance company will perform actions A_sendClaimForm (as *CF2*) and A_forwardClaim (as *DS2*) according to rules "Records2 → CF_2" and "Records2 → DS_2" respectively that are joined by "and-join" connector. After finishing action A_sendClaimForm (as *CF2*), "Clam from" is sent. After performing action A_forwardClaim, "Records3" is recorded.

As time passes (from top to down) and the parties' parameters get satisfied, each participant takes actions and the business process moves forward. A complex multi-party business process is divided into multiple commitments. Furthermore, business process steps are represented as the actions exchanged between the parties.

In this section, we presented multi-party business collaborations from three aspects. In the collaboration structure model, we provide a view on the interconnections of the business parties. Different connections can determine different ways to collaborate. In the commitment model, the responsibilities of all involved parties are presented. Finally, the behavior model provides more details of commitment fulfillment.

RELATED WORK

Much work is available concerning representation of computer processes. Processes for computer systems are commonly represented using modeling languages such as flow charts, data flow diagrams, state transition diagrams (which define finite state machines, push down machines, or even Turing machines), Petri Nets, and specialization.

A flow chart (Böhm & Jacopini, 1966) represents a process as a series of steps, with arrows between them, which represents an order in which the steps are to be performed. Some of the steps are decision points, so depending on the circumstances, different sets of steps might be performed. A data flow diagram is similar but represents how modules of a system are interconnected to perform the steps of a process but focuses on the ordering relationships imposed by the fact that data produced by some modules is used by other modules.

A state transition diagram represents a process in terms of the possible states of the system. The steps taken in the process are the transitions that move the system from one state to another. The most powerful representation which included a state transition diagram is a Turing machine, which can be used to describe any computer executing any computer program written in any computer programming language. A Petri net is similar to a finite state machine, but allows multiple states to be marked simultaneously. Transitions between states may be synchronized, since multiple states have to be marked at the same time for a particular transition to occur.

There are few works concerning multi-party business collaborations. We discuss the limitations of UML and Petri Nets for multi-party business collaboration modeling, as well as other models such as ebXML BPSS, web services choreography and SAP C-Business Scenarios.

UML, primarily designed as a language for software design, has been used in enterprise and business process modeling (Eriksson & Penker, 2000; Jacobson et al., 1995; Marshall, 1999). According to (Steen et al., 2002), however, the UML is not suitable for modeling business. The UML does not well support all the concepts needed for business collaborations. Modeling business collaborations is mainly concerned with what happens at the business level and how it is organized. First, the UML does not support expressing responsibilities. In the business world, parties permit the commitments to each other to execute a business activity. In our approach, the commitment model represents collaborations between business parties and provides the relations of the commitments. Second, for business party behavior, business processes are normally not confined to single actions. Therefore, state diagrams (also for Petri Net) are not really useful here. Most business collaborators do not reason about processes in terms of states but rather in terms of the activities performed and results produced. Although UML can be extended with stereotypes and profiles, the stereotyping mechanism just makes it possible to introduce new subtypes of existing concepts and profiles cannot introduce new concepts either (Henderson-Sellers, 2001).

Using the Petri Nets to specify a multi-party business collaboration process, the amount of states of the Petri Net can be significantly increased. Especially, because the multi-party business collaboration process focuses on when and who did, is doing or will do what. A Petri Net representation can be too trivial, even by using state-based workflow patterns (van der Aalst et al., 2003) because of a big amount of possible combinations of multi-party's behavior.

Two models for ebXML BPSS multi-party collaboration and web services choreography are presented in (Dubray, 2002; Webber, 2004) respectively. Other research (Haugen, 2002) on multi-party collaboration tries to break down a multi-party collaboration into a number of bilateral relations. A principle cause behind this is that current e-commerce environments only support bilateral executions. In some simple cases, the approach to support multi-party collaboration execution in current e-commerce environments is to assume the whole business process runs correctly according to a number of bilateral relations. However, in complicated multi-party collaborations this conversion results in information of relations being lost or hidden. Consequently this option to split the multi-party collaborations up into several two-party relations will not work for these complex multi-party collaborations (Dubray, 2002; Haugen, 2002).

SAP's collaborative business scenarios describe inter-enterprise business processes from three different perspectives (SAP, 2000), namely business view, interaction view and component view. The purpose of the business view is showing the business advantages of implementing a collaborative business scenario. Business relations per se are out of the scope of our research through. The interaction view describes the process design and detailed dependency relationship between the different activities and responsibilities of the participants. It is too simple to describe the relationship like the action relations with conjunctive and disconjunctive "splits" and "joins". The component view describes the logical application components needed to support the business process. Different channels in a collaboration structure model can determine different ways to implement a multi-party collaboration. Commitment model and interaction model provide enough details of interactions between multi-parties. Those three collaboration models can easily map into a component level model by using specifically software implementation packages.

CONCLUSION

We have looked at a multiple supplier business process outsourcing case. In a business process outsourcing case, the outsourcing initiator should be able to get control of the whole business process and its co-operators should also be able monitor the business process.

Moreover, in the modern business world, we see that explicit structural collaboration between organizations is becoming more and more important. This is reflected in the emergence of tightly-coupled supply chains, the service outsourcing paradigm, complex co-makerships, etceteras. Collaboration is not limited by geographical proximity, but is of an increasingly international character. As a result explicit multi-party business collaboration is becoming global. The need for a multi-party collaboration model for a business process is thus becoming evident. Our modeling approach can be applied in those cases.

Nevertheless most of the past initiatives have addressed only partial aspects of the problem, failing to understand and properly support the various business entities and their inter-relationships in complex and fast evolving business environments. In this chapter, we have present multi-party business collaboration models from three perspectives for supporting monitoring multi-party business process. In the collaboration structure model, we provide a view of how business parties are linked. Different links can determine different ways of collaboration. In the commitment model, the responsibilities of all involved parties are presented. Finally, the behavior model provides details of commitment fulfillment. Further research has to map our multi-party business collaboration model to specific implementations like SAP or Baan' ERP systems. This would allow the semantics of the web of collaborating parties to be validated. This chapter introduced the approach and current development towards the stated goals.

ACKNOWLEDGMENT

Part of work has been performed at the CSIRO ICT Centre, Australia.

REFERENCES

Austin, J. L. (1975). *How to do things with words*. Oxford University Press, 2 edition.

Biemans, F., Lankhorst, M., Teeuw, W., and van de Wetering, R. (2001). Dealing with the complexity of business systesm architecting. *System Engineering*, 4(2).

Böhm, C. and Jacopini, G. 1966. Flow diagrams, turing machines and languages with only two formation rules. Commun. ACM 9, 5 (May. 1966), 366-371. DOI= http://doi.acm.org/10.1145/355592.365646

Booch, G., Rumbaugh, J., and Jacobson, I. (1999). *The Unified Modeling Language User Guide*. AddisonWesley, Inc.

Browne, S. and Kellett, M. (1999). Insurance scenario description. Technical Report Cross-Flow project deliverable: D1.a, CrossFlow consortium.

Cohen, P. R. and Levesque, H. J. (1995). Communicative actions for artificial agents. In Lesser,V. and Gasser, L., editors, *Proceedings of the First International Conference on Multi-Agent Systems*, pages 65–72, San Francisco, CA, USA. The MIT Press: Cambridge, MA, USA.

Dooley, R. (1976). *Repartee as a Graph*. Appendix B in [Longacre, 1976].

Drucker, P. (1992). The new society of organizations. *Harvard Business Review*.

Dubray, J.-J. (2002). A new model for ebxml bpss multi-party collaborations and web services choreography. http://www.ebpml.org/ebpml.doc.

ebXML (2001). Uncefact and oasis, ebxml business process specification schema v1.01.

Eriksson, H.-E. and Penker, M. (2000). *Business Modeling with UML: Business Patterns at Work*. John Wiley & Sons.

Ervin, R. (2002). Chains of commitment software architecture. *ACM SIGecom Exchanges*, 3(1).

Gary Gereffi and Timothy J. Sturgeon (2004). Globalization, employment and economic development. *Sloan Workshop Series in Industry Studies Rockport Massachusetts*, June 14-16, 2004.

Haerder, T. and Reuter, A. (1983). Principles of transaction-oriented database recovery. *ACM Computing Surveys*, 15(4):287–317.

Haugen, B. (2002). Multi-party electronic business transactions. http://www.supplychainlinks. com/MultiPartyBusinessTransactions.PDF.

Henderson-Sellers, B. (2001). Some problems with the uml v1.3 metamodel. In *the 34th Annual Hawaii International Conference on Systems Sciences (HICSS-34).*

ISO/IEC (1997). 14662, information technologies-open-edi reference model.

Jacobson, I., Ericsson, M., and Jacobson, A. (1995). *The object advantage: business process reengineering with object technology.* Addison-Wesley.

Jude Pinto and Brigitte Harms (2005). Soucing of it-services to offsoure destinations. 3A Strategy.

Longacre, R. E. (1976). *An anatomy of speech notions.* Lisse: de Ridder.

Marshall, C. (1999). *Enterprise Modeling with UML: Designing Successful Software through Business Analysis.* Addison-Wesley.

Rechtin, E. and Maier, M. (1997). *The Art of Systems Architecturing.* CRC Press.

SAP (2000). mysap.com collaborative business scenarios,whitepaper. In *Walldorf.*

Steen, M., Lankhorst, M., and van de Wetering, R. (2002). Modelling networked enterprises. In *the sixth international Enterprise distributed Object Computing Conference (EDOC'02).*

van der Aalst, W., ter Hofstede, A., B., K., and Barros, A. (2003). Workflow patterns. *Distributed and Parallel Databases*, (3):5-51.

Van Dyke Parunak, H. (1996). Visualizing agent conversations: Using enhanced dooley graphs for agent design and analysis. In *The Second International Conference on Multi-Agent System (ICMAS'96).*

Verdicchio, M. and Colombetti, M. (2002). Commitments for agent-based supply chain management. *ACM SIGecom Exchanges, 3(1).*

Webber, D. (2004). The benefits of ebxml for e-business. *In International Conference on XML (XML'04).*

Wolstenholme, E. F. (1990). *System enquiry: a system dynamics approach.* John Wiley & Sons, Inc., New York, NY, USA.

Xu, L. (2004). *Monitoring Multi-party Contracts for E-business.* PhD thesis, Tilburg University.

Xu, L. and Jeusfeld, M. A. (2003). Pro-active monitoring of electronic contracts. In *The 15th Conference On Advanced Information Systems Engineering in Lecture Notes of Computer Science*, volume 2681, pages 584–600. Springer-Verlag.

Xu, L. and Jeusfeld, M. A. (2004). Detecting violators of multi-party contracts. In *The Conference on CoopIS/DOA/ODBASE in Lecture Notes of Computer Science*, volume 3290, pages 526–543. Springer-Verlag.

Xu, L., Jeusfeld, M. A., and Grefen, P. (2005). Detection tests for identifying violators of multiparty contracts. *ACM SIGecom Exchanges, 5(3).*

Chapter XII
Innovative Technological Paradigms for Corporate Offshoring

Tapasya Patki
GGSIP University, India

A. B. Patki
Department of Information Technology, India

ABSTRACT

Internet technology has impelled us to develop faith in the modern practices of business, commerce, and trade. Offshoring has been viewed as a global phenomenon on the economic frontier. While new technologies need to be framed, stopgap arrangements in the form of transient solutions to upgrade the current systems are also desired. Newer regulations and multi-jurisdictional compliance have profound impacts on the growth of outsourcing projects. The development of new technological solutions must challenge the myth that legislation and statutory practices are the only possible mechanisms to counter the unscrupulous activities in the context of outsourcing. A change in the outlook toward such methodologies is essential to shed away the technological inertia and latency. This article opens up discussion issues in the perspective of hardware and software requirements for efficient offshoring. The aim is to achieve higher precision, protection, and throughput by applying core-computing techniques to the existing practices of outsourcing.

INTRODUCTION

The information and communications technology (ICT) revolution has triggered the economic development at collaborative and cooperative levels. Internet-based infrastructure provided impetus for outsourcing projects to hubs such as India, China, and the Philippines. Bednarzik (2005) indicates that due to its emerging nature, there is no universally accepted definition of offshoring. While the industry professionals use outsourcing and offshoring terms interchangeably, IEEE and ACM believe that when a U.S. company gives work to companies in other nations like India, it is outsourcing (and not offshoring). A general business expansion trend, including an outreach program, is to explore potentials of other nations for widening an organization's horizons (Friedman, 2005). Considering this general view, offshoring, outsourcing, and *subcontracting* need to be distinguished. A report of the ACM Job Migration Taskforce (Aspray, Mayadas, & Vardim, 2005) looked at the issue from a global perspective, as compared to a country-centric one in the context of rapid globalization of IT and the migration of jobs resulting from outsourcing and offshoring. The report clearly defines the following two terms:

- Outsourcing refers to having work for a company done by another organization.
- Offshoring refers to having this work done in another country, whether or not it is done by part of the same company.

This leads to a partially overlapping definition of outsourcing and offshoring. Transferring a part of the workload from a host location to another adjunct destination can broadly represent the meaning of these two terms. Predominantly, the host and the destination locations are in different countries. The authors explore the possibility of such situations from the previous perspective, that is, not adhering to a fixed definition. Such an approach is necessary for a global outlook, wherein the participation of developed and developing nations is at equal stake levels (Farrell, Kaka, & Sturze, 2005). Both subcontracting and offshoring/outsourcing have impact on work force realignment. The fears, however, are disjoint. Subcontracting may result in a partial relocation of the workforce with ensured job security. Such a possibility is absent in offshoring/outsourcing. In this context, the *theory of comparative advantage*, propagated by the economics of offshoring cannot be applied to subcontracting.

With the introduction of business models in the developing nations for managing the available workforce and the infrastructure, the ICT industry paved the way for the foundation of first generation outsourcing oriented corporate models (FG-OOCM) for expanding commerce. The FG-OOCM has opened up various issues for outsourcing-based research, and a need for deploying technological solutions to offshoring activities is being felt. For example, consider a situation where Mexican, Indian, Chinese, and American people work together in an outsourcing-based system. In such cases, knowledge management is a challenge and a need for introducing technological solutions is felt. Although distinct units, rules, and documents of each participating organization can be considered as *explicit knowledge*, these do not make knowledge for the entire outsourcing system. Information and knowledge are interdependent, but information per-se contains no knowledge. Some of the issues of knowledge management in software engineering (Desouza, 2003) are applicable to outsourcing. In general, outsourcing system operations are performed by outside contractors, and the terms of understanding between the client and the contractor for outsourced services are defined based on distribution of responsibility, liability sharing, and performance monitoring. These issues require managing of electronic records and evidence, impose legal compliance requirements, and need to be viewed from the perspective of technology as opposed to that of mere administration.

Internet Technology Framework

Outsourcing is a multistage phenomenon involving *individual* (usually management/technical positions), *functional* (knowledge and responsibility orientated), and *process* (flow of product or services) level activities (Greaver, 1998). Depending on the process requirements, outsourcing can be classified as tactical, strategic, and transformational (Brown & Wilson, 2005). The mindset of considering tactical outsourcing for reducing financial costs is assuming new dimensions to make business capabilities portable on a global basis. Detailed analysis of case studies in a research-based manner establishes the success pattern using transformational outsourcing (Linder, 2004). Conventional outsourcing approaches that focus on incremental cost savings have outlived and business process offshoring (BPO) as well as emerging knowledge process offshoring (KPO) are the likely next generation outsourcing activities. At present, the Internet technology-based computing deployed for Web services and outsourcing comprises of a broad range of processors, communication networks, and *information reservoirs*. The trustworthy computer systems encompassing a spectrum of information processing technologies will play a major role in the impressive growth of the BPO sector. The technology to support next generation outsourcing is likely to witness *large scope computing* instead of *large scale computing* to withstand attacks and to ensure greater security, dependability, and reliability. Multimedia, mul-

Figure 1. Problems triggered by outsourcing

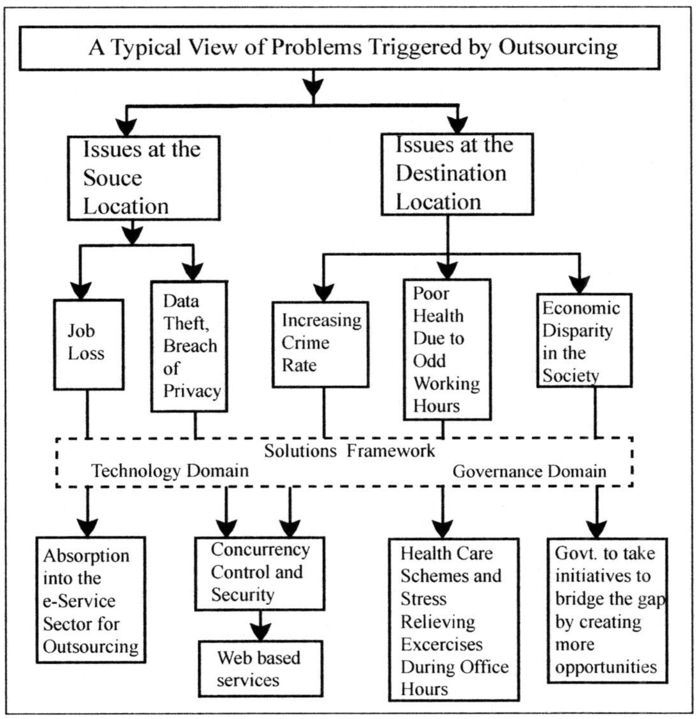

tilingual network operating software (MISNOS) supports large scope computing permitting application semantics (Bandyopadhyay, 1996). It has potential for context-sensitive and secure OS architectures to facilitate e-services needs of conventional and emerging ubiquitous embedded systems deployed in BPO sectors. Outsourcing, in the past, has evoked a response, which is a combination of excitement for corporate management and fear/worries like loss of jobs for employees in the host country. In addition to these social issues, the technological issues like data thefts, privacy protection, and timely deliveries have been concerns in the past few years. Figure 1 depicts problems triggered by outsourcing. The Internet must also provide substantive benefits to the various stakeholders of outsourcing business community as opposed to merely offering traditional subcontracting disguised with technology. The early management-oriented outsourcing studies focused on employment issues instead of productivity aspects. The job losses due to direct impact of offshoring and indirectly due to productivity enhancements are concerns of transient nature (Bednarzik, 2005). Lo (2005) has demonstrated using a mathematical approach that the international outsourcing trade and technology improvements have potentials to make the world better off with higher real wage and more product variety.

Outsourcing failure is termed as a situation when a deal is either terminated or re-negotiated (Brudenall, 2005). High rate of outsourcing failure is attributed to factors like poor planning, choice of partner, or lack of proper strategy. The importance of identifying short-term and long-term goals to prevent outsourcing failures is discussed in the context of vendor selection and cultural match (Chandrasekar, 2005). Lee, Huynh, Chi-Wai, and Pi (2000) identify key research areas for deeper understanding on outsourcing as a *two-phase* exercise. Evolution of several identified outsourcing issues from motivation, performance angle, to management control has been the focus of first phase. The second phase describes partnership-based outsourcing trend. A management checklist (Kobayashi-Hillary, 2004) focuses on preparation as a critical part of transition and redundancy process for managerial commitments. However, the preference of the "touch-and-feel" factor over the impersonal virtual environment and the lack of adequate security systems to safeguard strategic information may limit the extent and pace of outsourcing.

A need to structure and equip the outsourcing business community for content sharing and control has arisen in the Internet technology framework. With the continued globalization and technology push, outsourcing is seen as the growth engine of the global economy (Roger, Smith, & Kidd, 1999). The IT infrastructure currently available to small- and medium-sized enterprises (SMEs) does not provide sufficient integration amongst different application components of business to support trustworthy inter-organizational outsourcing process. As a stopgap arrangement to improve trustworthiness, we suggest an e-service-oriented methodology for outsourcing for addressing trustworthiness concerns. The approach suggested in the section on *establishing concurrency control and security* is on the lines of TIOBE programming community index that is updated once a month (TIOBE, n.d.). Flexibility in arranging trans-organizational BPO is a key requirement for a common middleware. Shifting of skill set up the value chain is useful (Fowler, 2005). As a long-term goal, underutilized skill sets arising out of job losses due to outsourcing must be deployed for assessing global methodologies for benchmarking BPO/KPO infrastructure on the lines of supercomputer ranking initiatives (Top 500 supercomputer Sites, n.d.) that are updated half yearly. Technological approaches suggested in this article are useful from this perspective.

Status of Initiatives Taken by Developing Nations to Support Outsourcing

In order to gain economic benefits of the BPO boom, a number of developing nations responded in a multipoint fashion. This included focus on the science and technology policy, introduction of cyber legislation, the creation of supportive legal infrastructure, and reforming academic/educational courses (Matsuura 2002; NASSCOM & BCG, 2001; Patki, 2004). Outsourcing principles and practices never addressed the cybernetic angle of the process. Issues of the cyber-legislative status and the cyber-crime rate of the outsourced/outsourcing nation were not given due attention. Community centers, Internet kiosks, cyber cafés, cyber marts that are the Internet access points in metropolitan cities, and townships are the objects of attack (Matsuura, 2002). The profile of cyber café usage, types of browsers used, and time of day vis-à-vis the physical locations are among the major criteria for assessing cyber crimes through the potentially *floating* user population. In the present form, cyber forensic tools concentrate merely on electronic records and need to extend their scope to network forensics. This is one issue that is an impediment in the growth of the BPO industry, and needs to be handled at the research and implementation levels. While statistical data on the quantum of business of BPO sector are published to encourage investments, no data are readily available in open source for assessing legislative potential prior to the commencement of any outsourcing contract-based project. The print media offers some basic narrative information and completely overlooks the analytical and technological aspects of outsourcing. These areas call for further detailing and need to be addressed at the national and international levels. Previous studies related to offshoring have concentrated on a developed nation (primarily U.S.) offshoring to a developing nation (India/China), resulting in an economically win-win situation for both the participating nations. The ACM report (Aspray et al, 2005), has, to some extent, succeeded in overcoming such constraints by addressing broader issues from both national and company perspectives, including the globalization of research, and educational changes. Thus, the initial concept of establishing an offshoring base in a developing nation needs to be altered for the sustained growth, especially for partnership-based outsourcing.

TECHNOLOGICAL ISSUES

Reifer (2004) brings out the views of both sides of the outsourcing debate and highlights that in order to succeed in outsourcing, it is necessary to avoid *conflict* arising out of lawyers and contract administrators. In this article, we discuss the technology aspects (viz. hardware/software) to avoid the *conflict*. The present day information systems designed on von Neumann philosophy and the applications tailored for such architectural platforms are successfully running on various hardware/software platforms. Electronic data processing (EDP) was the sole purpose of the early generation of computers. Their extensions to scientific and commercial applications paved the way for new avenues using high-speed computation and DBMS. All through, the Boolean-logic based data items continued to be a basic micro unit and the concepts of raw data, processed data, raw information, and processed information were implemented at application-level instead of CPU hardware (instruction set level) or system software level. This mindset resulted into OS commands of *delete* type for removal of data as well as information. However, the *information weeding* is much different than simply deleting a file or the contents of a directory from a computer system. Subsequently, algorithms were developed for data compression to overcome storage, transmission, and retrieval problems. With the introduction of information transfer through the Internet (video graphics, sound, and images), the data compression algorithms grew more popular. Such patchwork approach was acceptable for in-house, networked IT installations. However, the lack of built-in cognitive supports at computational/operational levels adversely influenced outsourcing. It has led to situations of outcry toward outsourcing ranging from labour dissatisfaction to data thefts, forcing countries to resort to legislation. The authors identify the limitations of the current outsourcing technologies and focus on using soft computing based solutions.

Cognitive Support for Data Processing

With the availability of Internet, EDP-oriented methodology has been directly extended to the BPO sector for establishing dedicated application-oriented servers (e.g., ftp, mail, and dbms) to preclude the intermixing of data and information. However, concept modeling as per the user specifications and requirements is not incorporated in these dedicated servers. Unlike the EDP applications of the bygone century, the future information systems will require computers with capabilities to handle imprecise and partial information, approximate reasoning, and learning, both for scientific and commercial applications. Capturing and representing knowledge and inferencing are major challenges in classical computing techniques due to the imprecise or *gray* nature of real-life decisions. Since computer programming is the ultimate vehicle for the practical realization of outsourcing plans, it is necessary to cater to imprecision and context through software construction approach (Hunt & Thomas, 2003; Patki, 2004). Fuzzy logic (Zadeh, 1965, 1976) techniques allow system modeling using *linguistic hedges* for handling imprecision, partial truth, uncertainty, and approximations. The focus should be on reducing the cognitive load of the end user leading to the simplification and ease of use of the data processing framework. We provide a brief review of the basic concepts of fuzzy logic (FL) next.

Fuzzy Logic

The theory of binary logic is based on the assumption of crisp membership of an element to a certain set. An element x thus either belongs to (i.e., has a membership value of 1) or does not belong to (i.e., has a membership value of 0) a particular set X. Conventional logic systems can be extended to encompass normalized values in the range of [0,1]; thus introducing the notion of partial membership of an element to a particular set. The variable in a fuzzy system is generally described linguistically prior to its mathematical description, as it is more important to visualize a problem in totality to devise a practical solution.

A fuzzy set F, on a collection of objects, X, is a mapping

$$\mu_F(x): X \rightarrow [0,a]$$

Here, $\mu_F(x)$ indicates the extent to which $x \in X$ has the attribute F, thus it is the membership function. In general, we use a normalized fuzzy domain set, for which

$$a = \sup \mu_F(x) = 1$$

The membership function can be generated with the help of mathematical equations. Typically, it can be in trapezoidal, triangular or in the form of S or π - curve.

The support of a fuzzy set, F, $S(F)$ is the crisp set of all $x \in X$ such that $\mu(x) > 0$.

The three basic logical operations of intersection, union, and complementation can be performed on fuzzy sets.

1. The membership $\mu_C(x)$ of the intersection $C = A \cap B$ satisfies for each $x \in X$,

   $$\mu_C(x) = \min\{\mu_A(x), \mu_B(x)\}$$

2. The membership $\mu_C(x)$ of the union $C = A \cup B$ satisfies for each $x \in X$,

   $$\mu_C(x) = \max\{\mu_A(x), \mu_B(x)\}$$

3. The membership $\mu_C(x)$ of the complementation $C = \overline{A}$ satisfies for each $x \in X$,

   $$\mu_C(x) = 1 - \mu_A(x)$$

Example: Fuzzy logic hardware modules (Alag & Patki, 1996; Hung, 1995; Watanabe, 1991) as well as disk operating system (DOS) level FL software (Patki, Raghunathan, & Khurshid, 1997) have potential for ameliorating outsourcing/offshoring infrastructure. Basic DOS level commands like *dir, list, copy, move,* and *del* have been provided with FL support. The use of variables like *old* and *recent* in the time domain and *large*, *average,* and *small* in the size domain have been used to modify the existing DOS commands. A further support using hedges such as *very, moreorless*, and *not* is demonstrated in the fuzzy logic-based operating system, FUZOS© (Patki et al., 1996). This concept can be extended to the data processing unit of a BPO, in which the FL based browsers, text editors, call support utilities etc., can be incorporated. For real time response, software approaches are not adequate and there is a need for fuzzy hardware support. Although, add-on cards for computing hardware have been suggested, the practical solution calls for instruction set based processors with hardwired or micro-programmed implementations (Patki, 1997; Watanabe, 1991).

Machine Intelligence Quotient

In the past, the performance of computing systems was judged purely by its constituent hardware. Thus, MIPS (million instructions per second), GFLOPS (giga floating point operations per second), and Gibson mix were the metrics for the computer performance assessment. Subsequently, with the developments in the fields of artificial intelligence and fuzzy logic, the software performance index like FLIPS (fuzzy logic inferences per second) appeared in the hardware dominated era to determine the combined hardware and software (i.e., integrated technological performance). FLIPS did not become as popular as MIPS since there were not many occasions to benchmark fuzzy logic hardware/software systems. MIPS rating for benchmarking computing hardware is slowly being replaced with machine intelligence quotient (MIQ) and is likely to have potential impact on offshoring. MIQ permits the understanding of any machine through multiple perspective analysis (Jamshidi, Titli, Zadeh, & Boveriv, 1997). Any numerical or linguistic index/structure indicating the degree of autonomy of an intelligent system module can be regarded as MIQ. Although it is difficult to obtain an absolute measure of MIQ in the strictest sense, a relative value based on a comparison of the system with an existing baseline machine in use can be determined. This allows us to rate a particular system with respect to an already established machine in use, thus, allowing us to determine its efficiency and effectiveness that can be deployed to tackle a certain problem.

MIQ differs significantly from indices like control performance, reliability, fault-diagnosis (Park, Kim, & Lim, 2001). MIQ has been defined as the measure of autonomy and performance for *unanticipated* events. The MIQ approach can link the infrastructural needs of an offshoring/outsourcing institution with its throughput. Issues regarding the measurement of MIQ have been discussed by analyzing human-machine cooperative systems. MIQ (M) can be considered as a union of machine control intelligence (M_C) and machine interface intelligence (M_F).

$$M = M_C + M_F$$

Engineering systems or products that are said to be intelligent have been analyzed and a three-dimensional construct space representation as entities has been suggested (Zeungnam, Bang, Kim, & Han, 2002). In order to determine the numeric value of MIQ, Sugeno fuzzy integral and Choquet fuzzy integral have been adopted.

An important characteristic of the future outsourcing information systems will cater to a situation in which information needs are not defined precisely at the time of the system design and awarding the contract. This brings the focus on dynamically integrated intelligent information systems instead of the computer hardware and software as disjoint infrastructure entities for service sectors. In the near future, when we consider outsourcing, we shall also encompass the broad category of information producing and information lending industries that are likely to usher in a new type of global market. Thus, MIQ will occupy special significance since the outsourcing contract awarding and project-executing organizations will be part of same MNC where current trend of country-oriented legislation will serve no purpose.

Example*:* The offshoring procedure poses an operational threat in deploying commercial off-the-shelf (COTS) product procuring strategies for building IT based critical infrastructure. Such a view is expressed (Aspray et al., 2005) in the context of source and application code of COTS products procured through offshoring. This situation can be improved by introducing MIQ evaluation of subassemblies/assemblies using individually certified COTS products. Recommended methodology could include in-depth research in introducing the concept of MIQ authorization and type approval of the COTS products and the evaluation of the host and the destination companies by an international agency.

Establishing Concurrency Control and Security

As brought out in the previous sections, there is a strong need to assess the figure of merit from the security point of view for any city-based infrastructure in an outsourcing/outsourced nation where the project is being executed. The infrastructure does not merely refer to the physical hardware/software setup; but also encompasses dynamic parameters like the cyber crime index (CCI), customer satisfaction rate (CSR), and civil infrastructure status (CIS). These parameters are extremely important to compute cyber *trustworthiness* of a particular service unit, and to assess how far the unit succeeded in reaching its targets. This approach calls for a technological development and is not possible by merely adhering to standards and/or certification practices like the ISO. The CCI, CSR, and CIS term set has been briefly described next, as elaborate explanations are beyond the scope of this article. This methodology is on the lines of TIOBE programming community index, which is updated every month (TIOBE, n.d.). However, unlike TIOBE, the trustworthiness assessment requires online project data collection based on inherent cognitive styles prevailing in offshoring. In order to illustrate a cognition-based approach for such situations, we discuss how rough set theory (RST) can be applied for assessing CCI. Independent agencies should be setup centrally that provide a Web-based portal for these parameters and also provide periodic updates on a regular basis for assessing cyber trustworthiness. The data access to such an e-service must be standardized so that processing of requests for proposals (RFPs) is more effective.

- **Cyber crime index (CCI):** It is the cumulative measure of the various cyber crimes that occur at a particular service unit in a city where the outsourcing infrastructure has been installed and involves inter-nation as well as intra-nation successful *illegal attempts* that have taken place in the time period of observation. The term illegal attempt is based on a cognitive factor and cannot be determined directly.
- **Customer satisfaction rate (CSR):** It determines the percentage-based value of the number of satisfied customers per unit time (this time is the time-period of observation). The CSR value determines the reliability and the serviceability of the infrastructure unit. Weekly project progress of the targets as per the PERT chart serves as an important parameter. This value is fuzzy in nature as it is used to plot a membership function of CSR with the help of parameters like satisfied and dissatisfied. Furthermore, hedges like *moreorless* and *very* can be applied to these values. This membership curve can be used to determine the efficiency and the effectiveness of a service center unit.
- **Civil infrastructure status (CIS):** This is a value that is computed from the join of various other factors like the present population of the city, the administrative status of the city, the present need and urgency of a request, and several such related factors. This factor uses type-II fuzzy sets representation. This is a highly variant quantity and it generally fluctuates with parameters like the current climate/season, the socio-economic condition of the city, the language and culture of the people, the percentage of academicians in the city, the business base of the city etc. This is a very important value as it determines the usability and accessibility of a service unit for offshoring, and needs to be consulted before investing in a particular location prior to the finalizing of the outsourcing project.

In the context of the previous discussions, when we talk of outsourcing at the most fundamental level, we refer to a collection of operations that form a single logical unit that need to be executed to perform a specified task to fulfill a particular request. This collection of operations is referred to as a *transaction*. Transaction management (TM) and concurrency control (CC) are thus evolving issues in outsourcing. To support such schemes, technological solutions have to be provided in the form of *cognition-based protocols* for TM and CC. Some important considerations with regard to TM include atomicity, consistency, isolation, and durability, popularly referred to as ACID properties. When several transactions take place simultaneously, the isolation property may not necessarily be preserved and to ensure that it holds, a separate CC algorithm must be designed to control the interaction between simultaneous transactions. *Serialization* of transactions is one such method to establish CC. We can do this by the use of protocol-oriented techniques. Techniques such as lock-based, timestamp-based, graph-based, and validation-based protocols have been previously employed for database systems (Elmasri & Navathe, 2004; Silberschatz, Korth, & Sudarshan, 2002). However, these techniques fail to deliver a good output, as they are not based on the real-life problems. A major limitation of these protocol-oriented solutions is that they have been founded on the grounds of example situations, and they do not by any means address the grass-root reality of outsourcing/offshoring setup, as they cannot take *intelligent* decisions. In order to develop more practically efficient solutions, we have to move to the soft-computing based options (Kapoor, Patki, & Khurana, 2005). Proposed TM could be implemented using rough set theory (RST) approach, which also supports the powerful concept of information systems (IS). We provide a brief introduction to RST (Pawlak, 1982, 1984) as well as IS in this article and then discuss how these can be applied for security and concurrency control.

Information Systems

A system that is capable of storing information for archival and reference purposes can be thought of as an IS. It is quite similar to a relational database (Silberschatz et al., 2002) in terms of its physical structuring. The difference lies in the powerful concepts of *reduction* and *abstraction* that it uses. It can also perform the task of a decision making system, allowing us to select a few attributes as decision parameters. The attributes can also be classified as relevant and irrelevant.

Mathematically, an IS is defined as a 4-tuple system (Marek & Pawlak, 1976; Pawlak, 1984)

$S = \{U, D, V, \rho\}$

where

- U is a non-empty finite set of objects known as the Universe of Discourse;
- D is a non-empty finite set of attributes or descriptors used to represent the objects;
- V is the set of values, such that for every $a \in D$, we associate a set V_a, called the domain of attribute a; and
- ρ is the mapping function such that $\rho : U \times D \rightarrow V_a$

Rough Set Theory

Rough set theory, as the name suggests, is based on the concept of roughness or approximation of the crisp sets. It extends the conventional set theory to include a concept known as an *approximation space*, which can be defined mathematically as an ordered pair, $A = (U, R)$ where U refers to the universe of discourse, and R refers to a binary relation over U, also called the *indiscernibility* relation of the IS (Marek et al., 1976; Pawlak, 1984).

We assume R to be an equivalence relation, thus broadly classifying R as reflexive, symmetric, and transitive. Thus, if an ordered pair $(x, y) \in R$, we say that x and y are indiscernible or indistinguishable in A. Equivalence classes of relation R are often called *elementary* sets or *atoms* in rough set theory. An empty set (i.e., φ) is assumed to be the elementary set for every A. When the union of elementary sets for a set X is finite, we say that the set X is definable or composed. Essentially, for a quantifiable set X, we can talk of two approximations in general, a *lower approximation* (LA or $\underline{A}$), which refers to the greatest definable set in A of which X is a superset, and an *upper approximation* (UA or $\overline{A}$), which refers to the least definable set in A of which X is a subset. The *positive region* is the union of the lower approximations (Pawlak, 1982). The boundary of X in A is mathematically the set difference of the upper approximation and the lower approximation. Thus, BND(X)= $\overline{A} - \underline{A}$. Figure 2 illustrates these operations. The *negative region* (or NEG (X)) is the difference between the universe of discourse and the positive region. A set can also be referred to as *definable* when its LA and UA represent the same set, i.e., when $\underline{A} = \overline{A}$. In all other cases, the set X is said to be *undefinable*.

Undefinable sets in a given approximation space A are of the following four types:

- Roughly Definable: When for a given set X, $\underline{A} \neq \varphi$ and $\overline{A} \neq U$
- Externally Undefinable: When for a given set X, $\underline{A} \neq \varphi$ and $\overline{A} = U$
- Internally Undefinable: When for a given set X, $\underline{A} = \varphi$ and $\overline{A} \neq U$
- Totally Undefinable: When for a given set X, $\underline{A} = \varphi$ and $\overline{A} = U$

Figure 2. Basics of rough sets

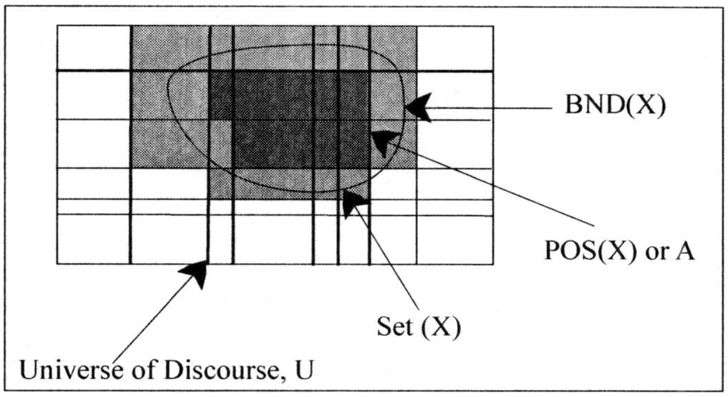

Example: RST can be effectively applied for determining and analyzing the CCI. To find CCI, we need to follow up a given service unit and approximate its *illegal activities/attempts*. This approximation can be done in a suitable time frame, which depends on the traffic load of that particular unit. In case of a heavy traffic, we can approximate the attempts every half-an-hour; and in case of low traffic, the procedure can be carried out every 12 hours. The approximated results would give us a *rough* idea of the illegal attempts that are taking place. We can thus formulate two extreme limits, given by the upper and the lower approximations. These limits can be overlapped in a cumulative fashion to gather information about that particular service unit. The number of *successful* illegal attempts can also be determined. This value however, will not be an approximated value, as the number of crimes that have actually taken place, i.e. the number of successful illegal attempts can be determined finitely. The CCI can then be computed by considering the ratio of these two values.

RST can also be applied in case of the security of transactions that are taking place in a service unit on an outsourced enterprise. This is done through the development of an intrusion detection system (IDS) for protection of a networked link (Peng, Yun, Douglas, & Dingbang, 2004). An IDS evaluates suspected intrusions and signals an alarm once a suspected intrusion happens. It also watches for attacks that originate from within the setup. The basic process extracts predictive features from the raw data stream being monitored to produce formatted data that can be used for detection. Following this, a detection model determines whether the data is intrusive. RST based methods for the development of IDS is promising in terms of detection accuracy, requirement of training data set and efficiency. In a classical RST based approach, the new attack records are combined with the original training data, and a process of rule generation is employed. The rules generated are used for detection and analysis of further similar attacks. However, this process is not very practical as the entire existing knowledge base has to be re-examined. To solve this problem, an *incremental* learning procedure is required to approximate the attacks in a more efficient manner in a real-time environment (and not in a post-mortem style of cyber forensics' analysis). A rough set based incremental knowledge acquisition algorithm requires that whenever a new attack type or a new variation of attack appears, the rule generation process with the entire training data need not be repeated. The only computation required is that new rules should be generated from the new attack records and these should be used in conjunction with the existing rules. This algorithm has higher speed and recognition rate and can be appropriate for processing huge amounts of data/transactions. Handheld portable gadgets for cyber police patrolling have already been proposed based on the previous ideas (Patki, Patki, Khurana, & Sivasubramanian, 2005).

LIMITATIONS OF EXISTING SOFTWARE PRACTICES

Offshoring operations are heavily dependent on networked computer systems, making it essential to address software and hardware issues. The existing *software practices*, their limitations, and the scope for improvements are rarely studied in this context. Methodologies focused on producer/consumer philosophy for software development, upkeep, and maintenance are no longer adequate for outsourcing as they lack of monitoring flexibility. Outsourcing practices have requirements for frequent *cognitive* interactions. In the absence of technological solutions, retrofit measures in the form of management and administrative directives are adopted.

We broadly classify and discuss software issues in order of their immediate significance: operating systems, file systems, database management systems, and computer programming languages.

Issues at the Operating System Level

The traditional approaches to OS focus on memory management (paging/segmentation/overlays), process scheduling, multiprocessing environment, and networking (Stallings, 2004). Not only for offshore work assignments, but also in general, OS is considered to be an extension of computer hardware, and as an interface to the users. This has led to an agglomeration of system level calls in OS implementations, to cater to each requirement. The batch processing and multiprogramming oriented approaches need to be modified to support and strengthen outsourcing. In the strictest sense, there is no accepted universal practice for measuring the performance of an OS in an outsourcing environment. On the lines of reduced instruction set computing (RISC) philosophy of microprocessors, OS will have to shed off some of its existing burden onto hardware. Some of the salient points in the context of outsourcing are presented below.

- Emergence of application specific processor architecture (ASPA) that permits dynamic loading, configuring and remote monitoring of the software environments by the originator on the outsourced contractor's infrastructure, should be supported by OS. Thus, the concept of *information disposal* arising out of this will open up issues like weeding of information records (text, graphics, images, video clips, movies, audio sounds, program code--both source and binary executables). Information weeding is different from the *delete* commands of OS or the data compression methods for storage and retrieval as viewed by cyber forensic professionals. The cognitive aspects of raw data, processed data, raw information, and processed information will gain special significance in outsourcing to overcome today's data theft problems and associated legislation practices.
- The conventional approach adopted for servers for different purposes (e.g., application-oriented servers providing ftp, mail, and database will undergo transformations using concept modeler techniques both at hardware/software modules). This will call for generation of information, determining its contents using fuzzy information inference, and processing of partial/imprecise information. Today's OS shell programming does not permit such constructs. Thus, if we have to execute an iterative loop for *few* times, there is no *context* available or

created by programming environment to map the fuzzy term *few*. We have to state the quantity explicitly--loop 100 times. In an outsourced scenario, to avoid misuse of resources (user's data is also a resource for unscrupulous people as they can misuse or abuse it), *resource aware programming* support requires to be incorporated for OS shell programming itself, instead of library support since either deliberately or inadvertently, library support can be switched off in an outsource job processing infrastructure.

Issues at the File System and Database Levels

Outsourcing at the primary level is data-dependent and calls for efficient information systems, which can endorse search and information mining operations. Traditionally, partial information systems were adopted and configured for outsourcing resulting into situations leading to *conflict* management (Reifer, 2004).

File system organization and databases are linked up and we describe them from the perspective of problems associated with data-theft in outsourcing. We suggest a fuzzy logic-based approach to overcome the existing lacuna. Two mechanisms for file systems have been proposed next:

1. The files can be grouped fuzzily in a dynamic manner according to guidelines inherent to the system installation (or configured by the user), taking into account security policies. Membership function values and fuzzy relations can be computed using following considerations.
   a. Files open at the same time or in the same session by a single user will be strongly related.
   b. User as well as system profiles (including privileges) in multi-user systems deployed in BPO installations.
   c. File extensions and categorization like .cpp, .exe, .jpeg in the case of non-compilatory tasks.
2. The user will specially create types of directories with certain crisp (or fuzzy) attributes for all the files associated with the directory, so that these may be updated dynamically as per the previous principle.

Example: Consider the directory structure in Figure 3. The directory Medical_data_papers under MrX\Restricted contains laboratory investigations examined by pathologist DrY. Although it is desired that DrY may share rights to access MrX\Restricted\Medical_data_papers, the files under MrX\Restricted\Insurance are not to be shared with DrY.

In the existing directory structure, organizational policies may lead to complex access restrictions as well as wastage of disk storage. The present software practices handle such situations and protect information through password-based authorization schemes, which make the system prone to attacks bordering on hacking/password cracking. Generally, there exist fuzzily definable relationships between files like pathological data and medical insurance; hence, a model based on the *role theory* (Kandel & Lee, 1979) must be employed to handle the complexities. Consider the case of five fuzzily related directories (D1 to D5), having degrees of association ranging from 0 to 1 (membership values), which have been listed in Table 1.

A degree of association with the value unity indicates self and direct hierarchical subdirectories, while any real value less than unity means informal influence. Similar maps of associations may be generated among the users of the system logged on during a particular session. Such a ses-

Figure 3. Directory structure for example

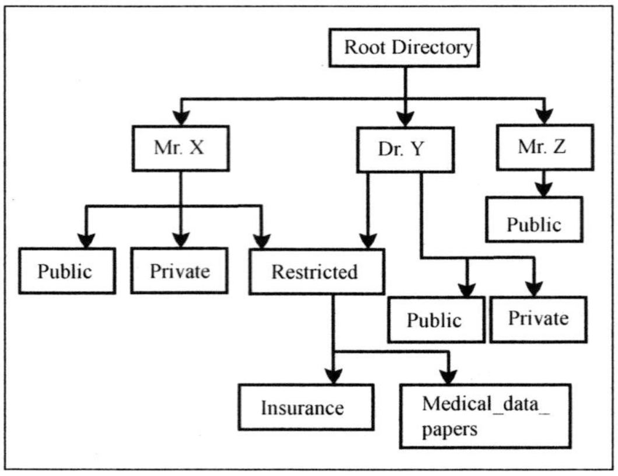

Table 1. Degrees of association amongst various directories

	D1	D2	D3	D4	D5
D1	1	0	1	0.6	0.9
D2	0	1	0.4	0.2	0.5
D3	0	0	1	0.5	0.4
D4	0.5	0.6	0	1	0.1
D5	0.8	0.4	0	0.7	1

sion must be dynamically updated in accordance to the logging in and logging out of any user.

Matrices to map the relationships between (a) directory/subdirectory, (b) directory/user, and (c) group/user are created in the system to analyze the attribute-value domains. Then, with the help of fuzzy equations and recursive matrix operations, the influence of different users on each other as well as influence of different directories on the users and system is computed. The time and date of creation in fuzzy format will enable processes to make inferences by considering hedges regarding the file being *new*, *very new*, *old*, *moreorless old*, etc. This is useful for detecting tampering of files and assessing the damage due to unauthorized access using fuzzy role theory (Kandel et al., 1979).

Unlike the text-oriented databases of the current decade, future information systems would primarily use multimedia and non-multimedia databases. The current efforts in the multimedia databases have been restricted to audio, video, and textual stimuli. In order to give them true power of expression, a concept mapping system needs to be viewed as a core, instead of considering these objects merely as collection of symbols, bitmaps, or audio signals. With provision for open ended queries comprising of textual and an ordered group/ring/field-based composition of audio/image/video clippings as language symbols displayed on the small screen of an optical keyboard (Bandyopadhyay, 1997), multimedia database systems can play a significant role in providing information for the masses (Bandyopadhyay,

1996). It is envisaged that for building large-scope information systems using outsourcing methodology, the data entry, query, and retrieval nodes would naturally be distributed. The data in the form of textual reports, audio/video clippings, and images arriving in all these information reservoir nodes would be un-modeled raw data. The existing password-protected schema *view* methods of SQL/DBMS environments can be modified to incorporate encryption and decryption methodologies operative through ASPA for sensitive data. Software tools would be required to analyze and aid modeling using raw data for concept generation.

Programming Language Considerations

The conventional programming languages from the era of FORTRAN/LISP to the present day C/C++/Java are based on the following building blocks:

- Iterative statements (*for* loop, *do* loop).
- Conditional and non-conditional executions (*If-then-else, Goto*).
- Recursion oriented structures (Stack oriented).
- Assignments with associated enhancements (i= i +1, c+= 5).

A need for an effective *programming medium* in place of a *programming language* was sensed while examining various issues of information banking related activities in the development phases for SIIS (Sivasubramanian & Patki, 1996) and FUZOS© (Patki et al, 1997). We discuss the programming medium approach, which encompasses programming languages as one of the building blocks around which other modules for monitoring information disposal, fraudulent attempts, resource aware, and context-based data collections are dynamically configured. In order to facilitate ASPA to load instruction set modules to improve trustworthiness of outsourcing projects, object-oriented programming systems (OOPS) need to include *synthesis* support. The existing programming languages are more in the form of large suite of tools (with associated integrated development environment IDE), which support algorithmic methodology constructs like iterative loops, multiple branch (switch-case), and conditional controls (if-then-else). These languages emphasize algorithmic programming using an *iterative* philosophy instead of design using synthesis approach. At present, the existing programming languages used in information systems design do not support synthesis constructs prevailing in the hardware engineering design practice like VHDL for digital VLSI circuit design. This calls for introducing basic primitive modifications at object-oriented programming languages. *Ruby* programming language has attempted to bring programming closer to the application space of the user (Thomas, Fowler, & Hunt, 2004). *Ruby's* object-oriented features are designed to add an instance during runtime, allowing this instance of a class to behave differently from the other instances of the same class. This feature is useful in combination with ASPA loaded partial instruction set to monitor security concerns and prohibit data thefts in real time environment at outsourcing infrastructure. However, *Ruby* does not address features required for outsourcing. In order to address issues ranging from sharing code development across the globe to asynchronous interactions amongst developers and/or supervisors, it is essential to deploy cognition-based algorithms. We illustrate a case of document support in programming language for outsourcing environment.

The debugger and documentation capabilities of object-oriented programming languages (e.g., Java) are not much useful after the software-testing phase is over. Program understanding and documentation, which is useful for software designers, code developers, and testing personnel keeps the end-user out of loop. This bottleneck leads to *conflict* creation, which should be avoided (Reifer, 2004). The information retrieval and documentation approaches in the past had been traditionally configured for *isolated* activity and had never been considered for a *group* activity like outsourcing. The scope for utilizing document features is very limited in the software maintenance and practically no scope exists for its usage by the end users who use such software at their computer installations. We should concentrate on group performance in the outsourcing environment (Damian & Eberlein, 2000). Since existing documentation is not tailored for multiple perspectives, there is no provision to configure the documentation application module on a user selection basis.

An end user in an outsourcing scenario rarely uses the software documentation supplied with the systems since it does not provide any cognitive assistance. Thus, OOPS should provide application semantic support on documentation so that cognitive assistance is provided individually to every category of user community consisting of management controllers, cyber forensic analysts, security supervisors, and client managers. Thus, existing *broadcasting* modes of documentation should be replaced by an interactive category-specific mode for users. Intelligent software agents can help to simulate such studies. Support documentation for outsourcing infrastructure should answer cognitive queries and not function as *help* menus or *FAQs*. The text analysis orientation in traditional documentation retrieval leads to the situation that two words with same underlying meaning/stem refer to the same concept for indexing, e.g. neutron and neutralize. The *index* terms that are derived from the text of the document use pre-coordinate or post-coordinate principles. The controversy about index language for document retrieving (Farradane, Russell, & Yates-Mercer, 1973) is primarily due to text analysis approaches adopted and can be overcome using synthesis principle.

Conventional documentation retrieval techniques do not address *mid-operation* support and the scope of fuzzy logic and rough set techniques is promising (Bandyopadhyay, 1996; Goguen, & Lin Kai, 2000). A fuzzy logic-oriented documentation support system for programming language that will permit offshoring community to develop a dynamic view of the same output from multiple perspectives like software code obfuscation, trustworthy computing, and forensic examinations to improve the overall group performance has been proposed (Patki & Khurana, 2006). By using the lower and upper approximation techniques of rough set theory, along with fuzzy relational data view, different projections of the same information are feasible for different information consumers (Kapoor et al., 2005). This capability is a must for efficient outsourcing to restrict and partially overcome the data thefts and similar problems.

MULTIPLEXING OF BPO INFRASTRUCTURE

At present, BPO infrastructure is being used in *absolute* terms with respect to the consumer community. There is a need to think on the lines of *relative* BPO houses where scheduling of jobs is carried out in a manner corresponding to the demands as well as the feedback of the user. Multiplexing of infrastructure on the basis of geographical locations to provide and serve a larger user community to the fullest extent is a novel idea. Such a scheme may use a three-schema architecture at the grass root level, comprising of a physical (internal) schema, a conceptual (logical) schema, and an application (external) schema. This architecture will aid the development of secure systems and will thus revolutionalize the concept of data protection and safe transfer. The OSI reference model for the TCP/IP network protocol can be extended to accommodate such multiplexed BPOs. Resource allocation should be carried out using platform independent integrated development environment (IDE). This will also cater to the increasing traffic through the network at the peak hours due to the availability of efficient resources, resulting into the optimal utilization of the BPO infrastructure.

In order to provide a makeshift arrangement to incorporate concept modeling as per the client requirements, we introduce the concept of an inter-dialoguing processor (IDP).

The IDP infrastructure could be based on a simple microcomputer, which takes in machine level inputs (instructions as well as data packets). The IDP acts as a transfer-establishing a resource link between the service center and the customer interface array dynamically. The main task of the IDP is to merge and route the traffic of the N service centers via a single transfer path to the customer interface array, which is responsible for interactions with the actual customer. The CCI value is computed for each service center. This value is used for handling the security issues. At the IDP level, the CIS value is calculated. The customer interface array uses the CIS value for routing information to various customers. It is also responsible for finding the CSR with the help of user feedback. Such an arrangement is depicted in Figure 4. The arrangement shown here is very fundamental in nature and is not necessarily a final solution to the multiplexing concept. It can however be used as a makeshift pattern in this transient phase of offshoring. Since some special customized hardware needed for such a system is not yet available, this section of the article may be considered as a precursor. Refinements of this design are expected. We discuss fuzzy logic-based algorithm for BPO multiplexing in the following subsection.

Algorithmic Steps for BPO Multiplexing

1. Create a global FMAP of service centers available to the customers, mapping customers to the multiplexed infrastructure based on the membership function value. FMAP is a resource relation that allows customers to determine which service center stores or

Figure 4. Multiplexing architecture

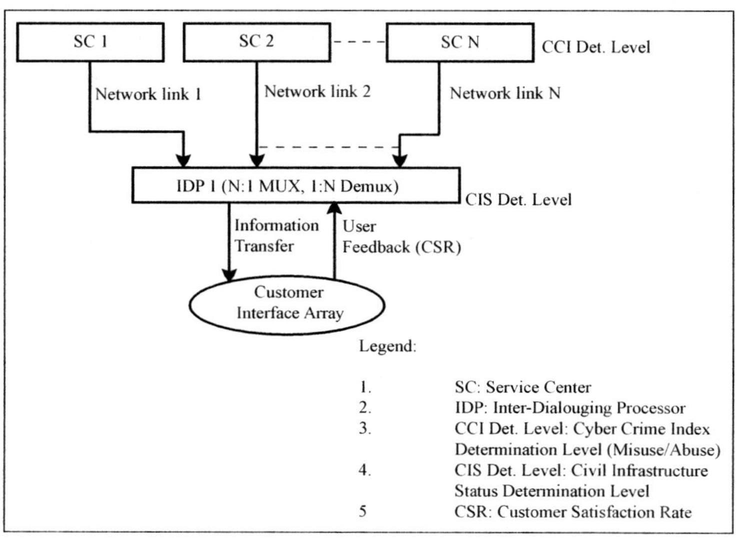

Table 2. Fuzzy control for BPO multiplexing

CIA Index	Service Center I	Service Center II	…	Service Center N
0X00	0.5	0.9		0
0X01	1	0		0.1
….	..	..	..	..
0XFF	0	0		0.5

caches which files. The structure of a typical FMAP is given in Table 2 where customer interface array (CIA) index of figure 4 is used.

2. Manage metadata through proxy servers that reference the locations where data blocks of different files are placed in an encrypted format.
3. Maintain a cache block so that some *permitted, registered* requests can be handled without accessing the machine disks and resources directly.
4. Maintain cache consistency metadata (i.e., version information so that no writes can be done on obsolete data) however, read requests for this data are permitted.

The control-system-managing module of inter-dialoguing processor (IDP) of BPO multiplexer acts as a *load balancer* and changes the FMAP by increasing the membership value of *lesser-used* BPO infrastructure machines and reducing those of heavily loaded machines. This representation and replication (FMAP is globally replicated and present in different machines with different entries) of FMAP enables the customers to be serviced with minimum number of network hops using BPO multiplexing, by taking into account parameters like link speed, bandwidth, and load status when assigning membership values in the FMAP. This helps in preventing network congestion. As and when a new machine joins the multiplexing infrastructure, the FMAP of the closest link is read, and the system-updating module of IDP modifies its own map accordingly. Updating of FMAPs takes place synchronously. The system can also be expanded using multiple fuzzy variables like distance between client and BPO, cyber trustworthiness, and cost factor to provide other advantages. Such an approach helps in reducing the cognitive load. It is important to observe that the conventional von Neumann architecture is not efficient for handling fuzzy logic processing and IDP can be only simulated in software environment for demonstrating the effectiveness. ASPA based instruction sets can be introduced for modeling such a system. Instead of general-purpose processors, digital fuzzy hardware is required for acceptable real-time performance. In the absence of such dedicated fuzzy hardware, either the limited scaled down software solutions will be used or the approach may be abandoned altogether, as it requires very high fuzzy inference speeds (Alag et al., 1996; Hung, 1995; Patki 1996; Watanabe, 1991).

CONCLUSION

In the past, computing technologies were framed by developed nations and were deployed domestically as well as internationally. This view of technology *producers* and *consumers* must be understood in the context of offshoring by integrating consumer experiences rigorously. Data collected at the outsourced infrastructure destinations will be a useful technology driving parameter. This is now feasible as many MNCs have set up their own infrastructure units in various countries, which are routinely undertaking outsourcing work. Thus, the trend will focus on the transformation of human resources, ethics, practices, and motivations into software intelligent agents involving cognitive processing. The present practice of isolated country specific solutions needs to be replaced with global initiative, as outsourcing is emerging as new trade and commerce vehicle for world economic growth.

The exploratory and development work carried so far has validated the initial assumption that better integration using MIQ approach at hardware and software module level along with the multiplexing of BPO infrastructure is central to the *next generation offshoring technology.* Soft computing techniques such as the fuzzy logic and the rough set theory are vital to the expansion of such ideas. The recent announcement of the National Science Foundation of planning an effort to fundamentally re-engineer the Internet and overcome it's shortcomings, and thus creating a network more suited to the computerized world of the next decade, indicates the willingness to redesign the net for future. The technological paradigms suggested in this article can be thought of as a stepping-stone in this direction.

ACKNOWLEDGMENT

Authors wish to acknowledge their discussions with industry representatives, academic community, and government policy makers. The experimental work undertaken by various students has been the driving force to consolidate the issues to face the challenges of outsourcing technological revolution. Interactions with Mr. Mahesh Kulkarni, Group Coordinator, Center for Development of Advanced Computing (CDAC), Pune and Mr. S. Sivasubramanian, Scientist-E, Department of Information Technology, New Delhi, have been enlightening. Suggestions from editors have been useful in shaping the article effectively.

REFERENCES

Alag, S., & Patki, A. B. (1996). Fuzzy logic integrated circuits. In *Proceedings of the 1st Online Workshop on Soft Computing* (pp. 187-191), Nagoya, Japan.

Aspray, W., Mayadas, F., & Vardim, Y. (2005). *Globalization and offshoring of software: A Report of the ACM Job Migration Task Force*, Association for Computing Machinery.

Bandyopadhyay, R. (1997). *Engineering schematics and draft specification for multilingual optical keyboard (MLOPKB).* SDD Technical Report, DOE, May 1997.

Bandyopadhyay, R. (1996). MISNOS—Multimedia, multilingual, information services network operating systems software. *Electronics, Information, and Planning Journal, 23*(4), 205-230.

Bednarzik, R. W. (2005). Restructuring information technology: Is offshoring a concern? *Monthly Labor Review*, August 2005, p. 11-21, Bureau of Labor Statistics, US Department of Labor.

Blunden, R. B. (2004). *Offshoring IT: The good, the bad, and the ugly.* Apress Publication.

Brown, D., & Wilson, S. (2005, May). *The black book of outsourcing: How to manage the changes, challenges, and opportunities.* Wiley Publication.

Brudenall, P. (2005, May). *Technology and offshore outsourcing strategies.* Palgrave Macmillan Ltd.

Chandrasekar, P. R. (2005). Tips for outsourcing. *IEE Engineering Management Journal, 6*, 24, Dec 2004-Jan 2005.

Damian, D., & Eberlein (2000). The effect of communication media on group performance in RE. In *Proceedings of the 4th International Conference on Requirements Engineering (ICRE 00)* (pp. 91), IEEE CS Press.

Desouza, K. C. (2003). Barriers to effective use of knowledge management systems in software engineering. *Comm. ACM, 4691*, 99-101.

Elmasri, R., & Navathe, S. B. (2004). *Fundamentals of database systems*. PearsonEducation.

Farradane, J., Russell, J. M., & Yates-Mercer, A. (1973). Problems in information retrieval: Logical jumps in the expression of information. *Information Storage and Retrieval, 9*, 65-77.

Farrell, D., Kaka, N., & Sturze, S. (2005). *Ensuring India's offshoring future, The McKinsey Quarterly*, 2005 Special Edition: Fulfilling India's Promise.

Fowler, C. (2005). *My job went to India*. Pragmatic bookshelf Publisher.

Friedman, T. L. (2005). *World is flat: Brief history of the globalized world in twenty-first century*. London: Penguin.

Goguen, J. A., & Lin, K. (2000). Web-based multimedia support for distributed cooperative software engineering. In *Proceedings of International Symposium on Multimedia Software Engineering* (pp. 25-32), December 11-13, 2000.

Greaver II, M. F. (1998). *Strategic outsourcing: A structured approach to outsourcing decisions and initiatives*. American Management Association.

Hung, D. L. (1995, August). Dedicated digital fuzzy hardware. *IEEE Micro, 15*(4), 31-38.

Hunt, A., & Thomas, D. (2003). Preparing the raw material. *IEEE Software, 20*(5), 97-98.

Jamshidi, M., Titli, A., Zadeh, L. A., & Boveriv, S. (1997). *Applications of fuzzy logic—towards high machine intelligence quotient systems*. NJ: Prentice Hall.

Kandel, A., & Lee, A. (1979). *Fuzzy switching and automata*. Crane Russak, New York.

Kapoor, A., Patki, T., & Khurana, S. (2005). *Part-I: Analytical methodologies in soft computing, Part II: Exposure to cyber forensic software tools*. Technical Report Submitted to DIT, New Delhi.

Kobayashi-Hillary, M. (2004). *Outsourcing to India--The offshore advantage*. Berlin: Springer-Verlag.

Lee, J., Huynh, M. Q., Chi-Wai, K. R., & Pi, S. (2000). The evolution of outsourcing research: What is next issue? In *Proceedings of the 33rd Hawaii International Conference on Systems Sciences-2000*.

Linder, J. C. (2004). *Outsourcing for radical change*. American Management Association.

Lo, C. (2005). International outsourcing and intra-industrial trade. *International Journal of Applied Economics, 2*(2), 69-82, September 2005

Marek, V. W., & Pawlak, Z. (1976). Information storage and retrieval system. *Mathematical Foundations, Theoretical Computer Science, 1*(4), 331-354.

Matsuura, J. H. (2002). *Security, rights, and liabilities in e-commerce*. Artech House.

NASSCOM, & BCG. (2001). *e-commerce opportunities for India Inc*. Study Report prepared by NASSCOM and The Boston Consultancy Group Report.

Park, H. J., Kim, B. K., & Lim, K.Y. (2001). Measuring the machine intelligence quotient (MIQ) of human-machine cooperative systems. *IEEE Transactions on Systems, Man, and Cybernetics—Part A: Systems and humans, 31*(2), 89-96.

Patki, A., Lakshminarayanan, S., Sivasubramanian, S., & Sarma, S. (2003b). Cyber crime information system for cyberethics awareness. In *Proceedings of the International Conference on Cyberworlds* (pp. 46-52), Singapore.

Patki, A.B. (2004). *Offshoring and outsourcing opportunities.* Lecture Notes for Engineering Student Internship Programme, Department of Information Technology, New Delhi.

Patki, A. B. (1996). Fuzzy logic based hardware: Some experiences. In *Proceedings of the 1st International Discourse on Fuzzy Logic and the Management of Complexity (FLAMOC'96)* (Vol. 3, pp. 247-251), January, 15-18, 1996, Sydney, Australia.

Patki, A. B., Kulkarni, M., Sivasubramanian, S., & Patki, D. D. (2003a). Technology development trends for cyber civilization. In *Proceedings of the International Conference on Cyberworlds* (pp. 40-45), Singapore.

Patki, A. B., Patki, T., Khurana, S., & Sivasubramanian, S. (October 17-19, 2005). Product development for female cyber police programme. In *Proceedings of Conflux, 2005*, New Delhi, India.

Patki, A. B., Raghunathan, G. V., & Khurshid, A. (1997). FUZOS—Fuzzy operating system support for information technology. In P. K. Chawdhry, R. Roy, & R. K. Pant (Eds.), *Soft computing in engineering design and manufacturing* (pp. 131-140), Springer.

Patki, T., & Khurana, S. (2006). *Software cost estimation and software obfuscation: A fuzzy logic perspective.* Technical Report Submitted to Department of Information Technology, New Delhi.

Patki, T., Khurana, S., & Neha (2005b). Cyber civilization: Advantages and shortcomings. *VISION MSIT*, New Delhi.

Pawlak, Z. (1984). Rough classification. *Man-Machine Studies*, 469-483.

Pawlak, Z. (1982). Rough sets. *International Journal of Computer and Information Sciences, II*(5), 342-356.

Peng, N., Yun, C., Douglas, R., & Dingbang, X. (2004). Tools and techniques for analyzing intrusion. *ACM Transactions on Information and System Security, 7*(2), 273-318, May 2004.

Reifer, D. J. (2004). Seven hot outsourcing practices, *IEEE Software*, 14-16.

Roger, J. Y., Smith, B., & Kidd, P. T. (1999). *Business and work in the information society: new technologies and applications.* IOS Press.

Silberschatz, A., Korth, H.F., & Sudarshan S. (2002). *Database system concepts.* NY: McGraw-Hill.

Sivasubramanian, S., & Patki, A. B. (1996). Software industry intelligent information system. *Electronics Information and Planning Journal, 23*(9), 513-518.

Stallings, W. (2004). *Operating systems* (4th ed.). Pearson Education.

TIOBE Programming Community Index. (n.d.). Retrieved September 15, 2006, from http://www.tiobe.com/tpci.htm

Thomas, D., Fowler, C., & Hunt, A. (2004). *Programming ruby: A pragmatic programmer's guide* (2nd ed.). O'Reilly Media Inc.

Top 500 supercomputer Sites. (n.d.). Retrieved September 15, 2006, from http://www.top500.org

Watanabe, H. (1991). Some consideration on design of fuzzy information processors--from a computer architectural point of view. In *Proceedings of Fuzzy Engineering Towards Human Friendly Systems, IFES' 91* (pp. 387-398).

Zadeh, L. A. (1976). A fuzzy-algorithmic approach to the definition of complex or imprecise concepts. *International Journal of Man-Machine Studies*, (8), 249-291.

Zadeh, L. A. (1965). Fuzzy sets. *Information and Control*, (8), 338-353.

Zeungnam, B., Bang, W., Kim, D., & Han, J. (2002). Machine intelligence quotient: Its measurement and applications. *Fuzzy Sets and Systems, 127*(1), 3-16.

This work was previously published in Journal of Electronic Commerce in Organizations, Vol. 5, Issue 2, edited by M. Khosrow-Pour, pp. 57-76, copyright 2007 by IGI Publishing, formerly known as Idea Group Publishing (an imprint of IGI Global).

Chapter XIII
Factors Influencing the Extent of Deployment of Electronic Commerce for Small- and Medium-Sized Enterprises

Sandy Chong
Curtin University of Technology, Australia

Graham Pervan
Curtin University of Technology, Australia

ABSTRACT

This study surveys the perceptions and experiences of Australian small- and medium-sized enterprises (SMEs) in the implementation of Internet-based Electronic Commerce (EC) as seen from the perspective of the extent of deployment. With a sample of 115 small businesses in Australia, this article uses regression modelling to explore and establish the factors that are related to the extent of deployment in EC. A multiple regression analysis shows that seven factors: perceived relative advantage, trialability, observability, variety of information sources, communication amount, competitive pressure, and non-trading institutional influences, significantly influence the extent of EC deployment by SMEs in Australia. The managerial implications are discussed.

INTRODUCTION

The commercialization of the Internet and World Wide Web (WWW) has driven electronic commerce (EC) to become one of the most promising channels for inter-organizational business processes. Despite the economic downturn and the burst of the "dot-com" bubble, EC is expected to continue its significant growth. EC has emerged as a whole business strategy that enables organizations to improve business processes and communication, both within the organization and with trading partners. In the U.S. alone, the second decade of EC would boost online sales from $172 billion in 2005 to $329 billion in 2010 (Forrester Research, 2005), while Asia Pacific's B2B EC is forecasted to grow rapidly at a Compound Annual Growth Rate (CAGR) of 59% percent (IDC, 2004). Specifically in Australia, EC is estimated to be worth $11.3 billion dollars annually (Australian Government Information Management Office, 2005).

RESEARCH PROBLEM

According to the report of the Information Economy (NOIE, 2002), Australia is well positioned to benefit from the emerging information economy. On a number of metrics, Australia is among the leading nations in terms of measures of Internet infrastructure, penetration and activity. In fact, Australia is ranked the top second country in Asia Pacific region by EC infrastructure (eMarketer, 2005). However, in comparison with other countries and larger Australian businesses, small- and medium-sized enterprises (SMEs) [1] have been relatively slow in adopting EC (The Age, 2002; NOIE, 2002; Sensis, 2005). Even if SMEs were able to overcome the barriers of initial adoption, they still face challenges when trying to implement the new system into their business. Most SMEs perceive the challenge of integrating EC into their business operations as risky, complex, time-consuming, and an expensive initiative (NOIE, 2002). Yet it should be noted that if EC implementations are successful, the potential benefits to small businesses can include increased sales, improved profitability, increased productivity, reduced costs associated with inventories, procurement and distribution, improved quality of service, and secured competitive positions (see Dholakia & Kshetri, 2004; Grandson & Pearson, 2003a; Purao & Campbell, 1998; Stockdale & Standing, 2004; Whiteley, 2000).

The need to adopt EC for survival in the international marketplace, especially due to physical and economic distance faced by Australian SMEs is imperative. An awareness of the critical success factors of EC implementation also becomes essential for SMEs to appropriately address the relevant issues and move forward, since failed implementation may have severe repercussions on small businesses with their limited resources. Despite the salience of these issues, there is little empirical research that examines the success of EC deployment after the technology has been implemented. In addition to that, there is little of the prior information systems (IS) and information technology (IT) literature, and none from EC literature, that has investigated the relative importance of the identified factors of extent of deployment. Without knowing the relative importance of these factors, SMEs may be expending their limited resources and energy on less important factors which have limited contribution to EC implementation success. Hence, the principal contribution of the current report can be asserted to be its provision of a model for EC adoption that takes into account the relative importance of various factors that encourage or inhibit the extent to which it is deployed. It may also provide a theoretical tangent that authors and facilitators of future research may wish to follow.

SCOPE OF STUDY

In this study, the term Electronic Commerce principally includes, but is not limited to, Internet-based EC. The scope of EC applications is limited to the utilization of the Internet as the technological infrastructure to communicate, distribute, and conduct information exchange and transactions with business partners. The overwhelming growth rate of the Internet since the commercialization in the mid-1990s makes it the most utilized Wide Area Network platform even for business-to-business communications, and makes the further substitution of previous platforms highly likely throughout the next decade. It is estimated that 53% of EC capabilities will be based on business-to-business relationship, and the Forrester Research predicted that B2B EC was to hit US$12.2 billion in 2006 worldwide (Forrester Research, 2002). It is now universally recognized that B2B EC possesses the largest potential in the EC segment (Gibbs, Kraemer & Dedrick, 2003), which is supported by a growing trend of companies incorporating one or more of its business initiatives in e-procurement, CRM, online sales and supply chain management. This study is purposely focused on organizations that use business-to-business EC to carry out transactions and interactions that affect existing business relationships or preexisting contractual relations between trading partners.

RESEARCH OBJECTIVES

In response to the current issues faced by SMEs, an awareness of the critical success factors of EC implementation would provide these organizations with the required knowledge to appropriately address the relevant concerns and move forward in the area of EC. Using the *Extent of Deployment* as the indicator of implementation success, the study aims to address the following research questions:

- What factors influence of the extent of EC deployment for SMEs?
- To what degree do these individual factors influence the success of EC implementation?

Theoretical Perspective of this Study

It should be noted that this study has been informed by a substantial variety of previous research on adoption, implementation, and innovation diffusion theories applied to technology in general: information systems, information technology, Electronic Data Interchange (EDI), Interorganizational System (IOS), and Management of Information Systems (MIS). Clearly, EC is not identical with any of them. It necessarily involves IT which it shares with IS and MIS, and at more sophisticated levels is likely to enable EDI. It is also undeniably "Interorganizational." It may therefore be argued that any factor that has been shown to influence the adoption and implementation of technology or application in general is worthy of consideration as a potential explanatory variable with respect to EC. To ensure thoroughness, wherever previous research or reasoning suggested a relationship between a factor and one of the variables, its possible influence on the focal variables will also be hypothesized. Innovation diffusion theories have been particularly useful for understanding the facilitators and inhibitors of EC, which can be asserted to be a subtype of innovation. After a critical analysis of existing models, their influencing factors, stages, and process, the theoretical framework is extended to incorporate important organizational and contextual aspects of adoption and implementation in the development of a research model.

EC Adoption and Implementation

As defined in Roger's diffusion theory (1995), *adoption* is a decision to define the full use of an innovation as the best course of action, and *implementation* is taking the necessary steps to facilitate and execute that innovation into business practice or process. For several reasons, there is rarely any clear separation between adoption and implementation in EC. In other words, EC is not "one simple or single innovation" that a firm either does or does not adopt, but should be considered as consisting of a number of combinations of innovations of varying complexity and sophistication on a continuum requiring lesser to greater levels of commitment. While conceptually distinct, there is no temporal dividing line between all the dependent variables in this study for they merge into one another (i.e., *State of Adoption*, *Extent of Deployment*, *Level of Usage*, and *Overall Satisfaction*). Rather, their hierarchy is logical in that each is a necessary condition for the next: while one feature is becoming more utilized, another is being explored and a third is being considered or enabled. Thus, in any firm EC is never "adopted" or "not adopted," but always in one of a large number of possible "states of adoption". The following section focuses on discussing the significance of *Extent of Deployment* as a measure of implementation success. The other three dependent variables are beyond the scope of this article.

Extent of Deployment

While most IS adoption studies are inwardly oriented (due to the internal deployment of systems architectures or software within a specific firm), the current study utilizes *Extent of Deployment* as an externally-oriented measure. Hence, the definition of *Extent of Deployment* can be designated as the degree to which a firm is successful in linking with external partners and converting its transaction documents into electronic form. The construct borrows three concepts and definitions from diffusion and integration studies by Massetti and Zmud (1996). A weighted index was developed to measure *Extent of Deployment* by multiplying all the three components of deployment (or the "extent of integration" or "diffusion" as defined by previous studies—see Massetti & Zmud, 1996; Premkumar, Ramamurthy & Nilkantan, 1994; Ramamurthy, Premkumar & Crum, 1999; Raymond & Bergeron, 1996). Although it is an adaptation of concepts from previous research, the current report has tailored these for an EC context. Thus, the variable *Extent of Deployment* combines the notions of **volume**, **diversity**, and **breadth**. As for the aspect of **depth**, this is captured in the other dependent variable not covered in this article—the *Level of Usage*.

- **Volume**—the proportion of business that the firm derives from Internet-based EC is defined as the "*Percent of Business Conducted Online*" in this study.
- **Diversity**—the variety of documents exchanged via Internet-based EC with their external partners. It is defined as "*Application Diversity*" in this study.
- **Breadth**—the extent to which a firm has developed EC connections with its trading partners. It is defined as "*Number of Linkages*" in this study.

Unlike traditional information systems, EC is an IOS, and therefore requires the organization to expand its external electronic links to gain economies of scale and be cost effective. Previous studies have demonstrated that there is a need for "inter-exploitation" between partners through expansion of IOS in order to sustain strategic advantage (Computerworld, 1992; Vitale, 1985). Firms could utilize the electronic links to a greater extent by including more transactions or documents. Such an expansion of electronic exchange would enable firms to experience the full benefits of EC and an improvement in organizational effectiveness in the long run.

RESEARCH MODEL

In this study, it is proposed that several factors influence different levels of EC adoption for the organization. To assist in the selection of the most significant variables for EC adoption and

Figure 1. Conceptual model of factors that influence the extent of deployment of EC

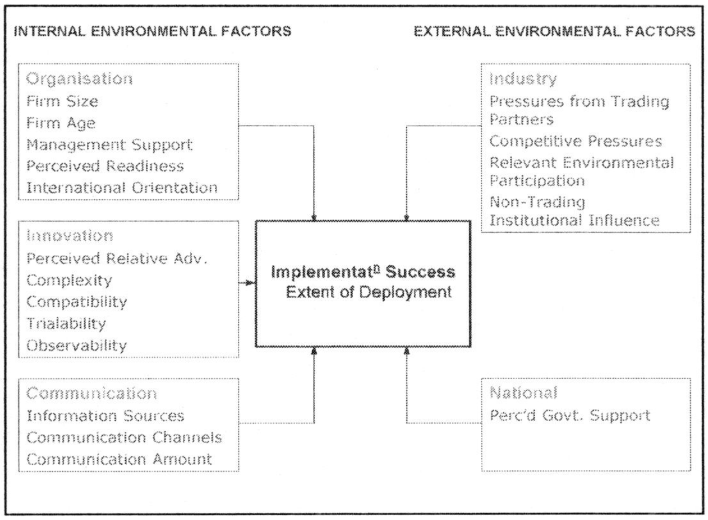

implementation, a number of possible relevant factors have been identified and grouped into broad categories of *internal* and *external environmental factors*. The principal reason for separating internal from external influences is to distinguish between organization-derived factors and other motivations that may arise from the overall business environment (or outside the organization). Figure 1 presents the research model in which the relationship between the influencing factors and the *Extent of Deployment* was examined.

INFLUENCING FACTORS OF EC ADOPTION AND IMPLEMENTATION

Internal Environmental Factors

Despite the advantages of EC, SMEs around the world are not adopting it as rapidly as originally anticipated (The Age, 2002; Dholakia & Kshetri, 2004; Grandon & Pearson, 2003b; McCole & Ramsey, 2005; Mirchandani & Motwani, 2001; Poon & Swatman, 1998; Purao & Campbell, 1998; Rao, Metts & Monge, 2003; Van Beveren & Thomson, 2002; Wagner, Fillis & Johansson, 2003). Several *organizational factors* that inhibit IT and EC adoption were identified after conducting preliminary interviews and an extensive literature search. Among these were the cost of technology, a lack of managerial and technological skills, a lack of system integration and a lack of financial resources (Cragg & King, 1993; Iacovou, Benbasat & Dexter, 1995; McCole & Ramsey, 2005; Nilankanta & Scamell, 1990; Stockdale & Standing, 2004). These inhibitors are expected to play a major role in the context of small organizations, where resources and the level of computer sophistication are limited (Dholakia & Kshetri, 2004; Grandon & Pearson, 2003b; Lertwongsatien & Wongpinunwatana, 2003; Riemenschneider & McKinney, 2001-2002; Stockdale & Standing, 2004; Van Beveren & Thomson, 2002; Zhu, Kraemer & Xu, 2003), thus *firm size* and *perceived readiness* are included in the category of internal environmental factors. Another recurrent observation is that EC adoption seems to be more of a management issue than a technical one (Corbitt, Behrendorf & Brown-Parker, 1997). Many researchers have found that if there is a lack of support amongst top executives, technology cannot be successfully adopted (Cooper & Zmud, 1990; Gagnon & Toulouse, 1996; Grandon & Pearson, 2003a; Igbaria, Zinatelli & Cavaye, 1998; Lertwongsatien & Wongpinunwantana, 2003; Premkumar & Ramamurthy, 1995). It is therefore reasonable to assume that *management support* is a critical factor to the successful adoption of EC. Previous scholars also anticipated that the *age of the firm* could either foster or impede technology adoption in terms of resistance to change, a track record of successfully overcoming hurdles, and experience in adopting prior technological advances (Germain, Droge & Daugherty, 1994). The *international orientation* of the company is also examined in this study, as previous research within the area of Internet adoption demonstrates that firms that are operating in the international markets are more likely to conduct EC through portals than those that do not have foreign collaborations (see Daniel & Grimshaw, 2002; Lal, 2002; Wagner, Fillis & Johansson, 2003).

Several factors that influence the adoption of innovation are deduced since EC is treated as the innovative business practice in this study. Of most commonly investigated characteristics that promote the adoption of innovation, the best known may be those developed by Rogers (1995). These *innovation factors* have also been the key feature of several other IT adoption studies (Iacovou et al., 1995; Kwon & Zmud, 1987; Moore & Benbasat, 1991; Sharif, 1994; Tornatzky & Klein, 1982) and EC studies (Kendall, Tung, Chua, Ng & Tan, 2001; Lertwongsatien & Wongpinunwatana, 2003; McCole & Ramsey, 2005; Van Slyke, Belanger & Comunale, 2004; Wagner et. al., 2003). In this study, they are adapted for the current report as follows: *perceived relative advantage* (i.e., the perceived EC benefits and impact relative to its existing practice or system), *compatibility* (how well EC fits in both technical and organizational processes), *trialability* (the degree to which EC can be pilot tested or experimented without high start-up costs), *complexity* (ease of use or the ease with which EC can be learned), and *observability* (the extent to which EC advantages or gains are visible to firms).

During the early stage of the study, preliminary interviews and extensive literature search conducted indicated limited sources of information that SMEs can exploit in order to gain knowledge of EC. This may serve to hinder the smooth adoption of EC in many cases. Moreover, following the work of Rogers (1995), other scholars argue that the adoption of a new technology is influenced by *communication channel types* (mass media vs. interpersonal channels), *information source* (external source vs. internal source), and *communication amount* (Brancheau & Wetherbe, 1990; Nilankantan & Scamell, 1990). Hence *communication factors* were added to the EC adoption model.

External Environmental Factors

SMEs are usually characterized by a high level of environmental uncertainty that includes fluctuations in interest rates, reliability of supply, and competition. Related to this factor, the use of IT and EC is often imposed on SMEs by major customers or suppliers. Such pressure from trading partners plays a critical role in encouraging small firms to adopt IT and EC, as evidenced in previous studies (Daniel & Grimshaw, 2002; Grandon & Pearson, 2003b; Iacovou et al., 1995; McCole & Ramsey, 2005; Stockdale & Standing, 2004; Thong, 1999; Wagner et al., 2003; Zhu et al., 2003). In addition, the competitive pressure that firms face within the industry also has an influence on the company's decision to adopt IT or EC (Crum, Premkumar & Ramamurthy, 1996; Grandon & Pearson, 2003a, b; Iacovou et al., 1995; McCole & Ramsey, 2005; Wagner et al., 2003; Zhu et al., 2003). As more competitors adopt EC, small firms are more inclined to follow suit in order to maintain their own competitive positions. Even though it should also be noted that the influence of nontrading institutions such as industry associations, government, financial institutions, the media and universities may not be as strong as that of the entities the firm trades with, they may still influence the adoption of EC to a certain extent. Thus, the aforementioned justifications lead to the inclusion of *trading partner's pressure*, *competitive pressure* and *nontrading institutional influence* under the category of *industry factors*. *Relevant environmental participation* is also an important factor for any firm that is trying to employ new technology or systems to their fullest potential. Without the wide acceptance of applications or systems, current or potential customers may resist the adoption of EC because of the lack of infrastructure, suitable platform, or compatible technological standards (Lertwongsatien & Wongpinunwatana, 2003; McCole & Ramsey, 2005; Wagner et al., 2003). It should be noted that although relevant environmental participation recognizes the existence of a possible critical mass, it is not synonymous with that term. While the concept of critical mass may be appropriate to studying the movement of a single innovation through a large social system, its usefulness when applied to innovations that lie on a continuum (such as EC in SMEs) is limited.

Finally, the *national factor* is included in the adoption model in order to provide a macro country-level view of EC, its adoption behaviour and the business environment. This study demonstrates that in addition to the private sector, the governmental sector can also act as a crucial catalyst in stimulating a successful adoption experience for the SMEs (see Grandon & Pearson, 2003a; Wagner et al., 2003). Previous studies have illustrated that governmental support in funding infrastructure projects, adoption schemes and initiatives have provided direct and indirect stimulation to the supply of information which—as a consequence—produces faster technology diffusion (Kettinger, 1994; Tan, 1998). Governmental subsidy and supports have been demonstrated to have a positive impact on the uptake of IT use and innovative business practice by organizations, especially SMEs (Anderson, Aydin & Jay, 1994; Payton & Ginzberg, 2001; Wagner et al., 2003). Institutional regulations that promote electronic interactions and transactions may also encourage EC or future IT adoption in small businesses (King, Gurbaxani & Kraemer, 1994; Rao et al., 2003). In this study, we examine the influence of *governmental support* and its propensity to shape the push for EC in SMEs.

Research Methodology

At the time of the study, an exploratory approach was taken to consider a comprehensive scope of factors that may influence the implementation success of EC. Thus, a cross sectional approach was undertaken and a framework was enacted to measure firms' responses with respect to the implementation of EC. The desired result in testing the model is the identification of factors **associated** with the *Extent of Deployment*.

Data Collection

The study was conducted in Australia in three phases: a preliminary investigation, pilot study, and questionnaire survey. Preliminary interviews with five Australian SMEs alongside with extensive literature review were conducted to provide direction as to what implementation factors are imperative to SMEs, all of which contributed to the design of the proposed research model. Firstly, a survey instrument with questions and multiple-item scales was developed and then a pilot study was conducted to capture the information reflecting the perceptions and practice of those adopting EC. This was helpful in refining the survey instrument as the questions aimed to identify specifically the internal or external environmental factors that influence the adoption of EC and the degrees of their influence. In order to focus on SMEs, assistance was sought from governmental and research institutions in Austra-

Table 1. Summary of response rate

	Usable	Unusable	Undeliverable	Unreturned	Total
AUSTRALIA					
1st Round					
Number	68	18	85	314	485
Percent %	*14.0*	*3.7*	*17.5*	*64.7*	*100*
2nd & 3rd Round (Follow-up)					
Number	47	7	29	231	314
Percent %	*15.0*	*2.2*	*9.2*	*73.6*	*100*
Total Number of Usable Responses[1]	115				
Percent %	23.7				

lia to develop a database of such companies and contact details of target respondents. A systematic random sampling method was conducted and a total of 485 records were derived from a database of 3,232 companies. As the survey was intended to apply to a wide geographical area, the chosen method of delivery was a combination of e-mail, Web, and mail survey, and 485 questionnaires were disseminated. A cover letter stating the objective of the study and the web address of the online version of the survey was included. The questionnaires were personally addressed to the director or owner of the firms. In order to improve response rate, reminders were sent out to target respondents two weeks after the commencement of first and second-wave of mail-outs. A total of 115 usable responses were collected.

In the first round of distribution, 68 responses were returned in a usable format, 18 were unusable, and 85 were marked as undeliverable. Three weeks after the first round, a second round was sent out. For those surveys delivered electronically, the returned responses contained the e-mail addresses of respondents, and reminders were not sent to them on the follow-up rounds. New e-mail addresses, mailing addresses, and fax numbers were identified for some of the undeliverable responses. Of the 314 remaining surveys sent the second and third rounds, 47 were returned in a usable format, and 7 were identified as unusable. Overall, the total number of usable questionnaires elicited from the Australian SMEs was 115, amounting to an acceptable rate of 23.7% of responses.

Nonresponses Bias Assessment

In order to encourage SMEs' participation in the study, more than two mailings of the questionnaire were conducted. To further increase the response rate, each of the cover letters accompanying the questionnaire was personally addressed to the Director or Chief Executive Officer (where such information was available). For those businesses for which no details were supplied, the covering letter was addressed to the position title of Director or Chief Executive Officer. A reply paid envelope was also issued and this was an effort to encourage responses even further. A copy of summary findings was yet another incentive offered to ensure a high response rate. To arrive at the estimate of total nonresponse error, a comparison of the data obtained from the two mailing rounds was conducted. The basic assumption behind this approach is that subjects that respond only after further prompting were potential nonrespondents. Analyses from the first round of respondents are compared with results from later rounds. If no statistically significant difference between the two groups is found, then it is reasonable to assume that nonresponse error is not present and that the remaining nonrespondents exhibit similar characteristics to the respondents (Churchill, 1991).

In summary, the two-step response assessment process that was utilized, together with the personally addressed covering letters, reply paid facility, and an offer of summary findings, were put into practice in order to counteract the disadvantages normally associated with a mail survey: namely, low response rates and the problem of non-response error. It was therefore safe to make the assumption that the data obtained from the respondents was representative of the sample and that, as a consequence, any findings derived from this data were generalizable to the sample frame in its entirety.

INSTRUMENT DEVELOPMENT

The questionnaire used in this study was designed to measure variables in the theoretical model illustrated previously. Some of the indicators were developed by the researcher, while some were adopted or modified from previous scholars. In some cases in which a previous measure is adequate, sources and proper credit were cited. In other cases, new indicators were added and compared with the previous measures to help improve the explanatory power of the research model. Slight modifications of the wordings were made to reflect the business-to-business EC nature of the study and any further changes to the instrument were retested and then included in the final survey.

Individual survey items that are presented in Appendix A represent a comprehensive list of the variables used in the current study. These variables are presented with the corresponding indicators, the types of scales used, and an indication of whether they were researcher-defined or, if not, the sources from which they were adopted or adapted. Researcher-defined variables are developed according to Neuman's (1999) suggestions for constructing new measure. In the current report, all variables were measured as attitudinal perception items on five-point Likert scales (e.g., 1 to 5 = *very unimportant* to *very important*; *strongly agree* to *strongly disagree*). The research instrument was based on many multiple-item scales, as incorporating several items results in a more realistic and comprehensive indicator (Neuman, 1999). To ensure the validity of the dependent measure, this study also incorporates a single rating scale so as to provide a comparison of results.

DEPENDENT VARIABLE: EXTENT OF DEPLOYMENT

It was stated in the previous section that *Extent of Deployment* measures the degree to which the firm is successful in linking with external partners and converting its transaction documents into electronic form. Thus, *Extent of Deployment* is measured by multiplying all the three components of deployment—volume, diversity and breadth of EC application as implemented within the business practice.

Owing to the exploratory nature of the research at the time the current study was conducted, the relationships that emerged as significant at the 10% level may or may not eventually prove to be valid in a more intensively formed undertakings. However, they were deemed to be worthy of serious consideration in this report as a basis for further exploration. In addition, due to the sample size limitation of this study, a rigid imposition of the traditional 5% level of significance level ($p < 0.05$) entailed an unwarranted risk of rejecting possible valid relationships (i.e., type II error). As indicated by Hair, Anderson, Tatham, and Black (1998), the recommended minimum ratio of cases to variables in regression is five to one. The criterion of sample size adequacy was met in this study.

Instrument Validation

As recommended by Nunnally (1978), the reliability and validity of the measures for this study were tested to ascertain the suitability and rigour of the study instrument. The Cronbach's (1951) coefficient alpha has been used in the present research to examine the internal consistency of the scales relating to all the independent variables of this study. This reliability measure of two or more construct indicators produces values between 0 and 1. Higher values indicate greater reliability among the indicators (Hair et al., 1998, p. 618). The amount of scale reliability could have been improved by repeating or requesting the same essential question in a disguised or reoriented form in another part of the questionnaire. However, this would have substantially lengthened the questionnaire and very likely decreased the response rate. The following are the practical considerations and principles (Neuman, 1999) that were taken to ensure the reliability of the current study:

- Clarity of most constructs was carefully examined. Most of which have already been established in previous literature.
- Pretests and pilot studies were used.
- The most precise level of measurement was used in each question within the constraints of meaningful discernibility of values. A 5-point scale is used in the questionnaire.
- Multiple indicators were used where any possibility of ambiguity existed on the part of the respondents.

It should be noted that methods of testing the stability of any measurement becomes relatively meaningless and unnecessary when a concept or construct has defined the essential components, each of which is measured using an appropriate item (Jacob, 2000). Here, the items are not expected to be homogenous, nor are they selected at random.

A test of internal consistency amongst each set of items representing the Internal and External Environmental Factors was conducted. These tests reveal that the *Innovation Factors—Perceived Relative Advantage* (0.73), *Compatibility* (0.77) and *Complexity* (0.72), and *Observability* (0.79), all had Cronbach Alpha values greater than the 0.7 benchmark suggested by Nunnally (1978). The value for *Trialability* (0.56) was marginally below the cut off value of 0.6, acceptable in the early stages of research (Tan & Teo, 2000). The reliability coefficient for the new variables, *Management Support* (0.94), and *Nontrading Institutional Influence* (0.98) all exceeded 0.7. Thus, overall the results appeared robust enough to carry out further analysis. It must be acknowledged however, that since the items comprising some of these scales were not heterogeneous collections drawn from a large number of possible candidates but specifically designed to cover distinct components, the appropriateness of equivalence reliability measures such as Cronbach Alpha may be debated. The lists of items for the variables concerned are not created by a large sample of possible phenomena. They are almost an exhaustive list but not a complete one. The applicability of the standard reliability score (0.70) by Cronbach Alpha is limited for the following reasons:

- The list does not consist of a small heterogeneous collection of items drawn from a large number of potential candidates.
- However, for those who insist on Cronbach Alpha, the results are presented above. The Cronbach Alpha indicates that the list of items is internally homogeneous.

- These methods of reliability analysis are of limited ability. However, in each case Cronbach Alpha does at least indicate a satisfactory level of internal consistency.

The issue of face validity in the case of previously recognized concepts is taken as established. The researcher-defined concepts naturally awaits general acceptance. Content validity is achieved during the planning and construction stages of the scale and not when the scale is completed, hence procedures that are used to develop the instrument are the key to content validity (Churchill, 1991). The key issues to be addressed in this study regarding content validity include: (1) Whether the full set of items being measured covers all the relevant variables and (2) whether each specific set of items cover the intended range of components in a given variable. Various indexes such as the *Management Support, Organizational Readiness, Innovation Factors,* and the *Communication Factors* have already been tested, as many of these measures contain items or components that have been borrowed or adopted from previous studies. As dependent variable like the *Extent of Deployment* have not previously been used in studies of this kind, it was appropriate that its content validity be given some consideration. Guided by the procedures suggested by Davis (1996), the following steps were taken to address the issue for the variables mentioned above:

1. A literature search to examine all possible items to be included.
2. The utilization of multiple judges to assess the appropriateness of the items included.
3. Pretesting the scale on a small sample of target respondents so as to identify potential flaws with the contents and/or wording.
4. Any potentially questionable item was discussed with a range of experts and practitioner in the area of EC for clarification.
5. The modification of the scales based on suggestions developed from steps (2) and (3).

Criterion-related validity is an important issue where latent variables are involved. No variable in this study can be regarded as truly latent. While several measures involve subjective perceptions on part of the respondents, it is the actual perception which is the focal variable and not the latent reality behind it. One such variable is the *Perceived Readiness*. The perception of one's own readiness is a potential influencing factor related to, but nonetheless distinct from, the actual readiness; and has an influence on decisions in its own right. To assess whether the various indicators of the concept operate in a consistent manner, construct validity was tested. Very few variables in this study fall into the category of abstract concepts that possess serious ambiguity. Those that did, namely, the *Innovation Factors*, were extensively investigated. The issue of construct validity was addressed in the pilot study and resulted in the removal or modification or some potentially ambiguous items which further ensures clear measurement and consistency.

Despite all endeavour to ensure the validity of each measure in this study, it should be noted that it is not possible to achieve it in an absolute sense, as constructs are abstract ideas while indicators are concrete observations. As argued by Bohrnstedt (1992), validity is a matter of degree and is a part of a dynamic process that grows by accumulating evidence over time, and without it all measurement becomes meaningless.

Assumption Testing and Multicollinearity

As noted in Table 2, this study exceeds the standards of regression by scoring less than 10 for its Variance Inflation Factor (VIF), which is a minimum of Tolerance value of 1.0. In addition, the Durbin Watson statistics fell within the range of 1.5 to 2.5.

The existence of outliers was queried and none were found. All assumptions were satisfied, suggesting no serious deviations from normality and no serial correlation of errors in this study, with the exception of the partial regression plot that examined the relationship between *Extent of Deployment* and *Communication Amount*. In this case there was evidence of a slight upward curvature and attempts were made to compensate for this by introducing the square of this variable. This resulted in the latter becoming significant at the expense of the former, but no change in the inclusion or the exclusion of other variables. In other words, no additional advantage was gained and thus, for the purposes of identifying *Communication Amount* as a factor related to the *Extent of Deployment* and confirming the direction of its relationship, the original formulation was retained.

RESULTS

Of the 485 survey questionnaires distributed to target respondents within Australia, a total of 115 usable responses were collected. More than 50% of the responding firms employ less than 50 workers. The distribution of respondents was consistent with the overall community distribution. The majority of those who responded in this study held Managing Director positions in their respective companies and three quarters of them had tertiary education or above. This suggests that the level of language used in the survey is unlikely to have been any hindrance to its proper interpretation by the respondents.

Multiple linear regression was used to generate the results illustrated in Table 3. It represents the results of the stepwise-backward elimination, whereby those factors that are statistically significant in the model for the *Extent of Deployment*, are retained.

An adjusted R-squared value of 47% of the variation in *Extent of Deployment* by Australian SMEs is explained by the variation of *Communication Amount, Variety of Information Sources, Perceived Relative Advantage, Observability, Trialability, Competitive Pressure,* and *Non-Trading Institutional Influences* (F-significance < 0.000). All variables are significant at the 0.10 level or better. The figure below shows factors that are supported by significant evidence.

DISCUSSION

Communication Amount

Communication Amount is the most significant factor related to the Extent of Deployment thus

Table 2. Assumption testing: Coefficients of extent of deployment

	Collinearity Statistics	
Model	***Tolerance***	***VIF***
(Constant)		
MGMT.SUPP	0.933	1.072
INTL.ORIENT	0.876	1.142
PCD.REL.ADV	0.857	1.167
TRIALAB	0.876	1.142
INFO.SRC	0.867	1.153
COMM.AMT	0.895	1.117
COMP.PRES	0.716	1.396
NON.TRD.INFL	0.719	1.391

Table 3. Final model estimation (stepwise-backward method) for the Extent of Deployment

Influencing Factors	Standardized Coefficient (beta)	t-value	Significance
(Constant)		-3.270	0.002
PCD.REL.ADV	0.301	2.947	0.005**
TRIALAB	-0.240	-2.315	0.025*
OBSERV	0.267	2.466	0.017*
INFO.SRC	0.316	3.039	0.004**
COMM.AMT	0.322	3.271	0.002**
COMP.PRES	0.183	1.739	0.088
NON.TRD.INFL	-0.172	-1.737	0.088

$R^2 = 0.533$ Adjusted $R^2 = 0.470$ F-significance = 0.000 Observations = 115
* Significance at 0.05 level
** Significance at 0.01 level

suggesting that the more a firm increases its intensity of communication with other organizations, the higher its extent of deployment is likely to be. It can also be rationalized that the greater the amount of information a small firm shares with its trading partners, the greater the diversity and depth of integration of EC will be between firms. Since EC can be regarded as another interorganizational system, more frequent communication between trading partners will help them coordinate policies, provide technical information, and answer questions. Such collaborative approaches may assist, in a fairly unobtrusive manner, in bringing the trading partners "on-board" to the EC network. This would in turn help them in the uptake of new systems, which would eventually motivate the adopting firms to improve the extent of their EC deployment.

Variety of Information Sources

The *Variety of Information Sources* used to attain information pertaining to EC, is found to be positively related to the Extent of Deployment. This suggests that the larger the variety of sources a firm used in acquiring information about EC, the higher the Extent of Deployment. This can be explained in the following way: as firms are getting ready to implement EC, they are likely to seek advice and information from a large variety of sources in order to familiarize themselves with the different functions, applications, or benefits of EC. The larger the variety of the sources the firm consults, the higher possibility will be that the firm would seek diversification of applications and external participants for higher levels of deployment. It may also be suggested that the diligence on the part of the firm that seeks information from a greater variety of sources will result in them being better informed than those relying on a smaller sample of sources. Since those companies that have consulted widely are likely to have more knowledge in the requisite areas of EC, they are more likely to apply their knowledge to practical functions and applications. This would conceivably lead to a higher ability to trade with a variety of participants in the market, thus encouraging them to attain a higher proportion of business online.

Perceived Relative Advantage

Perceived Relative Advantage appears to be significantly related to the Extent of Deployment. This contradicts the results of a study by Premkumar, Ramamurthy and Nilkantan (1994) in which they found that perceived relative advantage only influences the adoption decision and not the implementation success of EDI. The high relative importance of this variable indicates that the benefits of EC perceived by SMEs have led to a high extent of deployment. This can be logically explained in so far as it is akin to assessing the benefits and costs of adopting any type of innovation. In this case it can be seen that SMEs are most motivated by the prospects of gaining a relative advantage over competitors, or by the likelihood that EC can put them ahead of the "status quo" or existing business practice in as much as it might open up new markets for them or lower their business costs. On the other hand, it could be suggested that if companies do not believe that EC can provide them with relative advantage after they have already adopted it, it is likely that the implementation would be discontinued.

Although one cannot forcibly increase ones' perception of relative advantage where it does not genuinely exist it is nevertheless possible to be more proactive in investigating and exploring possible advantages that could lead to increased success (Chong & Pervan, 2001). SMEs should evaluate their implementation of EC on a regular basis in order to integrate and expand its application to other business functions effectively. After making the decision to adopt EC, it also needs to be perceived by SMEs as a better alternative to existing practices in the business. However, very often the lack of knowledge of the advantages that EC offers can cause impatient firms to give up and discontinue the adoption and implementation. Therefore, the use of promotional efforts and noncoercive influence tactics is suggested for increasing the levels of awareness for EC benefits. Perhaps both government and industry associations can also play a more active role raising

Figure 2. Factors related to the Extent of Deployment among Australian SMEs

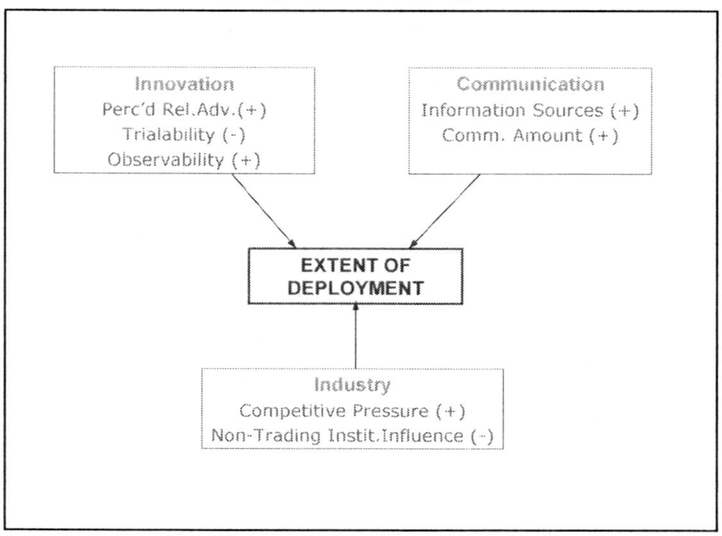

participation, pointing SMEs to the opportunities and benefits of EC, providing them with support, and working with them to overcome their doubts regarding the implementation of EC.

Observability

For Australian SMEs, *Observability* appears to be significantly related to the Extent of EC Deployment. A two-way causation is likely to be operating in this instance. First, there is a logical relationship between confidence and Extent of Deployment. When a firm can observe the benefits that EC has brought to the business, it is very likely that the firm will increase the depth and breadth of EC implementation. In the case of doing business online, effects such as quicker access to and dissemination of information and savings in costs (e.g., printing, advertizing, communication, and overheads) are more immediate and easier to acknowledge. The implication for SMEs is therefore to highlight the easily and quickly demonstrable benefits and usage in the first instance, such that the short term visible effects of EC can help promote its continued adoption and hence facilitate the long-term goals of the initiative. It is sometimes not enough to assume that people will automatically realize the impact of an innovation. Indeed, it may be necessary to insist that firms reflect on their EC implementation in order to increase their awareness and observation of the regimen's impact. This could include the requirement of a formal review procedure involving both owner/managers and employees of a given company, in order to elicit the end user observations of how well the application of the EC systems is progressing. During the course of implementing EC a degree of pessimism may be exhibited amongst key personnel, and this may be a justifiable reaction to a certain extent. Nonetheless, every effort must be made to counter unjustified and groundless pessimism because this could serve as a needless inhibitor in the deployment of EC. This may well require a more proactive approach in which SMEs will need to be courageous enough to implement an EC system, even if its tangible benefits are not readily observable from the outset.

Another possible explanation for the significant relationship between observability and extent of deployment could lie in reversing the chain of causality as follows: the higher the extent of EC deployment, the greater the likelihood that the regimen's advantages will be observable. It is logical to expect that the more extensive the deployment of EC is in terms of its application to a given firm's business practices, the more benefits the firm is going to reap. These benefits will in turn become more observable to the adopting firms and confidence in EC will thus be self-perpetuating. To improve the extent of EC deployment, firms should not only increase the variety of documents exchanged via the Internet, but also seek to increase external links with trading partners. This can be done by providing incentives and assistance to encourage these partners to get involved in the electronic network. Such incentives may include, for instance, bulk discounts or special rates for trading online.

Trialability

It was interesting to note that *Trialability* appears to be inversely related the Extent of Deployment. It is possible to suggest that when adopting firms perceived EC to be less trialable, they are more likely to push for higher levels of commitment. Such firms would thus apply more urgency to learning and experimenting with the new system, which normally leads to greater preparedness as most companies want to ensure that their investment will not be wasted. This also indicates that such firms would have a higher ability to deploy extensively. Another possible explanation, however, is that the perception of trialability may be a sign of lack of commitment. Because deployment requires some degree of commitment, it can only truly begin when the trialing mentality stops. This serves as a reminder to would-be or hesitant adopters that even though preparation and keen attitude in experimenting may be essential, SMEs should not take too long to deploy EC. For a start, rather than purchasing more expensive, custom-developed EC software or applications, well-tested dedicated packages may well suit the needs of the company.

Competitive Pressure

Competitive Pressure was positively related to the Extent of Deployment, suggesting that the higher the level of pressure experienced to the firm from its competitors, the greater the extent of its EC deployment is likely to be. This means that the competitiveness of the environment has been found to provide the "push" for SMEs to deploy their existing capabilities. Firms that fear losing customers or market share may expedite their learning process or expand the use of new systems in order to keep up with what their competitors are doing. The emergence of competitive pressure as a key variable also underscores the need to electronically integrate business operations both internally and externally with trading partners. Formalization of these functions and trading processes is essentially a matter of deployment. SMEs are advized that early formalization of a system between the firm and its trading partners may decrease the likelihood of the trading partners finding a competitive relationship more attractive. By being more efficient in business transactions with their partners through faster and more accurate processing, the competitiveness of a given firm would naturally be strengthened, and better links with its customers would be formed.

Nontrading Institutional Influence

Nontrading Institutional Influence was found to have an inverse relationship with the Extent of Deployment. This suggests that those autonomous early adopters that are less likely to be influenced by the publicity and persuasion of certain institutions (such as governments, banks, telecommunication corporations, media, consulting firms or universities), may tend to explore the possibilities more widely and with greater initiative. Alternatively, those that tend to follow what others prescribe (e.g., laggards or non-initiators) tend to lack the characteristics or incentives to explore, take risks, adapt to new change, and to venture into different avenues for maximizing the potential of new business practices (in this case, adopting EC). It may also be true that when firms react to pressure from the external environment, it is more likely that they are limiting their deployment in the direction from which the pressure is arising instead of exploring the fuller extent of possibilities that the innovation (EC) offers. This can impede wider deployment as some firms may see it as a chore to keep following others, while some may be discouraged to further the adoption due to unreadiness or unclear objectives. Thus, SMEs are strongly encouraged not to restrict their exploration of possibilities as a result of the dominance of narrow influencing sources. Nonetheless, it should be noted that despite the relationship between *Nontrading Institutional Influence* and *Extent of Deployment* being statistically significant, it is a comparatively weak relationship.

Managerial Implications

To achieve a greater extent of EC deployment, it is imperative for SMEs to possess an enduring perception of EC as being advantageous over preceding legacy systems and that its implementation can give them an advantage over their competitors. In fact, Grandon and Pearson (2003a) even asserted that late adopters may not gain *competitive advantage* as much as they may gain *competitive parity* because most of the surplus value of EC implementation would be ceded to the earlier adopters. Thus, apart from encouraging hesitant firms to stop procrastinating and begin making a commitment, it is also essential for SMEs to possess a sufficient degree of optimism and confidence such that a habit of continued deployment becomes the norm for future adoptions of innovation. When obtaining information about EC, SMEs should consult more than one source of information to better its knowledge about its applications and benefits, as well as its potential pitfalls. However, while external information sources are valuable, a thorough assessment of a firm's own business needs may still be required to prevent the type of unfounded influence which commonly leads to limited deployment or discontinuity of implementation. It was also found to be beneficial for SMEs to increase the frequency of communication with their trading partners. This often enhances collaboration between the firms, establishes trust, and integrates future online business more extensively. The current study also suggests that SMEs should take more initiative in their deployment strategies, as an impulsive reaction to pressures coming directly from competitors and non-trading institutions tend to limit the fuller potential of what EC has to offer.

CONCLUSION, LIMITATIONS, AND FURTHER RESEARCH

It is clear that in the implementation of EC, most SMEs in Australia face a range of challenges including a lack of perceived relative advantage over current systems, lack of visible improvement or benefits, competitive pressure, and insufficient sources of information for further deployment. This study offers a comprehensive framework and knowledge of the relative importance of factors that influence EC deployment which would assist SMEs to better plan their continuous IT and resource investments. It is found in this study that communication factors are more vital than other influencing factors in order to achieve successful implementation of EC. The reasons why organizational factors were not found to have any influence on implementation success may be due to the fact that once most SMEs got a clear push from its management to adopt this initiative, readiness, age of the firm or even its international orientation become less of an issue when striving to achieve implementation success. The same is also true for governmental support—for most SMEs, incentives and assistance would be most appreciated and needed in the initial stage when firms are new to the idea of conducting business electronically. Once the inertia has been overcome, the issue of governmental support becomes less of an importance for the adopters.

The study found that it is important for SMEs to seek information from a greater variety of sources to be better informed in the area of EC. During the implementation of highly advanced or sophisticated applications, SMEs are advised to evaluate its integration with other business functions on a regular basis. The study also revealed that SMEs need to take a more proactive approach in disseminating success cases of implementation to encourage continued and further deployment. This also requires the firm to take a more committal approach rather than an experimental one towards such initiatives as it ensures likelihood of implementation success.

Apart from conceptualizing the theoretical framework of EC implementation success for SMEs, the current study has also helped to clarify the definition of the concept "adoption" and most importantly, the measurement of *Extent of Deployment*. Moreover, it encapsulates a multi-dimensional measure of implementation success combining the notions of volume, diversity, and breadth, while encompassing both an external and internal orientation.

Despite the above contribution, it should be noted that this study focuses on theory development rather than theory confirmation. This, with the cross sectional nature of data, also limits the ability of this study to draw causal implications in the findings. Owing to the inherent time constraints in a study of this kind, the adoption decision, which would have required a longitudinal perspective, was not investigated. As such, adoption is only observed in hindsight. Furthermore, the positivist approach undertaken assumes that all variables relevant to the study are established prior to the collection of any data. This approach, while economical and focused from the data collection perspective, also deprives the researcher of potentially new relevant information that might emerge during the data collection process itself. While it would be insightful to have the research model tested in more countries, the study was only conducted in Australia and Singapore (reported elsewhere), due to time and resource constraints. Thus, in making generalization from the research sample, one has to take into consideration the context of Australia. The findings may not be universally true, but they are likely to be applicable in similar cultural contexts. Lastly and most importantly, having established the soundness of the theoretical framework of extent of deployment for SMEs, other researchers may investigate its applicability to a wider range of business communication technologies and further innovations in the future.

REFERENCES

The Age. (2002, October 23). Australian net economy worth $43b: Cisco study. Retrieved September 10, 2006, from http://www.theage.com/au/articles/2002/10/23/1034561542812.html

Anderson, J., Aydin, C., & Jay, S. (1994) *Evaluating health care information systems: Methods and applications*. Sage Publications.

Australian Government Information Management Office. (2005, July 28-29). E-government: Australia's Approach (Keynote Address, Special Minister of State Senator The Hon Eric Abetz, Commonwealth of Australia). In *Proceedings of the Nikkei Fifth Strategic Conference on e-Government*, Tokyo, Japan.

Bohrnstedt, G. (1992). Validity. In E. Borgatta & M. Borgatta (Eds.), *Encyclopaedia of sociology* (Vol. 4, pp. 2217–2222). New York: Macmillan.

Brancheau, J., & Wetherbe, J. (1990). The adoption of spreadsheet software: Testing innovation diffusion theory in the context of end-user computing. *Information Systems Research., 1-2*, 115–143.

Cannon, J. P., & Homburg, C. (2001, January). Buyer-supplier relationships and customer firm costs. *Journal of Marketing*, pp. 29–43.

Chong, S., & Pervan, G. (2001, July 2-3). Implementation success of Internet-based electronic commerce for small- and medium-sized enterprises in Singapore. In *Proceedings of the International Telecommunications Society Asia-Indian Ocean Regional Conference,* July 2-3, Perth, Western Australia, pp. 243-259.

Churchill, G. A. (1991). *Marketing research: Methodological foundations* (5th ed.). Chicago: Dryden Press.

Computerworld. (1992). *Electronic data interchange* (White Paper). Author.

Cooper, R., & Zmud, R. (1990). Information technology implementation research: A technological diffusion approach. *Management Science, 36*(2), 123–139.

Corbitt, B., Behrendorf, G., & Brown-Parker, J. (1997). SMEs and electronic commerce. *The Australian Institute of Management, 14*, 204-222.

Cragg, P., & King, M. (1993). Small-firm computing: Motivators and inhibitors. *MIS Quarterly, 17*(1), 47-60.

Cronbach, L. J. (1951, September). Coefficient alpha and internal structure of tests. *Psychometrika, 16*, 297–334.

Crum, M., Premkumar, G., & Ramamurthy, K. (1996, Summer). An assessment of motor carrier adoption, use, and satisfaction with EC. *Transportation Journal*, pp. 44–57.

Damanpour, F. (1991, September). Organizational innovation: A meta-analysis of effects of determinants and moderators. *Academy of Management Journal, 34*(3), 555–590.

Daniel, E. M., & Grimshaw, D. J. (2002). An exploratory comparison of electronic commerce adoption in large and small enterprises. *Journal of Information Technology, 17*, 133–147.

Davis, D. (1996). *Business research for decision making* (4th ed.). Duxbery Press.

Dholakia, R. R., & Kshetri, N. (2004). Factors impacting the adoption of the Internet among SMEs. *Small Business Economics, 23*(4), 311–322.

eMarketer. (2005, January 17). *IT and e business in the Asia-Pacific region.*

Forrester Research. (2002, April). *E-commerce next wave: Productivity and innovation.* Paper presented at a seminar on Revenue Implications of E-commerce: Trends in E-commerce by Julie Meringer, WTO Committee on Trade and Development.

Forrester Research. (2005, September 14). *US eCommerce forecast: Online retail sales to reach $329 billion by 2010.* Retrieved September 10, 2006, from http://www.forrester.com/Research/Document/Excerpt/0,7211,3726,00

Gagnon, Y., & Toulouse, J. (1996). The behaviour of business managers when adopting new technologies. *Technological Forecasting and Social Change, 52*, 59-74.

Gatignon, H., & Robertson, T. (1989). Technology diffusion: An empirical test of competitive effects. *Journal of Marketing, 53*(1), 35–49.

Germain, R., Droge, C., & Daugherty, P. (1994). A cost and impact typology of logistics technology and the effect of its adoption on organisational practice. *Journal of Business Logistics, 15*(2), 227–248.

Gibbs, J., Kraemer, L., & Dedrick, J. (2003, January-March). Environment and policy factors shaping global e-commerce diffusion: A cross-country comparison. *The Information Society, Special Issue on Globalization of Electronic Commerce, 19*(1), 5–18.

Grandon, E., & Pearson, J. M. (2003a). Strategic value and adoption of electronic commerce: An empirical study of Chilean small and medium businesses. *Journal of Global Information Technology Management, 6*(3), 22–43.

Grandon, E., & Pearson, J. M. (2003b). Electronic commerce adoption: An empirical study of small and medium US businesses. *Information & Management, 42*, 197–216.

Hair, J. F., Anderson, R. E., Tatham, R. L., & Black, W. C. (1998). *Multivariate data analysis with readings* (5th ed.). Englewood Cliffs, NJ: Prentice Hall.

Iacovou, C., Benbasat, I., & Dexter, A. (1995). Electronic data interchange and small organisations: Adoption and impact of technology. *MIS Quarterly, 19*(4), 465-485.

IDC. (2004, August 6). IDC predicts double digit growth of Asia/Pacific Internet buyers from 2003 to 2008. IDC Australia. Retrieved September 10, 2006, from http://www.idc.com.au/newsletters/idcpulse/detail.asp?intID=43

Igbaria, M., Zinatelli, N., & Cavaye, A. (1998). Analysis of information technology success in small firms in New Zealand. *International Journal of Information Management, 18*, 103–119.

Jacob, C. (2000). *Advanced data analysis* (Lecture Series). Curtin University of Technology, Western Australia.

Kendall, J., Tung, L., Chua, K. H., Ng, C. H., & Tan, S. M. (2001). Receptivity of Singapore's SMEs to electronic commerce adoption. *Journal of Strategic Information Systems, 10*, 223–242.

King, J., Gurbaxani, V., & Kraemer (1994). The institutional factors in information technology innovation. *Information Systems Research, 5*(2), 139–169.

Lal, K. (2002). E-business and manufacturing sector: A study of small and medium-sized enterprises in India. *Research Policy, 31*, 1199–1211.

Lertwongsatien, C., & Wongpinunwatana, N. (2003). E-commerce adoption in Thailand: An empirical study of small and medium enterprises (SMEs). *Journal of Global Information Technology Management, 6*(3), 67–83.

Massetti, B., & Zmud, R. (1996). Measuring the extent of EDI usage in complex organisations: Strategies and illustrative examples. *MIS Quarterly, 20*(3), 603–640.

McCole, P., & Ramsey, E. (2005). A profile of adopters and non-adopters of eCommerce in SME professional service firms. *Australasian Marketing Journal, 13*(1), 36–48.

Mirchandani, D. A., & Motwani, J. (2001). Understanding small business electronic commerce adoption: An empirical analysis. *The Journal of Computer Information Systems, 41*(3), 70–73.

Mohr, J., Fisher, R., & Nevin, J. (1996, July). Collaborative communication in interfirm relationships: Moderating effects of integration and control. *Journal of Marketing, 60*, 349–370.

Moore, G., & Benbasat, J. (1991). Development of an instrument to measure the perceptions of adopting an information technology innovation. *Information System Research, 2*(3), 191–222.

Neuman, L. W. (1999). *Social research methods: Qualitative and quantitative approaches* (4th ed.). Allyn & Bacon.

Nilakanta, S., & Scamell, R. (1990). The effect of information sources and communication channels on the diffusion of innovation in a data base development environment. *Management Science, 36*(1), 24-40.

NOIE. (2002, December). E-business for small business. Retrieved September 10, 2006, from http://www.noie.gov.au/projects/ebusiness/Advancing/SME/index.htm

Nunnally, J. (1978). *Psychometric theory.* New York: McGraw-Hill.

Payton, F., & Ginzberg, M. (2001). Interorganisational health care systems implementations: An exploratory study of early electronic commerce initiatives. *Health Care Management Review, 26*(2), 20–32.

Poon, S., & Swatman, P. (1998, June 8-10). Small business Internet commerce experiences: A longitudinal study. In *Proceedings of the Eleventh International Bled Electronic Commerce Conference* (pp. 295-309), Bled, Slovenia.

Premkumar, G., & Ramamurthy, K. (1995). The role of interorganisational and organizational factors on the decision mode for adoption of interorganisational systems. *Decision Sciences, 26*(3), 303-336.

Premkumar, G., Ramamurthy, K., & Nilakanta, S. (1994). Implementation of electronic data interchange. *Journal of Management Information Systems, 11*(2), 157–186.

Premkumar, G., & Roberts, M. (1999). Adoption of new information technologies in rural small businesses. *Omega, The International Journal of Management Science, 27*, 467-484.

Purao, S., & Campbell, S. (1998). Critical concerns for small business electronic commerce: Some reflections based on interviews of small business owners. In *Proceedings of the AIS Conference*, Baltimore, Maryland, pp. 325-327

Ramamurthy, K., Premkumar, G., & Crum, M. (1999). Organisational and interorganisational determinants of EDI diffusion and organisational performance: A casual model. *Journal of Organisational Computing and Electronic Commerce, 9*(4), 253–285.

Rao, S. S., Metts, G., & Monge, C. A. M. (2003). Electronic commerce development in small and medium sized enterprises. *Business Process Management Journal, 9*(1), 11–32.

Raymond, L., & Bergeron, B. (1996). EDI success in small and medium sized enterprises: A field study. *Journal of Organisational Computing and Electronic Commerce, 6*(2), 161–172.

Riemenschneider, C. K., & McKinney, V. R. (2001/2002). Assessing belief differences in small business adopters and non-adopters of Web-based e-commerce. *The Journal of Computer Information Systems, 42*(2), 101–107.

Rogers, E. M. (1995). *Diffusion of innovations* (4th ed.). New York: The Free Press.

Sensis. (2005, August). *e-Business report: The online experience of small and medium enterprises*. Author.

Sharif, N. (1994). Technology change management: Imperatives for developing economies. *Technological Forecasting and Social Change, 47*, 103-114.

Soh, C., Mah, Q. Y., Gan, F. Y., Chew, D. & Reid, E. (1997). The use of the Internet for business: The experience of early adopters in Singapore. *Internet Research, 7*(3), 217-228.

Stockdale, R., & Standing, C. (2004). Benefits and barriers of electronic marketplace participation: An SME perspective. *Journal of Enterprise Information Management, 17*(4), 301–311.

Tan, M., & Teo, T. S. H. (2000). Factors influencing the adoption of Internet banking. *Journal of the AIS, 1*(5), 1-42.

Thong, J. Y. L. (1999). An integrated model of information systems adoption in small businesses. *Journal of Management Information Systems, 15*(4), 187-214.

Tornatzky, L., & Klein, K. (1982). Innovation characteristics and innovation adoption-implementation: A meta analysis of findings. *IEEE Transactions on Engineering Management, 29*(11), 28–45.

Van Beveren, J. V., & Thomson, H. (2002). The use of electronic commerce by SMEs in Victoria, Australia. *Journal of Small Business Management, 40*(3), 250–253.

Van Slyke, C., Belanger, F., & Comunale, C. (2004). Factors influencing the adoption of Web-based shopping: The impact of trust. *Database for Advances in Information Systems, 35*(2), 32–49.

Vitale, M. (1985). *American Hospital Supply Corp.: the ASAP system* (Harvard Business School Case Services No. 9-186-005). Boston: Harvard University.

Wagner, B. A., Fillis, I., & Johansson, U. (2003). E-business and e-supply strategy in small and medium sized businesses (SMEs). *Supply Chain Management, 8*(4), 343–354.

Whiteley, D. (2000). *E-commerce: Strategy, technologies and applications*. Berkshire, UK: McGraw-Hill.

Zhu, K., Kraemer, K., & Xu, S. (2003). E-business adoption by European firms: A cross-country assessment of the facilitators and inhibitors. European Journal of Information Systems, *12*(4), 251-268.

ENDNOTE

1. Definition of Small- and Medium-sized Enterprises (SMEs) in Australia is any business employing less than 20 people; and 20 or more but less than 200 people for medium business. For further definitions of SMEs, please refer to http://sbdc.gov.au

This work was previously published in Journal of Electronic Commerce in Organizations, Vol. 5, Issue 1, edited by M. Khosrow-Pour, pp. 1-29, copyright 2007 by IGI Publishing, formerly known as Idea Group Publishing (an imprint of IGI Global).

APPENDIX A: ANNOTATED INSTRUMENT

Introduction

Please complete this questionnaire with reference to your company's experience in the adoption of Internet-based Electronic Commerce (EC). The study is designed to investigate users' perceptions of the utilization of Internet as the medium to communicate, distribute and conduct information exchange and business transaction with other organizations or businesses. You could expect to complete this questionnaire in about ten to fifteen minutes. There are no right or wrong answers—all we are interested in is a number that truly reflects your thoughts. Thank you again for your time.

Demographic Information (Damanpour, 1991; Gatignon & Robertson, 1989)

1. What is the nature of your business? Please choose from the industry sectors provided.
2. Please indicate the size of your firm based on the number of employees in the company?
3. What is your position in the company?

Dependent Variable: Extent of Deployment (Massetti & Zmud, 1996)

If you use Internet-based EC applications/methods to exchange documents or business information with your trading partners, please answer the following questions.

4. What types of documents or information do you exchange via Internet-based EC? (You may tick more than one box).

- ❑ Transaction & shipping documents (order statements, receipts, etc.)
- ❑ Financial documents
- ❑ Technical information
- ❑ Word documents (reports, proposals, etc.)
- ❑ Marketing information
- ❑ Electronic mails
- ❑ Legal documents
- ❑ Other, please specify: ______________________________

5. With whom do you currently participate in EC (external partners)? (You may tick more than one box).

- ❑ Suppliers
- ❑ Buyers
- ❑ Online recruitment & personnel agencies
- ❑ Telecommunication Companies
- ❑ Financial Institutions (banks, finance co.)
- ❑ Other, please specify: ______________________________

6. What percentage of the total business that your company exchanges with its trading partners are transacted via the Internet?

ORGANIZATIONAL FACTORS

Management Support (Iacouvou, Benbasat & Dexter, 1995)

7. Please indicate your level of agreement on a scale of 1 to 5 (Strongly Disagree to Strongly Agree) with the following statements about the support for EC implementation by the top management in your company (where top management includes yourself and other directors).
   a. Educational support (e.g., training, seminars)
   b. Advisory support
   c. Financial support
   d. Human Resources support
   e. Technical support

Perceived Readiness (Iacouvou et al., 1995)

8. How prepared was your company for the implementation of EC? Please indicate your opinion on the scale of 1 to 5 (Not Prepared to Fully Prepared).

Age of Firm

How long has this company been established? *(Researcher Defined)*

International Orientation (Lal, 2002)

9. What proportion or percentage of your company's turnover is derived from international trade?

Innovation Factors (Rogers, 1995; Soh, Mah, Gan, Chew & Reid, 1997)

10. Please state your opinions to the following statements on a scale of 1 to 5 (Strongy Disagree to Strongly Agree)

Perceived Relative Advantage (over current or other systems)

a. Your company is satisfied with the use of EC in the business
b. Internet has enhanced the corporate image of your company
c. Internet has helped establish stronger links with your clients or other organizations
d. Internet has helped your company develop new business opportunities
e. Internet has helped reduce the costs of information marketing and advertising, customer service and support, information gathering and telecommuting
f. Internet has helped increase sales in your company
g. Internet has enlarged market share of your company

Compatibility (technical and organizational)

h. The adoption of EC is consistent with the values, beliefs, and business needs of your company.
i. There is sufficient support for the adoption of EC from your top management.
j. There is no or only minimal resistance to change from your staff.

Complexity (difficulties in using EC applications)

k. Your company has encountered problems with locating desired information in relation to EC
l. There are rapid changes and technological advances in EC
m. There are technical constraints about adopting EC
n. There are problems relating to the complexity of the application of EC, the skills and training required

Trialability (the ability to test or trial the applications)

o. Your company has no fear of time slippage when experimenting with Internet-based EC
p. Your company faces no financial constraints in experimenting with Internet-based EC
q. Your company perceived Internet-based EC to be trialable before committing more resources to it

Observability (the ability to observe the benefits of EC)

r. Your company believes that the use of Internet-based EC will be highly valued
s. Your company thinks that most firms will adopt the use of EC
t. Your company does not face limitations to the use of the Internet-based EC for business
u. Your company observes the success of similar initiatives by other companies
v. Your company finds that the use of Internet-based EC will become essential

COMMUNICATION FACTORS

Information Sources (Researcher Defined)

11. a. Where does your firm get its information about EC from? (you may tick more than one box):

- ❑ Journal articles
- ❑ Conference papers
- ❑ Sales data
- ❑ Newspaper
- ❑ Government reports
- ❑ Technical or research reports
- ❑ Bulletins/ circulars
- ❑ Books in general
- ❑ Marketing survey reports
- ❑ Reference materials (e.g., handbooks, manuals, etc.)
- ❑ Talks given at meetings, conferences, seminars, etc.
- ❑ Trade or supplier's publications
- ❑ Internet
- ❑ Others, please specify: ______________________

b. Which outside sources of advices would your company use for identification or supply of information about EC? (you may tick more than one box):

- ❑ Trade & industry association
- ❑ Universities or college
- ❑ Personal contacts
- ❑ Professional bodies
- ❑ Small business advisory centres
- ❑ Accountants
- ❑ Research organizations
- ❑ Consultants
- ❑ Financial institutions, banks.
- ❑ Public libraries
- ❑ Suppliers
- ❑ Government depts. or agencies
- ❑ Other, please specify: ______________________

Communication Channels (Researcher Defined)

12. What forms of communication channel does your company employ to disseminate EC-related information <u>to your business partners</u>:

- ❑ Presentation & seminars
- ❑ Print medias (e.g., brochures, newsletters, etc.)
- ❑ On-the-job training
- ❑ Electronic means (e.g., e-mails, discussion board, etc.)
- ❑ Social events or activities
- ❑ Mass training sessions
- ❑ Company or project meetings
- ❑ Intranet
- ❑ Other, please specify: ______________________

Communication Amount (Cannon & Homburg, 2001; Mohr, Fisher & Nevin, 1996)

13. What is the average number of documents communicated Internet-based between your company and other organizations? Types of Relationship—Inter-organizational: Business-related communication with other organizations (e.g., suppliers, customers). Please choose the most appropriate answer from the following choices on the scale of 1 to 7 (1 = Once every year, 2 = Twice a year, 3 = Once every month, 4 = Once every two weeks, 5 = Once a week, 6 = Once every two days, 7 = More than once a day).

INDUSTRY FACTORS

Trading Partners' Pressure (Iacouvou et al., 1995; Premkumar & Roberts, 1999)

14. Was your company under any pressure from your trading partners to implement EC? Please indicate your opinion from the scale of 1 to 5 (Under Very Little Pressure to Under Very High Pressure, 0 = Not affected at all).

    a. Customers
    b. Suppliers

Competitive Pressure (Gatignon & Robertson, 1989; Iacouvou et al., 1995)

15. To what extent did the EC capability of any of your competitors influence your decision to implement EC? Please indicate your opinion from the scale of 1 to 5 (Under Very Little Pressure to Under Very High Pressure, 0 = Not affected at all).

Relevant Environmental Participation (Researcher Defined)

16. Please estimate the percentage of the following participants in your industry that currently use EC to conduct business.

    a. Customers
    b. Suppliers
    c. Competitors
    d. Partners or affiliated organization
    e. Governmental departments & offices

Non-Trading Institutional Influence (Researcher Defined)

17. There may be other organizations, associations, or agencies in Australia that influenced your decision to implement EC. What was the level of influence posed by the following? Please indicate your opinion from the scale of 1 to 5 (Under Very Little Pressure to Under Very High Pressure, 0 = Not affected at all):
    a. Department of Commerce & Trade
    b. Small Business Development Corporation (SBDC)
    c. Business Enterprise Centres
    d. National Office for the Information Economy (NOIE)
    e. Federal Government Office of Small Business
    f. Western Australian Electronic Commerce Centre
    g. Australian Electronic Business Network (AUSeNET)
    h. Financial Institutes (banks, finance co.)
    i. Consulting firms or centres
    j. Telecommunication company
    k. Media
    l. Universities

NATIONAL FACTORS

Perceived Governmental Support (Researcher Defined)

18. What kinds of governmental support have you found available to your company to implement EC? How helpful has the support been? Please indicate your opinion from the scale of 1 to 5 (Least Helpful to Most Helpful, 0 = Not aware at all).

a. Educational support (e.g., training, seminars)
b. Advisory support
c. Financial support
d. Human Resources support

FOOTNOTE

1 Total number of responses was calculated out of 485 target respondents.

Chapter XIV
Barriers to E-Commerce Adoption in SMEs:
A Comparison of the Perception of Barriers in a Developed and a Developing Country

Robert C. MacGregor
University of Wollongong, Australia

Mira Kartiwi
University of Wollongong, Australia

ABSTRACT

It has long been known that small businesses have realised enhanced profits through the adoption of e-commerce. However, a number of recent studies have suggested that it is the larger businesses that are reaping the rewards of e-commerce rather than the smaller businesses. This slow growth of e-commerce adoption in SMEs has been attributed to various adoption barriers that are faced by small business owners/managers. These barriers have been well documented in numerous research studies. However, the relationship between these barriers has not been fully examined, particularly in developing countries. Of particular concern is the fact that the conclusions concerning the nature and role of barriers to e-commerce adoption have simply been transferred from studies in developed economies to those in developing ones. 96 non-adopting SMEs in Indonesia are compared to 129 in Sweden to determine whether the perception of importance of barriers differs between the two locations. The data is also analysed to determine whether the underlying factors of these barriers differs across the two locations.

INTRODUCTION

The importance of the small to medium enterprise (SME) sector as the cornerstone of most economies is widely recognised (Abdullah and Bakar, 2000; Hall, 2002; NOIE, 2002). This is not only borne out by the number of SMEs (almost 90% of the total number of businesses across the world), but also by their significant role in creating employment opportunities (Hall, 2002). This is no less the case in developing countries. A number of studies (Abdullah & Bakar 2000, Urata 2000, Kartiwi & MacGregor 2007) suggest that SMEs are vital to the emergence of healthy private sectors in developing countries. However, research has indicated that the SME contribution to the GDP of many nations has fallen over the past few years (Abernethy, 2002). While the reasons for this decrease are diverse, SMEs, both in developing and developed countries are attempting to reverse the trend by turning to global markets. This development has been enabled by the advent of electronic commerce (E-commerce) technology. E-commerce, defined as "the buying and selling of information, products, and services via computer networks" (Kalakota and Whinston, 1997) is radically changing the dynamics of the business environment and the way in which people and organizations are conducting business with one another. There are numerous studies suggesting that, for SMEs, e-commerce has the potential to provide competitive advantage. However, Molla & Heeks (2007) suggest that many of these studies, particularly those focused on developing economies, often lack an empirical basis and simply assume that the adoption and use of internet technologies is the same for all users.

While clearly many small businesses have realised enhanced profits through the adoption of e-commerce (Scupola 2003, Khiang & Chye 2002, MacGregor & Vrazalic 2007), studies (Macgregor & Vrazalic 2005, 2007, IEI 2003, Magnusson 2001) suggest that it is the larger businesses that are reaping the rewards of e-commerce rather than the smaller businesses. This slow growth of e-commerce adoption in SMEs has been attributed to various adoption barriers that are faced by small business owners/managers. These barriers have been well documented in numerous research studies. However, the relationship between these barriers has not been fully examined, particularly in developing countries. A number of studies (Kaynak et al., 2005; Stockdale and Standing, 2004; Taylor and Murphy, 2004) have suggested that much of literature concerned with e-commerce use (or lack of use) in SMEs have been undertaken in developed countries (particularly, but not exclusively US, Europe and Scandinavia). They argue that the wholesale application of these findings to developing economies is not justifiable because the driving forces for SMEs to adopt E-commerce, as well as the barriers preventing adoption differ widely from location to location (UNCTAD 2004, Molla & Heeks 2007, Molla & Licker 2005).

In line with these criticisms, the aim of this chapter is threefold: to analyse the correlation between various e-commerce adoption barriers in order to identify any underlying factors; to examine whether there are any significant differences in the rating of importance of barriers to E-commerce between SMEs that are located in a developing country (Indonesia) and those located in a developed country (Sweden); and to determine whether the underlying factors themselves differ between SMEs in a developed and a developing economy.

This chapter begins by examining the nature of SMEs and identifying features that are unique to SMEs. This is followed by a discussion of factors pertaining specifically to developing countries. As the study compares the perception of barriers to e-commerce adoption in a developing country (Indonesia) and a developed country (Sweden), a brief synopsis of the role of SMEs in each location is provided. A discussion of barriers to e-commerce adoption based on previous research is then presented and the barriers are mapped to the unique SME features. This is followed by a correlation and factor analysis of the combined Swedish and Indonesian data. A series of two-tailed t-tests is then applied to determine whether there are any significant differences between the ratings of importance of the barriers to E-commerce adoption (Indonesia – Sweden). Finally a factor analysis of the data is undertaken for each location. A discussion of similarities and differences is then presented. The limitations of the study are presented and conclusions drawn.

THE NATURE OF SMEs

There are a number of definitions of what constitutes an SME. Some of these definitions are based on quantitative measures such as staffing levels, turnover or assets, while others employ a qualitative approach. Meredith (1994) suggests that any description or definition must include a quantitative component that takes into account staff levels, turnover, assets together with financial and non-financial measurements, but that the description must also include a qualitative component that reflects how the business is organised and how it operates. In terms of employee numbers, the definition of an SME in Sweden is 50 employees or less (EIRO 2006), while for Indonesia the figure is 20 employees or less (DEPKOP 2005). In an effort to maintain uniformity, the study has adopted the wider, Swedish model (50 employees or less) as the quantitative component.

Qualitatively, any description of a small business must be premised on the notion that they are not simply scaled down large businesses and although size is a major distinguishing factor, small businesses have a number of unique features that set them apart from larger businesses.

There have been numerous studies carried out in order to isolate the features unique to SMEs. Brigham & Smith (1967) found that SMEs tended to be more prone to risk than their larger counterparts. This view is supported in later studies (Walker,1975, Delone,1988). Cochran (1981) found that SMEs tended to be subject to higher failure rates, while Rotch (1987) suggested that SMEs had inadequate records of transactions. Welsh & White (1981), in a comparison of SMEs with their larger counterparts found that SMEs suffered from a lack of trained staff and had a short-range management perspective. They termed these traits 'resource poverty' and suggested that their net effect was to magnify the effect of environmental impact, particularly where information systems were involved.

These early suggestions have been supported by more recent studies that have found most SMEs lack technical expertise (Barry & Milner 2002), most lack adequate capital to undertake technical enhancements (Gaskill et al (1993, Raymond 2001), most SMEs suffer from inadequate organisational planning (Tetteh & Burn 2001, Miller & Besser 2000) and many SMEs differ from their larger counterparts in the extent of the product/service range available to customer (Reynolds et al, 1994).

A number of studies (see Reynolds et al (1994), Murphy (1996), Bunker & MacGregor 2000), MacGregor & Vrazalic (2005, 2007)) have examined the differences in management style between large businesses and SMEs. These studies have shown that, among other characteristics, SMEs tend to have a small management team (often one or two individuals), they are strongly influenced by the owner and the owner's personal idiosyncrasies, they have little control over their environment (this is supported by the studies of Westhead & Storey (1996) and Hill & Stewart (2000) and they have a strong desire to remain independent (this is supported by the findings of Dennis 2000 and Drakopolou-Dodd et al 2002).

Based on an extensive review of the literature, a summary of the features unique to SMEs is shown in Table 1. An analysis of the features revealed that they could be classified as being internal or external to the business. Internal features include management, decision-making

Table 1. Features unique to small to medium enterprises (SMEs) (Adapted from MacGregor & Vrazalic 2004)

ID	FEATURES UNIQUE TO SMEs	REPORTED BY
	Features Related to Management, Decision Making and Planning Processes	
INT 1	SMEs have small and centralised management with a short range perspective	Bunker & MacGregor (2000) Welsh & White (1981)
INT 2	SMEs have poor management skills	Blili & Raymond (1993)
INT 3	SMEs exhibit a strong desire for independence and avoid business ventures which impinge on their independence	Dennis (2000) Reynolds et al (1994)
INT 4	SME Owners often withhold information from colleagues	Dennis (2000)
INT 5	The decision making process in SMEs is intuitive, rather than based on detailed planning and exhaustive study	Reynolds et al (1994) Bunker & MacGregor (2000)
INT 6	The SME Owner(s) has/have a strong influence in the decision making process	Reynolds et al (1994) Bunker & MacGregor (2000)
INT 7	Intrusion of family values and concerns in decision making processes	Dennis (2000) Bunker & MacGregor (2000) Reynolds et al (1994)
INT 8	SMEs have informal and inadequate planning and record keeping processes	Reynolds et al (1994) Tetteh & Burn (2001) Miller & Besser (2000) Markland (1974) Rotch (1967)
	Features Related to Resource Acquisition	
INT 9	SMEs face difficulties obtaining finance and other resources, and as a result have fewer resources	Cragg & King (1993) Welsh & White (1981) Gaskill & Gibbs (1994) Reynolds et al (1994) Blili & Raymond (1993)
INT 10	SMEs are more reluctant to spend on information technology and therefore have limited use of technology	Walczuch et al (2000) Dennis (2000) MacGregor & Bunker (1996) Poon & Swatman (1997) Abell & Limm (1996)
INT 11	SMEs have a lack of technical knowledge and specialist staff and provide little IT training for staff	Martin & Matlay (2001) Cragg & King (1993) Bunker & MacGregor (2000) Reynolds et al (1994) Welsh & White (1981) Blili & Raymond (1993)

INTERNAL FEATURES

continued on following page

Table 1. continued

	Features Related to Products/Services and Markets		EXTERNAL FEATURES
EXT 1	SMEs have a narrow product/service range	Bunker & MacGregor (2000) Reynolds et al (1994)	
EXT 2	SMEs have a limited share of the market (often confined towards a niche market) and therefore heavily rely on few customers	Hadjimonolis (1999) Lawrence (1997) Quayle (2002) Reynolds et al (1994)	
EXT 3	SMEs are product oriented, while large businesses are more customer oriented	Reynolds et al (1994) Bunker & MacGregor (2000) MacGregor et al (1998)	
EXT 4	SMEs are not interested in large shares of the market	Reynolds et al (1994) MacGregor et al (1998)	
EXT 5	SMEs are unable to compete with their larger counterparts	Lawrence (1997)	
	Features Related to Risk Taking and Dealing with Uncertainty		
EXT 6	SMEs have lower control over their external environment than larger businesses, and therefore face more uncertainty	Westhead & Storey (1996) Hill & Stewart (2000)	
EXT 7	SMEs face more risks than large businesses because the failure rates of SMEs are higher	Brigham & Smith (1967) DeLone (1988) Cochran (1981)	
EXT 8	SMEs are more reluctant to take risks	Walczuch et al (2000) Dennis (2000)	

and planning processes, and the acquisition of resources, while external features are related to the market (products/services and customers) and the external environment (risk taking and uncertainty).

E-COMMERCE IN DEVELOPING COUNTRIES

Any examination or comparison of e-commerce adoption in developed and developing countries must be premised on the understanding that many developing countries face many challenges that are not found in developed countries (Kartiwi & MacGregor 2007, Molla & Licker 2005, Molla & Heeks 2007). These include the notion of accessible and affordable infrastructure (Humphrey et al 2005). Molla & Heeks (2007) suggest that the notion of infrastructure includes the level of diffusion of technology and awareness, noting that where these are taken for granted in developed economies, this is not necessarily the case in developing environments. Oxley & Yeung (2001) take this a step further suggesting that not only does technology and awareness need to reach a critical mass before network externalities and e-commerce can take effect, but that there needs to be a willingness by participants to regulate and govern its use.

Aside from the availability of infrastructure, studies by Goode & Stevens (2000) and Hempel & Kwong (2001) suggest that there is a far lower level of IS and business sophistication in many SMEs in developing economies. They add that where the adoption of e-commerce requires modification to organisational structure, product characteristics or business culture, this is often a far larger 'stumbling block' for SMEs in developing countries.

SMEs in Sweden

The European Union views SMEs as a catalyst for regional development (Europa, 2003). SMEs have been earmarked as playing an important role in promoting growth because they are seen as a key source of jobs and employment prospects (Keniry et al., 2003; Larsson et al., 2003). For the purposes of its various support programs and measures, the European Commission has constructed a single set of definitions of SMEs (EIRO, 2006).

Two major interconnected policies exist in Sweden. These are termed the SME policy and the Enterpreneurship policy. Both policies pursue several major objectives – to stimulate employment creation, to stimulate regional development, to stimulate innovation and to expand economic growth. Lundström and Stevenson (2002) suggest, amongst other things, the two policies support the creation of new firms, the delivery of education and support to newly established firms, the promotion of women as owner/manager, the spread of technology to SMEs and the streamlining of financial, organisational and exporting support for SMEs.

At a practical level, Boter and Lundström (2005) point to 2 National agencies (Almi Busieness Partner and Swedish Trade Council) and 2 regional agencies (the National Labour Market Board and the County Administration Board) whose tasks include the development of entrepreneurship curricula, the development of business – education partnerships, the development of community support, the administration of funding for new initiatives and the involvement the students in technical and organisational analysis of SME firms and ventures.

SMEs in Indonesia

During the last twenty years, there has been a considerable growth in terms of the number of SMEs throughout Asian economies, and Indonesia in particular. Indonesian SMEs have proven to be the most dynamic and vibrant sector, especially during the time of financial crisis in 1997 (Urata, 2000).

There is no consensus on the definition of SMEs in Asia Pacific region. The definitions differ from country to country depending on the phase of economic development as well as their existing social conditions. As the focus of this study is on the Indonesian economic setting, the official definitions from two Indonesian govern-

Table 2. A comparison of SMEs in Sweden and Indonesia

Country	Small Business	Medium Business
Sweden	Employees : Fewer than 50 people *and* Annual turn-over : EUR 7 million *or* Annual balance-sheet total: Not exceeding EUR 5 million	Employees : 50-250 people *and* Annual turn-over : EUR 40 million *or* Annual balance-sheet total: Not exceeding EUR 27 million
Indonesia	Employees: 5 – 19 people *And/or* Annual turn-over < Rp 1 billion (EUR 8.5 million) *And* Assets < Rp 200 million (excluding land and buildings)	Employees: 20 – 99 people *And/or* Annual turn-over >Rp 1 billion (EUR 8.5 million) *And* Assets < Rp 10 billion (excluding land and buildings)

ment bodies The Central Bureau of Statistics (CBS, 2004) and the Ministry of Cooperatives and Small Medium Enterprises (DEPKOP, 2005a) will be adopted.

There are currently more than 40 million SME establishments in Indonesia. They account for 99.99% of the total number of business enterprises. Based on the latest data (DEPKOP, 2005b), the largest percentage is in the agriculture sector (58.9%), followed by trade (22%) and manufacturing (6.3%) sectors with transportation and services also significant. The significance of SMEs to the Indonesia economy is further highlighted by their contribution to national development and by the fact that, as a sector, they provide and create jobs especially during times of recession (Asian Development Bank., 2003; DEPKOP, 2005a). Table 2 provides a comparison of SMEs in Sweden and Indonesia.

BARRIERS TO E-COMMERCE ADOPTION IN SMES

It has been demonstrated previously that the rate of e-commerce adoption in SMEs has been low. This slow paced uptake of e-commerce technologies has been documented and researched widely, with results indicating that SMEs face inhibitors or barriers that prevent them from implementing and fully reaping the benefits of e-commerce. In their study of 27 SME manufacturing firms, Cragg and King (1993) identified the lack of financial and managerial resources, and inadequate levels of technical expertise as the major inhibitors of IT grown in small businesses. These three factors were also identified by Welsh and White (1981) as being symptomatic to SMEs. However, other barriers have also been identified.

Like the unique features of SMEs, the barriers to e-commerce adoption can be classified as external or internal to the business. Hadjimonolis (1999), in a study of e-commerce adoption by SMEs in Cyprus, found that external barriers could be further categorised into supply barriers (difficulties obtaining finance and technical information), demand barriers (e-commerce not fitting with the products/services or not fitting with the way clients did business) and environmental barriers (security concerns). Internal barriers were further divided into resource barriers (lack of management and technical expertise) and system barriers (e-commerce not fitting with the current business practices). A summary of e-commerce adoption barriers in SMEs is presented in Table 3. An analysis was undertaken to examine the relationship between these barriers and unique features of SMEs listed in Table 1. Table 3 shows this relationship by indicating which unique features can be mapped to which barriers. For example, one of the most commonly cited barriers to e-commerce adoption is that it is too expensive to implement, a barrier that arises from the fact that SMEs face difficulties obtaining finance, unlike their larger counterparts. If the finance was readily available to SMEs, high cost may not be a barrier to e-commerce adoption. Table 3 is an initial, exploratory attempt at determining the relationship between unique features and barriers. Further research is required to establish the nature of this relationship.

METHODOLOGY

An empirical study was designed to collect data from two countries representing develop and developing economies. Sweden was selected as an example of a developed country, and Indonesia as an example of a developing country (World Bank Group, 2006).

Ten barriers to E-commerce adoption were gathered from the literature. For the Swedish study, 6 in-depth interviews were undertaken with SME owner/managers to determine whether the barriers were applicable and complete. In order to validate the barriers to the Indonesian setting, a series of 8 in-depth interviews with SMEs

Table 3. Summary of e-commerce adoption barriers and their relationship to the features unique to SMEs

BARRIERS TO E-COMMERCE ADOPTION	REPORTED BY	TO UNIQUE
High cost of e-commerce implementation; Internet technologies too expensive to implement	Iacovou et al (1995); Quayle (2002); Purao & Campbell (1998); Lawrence (1997); Riquelme (2002); Van Akkeren & Cavaye (1999)	INT 9
E-commerce too complex to implement	Quayle (2002)	INT 11
Low level of existing hardware technology incorporated into the business	Lawrence (1997)	INT 10
SMEs need to see immediate ROI and e-commerce is a long-term investment	Lawrence (1997)	INT 1
Organisational resistance to change because of the fear of new technology amongst employees	Lawrence (1997); Van Akkeren & Cavaye (1999)	INT 2; INT 11
Preference for and satisfaction with traditional manual methods, such as phone, fax and face-to-face	Lawrence (1997); Venkatesan & Fink (2002); Poon & Swatman (1998)	INT 10; EXT 3
Lack of technical skills and IT knowledge amongst employees; Lack of computer literate/specialised staff	Quayle (2002); Lawrence (1997); Riquelme (2002); Van Akkeren & Cavaye (1999); Iacovou (1995); Damsgaard & Lyytinen (1998); Chau & Turner (2002)	INT 11
Lack of time to implement e-commerce	Walczuch et al (2000); Lawrence (1997); Van Akkeren & Cavaye (1999)	INT 5; INT 2; INT 1
E-commerce is not deemed to be suited to the way the SME does business	Abell & Limm (1996); Hadjimanolis (1999); Iacovou et al (1995); Poon & Swatman (1997)	INT 5; INT 8; EXT 3;
E-commerce is not deemed to be suited to the products/ services offered by the SME	Walczuch et al (2000); Kendall & Kendall (2001); Hadjimanolis (1999)	EXT 1; EXT 5
E-commerce is perceived as a technology lacking direction	Lawrence (1997)	INT 1; INT 10; EXT 8
Lack of awareness about business opportunities/ benefits that e-commerce can provide	Iacovou et al (1995); Quayle (2002)	INT 1; INT 2; INT 5; INT 8; EXT 3; EXT 4
Lack of available information about e-commerce	Lawrence (1997)	EXT 8
Concern about security of e-commerce	Quayle (2002); Purao & Campbell (1998); Abell and Limm (1996); Riquelme (2002); Van Akkeren & Cavaye (1999); Poon & Swatman (1999); Hadjimanolis (1999)	EXT 6; EXT 7; EXT 8
Lack of critical mass among customers, suppliers and business partners to implement e-commerce	Abell and Limm (1996); Hadjimanolis (1999)	EXT 2
Heavy reliance on external consultants (who are considered by SMEs to be inadequate) to provide necessary expertise	Lawrence (1997);Van Akkeren & Cavaye (1999); Chau & Turner (2002)	INT 11
Lack of e-commerce standards	Tuunainen (1998); Robertson & Gatignon (1986)	INT 11

owner/manager and consultants was undertaken to determine whether the barriers were applicable and complete. The interviews in both Sweden and Indonesia showed that all of the barriers were applicable and no extra barriers were forthcoming. Based on the interviews a survey instrument was developed for SME managers. The survey was used to collect data about the barriers to e-commerce adoption in SMEs. The respondents who had not adopted e-commerce were asked to rate the importance of each barrier to their decision not to adopt e-commerce. A standard 5 point Likert scale was used to rate the importance with 1 meaning very unimportant and 5 meaning very important. Figure 1 shows the English equivalent of the question.

Karlstad was the chosen location in Sweden. Karlstad is described as a regional 'developed' city, both by the OECD and the World Bank, and it contained personnel who could assist with the distribution and re-gathering of the survey materials.

A total of 1170 surveys were distributed by post in four regional areas of Sweden: Karlstad, Filipstad, Saffle and Arvika.

The same procedure with data collection in Sweden was undertaken in Indonesia. The respondents who had not adopted e-commerce were asked to rate the importance of each of the barriers to their decision not to adopt e-commerce. A standard 5 point Likert scale was used to rate the importance with 1 meaning very important and 5 meaning very unimportant.

Seven locations were chosen across the three provinces in Indonesia, as they were deemed to have sufficient numbers of adopters as well as non-adopters. These were:

Figure 1. Question about barriers to e-commerce adoption used in survey

23. This question relates to the reasons why your organisation is not be using e-commerce. Below is a list of statements indicating possible reasons. Based on your opinion, please rank each statement on a scale of 1 to 5 to indicate how important it was to your decision NOT to use e-commerce, as follows:

1 = the reason was very unimportant to your decision not to use e-commerce
2 = the reason was unimportant to your decision not to use e-commerce
3 = the reason was neither unimportant nor important to your decision not to use e-commerce
4 = the reason was important to your decision not to use e-commerce
5 = the reason was very important to your decision not to use e-commerce

Our organisation does not use e-commerce because:	Rating				
E-commerce is not suited to our products/ services.	1	2	3	4	5
E-commerce is not suited to our way of doing business.	1	2	3	4	5
E-commerce is not suited to the ways our clients (customers and/or suppliers) do business.	1	2	3	4	5
E-commerce does not offer any advantages to our organisation.	1	2	3	4	5
We do not have the technical knowledge in the organisation to implement e-commerce.	1	2	3	4	5
E-commerce is too complicated to implement.	1	2	3	4	5
E-commerce is not secure.	1	2	3	4	5
The financial investment required to implement e-commerce is too high for us.	1	2	3	4	5
We do not have time to implement e-commerce.	1	2	3	4	5
It is difficult to choose the most suitable e-commerce standard with so many different options available.	1	2	3	4	5

- West Java: Bandung, Sukabumi, Tasikmalaya
- Bali: Denpasar, Kuta, Gianyar
- DKI Jakarta

These locations are also chosen as they were determined to represent a 'developing' economy, and again, they contained personnel who could assist with the distribution and re-gathering of the survey materials. A total 330 surveys were distributed by post.

RESULTS

Responses were obtained from 313 SME organisations in Sweden giving a response rate of 26.8%. 129 of these responses were from non-adopter SMEs. 179 responses were obtained from Indonesia, giving a response rate of 54.2%. 96 of these responses were from non-adopter SMEs. A test for reliability was applied to both sets of data. The Cronbach's Alpha for the Swedish responses was .910, while for the Indonesian data it was .780.

Table 4 shows the 5 highest rated barriers for both Sweden and Indonesia.

The first aim of the study was to determine whether there were any underlying factors for the barriers to E-commerce adoption in SMEs. The rating of the barriers was combined. The results of the Kaiser-Meyer-Olkin MSA (.887) and Bartlett's Test for Sphericity ($\chi^2 = 1347$, p=.000) indicated that the data set satisfied the assumptions for factorability. Principle Components Analysis was chosen as the method of extraction in order to account for maximum variance in the data using a minimum number of factors. A two-factor solution was extracted with Eigenvalues of 5.145 and 1.856 and was supported by an inspection of the Scree Plot. The two factors accounted for 70.012% of the total variance as shown in Table 5.

The two resulting components were rotated using the Varimax procedure and a simple structure was achieved as shown in the Rotated Component Matrix in Table 6. Six barriers loaded highly on the first component. These barriers are related to the complexity of implementation techniques, range of e-commerce options, high investments

Table 4. The 5 highest rated barriers to e-commerce

Sweden	Indonesia
E-commerce is not suited to our products/ services.	E-commerce is not suited to our products/ services.
E-commerce is not suited to our way of doing business.	E-commerce does not offer any advantages to our organisation.
We do not have the technical knowledge in the organisation to implement e-commerce	E-commerce is not suited to our way of doing business.
E-commerce is not suited to the ways our clients (customers and/or suppliers) do business.	E-commerce is not suited to the ways our clients (customers and/or suppliers) do business.
We do not have time to implement e-commerce.	E-commerce is not secure.

Table 5. Total variance explained

Rotation Sums of Squared Loadings			
Component	Eigenvalue	% of Variance	Cumulative %
1 (Too Difficult)	5.145	51.451	51.451
2 (Unsuitable)	1.856	18.561	70.012

Table 6. Rotated component matrix

Barriers	N Sweden	Mean Sweden	N Indonesia	Mean Indonesia	t-value	Signif.
E-commerce is not suited to our products/ services.	129	2.72	96	3.70	5.117	.000
E-commerce is not suited to our way of doing business.	129	2.61	96	3.49	4.649	.000
E-commerce is not suited to the ways our clients (customers and/or suppliers) do business.	129	2.55	96	3.38	4.317	.000
E-commerce does not offer any advantages to our organisation.	129	2.34	96	3.66	7.250	.000
We do not have the technical knowledge in the organisation to implement e-commerce.	129	2.57	96	2.16	-2.268	.024
E-commerce is too complicated to implement.	129	1.97	96	2.26	1.655	.099
E-commerce is not secure.	129	2.08	96	2.58	2.937	.004
The financial investment required to implement e-commerce is too high for us.	129	2.23	96	2.05	-1.022	.308
We do not have time to implement e-commerce.	129	2.46	96	2.33	-.654	.514
It is difficult to choose the most suitable e-commerce standard with so many different options available.	129	2.28	96	2.07	-1.158	.248

Table 7. Two-tailed t-tests

	Component 1 (Too Difficult)	Component 2 (Unsuitable)
E-commerce is not suited to our products/ services.		.882
E-commerce is not suited to our way of doing business.		.894
E-commerce is not suited to the ways our clients (customers and/or suppliers) do business.		.786
E-commerce does not offer any advantages to our organisation.		.817
We do not have the technical knowledge in the organisation to implement e-commerce.	.721	
E-commerce is too complicated to implement.	.844	
E-commerce is not secure.	.662	
The financial investment required to implement e-commerce is too high for us.	.810	
We do not have time to implement e-commerce.	.785	
It is difficult to choose the most suitable e-commerce standard with so many different options available.	.804	

and the lack of technical knowledge and time. This component has been termed the "Too Difficult" factor. Four barriers highly loaded on the second component are termed the "Unsuitable" factor and are related to the suitability of e-commerce to the respondent's business, including the extent e-commerce matched the SME's products/services, the organisation's way of doing business, their client's way of doing business and the lack of advantages offered by e-commerce implementation. These two factors are independent and uncorrelated, as an orthogonal rotation procedure was used.

The second aim of the study was to determine whether there were any significant differences in the rating of importance of any of the barriers (Sweden vs. Indonesia). A series of two-tailed t-tests was applied to the data (see Table 7).

Six of the ten barriers showed a statistically significant difference (Sweden – Indonesia). With the exception of the barrier "We do not have the technical knowledge in the organisation to implement e-commerce", all the significant barriers were rated higher by the Indonesian respondents. Four barriers showed a significant difference at the .001 level. These were E-commerce is not suited to our products/ services, E-commerce is not suited to our way of doing business, E-commerce is not suited to the ways our clients (customers and/or suppliers) do business and E-commerce does not offer any advantages to our organisation.

The final aim of the study was to determine whether the factors underlying the barriers to e-commerce differed between developing and developed economies. Prior to any factor analysis being undertaken, a series of correlations was carried out (see Tables 8 and 9). The Correlations which were significant at the .001 level are shown in bold lettering.

Table 8 shows an interesting pattern of results. The first four barriers seem to all correlate with each other, but show weak or no correlations with the last set of barriers. Similarly, it appears that correlations exist between the last five barriers in the Correlation Matrix. Therefore, two distinct groupings of results can be identified in the Correlation Matrix. In the first grouping, there is a strong positive correlation between the barriers "E-commerce is not suited to our products/ services" and "E-commerce is not suited to our way of doing business" (Pearson's $r = .746$, $p < .000$). These two barriers also show moderately strong positive correlations with the barriers "E-commerce is not suited to the ways our clients (customers and/or suppliers) do business" and "E-commerce does not offer any advantages to our organisation". In the second grouping, the barriers relating to the investment, time, number of options, complexity and security aspects of e-commerce adoption generally show moderately strong positive correlations with each other. However, the barriers within these two groupings appear to be unrelated to the barriers in the alternate group, with the exception of very weak correlations for the barrier relating to security and time.

Table 9 also shows an interesting pattern of results. Again, the first four barriers seem to all correlate with each other, but show weak or no correlations with the last set of barriers. Similarly, it appears that correlations exist between the last five barriers in the Correlation Matrix. Therefore, two distinct groupings of results can be identified in the Correlation Matrix. In the first grouping, there is a positive correlation between the barriers "E-commerce is not suited to our products/ services" and "E-commerce is not suited to our way of doing business" (Pearson's $r = .715$, $p < .05$). These two barriers also show moderately strong positive correlations with the barriers "E-commerce is not suited to the ways our clients (customers and/or suppliers) do business" and "E-commerce does not offer any advantages to our organisation". In the second grouping, the barriers relating to the investment, time, number of options, complexity and security aspects of e-commerce adoption generally show moderately strong positive correlations with each other. The correlation matrices suggested the use of factor analysis for both sets of data. The Kaiser-Meyer-Olkin MSA (.895 Sweden, .720 Indonesia) and Bartlett's Test for Sphericity ($\chi^2 = 845$ $p = .000$ Sweden, $\chi^2 = 448$ $p=.000$ Indonesia) indicated that the data set satisfied the assumptions for factorability. Principle Components Analysis was chosen as the method of extraction in order to account for maximum variance in the data using a minimum number of factors. A two-factor solution was extracted with Eigenvalues of 5.615 and 1.556 for Sweden. This was supported by an inspection of the Scree Plot. These two factors accounted for 71.717% of the variance. A three-factor solution was extracted with Eigenvalues of 3.439, 2.586 and 1.014 for Indonesia. Again, this

Table 8. Correlation matrix of e-commerce adoption barriers, Sweden

Correlation Matrix

	Not match prod/serv	Not fit our way of working	Not fit cust way of working	No advantage	No knowledge	Complicated techniques	Doubt security	Investment too high	No time
fit our way /orking	**.746**								
fit cust way /orking	**.462**	**.530**							
advantages	**.482**	**.547**	.280*						
knowledge	-.030	.054	-.097	.249*					
nplicated ıniques	-.009	.059	.065	.106	**.544**				
ıbt security	.184*	.303**	.096	.249*	.277*	**.516**			
ɜstment too ı	-.051	-.138	.092	-.104	**.445**	**.481**	.217*		
time	-.245*	-.261**	-.056	-.195*	**.432**	**.587**	.174	**.448**	
ıy choices	-.056	-.005	-.033	.062	**.514**	**.679**	**-.334**	**.494**	**.632**

** Correlation is significant at the 0.01 level (2-tailed). * Correlation is significant at the 0.05 level (2-tailed).

Table 9. Correlation matrix of e-commerce adoption barriers in Indonesia

Correlation Matrix

	Not match prod/serv	Not fit our way of working	Not fit cust way of working	No advantage	No knowledge	Complicated techniques	Doubt security	Investment too high	No time
fit our way /orking	**.718***								
fit cust way /orking	**.657****	**.736****							
advantages	.410**	.483**	.222						
knowledge	.050	.161	.251	.060					
nplicated ıniques	-.147	.029	.019	.005	**.570****				
ıbt security	.289	.350*	.364*	.131	.370*	.426**			
ɜstment too ı	.078	.074	.212	.090	.478**	**.680****	**.704****		
time	.218	.493**	.229	.300	.287	**.659****	.437**	**.534****	
ıy choices	.320*	.166	.347*	-.048	.332*	.415**	**.544****	**.692****	.455**

** Correlation is significant at the 0.01 level (2-tailed). * Correlation is significant at the 0.05 level (2-tailed).

Table 10. Total variance explained

Component	Sweden			Indonesia		
	Eigenvalue	**% variance**	**Cum. %**	**Eigenvalue**	**% variance**	**Cum. %**
Too Difficult	5.615	56.154	56.154	2.586	25.864	60.255
Unsuitable	1.556	15.562	71.717	3.439	34.391	34.391
Time/Choice				1.014	10.145	70.400

was supported by an inspection of the Scree Plot. These three factors accounted for 70.400% of the variance. Table 10 provides the details.

In both cases the resulting components were rotated using a Varimax procedure and a simple structure was achieved as shown in Table 11.

DISCUSSION

The first aim of the study was to analyse the correlation between various e-commerce adoption barriers in order to identify any underlying factors. An examination of Tables 5 and 6 shows that, as a composite group, adoption barriers can be grouped according to 2 factors termed unsuitable and too difficult. The "Too Difficult" factor is related to the barriers which make e-commerce complicated to implement, including barriers such as the complexity of e-commerce implementation techniques, the difficulty in deciding which standard to implement because of the large range of e-commerce options, the difficulty obtaining funds to implement e-commerce, the lack of technical knowledge and difficulty in finding time to implement e-commerce. The "Unsuitable" factor, on the other hand, is related to the perceived unsuitability of e-commerce to SMEs. These barriers include the unsuitability of e-commerce to the SME's products/services, way of doing business, and client's way of doing business, as well as the lack of perceived advantages of e-commerce implementation.

The second aim of the study was to examine whether there are any significant differences in the rating of importance of barriers to E-commerce between SMEs that are located in a developing country (Indonesia) and those located in a developed country (Sweden). An examination of Table 7 shows that 6 of the 10 barriers showed

Table 11. Rotated component matrix

Barrier	Indonesia			Sweden	
	Too Difficult	Unsuitable	Time/ Choice	Too Difficult	Unsuitable
E-commerce is not suited to our products/ services.		.876			.864
E-commerce is not suited to our way of doing business.		.926			.882
E-commerce is not suited to the ways our clients (customers and/or suppliers) do business.		.863			.729
E-commerce does not offer any advantages to our organisation.		.671			.803
We do not have the technical knowledge in the organisation to implement e-commerce.	.874			.714	
E-commerce is too complicated to implement.	.722			.864	
E-commerce is not secure.	.596			.699	
The financial investment required to implement e-commerce is too high for us.	.648			.798	
We do not have time to implement e-commerce.			.782	.829	
It is difficult to choose the most suitable e-commerce standard with so many different options available.			.850	.809	

a statistically significant difference between the two locations. However, the results of Table 6 are different to expectation. Where conventional wisdom would suggest that the greater difference would be seen in the technical barriers (with the developing economy respondents placing a greater level of importance on these than the developed economy respondents), it is the organisational barriers that show the greatest difference, with the developing economy placing a greater level of importance on these barriers. A number of authors (Hawk, 2004; Lim, 2002; Paul, 2002; Sheth and Sharma, 2005; Wood, 2004) have indicated that there are 'organisational difficulties' in many developing countries, including low income, low credit card penetration, cultural differences. The data from Table 7 seems to support these as being more important to developing economies. Indeed, it is interesting to note that the only barrier that showed any significant difference between the two sets of respondents, we do not have the technical knowledge to implement E-commerce, was actually rated more important by the Swedish respondents.

The final aim of the study was to determine whether the underlying factors themselves differ between SMEs in a developed and a developing economy. An examination of tables 10 and 11 show a number of interesting, and again unexpected results. Firstly, and most obviously, is that while the Swedish respondents loaded the barriers onto 2 factors, the Indonesian respondents loaded theirs onto 3. Perhaps even more interesting, however, is the fact that again the Swedish respondents were more concerned with technical barriers while the Indonesian respondents were concerned with organisational barriers. An examination of Table 9 shows that 2 barriers, We do not have time to implement e-commerce and It is difficult to choose the most suitable e-commerce standard with so many different options available were loaded onto a separate and uncorrelated factor by the Indonesians, while the Swedish respondents considered them to be part of the organisational factor.

The results of this study are significant in several ways. The analysis has shown that ten of the most common barriers to e-commerce adoption can be grouped in relation to two or three main factors. This gives researchers a powerful explanatory tool because it reduces the "noise" in the data. Instead of accounting for ten different barriers, the inhibitors to e-commerce adoption can be explained as a result of one of three factors: e-commerce is either too difficult, unsuitable to the business or we have a problem with time and choice. The Rotated Component Matrix also enables the prediction of the scores of each individual barrier based on the score of the two or three factors and vice versa, for an SME. This has implications for research into e-commerce barriers. Whereas before researchers have identified various barriers (such as the ones listed in Table 3), this is the first time a study has shown that certain barriers are correlated and can be logically grouped according to two or three factors. This makes it simpler not only to explain, but also predict barriers to e-commerce adoption in SMEs.

LIMITATIONS OF THE STUDY

It should be noted that this study has several limitations. The data used for this study was drawn from 4 areas in Sweden and 3 provinces in Indonesia. As is apparent, while conclusions can be drawn, they are not generalisable to SMEs in other locations. Also, the data for the study was collected from various industry sectors and it is not possible to make sector specific conclusions. Finally, this is a quantitative study, and further qualitative research is required to gain a better understanding of the key issues.

CONCLUSION

The aim of this study was threefold: to analyse the correlation between various e-commerce adoption barriers in order to identify any underlying factors; to examine whether there are any significant differences in the rating of importance of barriers to E-commerce between SMEs that are located in a developing country (Indonesia) and those located in a developed country (Sweden); and to determine whether the underlying factors themselves differ between SMEs in a developed and a developing economy. To this end, the unique features of SMEs were presented and mapped to e-commerce adoption barriers indicating a potential relationship between the two. Further investigation is required to identify the exact nature of this relationship. A factor analysis was performed on the composite data to determine whether there were underlying factors for the barriers to E-commerce adoption and use. A two-tailed t-test was applied to the data to determine whether there were differences in the perception of barriers to E-commerce between the two locations. The results showed that it was the organisational barriers that provided the most significant differences, with the Indonesian respondents rating these higher than the Swedish respondents. Finally the data was separated and a series of factor analyses was applied. The data showed that while the Swedish respondents were more concerned with technical issues, the Indonesian respondents were more concerned with organisational barriers.

The results of this study are important both for researchers as well as small business practitioners (including government agencies and owner/managers). While many studies have suggested (or at least predicted) that E-commerce 'levels the playing field', this study has shown that this may only be applicable at a technical level. Indeed, the study raises a number of interesting questions as to why it is the organisational barriers, rather than the technical barriers that are of paramount importance in the emerging SME economy of Indonesia. An examination of many governmental websites and brochures concerned with E-commerce adoption by SMEs suggest that they are more focussed on the technical problems that may beset a small business than organisational concerns. Indeed, Taylor & Murphy (2004) suggest that governments are 'besotted with technology', often to the detriment of organisational concerns. The data clearly shows that, particularly for developing economies, organisational impacts of E-commerce appear far stronger than technical concerns. For the owner/manager, the data clearly shows that it is essential to consider the organisational impacts of E-commerce adoption, including customers, suppliers, products/services and the methods employed within the small business.

The study presented in this paper is only one part of a larger long-term project investigating the drivers and barriers to e-commerce adoption in SMEs. Further research is currently being undertaken in order to overcome some of the limitations outlined above.

REFERENCES

Abdullah, M. A. and Bakar, M. I. H. (2000). *Small and medium enterprises in Asian Pacific countries.* Nova Science Publishers. Huntington, NY.

Abell, W. and Lim, L. (1996). *Business use of the internet in New Zealand.* Retrieved August 2004 from: http://ausweb.scu.edu.au/aw96/business/abell/index.htm

Abernethy, M. (2002). SMEs: Small World Order. *The Bulletin 120*(34).

Asian Development Bank. (2003). *Private sector development and finance.* Asian Development Bank.

Bajaj, K. K. and Nag, D. (1999). *E-commerce: The cutting edge of business.* Tata McGraw-Hill. New Delhi.

Barry H. & Milner B. (2002). SME's and Electronic Commerce: A Departure from the Traditional Prioritisation of Training? *Journal of European Industrial Training, 25*(7), 316-326.

Blili, S. and Raymond, L. (1993). 'Information Technology: Threats and opportunities for small medium-sized enterprises'. *International Journal of Information Management, 13*(6), 439-448.

Boter, H. and Lundström, A. (2005). 'SME perspectives on business support services'. *Journal of Small Business and Enterprise Development, 12*(1), 244-258.

Bringham, E. F. and Smith, K. V. (1967). The cost of capital to small firm. *The Engineering Economist, 13*(1), 1-26.

Bunker, D. and MacGregor, R. C. (2000). Successful generation of Information Teschnology (IT) requirements for Small/Medium Enterprises (SMEs)—Cases from regional Australia, in *Proceedings of SMEs in Global Economy.* Wollongong, Australia. pp. 72-84.

CBS (2004). *Survey usaha terintegrasi 2004.* Central Bureau of Statistics (CBS).

Chau, S.B. and Turner, P. (2001). A Four Phase Model of EC Business Transformation Amongst Small to Medium Sized Enterprises, *Proceedings of the 12th Australasian Conference on Information Systems*, Coffs Harbour, Australia.

Cochran, A. B. (1981). Small business mortality rates: A review of the literature. *Journal of Small Business Management, 19*(4), 50-59.

Cragg, P. B. and King, M. (1993). 'Small-firm computing: Motivators and inhibitors'. *MIS Quarterly, 17*(1), 47.

Damsgaard, J. and Lyytinen, K. (1998). Contours of Diffusion of Electronic Data Interchange in Finland: Overcoming Technological Barriers and Collaborating to Make it Happen, *Journal of Strategic Information Systems*, 7, 275-297.

DeLone, W. H. (1988). 'Determinants of Success for Computer Usage in Small Busines'. *MIS Quarterly, 12*(1) 51.

Dennis, C. (2000). 'Networking for marketing advantage'. *Management Decision, 38*(4), 287-292.

DEPKOP (2005a). *Peran Koperasi dan Usaha Kecil Menengah Dalam Pembangunan Nasional*, 2005. Departemen Koperasi dan Usaha Kecil Menengah.

DEPKOP (2005b). *Statistik Usaha Kecil Menengah*, 2005. Departemen Koperasi dan Usaha Kecil Menengah.

Drakopoulou-Dodd S. Jack S. & Anderson A.R. (2002). Scottish Entrepreneurial Networks in the International Context *International Small Business Journal, 20*(2), 219-219.

EIRO (2006). *Industrial relations in SMEs.* Retrieved March 2006 from http://www.eiro.eurofound.eu.int/1999/05/study/tn9905201s.html

Europa. (2003). *SME definition.* The European Commission. Retrieved December 15, 2003, from http://europa.eu.int/comm/enterprise/enterprise_policy/sme_definition/index_en.htm

Gaskill L.R., Van Auken H.E. & Kim H. (1993). The Impact of Operational Planning on Small Business Retail Performance *Journal of Small Business Strategy, 5*(1), 21-35.

Gaskill, L. R. and Gibbs, R. M. (1994). Going away to college and wider urban job opportunities take highly educated away from rural areas'. *Rural Development Perspectives, 10*(3), 35-44.

Goode S. & Stevens K. (2000). An Analysis of the Business Characteristics of Adopters and Non-Adopters of WWW Technology *Information & Management, 1*(1), 129-154.

Hadjimonolis, A. (1999). 'Barriers to Innovation for SMEs in a Small Less Developed Country (Cyprus)'. *Technovation, 19*(9), 561-570.

Hall, C. (2002). *Profile of SMEs and SME issues*

1990-2000. Asia-Pacific Economic Cooperation. Singapore.

Hawk, S. (2004). 'A Comparison of B2C E-commerce in Developing Countries'. *Electronic Commerce Research, 4,* 181-199.

Hempel P.S. & Kwong Y.K. (2001). B2B E-commerce in Emerging Economies: i-metal.com's Non-ferrous Metals Exchange in China *Journal of Strategic Information Systems, 10*, 335-355.

Hill, R. and Stewart, J. (2000). Human Resource Development in Small Organisations. *Journal of European Industrial Training, 24*(2/3/4), 105-117.

Humphrey J., Mansell R., Pare D. & Schimtz H. (2003). The Reality of E-commerce in Developing Countries *Media@LSE*

Iacovou C.L., Benbasat I. & Dexter A.S. (1995). Electronic Data Interchange and Small Organisations: Adoption and Impact of Technology *MIS Quarterly, 19*(4) 465-485.

IEI (2003). *Facts & Figures: The Internet and Business.* The Internet Economy Indicators. Retrieved June 4, 2003, from http://www.internetindicators.com/facts.html

Kalakota, R. and Whinston, A. B. (1997). *Electronic commerce: A manager's guide.* Addison-Wesley. MA.

Kartiwi M. & MacGregor R.C. (2007). Electronic Commerce Adoption Barriers in Small to Medium-sized Enterprises (SMEs) in Developed and Developing Countries: A Cross-country Comparisons. *Journal of E-commerce in Organizations, 5*(3), 35-51.

Kaynak, E., Tatoglu, E. and Kula, V. (2005). An analysis of the factors affecting the adoption of electronic commerce by SMEs: Evidence from an emerging market. *International Marketing Review, 22*(6), 623-640.

Kendall, J.E. and Kendall, K.E. (2001). A Paradoxically Peaceful Coexistence Between Commerce and Ecommerce. *Journal of Information Technology, Theory and Application, 3*(4), 1-6.

Keniry, J., Blums, A., Notter, E., Radford, E. and Thomson, S. (2003). *Regional business—A plan for action.* Department of Transport and Regional Services. Retrieved December 13, 2003, from http://www.rbda.gov.au/action_plan

Khiang, A. L. B. and Chye, G. N. K. (2002). Information technology and e-commerce for successful SMEs. *Malaysian Management Review, 37*(2).

Larsson, E., Hedelin, L. and Gärling, T. (2003). Influence of expert advice on expansion goals of small businesses in rural Sweden. *Journal of Small Business Management, 41*(2), 205-212.

Lawrence, K. L. (1997). Factors Inhibiting the Utilisation of Electronic Commerce Facilities in Tasmanian Small-to-Medium Sized Enterprises, in *Proceedings of 8th Australasian Conference on Information Systems.* pp. 587-597.

Lim, J. J. (2002). East Asia in the Formation of Economy: Opportunities and Challanges. *Info, 4*(5), 56-63.

Lundström, A. and Stevenson, L. (2002). *On the road to entrepreneurship policy: The entrepreneurship policy for the future series.*

MacGregor, R. C. and Bunker, D. (1996). The effect of priorities introduced during computer acquisition on continuing success with IT in small business environments, in *Proceedings of Information Resource Management Association International Conference.* Washington. pp. 271-227.

MacGregor, R. C., Bunker, D. and Waugh, P. (8-10 June 1998). Electronic commerce and small/medium enterprises in Australia: An EDI pilot study, in *Proceedings of Proceedings of 11th International Bled E-commerce Conference.* Bled Slovania. pp. 331-345.

MacGregor, R. C. & Vrazalic, L. (2007). *E-commerce in Regional Small to Medium Enterprises.* Hershey: IGI Global.

MacGregor, R.C. & Vrazalic, L. (2005). A Basic Model of Electronic Commerce Adoption Barriers: A Study of Regional Small Businesses in Sweden and Australia. *Journal of Small Business and Enterprise Development, 12*(4), 510-527.

Magnusson, M. (May 28-29, 2001). E-commerce in small businesses—focusing on adoption and implementation, in *Proceedings of the 1st Nordic Workshop on Electronic Commerce.* Halmstad, Sweden.

Markland, R. E. (1974). The role of the computer in small business management. *Journal of Small Business Management, 12*(1), 21-26.

Martin, L. and Matlay, H. (2001). "Blanket" approaches to promoting ICT in small firms: some lessons from DTI ladder adoption model in the UK'. *Internet Research: Electronic Networking Applications and Policy, 11*(5), 399-410.

Meredith G. G. (1994). *Small Business Management in Australia* McGraw Hill, 4th Edition

Miller, N. J. and Besser, T. L. (2000). The importance of community values in small business strategy formation: Evidence from rural Iowa. *Journal of Small Business Management, 38*(1), 68.

Molla A & Heeks R. (2007). Exploring E-commerce Benefits for Businesses in a Developing Country *The Information Society, 23,* 95-108.

Molla A. & Licker P.S. (2005). Ecommerce Adoption in Developing Countries: A Model and Instrument *Information & Management, 42,* 877-899.

Murphy J. (1996). *Small Business Management.* London: Pitman.

National Research Council (2000). *Surviving Supply Chain Integration: Strategies for Small Manufacturers.* Commission on Engineering and Technical Systems. Retrieved June 2, 2003 from http://books.nap.edu/books/0309068789/html/R1.html

NOIE (2002). *e-Business for Small Business.* The National Office of Information Economy. Retrieved May 25, 2003, from http://www.noie.gov.au/projects/ebusiness/Advancing/SME/

Oxley J.E. & Yeung B. (2001). E-Commerce Readiness: Institutional Environment and International Competitiveness *Journal of International Business Studies, 32*(4), 705-723.

Paul, J. (2002). Narrowing the digital divide: initiatives undertaken by the Association of South-East Asian Nations (ASEAN). *Program: electronic library and information systems, 36*(1), 13-22.

Poon, S. and Swatman, P. M. C. (1997). Small business use of the Internet: Findings from Australian case studies. *International Marketing Review, 14*(5), 385.

Poon, S. and Swatman, P. M. C. (June 8-10, 1998). Small Business Internet Commerce Experiences: A Longitudinal Study, in *Proceedings of the 11th International Bled Electronic Commerce Conference.* Bled, Slovenia.

Purao S. & Campbell B. (August 4-16, 1998). Critical Concerns for Small Business Electronic Commerce: Some Reflections Based on Interviews of Small Business Owners *Proceedings of the Association for Information Systems Americas Conference* Baltimore, MD, pp. 325 - 327

Quayle, M. (2002). E-commerce: The challenge for UK SMEs in the twenty-first century. *International Journal of Operations & Production Management, 22*(9/10), 1148.

Raymond L. (2001). Determinants of Web Site Implementation in Small Business. *Internet Research: Electronic Network Applications and Policy, 11*(5), 411-422.

Reynolds, J., Savage, W. and Williams, A. (1994). *Your own business: A practica; guide to success.* ITP.

Riquelme, H. (2002). Commercial internet adoption in China: Comparing the experiences of small, medium and large businesses. *Internet Research: Electronic Networking Applications and Policy, 12*(3), 276-286.

Robertson, T. and Gatignon, H. (1986). Competitive Effects on Technology Diffusion. *Journal of Marketing*, 50.

Rotch, W. (1967). *Management of small enterprises: Cases and readings.* University of Virginia Press.

Ruth, J.-P. S. (2000). So far small biz is only dabbling in E-commerce. *Business News New Jersey, 13*(23), 24.

Scupola, A. (2003). The adoption of Internet commerce by SMEs in the south of Italy: An environmental, technological and organizational perspective. *Journal of Global Information Technology Management, 6*(1), 52.

Sheth, J. N. and Sharma, A. (2005). International e-marketing: opportunities and issues. *International Marketing Review, 22*(6), 611-622.

Stockdale, R. and Standing, C. (2004). Benefits and barriers of electronic marketplace participation: an SME perspective. *Journal of Enterprise Information Management, 17*(4), 301.

Taylor, M. and Murphy, A. (2004). SMEs and e-business'. *Journal of Small Business and Enterprise Development, 11*(3), 280.

Tetteh, E. and Burn, J. M. (2001). Global strategies for SMe-business: applying the SMALL framework. *Logistics Information Management, 14*(1), 171-180.

Tuunainen, V.K. (1998). Opportunities of Effective Integration of EDI for Small Businesses in the Automotive Industry, *Information & Management, 36*(6), 361-375.

UNCTAD (2002). *Electronic Commerce Strategies for Development: The Basic Elements on an Enabling Environment for E-Commerce.* Commission on Enterprise, Business Facilitation, and Development. Retrieved from http://r0.unctad.org/ecommerce/event_docs/geneva_strategies_issues.pdf

Urata, S. (2000). *Outline of Tentative Policy Recommendation for SME Promotion in Indonesia.* JICA. Retrieved November 2003 from http://www.jica.or.id/FOCI_urata.html

Van Akkeren, J. and Cavaye, A. L. M. (December 1-3, 1999). Factors Affecting Entry-Level Internet Technology Adoption by Small Business in Australia: An Empirical Study, in *Proceedings of the 10th Australasian Conference on Information Systems.* Wellington, New Zealand.

Venkatesan, V.S. and Fink, D. (2002). Adoption of Internet Technologies and E-Commerce by Small and Medium Enterprises (SMEs) in Western Australia, *Proceedings of the Information Resource Management Association International Conference*, pp. 1136-1137.

Walczuch, R., Van Braven, G. and Lundgren, H. (2000). Internet adoption barriers for small firms in The Netherlands. *European Management Journal, 18*(5), 561-572.

Walker E.W. (1975). Investment and Capital Structure Decision Making in Small Business in Walker E.W. (ed.) *The Dynamic Small Firm: Selected Readings.* Texas: Austin Press.

Welsh, J. A. and White, J. F. (1981). A Small Business Is Not a Little Big Business. *Harvard Business Review, 59*(4), 18.

Westhead, P. and Storey, D. J. (1996). Management Training and Small Firm Performance: Why is the Link so Weak? *International Small Business Journal, 14*(4), 13-24.

Wood, C. M. (2004). 'Marketing and e-commerce as tools of development in the Asia-Pacific: a dual path'. *International Marketing Review, 21*(3), 301-320.

World Bank Group (2006). *Country groups.* World Bank Group. Retrieved March 2006 from http://web.worldbank.org/

Chapter XV
A Parallel Methodology for Reduction of Coupling in Distributed Business-to-Business E-Commerce Transactions

Anthony Mark Orme
Athens State University, USA

Letha H. Etzkorn
University of Alabama, USA

ABSTRACT

Recently, new standards for business-to-business (B2B) e-commerce transactions, to reduce extended record locking, relaxed standard database transaction properties. In this chapter, we provide a parallel methodology employing a mobile/intelligent agent framework to alleviate extended record locking, while adhering to standard database transaction properties. Our methodology provides a minimum 30% reduction of record locking compared to new B2B standards.

INTRODUCTION

The Internet boom of the last decade has led to the realization that business automation is possible on a wider scale than ever before. Prior to the B2B push of the 1990s, electronic data interchange (EDI) was the industry standard for business automation across organizational boundaries. EDI provided a standard set of messages that business partners used to pass data between their respective applications. The EDI solution suffered from limited reusability due to the high degree of coupling required between applications and a high cost of implementation (Weigand, Heuvel, & Dignum, 1998), which translates to a higher cost per transaction. These factors prohibited smaller businesses from implementing EDI-based solutions (Weigand et al., 1998). A key benefit of the research in business automation is a lower transaction cost; the lowered transaction cost has been the impetus that has driven the latest B2B e-commerce research. The result of early B2B automation was the development of several proprietary B2B frameworks1 that defined a set of services to provide pairwise interoperability between two companies for integration of their enterprise applications (Ariba Inc., 2006). However, the pairwise interoperability was limited by the development of many competing frameworks and a lack of interoperability between the competing frameworks.

There are many examples of B2B e-commerce transactions that parallel logistics management problems that require coordination of multiple interactions between many trading partners. These logistic management problems require distributed transaction support on relational database management systems (Riccardi, 2001) not provided in these B2B frameworks. Therefore, front-end applications provide the distributed transaction support required for many B2B and logistics management problems. If these front-end applications use traditional distributed transaction techniques, the possibility of extended record locking across organizational boundaries exists. In long-running transactions, these extended record locks may not be desirable and must be considered as a component in the cost of a B2B e-commerce transaction. Extended record locking can be illustrated with the following example: Suppose company A is building widgetA. In order to build widgetA, company A needs widgetB from company B and widgetC from company C. Suppose company B possesses exactly five widgetBs at the current time. Also, suppose company C has just sold its last widgetC and must receive a shipment from the factory before it has new widgetCs available for purchase. A transaction goes out from company A to both companies B and C. This transaction asks to purchase a widgetB from company B and a widget C from company C. The database in company B locks the record corresponding to one of its five widgetBs. This widget will be held until the overall transaction is complete. Meanwhile, company C is unable to complete its part of the transaction, because it has not received its shipment of widgetCs. The record in company B could be locked for hours or days, until the overall transaction completes. In the meantime, several hours or a day later, another transaction request from a different customer arrives at company B. This request is for five widgetBs. Company B is unable to satisfy this request, due to the locked record for one of its widgetBs.

Much of the current research on distributed, Internet–based, B2B e-commerce transactions focuses on the possibility of having transactions characterized by their long-running nature; a consequence of this is the possibility of extended record locks being held by an integrated application from an outside organization. Therefore, the autonomy of individual trading partners may be compromised (Dan et al., 2001), which may lead to a potential loss of sales under certain circumstances. Some have suggested easing the restrictions of the properties of standard transaction-based systems, "Atomic," "Consistent," "Isolated," and "Durable," known as the ACID properties (Riccardi, 2001), as a solution to the potential problem of extended record locking (Dan et al., 2001). However, easing the restrictions associated with the ACID properties is unsatisfactory in many ways. First, data anomalies may be introduced into transaction-based systems when relaxing the ACID properties (Attaluri & Salem, 2002). Second, all databases implement ACID (Riccardi, 2001); ignoring this feature limits reuse of investments, which results in achieving correctness via another method, which is therefore an additional cost. The only problem with retaining the ACID properties is the extended record locking and potential rollback of work that has been accomplished in a transaction when one system fails, when in some cases preserving the work would be preferable (Organization for the Advancement of Structured Information Standards, 2002a) (Organization for the Advancement of Structured Information Standards, 2002b).

For example, suppose the "Isolated" ACID property is not being supported. This means that, for example, one transaction could read temporary data occurring during another transaction; that data might not be valid later. In a similar example to the one given earlier, suppose company C buys more widgetCs to replenish its stock. It requests these widgetCs from company D and at the same time requests some widgetDs from company D because there is a discount if you buy both widgetCs and widgetDs at the same time. It initially receives some widgetCs, and those enter its database, but the entire transaction with company D has not yet completed. During this time, the transaction from company B comes through. Company B's request (running at company C) can see that there are widgetCs available, so it provides these widgetCs to company B. Unfortunately, the transaction with company D fails, since no widgetDs are available, and company C is unwilling to pay a higher price for widgetCs. Then company C has no widget Cs after all, and has erroneously sold a widgetC that it does not possess to company B.

We examine the possibility that B2B distributed transactions should adhere to the ACID properties for transaction-based systems. Also, we propose a mobile/intelligent agent2 framework that supports B2B, e-commerce, distributed transactions with a reduced record locking time compared to traditional distributed ACID-based transactions. As we mentioned earlier, a software framework provides a partial software solution. It defines the architecture for software systems that are further defined by the user to apply to a particular problem. Our methodology exploits the use of a parallel approach versus a linear sequential approach to B2B transactions. We use mobile/intelligent agents to implement the parallelism of ourapproach. A parallel methodology such as the one described in this chapter breaks a task into multiple subtasks, each of which can be executed simultaneously.

Our framework exploits the use of mobile agents (MA) working in parallel as one mechanism to achieve the reduction in record locking time. Trading partner agreements (TPA) are used to enable MAs to negotiate and finalize interactions with individual vendors. For the purpose of this chapter we use the term transaction to define a data manipulation in which a state change of one or more tuples (rows) in one or more relations (tables) occurs in a database. An autonomous transaction is a transaction that occurs on a single system. A distributed transaction refers to a transaction that effects a change on more than one system, meaning data changes on more than one database. Finally, we introduce the term trading partner interaction to encompass all of the messaging capabilities required in order to achieve a transaction between trading partners; therefore, a distributed transaction is a set consisting of one or more trading partner interactions.

The remainder of this chapter is organized as follows: first, the background necessary to understand the relationship between transactions and distributed transactions and a standard two-phase commit protocol3 (Riccardi, 2001) with respect to the ACID properties (Riccardi, 2001) is provided. Then the ACID properties are also described. This includes a brief description of B2B transactions and ebXML (a new standard for B2B distributed transactions). The Methodology section outlines our architecture to support a B2B distributed transaction that adheres to the ACID properties and reduces record locking. Also in the Methodology section are the results of our research when applied to a specific transaction scenario. In the Discussion section we discuss the results. Finally, a conclusion to our research is presented and topics for further investigation are outlined.

BACKGROUND

The background section is divided into the following subsections: the first explores the ACID properties and the two-phase commit protocol, and their relationship to autonomous transactions and distributed transactions. The next section provides a look at B2B transactions as they relate to our architecture. After that, the last section provides an overview of a few core components of ebXML and their relation to business.

Transaction Properties

Although the concept of a transaction is not unique to a database system, the ACID properties and two-phase commit protocol provide the basis for database systems transactions. The ACID properties that follow provide a level of certainty and assurance on the outcome of a transaction and define a set of restrictions placed on the data.

- **Atomic:** A transaction must execute exactly once and must be atomic—either all of the work is done or none of it is.
- **Consistent:** A transaction must preserve the integrity constraints of data, transforming one legal (consistent) state of data into another legal (consistent) state of data.
- **Isolated:** A transaction must be a unit of isolation, which means that concurrent transactions should behave as if each were the only transaction running in the system.
- **Durable:** If a transaction commits, the system guarantees that its updates can persist and will not be undone.

These ACID properties have formed a basis for transactions in both autonomous transactions and distributed transactions. These properties guarantee transaction system developers that transaction-related data adhered to well-defined semantics, and that the image of the data before, during, and after the transaction meets the defined criteria for each of the ACID properties. The Consistent and Isolation properties define a set of rules on both the data state and the visibility of data in the scope of a transaction. Both the Consistent and Isolation properties are similar in an autonomous and a distributed transaction. The Consistent property assures that, during a transaction, tuples modified by an insert, update, or delete statement in the scope of a transaction must be in agreement with the constraints that govern the validity of the relationships among the data defined by the assumptions of the designers of this system. The Isolation property makes assurances on the visibility of the changes made to

Table 1. ANSI isolation levels

Isolation Level	Dirty Read	Non-Repeatable Read	Phantom Read
Read Uncommitted	Possible	Possible	Possible
Read Committed	Not Possible	Possible	Possible
Repeatable Read	Not Possible	Not Possible	Possible
Seializable	Not Possible	Not Possible	Not Possible

a tuple with respect to other transactions. In other words, the Isolation property governs the readability of tuples by other transactions, when one transaction has modified that tuple in its scope previously. In most modern database management systems (DBMS), the implementation of the Isolation property provides different levels of granularity with respect to the visibility of modified data between transactions.

Table 1 Summarizes the ANSI isolation levels (American National Standard Institute, 1992) with respect to known data anomalies.

Table 1 shows three data anomalies, Dirty Read, Non-Repeatable Read, and Phantom Read, that are used to differentiate the four isolation levels of Read Uncommitted, Read Committed, Repeatable Read, and Serializable. Each data anomaly represents a potential problem for transactions in terms of data changing in the scope of a transaction. A dirty read allows a transaction to read uncommitted data from another transaction. A non-repeatable read occurs when a transaction rereads data committed by another transaction and sees the changes. A phantom reads occurs when a transaction executes a query again and sees data inserted by another transaction. Both the non-repeatable read and phantom read are point-in-time correct, meaning any read sees only committed data from other transactions. However, on the other hand, a dirty read allows data to be viewed, which may eventually be rolled back by the modifying transaction. Each of these data anomalies may affect transaction logic by potentially supplying seemingly inconsistent views of data as the transaction progresses.

The strictest isolation level, serializable, must execute in such a way that transactions appear to be executing one at a time (serially) rather than concurrently. Concurrent transactions executing in serialized mode can only make database changes that they could have made if the transactions ran one after the other. Concurrent transactions executing in serializable mode require record locking in each concurrent transaction and the DBMS must allow a transaction to view all tuples in the database, as they were when the transaction started. A serializable isolation level guarantees that none of the data anomalies can occur in the scope of a transaction, at the cost of high overhead to make concurrent transactions appear to execute one at a time. At the other end of the spectrum, a read uncommitted transaction requires less overhead than a serializable transaction; however, this reduction in overhead allows all anomalies to occur in the scope of a transaction. Most DBMS systems opt for a commonly accepted default isolation level of read committed, which allows the possibility of both a non-repeatable read and phantom read, but does not allow a transaction to read or modify uncommitted data from another transaction. It is important to note that the length of the record locking does not define the isolation levels of a transaction; they are defined in terms of the possible data anomalies that may occur in the scope of a transaction. Therefore, a DBMS is free to implement these isolation levels as it sees fit, using record locking as a mechanism to achieve these different isolation levels.

The durable and atomic properties define rules for implementation that guarantee the state of the data with regard to the transaction as a single unit. The durable property assures that once change to any tuple in an autonomous or distributed transaction is made permanent, the implementation guarantees these changes even in the event of a system failure. The guarantee of the Atomic property assures that all changes made to any tuple can be made permanent (committed) or undone (rolled back) in an all-or-nothing manner. A transaction with regard to the state of the data is defined as a logical unit or work in which tuples are modified, and these modifications are either all committed or rolled back. In an autonomous transaction the Atomic property defines a relationship between individual insert, update, and delete statements; therefore all statements must be able to be made permanent or undone as a unit. Distributed transactions have additional requirements to ensure the atomicity property; all participants need to be assured as to the final outcome of the transaction.

The two-phase commit protocol is a standard that provides distributed transaction coordination. The coordination is achieved by defining one system as the distributed transaction coordinator (DTC), and the other participants become resource managers (RM). Attaluri and Salem (2003) provide a detailed account of the two-phase commit protocol; in general, there are a series of messages that are passed between the DTC and the RMs that demarcate a transaction, and allow a transaction to progress towards a finalized state, either committed or aborted. The distributed two-phase commit provides the mechanism for each RM to assure that its data state is consistent with respect to the finalized state of the distributed transaction. The DTC and RMs work together via the two-phase commit protocol to assure the atomicity and consistency properties; however, the Consistent, Isolation, and Durability properties are generally considered the responsibility of the RMs to assure within their local context.

The two-phase commit has two distinct phases:

- **Prepare Phase:** Prepare phase is where the DTC requests that all RMs will promise to commit or rollback the transaction. All participants respond to the DTC that they are prepared or not prepared.
- **Commit Phase:** Commit phase is where the DTC asks all RMs to commit the transaction.

If all participants cannot prepare or there is a system component failure, the coordinator asks all databases to roll back the transaction.

B2B TRANSACTIONS

One B2B transaction approach popularized during the Internet expansion was the concept of the B2B frameworks. These B2B frameworks took a services-oriented approach to providing interoperability between trading partners that have implemented the same B2B framework. Several competing frameworks have been developed such as eCo, commerce XML (cXML), and RosettaNet; each provides a solution that allows businesses to take advantage of e-commerce transactions. Business partners wishing to benefit from a B2B framework would integrate their enterprise applications as shown in Figure 1. Several advantages have been realized in these B2B frameworks, such as real-time access products and services. However, as a whole, B2B frameworks do not address interoperability between competing frameworks. The lack of interoperability between frameworks requires that front-end logistics management applications provide distributed transaction support to achieve an atomic transaction. The application acts as the DTC performing the synchronization task for a distributed transaction. A linear sequential approach to transaction management is used to accomplish the individual interactions with each trading partner participating in the distributed transaction. As with its predecessor, EDI, B2B framework messaging facilities are large and loaded exclusively for an individual trading partner interaction. Trading partner interactions are handled on an individual basis: one after another all requirements for the distributed transaction are fulfilled. This linear progression coupled with the ACID properties form a basis for the problem of extended record locking. The isolation property guarantees that no transaction can see the effect of another's transaction before the distributed transaction comes to a final state. Therefore, the isolation property requires each trading partner to hold locks on records being updated until the distributed transaction is complete. These locks are held indefinitely on a trading partner's system as the application moves on to the next trading partner while the distributed transaction progresses. The Atomic property, when applied to a distributed transaction, requires

Figure 1. B2B framework

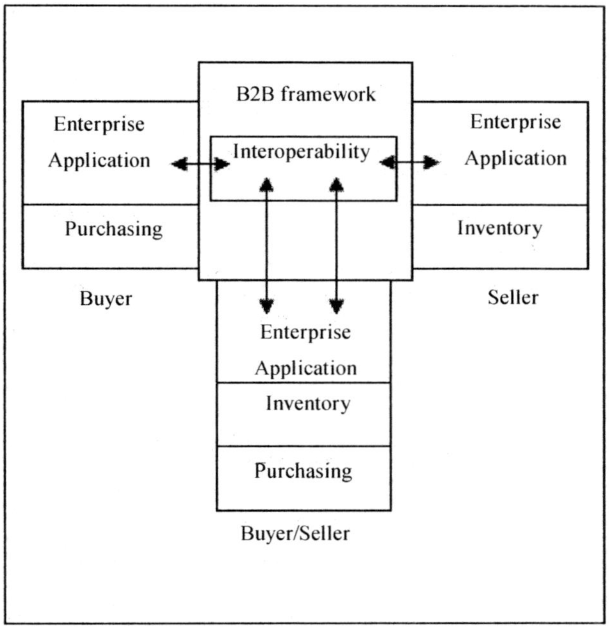

that all trading partners that participate come to an agreement on the final state of the distributed transaction. The distributed transaction is either committed or aborted based upon the two-phase commit protocol.

If all trading partners acknowledge that they are in a prepared state, the logistics management application acting as the DTC signals each trading partner to commit; otherwise, it sends the signal to abort. When the trading partner commits or aborts its respective transaction; the record locks are released and the effects of the distributed transaction become visible to other applications. This linear progression approach follows from a mindset based on modular sequential programming techniques. It is this linear progression that is the potential cause of extended record locking. Therefore, further research based on a nonsequential and nonlinear paradigm is needed to provide real-time collaboration in the e-commerce market.

ebXML Core Components

The Organization for the Advancement of Structured Information Standards (OASIS) is a global consortium that drives the development, convergence, and adoption of e-business standards (OASIS, 2002a). OASIS and the United Nations jointly sponsor ebXML, a global framework for e-business data exchange. In the past (for up to 20 years), most large companies have used EDI. As discussed earlier in the introduction, EDI is management intensive and also requires expensive software. This puts EDI out of reach for many smaller companies (Weigand et al., 1998). More recently, the advance of the Internet has made lower cost, Internet-based, e-business solutions popular. Many early Internet e-business solutions were proprietary solutions expressed in a format called Extensible Markup Language (XML). XML is a simple information exchange format and does not have, in itself, any e-business capabilities, so each new e-business solution based on XML alone was a unique solution, unstandardized. Thus, ebXML is intended to solve two problems. It replaces the high cost of EDI with a relatively inexpensive Internet-based solution. It also addresses the spread of incompatible XML-based B2B frameworks. One way ebXML addresses these incompatibilities is by defining a set of core components that are reusable across all industries. OASIS (2002b) contains a complete reference for all core components of ebXML.

A TPA, developed by IBM, defines how trading partners interact by defining the general contract terms and conditions; participant roles (buyers, sellers); communication and security protocols; and business processes (Dan et al., 2001). Therefore, the XML-based TPA documents capture the essential information upon which trading partners must agree in order for their applications and business processes to communicate.

The specification for a TPA (Dan et al., 2001) includes:

- Identification to uniquely identify the TPA document, and the parties.
- Communication to specify the transport protocol(s), electronic addresses of the parties.
- Security, to define the certificates used for authentication, including no repudiation, and a digital envelope.
- Invocation-independent properties, for example, the valid duration of the TPA.
- Data definition for describing formats of the data being passed around.
- Role definition that describes each of the roles specified in the TPA filled by specific parties.
- Action list to describe the requests each party can issue to the other. These actions are the independent units of work (The action definitions define the associated message flows between the invoker and the service provider, responsiveness, failure handling, and other attributes.).
- Sequencing rules to describe valid action invocation sequences in each party.
- Global properties to describe default properties of various fields in the TPA.
- Comments to describe handling of disputes, termination of the TPA as a whole, and other exceptional conditions.

One core component of ebXML, the Collaboration Protocol Agreement (CPA), automates the technical aspects of a TPA. In ebXML, all trading partners publish a Collaboration Protocol Profile (CPP) that states a basic description of the ebXML business processes, as defined by an industry that it supports, together with the industry's e-business systems points of access and technologies. Companies developing a CPA will match the business process they support to prospective trading partners. The CPA allows trading partners to agree on a set of common processes and the messages that need to be exchanged to accommodate these business processes. Therefore, the CPA provides for the automatic generation of the TPA.

Another initiative of ebXML was to address distributed B2B transactions in a heterogeneous environment, focusing on the extended record locking across organizational boundaries in long–running, distributed transactions. The long-running transaction is defined by (Dan et al., 2001) as a long-running conversation in which trading partners negotiate and create an electronic contract that stipulates the terms of the transaction. The scope of the transaction state has been broadened to encompass requirements and semantics of the state of a business transaction as a measure of the transaction's progress and outcome. A key benefit of this approach is that it provides an extensible model of a transaction that is well suited for the advance transaction models, such as Flexible transactions, Interoperable transactions, and Mobile transactions. Here, "model" refers to a methodology or sequence of operations. Although other benefits attributed to the ebXML approach include a solution for extended record locking, the ebXML approach does not define a transaction based upon standard ACID properties. The ebXML solution is a heterogeneous solution that does not place requirements on the RM as to the state of its data during the scope of the transaction. The result of not basing a transaction on the state of its data has an effect on the atomicity and isolation properties of ACID. In ebXML, atomicity in a transaction can no longer be preserved via the standard two-phase commit protocol. The two-phase commit relies on specific constraints placed on the state of transactional data via the protocol during the transaction. The ebXML solution utilizes a two-phase agreement protocol, which is much like the two-phase commit protocol, in that it coordinates the messaging required to allow a contractual agreement to be reached as to the outcome of the transaction. The agreement on the outcome of the distributed transaction is more contractual in nature, via the TPA, rather than being tied to transactional data states as in the standard two-phase commit protocol.

Research had suggested relaxing the isolation property of ACID as an appropriate procedure in reduction of record locking (Weigand, Verharen, Dignum, 1997). In the ebXML solution there exists no guarantee on the isolation property of the transaction data in the scope of a transaction. This lack of isolation in the ebXML solution is by design and is directly attributed to the fact that an ebXML implementation makes no requirements on RMs as to its' data state during a transaction.

METHODOLOGY

This section provides details of our mobile/intelligent agent framework: the goal of the framework is to directly address the issue of extended record locking by removing the linear progressive nature of current solutions to B2B distributed transaction (described in the background section). As mentioned in the introduction, a MA is software that moves itself from place to place in a network. An intelligent agent (IA) is software that has a particular goal and can act autonomously in certain situations.

Our research shows that removing this linear progression substantially reduces the average record locking time of the B2B distributed transaction. The framework uses a two-phase commit protocol (Attaluri & Salem, 2002) to guarantee the atomicity property of the transaction. First, we provide an architectural overview of the framework and describe for each component its general properties as they relate to the business transaction. The following section details a typical trading partner interaction.

Mobile/Intelligent Agent Framework

First, we formalize the trading partner interaction to assure that this process is complete and meets the requirements of the business transaction. Weigand et al. (1997) formalize the interaction process between supplier and consumer into the following four stages.

1. Inquiry and negotiation stage
2. Contractual stage
3. Fulfillment stage
4. Satisfaction stage

We have adopted this model as a basis for trading partner interaction in our framework. Our inquiry and negotiation stage is a set of messages that facilitate an initial understanding of the scope and parameters of the trading partner interaction. This stage is the electronic counterpart of a bartering system in which humans interact to determine the parameters of a trade. The contractual stage provides a mechanism for an e-document exchange that provides all the e-documents necessary to finalize the business interaction. The contractual phase is the electronic

Figure 2. Mobile /intelligent agent framework

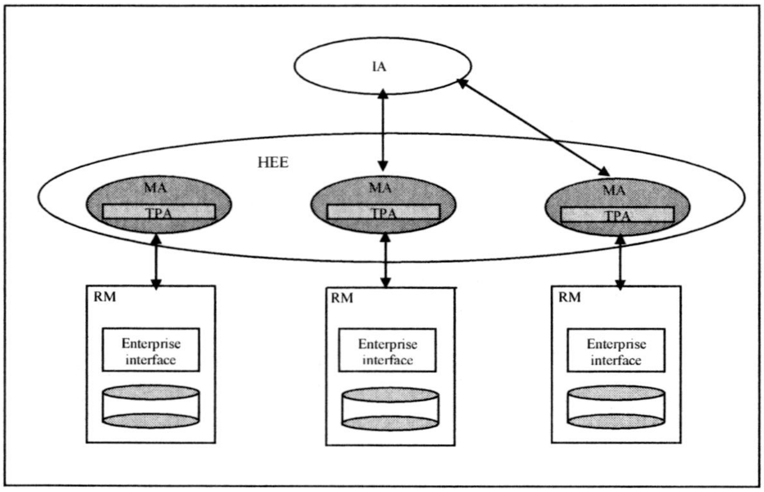

counterpart to a paper trail. The fulfillment stage actually provides the business transaction with the ability to exchange documents that state the transaction is completed and that resources have been allocated on each side to provide physical services. The satisfaction stage is a feedback mechanism design for process improvement. The TPA aids the MA to conduct the interactions necessary to accomplish the first three stages in the business transaction. How this interaction model is implemented in our mobile/intelligent agent framework is discussed further.

Our mobile/intelligent agent framework design addresses the need to reduce record locking without relaxing the ACID properties of transaction-based systems. Although (Dan et al., 2001) points out that we should not make assumptions on behalf of a trading partner's abilities, for many areas such as e-banking, the need for a trading partner to ensure that a transaction has truly completed as required leads to a desire for more insight into a trading partner's capabilities. Traditionally, having a trading partner implement the ACID properties was how such assurance was achieved.

This architecture assumes that each trading partner provides an interface to its enterprise applications and that the trading partners' systems are capable of ACID transactions. The focus of this research is to show that a reduction in record locking is possible for long-running distributed transactions without relaxing the ACID properties. This reduction in record locking is accomplished by allowing a set of MAs to work in a parallel manner to achieve each trading partner interaction required for the B2B distributed transaction. Our mobile/intelligent agent architecture, shown in Figure 2, has the following components: IA, MA, TPA(s), and a host execution environment (HEE).

In the business transaction the IA acts on behalf of the purchaser to fulfill all of the requirements of the distributed transaction. The purchaser describes, through a front-end application, the requirements for all interactions with each trading partner that are contained in the transaction. The IA uses ebXML

CPAs) to match the services needed by potential trading partners. When all requirements have been matched with potential trading partners, the

IA spawns a set of MAs, one for each interaction with a potential trading partner. These MAs are spawned to a shared distributed memory where each MA proceeds autonomously with its task. Each MA uses the TPA to carry out the interaction with this trading partner. The use of MAs allows us to remove the linear sequential aspect of most distributed B2B interactions. The parallel execution of MAs provides a significant improvement over sequential transactions.

Mobile/Intelligent Agent Framework Business Transaction Flow

This section details the transaction messaging required to allow an MA, working autonomously, to successfully complete a trading partner interaction. The IA creates the MA to conduct an individual trading partner interaction. The MA interacts with the enterprise application interface of the specified trading partner. The MA acting autonomously must carry out all stages of the trading partner interaction model defined in Figure 3. The trading partner business interaction model includes the following stages: initial/negotiation, contractual, and fulfillment.

Implementation, Testing, and Results

Our mobile/intelligent agent framework does not specify implementation-specific details for its core components; therefore, there are many ways to implement each component. We chose Sun Microsystems Java tm as the language for the framework core components' implementation of the MA and the enterprise application interface. Sun Microsystems Jini tm is used as the distributed computing platform to facilitate the required message passing between all components. The tested framework also uses Oracle 9i DBMS as the chosen platform to represent the implementation of a trading partner's enterprise application storage. Oracle 9i is capable of providing the requirements of the ACID properties in a distributed transaction. The Oracle XA library conforms to the X/Open Distributed Transaction Processing (DTP) software architecture's XA interface specification. The Oracle XA library is an external interface that allows distributed transactions to be coordinated by a transaction manager. In this section we describe the specific details of the test performed to quantify our hypothesis that on average the mobile/intelligent agent framework will significantly reduce record locking when compared with a linear progressive implementation. A description of the mobile/intelligent agent framework implementation used to test our hypothesis is provided for completeness.

Figure 3. Trading partner interaction model

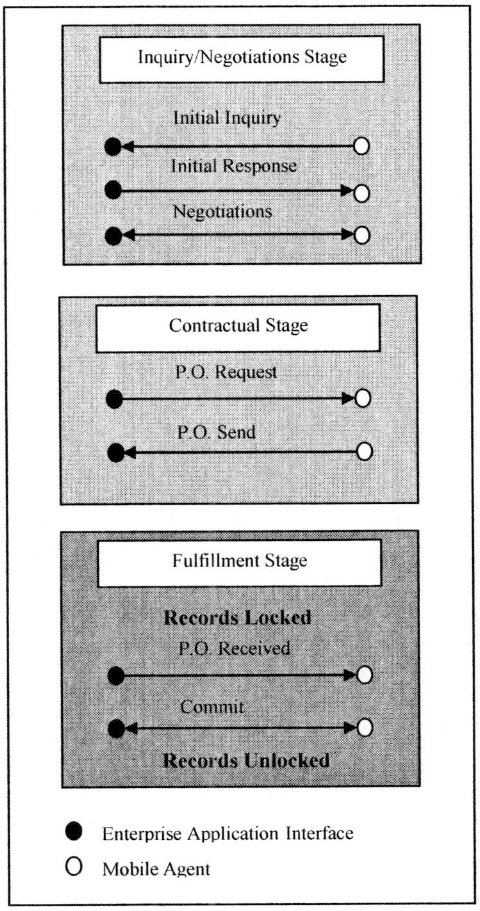

Testing the hypothesis requires a test scenario that simulates each method of record locking, while capturing the amount of time records are locked on each trading partners' system. The focus of each test scenario is to simulate all aspects of the specific approach that have an impact on the length of time records are locked in the distributed transaction without relaxing the ACID properties. Therefore, for the purpose of this analysis, the implementation of the linear progressive method and the mobile/intelligent agent framework need only address the record locking: other higher level B2B interactions are irrelevant for the purpose of this experiment. The implementation that follows is intended to simulate all the message-passing requirements between the IA, MA, and a trading partners' enterprise application necessary to implement an XOPEN two-phase commit.

The simulation of the linear progressive method for distributed B2B transactions uses the native ability of the Oracle 9i database to perform distributed transactions, as it captures the true essence of the linear progressive approach. The simulation uses the Oracle database's ability to perform a two-phase commit, in which one database acts as the DTC while the remaining databases act as RMs in the transaction. To simulate the linear progressive approach, a Structural Query Language (SQL) script is invoked on one database server. The SQL script locks records on each database by performing an update to a set of records. The SQL script required to achieve record locking is propagated in a linear fashion to each participant using Oracle 9i's Database Link mechanism. When the last participant in the transaction achieves its record lock, the script issues a commit and the DTC performs the two-phase commit. Figure 4 depicts the test scenario for the linear progressive simulation.

This test implementation of the mobile/intelligent agent framework simulates the same distributed transaction previously accomplished by the linear progressive method. In the test implementation, the IA communicates with the enterprise application using Sun Microsystem's Javaspace technology, a core component of Jini 2.0. The Javaspace is a Linda-like4 (Freeman, Hupfer, & Arnold, 1999) shared distributed memory that provides a synchronized message facility for this framework implementation. The Javaspace also provides an implementation of the Jini distributed events model that aids with synchronization of the message passing. The Javaspace can be used to implement a mobile-agent-based messaging requirement.

A typical distributed transaction in this implementation of the framework would flow as follows (a more business level algorithmic description is provided in Appendix A):

Figure 4. Simulation of the linear progressive methods for distributed B2B transactions

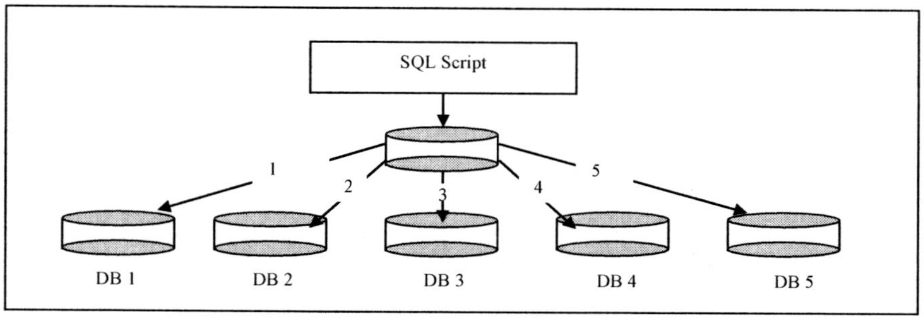

1. The Javaspace MA signals that the IA is ready to fulfill.
2. Upon receiving a fulfill message from all MAs the IA writes one entry into the Javaspace for each trading partner interaction. These entries represent the fulfill/acknowledge message.
3. The Javaspace MA signals each enterprise application via Jini's distributed event mechanism.
4. After completion of the record locking and the prepare phase of the XOPEN two-phase commit, each enterprise application writes its entry into the Javaspace. This entry represents the acknowledge message of the two-phase commit protocol.
5. The Javaspace MA signals the IA via Jini's distributed event mechanism. The Javaspace signals once for each business interaction
6. The IA waits to receive an acknowledge signal from each business partner participating in the distributed transaction. If the IA receives all acknowledgments within a specified time limit, the IA writes the commit entry to the Javaspace.
7. The Javaspace MA signals each enterprise application via Jini's distributed event mechanism.
8. Each enterprise application commits and releases its respective record locks.

As discussed earlier, in the test implementation the Javaspace and Jini's distributed events combine to perform the messaging requirement of an MA in the mobile/intelligent agent framework.

Testing our hypothesis required measuring the lock time required by the linear progressive transaction method and comparing this to the lock time required by the mobile/intelligent agent framework transaction. In our test, we sampled 50 distributed transactions using each method. Each distributed transaction consisted of five trading partner interactions. The trading partner interaction required the locking of a single record on the Oracle 9i database that provided storage for the enterprise applications. Using Oracle's LogMiner Utility, we were able to recover the amount of time in seconds each record was locked on the five Oracle 9i databases from the active redo log files. The total lock time for the distributed transaction was the sum of the five partner interactions. The 50 distributed transactions were averaged to compute a mean for each method.

To simulate both methods there were a total of six test machines, with one machine used to initiate the transaction, while the other five machines were running Oracle 9i. Each machine was running Windows 2000 Professional edition. Each of the test machines was a Pentium 4, with 512 megabytes of random access memory (RAM), running at 2.0 gigahertz. Table 2 shows a typical measurement for the distributed transaction using the linear progressive (Linear P) method and the mobile/intelligent agent framework (Mobile A).

A two-sample t-test was used to compare the rating of the two sample means (the linear progressive transaction and the parallel MA). This tested the following hypothesis.

Table 2. Record lock time measurements

Method	DB1	DB2	DB3	DB4	DB5
Linear P	6	5	5	4	3
Mobile A	3	3	4	3	3

Table 3. MINITAB two-sample t-test for linear progressive method versus mobile/intelligent agent

Two-sample T for linear progressive vs. Mobile/ Intelligent Agent				
	N	Mean	StDev	SE Mean
Linear P	50	23.64	3.30	0.47
Mobile A	50	15.40	1.03	0.15

Hypothesis

- **H0 :** $\rho = 0$ (Null hypothesis) There is no significant difference between the linear progressive transaction and the mobile/intelligent agent framework transaction.
- **H1:** $\rho \neq 0$ (Alternative hypothesis) There is a significant difference between the linear progressive transaction and the mobile/intelligent agent framework transaction.

The two-sample t-test was used to indicate if there is a significant difference (at a 95% confidence level) between the two sample means. When the means test indicates there is no significant difference between the linear progressive transaction and the mobile/intelligent agent framework transaction, this means that, on average, neither of the two transaction methods are different, subject to the confidence level of the test. When a test has a 95% confidence level, it means that if there were 100 comparisons between the linear progressive transaction and the mobile/intelligent agent framework transaction, there would be no significant difference in 95 out of the 100 comparisons.

The two-sample t-test was run with MINITAB statistical software. Table 3 shows the MINITAB output for the two-sample t-test . The sample mean for the linear progressive (Linear P) and the mobile/intelligent agent (Mobile A) is 23.64 s and 15.40 s respectively. Subtracting the sample means yields an estimate of the difference of sample means of 8.240.

The MINITAB output also shows that we are running the t-test with difference = 0, meaning that there is no significant difference between sample means (null hypothesis) versus the (alternative hypothesis) there is a significant difference between the sample means. The computed t-value of 16.86 with 58 df shows that there is less than .001 probability (p-value) that the population means are equal. Therefore, we must reject the null hypothesis, that the sample means are equal at a level of signficance of .05% and accept the alternative hypothesis that there is a significant difference in the population means.

Using a confidence interval (CI) to estimate the difference of the population means given these samples, the MINITAB output shows a 95% CI on the difference of 7.261 and 9.219. This CI states there is a probability of .95 that the difference

Figure 5. Simulation of mobile/intelligent agent frame for distributed transaction

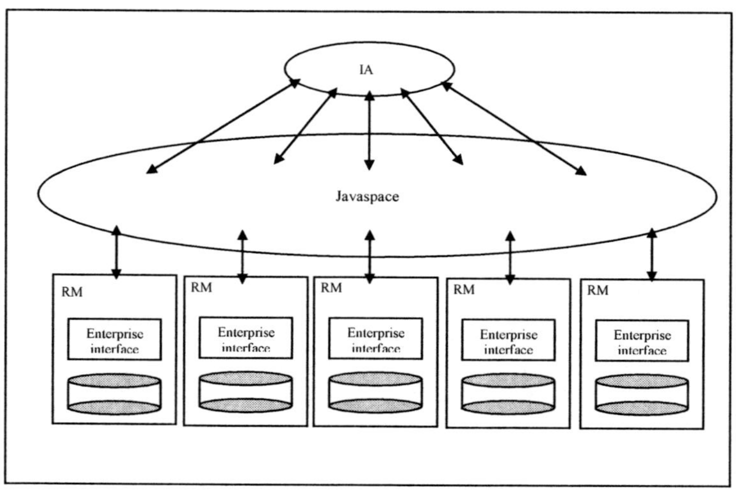

between the means will be between 7.261 and 9.219. The CI agrees with our rejection of the null hypothesis that there is no significant difference between the sample means, therefore we accept the alternative that there is a significant difference in the population means. To note that the difference between means is significantly different from 0, $\mu 1-\mu 2\neq 0$, the 95% CI of (7.261, 9.219) does not contain 0, therefore the difference of the means is significantly different from 0.

DISCUSSION

These results show that there is a significant difference between the linear progressive method and the mobile/intelligent agent framework method. Estimating the time saved to be 7.261, the lower end of the CI, suggests that in the worse case an average savings of 30% on the record locking time was achieved by our framework, compared to the linear progressive method The best case average saving shown by this test using the upper end of the CI, 9.219, suggests that a saving of 60% is possible under the tested scenario. However, one assumption of the test scenario for the linear progressive method was that all individual business interactions are fully specified by the front-end logistics application before any business interaction takes place. However, if the front-end application approaches each interaction one at a time, meaning the user specifies interaction 1, and the records are locked on vendor 1's system, then interaction 2 is specified by the user and records are locked on vendor 2's system and so on, the worse case and best case average saving would increase in proportion to the time it takes to specify all interactions other than the first.

CONCLUSION

In summary, our research shows that retaining ACID properties in transactions is possible in a distributed B2B scenario by employing a method that greatly reduces record lock time. The record-lock test conducted with our framework proved to be a significant improvement over the traditional linear approach to distributed transactions. In the worst case, a 30% improvement was shown; in the best case, the improvement could be as much as 60%. The noted improvement is a result of the framework's use of MAs working in parallel to accommodate individual trading partner interactions. Our mobile/intelligent agent framework makes use of ebXML's CPA in order to allow MAs to autonomously negotiate individual business interactions. As agents complete the negotiation, each agent signals the IA, which is standing by, ready to fulfill the intended transaction with its trading partner. When all MAs have signaled they are ready to fulfill the transaction, the IA starts a standard two-phase commit.

One benefit of our framework is that it reuses existing infrastructure such as databases that are capable of the two-phase commit. Therefore, companies would not need to implement a new distributed transaction protocol such as provided in the ebXML standard. In our implementation of the framework, this reuse is seen in the XOPEN distributed two-phase commit feature in the Oracle database. A secondary benefit attributed to the use of MAs and IAs in our framework is the ability to have a late binding to the atomicity property of the transaction. This is similar to ebXML's ability to do a partial transaction with respect to the originating request. Therefore, the framework is capable of saving partial work that has been accomplished towards the goals of the transaction.

Our current experiment was chosen so that the improvement would be the least possible improvement in record locking from using our methodology—our expectation would be that a typical operation in practice, as well as any other experiments using our methodology, would actually achieve better results than was possible in our chosen experiment. However, we would be interested to see further experiments by other researchers validating our results.

Although the mobile/intelligent agent framework has shown significant results in these test scenarios, future research will concentrate on the advanced transaction models. Our research suggests that it is possible to reduce record locking without compromising the ACID properties. However, in the cases where extended record locks would not be allowed from a business prospective, we suggest setting an isolation level for these transactions as a possible alternative. Isolation levels are a standard part of an SQL transaction that allow different levels of read access to records that are currently locked. In order to accommodate the use of isolation levels in these transactions there are two options: first, we should consider the static binding that is achievable if we modify the CPA to allow the addition of an isolation level property as part of its specification. A second method for achieving dynamic isolation levels would be to allow this property to be incorporated as a Web service to be negotiated during the appropriate phase of the business transaction.

REFERENCES

American National Standards Institute. (1992). *American national standards for information systems-database language- SQL. ANSI X3.135-1992.* Washington, D.C.: U.S. Government Printing Office.

Ariba Inc. (2006). *cXML version 1.0 specification.* Retrieved December 1, 2006, from http://www.cxml.org

Attaluri, G., & Salem, K. (2002). The presumed-ether two-phase commit protocol. *IEEE Transactions on Knowledge and Data Engineering, 14*(5), 1190-1196.

Dan, A., Dias, D., Kearny, R., Lau, T., Nguyen, R., Parr, F., et al. (2001). Business-to-business intergration with tpaML and a business-to-business protocol framework. *IBM Systems Journal, 40*(1), 68-90.

Freeman, E., Hupfer, S., & Arnold, K. (1999). *Javaspaces principles: Patterns and practice.* Reading, MA: Addison-Wesley.

Organization for the Advancement of Structured Information Standards (OASIS). (2002a). *Business transaction protocol primer [Version 1.0*]. Billerica, MA: Author.

Organization for the Advancement of Structured Information Standards (OASIS). (2002b). *Business transaction protocol [Version 1.03].* Billerica, MA: Author.

Riccardi, G. (2001). *Principles of database systems with Internet and Java applications.* Reading, MA: Addison-Wesley.

Weigand, H., Heuvel, W. J., & Dignum, F. (1998). Modeling electronic commerce transactions: A layered approach. In *Proceedings from LPCM '98: Third International Workshop on the Language/Action Perspective on Communication Modeling* (pp. 47-58).

Weigand, H., Verharen, E. M., & Dignum, F. (1997). Dynamic business models as a basis for interoperable transaction design. *Information Systems, 22*(2,3), 139-154.

Wooldridge, M. J., & Jennings, N. R. (1995). Intelligent agents: Theory and practice. *Knowledge Engineering Review, 10*(2), 115-152.

APPENDIX A.

The following algorithm describes a typical B2B distributed transaction using our framework for a vendor/purchaser interaction. See Figure 5 for a diagram illustrating this algorithm.

Step 1: Vendor/Purchaser negotiation
Step 2: Send acknowledgement to the Distributed Transaction Coordinator (the IA in Figure 5).
Step 3: Each of the distributed Resource Managers (the RMs in Figure 5) waits for the Distributed Transaction Coordinator to send the Prepare message for the two-phase commit.
Step 4: When the distributed Resource Managers receive the Prepare message, they lock records.
Step 5: The Resource Managers send the ACK-Prepare message to the Distributed Transaction Coordinator stating that this interaction is prepared to commit.
Step 6: The two-phase commit, or alternatively the rollback of the B2B transaction, finalize the business interaction.

1. A software framework provides a partial software solution. It defines the architecture for software systems that are further defined by the user to apply to a particular problem.
2. A mobile agent is software that moves itself from place to place in a network. An intelligent agent is software that has a particular goal and can act autonomously in certain situations (Wooldridge & Jennings, 1995).
3. The two-phase commit protocol is used to guarantee the Atomic ACID property in distributed transactions.
4. Linda is a well known coordination language (plus tools) that provides a virtual space where processes can communicate without regard to location (Freeman et al., 1999).

This work was previously published in Journal of Electronic Commerce in Organizations, Vol. 5, Issue 3, edited by M. Khosrow-Pour, pp. 52-67, copyright 2007 by IGI Publishing, formerly known as Idea Group Publishing (an imprint of IGI Global).

Chapter XVI
E-Business Triggers:
Further Insights into Barriers and Facilitators amongst Ghanaian Non-Traditional Exporters (NTEs)

Olav Sorensen
Aalborg University, Denmark

Robert Hinson
Aalborg University, Denmark

ABSTRACT

E-business is key to export development for developing economy firms. There are however key barriers and facilitators to e-business adoption for small and large internationalizing firms the world over. This chapter sets to find out, by means of the testing of key hypothesis, the main barriers and facilitators of e-business adoption by Ghanaian export firms. We adopt a quantitative approach to this study and draw our study sample from a directory of active non-traditional exporters (NTEs) in Ghana. We find that an export firm's international orientation, owner/management idiosyncrasies, e-sophistication of partners, export firm's characteristics (age, number of employees and location) and weak government regulation have no significant influence on e-business adoption by Ghanaian NTE firms. On the other hand, competitive pressure (as measured by competition from Ghanaian export firms and growth in size of export operations) significantly facilitates e-business adoption. Internal resource constraints (measured by technological and financial resources for e-business adoption and business culture) and environmental bottlenecks (measured by lack of support from export sector regulators and export associations and high internet access fees carged by ISPs) also reduce the likelihood of e-business adoption by Ghanaian NTE firms. We find interestingly that Export facilitation (measured by pressures from GEPC and FAGE) and digitalization (measured by perceived importance of e-business in digitalizing export operations and improving export competitiveness) perceived to facilitate e-business adoption however exhibit significant negative relationships with adoption. We proffer some explanations for this unusual finding and provide general management implications for improving e-business practices amongst the various players in Ghana's non-traditional export sector.

INTRODUCTION & STUDY OBJECTIVES

Issues surrounding the adoption of e-business for firm development have received extensive coverage in the e-commerce, international marketing, business development, strategy and entrepreneurship literature. Several other disciplines like supply chain management; marketing communication, finance etc. have all applied various theoretical and empirical treatments to the phenomenon of e-business/Internet adoption. The Internet itself has been heralded for over two decades as some sort of panacea to the various problems encountered by small businesses (Kalakota and Whinston, 1996). In the context of firms engaged in international business, it has been positioned by scholars like Levitt (1983) that embracing technology can result in gaining competitive advantage and capitalization of the opportunities resulting from the globalization of business. Fillis et al (2003), arguing from the work of earlier scholars (Keogh et al, 1998; Coviello and McAuley, 1999) posit that technology offers vast opportunities for instant international market access for SMEs.

The internet has been described as a global network of interlinked computers offering several commercial applications for most firms around the world (Hamill, 1997). The Internet acts as a major platform for the conduct of e-business and the astute deployment of Internet technologies holds promise for improvement in the management and organization of small export firms. Hornby et al (2002) argue that theoretically, exporting SMEs engaged in exporting should have a higher propensity for Internet uptake. Khoo et al (1998) have advanced arguments that small exporters are able to compete in foreign markets as a result of their technological capabilities. Bennet (1997) in a study on experiences of website use and perceptions of export barriers among UK businesses found that exporters held favourable views of the Internet's contribution to the facilitation of export. The study also found that Internet use was advantageous to the extent that it assisted in sales leads generation, ability to sell in remote countries, penetration of unfamiliar markets and creation of international awareness of the enterprise. Other proponents of the benefits of e-business to small firms have noted inter alia that some of the benefits include on-line sales and transactions (Poon and Swatman, 1997), acquisition of know-how through discussion with others on the Internet (Poon and Swatman, 1997), speedy and timely access to information from websites (Poon and Swatman, 1997), lower cost of obtaining supplies (Abell and Limm 1996), availability of expertise regardless of location (Abell and Limm, 1996), improved communication between customers and suppliers (Leadbeater, 2000). In addition, the small firm has the potential for gaining competitive advantage by being much quicker and flexible in connecting to the Internet (Durkin and McGowan, 2001).

Despite all the proposed benefits for small export firms outlined above, there is recorded in the literature, several constraints to e-business adoption by small export firms. Some of these constraints discussed from a more conceptual standpoint have included conservatism; fear of change/technology; inertia in decision making, security concerns, financial constraints and other resource constraints like the challenge of learning new skills and performing new tasks (Fillis et al, 2003). More empirical contributions to our understanding of the barriers to e-business adoption have included contributions by Eid (2005), Stockdale and Standing (2004) and Kaynak et al (2005). Eid (2005) found significant barriers to e-business adoption among 123 UK companies but posited that "powerful drivers of internet-based marketing in business-to-business firms will generally outweigh significant barriers to its adoption in the future". Chau and Pederson (2000) also noted some barriers to e-commerce adoption such as lack of resources, complications in implementing change, lack of cost-effective e-commerce enabled software, lack of technical skills and training, computer apprehension, inter-organisational motivation and prioritization of e-commerce initiatives. Our interest in this chapter is to develop a more comprehensive understanding of the range of perceived facilitators and barriers to e-business adoption in Ghana's export sector. The export sector is crucial to Ghana's development agenda and the uptake of ICT and Internet usage has been a matter of critical concern for policy-makers and researchers (Sorensen and Buatsi, 2002) and this study builds on earlier studies in this sector (Hinson and Sorensen, 2006; Hinson and Sorensen, 2007). The rest of the chapter is set out as follows: section two will give a general overview of Ghana's export sector; section three will address a literature review and the attendant hypothesis generated for the study whilst section four to six will address the study methodology, presentation and discussion of findings; as well as conclusions and recommendations for future research.

AN OVERVIEW OF GHANA'S NON-TRADITIONAL EXPORT SECTOR

In 2005, the Ghana Export Promotion Council (GEPC) set up a web portal (www.gepcghana.com) to begin improving the e-readiness of Ghanaian non-traditional exporters. The head of GEPC notes that "international trade was increasingly becoming global and highly competitive as a result of technological advancements...and information and communications technology" (www.myjoyonline.com) and that the Export Promotion Council had endeavoured to set up a trade information centre to assist in schooling exporters on e-business, which meant the importance of Information and Communication Technology (ICT)/e-business in dynamizing the sector is also not in doubt.

In reporting on the performance of his government, the President of Ghana in February 2008; noted inter alia that:

...the World Bank in 2007 rated Ghana as the most attractive place to do business in emerging markets in 2007...

...government is endeavouring to make information and communication technology available to available to large sections of society. The National Communicators Backbone Infrastructure Network is being pursued vigorously to provide open access broadband connectivity...

...all sectors of our society including commerce, health and government will access information speedily for decision-making...

...a number of world class companies are vying to partner the country to invest in the bauxite industry for both upstream and downstream procession locally...

...farmers in twenty three districts in five regions of the country are being assisted to undertake commercial agriculture, mainly in the cultivation of horticultural produce.

It has been the clarion call of the president and several policy makers that increased non-traditional export and the increasing dynamism of the same sector is key to improving the foreign exchange fortunes of Ghana. Export values according to an article on www.myjoyonline.com entitled "Non-traditional exports to cross billion dollar mark" rise from 705.4 million dollars in 2004 to 893 million in 2006. On a country –by-country basis the United Kingdom is the leading market for Ghana's non-traditional exports, followed by France, Burkina Faso and Nigeria. The article notes that those officials of the Ghana Export Promotion Council were optimistic that the value of non-traditional exports will traverse the 1 billion dollar mark in 2007; and this is precisely what happened. Currently, there are over 383 different Non-Traditional Export products categorized into Agricultural, Processed / Semi Processed and Handicrafts.

GEPC has a clientele base of over 3000 registered private sector exporting companies organized into 15 Product Associations, which she relates to both on individual corporate basis and as groups/associations. To create an enabling environment for e-business adoption among their clientele, the Ghana Export Promotion Council (GEPC), in January 2008, launched the Ghana Export Trade Information System to provide the business community in Ghana with resources to access and use trade information. Exporters registered with the Ghana Export Promotion Council and other members of the exporter community can now access *Trade Map, Product Map, Market Access Map* and *Investment Map* through a Common Management User System. We set out in this chapter to ascertain the adoption and facilitation triggers of e-business amongst a cross-section of Ghanaian NTEs.

The objectives of this study are:

a. An ascertainment of key facilitators of e-business for Ghanaian export firms.
b. An ascertainment of key barriers to e-business adoption amongst Ghanaian non-traditional export firms.

CONCEPTUAL FRAMEWORK & STUDY HYPOTHESES

We draw on the small exporter e-business development conceptual framework (Figure 1) developed by Hinson and Sorensen (2006). The framework posits that there are some internal and external forces/triggers that act on export firms at the disadvantaged end of the global digital divide to adopt the Internet in the conduct of their export businesses. Triggers like an international orientation and/or the level of international competition the firm faces, might constitute triggers for e-business adoption. Additionally, there are a set of triggers, like the level of infrastructural networks and the work of various business associations including FAGE (Federation of Association of Ghanaian Exporters) and export promotion agencies like the Ghana Export Promotion Council in creating a favourable climate for small exporter e-business adoption. Some elements of a favourable climate might include, for instance, helping to procure affordable PCs for the exporters, or setting up a trade information system that the small exporters can connect to.

Micro triggers for e-business adoption are hypothesized to include the business culture (measured by organization resistance/acceptance to technological change) and the type of export organization. It is hypothesized that a handicraft exporting firm might find the web strategy component of e-business more exciting than a tomato exporter and might therefore be incentivized to adopt e-business faster). Other e-business adoption triggers might include resource (financial and skill) constraints, and the age of the exporting firm. Owners/top management of small firms wield a lot of power in organizational direction, so in instances where such owner/managers tend to be technology averse, then e-business might be delayed or might even remain a perpetual mirage for the small firm in question.

E-business adoption in the conceptual framework is also expected to deliver certain benefits to export firms that adopt it. The focus of this chapter is however on the facilitators and inhibitors to e-business adoption in Ghanaian export firms and builds on the work on Hinson and Sorensen (2006 & 2007). We develop hypothesis to test what key facilitators and barriers exist in the e-business adoption bid of Ghanaian non-traditional export firms.

One of the greatest benefits of having an Internet presence could be said to be the instant access a small exporting business has to a global market. Evans and King (1999) note that the key deliverable benefits of the internet is global reach firm. It would stand to reason then that a developing country that is internationally oriented in its outlook will tend to adopt e-business. We therefore hypothesize that:

H1: The more internationally oriented the export firms, the more likely they are to adopt e-business.

Export facilitation institutions are meant to be key to improving the electronic competencies of export firms especially in developing country context. According to an article entitled "e-challenges: Countries in Action", it was noted that Ghana's national strategy is to aggressively facilitate export development; primarily in the non-traditional export sector and in this vein, the Ghana Export Promotion Council coordinates the implementation of this strategy. It was further noted that one of the strategic objectives of the council was that all registered Ghanaian exporters should become e-competent by 2003. We therefore hypothesize that:

Figure 1. Small firm exporter e-business development framework

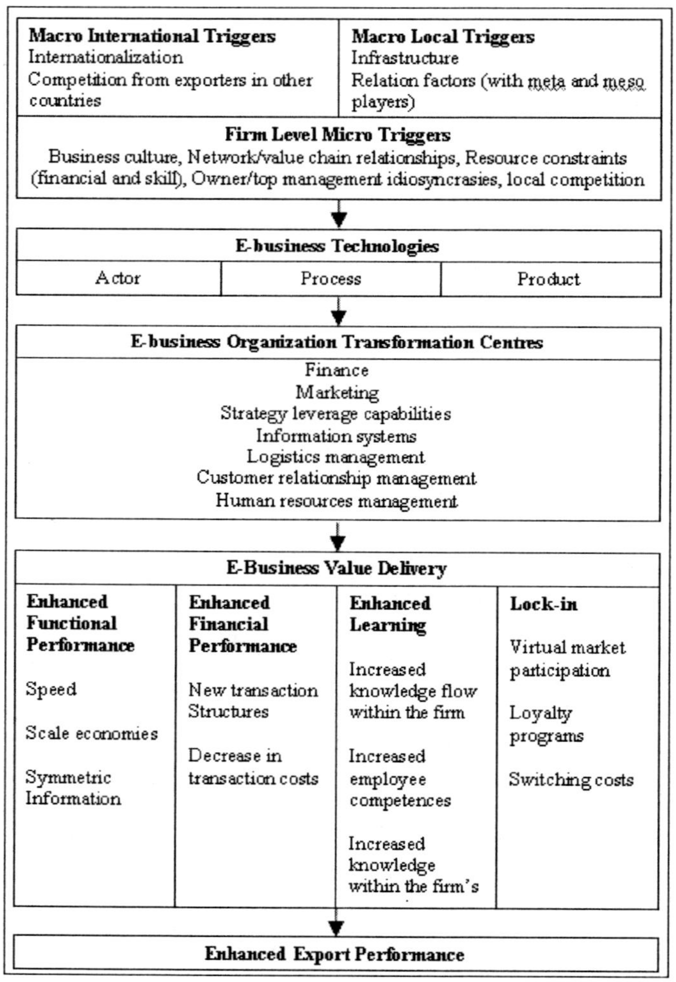

H2: The higher the level of export facilitation, the more likely a developing economy export firm is, to adopt e-business.

Digitalization can be understood to be the increasing application of electronic practices in the conduct of an export firm's business. Digitalization could therefore mean that the higher the compatibility of the export operation (task) with electronic processes (technology), the higher the likelihood of the adoption of e-business innovations (Cooper and Zmud, 1990). We therefore hypothesize:

H3: That the higher the level of digitalization, the higher the likelihood of e-business adoption.

Competitive pressure usually leads export firms along the path of unearthing strategies to outmanoeuvre their competition and maintain a competitive edge. The adoption of e-business practices represents one of the tools to the attainment of sustainable competitive advantage. The perceived benefits of e-commerce in fighting competitive pressure and facilitating export firm growth (Iacovou et al, 1995) could be an important factor in the adoption of e-business technologies. Khoo et al (1998) have also noted that small exporters are able to better compete in foreign markets because of their technological capabilities. Abell and Limm (1996) also posit that e-commerce adoption delivers and Epstein (2004) has also argued that e-commerce can potentially influence an organization's advantages of increase in market share of products/ services competitive position. We hypothesize that:

H4: The higher the level of competitive pressure, the higher the likelihood of e-business adoption.

In a developing economy (including African) context, owners/managers of small (including export) firms tend to be extremely powerful in the decision to adopt/not adopt new technologies. Small business owners do not usually have sophisticated governance structures and therefore any decision that requires substantial capital outlay; usually have to be decided by the owner/manager. In certain cases owner/managers fall on the advice of a management team. Orlikowski (1993), Rai and Patnayakuni (1996) have all identified top management support as crucial to the adoption of new innovation like e-business technologies. We therefore hypothesize that:

H5: Top management support and commitment will be positively related to e-business adoption.

Developing economy firms usually face resource constraints and this could have a direct bearing on their capacity to adopt e-business. The ability to purchase computers and put in simple technology applications like local area and wide area networks could be a major determinant of the adoption of e-business. Newcomer and Candle (1991) note that access to adequate equipment could hamper or facilitate the adoption of new technologies like e-business. The business culture within an export firm as well as the presence of staff with ICT exposure and related business strategy skills to harness and use e-business (Molla and Licker, 2005); also have a significant effect on the adoption or otherwise of e-business. Thus, we hypothesize that:

H6: The less resourced an export firm is, the less likely they are to adopt e-business.

Environmental bottlenecks in respect of e-business adoption for a developing country export are real and these could range from lack of support from export industry associations and regulations and the high cost of Internet access. In an international trade centre article on e-challenges: Countries in Action, it was noted that the Ghana Export Promotion Council had developed an e-competency strategy which sought to amongst others:

i. arrange soft loans...for the purchase of computer systems
ii. encourage computer companies and Internet Service Providers (ISPs) to participate directly in the e-competency programme
iii. encourage exporters to "connect" to the Internet, develop enterprise websites and devise e-trade strategies

Molla and Licker (2005) have argued that for electronic practices to be better assimilated there should be the presence of support-giving institutions; which we argue in this case could comprise export industry associates and ISPs. We hypothesize that:

H7: The higher the level of environmental bottlenecks/ lack of industry support, the less likely they are to adopt e-business.

Technological sophistication of the business networks in which an export firm operates in, has a bearing on their decision to adopt/ not adopt e-business. Chan et al (2000) have noted that the internet has now been adopted to facilitate greater supplier involvement in the activities of the firms. Turban et al (2004) have also noted that for e-commerce to thrive, sellers and buyers have to be willing to exchange goods and services for money online. We thus hypothesize that:

H8: The less technologically sophisticated the parties in the export/ international network of the export firm, the less likely they are to adopt e-business.

Exporting is a herculean challenge for developing economy export firms because of the financial and technical investments that need to be made into the export operation before it becomes a success. Sorensen and Buatsi, in a 2002 article on "The internet and exporting in Ghana" found that lack of means to finance equipment was one of the hindrances to internet adoption amongst Ghanaian non-traditional exporters. Since it takes quite a while for export firms from developing economies to become profitable, we posit that younger export firms may be not be as endowed (finance) as older exporters. Following on, we also believe that larger exporter firms and firms located into larger internet-ready cities may possess a higher level of I.T. resources and personnel I.T. knowledge (Akbulut 2002) as well as financial resources required to adopt e-business. We thus hypothesize that:

H9: The younger and more remotely located the export firm, the less likely they are to adopt e-business.

Molla and Licker (2005), Sorensen and Buatsi (2002), Pucihar (2006) and Kamel (2006) all agree that governments and their various ICT regulatory agencies are extremely crucial in facilitating the uptake of e-business in developing economy contexts. Sorensen and Buatsi posit for instance that the government of Ghana must increase infrastructural investments in order to improve the uptake of e-business whilst Pucihar (2006) notes that government activities played an important role in accelerating e-commerce adoption in Slovenia. We thus hypothesize that;

H10: The weaker ICT and export-related government regulation is, the less likely an export firm is to adopt e-business.

METHODOLOGY

The data for this study was collected from a sample of NTEs drawn from the agricultural processed & semi-processed and handicraft sectors. These are the broad categories of the NTEs usually delineated by the Ghana Export Promotion Council, the apex body for NTE export development in Ghana. We employed a convenience sampling technique and contacted 120 NTEs located/headquartered in Accra (the capital of Ghana). A six section questionnaire predominantly constructed using a five-point Likert scale with the responses for a majority of the questions ranging from "strongly disagree to strongly agree'. The sample was made up of 94 NTE firms located in Accra, the capital of Ghana. Majority (67%) of them are private and locally owned. The firms mostly employ less than 100 people and 81% have annual sales less than $500,000. Nearly half (46.5%) are involved in agriculture, 32.6% are in the processed & semi-processed sector and 20.9% are into export of handicrafts. Table 1 below presents descriptive statistics on the sample.

RESULTS

E-Business Adoption

The level of e-business adoption in this study has been measured in three levels – possession and use of computer, internet and website. Two items,

Table 1. Sample Characteristics

Nature of Organisation	**%**
Government	2.1
Private/Locally owned	67.0
Private/Foreign owned more than 50%	10.6
Private /Foreign owned less than 50%	3.2
Joint Venture partnership	10.6
Other	6.4
Size of Organization by Annual Sales	**%**
up to $50,000	35.7
$50,001-$250,000	28.6
$2,5001-$500,000	16.7
$500,001-$1,000,000	8.3
$1,000,001-$5,000,000	6.0
$10,000,000+	4.8
Size of Organization by Employees	**%**
0-10	55.6
11-100	30.0
101-250	4.4
251-1000	10.0
Export by Volume	**%**
0-19%	39.7
20-39%	12.1
40-59%	6.9
60-79%	22.4
80-99%	19.0

Size of Top Management	**%**
0-4	70.0
5-9	21.1
10-14	6.7
15-19	1.1
20+	1.1
Industry of Operation	**%**
Agric	46.5
Processed/ semi processed	32.6
Handicrafts	20.9
How Old Is Your Firm	**%**
0-5	31.3
5-10	33.7
10-15	15.7
15-20	3.6
20+	15.7
Is Your Export Firm a Division/Subsidiary of a Larger Organization	**%**
No	62.3
Yes	37.7

number of computers and number of full-time IT staff, each scored on a scale of 0 - 5, were used under computer. Internet adoption was measured with four items: possession of internet connection (0-no, 1-yes), percentage of computers with internet access, percentage of employees with internet access and percentage of employees with corporate email address, each scored 0 – 5. Adoption under website was measured by the nature of website (0-static, 1-dynamic), uses to which website is put (0 – 3) and the frequency of website update (0 – 7). A composite index of e-business adoption was then developed by summing the scores for the nine items. Scores thus range between 0 where none of the items is adopted to 37 where all are adopted. This scale has a Cronbach's Alpha of 0.605 which indicates a satisfactory level of construct reliability. The Friedman ANOVA test indicates that scores are significantly different ($p<0.001$) and Tukey's Test of Additivity is significant ($p < 0.001$).

Descriptive statistics on the various items comprising the e-business adoption index are shown in Table 2 below. Majority (93.3%) of firms have between 1 to 49 computers with about 1 to 4 full-time IT staff (70.1%). The average score for computer is 2.234 with a maximum of 6 out of the possible 10. About 70% of firms have internet connection with 59.5% having connections on less than 20% of computers in their firms. In 52% of firms, less than 20% of employees have corporate email addresses. The average score for internet adoption is 6.95, the highest being 16 out of the possible 16. Of the 53.2% of firms which have websites, nearly 65% described them as dynamic with between daily to yearly updates. The average score for website is 3.47 and the highest is 11 out of the possible 11. The observed adoption index ranged between 5 and 30 with an average of 13.42.

Table 2. E-business adoption Index

Number of computers within the firm	**%**
1-49 (1)	93.3
50-99 (2)	4.5
100-149 (3)	1.1
150-199 (4)	1.1
Full time IT staff	**%**
1-4 (1)	70.1
5-9 (2)	22.1
10-14 (3)	2.6
Internet connectivity	**%**
No (0)	29.3
Yes (1)	70.7
Percentage of PCs with internet access	**%**
<20% (1)	59.5
20-39% (2)	8.3
40-59% (3)	6.0
60-79% (4)	4.8
80-99% (5)	21.4
Employees with corporate e-mail address	**%**
<20% (1)	51.8
20-39% (2)	16.5
40-59% (3)	11.8
60-79% (4)	7.1
80-99% (5)	12.9
Description of website	**%**
Static (0)	35.4
Dynamic (1)	64.6
Website Uses	**%**
1 – 3 (1)	43.6
4 – 6 (2)	27.3
6+ (3)	29.1
Frequency of website update	**%**
Yearly (1)	12.2
Half-yearly (2)	20.4
Quarterly (3)	20.4
Monthly (4)	10.2
Fortnightly (5)	2.0
Weekly (6)	10.2
Daily (7)	24.5

Adoption Facilitators

The respondents were asked for their levels of agreement on a set of 13 items perceived to be possible triggers of e-business adoption. The perceived facilitators are set out in Table 3 below on the basis of the mean level of agreement with statements about the items. All items except those concerning pressures from the GEPC and FAGE have mean scores above the median scale of 4. In particular, strong agreement was expressed with "operating in international markets" (6.19), "competency to adopt e-business technologies" (5.95), "growth in size of export operations" (5.84), "vision of top management to adopt e-business" (5.74) and "competition with Ghanaian exporters" (5.4). The others are "level of infrastructural development in the ICT sector" (5.25), "adoption of e-business as a strategic option to enhancing export competitiveness" (5.05) and "competition from non-Ghanaian exporters" (5.0). Lower levels of agreement were expressed with the others ranked from 9 to 11. Respondents quite disagreed with pressures from the GEPC and FAGE as triggers for e-business adoption.

Moderate inter-item correlations were observed among the facilitators. We therefore employed factor analysis to produce distinct underlying facilitators for our analysis. Principal axis factoring with varimax rotation was used to extract four factors accounting for 71.2% of the variance observed among the items. The procedure was started with all 13 items but 4 were dropped because of inappropriate loading. The construct exhibited internal reliability with Cronbach's Alpha values ranging from 0.551 to 0.875. KMO-MSA was 0.566 and Bartlett's test of sphericity was significant. The factors were

Table 3. Perceived Adoption Facilitators

Item	Rank	Mean	Std. Deviation
Operating in international markets	1	6.19	1.252
Your firm has the competencies to use Internet/e-business technologies	2	5.95	1.353
Growth in the size of your export operation	3	5.84	1.344
Top management has the vision to adopt e-business	4	5.73	1.660
Competition from Ghanaian exporters	5	5.40	1.580
The level of infrastructural development in Ghana's ICT sector has a direct influence in our level of e-business adoption	6	5.25	1.882
Your company adopted e-business as a strategic option to enhancing its export competitiveness	7	5.05	1.972
Competition from non - Ghanaian exporters	8	5.00	1.945
importance of e-business in improving export competitiveness	9	4.98	2.281
Your export firm has embraced e-business as a value delivery tool	10	4.94	1.949
importance of e-business in digitizing your export operations	11	4.91	1.984
The Ghana Export Promotion Council (GEPC) has been pressurizing your firm to adopt e-business practices in your export promotion	12	3.63	1.886
The Federation of Association of Ghanaian Exporters (FAGE) has been pressurizing your firm to adopt e-business	13	3.08	2.139

labeled as international orientation, export facilitation, digitalization and competitive pressure. The results are shown in Table 4 below.

Adoption Barriers

Similar to the approach adopted for assessing adoption facilitators, the level of agreement of respondents were sought on a set of 19 items perceived to be e-business adoption barriers (internal and external to the firm). The scores on levels of agreement observed for the barriers were generally lower than those observed for the facilitators. Mean scores across the 19 items ranged between 3.33 and 4.81. Eleven items had scores above the median scale value of 4, indicating low agreement while eight items had mean scores between the indifference score and the median score. Table 5 below presents the ranks of the barriers.

Again, because of inter-item correlations among the over 25 internal and external barrier items measured by the instrument, factor analysis was used to extract distinct non-overlapping underlying factors. Principal axis factoring with varimax rotation produced six factors from 19 items after items with inappropriate loadings were dropped. This explained 72.9% of the observed variance. Satisfactory construct reliability and internal consistency is exhibited with Cronbach's Alpha values ranging from 0.60 to 0.93. KMO-MSA is 0.633 and Bartlett's test of sphericity is significant. The extracted factors were labeled

Table 4. Factors of perceived facilitators

Factors	Factor Loads	Eigen Values	% of Var. Explained	Cumulative % of Variance	Cronbach's α
Factor 1 (International orientation)		*3.032*	*24.923*	*24.923*	*.825*
E-business adopted as a strategic option to enhancing export competitiveness	.956				
Growth in the size of your export operation	.666				
Your export firm has embraced e-business as a value delivery tool	.649				
Operating in international markets	.637				
Factor 2 (Export Facilitation)		*1.859*	*18.914*	*43.837*	*.866*
Pressures from the Federation of Association of Ghanaian Exporters (FAGE)	.945				
Pressures from the Ghana Export Promotion Council (GEPC)	.814				
Factor 3 (Digitalization)		*1.527*	*16.672*	*60.509*	*.875*
importance of e-business in digitizing your export operations	.883				
importance of e-business in improving export competitiveness	.829				
Factor 4 (Competitive Pressure)		*1.118*	*10.717*	*71.226*	*.551*
Competition from Ghanaian exporters	.677				
Growth in the size of export operation	.446				
Notes: Principal axis factoring with varimax rotation, KMO-MSA = 0.566, Bartlett's test of sphericity = 163.723 ($p < .00001$)					

Table 5. Adoption barriers

Barriers	Rank	Mean	SD
Poor service from Internet service providers	1	4.81	1.407
High Internet Access fees charged by ISPs	2	4.67	1.583
Lack of support from export associations like Federation of Associations of Ghanaian Exporters	3	4.66	1.617
Poor infrastructural support for e-business development	4	4.56	1.350
Technological resources to adopt e-business.	5	4.48	1.712
Lack of support from export sector regulators like the Ghana Export Promotion Council	6	4.45	1.588
Network/Value Chain relationships	7	4.25	1.430
Our business culture	8	4.25	1.843
Financial resources to adopt e-business.	9	4.08	1.716
Educational level of employees	10	4.05	1.692
Inadequate Trading Volume to justify e-business	11	4.02	1.727
Strategic Direction of export company	12	3.97	1.760
Type of product exported	13	3.89	1.684
Non-Automated/Non-sophisticated Trading Partner(s).	14	3.85	1.787
Age of Employees	15	3.74	1.702
Top Management reluctance to adopt e-business	16	3.73	1.833
Age of export firm	17	3.52	1.652
Location of Export Firm	18	3.46	1.718
Reluctance of export firm owner to adopt e-business	19	3.33	1.704

as owner/management idiosyncrasies, internal resource constraints, environmental bottlenecks, e-sophistication, export firm characteristics and weak government regulation. Table 6 below presents the results.

E-Business Adoption, Perceived Facilitators and Barriers

Both perceived facilitators and barriers are expected to influence e-business adoption among firms. We therefore employ multiple regression analysis to investigate the possible functional relationship between adoption of e-business and the perceived facilitators and barriers among NTE firms in Ghana. The model is built using the composite adoption index developed as the dependent variable and the 10 extracted factors of perceived facilitators and barriers as independent variables. Pair wise correlation coefficients were low and thus cleared concerns about multicollinearity. The following hypotheses were tested.

- **H1.** The more internationally oriented the export firm is, the more likely they are to adopt e-business.
- **H2.** The higher the level of export facilitation, the more likely the export firm is to adopt e-business.
- **H3.** The higher the level of digitalization, the higher the likelihood of e-business adoption.
- **H4.** The higher the level of competitive pressure, the higher the likelihood of e-business adoption.

Table 6. Factors of perceived barriers

Factors	Factor Loads	Eigen Values	% of Var. Explained	Cumulative % of Variance	Cronbach's A
Factor 1(Owner/Mgt Idiosyncrasies)		*6.689*	*20.747*	*20.747*	*.933*
Strategic direction of export firm	.867				
Reluctance of export firm owner to adopt e-business	.788				
Type of product exported	.772				
Educational level of employees	.740				
Top Management reluctance to adopt e-business	.701				
Factor 2 (Internal Resource Constraints)		*3.191*	*12.424*	*33.171*	*.907*
Technological resources to adopt e-business.	.950				
Financial resources to adopt e-business.	.863				
Our business culture	.649				
Factor 3 (environmental bottlenecks)		*1.683*	*12.240*	*45.411*	*.864*
Lack of support from export sector regulators like the GEPC	.860				
Lack of support from export associations like FAGE	.812				
High Internet Access fees charged by ISPs	.716				
Factor 4 (e-sophistication)		*1.454*	*10.972*	*56.383*	*.789*
Inadequate Trading Volume to justify e-business	.642				
Network/Value Chain relationships	.615				
Non-Automated/Non-sophisticated Trading Partner(s).	.611				
Factor 5 (Export Firm Characteristics)		*1.421*	*9.635*	*66.018*	*.846*
Age of Employees	.777				
Age of export firm	.695				
Location of Export Firm	.604				
Factor 6 (Weak Government Regulation)		1.043	6.881	72.899	0.600
Poor infrastructural support for e-business development	.721				
Poor service from Internet service providers	.620				
Notes: Principal axis factoring with varimax rotation, KMO-MSA = 0.633, Bartlett's test of sphericity = 680.711 ($p < .0001$)					

- **H5.** The more favourable owner/management idiosyncrasies are to e-business the more likely the firm is to adopt e-business.
- **H6.** The more under-resourced the export firm is, the less likely it is to adopt e-business.
- **H7.** The higher the level of environmental bottlenecks, the less likely the export firm is to adopt e-business.
- **H8.** The less technologically sophisticated the partners in the export/international network of the export firm, the less likely they are to adopt e-business.
- **H9.** The younger the export firm with fewer employees and rural location, the less likely it is to adopt e-business.
- **H10.** The weaker ICT and export related government regulation is, the less likely an export firm is to adopt e-business.

The regression model is significant at the 0.01 level (F = 6.72, Adjusted R^2 = .397). Residual plots suggest there are no serious violations of error term assumptions. The coefficients of five factors (3 perceived facilitators and 2 perceived barriers) are significant. These are export facilitation, digitalization, competitive pressure, internal resource pressure and environmental bottlenecks. However, of the 3 significant perceived facilitators, only one (competitive pressure) has a positive sign. The implication of the two perceived facilitators with negative coefficients (export facilitation and digitalization) is that the higher the level of those factors, the less likely it is for the firms to adopt e-business. Both significant perceived barriers (internal resource constraints and environmental bottlenecks) have negative signs. Thus, the higher the levels of those perceived barriers, the less likely it is for firms to adopt e-business. From the results it can be concluded that an export firm's international orientation, owner/management idiosyncrasies, e-sophistication of partners, export firm's characteristics (age, number of employees and location) and weak government regulation have no significant influence on e-business adop-

Table 7. Regression model for e-business adoption

				95% Confidence Interval for Coefficients	
Variable	Coefficient	T	Significance	Lower Bound	Upper Bound
(Constant)	13.392	26.410	.000**	12.382	14.402
International orientation	-.011	-.018	.985	-1.210	1.187
Export facilitation	-1.552	-2.758	.007**	-2.672	-.431
Digitalization	-1.297	-2.154	.034*	-2.496	-.098
Competitive pressure	1.405	2.306	.024*	.192	2.619
Owner/management idiosyncrasies	-.823	-1.405	.164	-1.989	.343
Internal resource constraints	-2.771	-5.149	.000**	-3.842	-1.699
Environmental bottlenecks	-2.256	-3.962	.000**	-3.389	-1.122
E-sophistication	-.559	-.906	.368	-1.789	.670
Export firm characteristics	.157	.274	.785	-.984	1.298
Weak government regulation	-1.043	-1.867	.066	-2.155	.069

Dependent Variable: Adoption Index
** Significant at the 0.05 level*
*** Significant at the 0.01 level*

tion by Ghanaian NTE firms. On the other hand, competitive pressure (as measured by competition from Ghanaian export firms and growth in size of export operations) significantly facilitates e-business adoption. Export facilitation (measured by pressures from GEPC and FAGE) and digitalization (measured by perceived importance of e-business in digitalizing export operations and improving export competitiveness) perceived to facilitate e-business adoption however exhibit significant negative relationships with adoption. Internal resource constraints (measured by technological and financial resources for e-business adoption and business culture) and environmental bottlenecks (measured by lack of support from export sector regulators and export associations and high internet access fees charged by ISPs) also reduce the likelihood of e-business adoption by Ghanaian NTE firms. Thus, while H4, H6 and H7 are accepted, H1, H2, H3, H5, H8, H9 and H10 are rejected.

DISCUSSION

We found the two perceived facilitators with negative coefficients (export facilitation and digitalization) to be rather fascinating so we did a follow up with ten export firms to ascertain from them what the likely reasons for this finding might be. We discovered that non-traditional export firms perceive a lack of clarity on terms of e-business policy direction from the major export policy makers and therefore the more e-commerce or e-business advocacy noises they make, the less likely NTEs are to adopt e-business. This finding is consistent with Reid (1984) who found in a study on export assistance that institutional sources (for export assistance) tend to be the least used information source because exporters tend to perceive this as not being specific enough or not having accurate data. In separate research being conducted by us, we discovered 99 of the 438 exporters listed on the GEPC web portal in 2007 had wrong email addresses. From an institutional perspective therefore the policy maker (GEPC) must itself seek to become an e-business champion in order to begin to create norms that export firms can aspire to.

On the issue of digitalization, we found that it was closely related to the issue of export facilitation since most of the crusade about e-business adoption has come again from the facilitating institutions and therefore the more of the crusade they hear, the less likely they are adopt e-business. Competitive pressure (as measured by competition from Ghanaian export firms and growth in size of export operations) significantly facilitates e-business adoption and this was significant to the extent that it would seem that peer pressure is a more predictable adoption factor than pressure from facilitating institutions. The facilitating institutions might want to create training fora to get the best adopters to come and explain e-business adoption benchmarks to laggards so that the whole export sector e-business adoption propensities can be enhanced.

CONCLUSION

This chapter has attempted to delineate the main barriers and facilitators to e-business adoption by Ghanaian export firms. A quantitative approach was adopted, which involved selecting 120 Non-traditional exporters (NTEs) from a directory of active NTEs in Ghana. The results revealed that e-business adoption by small exporting firms was facilitated by pressure from other local firms, internet resourcefulness of the firm and a conducive business environment. It is recommended that facilitation institutions like the GEPC and FAGE get their e-business act together first; and then enhance these facilitators for export firms to move towards more internet-based operations. From an institutional theory perspective, it is posited that structures, rules, norms and routines become established as authoritative guidelines for social behaviour (Scott, 2004). For an e-business culture to become more diffuse in Ghana's NTE sector therefore, facilitation institutions themselves must aspire to higher levels of e-business excellence so they can take the appropriate lead in creating and diffusing this culture. Adoption and adaptation will eventually better take place over space and time (Scott, 2004).

REFERENCES

Abell, W. and Limm, L. (1996). *Business use of the internet in New Zealand: an exploratory study.* Retrieved from http://www.scu.edu.au/sponsered/ausweb96/business/abell/paper.html.

Akbulut, A. (2002). *An investigation of the factors that influence electronic information sharing between state and local agencies.* Dallas, Texas, USA: Proceedings of 8th American Conference on Information Systems. (2454-2460).

Bennett, R. (1997). Export marketing and the Internet. *International Marketing Review, 14*(5), 324-355.

Chan, C. and Swatman, P. (2000). Firm EDI to internet commerce: the BHL Steel Experience. *Internet Research: Electronic Networking Applications and Policy, 10*(1), 72-82.

Chau, S. and Pederson, S. (2000). *The Emergence of New Micro Businesses Utilizing Electronic Commerce.* Australia: Proceedings of the 11th Australian Conference of Information Systems (ACIS).

Cooper, R.B. and Zmud, R.W. (1990). Information technology implementation research; a technological difference approach. *Management Science, 36*(2), 123-139.

Coviello, N.E. and McAuley, A. (1999). Internationalization and the smaller firm: a review of contemporary empirical research. *Management International Review, 39*(3), 223-256.

Durkin, M. and McGowan, P. (2001). Net effect – views from the periphery: exploring the role and importance of the internet on marketing activity in entrepreneurial firms. *Irish Marketing Review, special issue, 14*(1), 15-25.

Eid, R. (2005). International Internet Marketing: A Triangulation study of drivers and barriers in the business-to-business context in the United Kingdom. *Marketing Intelligence and Planning, 23*(3), 266-280.

Epstein, M.J. (2004). *Implementing E-commerce strategies: A guide to corporate success after the dot.com bust.* Westerport: Praeger Publisher.

Evans, J. R. and King, V.E. (1999). Business-to-business marketing on the World Wide Web: planning, marketing and assessing websites. *Industrial Marketing Management, 28*(4), 343-358.

Fillis, I., Johansson, U. and Wagner, B. (2003). A conceptualization of the opportunities and barriers to e-business development in the smaller firm. *Journal of Small Business and Enterprise Development, 10*(3), 336-344.

Hamill, J. (1997). The internet and international marketing. *International Marketing Review, 14*(5), 300-323.

Hinson, R. and Sorensen, O. (2006). E-business and small Ghanaian Exports: Preliminary micro firm explorations in the light of a digital divide. *Online Information Review, 30*(2), 116-138.

Hinson, R. and Sorensen, O. (2007). Macro E-business Triggers: A Study of Small Ghanaian Exporters. *Journal of Electronic Commerce in Organizations, October-December, 5*(4), 55-69.

Hornby, G., Goulding, P. and Poon, S. (2002). Perceptions of export barriers and cultural issues: the SME e-commerce experience. *Journal of Electronic Commerce Research, 3*(4), 213-226.

Iacovou, C., Benbasat, I. and Dexter, A. (1995). Electronic data interchange and small organizations: Adoption and impact technology. *MIS Quarterly, 19*(4), 465-485.

International Trade Forum Issue I (2001). *E-challenges: Countries in Action*, p. 22.

Kalakota, R. and Whinston, A.B. (1996). *Frontiers of Electronic Commerce*. Reading: Addison-Wesley Publishing.

Kamal, S. (Ed.) (2006). *Electronic Business in Developing Countries: Opportunities and Challenges.* Hershey: Idea Group.

Kaynak, E., Tatoglu, E. and Kula, V. (2005). An analysis of the factors affecting the adoption of electronic commerce by SMEs: Evidence from an emerging market. *International Marketing Review, 22*(6), 623-40.

Keogh, W., Jack, S.L., Bower, J. and Crabtree, E. (1998). Small, Technology-based firms in the UK oil and gas industry: innovation and internationalization strategies. *International Small Business Journal, October, 17*(1), 57-68.

Khoo, D., McGill, T.J. and Dixon, M.W. (1998). *Use of the Internet by Small to Medium Enterprises in Singapore*. Murdoch University, Perth, Australia.

Leadbeater, C. (2000). *Living on Thin Air, The New Economy.* London: Penguin Books.

Levitt, T. (1983). Globalization of markets. *Harvard Business Review, 61*(May/June), 92-102.

Molla, A. and Licker, P. (2005). E-commerce adoption in developing countries: a model and instrument. *Information and Management, 42*, 877-899.

Newcomer, K.E. and Caudle, S.L. (1991). Evaluating Public Sector Information Systems: More than Meets the Eye. *Public Administration Review, 51*(5), 377-84.

Olikowski, W. (1993). CASE tools as organizational change: Investigating incremental and radical changes in systems development. *MIS Quarterly, 17*(3), 309-340.

Poon, S. and Swatman, P. (1997). *The Internet for small businesses: an enabling infrastructure*. Fifth Internet Society Conference, 221-231. Retrieved from Chon, K., HI, http://www.isworld.org/ais.ac.98/.

Pucihar, A. (2006). E-marketplace Adoption Success Factors: Challenges and Opportunities for a Small Developing Country. In Kamal, S. (Ed.), *Electronic Business in Developing Countries: Opportunities and Challenges* (pp. 88-117). Hershey: Idea Group.

Rai, A. and Patnayakumi, R. (1996). A Structural Model for CASE Adoption Behaviour. *Journal of Management Information Systems, 13*(2), 205-34.

Scott, W.R. (2004). Institutional theory. In Ritzer, G. (Ed.), *Encyclopedia of Social Theory.* Thousand Oaks, CA: Sage.

Sorensen, O. and Buatsi, S. (2002). Internet and Exporting: the case of Ghana. *Journal of Business & Industrial Marketing, 17*(6), 481-500.

Stockdale, R. and Standing, C. (2004). Benefits and Barriers of Electronic Marketplace Participation: An SME Perspective. *Journal of Enterprise Information Management, 17*(4), 301-11.

Turban, E., King, D., Lee, J. and Vienland, D. (2004). *Electronic Commerce: A Managerial Perspective*. New Jersey: Pearson/Prentice Hall.

WEBOGRAPHY

www.myjoyonline.com

Chapter XVII
Organizational Motivation and Interorganizational Systems Adoption Process:
Empirical Evaluation in the Australian Automotive Industry

Md. Mahbubur Rahim
Monash University, Australia

Graeme Shanks
Monash University, Australia

Robert Johnston
The University of Melbourne, Australia

Pradip Sarker
RMIT University, Australia

ABSTRACT

Interorganizational systems (IOS) play a critical role in today's e-commerce environment. These systems are introduced by different organizations following different adoption processes. Existing literature on IOS adoption, however, does not explain the variations in the IOS adoption processes initiated by different organizations. A theory of IOS adoption known as IOS Motivation Model (IMM) has recently been developed by the authors that explains the differences in IOS adoption processes in terms of differences in organizations' adoption motivations for any given IOS project. This chapter reports an application of the model in the Australian automotive industry. The findings provide support for the model and are useful for IT managers.

INTRODUCTION

IOS are important applications that support key boundary-spanning activities of many organizations (Saeed, Malhorta, & Grover, 2005). These systems play a critical role in today's e-commerce environment (Han, Kauffman, & Nault, 2004; Subramaniam & Shaw, 2004) because they provide significant business benefits to supply chain partners (Garfield, Kamis, & LeRouge, 2004). However, IOS benefits are likely to be experienced when these systems are carefully introduced by following appropriate adoption processes (Rahim, 2004; Rahim, Shanks, & Johnston, 2002). Regrettably, little is reported in the existing IOS adoption literature about how organizations determine IOS adoption processes. An exception is the work of Rahim, Shanks, & Johnston (2001a) that has recently developed IMM. The IMM relates IOS adoption processes to the organizational motivations for IOS adoption, classifies organizations into four generic motivation scenarios, and predicts different adoption processes to be initiated by organizations representing different motivation scenarios. The model was tested in the Australian pharmaceutical industry where it received considerable support (Rahim, Shanks, & Johnston, 2001b; Rahim et al., 2002); the model thus requires further validation in other industry contexts in order to evaluate its usefulness across industry segments. To address this, the IMM is applied in this article to examine electronic data interchange (EDI) adoption processes in the context of the Australian automotive industry.

Two organizations that are members (i.e., automotive assembler company and a first-tier automotive parts supplier) of an automotive assembling supply chain were thus chosen for case study in this research project. They have both experienced two distinct stages of EDI adoption. For the automotive assembler company, the first stage of IOS adoption was initiated with the introduction of a traditional EDI system, and the second stage focused on the adoption of an Internet-based EDI system. Similarly, in the first stage the supplier company introduced a stand-alone EDI system to communicate with the automotive assembly company; and at a latter stage the company adopted a fully integrated EDI system with its own suppliers (i.e., tier two suppliers) and as well as the automotive assembly company. Interestingly, the motivation for EDI adoption did not change between the two implementation episodes for the automotive assembler company, but did so for the automotive parts supplier. Thus the IMM predicts that the IOS adoption processes initiated by the manufacturing assembler company should be similar in nature at both stages; and by contrast, the IOS adoption processes undertaken by the automotive parts supplier should differ in specific ways between adoption episodes. Empirical evidence from the two cases suggests that the similarities/differences in the IOS adoption processes between the two stages of each company can be explained in terms of the corresponding similarities/differences in its motivations for EDI adoption. This finding provides support for the proposition that an organization that demonstrates different motivation for adopting an IOS solution at two different time periods will initiate dissimilar adoption processes and that the particular circumstances within which the motivation is formed do not affect significantly the adoption processes initiated. Thus, this study contributes to the literature by confirming the explanatory power of IMM and also demonstrating the applicability of IMM to an industry setting other than the one for which it was initially developed.

This article is organized as follows. First, past approaches to IOS adoption are critically reviewed and their limitations are pinpointed. Second, the IMM is briefly described and its relation to past research is explained. Third, the research approach is narrated. Empirical evidence is then produced to classify the motivations observed in each EDI stage and actions initiated by the case companies to introduce EDI in each stage. Next, the case study findings are discussed. Finally, the research contributions are highlighted and areas of further investigations are indicated.

EXISTING IOS ADOPTION LITERATURE: A CRITICAL EXAMINATION

Existing IOS adoption literature can be divided into two broad streams: (1) factor-based IOS research and (2) process-oriented IOS research. Factor-based studies posit that the presence or absence, or perhaps the level, of certain conditions (commonly known as factors) at some point in time predict IOS adoption. In general, three broad categories of factors are identified: (1) the properties of the IOS being adopted, (2) the characteristics of the adopting organization, and (3) the conditions prevailing in the environment of the organization. The works of Premkumar, Ramamurthy, and Nilakanta (1997) and Lee, Clark, and Tam (1999) represent the influence of the first factor group. On the other hand, Lee et al. (1999) and Chwelos, Benbasat, and Dexter (2001) have examined the influence of the second factor group. Finally, Kuan and Chau (2001); Chau and Hui (2001); and Soliman and Janz (2004) have looked at the influence of the third factor group. Reasonably strong empirical evidence has emerged that suggests such factors are predictive of the decision to adopt IOS. These studies are useful as they offer important guidelines facilitating successful IOS adoption decisions. They, however, do not discuss the conditions relating to initiating IOS adoption processes. Process-oriented IOS adoption studies, on the other hand, posit that outcomes of IOS adoption cannot be predicted from the level of factors, but can be partially predicted from knowledge of IOS adoption processes. These studies describe the processes used in adopting an IOS solution by organizations and explain the benefits achieved as a result of IOS adoption. The works of Kurnia and Johnston (2000) and Kautz and Henriksen (2002) represent this stream of research. Process-oriented studies generally provide a better understanding of IOS adoption benefits by explaining the role of adoption processes. However, although the connection between process and benefits is often quite convincingly demonstrated, these studies do not discuss how the processes are determined in organizations.

In recent years, Rahim et al. (2001b) and Rahim (2004) have proposed the IMM, which explains the role of organizational motives in determining the particular IOS adoption processes followed by organizations. While recognizing the role of traditional factors for the decision to adopt, the IMM rejects factors as predictors of benefits because IOS benefits can be predicted from knowledge of the processes followed by organizations to introduce an IOS. According to the model, traditional factors do not directly affect the attainment of IOS benefits; their influence is mediated through the selection of appropriate processes chosen by the organizations based on their motivations for a given IOS project. In their previous works (Rahim, 2004; Rahim et al., 2001a) the predictive ability of IMM was successfully demonstrated in explaining single EDI adoption initiatives in selected companies chosen from the Australian pharmaceutical industry. However, as the model is new it needs to be applied in other industry segments in order to evaluate its usefulness.

THE IOS MOTIVATION MODEL & RESEARCH PROPOSITIONS

The IMM (shown in Figure 1) is based on the fundamental premise that organizational motivations determine IOS adoption processes. The model classifies organizational motivation along two dimensions: (1) locus of motivation and (2) type of motivation, and identifies four distinct motivation scenarios (shown in the left hand side of Figure 1). These scenarios are proposed in recognition of the existence of various types of

Figure 1. IOS motivation model (IMM)

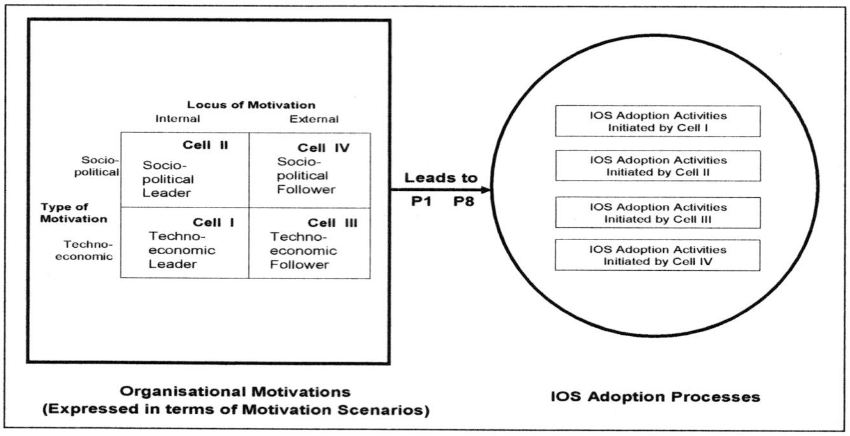

organizational motives (e.g., coercion, normative relations, economic gains, gaining status) and the source (e.g., internal or external) from which such motives may originate. IMM predicts different adoption processes to be initiated by organizations representing different motivation scenarios. The model also identifies eight key activities (shown in the rightmost column of Table 1) that constitute IOS adoption processes. Detailed discussion of these activities is reported in Rahim (2004). According to the model, the subset of these activities that will be initiated by an organization for introducing an IOS application is driven by its motivation scenario for a given IOS project.

According to the IMM, cell I defines the "Techno-economic Leader" scenario that occurs when organizations develop a direct economic motive internally and invest in an IOS project voluntarily, believing that the investment will improve organizational performance with regard to internal efficiency and competitiveness in the marketplace. Cell II defines the "Sociopolitical Leader" scenario that occurs when organizations invest in IOS voluntarily to realize their own sociopolitical motives. These organizations initiate an IOS project for reasons other than immediate efficiency gains, but nevertheless with a clear intention of perhaps portraying either a "progressive" or "customer caring" image in the industry, or with the realization that there is no other way forward, given its trading partner's IOS adoption strategies. However, the motivation to adopt IOS is conceived internally. Cell III refers to the "Techno-economic Follower" scenario that occurs when an organization is approached either by its business partners or by any other influential organization about IOS adoption and, having evaluated the potential economic benefits of the IOS, invests in it voluntarily. Although the motivation to adopt IOS is generated from external sources, the decision is made based on an economic motive. These followers generally do not build an IOS and simply embrace a standard IOS but remain proactive users of IOS. Cell IV represents the "Sociopolitical Follower" scenario that occurs when an organization is approached by its trading partner or a third-party organization to adopt an IOS, and a decision is made based on a sociopolitical motive. These followers do not develop an IOS, but embrace an existing IOS solution, and generally remain as passive users of IOS. IMM also includes a set of propositions

Table 1. Propositions relating to IOS adoption processes

Propositions	IOS Motivation Scenarios				Activities
	Techno-economic leaders	Sociopolitical leaders	Techno-economic followers	Sociopolitical followers	
P1	Likely	Likely	Likely	Unlikely	To prepare an IOS implementation plan
P2	Likely	Unlikely	Likely	Unlikely	To initiate cost-benefit analysis of IOS
P3	Likely	Unlikely	Likely	Unlikely	To perform a post-implementation review of IOS
P4	Likely	Unlikely	Likely	Unlikely	To integrate IOS with back-end IT systems
P5	Likely	Unlikely	Unlikely	Unlikely	To introduce changes in the business practices
P6	Likely	Likely	Likely	Likely	To organize IOS training
P7	Unlikely	Likely	Likely	Unlikely	To apply pressure on partners
P8	Likely	Likely	n/a	n/a	To market IOS concept

Note.: n/a means not applicable

(shown in Table 1) relating to the IOS adoption processes initiated by organizations belonging to each motivational scenario. Detail deductions of these propositions are not included here due to page constraints. They are reported in Rahim (2004).

RESEARCH DESIGN

A scientific case study approach was selected to empirically evaluate the IMM. This is because IOS adoption generally takes place in a complex environment since these systems have dependency on infrastructure, which may not be within the control of a single organization (Premkumar et al., 1997). Moreover, the complex interplay of resource dependencies and distribution of power along supply chain members also add complexity to the IOS adoption, decision-making process (Damsgaard & Lyytinen, 2000). Hence, it is critical to capture the experiences of the relevant people and the context of their actions to understand IOS adoption. Case studies are suitable for understanding phenomena within their organizational context (Yin, 2003). The automotive industry was selected because the contextual details within which IOS adoption takes place differ significantly from the pharmaceutical industry within which the IMM was previously tested. These two industry segments differ significantly in terms of type of products produced and distribution of power among supply chain members.

The case study was conducted using the rigorous principles of Yin (2003) and Sarker and Lee (2000), which are grounded in the positivist tradition. The positivist tradition is used because the aim is to test a preexisting theoretical model (i.e., IMM) to explain the behavior of organizations for IOS adoption. Drawing upon the model, it was also possible to deductively test concepts pertaining to organizational motives and adoption processes for adopting IOS. Data were collected using in-depth interviews from several senior executives from each case site. Each interview lasted for an hour, was tape-recorded, and subsequently transcribed in full. A coding scheme was developed based on the interview protocol suggested by Rahim (2004). Using this coding scheme, each interview script was examined by two members of the research team. Any differences were resolved through mutual discussion.

Established methodological guidelines were applied to generate reliable findings. Reliability was addressed by clearly conceptualizing research variables, using previously pilot-tested protocol and using multiple coders. The variables involved in the research propositions were clearly defined, and a summary of these definitions was provided to the interviewees prior to commencing the interviews. This was done in order to ensure that all the interviewees were able to interpret the research variables in a consistent manner. Additionally, following Yin's (2003) guidelines, a case-study protocol was developed, which together with a copy of the summary of definition of research variables, was sent to the interviewees one week prior to the actual date of the interview. The protocol included questions asking about the nature of the motives that persuaded the case organization to invest in IOS solutions, the activities undertaken during adoption, and explanations for initiating those activities. The protocol was developed based on the concepts involved in IMM and the propositions shown in Table 1 and was evaluated by academics who are actively engaged in e-commerce research. The interviewees on many occasions granted access to relevant company documents that helped the researchers to corroborate the information provided during interviews. The interview transcripts as well as a draft report on EDI adoption were prepared and were sent to the interviewees for review. Data collected from the company were analyzed using the pattern matching logic (Yin, 2003) which enabled the researchers to compare the pattern of outcomes of the dependent variable (i.e., IOS adoption processes) predicted from the theoretical model with the pattern of outcomes deduced from the case data collected through verbal interviews and other documentary sources of the company. However, consistent with the notion of analytical generalization (Yin, 2003), attempts were also made to check that the expected processes were initiated for the *same reasons* as those used in the logical deduction of the propositions reported in Rahim (2004). Additionally, in order to facilitate data analysis process, the following three strategies were applied: (1) a number of key themes and subthemes were identified, (2) each subtheme was captured using a number of questions that appeared in the interview protocol, and (3) a coding scheme was used to label a chunk of a "descriptive paragraph or part of" to categorize empirical data into subthemes.

DESCRIPTION OF CASES

Case A is a well-known automotive assembly company located in a large capital city, Australia. It wholly designs, develops, and builds a range of vehicles, many of which are exported to Asian countries. The company has several thousand staff and has introduced a wide range of IT-enabled applications in support of all the major business processes. The company uses an enterprise resource planning (ERP) system which is well integrated with its materials planning system. On the other hand, Case B is a an established first-tier supplier that produces various types of filters and delivers them to both the production division and parts accessories division of all four automotive assembly companies located in Australia. It also supplies filters direct to hundreds of small spare parts retailers. The supplier is a medium-sized enterprise and has only two IT managers. It currently uses the MFGPRO ERP system that runs on a UNIX platform in support of all its key business processes.

CASE STUDY FINDINGS

Case A: EDI Adoption in Automotive Assembly Company

The automotive assembly company has undertaken two distinct initiatives in adopting EDI systems which are discussed next.

- **Stage 1:** Adoption of traditional EDI systems.

In the late 1980s, the automotive industry underwent considerable changes. The Australian government decided to withdraw tariff protection as outlined in the Button Car Plan (Mackay, 1993) in order to make the industry more internationally competitive. As part of an industry-wide response to this situation, the automotive company then took an initiative to adopt a traditional EDI system to transact electronically with its large suppliers in order to improve its efficiency and develop the ability to compete effectively in the global market. The idea of conducting electronic transactions through EDI was initially conceived by the IT department. The materials planning department of the company then expressed a strong interest in the idea of EDI-enabled electronic transactions as EDI was considered as a means to become more competitive. The materials planning department prepared a project proposal with the assistance of the IT department to streamline the materials ordering process, which later received full support from the senior management of the company. Hence, the locus of motivation for EDI adoption can be classified as internal.

The materials planning department was attracted to the novelty of EDI technology and considered EDI technology to have the potential for bringing a reduction in data entry errors and order-document preparation time. The department wanted to send Material Requirements Schedules (MRS) to the suppliers who would then return Advanced Shipping Notices (ASN). The electronic exchange of these documents was believed to result in substantial time and cost savings. EDI was also expected to take some costs out of the ordering process by reducing mismatched ASNs. In addition, the department looked at EDI as a means of gaining competitive advantages over its rivals by locking in major suppliers. Hence, the type of motivation is techno-economic in nature. Considering the locus and type of motivation, the automotive company can be regarded as an instance of a techno-economic leader.

Prior to introducing the EDI system, the company framed a carefully crafted implementation plan to seek an approval from the senior management (P1). The plan included a detailed justification for introducing the EDI technology, a time table for implementing EDI, and an overview of the critical issues relating to communication and EDI standards. The company also conducted a cost-benefit analysis (P2) and clearly specified benefits in terms of immediate efficiency gains and long-term advantages over its competitors. Furthermore, it reviewed the situation in its internal operations as well as in the supply chain after having undertaken the implementation of the EDI system (P3). The company integrated EDI systems with its back-end, materials planning system in order to avoid manual data entry about MRS and ASN (P4). In the words of the materials planning manager:

In the pre-EDI days, our staff in the materials control division printed out the schedules and faxed them out to our suppliers. At the other end, when parts arrived at the gate, if the ASN had already reached the materials handling system via EDI when our staff can see the particular conveyance coming in, they can say - yes, I've got this conveyance…the screen's already populated…we've received all those parts.

The company streamlined its ordering process prior to introducing the traditional EDI system (P5) as indicated by the senior analyst:

...EDI implementation was preceded by the examination and enhancement of relevant business processes.

The company organized training for its IT staff, which enabled them to build an electronic interface between the EDI system and the back-end materials planning systems and greatly facilitated the seamless exchange of MRS and ASN data with its suppliers (P6). The company also took a strong stance in support of forcing its suppliers into joining the EDI network (P7). Suppliers risked losing their business relationship with the car manufacturer if they failed to adopt EDI, while potential non-EDI partners lost out in their competitiveness to the EDI-willing counterparts in their bid to join the supply chain network. Suppliers had no choice but to join the network, which eventually proved to be an expensive venture for them, both in terms of their own investment in EDI as well as technical proficiency required to send and receive documents through the EDI network. Even though EDI had the potential to provide benefits to suppliers by bringing a reduction in transaction errors, no serious attempt was made by the company to promote EDI based on its technological novelty (P8). Rather, the company indicated that the failure of the suppliers to comply with the company's requirement of doing business via EDI would unfavorably affect their performance ratings.

- **Stage 2:** Adoption of a Web-based EDI system.

In the year 2002, the company decided to migrate to the global manufacturing resource planning (MRP) system that had already been running for about 20 years in its headquarters. This decision was made due to its parent company's desire to standardize and streamline internal operations across its chapters worldwide. The migration to the global MRP, however, instigated changes to coding patterns and mailboxes in the company's EDI transactions with its suppliers. Thus, an EDI upgrade was undertaken that called for a revision of coding schemes and mailboxes with suppliers. At that time, the automotive company conducted a survey of its local suppliers to find out more about their EDI capability. It identified that somewhere down the line its purchasing department had "signed in" with suppliers with no EDI capability whatsoever, as these suppliers were delivering parts at a low cost. However, the noncompliance of EDI by these small suppliers had an ill effect on the company that was not identified before. Therefore, bringing these non-EDI enabled suppliers onto an EDI network presented an opportunity to obtain further efficiency improvement.

The automotive company further recognized that many of the non-EDI-enabled suppliers were small companies with limited financial resources and IT expertise. The company thus decided to invest in Web-enabled EDI application but outsourced its development to a third-party service provider. Using the Web-based EDI systems, the company could then send MRS to the third-party provider via a proprietary network. Suppliers could then log in and view the list of MRS using a standard Web interface. The Web application also allowed the suppliers to view a particular MRS, automatically convert it into an ASN, and send it off to the service provider. Upon receiving an ASN from the suppliers, the service provider would then translate it into a traditional EDI format and forward the EDI message to the automotive company via the proprietary network. Thus, the intent of the automotive company to invest in the Web-based EDI system was to realize further efficiency gains by encouraging the small suppliers to adopt an electronic medium. However, the Web-based EDI was not considered as a source of competitive advantage nor was the system intended to enhance the company's bargaining power over the small suppliers. Hence, the company was still being driven by its techno-economic leadership motivation although the circumstances under which this motive was formed were different from those in stage 1.

The automotive company framed an in-depth implementation plan in close collaboration with the third-party service provider (P1). It also conducted a cost-benefit analysis and decided to outsource the development of the system in order to minimize the development costs (P2). Furthermore, the company reviewed its internal operations after having undertaken the implementation of the Web EDI system (P3). It found out that further manual work was reduced as non-EDI suppliers were now able to transmit documents electronically via the Web. The company also integrated Web-based EDI systems with its back-end systems to avoid manual intervention for triggering the exchange of MRS and ASN at the company's side (P4).

The company did not streamline its ordering process while introducing the Web-based EDI system (P5) because the task of translating documents from EDI to Web formats and vice versa was now to be performed by the service provider. Therefore, the introduction of Web EDI services did not bring about any major changes in the internal business processes of the automotive company as it continued to send and receive documents in the usual EDI format. As the Web solution was actually developed by the third-party service provider, the automotive company did not conduct any training programs for its own personnel. However, the company instructed the third-party service provider to organize demonstration programs and online training programs for the small suppliers to train their staff in operating the application (P6).

The automotive company did not exert any pressure on the small suppliers (P7). Instead, it provided financial assistance to the Web EDI provider to develop a Web-based solution that was user friendly, Internet based, and required lower subscription fees from suppliers. The Web-based EDI eliminated the need for small suppliers to possess a high degree of technical proficiency and thus encouraged them to carry out transactions with the automotive company electronically.

The introduction of the Web EDI system was accompanied by a much more cooperative approach from the automotive company. Apart from investing in the development of the Web-based solution, the automotive company did not issue any explicit threats to non-EDI suppliers. Moreover, technical assistance and guidance were offered to the suppliers by the third-party service provider. In particular, as the translation of documents from the proprietary EDI network into a Web-based format and vice versa was being looked after by the Web EDI provider, small suppliers subscribing to the Web services did not have to worry about EDI codes and formats.

Case B: EDI Adoption in Automotive Parts Supplier

The automotive parts supplier has also undertaken two distinct initiatives in adopting EDI systems. The first initiative was concerned with introducing a DOS-based EDI system and the second initiative focused on introducing a fully integrated EDI system.

- **Stage 1:** Adoption of a DOS-based EDI system.

In the early 1990s, the supplier was approached by a large automotive assembly company (i.e., case A), which expressed its strong desire to be able to communicate with all its first-tier suppliers through EDI. The automotive assembly company also asked the supplier to conduct EDI transactions through its preferred third-party, value-added network (VAN) provider, which it appointed to provide EDI communication support for all its first-tier suppliers. The manufacturing company further suggested that the supplier use its proprietary EDI format to exchange documents with them through the preferred VAN provider. Hence, the locus of motivation for EDI adoption is external. The primary desire of the supplier in adopting EDI was to comply with the strong demand from its major customer (i.e., automotive assembler company) that it receives documents in EDI format for the customer's convenience. The supplier expected that its compliance with the customer's request would make them satisfied, and thus the supplier would be able to avoid any disadvantage caused by not adopting an EDI system. Additionally, the supplier also wanted to be seen as more responsive to its customer needs. Hence, developing an EDI capability was considered to be the right option for building a "customer-oriented image" in the eye of the powerful customers. Also, the EDI capability was not introduced to address supply chain inefficiency problems from the supplier perspective. Hence, the type of motivation for EDI adoption can be classified as sociopolitical in nature. Based on the aforementioned arguments, the EDI adoption of the supplier at this stage can be considered to represent an instance of the sociopolitical follower scenario.

The supplier did not prepare an EDI implementation plan (P1) because it simply wanted to comply with the customer's request to adopt EDI and hence considered it unnecessary to spend time and effort in rigorous EDI project planning. The supplier also did not initiate a cost-benefit analysis prior when introducing the EDI system (P2). Two reasons were identified: first, a DOS-based, stand-alone EDI system was introduced—the cost of which was less than $5,000, and this cost was absorbed as a necessary IT operating expense; second, the supplier had no expectations of economic returns from its investment in EDI. Likewise, a post-implementation review of EDI was not initiated (P3) because such a review was considered as a waste of time as the supplier had no intention of investing more resources in an EDI project for further improvement.

The supplier had a very low volume of EDI transactions. It received only one weekly production schedule from its customer and in response sent back several ASNs to the customer. Therefore, senior management did not see any visible benefits that EDI integration could provide to the company. Hence, no electronic integration was established between EDI and the back-end ERP system (P4). The supplier also did not introduce any major changes to its existing supply chain management practices (P5) as a result of EDI adoption. Senior management did not perceive a need for process changes because EDI was not seen as a strategic application nor did EDI help them to determine how many of their filters were used in the production line of the customer. The customer became satisfied when they learned about the compliance of the supplier in introducing the EDI system. In other words, EDI was basically regarded as a tool that helped the supplier to maintain good business relations with the customer that requested EDI connectivity.

The supplier trained its IT personnel (P6) which facilitated them in implementing EDI with few difficulties. The training was provided by the EDI vendor. Interestingly, neither the influential customer that requested EDI connectivity nor the EDI VAN provided any training. Training was also given to the customer service staff; they learned how to operate the EDI system in order to receive and print weekly production schedules and send ASNs.

The supplier did not put any pressure (P7) on the customer to expand the use of EDI in other functional areas. Basically, the supplier adopted a conservative approach; it did not look at EDI as a source of gaining economic advantage, and consequently, did not take any initiative to use EDI to share other important information with the customer. This view is expressed by senior business manager as follows:

Our management did not consider EDI to be a strategic application. Hence, we did not exert any influence on the customer to use the system for sharing additional information with us.

Proposition P8, which is about the promotion of the IOS solution, was not examined because, as argued in the previous section, it is not applicable for sociopolitical followers.

- **Stage 2:** Adoption of a fully integrated EDI system.

In the late 1990s, when the Y2K problem received huge attention from the media and popular trade magazines, the senior management of the supplier took a fresh look at their existing portfolio of IT applications. In doing so, they became aware of the difficulties encountered by the customer service staff in dealing with the DOS-based, stand-alone EDI system. The EDI system was not user friendly and because it was not integrated with the back-end ERP system, duplicate data entry was required, thus causing data inconsistency problems. The management realized that the EDI system did not bring any economic benefits to the company other than complying with its customers' request. Around that time, a new, young, highly educated and dynamic IT manager joined the company and was soon appointed as the head of the IT department. The IT manager was familiar with the notion of interorganizational systems. Thus, he brought in fresh ideas and explained to the senior management about how a fully integrated EDI system could address their chronic data inconsistency problems. He suggested that the company needed to exploit the full potential of new generation EDI systems in trading with their customers. The suppliers had about 500 small customers (which are basically retailers of spare parts) located throughout the country. Electronic transactions, through the new generation of EDI systems, with those customers had the potential to bring significant reduction in transaction costs and improve data accuracy. Being convinced of these arguments, a decision was made to replace the aging DOS-based EDI system. A new EDI application was chosen from a vendor in the year 2001 taking into consideration its integration capabilities with the back-end ERP system and its user-friendliness. These observations show that the locus of motivation for the new EDI system is internal and the type of motivation was techno-economic in nature. Hence, the EDI adoption at the second stage can be considered to represent an instance of the techno-economic leader scenario.

Prior to making a decision to adopt the new EDI system, the IT department conducted a formal implementation plan (P1). The plan included preparing a detailed justification for the new EDI system, specifying a time frame for EDI implementation, organizing a series of presentations by four leading EDI vendors, and establishing criteria for evaluating rival EDI products. A cost-benefit analysis was also conducted (P2), which took into account potential immediate cost savings due to the elimination of data entry errors and reduction in paper-based transactions. Upon deployment, a post-implementation review also took place (P3) involving discussing implementation problems and identifying corrective actions. Following the acquisition of the new EDI system, the IT department spent the next 2 months integrating the new EDI system with the back-end ERP system (P4). The integration began to yield benefits as data entry errors and paperwork were reduced. In addition, cost savings were also achieved by being able to limit the number of administrative personnel processing EDI documents.

The establishment of integration between the new EDI system and the back-end ERP system eliminated the need for the customer service staff to manually process EDI documents. However, the new EDI system did not bring about additional changes to the supplier's business processes (P5). The supplier faced difficulties in persuading the automotive assembly companies to agree on a uniform standard for exchanging EDI messages.

Consequently, considerable effort had to be devoted to the development of EDI templates and maps for each automotive assembly company. Furthermore, senior management did not perceive a need to improve their existing ordering process.

The IT team attended a training program organized by the EDI vendor that helped them to develop an electronic interface between the EDI system and the back-end ERP system (P6). The cost of the training was absorbed as a part of the EDI implementation project. No training was offered, however, to the customer service people because they did not need to view the EDI-based documents.

The supplier did not coerce the small retailers into trading with them through EDI (P7). The supplier rather explained the possible improvement in data accuracy and savings in transaction costs that those retailers are likely to achieve if they embrace EDI. The supplier was also actively involved in promoting the notion of doing business through EDI to the retailers (P8). It identified that one of the barriers that was discouraging the small retailers was the absence of a standard EDI format. The supplier then led an initiative to standardize EDI formats for electronic transactions with retailers in the aftermarket. The managing director of the supplier was also involved at the executive committee level of the Australian Automotive Aftermarket Association (AAAA).

DISCUSSION

The motivations that led the automotive manufacturing company to adopt EDI systems did not change during the course of the two stages. Its

Table 2. Outcomes of the propositions relating to IOS adoption processes initiated in case A

Propositions for Techno-economic Leader Motivation Scenario		Stage 1: Traditional EDI	Stage 2: Web-based EDI	Remarks
P1	Techno-economic leaders are likely to prepare an IOS implementation plan	Supported	Supported	
P2	Techno-economic leaders are likely to initiate cost-benefit analysis of IOS	Supported	Supported	
P3	Techno-economic leaders are likely to perform a post-implementation review of IOS	Supported	Supported	
P4	Techno-economic leaders are likely to integrate IOS with back-end IT systems	Supported	Supported	
P5	Techno-economic leaders are likely to introduce changes in the business practices	Supported	*Not supported*	*P5 at Stage 2 is explained by situational factor*
P6	Techno-economic leaders are likely to organize IOS training	Supported	Supported	
P7	Techno-economic leaders are unlikely to apply pressure on partners	*Not supported*	Supported	*P7 at Stage 1 is explained by situational factor*
P8	Techno-economic leaders are likely to market IOS concept	*Not supported*	Supported	*P8 at Stage 1 is explained by situational factor*

motivation in both stages remained techno-economic in nature. Thus, the automotive company is classified as a techno-economic leader in both episodes. By contrast, the motivations that influenced the automotive parts supplier to adopt EDI systems changed over the course of time. In the first stage, the initiative to introduce a DOS-based EDI system originated from an influential customer and the supplier adopted EDI to make that customer happy. In the second stage, the opportunity of achieving efficiency gains using new generation EDI technologies inspired the supplier to embrace a fully integrated, window-based EDI system. In the light of these observations, the supplier company was found to have migrated from the sociopolitical follower motivation scenario to the techno-economic leader scenario.

The outcomes of propositions with regard to EDI adoption at the automotive manufacturing company are summarized in Table 2, which shows that a total of six research propositions out of eight have received full support at the first stage of EDI adoption. Propositions P7 and P8 which did not receive empirical support however could be interpreted in terms of situational factors. For instance, the lack of EDI maturity and inadequate understanding of the assembling company about suppliers' difficulties in using EDI significantly contributed to the assembly company's strong coercive stance for promoting EDI to its suppliers. In the second stage, all but one proposition were supported. Proposition P5, which is about introducing changes in existing business processes, was not supported because the company had already streamlined its ordering process when it introduced the traditional EDI system at the first stage. Hence, there was no need to further alter the existing process. Interview data concerning those propositions that did not receive empirical support were revisited, and the deviations between the predictions of the propositions and actual experiences of the company could be satisfactorily interpreted in terms of situational factors unique to this company. Therefore, it can be safely suggested that the logical arguments used in developing these propositions were not challenged in a broad sense.

Likewise, the outcomes of propositions of EDI adoption for the automotive parts supplier are summarized in Table 3. All the research propositions appropriate to the sociopolitical follower scenario received full support in the first stage of EDI adoption. In the second stage, all but one proposition appropriate to the new techno-economic motivation scenario was supported.

P5 did not receive support because the supplier failed to receive any cooperation from its large customer, which pursued its own agenda of using proprietary EDI formats for competitive reasons. This situational factor, however, needs to be examined in other organizational contexts to find out whether it is unique to the automotive industry segment.

An interesting finding is that the approach followed by the automotive company in diffusing the EDI innovation to its suppliers has shown some differences between the two stages. In the early stage, the company forced its suppliers to join the proprietary EDI network. However, during the course of EDI implementation, the automotive company became aware of the difficulties for the smaller suppliers with data mapping and document standards, which caused great inconvenience to the suppliers and acted in a cooperative way that is consistent with the predictions made by the propositions for the techno-economic leader motivation scenario. Its maturity in using EDI and the lessons learned from the initial stage helped the company in changing its attitude towards diffusing a new innovation with its supply chain members. The company thus paid greater attention to providing a system that not only improved its efficiency but also added value and improved convenience to its suppliers. As such, the company promoted the Web-enabled EDI through a cooperative approach and did not exert any pressure on its suppliers so that the system made it easy for the small suppliers to establish

Table 3. Outcomes of the propositions relating to IOS adoption processes in two distinct stage of IOS adoption in case B

Stage 1: DOS-based EDI adoption		Stage 2: Integrated EDI adoption		
Propositions for Sociopolitical Motivation Scenario	Outcome	Propositions for Techno-economic Motivation Scenario	Outcome	Remarks
P1: Sociopolitical followers are unlikely to prepare an IOS implementation plan	Supported	P1: Techno-economic leaders are likely to prepare an IOS implementation plan	Supported	
P2: Sociopolitical followers are unlikely to initiate cost-benefit analysis of IOS	Supported	P2: Techno-economic leaders are likely to initiate cost-benefit analysis of IOS	Supported	
P3: Sociopolitical followers are unlikely to perform a post-implementation review of IOS	Supported	P3: Techno-economic leaders are likely to perform a post-implementation review of IOS	Supported	
P4: Sociopolitical followers are unlikely to integrate IOS with back-end IT systems	Supported	P4: Techno-economic leaders are likely to integrate IOS with back-end IT systems	Supported	
P5: Sociopolitical followers are unlikely to introduce changes in the business practices	Supported	P5: Techno-economic leaders are likely to introduce changes in the business practices	Not Supported	P5 at Stage 2 is explained by situational factor
P6: Sociopolitical followers are likely to organize IOS training	Supported	P6: Techno-economic leaders are likely to organize IOS training	Supported	
P7: Sociopolitical followers are unlikely to apply pressure on partners	Supported	P7: Techno-economic leaders are unlikely to apply pressure on partners	Supported	
--	--	P8: Techno-economic leaders are likely to market an IOS concept	Supported	

electronic exchanges. This realization provided support for the propositions 7 and 8 at the second stage of EDI adoption.

Finally, most of the activities undertaken by the automotive company during the two stages of EDI adoption were found to be consistent with the predictions shown in Table 1; thus providing empirical support for the research proposition that organizations tend to follow similar adoption processes when they establish similar motivations for IOS adoption, despite differences in the circumstances within which the motivation was formed. Similarly, most of the activities performed by the automotive supplier during each of the two stages of EDI adoption are consistent with the predictions shown in Table 1. This supports the theory that organizations tend to characteristically follow different adoption processes when they establish different motivations for IOS adoption, even when other aspects of the adoption situation are the same. These empirical findings thus offer broad support for the IMM model in the automotive industry context.

CONCLUSION

This article has reported the experiences of two members of a single supply chain selected from the Australian automotive industry and analyzed their EDI adoption initiatives in terms of the IMM. The findings support the prediction that similarities in IOS adoption processes observed in organizations could be successfully explained in terms of their corresponding similarities in motives for IOS adoption (i.e., the automotive assembler company case), and different organizational motivations for IOS adoption projects lead to different IOS adoption processes. These findings further demonstrate that even if an organization introduces an IOS for a particular motive it is not necessary for it to cling to that motive for the adoption of subsequent IOS projects.

The implication is that it is possible to observe variations in IOS adoption processes even within one organization and such variations can be satisfactorily explained in terms of the differences in the organization's motives for IOS adoption. In summary, the empirical findings of the case companies together indicate that the predictions of the IMM are independent of the nature of industry from which case companies were selected, the nature of company, and the position of company within its supply chain. The findings reported in this article thus provide indicative evidence that the model of IOS motivation that was initially tested in the pharmaceutical industry applies to the automotive industry as well. The article thus contributes to the e-commerce and IOS literature by highlighting the role of motivation as a determinant of IOS adoption processes. The practical implication is that, by understanding their own motivations for IOS adoption, potential IOS adopter organizations can obtain insights about how to initiate adoption processes, which in turn can bring a reduction in the uncertainty associated with IOS adoption in organizations.

It is planned to extend this work in three ways. First, the IMM was applied to examine only two cases. Thus, the findings reported in this article cannot be generalized for the entire automotive industry. As such, these findings should be treated with caution. Additional case studies are required to find out whether automotive companies representing the techno-economic leader and sociopolitical follower scenarios demonstrate predicted differences in IOS adoption processes as found in the participating two cases. Second, the EDI adoption experiences of the participating two companies represent instances of techno-economic leader and sociopolitical follower motivation scenarios. Hence, only part of the IMM framework has been evaluated in this article. Therefore, the findings are still preliminary in nature. Further work is thus necessary to include more cases from the automotive industry that will serve as the instances of the remaining two generic motivation scenarios (shown in Figure 1) and only then the explanatory ability of IMM could be fully evaluated. Third, additional research is required to apply the model to other industry contexts (e.g., grocery) to examine more closely the possible significance of the confounding situational factors reported in the article.

REFERENCES

Chau, P. Y. K., & Hui, K. L. (2001). Determinants of small business EDI adoption: An empirical invstigation. *Journal of Organizational Computing and Electronic Commerce, 11*(4), 229-252.

Chwelos, O., Benbasat, I., & Dexter, A. S. (2001). Research report: Empirical test of an EDI Adoption Model. *Information Systems Research, 12*(3), 304-322.

Damsgaard, J., & Lyytinen, K. (1998). Contours of diffusion of EDI in Finland: Overcoming technological barriers and collaborating to make it happen. *Journal of Strategic Information Systems, 7*(4), 275-297.

Damsgaard, J., & Lyytinen, K. (2000). The dynamics of factors explaining EDI diffusion in Hong Kong in the late 1990s. In *Proceedings of the Fourth Pacific Asia Conference on Information Systems*, Hong Kong SAR.

Garfield, M. J., Kamis, A. A., & LeRouge, C. M. (2004). Champion networks in federated interorganizational systems: Case studies in telemedicine. *Communications for the Association for Information Systems, 14,* 596-615.

Han, K., Kauffman, R. J., & Nault, B. R. (2004). Information exploitation and interorganizational systems ownership. *Journal of Management Information Systems, 21*(2), 109-135.

Kaefer, F., & Bendoly, E. (2000). The adoption of electronic data interchange: A model and practical tool for managers. *Decision Support Systems, 30,* 23-32.

Kautz, K., & Henriksen, H. (2002). Brilliant idea? But it didn't do the trick: The role of a designed project in the adoption and diffusion process of inter-orgnisational information systems. In *Proceedings of the IFIP TC8 WG8.6 International Working Conference on Diffusion, Adoption and Implementation of Information Technology*, Sydney, Australia.

Kuan, K. K. Y., & Chau, P. Y. K. (2001). A perception-based model for EDI adoption in small businesses using a technology-organization-environment framework. *Information & Management, 38,* 507-521.

Kurnia, S., & Johnston, R. B. (2000). Understanding the adoption of ECR: A broader perspective. *Proceedings of the 13th International Bled Electronic Commerce Conference*, Bled, Slovenia.

Lee, H. G., Clark, T., & Tam, K. Y. (1999). Research report: Can EDI benefit adopters. *Information Systems Research, 10*(2), 186-195.

Mackay, D. R. (1993). The impact of EDI on the components sector of the Australian automotive industry. *Journal of Strategic Information Systems, 2*(3), 243-263.

Premkumar, G., Ramamurthy, K., & Nilakanta, D. (1997). Determinants of EDI adoption in the transportation industry. *European Journal of Information Systems, 6*(2), 107-121.

Rahim, M. (2004). *Understanding adoption of inter-organisational systems: The role of organisational motivations.* PhD thesis, University of Melbourne, Australia.

Rahim, M., Shanks, G., & Johnston, R. (2001a). Motivations for inter-organisational systems adoption: A framework and initial case study. In *Proceedings of the Sixth Annual CollECTeR Conference on Electronic Commerce (CollECTeR)*, Coffs Harbour, NSW, Australia.

Rahim, M., Shanks, G., & Johnston, R. (2001b). Understanding motivations for IOS adoption. In *Proceedings of the Australasian Conference on Information Systems (ACIS'2001)*, Coffs Harbour, NSW, Australia.

Rahim, M., Shanks, G., & Johnston, R. (2002). A framework for understanding the motivations for inter-organisational systems adoption: An empirical assessment. In *Proceedings of the Thirteenth Australasian Conference on Information Systems (ACIS'2002)*, Melbourne, Australia.

Saeed, K. A., Malhorta, M. K., & Grover, V. (2005). Examining the impact of interorganizational systems on process efficiency and sourcing leverage in buyer supplier dyads. *Decision Sciences, 36*(3), 365-396.

Sarker, S., & Lee, A. S. (2000). Using a positivist case research methodology to test three competing theories-in-use of business process redesign. In *Proceedings of the International Conference on Information Systems (ICIS)*, Brisbane.

Soliman, K. S., & Janz, B. D. (2004). An exploratory study to identify the critical factors affecting the decision to establish Internet-based inter-organizational information systems. *Information & Management, 41*(6), 697-706.

Subramaniam, C., & Shaw, M. J. (2004). The effects of process characteristics on the value of B2B e-procurement. *Information Technology & Management, 5,* 161-180.

Teo, H. H., Wei, K. K., & Benbasat, I. (2003). Predicting intention to adopt inter-organizational linkages: An institutional perspective. *MIS Quarterly, 23*(1), 105-132.

Yin, R. K. (2003). *Case study research: Design and methods* (3rd ed.). Thousand Oakes, CA: Sage.

This work was previously published in Journal of Electronic Commerce in Organizations, Vol. 5, Issue 3, edited by M. Khosrow-Pour, pp. 1-16, copyright 2007 by IGI Publishing, formerly known as Idea Group Publishing (an imprint of IGI Global).

Chapter XVIII
Inter-Organizational E-Commerce in Healthcare Services:
The Case of Global Teleradiology

Arjun Kalyanpur
Teleradiology Solutions, India

Firoz Latif
Teleradiology Solutions, India

Sanjay Saini
Harvard Medical School, USA

Surendra Sarnikar
University of Arizona, USA

ABSTRACT

Advances in healthcare information technology have enabled new models for electronic delivery of healthcare services. In this article, we present the case of electronic delivery of radiological services and describe the market-based and technological factors that have led to the development of Internet-based service models for flexible delivery of radiological services. Specifically, we describe the technical, regulatory, and security issues that affect teleradiology and propose a service delivery model for providing cost-effective and flexible radiological services.

INTRODUCTION

The continued wide-scale adoption of information technology in the healthcare industry is facilitating the electronic delivery of healthcare related services. Following the integration of medical infrastructure with information and communication technologies (ICT), patient-facing, and inter-organizational healthcare services can now be delivered using Internet-based applications and e-commerce platforms. In order to understand the factors influencing the evolution of e-commerce models in healthcare services, we present the case of global teleradiology.

Teleradiology refers to the electronic transmission of radiological images such as x-rays, computed tomograms (CTs), and magnetic resonance images (MRIs) across geographical locations for the purposes of interpretation and consultation. The digital radiological images are typically transmitted using standard telephone lines, satellite connections, or wide area networks (WANs). Teleradiology is an empowering technology and a facilitator for enhanced medical care. It enables a single radiologist to simultaneously provide services to several hospitals independent of their location and allows the exploitation of global time differences to provide emergency night coverage by personnel in a different time zone working a day shift. Additionally, the quality of care delivered by an alert physician working a day shift is far superior to that provided by a radiologist who is up all night. In addition, teleradiology also enables the delivery of subspecialty opinions to remote locations, where otherwise expertise is not available. In this article, we describe the current state-of-art in teleradiology, the benefits of the clinical practice of teleradiology, and the technical, regulatory, and security issues related to teleradiology. We begin by discussing relevant work in healthcare e-commerce and subsequently the evolution of global teleradiology.

E-Commerce in Healthcare Services

In the past decade, several new businesses have developed that deliver healthcare related services over the Internet. They can be broadly classified into four different forms of e-health business (Parente, 2000). These include portal, connectivity, B2B, and B2C applications. Portal, connectivity, and B2C commerce in healthcare typically involves either the provisioning of information to consumers via advertising supported Web sites, or the Web-based ordering services for prescription drugs (Zehnder, Bruppacher, Ruppanner, & Hersberger, 2004). In B2B e-commerce, the healthcare industry is mostly focused on the procurement and supply of medical devices and equipment (Arbietman, Lirov, Lirov, & Lirov, 2001; Smith & Correa, 2005). The exchange of services has been mostly limited to non-medical services such as billing and claims processing.

The exchange of medical services over the Internet has received little attention both in the industry and in academic literature. However, recent advances and developments in the healthcare industry and medical information technology are now enabling several new models for delivery of medical services over the Internet (Siau, 2003), primary examples of which include telemedicine and teleradiology. In addition, initiatives on data standardization and standardization of quality are also driving the development of outsourcing-based models in the healthcare industry (Segouin, Hodges, Brechat, 2005). Following the development of enabling technologies and the emergence of favorable market factors for medical service outsourcing, the outsourcing of medical services is now a major topic for discussion and research (Wachter, 2006). Among the first applications of medical service outsourcing and offshoring is the teleradiology service, and is now practiced by firms like NightHawk (http://www.nighthawkrad.net/), virtual radiologic (www.

virtualrad.com), teleradiology solutions (www.teleradsol.com), etc.

Although the concept of teleradiology was first tested and clinically utilized in the late 1950's (Gershon-Cohen & Cooley, 1950), the high cost of transmission and the variability in digital imaging protocols limited the widespread adoption and application of teleradiology applications. However, the rapid progress in digital communication technologies and the development of efficient Internet-based software for image transmission, storage, and display in the 1990s has significantly reduced the technical barriers to teleradiology adoption. In addition to the previous developments, the universal adoption of the DICOM standard, as required by the ACR-NEMA (American College of Radiology and the National Electronic Manufacturers Association), has enabled the wide spread adoption of teleradiology applications.

GLOBAL Teleradiology

Today, teleradiology has become both global and online. The precedent for globalization of teleradiology was set by the information technology services industry, which has pioneered the concept of the global office where the work "follows the sun" (i.e., divisions in different time zones are connected over a WAN to provide a 24-hour workforce without the need for having individuals to work a night shift at any location). Extended to teleradiology, this means that the interpreting radiologist for a given hospital can potentially be located anywhere on the globe and day-night time differences can be exploited to staff the emergency room (ER) night shift. A paper published by Kalyanpur, Weinberg, Neklesa, Brink, and Forman (2003) from Yale University showed that this was both technically and clinically feasible (Kalyanpur et al., 2003).

Several market-based factors such as staffing shortages (Sunshine, Maynard, Paros, & Forman, 2004), increases in imaging volumes (Bhargavan & Sunshine, 2002), new technology, and insurance and regulatory changes have also contributed to the growth and development of teleradiology. We briefly describe these factors next.

- **Radiologist Staffing Shortage:** A significant shortage of radiologists became apparent in the U.S. toward the turn of the millennium, with a large cohort of senior radiologists retiring from practice and training programs not having grown adequately to keep pace with the increased needs (Sunshine et al., 2004). In many other parts of the world, a similar shortage of trained/skilled radiologists exists. As might be expected in a time of staffing shortages, it is the night shift in the community hospital that is typically hit the hardest, although academic departments also stand to benefit from having their off-hours/overflow work done remotely by faculty based offshore (Kalyanpur et al., 2004).
- **Increase in Imaging Volumes:** The rapid evolution of faster imaging technologies such as multi-slice CT, faster MRI scanners, and sequences, coupled with an ageing population in the U.S. has led to a consistent per year increase in imaging volumes in recent years. A recent survey of radiology utilization in Medicare population indicates a 13% increase in the utilization of radiological imaging (Martin et al., 2003).
- **Increase in Trauma Imaging Utilization:** The development of newer applications of CT in the emergency setting has necessitated a large increase in 24-hour radiologist coverage at hospital emergency rooms (Spigos, Freedy, and Mueller, 1996). In addition, the Health Care Financing Administration (HCFA) requires that in order for the services to be billable, overnight coverage for radiological services has to be provided by a fully trained and certified radiologists, rather than residents/trainees (Federal Regulation 60:

63124). This has resulted in a large increase for overnight radiologist services.

A Service Delivery Model for Teleradiology

Recent advances in information and communication technologies such as Web services and workflow technologies enable new extensions to teleradiology that facilitate the delivery of radiological services across various time zones and geographical regions. The foremost application of teleradiology is in the emergency setting. In emergencies, teleradiology facilitates a prompt response by bringing the emergently performed images to the off-site radiologist that allows for timely diagnosis and the timely administration of appropriate treatment.

However, using secure Internet-based communication mechanisms and workflow technologies, several new applications of teleradiology can be developed. An overview of the service delivery model is presented in Figure 1. A key feature of the model is an e-commerce platform consisting of payment, communication, and workflow services. Under typical current arrangements for emergency teleradiology, the radiology group outsources its night calls to a teleradiology provider, somewhat like a locum relationship. The radiology group then reimburses the teleradiology provider at a predetermined rate for the preliminary emergency report provided by the latter and then bills the insurer for the final read that the former performs. By integrating a workflow system with the remote teleradiology service, all the previous payment, billing, and routing services can be automated.

In addition to automating the billing, payment, and routing services, an Internet-based service delivery model enables the delivery of radiological services to emergency departments, large hospitals, and remote rural clinics. We further describe these application areas next.

- **Emergency teleradiology services:** Teleradiology within the U.S. led to the development of the "nighthawk" concept wherein a radiologist is able to simultaneously provide services to multiple hospitals via teleradiology links to a central reading facility (often the radiologist's home). This enables a single radiologist to simultaneously staff the night shift at multiple hospitals. The process is cost-effective to hospitals, as the need to recruit night shift personnel is minimized.
- **Radiology to remote locations:** Teleradiology also enables the provision of radiologi-

Figure 1. A service delivery model for teleradiology

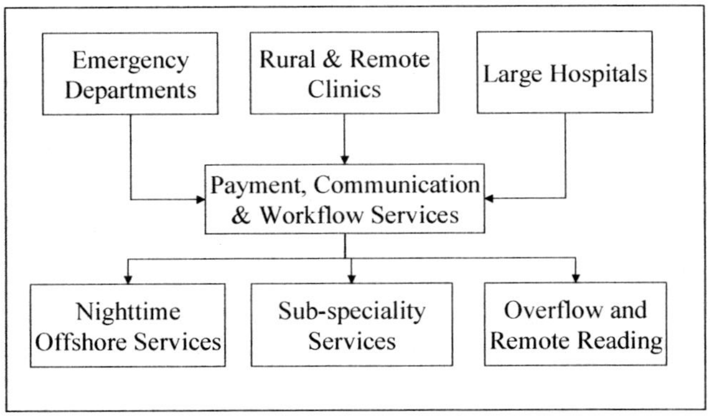

cal services to remote locations where the technical infrastructure for radiological scanning exists, but a radiologist is not available on site. Field studies indicate that teleradiology implementations at rural hospitals have been highly successful and cost-effective in providing radiological services even in real-time situations and have lead to improved patient care (Franken et al., 1995; Lee et al., 1998).

- **Optimization of workflow:** Teleradiology also increases the efficiency of a radiologist by ensuring that he or she spends the most part of his or her time delivering quality care to the maximum number of patients. This is achieved by bringing the images to the radiologist rather than vice versa, thereby saving physician commuting time and increasing the range and reach of the radiologists' expertise. Within large radiologist groups servicing multiple hospitals and imaging centers, teleradiology also permits the optimal distribution of work based on need and the availability of radiologists.
- **Subspecialty consultations**: Teleradiology enables the wider availability of subspecialty consultations wherein images of a specific body region/modality need to be referred to the radiologist with expertise in the interpretation of that type of study. Past studies indicate that opinions of subspecialty radiologists obtained through teleradiology have resulted in significant improvements in the quality of patient care (Franken et al., 1997; Kangarloo et al., 2000).

Technical Requirements for Teleradiology

The key components of a teleradiology system include a picture archiving and communications system (PACS), a radiology information system (RIS), and a reliable and secure high-speed connectivity between the remote sites. These put together with standards for imaging and systems/procedures for security and contingency practices complete the technical aspects of teleradiology. These are further discussed in the following sections.

Picture Archiving and Communications System

An efficient Web-based PACS is the cornerstone of a clinical teleradiology practice. PACS is the information system used for the acquisition, storage, communication, archival, viewing, and manipulation of radiological images and related data. We provide a brief discussion on each of these components next.

- **Acquisition devices:** Acquisition devices are modalities with digital output capabilities or devices such as frame grabber and digitizers that convert the analog output from imaging modalities to a digital format.
- **Storage:** The storage components in a PACS system include both short-term as well as long-term archival solutions. This allows radiologists to have easy access to relevant prior studies for comparison. Typical radiological images range from 0.5MB to 4 MB or higher in size and depending on the number of images storage requirements can run to several gigabytes of storage per month. Since long-term archives do not require instant accessibility, optical disks or tape drives could be used for this purpose. The duration for which images need to be stored is dependent on the image type and varies from organization to organization. In the emergency setting, images are not usually stored for longer than 30 days. However, if outpatient imaging is being performed where comparisons are required, longer periods of storage may be necessary.
- **Communication:** PACS requires high-speed connectivity to enable rapid transfer

of images to viewing workstations over LAN and WAN (the latter is what constitutes teleradiology). Transmission of images is based on protocols of imaging standards called DICOM. Transmission of non-image data like text uses HL7 standards. We further discuss DICOM and HL7 in later sections.

- **Software:** Image viewing and manipulation software are most often an integral part of PACS. Image viewers can be on a diagnostic workstation, review workstation, or could be done utilizing a Web-based module. Diagnostic workstations are high-end systems with high-resolution flat panel displays while standard desktop PCs can be used as review workstations or as Web viewers.
- **Image Compression:** Given the large file size of typical radiological images, an important feature required facilitating rapid image transfer and throughput in teleradiology is compression. Compression algorithms used may be industry standard like JPEG 2000 or could be proprietary to the vendor. It has been noted that compression settings of up to 10:1 can be tolerated in clinical teleradiology without the compromise or loss of clinically relevant data, for review of CT images (Kalyanpur, Neklesa, Taylor, & Daftary, 2000). In the case of plain radiographs, even higher settings may be tolerated.

Radiological Information Systems

RIS is often a subsystem of hospital information system (HIS), but can also be a stand-alone entity and may or may not be connected to PACS. While PACS mainly deals with images, RIS/ HIS deals with data associated with patient demography, studies, and reports. RIS is often what guides the workflow of a teleradiology practice. Though RIS was used as a report generation and distribution tool earlier, commercially available RIS packages currently have integrated many features like voice recognition, staff scheduling, work distribution, invoicing, etc. At teleradiology solutions, a RIS has been developed by an in-house software development team to meet the requirements of an offshore teleradiology practice.

Connectivity Requirements

An ideal connectivity solution for teleradiology providers includes dedicated commercial broadband connection. The high-speed connections allow teleradiology service providers to serve clients halfway around the globe, with report turnaround times comparable or even superior to the ones from local radiologists. A single radiologist working from home may use DSL connectivity, provided adequate throughput is confirmed prior to clinical use. For example, a single ultrasound image would take about 2 seconds to transfer over a typical DSL connection; however, larger plain film images can take between 1 and 4 minutes to transfer. Apart from bandwidth, one would also require other networking components such as routers, firewalls, VPN concentrators, and intrusion detection and prevention systems.

As the service being provided is a clinical service, typically in the emergency setting, a high level of communication between the site of origin and interpretation of the images is mandatory. This involves the utilization of fax systems capable of handling high volume data, direct telephonic contact and video and teleconferencing facilities.

Data Standards

DICOM is the industry standard used for transfer of radiological images between different hosts claiming conformance. DICOM is a standard developed by a joint committee set up by American College of Radiology (ACR) and National Electrical Manufacturers Association (NEMA). HL7 (Health Level Seven) is the standard for the exchange, management, and integration of electronic healthcare information like clinical and administrative data. Using HL7 compatible software streamlines the workflow considerably. For example, if PACS and RIS of a teleradiology practice are HL7 enabled, as soon as a new study is received by the PACS, a new order can be created on the RIS using patient demography and study details from the DICOM file, thereby eliminating duplication of work.

Securing Patient Data

Teleradiology providers are covered under the Health Insurance Portability & Accountability Act (HIPAA) and therefore need to implement adequate privacy and security practices as protected health information (PHI) and electronic protected health information (EPHI) are transmitted over public networks on a regular basis. While offshore teleradiology providers are not required to comply with HIPAA laws, the HIPAA act requires that "covered entities execute contracts that consist specific provisions for protection, use, and disclosure of health information" (Hilger, 2004). The privacy rule deals with all forms of patients' protected health information, whether electronic, written, or oral, while, the security rule covers only protected health information that is in electronic form, including EPHI that is created, received, maintained, or transmitted.

With the availability of a large number of commercial off the shelf network security solutions and technical safeguards, building and managing a secured network are relatively easy to implement. However, unauthorized access to patient data due to administrative breaches are difficult to monitor and implement, and hence the bulk of the HIPAA privacy rules have to do with administrative and physical safeguards. These breaches can only be prevented by educating employees about privacy and security practices followed by the organization and ensuring that these practices are implemented.

The security rule does not prescribe any specific technologies--being technology neutral allows the HIPAA covered entities to choose solutions based on their specific requirements. Technical safeguard standards include access control, audit controls, data integrity, person or entity authentication, and transmission security. Our in-house developed RIS solution (Tele-RIS) is used as a case in point here to illustrate/demonstrate how it complies with the above standards.

Access control mechanisms are used to ensure that a person or software can only access and modify resources for which the person is granted authorization. Access controls standard require the implementation of several features such as unique user identification, automatic logoff, and data encryption procedures. In addition, the following functionality also needs to be implemented:

- **Emergency access procedure:** This implementation specification requires a covered entity to establish procedures to retrieve EPHI during emergencies. Tele-RIS has a provision for adequate backup for power or network outages, but in case of a total outage, a backup procedure for the entire workflow from order entry to report distribution is well defined. Operating from different geographical locations also helps in dealing with contingencies.
- **Audit controls:** Are useful for recording and examining information system activity, especially when determining if a security violation occurred. Any addition, deletion, or remarkable modification on Tele-RIS is logged for audit purposes.
- **Data integrity:** Data could be altered during transit or in storage. "EPHI that is improperly altered or destroyed can result in clinical quality problems for a covered entity, including patient safety issues" (Health Insurance Portability & Accountability Act). This could happen by both technical and non-technical sources. A user can change the data, accidentally or maliciously. Tele-

RIS addresses this problem using audit logs and techniques like versioning and digital signing.

- **Person or entity authentication:** Authentication involves confirming that users are who they claim to be. Tele-RIS uses a username/password combination for authentication. Many applications now incorporate the use of biometrics for authentication.
- **Transmission security:** This standard requires a covered entity to "Implement technical security measures to guard against unauthorized access to electronic protected health information that is being transmitted over an electronic communications network" (Health Insurance Portability & Accountability Act).

Barriers to Adoption

Although teleradiology provides several benefits and can result in improved patient care and the technology exists for the large scale implementation of Internet-based radiological services, several barriers exist in the healthcare services industry that prevent the wide adoption of Internet-based radiological and medical service delivery. We briefly discuss these factors next.

- **Technology:** Although the technological capability to enable the delivery of medical services exists, the availability of the technology and trained technicians to operate them is a major barrier to wide-scale adoption. For example, the availability of reliable Internet connections in remote locations is a major barrier to the successful implementation of teleradiology and telemedicine projects. For a detailed discussion on the technological barriers to telemedicine, please refer to Paul, Pearlson, and McDaniel (1999).
- **Credentialing:** A major impediment to the rapid adoption of teleradiology services is the credentialing process. In addition to state-wise licensing requirements and board certifications, a hospital appointment for the consulting radiologist with the client hospital is necessary for providing radiological services. The current regulatory and credentialing structure is designed for a physical presence-based delivery model of radiological services, and needs to be redesigned for remote radiological or medical service delivery to develop.
- **Malpractice liability:** The medical malpractice liability laws differ from state to state and its implications to the practice of telemedicine are not clear. In addition, malpractice claims could also arise from improper use of equipment and errors in data transmission. For a detailed discussion on the legal issues related to the practice of telemedicine and teleradiology, the reader is referred to Gantt (1999).
- **Billing and reimbursement:** Although teleradiology consultations are now eligible for reimbursement under Medicare, HFCA rules limit the eligibility to patients who reside in a designated health professional shortage area (HPSA). In addition, regulations exist that prevent the billing of Medicare claims outside of United States, thus preventing the offshore reading services for Medicare related cases.
- **Health Insurance Portability & Accountability Act:** The confidentiality and security of patient information when transmitted across public networks is of major concern during the implementation of teleradiology solutions. Adequate safeguards need to be implemented in order to prevent unauthorized access to patient information at both local and remote locations. In addition to textual data, new encryption mechanisms need to be implemented to secure image data while maintaining their reliability (Cao, Huang, & Zhou, 2003).

- **Availability and work-satisfaction:** The availability and work-satisfaction of radiologist is a major factor in determining the success of teleradiology services. While a recent study of teleradiology satisfaction indicates a positive job-satisfaction for radiologists (Krupinski, McNeill, Haber, & Ovitt, 2003), the long effect of teleradiology on job satisfaction of radiologists needs to be evaluated.

CONCLUSION

In this article, we describe the state-of-art in teleradiology and present a service delivery model for providing cost-effective and flexible radiological services. The proposed model can enable the delivery of radiological services to several hospitals independent of their location and allows the exploitation of global time differences to provide emergency night coverage in emergency departments. In addition, we also describe the technical, regulatory, and security issues related to teleradiology and discuss barriers to the adoption of Internet-based teleradiology services. We conclude that while the technological capability exists to enable the remote delivery of radiological and other medical services, several legal, regulatory, and operational barriers remain that prevent the wide-scale adoption of Internet-based radiology and medical services.

REFERENCES

Arbietman, D., Lirov, E., Lirov, R., & Lirov, Y. (2001). E-commerce for healthcare supply procurement. *Journal of Healthcare Information Management, 15*(1), 61-72.

Bhargavan, M., & Sunshine, J. (2002). Workload of radiologists in the United States in 1998-1999 and trends since 1995-96. *American Journal of Roentgenol, 179*, 123-1128.

Cao, F., Huang, H. K., & Zhou, X. Q. (2003). Medical image security in a HIPAA mandated PACS environment. *Computerized Medical Imaging and Graphics, 27*(3), 185.

Franken, E. A., Berbaum, K. S., Brandser, E. A., D'Alessandro, M. P., Schweiger, G. D., & Smith, W. L. (1997). Pediatric radiology at a rural hospital: Value of teleradiology and subspecialty consultation. *American Journal of Roentgenology, 168*, 1349-1352.

Franken, E. A., Berbaum, K. S., Smith, W. L., Chang, P. J., Owen, D. A., & Bergus G. R. (1995). Teleradiology for rural hospitals: Analysis of a field study. *Journal of Telemed Telecare, 1*(4), 202-208.

Gantt, A. H. (1999). Telemedicine and healthcare e-commerce. *The Maryland Bar Journal, 32*(6).

Gershon-Cohen, J., & Cooley, A. G. (1950). Telognosis. *Radiology, 55*, 582-587.

Goldberg, M. A., Sharif, H. S., Rosenthal, D. I., Black-Schaffer, S., Flotte, T. J., Colvin, R. B., & Thrall, J. H. (1994). Making global telemedicine practical and affordable: Demonstrations from the Middle East. *American Journal of Roentgenol, 163*(6), 1495-500.

Health Care Financing Administration Medicare Program. (1995). Revisions to payment policies and adjustments to the relative value units under the physical fee schedule for the calendar year 1996 Fed Reg 60: 63124

Health Insurance Portability & Accountability Act, http://www.hhs.gov/ocr/hipaa/

Hilger, D. D. (2004). The HIPAA privacy rule and HR/benefits outsourcing: Does the business associate label belong on your recordkeeper? *Benefits Quarterly, 20*(1), 44-52.

Kalyanpur, A., Casey, S., & Michel, E. (2002). Impact of overnight staff coverage of a university hospital emergency room via international teleradiology. RSNA, Chicago, IL.

Kalyanpur, A., Neklesa, V., Brink, J., Pham, D., Stein, S., & Forman, H. (2004). Implementation of an international teleradiology staffing model. *Radiology, 232*, 415-419.

Kalyanpur, A., Neklesa, V. P., Taylor, C. R., & Daftary, A. (2000). Evaluation of JPEG and Wavelet compression for teleradiology transmission of direct-digital body CT images. *Brink Journal of Radiology, 217*, 772-779.

Kalyanpur, A., Weinberg, J., Neklesa, V., Brink, J., & Forman, H. (2003). Emergency radiology coverage: Technical and clinical feasibility of an international teleradiology model. *Emergency Radiology, 10*(3), 115-118.

Kangarloo, H., Valdez, J. A., Yao, L., Chen, S., Curran, J., Goldman, D., Sinha, U., Dionisio, J. D., Taira, R., Sayre, J., Seeger, L., Johnson, R., Barbaric, Z., & Steckel, R. (2000). Improving the quality of care through routine teleradiology consultation. *Acad Radiol, 7*(3), 149-55.

Krupinski, E., McNeill, K., Haber, K., & Ovitt, T. (2003). High-volume teleradiology service: Focus on radiologist satisfaction. *Journal of Digital Imaging, 16*(2), 203-209.

Lee J. K., Renner, J. B., Saunders, B. F., Stamford, P. P., Bickford, T. R., Johnston, R. E., Hsaio, H. S., Phillips, M. L. (1998). Effect of real-time teleradiology on the practice of the emergency department physician in a rural setting: Initial experience. *Acad Radiol, 5*(8), 533-8.

Maitino, A. J., Levin, D. C., Parker, L., Rao, V. M., & Sunshine, J. H. (2003). Practice patterns of radiologists and nonradiologists in utilization of noninvasive diagnostic imaging among the Medicare population 1993-1999. *Radiology, 228*, 795-801.

Parente, S. T. (2000). Beyond the hype: A taxonomy of e-health business models. *Health Aff, 19*(6), 89-102.

Paul, D. L., Pearlson, K. E., & McDaniel, R. R. (1999). Assessing technological barriers to telemedicine: Technology-management implications. *IEEE Transactions on Engineering Management, 46*(3).

Segouin, C., Hodges, B., & Brechat, P. H. (2005). Globalization in health care: Is international standardization of quality a step toward outsourcing? *International Journal of Quality Health Care, 17*(4), 277-9.

Siau, K. (2003). Health care informatics. *IEEE Transactions on Information Technology in Biomedicine*, 7(1), 1-7.

Smith, A. D., & Correa, J. (2005). Value-added benefits of technology: E-procurement and e-commerce related to the health care industry. *International Journal of Health Care Qual Assur Inc Leadersh Health Serv, 18*(6-7), 458-73.

Spigos, D., Freedy, L., & Mueller, C. (1996). 24-hour coverage by attending physicians: A new paradigm. *American Journal of Roentgenol, 167*, 1089-1090

Sunshine, J., Maynard, C. D., Paros, J., & Forman, H. P. (2004). Update on the diagnostic radiologist shortage. *AJR, 182*, 301-305

Wachter, R. M. (2006). The "dis-location" of U.S. medicine--The implications of medical outsourcing. *New England Journal of Medicine, 354*(7), 661-665.

Zehnder, S., Bruppacher, R., Ruppanner, H., & Hersberger, K. E. (2004). Swiss community pharmacies' on the Web and pharmacists' experiences with e-commerce: Longitudinal study and Internet-based questionnaire survey. *Journal of Med Internet Res. 6*(1).

This work was previously published in Journal of Electronic Commerce in Organizations, Vol. 5, Issue 2, edited by M. Khosrow-Pour, pp. 47-56, copyright 2007 by IGI Publishing, formerly known as Idea Group Publishing (an imprint of IGI Global).

Compilation of References

AbayomiPaul, T. (2005). Can a Ping Really Help Your Blog Get Top Search Engine Rankings?. *Search Engine Journal*, January 19, 2005. Retrieved July 17, 2006, from http://www.searchenginejournal.com/?p=1243

Abdullah, M. A. and Bakar, M. I. H. (2000). *Small and medium enterprises in Asian Pacific countries.* Nova Science Publishers. Huntington, NY.

Abell, W. and Limm, L. (1996). *Business use of the internet in New Zealand: an exploratory study.* Retrieved from http://www.scu.edu.au/sponsered/ausweb96/business/abell/paper.html.

Abernethy, M. (2002) SMEs: Small World Order. *The Bulletin 120*(34).

Adams, D.A.; Nelson, R.R.; & Todd, P.A. (1992). Perceived usefulness, ease of use, and usage of information technology: A replication. *MIS Quarterly*, 16(2), 227-247.

Adomavicius, G., & Tuzhilin, A. (2005). Toward the next generation of recommender systems: A survey of the state-of-the-art and possible extensions. *IEEE Transactions on Knowledge and Data Engineering, 17*(6), 734-749.

Agarwal, R. & Prasad, J. (1999). Are individual differences germane to the acceptance of new information technologies? *Decision Sciences*, 30(2), 361-391.

Agarwal, R., & Karahanna, E. (2000). Time flies when you're having fun: Cognitive absorption and beliefs about information technology usage. *MIS Quarterly, 24*(4), 665-694.

Agarwal, R., & Venkatesh, V. (2002). Assessing a firm's web presence: a heuristic evaluation procedure for the measurement of usability. Information Systems Research 13, 168–186.

Agrawal, R., & Srikant, R. (1994). Fast algorithms for mining association rules. In J. Bocca, M. Jarke, & C., Zaniolo (Eds.), *Proceedings of the 20th VLDB* (pp. 487-499). Morgan Kaufmann.

Agrawal, R., Imielinski, & T., Swami, A. (1993). Mining association rules between sets of items in large databases. In *Proceedings of the ACM SIGMOD International Conference on Management of Data* (pp. 207-216).

Agresti, A. (1996). *An introduction to categorical data analysis.* New York: John Wiley and Sons.

Ahmed, A. (2002). E-outsourcing cuts costs and risks. *National Underwriter/Property & Casualty/Risk & benefit Management Edition, 106*(34), 12-13.

Ajzen, I. & Fishbein, M. (1980). *Understanding attitudes and predicting social behavior.* Englewood Cliffs: Prentice Hall.

Ajzen, I. (1985). From Intentions to Actions: A Theory of Planned Behavior. in *Action Control: From Cognition to Behavior*, Kuhl, J., & Beckmann, J., Editors. Springer Verlag, New York, 11-39.

Ajzen, I. (1988). *Attitudes, Personality, and Behavior.* Chicago, IL: The Dorsey Press.

Akbulut, A. (2002). *An investigation of the factors that influence electronic information sharing between state and local agencies.* Dallas, Texas, USA: Proceedings of 8th American Conference on Information Systems. (2454-2460).

Alag, S., & Patki, A. B. (1996). Fuzzy logic integrated circuits. In *Proceedings of the 1st Online Workshop on Soft Computing* (pp. 187-191), Nagoya, Japan.

Albert, T.C., Goes, P.B., & Gupta, A. (2004). GIST: A Model for Design and Management of Content and Interactivity of Customer-Centric Web Sites. *MIS Quarterly*, 28(2), 161-182.

Al-Qerim, N. A., & Bathula, H. (2002). IT and eCommerce outsourcing in small to medium-size enterprises in New Zealand: An exploratory research. In *Proceedings of the 15th Bled Electronic Commerce Conference* (pp. 537-551).

Alzola, L. M., & Robaina, V. P. (2005). SERVQUAL: its applicability in electronic commerce B2C. *The Quality Management Journal, 12*(4), 46-57.

American National Standards Institute. (1992). *American national standards for information systems-database language- SQL. ANSI X3.135-1992*. Washington, D.C.: U.S. Government Printing Office.

Anderson, E.W., & Sullivan, M.W. (1993). The antecedents and consequences of customer satisfaction for firms, *Marketing Science* 12(2), 125--143.

Anderson, J. C., & Narus, J. A. (1990). A model of distributor firm and manufacturer firm working partnerships. *Journal of Marketing, 54*(1), 42-58.

Anderson, J., Aydin, C., & Jay, S. (1994). *Evaluating health care information systems: Methods and applications*. Sage Publications.

Ang, S. & Slaughter, S. (2004). Turnover of Information Technology Professionals: The Effects of Internal Labor Market Strategies. The DATA BASE for Advances in Information Systems 35(3), 11-28.

Ang, S. & Slaughter, S.A. (2001). Work Outcomes and Job Design For Contract versus Permanent Information Systems Professionals On Software Development Teams. MIS Quarterly 25(3), 321-350.

Ang, S., & Cummings, L. L. (1997). Strategic response to institutional influences on information systems outsourcing. *Organization Science, 8*(3), 235-256.

Anonymous. (2004). Six-Month Assessment of Workforce Globalization in Certain Knowledge-Based Industries. Technology Administration (July*)*. pp. 1-12.

Arbietman, D., Lirov, E., Lirov, R., & Lirov, Y. (2001). E-commerce for healthcare supply procurement. *Journal of Healthcare Information Management, 15*(1), 61-72.

Arbuckle, J.L. (1999). *Amos* [Computer Software]. Small Waters: Chicago.

Arbuckle, J.L., & Wothke, W. (1999). *Amos 4.0 User's Guide*. Small Waters: Chicago.

Ariba Inc. (2006). *cXML version 1.0 specification.* Retrieved December 1, 2006, from http://www.cxml.org

Arlitt, M., Krishnamurthy, D. & Rolia, J. (2001). Characterizing the scalability of a large web-based shopping system. ACM Transactions on Internet Technology, 1(1), 44-69.

Armstrong, A., & Hagel, J. (1996). The real value of on-line communities. *Harvard Business Review, 74*(3), 134-141.

Arnett, K.P. & Litecky, C. R. (1994). Career Path Development for the Most Wanted Skills in the MIS Job Market. Journal of Systems Management, February, 45(2), 6-11.

Asian Development Bank. (2003). *Private sector development and finance.* Asian Development Bank.

Aspray, W., Mayadas, F., & Vardim, Y. (2005). *Globalization and offshoring of software: A Report of the ACM Job Migration Task Force*, Association for Computing Machinery.

Attaluri, G., & Salem, K. (2002). The presumed-ether two-phase commit protocol. *IEEE Transactions on Knowledge and Data Engineering, 14*(5), 1190-1196.

Austin, J. L. (1975). *How to do things with words*. Oxford University Press, 2 edition.

Australian Government Information Management Office. (2005, July 28-29). E-government: Australia's Approach (Keynote Address, Special Minister of State Senator The Hon Eric Abetz, Commonwealth **of Australia). In** *Proceedings of the Nikkei Fifth Strategic Conference on e-Government*, Tokyo, Japan.

Ba, S., & Pavlou, P. A. (2002). Evidence of the effect of trust building technology in electronic markets: Price premiums and buyer behavior. *MIS Quarterly, 26*(3), 243-269.

Ba, S., Whinston, A. B., & Zhang, H. (2003). Building trust in online auction markets through an economic incentive mechanism. *Decision Support Systems, 35*(3), 273-286.

Bagozzi, R.P. (1980). *Causal methods in marketing.* New York: John Wiley and Sons.

Bagozzi, R.P. (2007). "The Legacy of the Technology Acceptance Model and a Proposal for a Paradigm Shift," *Journal of the Association of Information Systems*), 8, 244-254.

Bagozzi, R.P., & Yi, Y. (1988). On the Evaluation of Structural Equation Models. *Journal of the Academy of Marketing Science*, 16, 74-94.

Bajaj, K. K. and Nag, D. (1999). *E-commerce: The cutting edge of business.* Tata McGraw-Hill. New Delhi.

Balabanovic, M., & Shoham, Y. (1997). Fab: Content-based, collaborative recommendation. *Communications of the ACM, 40*(3), 66-72.

Bandyopadhyay, R. (1996). MISNOS—Multimedia, multilingual, information services network operating systems software. *Electronics, Information, and Planning Journal*, *23*(4), 205-230.

Bandyopadhyay, R. (1997). *Engineering schematics and draft specification for multilingual optical keyboard (MLOPKB).* SDD Technical Report, DOE, May 1997.

Banerjee, A. (1992). A simple model of herd behavior. *Quarterly Journal of Economics, 107*, 797–818.

Bapna, R., Goes, P., & Gupta, A. (2000). A theoretical and empirical investigation of multi-item on-line auctions. *Information Technology and Management, 1*(1-2), 1-23.

Bapna, R., Goes, P., & Gupta, A. (2001). Insights and analyses of online auctions. *Association for Computing Machinery. Communications of the ACM, 44*(11), 42-50.

Bapna, R., Goes, P., & Gupta, A. (2003). Analysis and design of business-to-consumer online auctions. *Management Science, 49*(1), 85-102.

Bapna, R., Goes, P., & Gupta, A. (2003). Replicating online Yankee auctions to analyze auctioneers' and bidders' strategies. *Information Systems Research, 14*(3), 244-268.

Bapna, R., Goes, P., Gupta, A., & Jin, Y. (2004). User heterogeneity and its impact on electronic auction market design: An empirical exploration. *MIS Quarterly, 28*(1), 21-43.

Bapna, R., Goes, P., Gupta, A., & Karuga, G. (2002). Optimal design of the online auction channel: Analytical, empirical, and computational insights. *Decision Sciences, 33*(4), 557-578.

Barnes D., Hinton, M, Mieczkowska. (2005). Enhancing Customer Service Operations in E-business: The Emotional Dimension. *Journal of Electronic Commerce in Organizations*. 3(2), 17-33.

Barron, D. N., West, E., & Hannan, M. T. (1994). A time to grow and a time to die: Growth and mortality of credit unions in New York City, 1914-1990. *American Journal of Sociology, 100,* 196-241.

Barry H. & Milner B. (2002). SME's and Electronic Commerce: A Departure from the Traditional Prioritisation of Training? *Journal of European Industrial Training, 25*(7), 316-326.

Barthelemy, J., & Geyer, D. (2005). An empirical investigation of IT outsourcing versus quasi-outsourcing in France and Germany. *Information & Management, 42,* 533-542.

Basilico, J., & Hofmann, Th. (2004). Unifying collaborative and content-based filtering. In *Proceedings of the 21st International Conference on Machine learning* (69: 9). New York: ACM Press.

Baskerville, R. L. & Wood-Harper, A. T. (1996). A Critical Perspective on Action Research as a Method for Information Systems Research, *Journal of Information Technology* (11:3), 1996, pp. 235-246.

Baty, J.B. & Lee, R.M. (1995). InterShop: enhancing the vendor/customer dialectic in electronic shopping. Journal of Management Information Systems, (11), 9-31.

Bauer, H. H., Falk, T., & Hammerschmidt, M. (2006). eTransQual: a transaction process-based approach for capturing service quality in online shopping. *Journal of Business Research, 59*, 866-875.

Beach, L. R. (1993). Broadening the definition of decision making: The role of prechoice screening of options. *Psychological Science, 4*(4), 215-220.

Bednarzik, R. W. (2005). Restructuring information technology: Is offshoring a concern? *Monthly Labor Review*, August 2005, p. 11-21, Bureau of Labor Statistics, US Department of Labor.

Benbasat, I., & DeSanctis, G. (2001). Communication challenges: A value network perspective. In G. W. Dickson & G. DeSanctis (Eds.), *Information technology and the future enterprise: New models for managers* (pp. 144-162). Upper Saddle River, NJ: Prentice-Hall.

Bennett, R. (1997). Export marketing and the Internet. *International Marketing Review, 14*(5), 324-355.

Bentler, P.M., & Bonnet, D.G. (1980). Significance tests and goodness of fit in analysis of covariance structures. *Psychological Bulletin*, 88, 588-606.

Berendt, B. (2001). Understanding Web usage at different levels of abstraction: Coarsening and visualizing sequences. In *Proceeding of the Mining Log Data Across All Customer TouchPoints*, San Francisco.

Berendt, B., Hotho, A., & Stumme, G. (2002). Towards semantic Web mining. In I. Horrocks & J. Hendler (Eds.), *Proceedings of the ISWC 2002* (pp. 264-278). Springer-Verlag.

Berners-Lee, T., Hendler, J., & Lassila, O. (2001). Semantic Web. *Scientific American, 284*(5), 34-43.

Best's key rating guide, life-health United States. (2002). Oldwick, NJ: AM Best.

Bharati, P. & Chaudhury, A. (2004). Using choiceboards to create business value. Communications of the ACM, 47(12), 77-81.

Bharati, P. and A. Chaudhury (2004). An Empirical Investigation of Decision-Making Satisfaction in Web-Based Decision Support Systems, *Decision Support Systems*, 37(2), 187-197.

Bhargavan, M., & Sunshine, J. (2002). Workload of radiologists in the United States in 1998-1999 and trends since 1995-96. *American Journal of Roentgenol, 179*, 123-1128.

Bhattacherjee, A. (2001). Understanding information systems continuance: An expectation confirmation model. *MIS Quarterly, 25*(3), 351-370.

Biemans, F., Lankhorst, M., Teeuw, W., and van de Wetering, R. (2001). Dealing with the complexity of business systesm architecting. *System Engineering*, 4(2).

Bikhchandani, S., Hirshleifer, D., & Welch, I. (1992). A theory of fads, fashions, custom and cultural change as information cascades. *Journal of Political Economy, 100*(5), 992-1026.

Blili, S. and Raymond, L. (1993) 'Information Technology: Threats and opportunities for small medium-sized enterprises'. *International Journal of Information Management.* vol. 13 no. 6. pp.439-448.

Blili, S. and Raymond, L. (1993). 'Information Technology: Threats and opportunities for small medium-sized enterprises'. *International Journal of Information Management, 13*(6), 439-448.

Blunden, R. B. (2004). *Offshoring IT: The good, the bad, and the ugly.* Apress Publication.

Böhm, C. and Jacopini, G. 1966. Flow diagrams, turing machines and languages with only two formation rules. Commun. ACM 9, 5 (May. 1966), 366-371. DOI= http://doi.acm.org/10.1145/355592.365646

Bohrnstedt, G. (1992). Validity. In E. Borgatta & M. Borgatta (Eds.), *Encyclopaedia of sociology* (Vol. 4, pp. 2217–2222). New York: Macmillan.

Booch, G., Rumbaugh, J., and Jacobson, I. (1999). *The Unified Modeling Language User Guide*. AddisonWesley, Inc.

Boter, H. and Lundström, A. (2005) 'SME perspectives on business support services'. *Journal of Small Business and Enterprise Development*. vol. 12 no. 1. pp.244-258.

Boter, H. and Lundström, A. (2005). 'SME perspectives on business support services'. *Journal of Small Business and Enterprise Development, 12*(1), 244-258.

Brancheau, J., & Wetherbe, J. (1990). The adoption of spreadsheet software: Testing innovation diffusion theory in the context of end-user computing. *Information Systems Research., 1-2*, 115–143.

Brin, S. & Page, L. (1998). The anatomy of a large-scale hypertextual Web search engine. *Proceedings of the 7th International World Wide Web Conference*, April 1998, Computer Networks and ISDN Systems, 30 (1998), 107 - 117. Available from http://www-db.stanford.edu/pub/papers/google.pdf

Bringham, E. F. and Smith, K. V. (1967) 'The cost of capital to small firm'. *The Engineering Economist*. vol. 13 no. 1. pp.1-26.

Bringham, E. F. and Smith, K. V. (1967). The cost of capital to small firm. *The Engineering Economist, 13*(1), 1-26.

Brint, A. T. (2003). Investigating buyer and seller strategies in online auctions. *The Journal of the Operational Research Society, 54*(11), 1177-1188.

Brooks, G. (2006, March 23). In-house or outsource? *New Media Age, Supplement,* 6-8.

Brown, D., & Wilson, S. (2005, May). *The black book of outsourcing: How to manage the changes, challenges, and opportunities.* Wiley Publication.

Browne, J., Higgins, P., & Hunt, I. (2003). E-business principles, trends, visions. In J. Gasos & K. D. Thoben (Eds.), *E-business Applications, Technologies for Tomorrow's Solutions* (pp. 3-16). Springer-Verlag.

Browne, M. W. & Cudeck, R. (1993). Alternative ways of assessing model fit. In: Bollen, K. A. & Long, J. S. (Eds.) *Testing Structural Equation Models*, Beverly Hills, CA: Sage, 136-162.

Browne, S. and Kellett, M. (1999). Insurance scenario description. Technical Report CrossFlow project deliverable: D1.a, CrossFlow consortium.

Bruce, N., Haruvy, E., & Rao, R. (2004). Seller rating, price, and default in online auctions. *Journal of Interactive Marketing, 18*(4), 37-51.

Brudenall, P. (2005, May). *Technology and offshore outsourcing strategies.* Palgrave Macmillan Ltd.

Brusilovsky, P. (2001). Adaptive hypermedia [Ten Year Anniversary Issue]. In A. Kobsa (Ed.), *User Modeling and User Adapted Interaction*, 11(1/2), 87-110.

Budish, E., & Takeyama, L. N. (2001). Buy prices in online auctions: Irrationality on the Internet? *Economics Letters, 72*(3), 325-334.

Bunker, D. and MacGregor, R. C. (2000). Successful generation of Information Teschnology (IT) requirements for Small/Medium Enterprises (SMEs)—Cases from regional Australia, in *Proceedings of SMEs in Global Economy.* Wollongong, Australia. pp. 72-84.

Burger, K. (2005). Laggards no more. *Insurance & Technology, 30*(7), 4.

Burnham, T. A., Frels, J. K., & Mahajan, V. (2003). Consumer switching costs: A topology, antecedents, and consequences. *Journal of the Academy of Marketing Science, 31*(2), 109-126.

Byrd, T. A. & Turner, D. E. (2001). An Exploratory Analysis of the Value of the Skills of IT Personnel:

Their Relationship to IS Infrastructure and Competitive Advantage. Decision Sciences, 32(1), 21-54.

Byrne, B.M. (1989). *A Primer of LISREL*. New York: Springer-Verlag.

Camison-Zornova, C., Lapiedra-Alcami, R., Segarra-Cipres, S., & Boronat-Navarro, M. (2004). A meta-analysis of innovation and organizational size. *Organization Studies, 25*(3), 331-361.

Cannon, J. P., & Homburg, C. (2001, January). Buyer-supplier relationships and customer firm costs. *Journal of Marketing*, pp. 29–43.

Cao, F., Huang, H. K., & Zhou, X. Q. (2003). Medical image security in a HIPAA mandated PACS environment. *Computerized Medical Imaging and Graphics, 27*(3), 185.

Cao, M., Zhang, Q., & Seydel, J. (2005). B2C e-commerce web site quality: an empirical examination. *Industrial Management & Data Systems, 105*(5), 645-661.

Cappel, J. J. (2001). Entry-Level IS Jobs Skills: A Survey of Employers. The Journal of Computer Information Systems 42(2), 76-83.

Carr, N. (2003). IT Doesn't Matter. Harvard Business Review 81(5), 41-49.

CBS (2004). *Survey usaha terintegrasi 2004*. Central Bureau of Statistics (CBS).

Chakrabarti, S. (2003). *Mining Web: Discovering knowledge from hypertext data*. Morgan Kaufmann.

Chakravarty, S., Feinberg, R., & Rhee, E. (2004). Relationships and individuals' bank switching behavior. *Journal of Economic Psychology, 25*(4), 507-527.

Chan, C. and Swatman, P. (2000). Firm EDI to internet commerce: the BHL Steel Experience. *Internet Research: Electronic Networking Applications and Policy, 10*(1), 72-82.

Chandrasekar, P. R. (2005). Tips for outsourcing. *IEE Engineering Management Journal, 6*, 24, Dec 2004-Jan 2005.

Chau, P. Y. K., & Hui, K. L. (2001). Determinants of small business EDI adoption: An empirical invstigation. *Journal of Organizational Computing and Electronic Commerce, 11*(4), 229-252.

Chau, S. and Pederson, S. (2000). *The Emergence of New Micro Businesses Utilizing Electronic Commerce*. Australia: Proceedings of the 11th Australian Conference of Information Systems (ACIS).

Chau, S.B. and Turner, P. (2001). A Four Phase Model of EC Business Transformation Amongst Small to Medium Sized Enterprises, *Proceedings of the 12th Australasian Conference on Information Systems*, Coffs Harbour, Australia.

Chen, L., Gillenson, M. L., & Sherrell, D. L. (2002). Enticing online consumers: an extended technology acceptance perspective. *Information & Management, 39*(8), 705-719.

Chen, P. Y., & Hitt, L. M. (2002). Measuring switching costs and the determinants of customer retention in Internet-enabled businesses: A study of the online brokerage industry. *Information Systems Research, 13*(3), 255-274.

Chen, Q., & Chen, H.M. (2004). Exploring the Success Factors of eCRM Strategies in Practice. *Journal of Database Marketing & Customer Strategy Management*, 11(4), 333-343.

Cheung, C., Chan, G., & Limayem, M. (2005). A Critical Review of Online Consumer Behavior: Empirical Research. *Journal of Electronic Commerce in Organizations*, 3(4), 1-19.

Choa, Y. H., & Kimb, J. K. (2004). Application of Web usage mining and product taxonomy to collaborative recommendations in e-commerce. *Expert Systems with Applications, 26*, 233-246.

Choi, J.D., Choi, J.S., Park, C. & Kim, D. (1998). A cell-based shared virtual world management mechanism in the cyber mall system. Computer Networks and ISDN Systems, 30, 1865-1874.

Chong, S., & Pervan, G. (2001, July 2-3). Implementation success of Internet-based electronic commerce for small- and medium-sized enterprises in Singapore. In *Proceedings of the International Telecommunications Society Asia-Indian Ocean Regional Conference,* July 2-3, Perth, Western Australia, pp. 243-259.

Chu, C., & Smithson, S. (2003). Organizational structure and e-commerce: A structurational analysis. In *Proceedings of the 5th International Conference on Electronic Commerce* (pp. 205-212).

Churchill, G. A. (1991). *Marketing research: Methodological foundations* (5th ed.). Chicago: Dryden Press.

Chwelos, O., Benbasat, I., & Dexter, A. S. (2001). Research report: Empirical test of an EDI AdoptionModel. *Information Systems Research, 12*(3), 304-322.

Cinemascreen. (2006). Retrieved December 20, 2006, from http://www.cinemacreen.co.uk

Cochran, A. B. (1981). Small business mortality rates: A review of the literature. *Journal of Small Business Management, 19*(4), 50-59.

Cohen, P. R. and Levesque, H. J. (1995). Communicative actions for artificial agents. In Lesser,V. and Gasser, L., editors, *Proceedings of the First International Conference on Multi-Agent Systems*, pages 65–72, San Francisco, CA, USA. The MIT Press: Cambridge, MA, USA.

Cohen, W. M., & Levinthal, D. A. (1990). Absorptive capacity: A new perspective on learning and innovation. *Administrative Science Quarterly, 35,* 128-152.

Computerworld. (1992). *Electronic data interchange* (White Paper). Author.

comScore. (2004). Marketers take note: The elusive 18-34 year-old is habitually online. Retrieved September 10, 2006, from http://www.comscore.com/press/release.asp?press=445

Cooper, R.B. and Zmud, R.W. (1990). Information technology implementation research; a technological difference approach. *Management Science, 36*(2), 123-139.

Corbitt, B., Behrendorf, G., & Brown-Parker, J. (1997). SMEs and electronic commerce. *The Australian Institute of Management, 14*, 204-222.

Coviello, N.E. and McAuley, A. (1999). Internationalization and the smaller firm: a review of contemporary empirical research. *Management International Review, 39*(3), 223-256.

Cragg, P., & King, M. (1993). Small-firm computing: Motivators and inhibitors. *MIS Quarterly, 17*(1), 47-60.

Cronbach, L. J. (1951, September). Coefficient alpha and internal structure of tests. *Psychometrika, 16*, 297–334.

Crosby, L.A., & Stephens, N. (1987). Effects of Relationship Marketing on Satisfaction, Retention and Prices in the Life Insurance Industry. *Journal of Marketing Research.* 24, 404-411.

Crum, M., Premkumar, G., & Ramamurthy, K. (1996, Summer). An assessment of motor carrier adoption, use, and satisfaction with EC. *Transportation Journal*, pp. 44–57.

Csikszentimihalyi, M. (1975). *Beyond boredom and anxiety.* San Francisco: Jossey-Bass.

Curran, Kevin. (2004). Tips for Achieving High Positioning in the Results Pages of the Major Search Engines, *Information Technology Journal* 3 (2): 202-205

CyberWyre. (2006) Updated: Highest Paying AdSense Keywords. Retrieved July 17, 2006, from *http://www.cwire.org/2006/03/23/updated-highest-paying-adsense-keywords/*

D'Angelo, J., & Little, S. K. (1998). Successful Web pages: What are they and do they exist? *Information Technology & Libraries, 17*(2), 71-80.

Daft, R.L., Lengel, R. H., & Trevino L. K. (1987). Message Equivocality, Media Selection and Manager Performance. *MIS Quarterly*, 11, 355-364.

Damanpour, F. (1991, September). Organizational innovation: A meta-analysis of effects of determinants and moderators. *Academy of Management Journal, 34*(3), 555–590.

Damanpour, F. (1996). Organizational complexity and innovation: Developing and testing multiple contingency models. *Management Science, 42,* 693-716.

Damas, Phillip. (2001). " E-shippers Kick the Paper Habit", American Shipper, February 2001. available at: http://www.tradecard.com/languages/EN/news/articles/AmericanShipper_022001.pdf

Damian, D., & Eberlein (2000). The effect of communication media on group performance in RE. In *Proceedings of the 4th International Conference on Requirements Engineering (ICRE 00)* (pp. 91), IEEE CS Press.

Damsgaard, J. and Lyytinen, K. (1998). Contours of Diffusion of Electronic Data Interchange in Finland: Overcoming Technological Barriers and Collaborating to Make it Happen, *Journal of Strategic Information Systems*, 7, 275-297.

Damsgaard, J., & Lyytinen, K. (1998). Contours of diffusion of EDI in Finland: Overcoming technological barriers and collaborating to make it happen. *Journal of Strategic Information Systems, 7*(4), 275-297.

Damsgaard, J., & Lyytinen, K. (2000). The dynamics of factors explaining EDI diffusion in Hong Kong in the late 1990s. In *Proceedings of the Fourth Pacific Asia Conference on Information Systems*, Hong Kong SAR.

Dan, A., Dias, D., Kearny, R., Lau, T., Nguyen, R., Parr, F., et al. (2001). Business-to-business intergration with tpaML and a business-to-business protocol framework. *IBM Systems Journal, 40*(1), 68-90.

Daniel, E. M., & Grimshaw, D. J. (2002). An exploratory comparison of electronic commerce adoption in large and small enterprises. *Journal of Information Technology, 17,* 133–147.

Davis, D. (1996). *Business research for decision making* (4th ed.). Duxbery Press.

Davis, F.D. (1989). Perceived usefulness, perceived ease of use, and user acceptance of information technology. *MIS Quarterly*, 13(3), 319-340.

Davis, F.D. Bagozzi, R.P., & Warshaw, P.R. (1992). Extrinsic and intrinsic motivation to use computers in the workplace. *Journal of Applied Social Psychology*, 22(14), 1111-1132.

Davis, F.D.; Bagozzi, R.P.; & Warshaw, P.R. (1989). User acceptance of computer technology: a comparison of two theoretical models. *Management Science*, 35(8), 982-1003.

Deci, E.L. (1971). Effects of externally mediated rewards on intrinsic motivation. *Journal of Personality and Social Psychology*, 18, 105-115.

Deloitte (2005). Calling a Change in the Outsourcing Market. Deloitte Consulting Report (April).

DeLone, W. H. (1988). 'Determinants of Success for Computer Usage in Small Busines'. *MIS Quarterly, 12*(1) 51.

DeLone, W. H., & McLean, E. R. (1992). Information systems success: the quest for the dependent variable. *Information Systems Research, 3*(1), 60-95.

DeLone, W. H., & McLean, E. R. (2003). The DeLone and McLean model of information systems success: a ten-year update. *Journal of Management Information Systems, 19*(4), 9-30.

DeLone, W. H., & McLean, E. R. (2004). Measuring e-commerce success: applying the DeLone & McLean information systems success model. *International Journal of Electronic Commerce, 9*(1), 31-47.

Dennis, A.R., & Kinney, S. T. (1998). Testing Media Richness Theory in the New Media: The Effects of Cues, Feedback, and Task Equivocality. *Information Systems Research*, 9(3), 256-274.

Dennis, C. (2000). 'Networking for marketing advantage'. *Management Decision, 38*(4), 287-292.

DEPKOP (2005). *Peran Koperasi dan Usaha Kecil Menengah Dalam Pembangunan Nasional*, 2005. Departemen Koperasi dan Usaha Kecil Menengah.

DEPKOP (2005). *Statistik Usaha Kecil Menengah*, 2005. Departemen Koperasi dan Usaha Kecil Menengah.

Desouza, K. C. (2003). Barriers to effective use of knowledge management systems in software engineering. *Comm. ACM*, *4691*, 99-101.

Devaraj, S., Fan, M., & Kohli, R. (2002). Antecedents of B2C channel satisfaction and preference: validating e-commerce metrics. *Information Systems Research, 12*(3), 316-333.

Devaraj, S., Fan, M., & Kohli, R. (2006). Examination of online channel preference: using the structure-conduct-outcome framework. *Decision Support Systems, 42*(2), 1089-1103.

Dholakia, R. R., & Kshetri, N. (2004). Factors impacting the adoption of the Internet among SMEs. *Small Business Economics, 23*(4), 311–322.

Dholakia, U. M. (2005). Concept discovery, process explanation, and theory deepening in e-marketing research: The case of online auctions. *Marketing Theory, 5*(1), 117-124.

Dholakia, U. M. (2005). The usefulness of bidders' reputation ratings to sellers in online auctions. *Journal of Interactive Marketing, 19*(1), 31-41.

Dholakia, U. M., & Soltysinski, K. (2001). Coveted or overlooked? The psychology of bidding for comparable listings in digital auctions. *Marketing Letters, 12*(3), 225-237.

Dibbern, J., Goles, T., Hirschheim, R., & Jayatilaka, B. (2004). Information systems outsourcing: A survey and analysis of the literature. *The Data Base for Advances in Information Systems, 35*(4), 6-102.

Ding, Y., Fensel, D., Klein, M., Omelayenko, B., & Schulten, E. (2004). The role of ontologies in ecommerce. In S. Staab & R. Studer (Eds.), *Handbook on Ontologies* (pp. 593-615). Springer-Verlag.

Doll, W.J. & Torkzadeh, G. (1988). The measurement of end-user computing satisfaction. *MIS Quarterly*, 12(2), 259-274.

Doll, W.J.; Hendrickson, A.; & Deng, X. (1998). Using Davis's perceived usefulness and ease of use instruments for decision making: A confirmatory and multi-group invariance analysis. *Decision Sciences*, 29(4), 839-869.

Dooley, R. (1976). *Repartee as a Graph*. Appendix B in [Longacre, 1976].

Dos Santos, B. L., & Peffers, K. (1995). Rewards to investors in innovative information technology applications: First movers and early followers in ATMs. *Organization Science, 6,* 241-259.

DoubleClick.com (2005). Search Before the Purchase - Understanding Buyer Search Activity as it Builds to Online Purchase. Retrieved July 17, 2006, from *http://www.doubleclick.com/us/knowledge_central/documents/RESEARCH/searchpurchase_0502.pdf*

Douglas, S.P., Morrin, M.A., & Craig, C.S. (1994). Cross-national consumer research traditions. In G. Laurent, G. Lilien, & B. Bras (Eds.), *Research traditions in marketing.* Boston: Kluwer.

Drakopoulou-Dodd S. Jack S. & Anderson A.R. (2002). Scottish Entrepreneurial Networks in the International Context *International Small Business Journal, 20*(2), 219-219.

Drennan, J., Mort, G. S., & Previte, J. (2006). Privacy, risk perception, and expert online behavior: an exploratory study of household end users. *Journal of Organizational and End User Computing, 18*(1), 1-22.

Drucker, P. (1992). The new society of organizations. *Harvard Business Review.*

Dubray, J.-J. (2002). A new model for ebxml bpss multi-party collaborations and web services choreography. http://www.ebpml.org/ebpml.doc.

Durkin, M. and McGowan, P. (2001). Net effect – views from the periphery: exploring the role and importance of the internet on marketing activity in entrepreneurial firms. *Irish Marketing Review, special issue, 14*(1), 15-25.

Easley, R. F., & Tenorio, R. (2004). Jump bidding strategies in Internet auctions. *Management Science, 50*(10), 1407-1420.

eBay. (2006). eBay Inc. announces fourth quarter and full year 2005 financial results. Retrieved September 11, 2006, from http://www.investor.ebay.com/news/Q105/ebay0420-2932ld.pdf

ebXML (2001). Uncefact and oasis, ebxml business process specification schema v1.01.

E-commerce Alert. (2006). *Surveys and reports.* Retrieved December 20, 2006, from http://blogs.library.ualberta.ca/ecommerce

Eder, L. B., & Igbaria, M. (2001). Determinants of intranet diffusion and infusion. *Omega, 29,* 233-242.

Eid, R. (2005). International Internet Marketing: A Triangulation study of drivers and barriers in the business-to-business context in the United Kingdom. *Marketing Intelligence and Planning, 23*(3), 266-280.

Eirinaki, M., & Vazirgiannis, M. (2003). Web mining for Web personalization. *ACM Transactions on Internet Technology, 3*(1), 1-27.

Eirinaki, M., Lampos, C., Paulakis, S., & Vazirgiannis, M. (2004, November, 12-13). Web personalization integrating content semantics and navigational patterns. In *Proceedings of 6th ACM International Workshop on Web Information and Data Management* (pp. 72-79). Washington.

Eirinaki, M., Vazirgiannis, M., & Varlamis, I. (2003). SEWeP: Using site semantics and a taxonomy to enhance the Web personalization process. In *Proceedings of 9th ACM Conference on Knowledge Discovery and Data Mining* (pp. 99-108). Washington.

EIRO (2006). *Industrial relations in SMEs.* Retrieved March 2006 from http://www.eiro.eurofound.eu.int/1999/05/study/tn9905201s.html

Elmasri, R., & Navathe, S. B. (2004). *Fundamentals of database systems.* PearsonEducation.

El-Shinnawy, M., & Markus, M. (1997). The poverty of media richness theory: explaining people's choice of electronic mail vs voice mail. *International Journal of Human-Computer Studies*, 46(4), 443-467.

eMarketer. (2005, January 17). IT and e business in the Asia-Pacific region.

Epstein, M.J. (2004). *Implementing E-commerce strategies: A guide to corporate success after the dot.com bust.* Westerport: Praeger Publisher.

Eriksson, H.-E. and Penker, M. (2000). *Business Modeling with UML: Business Patterns at Work.* John Wiley & Sons.

Ervin, R. (2002). Chains of commitment software architecture. *ACM SIGecom Exchanges*, 3(1).

Europa. (2003). *SME definition.* The European Commission. Retrieved December 15, 2003, from http://europa.eu.int/comm/enterprise/enterprise_policy/sme_definition/index_en.htm

Evans, J. R. and King, V.E. (1999). Business-to-business marketing on the World Wide Web: planning, marketing and assessing websites. *Industrial Marketing Management, 28*(4), 343-358.

Farradane, J., Russell, J. M., & Yates-Mercer, A. (1973). Problems in information retrieval: Logical jumps in the expression of information. *Information Storage and Retrieval, 9*, 65-77.

Farrell, D., Kaka, N., & Sturze, S. (2005). *Ensuring India's offshoring future, The McKinsey Quarterly,* 2005 Special Edition: Fulfilling India's Promise.

Farrell, D., Laboisiere & M.A., Rosenfeld, J. (2005). Sizing the Emerging Global Labor Market. The McKinsey Quarterly, 3, 93-103.

Feeny, D. (2001). Making business sense of the e-opportunity. Sloan Management Review, 42(2), 41-51.

Fillis, I., Johansson, U. and Wagner, B. (2003). A conceptualization of the opportunities and barriers to e-business development in the smaller firm. *Journal of Small Business and Enterprise Development, 10*(3), 336-344.

Filson, D. & Willimson, K. (2001). The impact of e-commerce strategies on firm value: lessons from Amazon.com, Working paper.

Fishbein, M. & Ajzen, I. (1975). *Belief, attitude, intentions and behavior: An introduction to theory and research.* Boston: Addison-Wesley.

Flavian, C., Guinaliu, M., & Gurrea, R. (2006). The role played by perceived usability, satisfaction and consumer trust on Website loyalty. *Information & Management, 43*(1), 1-14.

Foote, D. (2005). "Managing IT Organizations and Professionals" presentation to The Advisory Council, Foote Partners, LLC.

Fornell, C. & Bookstein, F.L. (1982). Two structural equation models: LISREL and PLS applied to consumer exit-voice theory, *Journal of Marketing Research*, 19(4), 440-452.

Fornell, C. (1982). *A second generation of multivariate analysis.* New York, NY: Praeger.

Fornell, C., & Larcker, D. F. (1981). Evaluating structural equations with unobservable variables and measurement error. *Journal of Marketing Research, 18*(1), 39-50.

Forrester Research. (2002, April). *E-commerce next wave: Productivity and innovation.* Paper presented at a seminar on Revenue Implications of E-commerce: Trends in E-commerce by Julie Meringer, WTO Committee on Trade and Development.

Forrester Research. (2005). Young consumers are the first "technology everywhere" generation. Retrieved September 10, 2006, from http://www.forrester.com/ER/Press/Release/0,1769,1051,00.html

Forrester Research. (2005, September 14). *US eCommerce forecast: Online retail sales to reach $329 billion by 2010.* Retrieved September 10, 2006, from http://www.forrester.com/Research/Document/Excerpt/0,7211,3726,00

Fowler, C. (2005). *My job went to India.* Pragmatic bookshelf Publisher.

Franken, E. A., Berbaum, K. S., Brandser, E. A., D'Alessandro, M. P., Schweiger, G. D., & Smith, W. L. (1997). Pediatric radiology at a rural hospital: Value of teleradiology and subspecialty consultation. *American Journal of Roentgenology, 168*, 1349-1352.

Franken, E. A., Berbaum, K. S., Smith, W. L., Chang, P. J., Owen, D. A., & Bergus G. R. (1995). Teleradiology for rural hospitals: Analysis of a field study. *Journal of Telemed Telecare, 1*(4), 202-208.

Franz, C.R. & Robey, D. (1986). Organizational context, user involvement and the usefulness of information systems. *Decision Sciences*, 17(3), 329-356.

Freeman, E., Hupfer, S., & Arnold, K. (1999). *Javaspaces principles: Patterns and practice.* Reading, MA: Addison-Wesley.

Friedman, T. L. (2005). *World is flat: Brief history of the globalized world in twenty-first century.* London: Penguin.

Gagnon, Y., & Toulouse, J. (1996). The behaviour of business managers when adopting new technologies. *Technological Forecasting and Social Change, 52*, 59-74.

Gallivan, M. J., Truex Iii D. P. & Kvasny, L. ((2004)). Changing Patterns in IT Skill Sets 1988-2003: A Content Analysis of Classified Advertising. Database for Advances in Information Systems 35(3), 64-88.

Ganesh, J., Arnold, M. J., & Reynolds, K. E. (2000). Understanding the customer base of service providers: An examination of the differences between switchers and stayers. *Journal of Marketing, 64*(3), 65-87.

Gantt, A. H. (1999). Telemedicine and healthcare e-commerce. *The Maryland Bar Journal, 32*(6).

Garbarino, E., & Johnson, M. S. (1999). The different roles of satisfaction, trust, and commitment in customer relationships. *Journal of Marketing, 63*(2), 70-87.

Garden, M. (2004). *On the use of semantic feedback in recommender systems.* Unpublished master's thesis, McGill University, Montreal, Canada.

Garfield, M. J., Kamis, A. A., & LeRouge, C. M. (2004). Champion networks in federated interorganizational systems: Case studies in telemedicine. *Communications for the Association for Information Systems, 14,* 596-615.

Garrity, E. J., Glassberg, B., Kim, Y. J., Sanders, G. L., & Shin, S. (2005). An experimental investigation of web-based information systems success in the context of electronic commerce. *Decision Support Systems,* 39(3), 485-503.

Garrity, E.J. & Sanders, G.L. (1998). Dimensions of information systems success measurement, in *Information Systems Success Measurement.* Garrity, E.J. & Sanders G.L (eds.), Hershey: Idea Group Publishing, 13-45.

Gary Gereffi and Timothy J. Sturgeon (2004). Globalization, employment and economic development. *Sloan Workshop Series in Industry Studies Rockport Massachusetts,* June 14-16, 2004.

Gaskill L.R., Van Auken H.E. & Kim H. (1993) The Impact of Operational Planning on Small Business Retail Performance. *Journal of Small Business Strategy 5*(1), pp. 21-35.

Gaskill, L. R. and Gibbs, R. M. (1994). Going away to college and wider urban job opportunities take highly educated away from rural areas'. *Rural Development Perspectives, 10*(3), 35-44.

Gatignon, H., & Robertson, T. (1989). Technology diffusion: An empirical test of competitive effects. *Journal of Marketing, 53*(1), 35–49.

Gefen, D., & Straub, D. (2000). The relative importance of perceived ease of use in IS adoption: a study of e-commerce adoption. *Journal of the Association for Information Systems, 1*(Article 8), 1-28.

Gefen, D., Karahanna, E., & Straub, D. (2003). Inexperience and experience with online stores: the importance of TAM and trust. *IEEE Transactions on Engineering Management, 50*(3), 307-321.

Gefen, D., Karahanna, E., & Straub, D. (2003). Trust and TAM in online shopping: An integrated model. *MIS Quarterly, 27*(1), 51-90.

Gentry, C. R. (2003). Recycled returns. *Chain Store Age, 79*(1), 72-73.

George, J.F., Valacich J.S. & Valor J. (2005). Does Information Systems Still Matter? Lessons for a Maturing Discipline. Communications of the Association for Information Systems 16, 219-232.

Gerbing, D.W., & Anderson, J.C. (1988). An Updated Paradigm for Scale Development Incorporating Unidimensionality and Its Assessment. *Journal of Marketing Research,* 25, 186-92.

Germain, R., Droge, C., & Daugherty, P. (1994). A cost and impact typology of logistics technology and the effect of its adoption on organisational practice. *Journal of Business Logistics, 15*(2), 227–248.

Gershon-Cohen, J., & Cooley, A. G. (1950). Telognosis. *Radiology, 55,* 582-587.

Ghani, J.A. & Deshpande, S.P. (1994). Task characteristics and the experience of optimal flow in human-computer interaction. *The Journal of Psychology.* 128(4), 381-391.

Ghani, J.A., Supnick, R., & Rooney, P. (1991). The experience of flow in computer-mediated and in face-to-face groups. J.I. DeGross, I. Benbasat, G. DeSanctis, & C.M. Beath, (eds.) *Proceedings of the 12th International Conference on Information Systems,* New York, 229-237.

Gibbs, J., Kraemer, L., & Dedrick, J. (2003, January-March). Environment and policy factors shaping global e-commerce diffusion: A cross-country comparison. *The Information Society, Special Issue on Globalization of Electronic Commerce, 19*(1), 5–18.

Gilkeson, J. H., & Reynolds, K. (2003). Determinants of Internet auction success and closing price: An exploratory study. *Psychology & Marketing, 20*(6), 537-566.

Goguen, J. A., & Lin, K. (2000). Web-based multimedia support for distributed cooperative software engineering. In *Proceedings of International Symposium on Multimedia Software Engineering* (pp. 25-32), December 11-13, 2000.

Goldberg, D., Nichols, D., Oki, B. M., & Terry, D. (1992). Using collaborative filtering to weave an information tapestry. *Communication of ACM, 35*(12), 61-70.

Goldberg, M. A., Sharif, H. S., Rosenthal, D. I., Black-Schaffer, S., Flotte, T. J., Colvin, R. B., & Thrall, J. H. (1994). Making global telemedicine practical and affordable: Demonstrations from the Middle East. *American Journal of Roentgenol, 163*(6), 1495-500.

Gomes P.J., Joglekar N.R. (2005). The Costs of Coordinating Distributed Software Development Tasks. Working Paper.

Goo, J., Kishore, R., & Rao, H. R. (2000). A content-analytical longitudinal study of the drivers for information technology and systems outsourcing. In *Proceedings of the Twenty First International Conference on Information Systems* (pp. 601-611).

Goode S. & Stevens K. (2000). An Analysis of the Business Characteristics of Adopters and Non-Adopters of WWW Technology *Information & Management, 1*(1), 129-154.

Goodhue, D.L. (1990). Developing a theory-based measure of user satisfaction: The task systems fit questionnaire. *Working Paper, Information and Decision Sciences, University of Minnesota.*

Google (2004). Google searches more sites more quickly, delivering the most relevant results. Retrieved July 17, 2006, from *http://www.google.com/technology/index.html*

Gordon, J. R., & Gordon, S. R. (2000). Structuring the interaction between IT and business units, Prototypes for service delivery. *Information Systems Management, 17*(1), 7-16.

Gottfredson, M., Puryear, R., Phillips, S. (2005). Strategic Sourcing: From Periphery to the Core. Harvard Business Review, February 2005.

Gounaris, S., & Dimitriadis, S. (2003). Assessing service quality on the Web: evidence from business-to-consumer portals. *Journal of Services Marketing, 17*(5), 529-548.

Grandon, E. E., & Pearson, J. M. (2004). Electronic commerce adoption: an empirical study of small and medium US businesses. *Information & Management, 42*(1), 197-216.

Grandon, E., & Pearson, J. M. (2003). Strategic value and adoption of electronic commerce: An empirical study of Chilean small and medium businesses. *Journal of Global Information Technology Management, 6*(3), 22–43.

Grant, R. (2003). Canadian approaches to e-commerce implementation. *Canadian Journal of Administrative Sciences, 20*(1), 3-20.

Grant, S., & McCalla, G. (2001). A hybrid approach to making recommendations and its application to the movie domain. In *Proceedings of the 14th Biennial Conference of the Canadian Society on Computational Studies of Intelligence: Advances in Artificial Intelligence* (LNCS 2056, pp. 257-266). London, UK: Springer-Verlag.

Greaver II, M. F. (1998). *Strategic outsourcing: A structured approach to outsourcing decisions and initiatives.* American Management Association.

Greenberg, P. *CRM at the speeed of light: capturing & keeping customers in Internet Real Time.* New York, NY: Osborne/McGraw-Hill, 2001.

Grow, B. (September 9, 2002). Exess inventory? Ebay to the rescue. *Business Week, 3798*, 8.

Gulati, R. & Garino, J. (2000). Get the right mix of bricks & clicks. Harvard Business Review, 78(3), 107-114.

Gupta, A., Su, B., & Walter, Z. (2004). An empirical study of consumer switching from traditional to electronic channels: A purchase-decision process perspective. *International Journal of Electronic Commerce, 8*(3), 131-161.

Hackbarth, G.; Grover, V.; & Yi, M.Y. (2003). Computer playfulness and anxiety: positive and negative mediators of the system experience effect on perceived ease of use. *Information and Management*, 40, 221-232.

Hadjimonolis, A. (1999). 'Barriers to Innovation for SMEs in a Small Less Developed Country (Cyprus)'. *Technovation, 19*(9), 561-570.

Haerder, T. and Reuter, A. (1983). Principles of transaction-oriented database recovery. *ACM Computing Surveys*, 15(4):287–317.

Hair Jr., J. F., Anderson, R. F., Tatham, R. L., & Black, W. C. (1998). *Multivariate data analysis* (5th ed.). Upper Saddle River, NJ: Prentice-Hall.

Hair, J. F., Anderson, R. E., Tatham, R. L., & Black, W. C. (1995). *Multivariate data analysis* (4th ed.). Upper Saddle River, NJ: Prentice Hall, Inc.

Hall, C. (2002). *Profile of SMEs and SME issues 1990-2000.* Asia-Pacific Economic Cooperation. Singapore.

Hamill, J. (1997). The internet and international marketing. *International Marketing Review, 14*(5), 300-323.

Han, K., Kauffman, R. J., & Nault, B. R. (2004). Information exploitation and interorganizational systems ownership. *Journal of Management Information Systems, 21*(2), 109-135.

Hand, D., Mannila, H., & Smyth, P. (2001). *Principles of data mining.* Cambridge, MA: MIT Press.

Harman, H. H. (1967). *Modern Factor Analysis.* Chicago: University of Chicago Press.

Harris, S., & Katz, J. (1991). Firm size and the information technology investment intensity of life insurers. *MIS Quarterly, 15,* 333-352.

Hart, P., & Saunders, C. (1997). Power and trust: Critical factors in the adoption and use of electronic data interchange. *Organization Science, 8*(1), 23-42.

Haubl, G., & Trifts, V. (2000). Consumer Decision Making in Online Shopping Environments: The Effects of Interactive Decision Aids. *Marketing Science*, 19(1), 4-21.

Haugen, B. (2002). Multi-party electronic business transactions. http://www.supplychainlinks. com/ MultiPartyBusinessTransactions.PDF.

Hawk, S. (2004). 'A Comparison of B2C E-commerce in Developing Countries'. *Electronic Commerce Research, 4,* 181-199.

Health Care Financing Administration Medicare Program. (1995). Revisions to payment policies and adjustments to the relative value units under the physical fee schedule for the calendar year 1996 Fed Reg 60: 63124

Health Insurance Portability & Accountability Act, http://www.hhs.gov/ocr/hipaa/

Heijden, H. (2003). Factors influencing the usage of websites: the case of a generic portal in the netherlands. Information & Management, 40, 541-549.

Hempel P.S. & Kwong Y.K. (2001). B2B E-commerce in Emerging Economies: i-metal.com's Non-ferrous Metals Exchange in China *Journal of Strategic Information Systems, 10*, 335-355.

Henderson, A. D. (1999). Firm strategy and age dependence: A contingent view of the liabilities of newness, adolescence, and obsolescence. *Administrative Science Quarterly, 44,* 281-314.

Henderson-Sellers, B. (2001). Some problems with the uml v1.3 metamodel. In *the 34th Annual Hawaii International Conference on Systems Sciences (HICSS-34).*

Hilger, D. D. (2004). The HIPAA privacy rule and HR/benefits outsourcing: Does the business associate label belong on your recordkeeper? *Benefits Quarterly, 20*(1), 44-52.

Hill, R. and Stewart, J. (2000). Human Resource Development in Small Organisations. *Journal of European Industrial Training, 24*(2/3/4), 105-117.

Hinson, R. and Sorensen, O. (2006). E-business and small Ghanaian Exports: Preliminary micro firm explorations in the light of a digital divide. *Online Information Review, 30*(2), 116-138.

Hinson, R. and Sorensen, O. (2007). Macro E-business Triggers: A Study of Small Ghanaian Exporters. *Journal of Electronic Commerce in Organizations, October-December, 5*(4), 55-69.

Hoffman, D.L. & Novak, T.P. (1996). Marketing in hypermedia computer-mediated environments: Conceptual foundations. *Journal of Marketing*, 60, 50-68.

Hollander, J. (1999). Dell and amazon link sites, and possibly fortunes. E-Commerce Times. Retrieved from http://www.ecommercetimes.com/story/281.html/

Holzwarth, M., Janiszewski, C. & Neumann, M.M. (2006). The influence of avatars on online consumer shopping behavior. Journal of Marketing, 70(4), 19-36.

Hornby, G., Goulding, P. and Poon, S. (2002). Perceptions of export barriers and cultural issues: the SME e-commerce experience. *Journal of Electronic Commerce Research, 3*(4), 213-226.

Howcroft, D. (2001). After the goldrush: deconstructing the myths of the dot.com market. Journal of Information Technology, 16(4), 195-204.

Hsu, M., Bhatt, M., Adolphs, R., Tranel, D., and Camerer, C.F. (2005) "Neural Systems Responding to Degrees of Uncertainty in Human Decision-Making.," *Science* (310:5754),, pp. 1680-1683.

Hu, X., Lin, Z., Whinston, A. B., & Zhang, H. (2004). Hope or hype: On the viability of escrow services as trusted third parties in online auction environments. *Information Systems Research, 15*(3), 236-250.

Humphrey J., Mansell R., Pare D. & Schimtz H. (2003). The Reality of E-commerce in Developing Countries *Media@LSE*

Hung, D. L. (1995, August). Dedicated digital fuzzy hardware. *IEEE Micro, 15*(4), 31-38.

Hunt, A., & Thomas, D. (2003). Preparing the raw material. *IEEE Software, 20*(5), 97-98.

Iacovou C.L., Benbasat I. & Dexter A.S. (1995). Electronic Data Interchange and Small Organisations: Adoption and Impact of Technology *MIS Quarterly, 19*(4) 465-485.

Iacovou, C., Benbasat, I. and Dexter, A. (1995). Electronic data interchange and small organizations: Adoption and impact technology. *MIS Quarterly, 19*(4), 465-485.

IDC. (2004, August 6). IDC predicts double digit growth of Asia/Pacific Internet buyers from 2003 to 2008. IDC Australia. Retrieved September 10, 2006, from http://www.idc.com.au/newsletters/idcpulse/detail.asp?intID=43

IEI (2003). *Facts & Figures: The Internet and Business.* The Internet Economy Indicators. Retrieved June 4, 2003, from http://www.internetindicators.com/facts.html

Igbaria, M., Zinatelli, N., & Cavaye, A. (1998). Analysis of information technology success in small firms in New Zealand. *International Journal of Information Management, 18*, 103–119.

International Trade Forum Issue I (2001). *E-challenges: Countries in Action*, p. 22.

Internet World Stats. (2006). *Internet usage statistics, the big picture, world Internet users and population stats.* Retrieved December 20, 2006, from http://www.internetworldstats.com/stats.htm

Introna, L. (2001). Defining the virtual organization, E-Commerce & V-Business, Barnes, S. & Hunt, B., (Eds.). Oxford: Butterworth-Heinemann, 143-152.

iProspect (2006). iProspect Search Engine User Behavior Study. Retrieved July 17, 2006, from *http://www.iprospect.com/premiumPDFs/WhitePaper_2006_SearchEngineUserBehavior.pdf*

Irwin, JR, & McClelland, GH (2003). Negative consequences of dichotomizing continuous predictor variables. Journal of Marketing Research, 40(3), 366-371

ISO/IEC (1997). 14662, information technologies-open-edi reference model.

ITAA (2004). Adding Value...Growing Careers - The Employment Outlook In Today's Increasingly Competitive It Job Market. Information Technology Association of America (ITAA) Annual Workforce Development Survey (September).

Ives, B., Valacich, J., Watson, R., Zmud, R., Et Al. (2002). What Every Business Student Needs to Know About Information Systems. Communications of the Association for Information Systems, 9, 467-477.

Jacob, C. (2000). *Advanced data analysis* (Lecture Series). Curtin University of Technology, Western Australia.

Jacobson, I., Ericsson, M., and Jacobson, A. (1995). *The object advantage: business process reengineering with object technology.* Addison-Wesley.

Jamshidi, M., Titli, A., Zadeh, L. A., & Boveriv, S. (1997). *Applications of fuzzy logic—towards high machine intelligence quotient systems.* NJ: Prentice Hall.

Jarvenpaa, S.L.; & Todd, P.A. (1997). Is there a future for retailing on the Internet? R.A. Peterson, (ed.) *Electronic Marketing and the Consumer*. Thousand Oaks, CA: Sage.

Jarvenpaa, S.L.; & Todd, P.A. (1997). Consumer reactions to electronic shopping on the World Wide Web. *International Journal of Electronic Commerce*, 1(2), 59-88.

Jarvenpaa, S.L.; Tractinsky, N.; & Vitale, M. (2000). Consumer trust in an Internet store. *Information and Technology Management*, 1(1), 45-71.

Jarvenpaa, S.L.; Tractinsky, N.; Saarinen, L.; & Vitale, M. (1999). Consumer trust in an Internet store: A cross-cultural validation. *Journal of Computer Mediated Communications*. 5(2) 1-35.

Jee, J., & Lee, W-N. (2002). Antecedents and Consequences of Perceived Interactivity: An Exploratory Study. *Journal of Interactive Advertising*, 3(1), Retrieved from http://jiad.org/vol3/no1/jee/index.htm.

Jiang, J. J., Klein, G., & Carr, C. L. (2002). Measuring information systems service quality: SERVQUAL from the other side. *MIS Quarterly, 26*(2), 145-166.

Johnson, R. A., & Wichern, D. W. (1992). *Applied multivariate statistical analysis* (3rd ed.). Upper Saddle River, NJ: Prentice Hall.

Jones, K., & Leonard, L. N. K. (2008). Trust in consumer-to-consumer electronic commerce. *Information & Management, in press.*

Joreskog, K. (1971). Statistical Analysis of Sets of Congeneric Tests. *Psychometrika*, 36, 109-133.

Joreskog, K., & Sorbom, D. (1988). *LISREL 1: A Guide to the Program and Applications*. SPSS: Chicago.

Jude Pinto and Brigitte Harms (2005). Soucing of it-services to offsoure destinations. 3A Strategy.

Jung, K., Na, Y., & Lee, J. (2003). *Creating user-adapted design recommender system through collaborative filtering and content based filtering*, (LNCS 2902, pp. 204-208).

K'necht, A. (2004). SEO and Your Web Site. *Digital Web Magazine*, August 4, 2004. Retrieved July 17, 2006, from *http://www.digital-web.com/articles/seo_and_your_web_site/*

Kaefer, F., & Bendoly, E. (2000). The adoption of electronic data interchange: A model and practical tool for managers. *Decision Support Systems, 30,* 23-32.

Kagel, J. H. (1995). A survey of experimental research. In J. H. Kagel & A. E. Roth (Eds.), *The handbook of experimental economics* (pp. 501-586). Princeton, NJ: Princeton University Press.

Kahneman, D., & Tversky, A. (1979). Prospect theory: An analysis of decision under risk. *Econometrica, 47*(2), 263-292.

Kaiser, K.M. & Hawk, S. ((2004)). "Evolution of Offshore Software Development: From Outsourcing to Cosourcing," MIS Quarterly Executive, 3 (2), June (2004), 69-81.

Kalakota, R. and Whinston, A. B. (1997). *Electronic commerce: A manager's guide.* Addison-Wesley. MA.

Kalakota, R. and Whinston, A.B. (1996). *Frontiers of Electronic Commerce*. Reading: Addison-Wesley Publishing.

Kalyanpur, A., Casey, S., & Michel, E. (2002). Impact of overnight staff coverage of a university hospital emergency room via international teleradiology. RSNA, Chicago, IL.

Kalyanpur, A., Neklesa, V. P., Taylor, C. R., & Daftary, A. (2000). Evaluation of JPEG and Wavelet compression for teleradiology transmission of direct-digital body CT images. *Brink Journal of Radiology, 217*, 772-779.

Kalyanpur, A., Neklesa, V., Brink, J., Pham, D., Stein, S., & Forman, H. (2004). Implementation of an international teleradiology staffing model. *Radiology, 232*, 415-419.

Kalyanpur, A., Weinberg, J., Neklesa, V., Brink, J., & Forman, H. (2003). Emergency radiology coverage: Technical and clinical feasibility of an international teleradiology model. *Emergency Radiology, 10*(3), 115-118.

Kamal, S. (Ed.) (2006). *Electronic Business in Developing Countries: Opportunities and Challenges.* Hershey: Idea Group.

Kandel, A., & Lee, A. (1979). *Fuzzy switching and automata.* Crane Russak, New York.

Kangarloo, H., Valdez, J. A., Yao, L., Chen, S., Curran, J., Goldman, D., Sinha, U., Dionisio, J. D., Taira, R., Sayre, J., Seeger, L., Johnson, R., Barbaric, Z., & Steckel, R. (2000). Improving the quality of care through routine teleradiology consultation. *Acad Radiol, 7*(3), 149-55.

Kapoor, A., Patki, T., & Khurana, S. (2005). *Part-I: Analytical methodologies in soft computing, Part II: Exposure to cyber forensic software tools.* Technical Report Submitted to DIT, New Delhi.

Karahanna, E., & Straub, D.W. (1999). The Psychological Origins of Perceived Usefulness and Ease of Use. *Information and Management*, 35(4), 237-250.

Kartiwi M. & MacGregor R.C. (2007). Electronic Commerce Adoption Barriers in Small to Medium-sized Enterprises (SMEs) in Developed and Developing Countries: A Cross-country Comparisons. *Journal of E-commerce in Organizations, 5*(3), 35-51.

Kautz, K., & Henriksen, H. (2002). Brilliant idea? But it didn't do the trick: The role of a designed project in the adoption and diffusion process of inter-orgnisational information systems. In *Proceedings of the IFIP TC8 WG8.6 International Working Conference on Diffusion, Adoption and Implementation of Information Technology*, Sydney, Australia.

Kaynak, E., Tatoglu, E. and Kula, V. (2005). An analysis of the factors affecting the adoption of electronic commerce by SMEs: Evidence from an emerging market. *International Marketing Review, 22*(6), 623-40.

Keaveney, S. M. (1995). Customer switching behavior in service industries: An exploratory study. *Journal of Marketing, 59*, 71-82.

Keaveney, S. M., & Parthasarathy, M. (2001). Customer switching behavior in online services: An exploratory study of the role of selected attitudinal, behavioral, and demographic factors. *Journal of the Academy of Marketing Science, 29*(4), 374-390.

Keil, M.; Beranek, P.M.; & Konsynski, B.R. (1995). Usefulness and ease of use: Field study evidence regarding task considerations. *Decision Support Systems*, 13(1), 75-91.

Kendall, J., Tung, L., Chua, K. H., Ng, C. H., & Tan, S. M. (2001). Receptivity of Singapore's SMEs to electronic commerce adoption. *Journal of Strategic Information Systems, 10*, 223–242.

Kendall, J.E. and Kendall, K.E. (2001). A Paradoxically Peaceful Coexistence Between Commerce and Ecommerce. *Journal of Information Technology, Theory and Application, 3*(4), 1-6.

Keniry, J., Blums, A., Notter, E., Radford, E. and Thomson, S. (2003). *Regional business—A plan for action.* Department of Transport and Regional Services. Retrieved December 13, 2003, from http://www.rbda.gov.au/action_plan

Keogh, W., Jack, S.L., Bower, J. and Crabtree, E. (1998). Small, Technology-based firms in the UK oil and gas industry: innovation and internationalization strategies. *International Small Business Journal, October, 17*(1), 57-68.

Kern, T., & Willcocks, L. (2002). Exploring relationships in information technology outsourcing: The interaction approach. *European Journal of Information Systems, 11*, 3-19.

Kettinger, W. J., & Lee, C. C. (1997). Pragmatic perspectives on the measurement of information systems service quality. *MIS Quarterly, 21*(2), 223-240.

Kettinger, W. J., & Lee, C. C. (2005). Zones of tolerance: alternative scales for measuring information systems service quality. *MIS Quarterly, 29*(4), 607-623.

Khiang, A. L. B. and Chye, G. N. K. (2002). Information technology and e-commerce for successful SMEs. *Malaysian Management Review, 37*(2).

Khoo, D., McGill, T.J. and Dixon, M.W. (1998). *Use of the Internet by Small to Medium Enterprises in Singapore.* Murdoch University, Perth, Australia.

Kim, C. & Galliers, R.D. (2006). The development and application of a configuration model of web-based shopping systems. International Journal of Electronic Business, 4(1), 1-17.

Kim, C., Galliers, R.D. & Yang, K.H. (2005). Comparison of web-based shopping systems in the UK and Korea. International Journal of Global Information Technology Management, 8(4), 49-66.

Kim, C., Galliers, R.D., Yang, K.H. & Kim, J. (2007). Evolution of web-based shopping systems: characteristics and strategies. Journal of Electronic Commerce in Organizations, 5(4), 70-87.

Kim, Y.J., E.J. Garrity, G.L. Sanders, and B.A. Sherman. (2004). A means-end model of IS success: Toward understanding the cognitive structure of IS users. *Working Paper State University of New York at Buffalo.*

King, J., Gurbaxani, V., & Kraemer (1994). The institutional factors in information technology innovation. *Information Systems Research, 5*(2), 139–169.

Kishore, R., Agrawal, M., & Rao, H. R. (2004). Determinants of sourcing during technology growth and maturity: An empirical study of e-commerce sourcing. *Journal of Management Information Systems, 21*(3), 47-82.

Kite, Shane (November, 2004). Trade Services: Banks Refocus On The EX/IM Business. *Bank Technology News.* http://findarticles.com/p/articles/mi_km2919/is_200411/ai_n8616615

Klein, S. (1997). Introduction to electronic auctions. *Electronic Markets, 7*(4), 3-6.

Kobayashi-Hillary, M. (2004). *Outsourcing to India--The offshore advantage.* Berlin: Springer-Verlag.

Kohli, R. & Kettinger, W.J. (2004). Informating The Clan: Controlling Physicians' Costs And Outcomes, *MIS Quarterly* (28:3), September 2004, pp. 363-394.

Koong, K. S., Liu, Lai C. & Liu, X. (2002). A Study of the Demand for Information Technology Professionals in Selected Internet Job Portals. Journal of Information Systems Education 13(1), 21-29.

Kosala, R., & Blockeel, H. (2000). Web mining research: Survey. *SIGKDD Explorations, 2*(1), 1-15.

Koufaris, M. (2002). Applying the technology acceptance model and flow theory to online consumer behavior. *Information Systems Research*, 13(2), 205-223.

Kowtha, N. R., & Choon, T. W. I. (2001). Determinants of Website development: A study of electronic commerce in Singapore. *Information & Management, 39*(3), 227-242.

Kraemer, K. & Wigand, R. T. (2004), "Introduction to Globalization and Electronic Commerce Special Issue," Electronic Markets, 14(1), January, 2-3.

Kraemer, K.L., Dedrick, J. & Yamashiro, S. (2000). Refining and extending the business model with information technology: Dell Computer corporation. Information Society, 16(1), 5-21.

Kramer, J., Noronha, S., & Vergo, J. (2000). A user-centered design approach to personalization. *Communications of the ACM*, 8, 45-48.

Krishnan, M.S., Ramaswamy, V., Meyer, M. C., & Damien, P. (1999). Customer Satisfaction for Financial Services: The Role of Products, Services, and Information Technology. *Management Science*, 45(9), 1194-1209.

Krupinski, E., McNeill, K., Haber, K., & Ovitt, T. (2003). High-volume teleradiology service: Focus on radiologist satisfaction. *Journal of Digital Imaging, 16*(2), 203-209.

Kuan, K. K. Y., & Chau, P. Y. K. (2001). A perception-based model for EDI adoption in small businesses using a technology-organization-environment framework. *Information & Management, 38,* 507-521.

Kurnia, S., & Johnston, R. B. (2000). Understanding the adoption of ECR: A broader perspective. *Proceedings of the 13th International Bled Electronic Commerce Conference*, Bled, Slovenia.

Lal, K. (2002). E-business and manufacturing sector: A study of small and medium-sized enterprises in India. *Research Policy, 31*, 1199–1211.

Larsson, E., Hedelin, L. and Gärling, T. (2003). Influence of expert advice on expansion goals of small businesses in rural Sweden. *Journal of Small Business Management, 41*(2), 205-212.

Lawrence, K. L. (1997). Factors Inhibiting the Utilisation of Electronic Commerce Facilities in Tasmanian Small-to-Medium Sized Enterprises, in *Proceedings of 8th Australasian Conference on Information Systems.* pp. 587-597.

Leadbeater, C. (2000). *Living on Thin Air, The New Economy.* London: Penguin Books.

Lederer, A.L., Maupin, D.J., Sena, M.P., & Zhuang, Y. (2000). The technology acceptance model and the World Wide Web. *Decision Support Systems*, 29(3), 269-282.

Lee J. K., Renner, J. B., Saunders, B. F., Stamford, P. P., Bickford, T. R., Johnston, R. E., Hsaio, H. S., Phillips, M. L. (1998). Effect of real-time teleradiology on the practice of the emergency department physician in a rural setting: Initial experience. *Acad Radiol, 5*(8), 533-8.

Lee, D.M.S., Trauth, E. M. & Farwell, D. (1995). Critical Skills and Knowledge Requirements of IS Professionals: A Joint Academic/Industry Investigation. MIS Quarterly 19(3), 313-341.

Lee, G., & Xia, W. (2006). Organizational size and IT innovation adoption: A meta-analysis. *Information & Management, 43*(8), 975-985.

Lee, G.-G., & Lin, H.-F. (2005). Customer perceptions of e-service quality in online shopping. *International Journal of Retail & Distribution Management, 33*(2), 161-176.

Lee, H. G., Clark, T., & Tam, K. Y. (1999). Research report: Can EDI benefit adopters. *Information Systems Research, 10*(2), 186-195.

Lee, J. N., Huynh, M. Q., Kwok, R. C., & Pi, S. (2003). IT outsourcing evolution-past, present and future. *Communications of the ACM, 46*(5), 84-87.

Lee, J., Huynh, M. Q., Chi-Wai, K. R., & Pi, S. (2000). The evolution of outsourcing research: What is next issue? In *Proceedings of the 33rd Hawaii International Conference on Systems Sciences-2000.*

Lee, Y., Kozar, K.A., & Larsen, K.R.T. (2003). The Technology Acceptance Model: Past, Present, and Future. *Communications of the Association for Information Systems*, 12(5), 752-780.

Lertwongsatien, C., & Wongpinunwatana, N. (2003). E-commerce adoption in Thailand: An empirical study of small and medium enterprises (SMEs). *Journal of Global Information Technology Management, 6*(3), 67–83.

Levitt, T. (1983). Globalization of markets. *Harvard Business Review, 61*(May/June), 92-102.

Lewis, D., & Weigert, A. (1985). Trust as a social reality. *Social Forces*, 63, 967-985.

Li, H., Kuo, C., & Russell, M. G. (1999). The Impact of Perceived Channel Utilities, Shopping Orientations, and Demographics on the Consumer's Online Buying Behavior. *Journal of Computer Mediated Communication*, 5(2), 1-20.

Liang, T.-P., & Huang, J.-S. (1998). An empirical study on consumer acceptance of products in electronic markets: a transaction cost model. *Decision Support Systems, 24*, 29-43.

Lim, J. J. (2002). East Asia in the Formation of Economy: Opportunities and Challanges. *Info, 4*(5), 56-63.

Lin, Z., Li, D., & Huang, W. (2007). Traders beware: an examination of the distribution of eBay sellers' online reputation. *International Journal of Electronic Business, 5*(5), 499-517.

Lin, Z., Li, D., Janamanchi, B., & Huang, W. (2006). Reputation distribution and consumer-to-consumer online auction market structure: an exploratory study. *Decision Support Systems, 41*(2), 435-448.

Linder, J. C. (2004). *Outsourcing for radical change.* American Management Association.

Litecky, C. R., Arnett, K. P. & Prabhakar, B. (2004). The Paradox of Soft Skills Versus Technical Skills in IS

Hiring. The Journal of Computer Information Systems, 45(1), 69-77.

Litecky, C.R., Prabhakar, B. & Arnett, K. P. (1996). MIS Job Market: Shaken But Not Stirred. Journal of Systems Management, 47(4), 50-54.

Livingston, J. A. (2005). How valuable is a good reputation? A sample selection model of internet auction. *The Review of Economics and Statistics, 87*(3), 453-465.

Lo, C. (2005). International outsourcing and intra-industrial trade. *International Journal of Applied Economics, 2*(2), 69-82, September 2005

Loh, L., & Venkatraman, N. (1992). Determinants of information technology outsourcing: A cross sectional analysis. *Journal of Management Information Systems, 9*(1), 7-24.

Longacre, R. E. (1976). *An anatomy of speech notions.* Lisse: de Ridder.

Looney, C.A. & Chatterjee, D. (2002). Web-enabled transformation of the brokerage industry. Communication of the ACM, 45(8), 75-81.

Lucking-Reiley, D. (1999). Using field experiments to test equivalence between auction formats: Magic on the Internet. *The American Economic Review, 89*(5), 1063-1081.

Lucking-Reiley, D. (2000). Auctions on the Internet: What's being auctioned, and how? *The Journal of Industrial Economics, 48*(3), 227-253.

Lucking-Reiley, D. (2000). Vickrey auctions in practice: From nineteenth-century philately to twenty-first-century e-commerce. *The Journal of Economic Perspectives, 14*(3), 183-193.

Lucking-Reiley, D., & Spulber, D. F. (2001). Business-to-business electronic commerce. *The Journal of Economic Perspectives, 15*(1), 55.

Lumpkin, G.T., Droege, S.B. & Dess, G.G. (2002). E-commerce strategies: achieving sustainable competitive advantage and avoiding pitfalls. Organizational Dynamics, 30(4), 325-340.

Lundström, A. and Stevenson, L. (2002). *On the road to entrepreneurship policy: The entrepreneurship policy for the future series.*

MacGregor, R. C. & Vrazalic, L. (2007). *E-commerce in Regional Small to Medium Enterprises.* Hershey: IGI Global.

MacGregor, R. C. and Bunker, D. (1996). The effect of priorities introduced during computer acquisition on continuing success with IT in small business environments, in *Proceedings of Information Resource Management Association International Conference.* Washington. pp. 271-227.

MacGregor, R. C., Bunker, D. and Waugh, P. (8-10 June 1998). Electronic commerce and small/medium enterprises in Australia: An EDI pilot study, in *Proceedings of Proceedings of 11th International Bled E-commerce Conference.* Bled Slovania. pp. 331-345.

MacGregor, R.C. & Vrazalic, L. (2005). A Basic Model of Electronic Commerce Adoption Barriers: A Study of Regional Small Businesses in Sweden and Australia. *Journal of Small Business and Enterprise Development, 12*(4), 510-527.

Mackay, D. R. (1993). The impact of EDI on the components sector of the Australian automotive industry. *Journal of Strategic Information Systems, 2*(3), 243-263.

Magnusson, M. (May 28-29, 2001). E-commerce in small businesses—focusing on adoption and implementation, in *Proceedings of the 1st Nordic Workshop on Electronic Commerce.* Halmstad, Sweden.

Maitino, A. J., Levin, D. C., Parker, L., Rao, V. M., & Sunshine, J. H. (2003). Practice patterns of radiologists and nonradiologists in utilization of noninvasive diagnostic imaging among the Medicare population 1993-1999. *Radiology, 228*, 795-801.

Marek, V. W., & Pawlak, Z. (1976). Information storage and retrieval system. *Mathematical Foundations, Theoretical Computer Science*, *1*(4), 331-354.

Markellou, P., Rigou, M., & Sirmakessis, S. (2005). Web personalization for e-marketing intelligence. In

S. Krishnamurthy (Ed.), *Contemporary research in e-marketing: Volume 1* (pp. 48-68). Hershey, PA: Idea Group Publishing.

Markellou, P., Rigou, M., & Sirmakessis, S. (2005). An online consumer purchase decision cycle. In I. Clarke III & Th. Flaherty (Eds.), *Advances in electronic marketing: Volume 1* (pp. 287-299). Hershey, PA: Idea Group Publishing.

Markellou, P., Rigou, M., & Sirmakessis, S. (2006). A closer look to the online consumer behavior. In M. Khosrow-Pour (Ed.), *Encyclopedia of e-commerce, e-government and mobile commerce* (pp. 106-111). Hershey, PA: Idea Group Reference.

Markellou, P., Rigou, M., Sirmakessis, S., & Tsakalidis, A. (2004, September, 3-11). Personalization in the semantic Web era: A glance ahead. In *Proceedings of the 5th International Conference on Data Mining, Text Mining and their Business Applications, Data Mining 2004* (pp. 15-17). Malaga, Spain. Wessex Institute of Technology (UK)

MarketingSherpa.com. (Sept. 20, 2005). MarketingSherpa Study Results: 3,271 Marketers Reveal Search Marketing Costs, Clicks, & Conversions. Retrieved October 3, 2005, from *http://www.marketingsherpa.com/sample.cfm?contentID=3078*

Markland, R. E. (1974). The role of the computer in small business management. *Journal of Small Business Management, 12*(1), 21-26.

Markus, M.L., Tora, K.B., Shinnawy, M., & Louise, L.S. (1993). Fragments of your communication: email, vmail, and fax. *Information Society*, 8, 207-226.

Marsh, H.W., Balla, J.R., & McDonald, R.P. (1988). Goodness-of-fit-indexes in confirmatory factor analysis: The effect of sample size. *Psychological Bulletin*, 103(March), 391-411.

Marshall, C. (1999). *Enterprise Modeling with UML: Designing Successful Software through Business Analysis*. Addison-Wesley.

Martin, L. and Matlay, H. (2001). "Blanket" approaches to promoting ICT in small firms: some lessons from DTI ladder adoption model in the UK'. *Internet Research: Electronic Networking Applications and Policy, 11*(5), 399-410.

Massetti, B., & Zmud, R. (1996). Measuring the extent of EDI usage in complex organisations: Strategies and illustrative examples. *MIS Quarterly, 20*(3), 603–640.

Mathieson, K. (1991). Predicting use intentions: Comparing the technology acceptance model with the theory of planned behavior. *Information Systems Research*, 2(3), 173-191.

Matsumoto, D. (1989). Cultural Influences on the Perception of Emotion. *Journal of Cross-Cultural Psychology*, 20(March), 92-105.

Matsuura, J. H. (2002). *Security, rights, and liabilities in e-commerce*. Artech House.

Mayer, R.C. & Davis, J.H. (1999). The effect of the performance appraisal system on trust for management: A field quasi-experiment. *Journal of Applied Psychology*, 84(1), 123-136.

McAfee, R. P., & McMillan, J. (1987). Auctions and bidding. *Journal of Economic Literature, 25*(2), 699-739.

McCloskey, D. W. (2006). The importance of ease of use, usefulness, and trust in online consumers: an examination of the technology acceptance model with older consumers. *Journal of Organizational and End User Computing, 18*(3), 47-65.

McCole, P., & Ramsey, E. (2005). A profile of adopters and non-adopters of eCommerce in SME professional service firms. *Australasian Marketing Journal, 13*(1), 36–48.

McDonald, C. G., & Slawson, V. C. (2002). Reputation in an Internet auction market. *Economic Inquiry, 40*(4), 633-650.

McFarlan, W., & Nolan, R. (1995). How to manage an IT outsourcing alliance. *Sloan Management Review, 36*(2), 9-23.

McLeod, S. (1987). Some Thoughts about Feelings The Affective Domain and the Writing Process. *College Composition and Communication* 38, 426-35.

McLeod, S. (1991). The Affective Domain and the Writing Process: Working Definitions. *Journal of Advanced Composition* 11, 95-105.

Mehrabian, A. & Russel. (1974). *An approach to environmental psychology.* Cambridge, MA.: MIT Press.

Mehta, K. (2002). *Understanding revenue drivers of electronic auctions.* Unpublished Doctoral Dissertation, University of Illinois at Chicago, Illinois.

Meinert, D. B., Peterson, D. K., Criswell, J. R., & Crossland, M. D. (2006). Privacy policy statements and consumer willingness to provide personal information. *Journal of Electronic Commerce in Organizations, 4*(1), 1-17.

Melbourne IT. (2005). *Website age and search engine rankings.* Retrieved January 13, 2007, from http://www.melbourneitcbs.com/news.php?article=9&title=Website%20age%20and%20search%20engine%20rankings&year=2005&month=12

Melnik, M. I., & Alm, J. (2002). Does a seller's ecommerce reputation matter? Evidence from Ebay auctions. *The Journal of Industrial Economics, 50*(3), 337-349.

Melville, P., Mooney, R., & Nagarajan, R. (2002). Content-boosted collaborative filtering for improved recommendations. In *Proceedings of the Eighteenth National Conference on Artificial Intelligence (AAAI-02)* (pp. 187-192).

Meredith G.G.: (1994), *Small Business Management in Australia* McGraw Hill, 4th Edition

Mesquita, C., Barbosa, S. D., & Lucena, C. J. (2002). Towards the identification of concerns in personalization mechanisms via scenarios.In *Proceedings of 1st International Conference on Aspect-Oriented Software Development.* Retrieved December 20, 2006, from http://trese.cs.utwente.nl/AOSD-EarlyAspectsWS/Papers/Mesquita.pdf

Middleton, S. E., De Roure, D. C., & Shadbolt, N. R. (2004). Ontology-based recommender systems. In S. Staab & R. Studer (Eds.), *Handbook on ontologies* (pp. 477-498). Springer-Verlag.

Middleton, S. E., Shadbolt, N. R., & De Roure, D. C. (2004). Ontological user profiling in recommender systems. *ACM Transactions on Information Systems, 22*(1), 54-88.

Milgrom, P. R., & Weber, R. J. (1982). A theory of auctions and competitive bidding. *Econometrica, 50*(5), 1089-1122.

Miller, N. J. and Besser, T. L. (2000). The importance of community values in small business strategy formation: Evidence from rural Iowa. *Journal of Small Business Management, 38*(1), 68.

Min, H., & Galle, W. P. (2001). Electronic commerce-based purchasing: A survey on the perceptual differences between large and small organizations. *International Journal of Logistics: Research and Applications, 4,* 79-95.

Minkoff, J. (2000). Outsourcing takes the worry out of the Web sites for financial services companies. *Web Finance, 4*(15), 9-10.

Mirchandani, D. A., & Motwani, J. (2001). Understanding small business electronic commerce adoption: An empirical analysis. *The Journal of Computer Information Systems, 41*(3), 70–73.

Mittal, V., Kumar, P., & Tsiros, M. (1999). Attribute-level performance satisfaction, and behavioral intentions over time: a consumption-system approach, *Journal of Marketing* 63 (2), 88– 101.

Mobasher, B., Jin, X., & Zhou, Y. (2004). Semantically enhanced collaborative filtering on the Web. In B. Berendt et al. (Eds.), *Proceedings of the European Web Mining Forum*(LNAI). Springer-Verlag.

Mohr, J., Fisher, R., & Nevin, J. (1996, July). Collaborative communication in interfirm relationships: Moderating effects of integration and control. *Journal of Marketing, 60*, 349–370.

Molenaar, C. (2002). The Future of Marketing: Practical Strategies for Marketers in the Post-Internet Age. London: Financial Times Prentice Hall.

Molla A & Heeks R. (2007). Exploring E-commerce Benefits for Businesses in a Developing Country *The Information Society, 23,* 95-108.

Molla A. & Licker P.S. (2005). Ecommerce Adoption in Developing Countries: A Model and Instrument *Information & Management, 42,* 877-899.

Möllenberg, A. (2004). Internet auctions in marketing: The consumer perspective. *Electronic Markets, 14*(4), 360-371.

Moon, J. & Kim, Y. (2001). Extending the TAM for a world wide web context. *Information and Management,* 38, 217-230.

Mooney, R., & Roy, L. (2000, June 2-7). Content-based book recommending using learning for text categorization. In *Proceedings of the 5th ACM Conference on Digital Libraries*, San Antonio, Texas (pp. 195-204).

Moore, G., & Benbasat, J. (1991). Development of an instrument to measure the perceptions of adopting an information technology innovation. *Information System Research, 2*(3), 191–222.

Morgan, M. & Hunt, B. (2005). Search engine optimization basics, Part 3: Get your Web pages into search indexes - A search engine can't find what it doesn't see. March 21, 2006. Retrieved July 17, 2006, from *http://www-28.ibm.com/developerworks/web/library/wa-seo3.html*

Morgan, R. M., & Hunt, S. D. (1994). The commitment-trust theory of relationship marketing. *Journal of Marketing, 58*(3), 20-38.

Morris, M., & Peng, K. (1994). Culture and Cause: American and Chinese Attributions for Social and Physical Events. *Journal of Personality and Social Psychology.* 67(December), 971.

Mulaik, S.A., James, L.R., Van Alstine, J., Bennett, N., Lind, S., & Stilwell, C.D. (1989). Evaluation of Goodness-of-Fit Indices for Structural Equation Models. *Psychological Bulletin*, 105, 430-445.

Mulvenna, M., Anand, S., & Bchner, A. (2000). Personalization on the net using Web mining. *Communications of ACM, 43*(8), 122-125.

Murphy J. (1996). *Small Business Management.* London: Pitman.

Nakamura, J., & Csikszentmihalyi, M. (2002). The concept of flow. In C. R. Snyder & S. J. Lopez (Eds.), *Handbook of Positive Psychology*: Oxford University Press US.

Nakayama, M. & Sutcliffe, N. G. (2001) "IT Skills Portfolio Research in SIGCPR Proceedings: Analysis, Synthesis and Proposals," ACM SIGCPR, 1-58113-361.

NASSCOM, & BCG. (2001). *e-commerce opportunities for India Inc.* Study Report prepared by NASSCOM and The Boston Consultancy Group Report.

National Research Council (2000). *Surviving Supply Chain Integration: Strategies for Small Manufacturers.* Commission on Engineering and Technical Systems. Retrieved June 2, 2003 from http://books.nap.edu/books/0309068789/html/R1.html

Neo, B. S. (1992). The implementation of an electronic market for pig trading in Singapore. *Journal of Strategic Management Systems, 1*(5), 278-288.

Neuman, L. W. (1999). *Social research methods: Qualitative and quantitative approaches* (4th ed.). Allyn & Bacon.

Newcomer, K.E. and Caudle, S.L. (1991). Evaluating Public Sector Information Systems: More than Meets the Eye. *Public Administration Review, 51*(5), 377-84.

Nilakanta, S., & Scamell, R. (1990). The effect of information sources and communication channels on the diffusion of innovation in a data base development environment. *Management Science, 36*(1), 24-40.

NOIE (2002). *e-Business for Small Business.* The National Office of Information Economy. Retrieved May 25, 2003, from http://www.noie.gov.au/projects/ebusiness/Advancing/SME/

NOIE. (2002, December). E-business for small business. Retrieved September 10, 2006, from http://www.noie.gov.au/projects/ebusiness/Advancing/SME/index.htm

Norman, D.A. (2002). Emotion and design: Attractive things work better. *Interactions: New Visions of Human-Computer Interaction IX*, 4, 36–42.

Nour, M.A. & Fadlalla, A. (2000). A framework for web marketing strategies: the e-commerce revolution. Information Systems Management, 17(22), 41-50.

Novak, T.P., Hoffman, D.L., & Duhachek, A. (2003). The influence of goal-directed and experiential activities on online flow experiences. *Journal of Consumer Psychology*, 13(1-2), 3-16.

Novak, T.P., Hoffman, D.L., & Yung, Y.F. (2000). Measuring the customer experience in online environments: A structural modeling approach. *Marketing Science*, 19(1), 19-42.

Nunnally, J. (1978). *Psychometric theory*. New York: McGraw-Hill.

Nunnally, J. C. (1967). *Psychometric Theory*. New York: McGraw-Hill.

Nunnally, J. C., & Bernstein, I. H. (1994). *Psychometric Theory* (3rd ed.). New York: McGraw-Hill Inc.

Nunnally, J.C. (1978). *Psychometric Theory*. New York: McGraw-Hill Inc.

O'Donnell, J.B.; Ferrin, D.L.; Glassberg, B.; & Sanders, G.L. (2004). The influence of web site characteristics on consumer trust and the purchase decision. *Working Paper, Canisius College*.

O'Keefe, R.M. & McEachern, T. (1998). Web-based customer decision support systems. *Communications of the ACM*, 41(3), 71-78.

Oh, W. (2002). C2C versus B2C: A comparison of the winner's curse in two types of electronic auctions. *International Journal of Electronic Commerce, 6*(4), 115-138.

Olikowski, W. (1993). CASE tools as organizational change: Investigating incremental and radical changes in systems development. *MIS Quarterly, 17*(3), 309-340.

Organization for the Advancement of Structured Information Standards (OASIS). (2002b). *Business transaction protocol [Version 1.03]*. Billerica, MA: Author.

Orman, L. V. (2006). Optimum design of electronic communities as economic entities. *Information Systems Frontiers, 8*, 179-194.

Oskamp, S. (1991). Attitudes and Opinions. 2nd ed. Englewood Cliffs, NJ: Prentice-Hall.

Ottaway, T. A., Bruneau, C. L., & Evans, G. E. (2003). The impact of auction item image and buyer/seller feedback rating on electronic auctions. *The Journal of Computer Information Systems, 43*(3), 56-60.

Oxley J.E. & Yeung B. (2001). E-Commerce Readiness: Institutional Environment and International Competitiveness *Journal of International Business Studies, 32*(4), 705-723.

Pace, S. A grounded theory of the flow experiences of web users. (2004). *International Journal of Human-Computer Studies*, 60(3), 327-363.

Papagelis, M. (2005). *Crawling the algorithmic foundations of recommendation technologies*. Unpublished master's thesis, University of Crete, Heraklion, Greece.

Paper, D., Pedersen, E. & Mulbery, K. (2003). An e-commerce process model: perspectives from e-commerce entrepreneurs. Journal of Electronic Commerce in Organizations, 1(3), 28-47.

Parente, S. T. (2000). Beyond the hype: A taxonomy of e-health business models. *Health Aff, 19*(6), 89-102.

Park, C., & Kim, Y. (2006). The effect of information satisfaction and relational benefit on consumers' online shopping site commitments. *Journal of Electronic Commerce in Organizations, 4*(1), 70-90.

Park, CH., & Kim, YG. (2006). The Effect of Information Satisfaction and Relational Benefit on Consumers' Online Shopping Site Commitments, *Journal of Electronic Commerce in Organizations.* 4(1), 70-91.

Park, H. J., Kim, B. K., & Lim, K.Y. (2001). Measuring the machine intelligence quotient (MIQ) of human-machine cooperative systems. *IEEE Transactions on Systems, Man, and Cybernetics—Part A: Systems and humans, 31*(2), 89-96.

Park, Y. H., & Bradlow, E. T. (2005). An integrated model for bidder behavior in internet auctions: Whether, who, when, and how much. *Journal of Marketing Research, XLII*, 470-482.

Parthasarathy, M., & Bhattacherjee, A. (1998). Understanding post-adoption behavior in the context of online services. *Information Systems Research, 9*(4), 362-379.

Patki, A. B. (1996). Fuzzy logic based hardware: Some experiences. In *Proceedings of the 1st International Discourse on Fuzzy Logic and the Management of Complexity (FLAMOC'96)* (Vol. 3, pp. 247-251), January, 15-18, 1996, Sydney, Australia.

Patki, A. B., Kulkarni, M., Sivasubramanian, S., & Patki, D. D. (2003). Technology development trends for cyber civilization. In *Proceedings of the International Conference on Cyberworlds* (pp. 40-45), Singapore.

Patki, A. B., Patki, T., Khurana, S., & Sivasubramanian, S. (October 17-19, 2005). Product development for female cyber police programme. In *Proceedings of Conflux, 2005*, New Delhi, India.

Patki, A. B., Raghunathan, G. V., & Khurshid, A. (1997). FUZOS—Fuzzy operating system support for information technology. In P. K. Chawdhry, R. Roy, & R. K. Pant (Eds.), *Soft computing in engineering design and manufacturing* (pp. 131-140), Springer.

Patki, A., Lakshminarayanan, S., Sivasubramanian, S., & Sarma, S. (2003). Cyber crime information system for cyberethics awareness. In *Proceedings of the International Conference on Cyberworlds* (pp. 46-52), Singapore.

Patki, A.B. (2004). *Offshoring and outsourcing opportunities.* Lecture Notes for Engineering Student Internship Programme, Department of Information Technology, New Delhi.

Patki, T., & Khurana, S. (2006). *Software cost estimation and software obfuscation: A fuzzy logic perspective.* Technical Report Submitted to Department of Information Technology, New Delhi.

Patki, T., Khurana, S., & Neha (2005). Cyber civilization: Advantages and shortcomings. *VISION MSIT*, New Delhi.

Paul, D. L., Pearlson, K. E., & McDaniel, R. R. (1999). Assessing technological barriers to telemedicine: Technology-management implications. *IEEE Transactions on Engineering Management, 46*(3).

Paul, J. (2002). Narrowing the digital divide: initiatives undertaken by the Association of South-East Asian Nations (ASEAN). *Program: electronic library and information systems, 36*(1), 13-22.

Pavlou, P. A. (2002). Trustworthiness as a source of competitive advantage in online auction markets. In *Academy of Management Proceedings* (pp. A1-A7).

Pavlou, P. A. (2002). What drives electronic commerce? A theory of planned behavior perspective. In *Academy of Management Proceedings 2002 OCIS* (pp. A1-A6).

Pavlou, P. A. (2003). Consumer acceptance of electronic commerce: integrating trust and risk with the technology acceptance model. *International Journal of Electronic Commerce, 7*(3), 101-134.

Pavlou, P. A., & Gefen, D. (2004). Building effective online marketplaces with institution-based trust. *Information Systems Research, 15*(1), 37-59.

Pavlou, P. A., & Gefen, D. (2005). Psychological contract violation in online marketplaces: Antecedents, consequences, and moderating role. *Information Systems Research, 16*(4), 372-399.

Pawlak, Z. (1982). Rough sets. *International Journal of Computer and Information Sciences, 11*(5), 342-356.

Pawlak, Z. (1984). Rough classification. *Man-Machine Studies*, 469-483.

Payne, J.W. (1982). Contingent decision behavior, Psychological Bulletin 92(2), 382– 402.

Payton, F., & Ginzberg, M. (2001). Interorganisational health care systems implementations: An exploratory study of early electronic commerce initiatives. *Health Care Management Review, 26*(2), 20–32.

Pazzani, M. (1999). A framework for collaborative, content-based and demographic filtering. *Artificial Intelligence Review, 13*(5-6), 393-408.

Pedhazur, E.J. (1997). *Multiple regression in behavioral research: Explanation and prediction.* Fort Worth: Harcourt Brace College Publishers.

Pei, Z., Zhenxiang, Z., & Chunping, H. (2007). An extended TAM modelor Chinese B2C websites design. *Journal of Global Information Technology, 10*(1), 51-66.

Peng, N., Yun, C., Douglas, R., & Dingbang, X. (2004). Tools and techniques for analyzing intrusion. *ACM Transactions on Information and System Security, 7*(2), 273-318, May 2004.

Peppers, D. & Rogers, M. (2004), *Managing Customer Relationship: A Strategic Framework.* Hoboken, New Jersey: John Wiley & Sons, Inc.,

Perloff, R.M. (1993). *The Dynamics of Persuasion.* Hillsdale, NJ: Lawrence Erlbaum and Associates.

Pew Internet Project. (2005). http://www.pewinternet.org/pdfs/PIP_Future_of_Internet.pdf

Pew.Internet.&.American.Life.Project. (2006). Demographics of internet users. Retrieved January 8, 2007, from http://www.pewinternet.org/trends/User_Demo_4.26.06.htm

Piercy, N.F. & Cravens, D.W. (1995). The network paradigm and the marketing organization. European Journal of Marketing, 29(3), 1995 7-34.

Pinker, E. J., Seidmann, A. & Foster, R. C. (2002). Strategies for transitioning 'old economy' firms to e-business. Communications of the ACM, 45(5), 77-83.

Pitt, L. F., Watson, R. T., & Kavan, C. B. (1997). Measuring information systems service quality: concerns for a complete canvas. *MIS Quarterly, June*, 209-221.

Poon, S. and Swatman, P. (1997). *The Internet for small businesses: an enabling infrastructure.* Fifth Internet Society Conference, 221-231. Retrieved from Chon, K., HI, http://www.isworld.org/ais.ac.98/.

Poon, S. and Swatman, P. M. C. (1997). Small business use of the Internet: Findings from Australian case studies. *International Marketing Review, 14*(5), 385.

Poon, S., & Swatman, P. (1998, June 8-10). Small business Internet commerce experiences: A longitudinal study. In *Proceedings of the Eleventh International Bled Electronic Commerce Conference* (pp. 295-309), Bled, Slovenia.

Porter, M. E. (2001). Strategy and the Internet. Harvard Business Review, 79(3), 63-76.

Porter, M.F. (1980). Competitive Strategy, New York: The Free Press.

Prabhakar, B., Litecky, C.R. & Arnett, K.P., (2005). IT Skills in a Tough Job Market, Communications of the ACM, 8(10), 91-104.

Premkumar, G., & Ramamurthy, K. (1995). The role of interorganisational and organizational factors on the decision mode for adoption of interorganisational systems. *Decision Sciences, 26*(3), 303-336.

Premkumar, G., & Roberts, M. (1999). Adoption of new information technologies in rural small businesses. *Omega, The International Journal of Management Science, 27*, 467-484.

Premkumar, G., Ramamurthy, K., & Nilakanta, D. (1997). Determinants of EDI adoption in the transportation industry. *European Journal of Information Systems, 6*(2), 107-121.

Premkumar, G., Ramamurthy, K., & Nilakanta, S. (1994). Implementation of electronic data interchange. *Journal of Management Information Systems, 11*(2), 157–186.

Pucihar, A. (2006). E-marketplace Adoption Success Factors: Challenges and Opportunities for a Small Developing Country. In Kamal, S. (Ed.), *Electronic Business in Developing Countries: Opportunities and Challenges* (pp. 88-117). Hershey: Idea Group.

Purao S. & Campbell B. (August 4-16, 1998). Critical Concerns for Small Business Electronic Commerce: Some Reflections Based on Interviews of Small Business Owners *Proceedings of the Association for Information Systems Americas Conference* Baltimore, MD, pp. 325 - 327

Quayle, M. (2002). E-commerce: The challenge for UK SMEs in the twenty-first century. *International Journal of Operations & Production Management, 22*(9/10), 1148.

Rackoff, N, Wiseman, C. & Ullrich, W. (1985). Information systems for competitive advantage: implementation of a planning process. MIS Quarterly, 9(4), 285-294.

Rafaeli, S. (1988). Interactivity: from new media to communication. in *Advancing communication science: merging mass and interpersonal processes*, R.P. Hawkins, Wieman, J.M., Pingree, S., Editor. Sage Perceived Usefulnessblications: Newbury Park, CA. pp. 110-134.

Rafaeli, S., & Noy, A. (2005). Soicial presence: Influence on bidders in Internet auctions. *Electronic Markets, 15*(2), 158-175.

Rafaeli, S., & Sudweeks, F. (1997). Networked Interactivity. *Journal of Computer Mediated Communication*, 2(4).

Rahim, M. (2004). *Understanding adoption of inter-organisational systems: The role of organisational motivations.* PhD thesis, University of Melbourne, Australia.

Rahim, M., Shanks, G., & Johnston, R. (2001). Motivations for inter-organisational systems adoption: A framework and initial case study. In *Proceedings of the Sixth Annual CollECTeR Conference on Electronic Commerce (CollECTeR)*, Coffs Harbour, NSW, Australia.

Rahim, M., Shanks, G., & Johnston, R. (2001). Understanding motivations for IOS adoption. In *Proceedings of the Australasian Conference on Information Systems (ACIS'2001)*, Coffs Harbour, NSW, Australia.

Rahim, M., Shanks, G., & Johnston, R. (2002). A framework for understanding the motivations for inter-organisational systems adoption: An empirical assessment. In *Proceedings of the Thirteenth Australasian Conference on Information Systems (ACIS'2002)*, Melbourne, Australia.

Rai, A. and Patnayakumi, R. (1996). A Structural Model for CASE Adoption Behaviour. *Journal of Management Information Systems, 13*(2), 205-34.

Raisinghani, Mahesh S. (2005). Future Trends in Search Engines, *Journal of Electronic Commerce in Organizations*; Jul-Sep 2005; 3, 3

Ramamurthy, K., Premkumar, G., & Crum, M. (1999). Organisational and interorganisational determinants of EDI diffusion and organisational performance: A casual model. *Journal of Organisational Computing and Electronic Commerce, 9*(4), 253–285.

Ranchhod, A. & Gurau, C. (1999). Internet-enabled distribution strategies. Journal of Information Technology, 14(4), 333-346.

Rao, S. S., Metts, G., & Monge, C. A. M. (2003). Electronic commerce development in small and medium sized enterprises. *Business Process Management Journal, 9*(1), 11–32.

Rapoport, R. (1970). Three dilemmas of action research, *Human Relations*, Vol. 23 No. 6, pp. 499-513.

Raymond L. (2001). Determinants of Web Site Implementation in Small Business. *Internet Research: Electronic Network Applications and Policy, 11*(5), 411-422.

Raymond, L., & Bergeron, B. (1996). EDI success in small and medium sized enterprises: A field study. *Journal of Organisational Computing and Electronic Commerce, 6*(2), 161–172.

Rechtin, E. and Maier, M. (1997). *The Art of Systems Architecturing.* CRC Press.

Reichheld, F. F., & Schefter, P. (2000). E-loyalty: Your secret weapon on the Web. *Harvard Business Review, 78*(4), 105-113.

Reifer, D. J. (2004). Seven hot outsourcing practices, *IEEE Software*, 14-16.

Resnick, P., & Varian, H. (1997). Recommender systems. *Communications of the ACM, 40*(3), 56-58.

Resnick, P., Iacovou, N., Suchak, M., Bergstrom, P., & Riedl, J. (1994). GroupLens: An open architecture for collaborative filtering of netnews. In *Proceedings of the ACM Conference on Computer Supported Cooperative Work*, (pp. 175-186).

Reynolds, J., Savage, W. and Williams, A. (1994). *Your own business: A practica; guide to success.* ITP.

Riccardi, G. (2001). *Principles of database systems with Internet and Java applications*. Reading, MA: Addison-Wesley.

Rice, R.E., & Shook, D.E. (1988). Access to, usage of and outcomes from electronic messaging. *ACM Transactions on Office Information Systems*, 6, 255-276.

Riemenschneider, C. K., & McKinney, V. R. (2001/2002). Assessing belief differences in small business adopters and non-adopters of Web-based e-commerce. *The Journal of Computer Information Systems, 42*(2), 101–107.

Rifkin, G. & Kurtzman, J. (2002). Is your e-business plan radical enough? Sloan Management Review, 43(3), 91-95.

Rindfleisch, A., & Heide, J. B. (1997). Transaction cost analysis: past, present, and future applications. *Journal of Marketing, 61*(October), 30-54.

Riquelme, H. (2002). Commercial internet adoption in China: Comparing the experiences of small, medium and large businesses. *Internet Research: Electronic Networking Applications and Policy, 12*(3), 276-286.

Robertson, T. and Gatignon, H. (1986). Competitive Effects on Technology Diffusion. *Journal of Marketing*, 50.

Roger, J. Y., Smith, B., & Kidd, P. T. (1999). *Business and work in the information society: new technologies and applications.* IOS Press.

Rogers, E. M. (1995). *Diffusion of innovations* (4th ed.). New York: The Free Press.

Rosenberg, M.J. (1960). An analysis of affective-cognitive consistency. in *Attitude Organization and Change*, C.I. Hovland, Rosenberg, M.J., Editor. Yale University Press: New Haven, CT. pp. 15-64.

Ross, J. W., Beath, C. M. & Goodhue, D. L. (1996). Develop Long-Term Competitiveness Through IT Assets. Sloan Management Review 3813; 38(1), 31–42.

Rotch, W. (1967). *Management of small enterprises: Cases and readings.* University of Virginia Press.

Rothkopf, M. H. (1969). A model of rational competitive bidding. *Management Science, 15*(7), 362-374.

Rottman, J.W. & Lacity, M.C. (2004). Proven Practices for IT Offshore Outsourcing, Cutter Consortium Executive Report, 5(12), 1-31.

Rousseau, D.M.; Sitkin, S.B.; Burt, R.S.; & Camerer, C. (1998), Not so different after all: A cross-disciplined view of trust. *Academy of Management Review*, 23(3), 393-404.

Runkel, P., & Runkel, M. (1984). *A guide to usage for writers and students in the social sciences.* Totawa, NJ: Rowman and Allanheld.

Rusbult, C. E., Martz, J. M., & Agnew, C. R. (1998). The investment model scale: Measuring commitment level, satisfaction level, quality of alternatives, and investment size. *Personal Relationships, 5*(4), 357-391.

Russell, J.A. (2003). Core affect and the psychological construction of emotion. *Psychological Review* 110, 1, 145–172.

Ruth, J.-P. S. (2000). So far small biz is only dabbling in E-commerce. *Business News New Jersey, 13*(23), 24.

Ryan, M.P., Farrell, M.C. & Doerflinger, T.M. (2005). Where Have All the Workers Gone?, UBS Financial Services Report, UBS Wealth Management, 27 June 2005.

Sadeh, N.M. & Lee, J.K. (2003). advances in b2b e-commerce and e-supply chain management. Journal of Organizational Computing & Electronic Commerce, 13(3/4), 163-165.

Saeed, K. A., Malhorta, M. K., & Grover, V. (2005). Examining the impact of interorganizational systems on process efficiency and sourcing leverage in buyer supplier dyads. *Decision Sciences, 36*(3), 365-396.

Salter, J., & Antonopoulos, N. (2006). CinemaScreen recommender agent: Combining collaborative and content-based filtering. *IEEE Intelligent Systems, 21*(1), 35-41.

Sanders, G.L. (1984). MIS/DSS Success Measure. *Systems, Objectives, Solutions*, 4, 29-34.

Santos, J. R. A. (1999). Cronbach's alpha: a tool for assessing the reliability of scales. *Journal of Extension, 37*(2), 1-5.

SAP (2000). mysap.com collaborative business scenarios,whitepaper. In *Walldorf.*

Sarker, S., & Lee, A. S. (2000). Using a positivist case research methodology to test three competing theories-in-use of business process redesign. In *Proceedings of the International Conference on Information Systems (ICIS)*, Brisbane.

Sarwar, B., Karypis, G., Konstan, J., & Riedl, J. (2001). Item-based collaborative filtering recommendation algorithms. In *Proceeding of the 10th World Wide Web Conference*, (pp. 285-295).

Sauer, C., & Willcocks, L. (2002). The evolution of the organizational architect. *MIT Sloan Management Review, 43*(3), 41-49.

SCCI (2006). Amazon timeline and history, Retrieved December 8, 2006, from http://phx.corporate-ir.net/phoenix.zhtml?c=176060&p=irol-corporateTimeline/

Schaaf, J. (2004). *Offshore outsourcing in financial industry.* Retrieved January 13, 2007, from http://www.dbresearch.com/prod/dbr_internet_en-prod/prod0000000000180100.pdf

Schafer, J. B. (2005, January 9). DynamicLens: A dynamic user-interface for a meta-recommendation system. *Beyond Personalization: A Workshop on the Next Stage of Recommender Systems Research*, in conjunction with the 2005 International Conference on Intelligent User Interfaces (IUI'05), San Diego, California, (pp. 72-76).

Schafer, J. B., Konstan, J. A., & Reidl, J. (2004). The view through MetaLens: Usage patterns for a meta-recommendation system. *IEE Proceedings Software, 151*(6), 267-279.

Schlosberg, H. (1952). The Description of Facial Expressions in Terms of Two Dimensions. *Journal of Experimental Psychology* (44), 229-237.

Scott, W.E., Farh, J., & Podaskoff, P.M. (1988). The effects of intrinsic and extrinsic reinforcement contingencies on task behavior. *Organizational Behavior and Human Decision Processes*, 41, 405-425.

Scott, W.R. (2004). Institutional theory. In Ritzer, G. (Ed.), *Encyclopedia of Social Theory.* Thousand Oaks, CA: Sage.

Scupola, A. (2003). The adoption of Internet commerce by SMEs in the south of Italy: An environmental, technological and organizational perspective. *Journal of Global Information Technology Management, 6*(1), 52.

Segev, A., Beam, C., & Shanthikumar, J. G. (2001). Optimal design of Internet-based auctions. *Information Technology and Management, 2*(2), 121-163.

Segouin, C., Hodges, B., & Brechat, P. H. (2005). Globalization in health care: Is international standardization of quality a step toward outsourcing? *International Journal of Quality Health Care, 17*(4), 277-9.

SEMPRO (2004). The State of Search Engine Marketing 2004 - Survey of Advertisers and Agencies Search Engine Marketing Professional Organization (SEMPO). Retrieved July 17, 2006, from *http://www.sempo.org/learning_center/research/sempo_trends/SEMPO-Market-Sizing-2004-SUMMARY-v1.pdf*

SEMPRO (2005). Press Release - Search Engine Marketers Spent $5.75 Billion in 2005, According to the Search Engine Marketing Professional Organization (SEMPO). Retrieved July 17, 2006, from *http://www.sempo.org/news/releases/Search_Engine_Marketers*

Sen, R. (2005). Optimal Search Engine Marketing Strategy, *International Journal of Electronic Commerce* (10:1), Fall 2005, pp. 9-25.

Sensis. (2005, August). *e-Business report: The online experience of small and medium enterprises.* Author.

SEOmoz (2005). 2005 Analysis of Google's Sandbox. Retrieved July 17, 2006, from *http://www.seomoz.org/articles/google-sandbox-analysis.php*

SEOmoz. Google's Patent: Information Retrieval Based on Historical Data. Retrieved July 17, 2006, from *http://www.seomoz.org/articles/google-historical-data-patent.php*

Shardanand, U., & Maes, P. (1995). Social information filtering: Algorithms for automating "Word of Mouth." *Human Factors in Computing Systems ACM CHI,* (pp. 210-217).

Sharif, N. (1994). Technology change management: Imperatives for developing economies. *Technological Forecasting and Social Change, 47,* 103-114.

Sherman, Chris. (Sept. 28, 2005). How are Search Marketers Performing?. Retrieved October 3, 2005, from *http://searchenginewatch.com/searchday/article.php/3551921*

Sheth, J. N. and Sharma, A. (2005). International e-marketing: opportunities and issues. *International Marketing Review, 22*(6), 611-622.

Shih, H.-P. (2004). An empirical study on predicting user acceptance of e-shopping on the web. *Information & Management, 41*(3), 351-368.

Short, J., Williams, E., & Christie, B. (1976). *The Social Psychology of Telecommunications.* London: Wiley.

Shugan, S.M. (1980). The cost of thinking, *Journal of Consumer Research* 7(2), 99–111.

Siau, K. (2003). Health care informatics. *IEEE Transactions on Information Technology in Biomedicine*, 7(1), 1-7.

Sibley, K. (2001). Outsourcing Web-hosting. *Computing Canada, 27*(9), 7.

Silberschatz, A., Korth, H.F., & Sudarshan S. (2002). *Database system concepts.* NY: Mc-Graw-Hill.

Simon, H. A. (1977). *The New Science of Management Decision.* Englewood Cliffs, NJ: Prentice-Hall.

Singelis, T.M. (1994). The Measurement of Independent and Interdependent Self-Construals. *Personality and Social Psychology Bulletin*, 20(October), 580-591.

Singelis, T.M., Bond, M.H., Sharkey, W.F., & Lai, C. (1999). Unpacking Culture's Influence on Self-Esteem and Embarrassability. *Journal of Cross-Cultural Psychology*, 30(3), 315-341.

Sivasubramanian, S., & Patki, A. B. (1996). Software industry intelligent information system. *Electronics Information and Planning Journal, 23*(9), 513-518.

Slaughter, S. & Ang, S. (1996). Employment Outsourcing in Information Systems. Communications of the ACM 39(7), 47-55.

Smith, A. D., & Correa, J. (2005). Value-added benefits of technology: E-procurement and e-commerce related to the health care industry. *International Journal of Health Care Qual Assur Inc Leadersh Health Serv, 18*(6-7), 458-73.

Smith, E. R (2000). e-Loyalty: How to keep Customers coming back to your website. NY, NY: HarperCollins Publishers Inc.

Soe, L.L., & Markus, M.L. (1993). Technological or social utility? Unraveling explanations of email, vmail, and fax use. *Information Society*, 9(3), 213-236.

Soh, C., Mah, Q. Y., Gan, F. Y., Chew, D. & Reid, E. (1997). The use of the Internet for business: The experience of early adopters in Singapore. *Internet Research,* 7(3), 217-228.

Soliman, K. S., & Janz, B. D. (2004). An exploratory study to identify the critical factors affecting the decision to establish Internet-based inter-organizational information systems. *Information & Management, 41*(6), 697-706.

Sorensen, J. B., & Stuart, T. E. (2000). Aging, obsolescence, and organizational innovation. *Administrative Science Quarterly, 45,* 81-112.

Sorensen, O. and Buatsi, S. (2002). Internet and Exporting: the case of Ghana. *Journal of Business & Industrial Marketing, 17*(6), 481-500.

Spence, M. (1973). Job market signaling. *Quarterly Journal of Economics, 87*, 355-374.

Spigos, D., Freedy, L., & Mueller, C. (1996). 24-hour coverage by attending physicians: A new paradigm. *American Journal of Roentgenol, 167*, 1089-1090

Spiller, P. & Lohse, G.L. (1998). A classification of internet retail stores. International Journal of Electronic Commerce, 2(2), 29-56.

Sproull, L., Subramani, M., Kiesler S., Walker J., & Waters, K. (1997). When the Interface Is a Face. in *Human Values and the Design of Computer Technology*, CSLI Lecture Notes, No. 72, B. Friedman, Editor. Cambridge University Press: Stanford, CA. pp. 163-190.

Stafford, M. R., & Stern, B. (2002). Consumer bidding behavior on Internet auction sites. *International Journal of Electronic Commerce, 7*(1), 135-150.

Stallings, W. (2004). *Operating systems* (4th ed.). Pearson Education.

Standifird, S. S. (2001). Reputation and e-commerce: eBay auctions and the asymmetrical impact of positive and negative ratings. *Journal of Management, 27*(3), 279-295.

Standifird, S. S., Roelofs, M. R., & Durham, Y. (2004). The impact of eBay's buy-it-now function on bidder behavior. *International Journal of Electronic Commerce, 9*(2), 167-176.

Steen, M., Lankhorst, M., and van de Wetering, R. (2002). Modelling networked enterprises. In *the sixth international Enterprise distributed Object Computing Conference (EDOC'02).*

Steiger, J.H. (1990). Structural model evaluation and modification: An interval estimation approach. *Multivariate Behavioral Research*, 25(April), 173-180.

Stevenson, J.S., Bruner, G.C., Kumar, A. (2000). Webpage background and viewer attitudes. *Journal of Advertising Research* 40, 29–34.

Stockdale, R. and Standing, C. (2004) 'Benefits and barriers of electronic marketplace participation: an SME perspective'. *Journal of Enterprise Information Management.* vol. 17 no. 4. pp.301.

Stockdale, R. and Standing, C. (2004). Benefits and Barriers of Electronic Marketplace Participation: An SME Perspective. *Journal of Enterprise Information Management, 17*(4), 301-11.

Stockdale, R. and Standing, C. (2004). Benefits and barriers of electronic marketplace participation: an SME perspective. *Journal of Enterprise Information Management, 17*(4), 301.

Stockdale, R., & Standing, C. (2004). Benefits and barriers of electronic marketplace participation: An SME perspective. *Journal of Enterprise Information Management, 17*(4), 301–311.

Strader, T. J., & Ramaswami, S. N. (2002). The value of seller trustworthiness in C2C online markets. *Communications of the ACM, 45*(12), 45-49.

Strader, T. J., & Ramaswami, S. N. (2002). The value of seller trustworthiness in c2c online markets. *Communications of the ACM, 45*(12), 45-49.

Straub, D. W. (1989). Validating instruments in MIS research. *MIS Quarterly*, 13(2), 147-169.

Straub, D.; Limayem, M.; & Karahanna-Evaristo, E. (1995). Measuring system usage: Implications for IS theory and testing. *Management Science*. 41(8), 1328-1342.

Street, C.T. & Meister, D.B. (2004). Small Business Growth and Internal Transparency: The role of information systems, *MIS Quarterly* (28:3), September 2004, pp. 473-506.

Subramaniam, C., & Shaw, M. J. (2004). The effects of process characteristics on the value of B2B e-procurement. *Information Technology & Management, 5*, 161-180.

Subramaniam, R., Mittal, V., & Inman, J. J. (2004). Revenue equivalence in online auctions: The case of yahoo and eBay. In P. Leszczyc (Ed.), *Advances in consumer research* (Vol. 31, pp. 1-2).

Sullivan, D. (2003). How Search Engines Rank Web Pages July 31, 2003. SearchEngineWatch. Retrieved July 17, 2006, from *http://searchenginewatch.com/webmasters/article.php/2167961*

Sullivan, D. (2006). The mixed message of paid inclusion. Search Engine Report, May 6, 2002. Retrieved July 17, 2006, from *http://searchenginewatch.com/sereport/02/05-inclusion.html*

Sunshine, J., Maynard, C. D., Paros, J., & Forman, H. P. (2004). Update on the diagnostic radiologist shortage. *AJR, 182*, 301-305

Susman, G. I., and Evered, R. D. (1978). An Assessment of the Scientific Merits of Action Research, *Administrative Science Quarterly* (23:4), 1978, pp. 582-603.

Tan, M., & Teo, T. S. H. (2000). Factors influencing the adoption of Internet banking. *Journal of the AIS, 1*(5), 1-42.

Tapscott, D. (2004). The Engine That Drives Success: The Best Companies Have the Best Business Models Because They Have the Best IT Strategies. CIO Magazine (May) 1-6.

Tas, J., & Sunder, S. (2004). Financial services business process outsourcing. *Communications of the ACM, 47*(5), 50-52.

Taylor, M. and Murphy, A. (2004). SMEs and e-business'. *Journal of Small Business and Enterprise Development, 11*(3), 280.

Taylor, S., & Todd, P. A. (1995). Understanding Information Technology Usage: A Test of Competing Models. *Information Systems Research*, 6(23), 144-176.

Teeni, D. (2001). Review: A Cognitive-Affective Model of Organizational Communication For Designing IT. *MIS Quarterly*, 25(2), 251-312.

Teo, H. H., Wei, K. K., & Benbasat, I. (2003). Predicting intention to adopt inter-organizational linkages: An institutional perspective. *MIS Quarterly, 23*(1), 105-132.

Teo, H.-H., Oha, L-B, Liua, C., & Wei, K-K. (2003). An empirical study of the effects of interactivity on web user attitude. *International Journal of Human-Computer Studies*, 58, 281-305.

Tetteh, E. and Burn, J. M. (2001). Global strategies for SMe-business: applying the SMALL framework. *Logistics Information Management, 14*(1), 171-180.

The Age. (2002, October 23). Australian net economy worth $43b: Cisco study. Retrieved September 10, 2006, from http://www.theage.com/au/articles/2002/10/23/1034561542812.html

Thomas, D., Fowler, C., & Hunt, A. (2004). *Programming ruby: A pragmatic programmer's guide* (2nd ed.). O'Reilly Media Inc.

Thomas, D., Ranganathan, C. & Desouza, K. C. (2005), "Race to Dot.com ad Back: lessons on E-Business Spin-Offs and Reintegration," Information Systems Management, 22(3), 23-30.

Thong, J. Y. L. (1999). An integrated model of information systems adoption in small businesses. *Journal of Management Information Systems, 15*(4), 187-214.

Thornhill, S., & Amit, R. (2003). Learning about failure: Bankruptcy, firm age, and the resource-based view. *Organization Science, 14*(5), 497-509.

TIOBE Programming Community Index. (n.d.). Retrieved September 15, 2006, from http://www.tiobe.com/tpci.htm

Tobias, R.D. (1999). *An introduction to partial least squares regression*. SAS Institute, Inc., 1-8.

Top 500 supercomputer Sites. (n.d.). Retrieved September 15, 2006, from http://www.top500.org

Torkzadeh, G. & Dhillon, G. (2002). Measuring factors that influence the success of internet commerce. Information Systems Research, 13(2), 187-204.

Tornatzky, L., & Klein, K. (1982). Innovation characteristics and innovation adoption-implementation: A meta analysis of findings. *IEEE Transactions on Engineering Management, 29*(11), 28–45.

Trauth, E.M., Farwell, D. & Lee, D.M.S.(1993). The I/S Expectation Gap: Industry Expectation vs. Academic Preparations, MIS Quarterly, 17(3), 293-308.

Trevino, L.K. & Webster, J. (1992). Flow in computer-mediated communication: Electronic mail and voice mail evaluation and impacts. *Communication Research*, 19(5), 539-573.

Trewyn, P. (2005). U.S. faces IT worker shortage. Milwaukee Business Journal, http://milwaukee.bizjournals.com/milwaukee/stories/2005/05/23/focus3.html, May 20, last viewed November 13, 2005.

Turban, E., King, D., Lee, J. and Vienland, D. (2004). *Electronic Commerce: A Managerial Perspective*. New Jersey: Pearson/Prentice Hall.

Turban, E., King, D., Lee, J., & Viehland, D. (2006). *Electronic Commerce 2006: A Managerial Perspective*. Upper Saddle River, NJ: Prentice-Hall.

Tuunainen, V.K. (1998) Opportunities of Effective Integration of EDI for Small Businesses in the Automotive Industry, *Information & Management*, 36(6), 361-375.

Tuunainen, V.K. (1998). Opportunities of Effective Integration of EDI for Small Businesses in the Automotive Industry, *Information & Management, 36*(6), 361-375.

UNCTAD (2002). *Electronic Commerce Strategies for Development: The Basic Elements on an Enabling Environment for E-Commerce.* Commission on Enterprise, Business Facilitation, and Development. Retrieved from http://r0.unctad.org/ecommerce/event_docs/geneva_strategies_issues.pdf

Upshaw, L. (1995). "The Keys to Building Cyberbrands," *Advertising Age*, May 29,

Urata, S. (2000). *Outline of Tentative Policy Recommendation for SME Promotion in Indonesia.* JICA. Retrieved November 2003 from http://www.jica.or.id/FOCI_urata.html

Van Akkeren, J. and Cavaye, A. L. M. (1999) Factors Affecting Entry-Level Internet Technology Adoption by Small Business in Australia: An Empirical Study, in *Proceedings of Proceedings of the 10th Australasian Conference on Information Systems.* 1-3 December. Wellington, New Zealand.

Van Akkeren, J. and Cavaye, A. L. M. (December 1-3, 1999). Factors Affecting Entry-Level Internet Technology Adoption by Small Business in Australia: An Empirical Study, in *Proceedings of the 10th Australasian Conference on Information Systems.* Wellington, New Zealand.

Van Beveren, J. V., & Thomson, H. (2002). The use of electronic commerce by SMEs in Victoria, Australia. *Journal of Small Business Management, 40*(3), 250–253.

van der Aalst, W., ter Hofstede, A., B., K., and Barros, A. (2003). Workflow patterns. *Distributed and Parallel Databases*, (3):5-51.

Van Dyke Parunak, H. (1996). Visualizing agent conversations: Using enhanced dooley graphs for agent design and analysis. In *The Second International Conference on Multi-Agent System (ICMAS'96).*

Van Dyke, T. P., Kappelman, L. A., & Prybutok, V. R. (1997). Measuring information systems service quality: concerns on the use of the SERVQUAL questionnaire. *MIS Quarterly, June*, 195-208.

Van Hasselt, Caroline (2004). Dump LC Headaches Overboard. *Treasury & Risk Management*. http://www.treasuryandrisk.com/issues/2004_01/supply_chain_management/256-1.html

van Heck, E., & van Damme, E. (1997). *New entrants and the role of IT: The teleflower auctions in the Netherlands.* Paper presented at the 30th HICSS, Hawaii.

Van Slyke, C. & Belanger, F. (2004). Factors influencing the adoption of web-based shopping: the impact of trust. Database for Advances in Information Systems, 35(2), 32- 49

Van Slyke, C., Belanger, F., & Comunale, C. (2004). Factors influencing the adoption of Web-based shopping: The impact of trust. *Database for Advances in Information Systems, 35*(2), 32–49.

Van Slyke, C., Comunale, C.L. & Belanger, F. (2002). Gender differences in perceptions of web-based shopping. Communications of the ACM, 45(7), 82-86.

Van Slyke, C., Kittner, M. & Cheney, P. (1998). Skill Requirements for Entry-Level Information Systems Graduates. Journal of Information Systems Education (Fall 1998), 6-10.

Varki, S., & Colgate, M. (2001). The role of price perceptions in an integrated model of behavioral intentions, *Journal of Service Research* 3(3), 232– 240.

Vaughan, L., & Wu, G. (2004). Links to commercial Websites as a source of business information. *Scientometrics, 60*(3), 487-496.

Vehovar, V., Manfreda, K.L., & Batagelj, Z. (2001). Sensitivity of electronic commerce measurement to the survey instrument. *International Journal of Electronic Commerce*, 6, 31-51.

Vehovar, V., Manfreda, K.L., Batagelj, Z. (2001). Sensitivity of Electronic Commerce Measurement to the Survey Instrument. *International Journal of Electronic Commerce* 6, 31–51.

Venkatesan, V.S. and Fink, D. (2002). Adoption of Internet Technologies and E-Commerce by Small and Medium Enterprises (SMEs) in Western Australia, *Proceedings of the Information Resource Management Association International Conference*, pp. 1136-1137.

Venkatesh, V. (1999). Creation of favorable user perceptions: exploring the role of intrinsic motivation. *MIS Quarterly, 23*(2), 239-260.

Venkatesh, V. (2000). Determinants of perceived ease of use: Integrating control, intrinsic motivation, and emotion into the technology acceptance model. *Information Systems Research*, 11(4), 342-365.

Venkatesh, V., Morris, M., Davis G., & Davis F. (2003). User Acceptance of Information Technology: Toward a Unified View. *MIS Quarterly,* 27(2), 425-478.

Verdicchio, M. and Colombetti, M. (2002). Commitments for agent-based supply chain management. *ACM SIGecom Exchanges, 3(1).*

Vickrey, W. (1961). Counterspeculation, auctions, and competitive sealed tenders. *Journal of Finance, 16*(1), 8-37.

Vijayasarathy, L. R. (2004). Predicting consumer intentions to use on-line shopping: the case for an augmented technology acceptance model. *Information & Management, 41*(6), 747-762.

Vitale, M. (1985). *American Hospital Supply Corp.: the ASAP system* (Harvard Business School Case Services No. 9-186-005). Boston: Harvard University.

Vogelstein, F., Boyle, M., Lewis, P., & Kirkpatrick, D. (2004). 10 tech trends to bet on. *Fortune, 149*(4), 75-81.

Wachter, R. M. (2006). The "dis-location" of U.S. medicine--The implications of medical outsourcing. *New England Journal of Medicine*, *354*(7), 661-665.

Wagner, B. A., Fillis, I., & Johansson, U. (2003). E-business and e-supply strategy in small and medium sized businesses (SMEs). *Supply Chain Management, 8*(4), 343–354.

Walczuch, R., Van Braven, G. and Lundgren, H. (2000). Internet adoption barriers for small firms in The Netherlands. *European Management Journal, 18*(5), 561-572.

Walker E.W. (1975). Investment and Capital Structure Decision Making in Small Business in Walker E.W. (ed.) *The Dynamic Small Firm: Selected Readings.* Texas: Austin Press.

Wall, Danny. (Feb. 22, 2005). An Insider's Secret To Seriously High Rankings With Yahoo. Retrieved October 3, 2005, from *http://www.seochat.com/c/a/Yahoo-Optimization-Help/An-Insiders-Secret-To-Seriously-High-Rankings-With-Yahoo*

Walther, J.B. (1996). Computer-mediated communication: impersonal, interpersonal and hyperpersonal interaction. *Communication Research*, 23, 3-43.

Wang, S. (2000). Managing the organizational aspects of electronic commerce. *Human Systems Management, 19,* 49-59.

Wang, Y.-S., & Tang, T.-I. (2003). Assessing customer perceptions of website service quality in digital marketing environments. *Journal of End User Computing, 15*(3), 14-31.

Ward, S. G., & Clark, J. M. (2002). Bidding behavior in on-line auctions: An examination of the eBay Pokemon card market. *International Journal of Electronic Commerce, 6*(4), 139-155.

Wareham, J., Zheng, J. G., & Straub, D. (2005). Critical themes in electronic commerce research: a meta-analysis. *Journal of Information Technology, 20*, 1-19.

Watanabe, H. (1991). Some consideration on design of fuzzy information processors--from a computer architectural point of view. In *Proceedings of Fuzzy Engineering Towards Human Friendly Systems, IFES' 91* (pp. 387-398).

Watson, R. T., Pitt, L. F., & Kavan, C. B. (1998). Measuring information systems service quality: lessons from two longitudinal case studies. *MIS Quarterly, March*, 61-79.

Web news you can use. (2003, January). *Best's Review, 103*(9), 80.

WebArrow (2006), http://www.webarrow.com.

Webber, D. (2004). The benefits of ebxml for e-business. *In International Conference on XML (XML'04).*

WebSideStory (2006). Press Release - New WebSideStory Study Reveals Conversion Rate for Each Major Search Engine. February 15, 2006. Retrieved July 17, 2006, from *http://www.websidestory.com/company/news-events/press-releases/view-release.html?id=319*

Webster, J., & Martocchio, J.J. (1992). Microcomputer playfulness: Development of a measure with workplace implications. *MIS Quarterly*, 16(2), 201-226.

Webster, J., & Watson, R. (2002). Analyzing the past to prepare for the future: Writing a literature review. *MIS Quarterly, 26*(2), xiii-xxiii.

Weick, K. (1995). What theory is not, theorizing is. *Administrative Science Quarterly, 40*(3), 385-390

Weigand, H., Heuvel, W. J., & Dignum, F. (1998). Modeling electronic commerce transactions: A layered approach. In *Proceedings from LPCM '98: Third International Workshop on the Language/Action Perspective on Communication Modeling* (pp. 47-58).

Weigand, H., Verharen, E. M., & Dignum, F. (1997). Dynamic business models as a basis for interoperable transaction design. *Information Systems, 22*(2,3), 139-154.

Welsh, J. A. and White, J. F. (1981). A Small Business Is Not a Little Big Business. *Harvard Business Review, 59*(4), 18.

Werts, C.E.; Linn, R.L.; & Joreskog, K.G. (1974). Interclass reliability estimates: Testing structural assumptions. *Educational and Psychological Measurement*, 34(1), 25-33.

Westhead, P. and Storey, D. J. (1996) 'Management Training and Small Firm Performance: Why is the Link so Weak?' *International Small Business Journal.* vol. 14 no. 4. pp.13-24.

Westhead, P. and Storey, D. J. (1996). Management Training and Small Firm Performance: Why is the Link so Weak? *International Small Business Journal, 14*(4), 13-24.

Whetten, D. (1989). What constitutes a theoretical contribution. *Academy of Management Review, 14*(4), 490-495.

White, T. B. (2004). Consumer disclosure and disclosure avoidance: A motivational framework. *Journal of Consumer Psychology, 14*(1-2), 41-52.

Whiteley, D. (2000). *E-commerce: Strategy, technologies and applications.* Berkshire, UK: McGraw-Hill.

Wilcox, R. T. (2000). Experts and amateurs: The role of experience in Internet auctions. *Marketing Letters, 11*(4), 363-374.

Wilson, D.T. (1995). An integrated model of buyer-seller relationships. *Journal of the Academy of Marketing Science, 23*(4), 335-345.

Wilson, R. B. (1969). Communications to the editor: Competitive bidding with disparate information. *Management Science, 15*(7), 446-449.

Wingfield, N. (2001). Ebay watch: Corporate sellers put the online auctioneer on even faster track: Goods from IBM, Disney help dot-com pioneer post a surge in profits: Why mom and pop are mad. *Wall Street Journal,* p. A.1.

Wingfield, N. (June 1, 2001). Ebay watch: Corporate sellers put the online auctioneer on even faster track: Goods from IBM, Disney help dot-com pioneer post a surge in profits: Why mom and pop are mad. Wall Street Journal, p. A.1.

Wixom, B.H. & Todd, P.A. (2005). A theoretical integration of user satisfaction and technology acceptance. *Information System Research,* 16(1), 85-102.

Wold, H. (1974). Causal flows with latent variables, *European Economic Review*, 5, 67-86.

Wold, H. (1985). Partial least squares, in *Encyclopedia of Statistical Sciences*, Kotz, S. & Johnson, N.L. (eds.), 6, New York: Wiley, 581-591.

Wolstenholme, E. F. (1990). *System enquiry: a system dynamics approach.* John Wiley & Sons, Inc., New York, NY, USA.

Wood, C. M. (2004). 'Marketing and e-commerce as tools of development in the Asia-Pacific: a dual path'. *International Marketing Review, 21*(3), 301-320.

Wooldridge, M. J., & Jennings, N. R. (1995). Intelligent agents: Theory and practice. *Knowledge Engineering Review, 10*(2), 115-152.

World Bank Group (2006). *Country groups.* World Bank Group. Retrieved March 2006 from http://web.worldbank.org/

Worthington, S.L.S. & Boyes, W. (2001). E-business in manufacturing: putting the Internet to work in the industrial enterprises, Research Triangle Park, NC: Instrumentation, Systems and Automation Society.

Xu, L. (2004). *Monitoring Multi-party Contracts for E-business.* PhD thesis, Tilburg University.

Xu, L. and Jeusfeld, M. A. (2003). Pro-active monitoring of electronic contracts. In *The 15th Conference On Advanced Information Systems Engineering in Lecture Notes of Computer Science*, volume 2681, pages 584–600. Springer-Verlag.

Xu, L. and Jeusfeld, M. A. (2004). Detecting violators of multi-party contracts. In *The Conference on CoopIS/DOA/ODBASE in Lecture Notes of Computer Science*, volume 3290, pages 526–543. Springer-Verlag.

Xu, L., Jeusfeld, M. A., and Grefen, P. (2005). Detection tests for identifying violators of multiparty contracts. *ACM SIGecom Exchanges, 5(3).*

Yamamoto, H., Ishida, K., & Ohta, T. (2004). Modeling reputation management system on online C2C market. *Computational & Mathematical Organization Theory, 10*, 165-178.

Yang, H., & Yoo, Y. (2004). It's all about attitude: revisiting the technology acceptance model. *Decision Support Systems*, 38(1), 19-31.

Yap, C. S. (1990). Distinguishing characteristics of organizations using computers. *Information & Management, 18,* 97-107.

Yin, R. K. (2003). *Case study research: Design and methods* (3rd ed.). Thousand Oakes, CA: Sage.

Zack, M.H. (1993). Interactivity and Communication Mode Choices in Ongoing Management Groups. *Information System Research*, 4(3), 207-239.

Zadeh, L. A. (1965). Fuzzy sets. *Information and Control*, (8), 338-353.

Zadeh, L. A. (1976). A fuzzy-algorithmic approach to the definition of complex or imprecise concepts. *International Journal of Man-Machine Studies*, (8), 249-291.

Zajonc, R., & Markus, H. (1982). Affective and Cognitive Factors in Preferences. *Journal of Consumer Research,* 9, 123-31.

Zajonc, R., & Markus, H. (1984). Affect and Cognition: The Hard Interface. *Emotions, Cognition, and Behavior.* Izard, C., Kagan, J. & Zajonc, R. Editors. Cambridge: Cambridge University Press, 73-102.

Zanjonc, R. (1980). Feeling and Thinking: Preferences Need No Inference. *American Psychologist*, 35(February), 152-171.

Zehnder, S., Bruppacher, R., Ruppanner, H., & Hersberger, K. E. (2004). Swiss community pharmacies' on the Web and pharmacists' experiences with e-commerce: Longitudinal study and Internet-based questionnaire survey. *Journal of Med Internet Res. 6*(1).

Zeithaml, V.A. (1981). How Consumer Evaluation Processes Differ Between Goods and Services. in *Marketing of Services*, Donnelly, J.H. & George, W. R., Editors. American Marketing Association: Chicago, IL. pp. 186-190.

Zeithaml, V.A. *Parasuraman*, A. & *Malhotra*, A. (2002). Service quality delivery through Web sites: A critical review of extant knowledge. *Academy of Marketing Science Journal,* 30(4), 362-76.

Zeithaml, V.A., Berry, L.L., & Parasuraman, A. (1981). The Behavioral Consequences of Service Quality. *Journal of Marketing*, 60, 31-46.

Zeungnam, B., Bang, W., Kim, D., & Han, J. (2002). Machine intelligence quotient: Its measurement and applications. *Fuzzy Sets and Systems, 127*(1), 3-16.

Zhang, A., & Reichgelt, H. (2006). Product complexity as a determinant of transaction governance structure: an empirical comparison of web-only and traditional banks. *Journal of Electronic Commerce in Organizations, 4*(3), 1-17.

Zhang, J. and Dimitroff, A. (2005). The impact of webpage content characteristics on webpage visibility in search engine results (Part I), *Information Processing and Management* 41: 665-690.

Zhang, J. and Dimitroff, A. (2005). The impact of metadata implementation on webpage visibility in search engine results (Part II), *Information Processing and Management* 41: 691-715.

Zhang, P., & Li, N. (2005). The importance of affective quality. *Communications of the ACM*, 48(9), 105-108.

Zhu, K., Kraemer, K., & Xu, S. (2003). E-business adoption by European firms: A cross-country assessment of the facilitators and inhibitors. European Journal of Information Systems, *12*(4), 251-268.

Zing, B. and Lin, Z. (2006). The Impact of Search Engine Optimization on Online Advertising Market, *Proceedings of the 8th international conference on Electronic commerce: The new e-commerce: innovations for conquering current barriers, obstacles and limitations to conducting successful business on the internet*, Fredericton, New Brunswick, Canada, pp. 519-529.

About the Contributors

Mehdi Khosrow-Pour, DBA, received his Doctorate in Business Administration (DBA) from the Nova Southeastern University (FL, USA). Dr. Khosrow-Pour taught undergraduate and graduate information system courses at the Pennsylvania State University – Harrisburg for 20 years where he was the chair of the Information Systems Department for 14 years. He is currently president and publisher of IGI Global, an international academic publishing house with headquarters in Hershey, PA and an editorial office in New York City (www.igi-global.com). He also serves as executive director of the Information Resources Management Association (IRMA) (www.irma-international.org), and executive director of the World Forgotten Children's Foundation (www.world-forgotten-children.org). He is the author/editor of over twenty books in information technology management. He is also the editor-in-chief of the Information Resources Management Journal, the Journal of Cases on Information Technology, the Journal of Electronic Commerce in Organizations, and the Journal of Information Technology Research, and has authored more than 50 articles published in various conference proceedings and journals.

* * *

Thomas Abraham is a professor and chair of the management department at Kean University. He received his PGDM (MBA) from the Indian Institute of Management, Bangalore and his PhD from the University of Massachusetts. He is a member of the New Jersey chapter of the Society for Information Management (SIM) and the association for information systems (AIS). His research interests include global supply chains and MIS education. He has been a consultant at various companies including Sony and BMG and his research has appeared in several journals.

Andreas Aresti is a graduate from the computer engineering and informatics department of the University of Patras. His research interests focus on algorithms and techniques for personalized recommendations in e-commerce systems and his diploma thesis dealt with the application of web mining techniques on a pilot e-shop's usage data for the production of recommendations.

Jeff Baker is a doctoral student in information systems and quantitative sciences at the Rawls College of Business Administration at Texas Tech University. His research interests include electronic commerce, visualization of multidimensional datasets, information systems strategy, and information technology tasks during corporate acquisitions.

Glenn J. Browne is an associate professor and the Wetherbe Professor of Information Technology at the Rawls College of Business Administration at Texas Tech University, where he is also director of the Institute for Internet Buyer Behavior. His research focuses on cognitive and behavioral issues in information requirements determination, systems development, e-business, and managerial decision making. His articles have appeared in *Management Science, the Journal of Management Information Systems, MIS Quarterly, Organizational Behavior and Human Decision Processes*, and other journals.

Christine V. Bullen joined Stevens Institute of Technology in August 2002, where she is coordinator for strategic issues in IT and director of the IT outsourcing concentration. Her current research focuses on IT workforce trends and the impacts of sourcing practices. Bullen was a distinguished lecturer at Fordham University and for 17 years she was the assistant director of the MIT Center for Information Systems Research where her research focused on strategic planning for the IT function, the organizational impact of IT, and the launching of the concepts of critical success factors and IT strategic alignment. She received her MS in Management from the MIT Sloan School and will shortly be awarded the PhD degree from Stevens Institute of Technology.

Teuta Cata is an assistant professor of MIS at Northern Kentucky University. She completed her PhD in MIS at the University of Nebraska-Lincoln. Her teaching and research interests include e-commerce in the financial industry, global IT, outsourcing, and enterprise solutions. Her papers have been published in several journals, and many research papers have been presented at national conferences.

Hong-Mei Chen is an associate professor of information technology management at the Shidler College of Business, the University of Hawaii at Manoa, and formally served as an associate dean for the College. She earned a PhD in business administration (majoring in MIS) from the University of Arizona. She conducts cross-disciplinary research including electronic customer relationship management, business-IT alignment, service engineering, business intelligence, and multimedia distributed database systems. She was a Fulbright grantee and has directed several multi-year, multi-million-dollar, multi-institution research projects in high performance telemedicine, data mining and data warehousing. She has published in such MIS journals as *Journal of Management Information Systems, Electronic Commerce Research, Journal of Database Marketing & Customer Strategy management, Journal of Electronic Commerce in Organizations, and Journal of Business Environment* as well as other computer science and software engineering journals.

Qimei Chen is an associate professor of marketing in the Shidler College of Business at the University of Hawaii at Manoa and an advisory professor at Fudan University, Shanghai, China. She received a BS in literature from Nanjing Normal University (JiangSu, China) and a MA and a PhD in mass communication from the University of Minnesota, Twin Cities. Her research interests include advertising effectiveness, online/offline consumer behavior, and innovation/knowledge. She has published in journals such as *Journal of Advertising, Journal of Advertising Research, and Journal of Retailing.*

Sandy Chong, PhD in information systems, is a lecturer in the School of Marketing at the Curtin University of Technology. She conducts research in the area of innovative business and technology adoption strategies, Web-based social marketing, business process management, collaborative organisational structures, costing model for IT procurement, as well as sustainability in supply chain management. She has presented papers at major conferences, and her research appears in information systems, marketing, and global business management journals. Her industry experience includes strategic marketing management in the credit card sector, advertising, consultancy and quantitative market research.

Letha H. Etzkorn is an associate professor in the computer science department at the University of Alabama in Huntsville. Her primary research interests are in software engineering (including program understanding, object-oriented software metrics, and artificial intelligence applications to software engineering) and mobile agents. She has a bachelors and masters degree in electrical engineering from the Georgia Institute of Technology, and a PhD in computer science from the University of Alabama in Huntsville.

Kevin Gallagher is an assistant professor in the business informatics department in the College of Informatics at Northern Kentucky University. He holds a PhD in management information systems from the Weatherhead School of Management at Case Western Reserve University in Cleveland, Ohio. Before his career in academia, he worked as an IT manager and consultant. His teaching, research and consulting interests include IT strategic planning, business agility, organization design, and workforce development.

Bob Galliers (rgalliers@bentley.ac.uk) is a provost of Bentley College, USA, formerly professor of information systems at the London School of Economics, UK, where he was research professor in the department of information systems. He retains his link with the LSE as a visiting professor. He was previously professor of information management at Warwick Business School, where he was Dean for the period 1994-1998. His research is transdisciplinary in nature and currently focuses on information technology and business innovation, knowledge creation and management, and intra- and extra-organisational impacts of the Internet. He is editor-in-chief of the *Journal of Strategic Information Systems* and co-author of a number of books.

Edward J. Garrity is professor of information systems in the Richard J. Wehle School of Business at Canisius College in Buffalo, New York. He holds a PhD in MIS and an MBA from the State University of New York at Buffalo. He has published research in a number of IS journals and also has co-authored a book of readings entitled Information *Systems Success Measurement*, published by Idea Group Publishing. His current research interests are system dynamics and systems thinking, information systems development issues, information systems success measurement, and the design of business and management systems.

Robert Hinson is a senior lecturer at the University of Ghana Business School. He is also studying for a doctoral degree at the Centre for International Studies in Aalborg University in Denmark under the supervision of Professor Olav Jull Sorensen. He has had papers accepted for publication in journals like the *Journal of Business* and *Industrial Marketing, Journal of African Business, Management Decision* and *the Place Branding Journal.*

Robert Johnston, BSc(Hons), MSc, PhD is an associate professor in the department of information systems. His research areas are electronic commerce, supply chain management and theoretical foundations of information systems. He has over 100 refereed publications, many in leading international journals including *Management Science, Journal of the Operational Research Society, OMEGA, International Journal of Production Economics, European Journal of Information Systems, International Journal of Electronic Commerce, Journal of Strategic Information Systems*, and *Supply Chain Management.* Before becoming an academic he was an IT consultant, designing and implementing about 25 large computer systems in a number of leading Australian manufacturing companies.

Kiku Jones is an assistant professor of management information systems at The University of Tulsa. Jones received her PhD from the University of Kentucky and is a member of the Association for Information Systems, Decision Sciences Institute, and Information Resources Management Association. Her research interests include knowledge management, electronic commerce, C2C commerce, trust, and human computer interaction. Her publications have appeared in *Knowledge and Process Management, International Journal of Knowledge Management, Journal of Computer Information Systems, International Journal of Information Management* as well as in various conference proceedings.

Kate M. Kaiser, associate professor of IT at Marquette University, researches future IT skill needs and the impact of offshore outsourcing from Ireland, Russia and India through research grants from the Sloan and 3M Foundations. Kaiser received her MBA from Kent State University and her PhD from the University of Pittsburgh.

Arjun Kalyanpur is CEO of Teleradiology Solutions, Bangalore. He obtained his medical education and initial radiology training from the All India Institute of Medical Sciences, New Delhi. He then obtained training in radiology at the Cornell University Medical Center in New York and at the Yale University School of Medicine, New Haven, Connecticut, leading to certification by the American Board of Radiology. In 1999, Dr. Kalyanpur founded Teleradiology Solutions, which currently provides online diagnostic teleradiology reporting services to over 50 hospitals and clinics in the U.S., Singapore and India. Dr Kalyanpur continues to be on the faculty at Yale University and has published several research papers in the field of teleradiology.

Mira Kartiwi is a PhD student in information systems at University of Wollongong. Her research interests include e-commerce, SMEs, women in IT, and IT in developing country. She has published several articles on proceedings and journals. She currently teaches at department of information systems, International Islamic University, Malaysia.

Rick Kazman is a professor in the Shidler College of Business at the University of Hawaii at Manoa and a visiting scientist at the software engineering Institute of Carnegie Mellon University. Kazman received a BA (English/music) and M.Math (computer science) from the University of Waterloo, an MA (English) from York University, and a PhD (computational linguistics) from Carnegie Mellon University. His research interests are software architecture, human-computer interaction and information retrieval. Kazman is the author of over 100 papers, and co-author of several books, including "*Software Architecture in Practice*," and "*Evaluating Software Architectures: Methods and Case Studies*."

Changsu Kim (c.kim@yumail.ac.kr) is an assistant professor at Yeungnam University, Korea. He received his PhD in Information Systems from London School of Economics (LSE). His research interests include ubiquitous computing, electronic commerce, ICT innovation diffusion and IS strategy.

Jaekyung Kim (kjkkej@gmail.com) is a PhD candidate in management at the University of Nebraska-Lincoln. He received his MBA from Miami University of Ohio. His research focuses on knowledge management, decision support systems, and electronic commerce. His work has been published in journals such as *Decision Support Systems, Omega, International Journal of Electronic Commerce, Expert Systems with Applications* and *International Journal of Knowledge Management.*

Yong Jin Kim is associate professor of management information systems at Sogang Business School and the School of Management at the State University of New York at Binghamton. He holds a PhD in MIS from the State University of New York at Buffalo. He participated in large IT consulting and development projects. His research interests are in knowledge management and innovation, IS success, e-commerce, and information technology valuation. He has published papers in outlets such as *MIS Quarterly, Communications of the ACM, Decision Support Systems, International Journal of Information Management, Information Systems Frontiers*, and *Knowledge and Process Management.* He also has published book chapters on IS Success and e-learning.

Firoz Latif is the senior manager for IT at Teleradiology Solutions. He has been working in the healthcare domain for over 3 years, mainly focusing on areas related to radiology like DICOM, PACS and RIS. He has also been involved in infrastructure management and security compliance at Teleradiology Solutions. He holds a bachelor's degree in instrumentation and electronics engineering.

Lori N. K. Leonard is an associate professor of management information systems at The University of Tulsa. Leonard received her PhD from the University of Arkansas and is a member of the Association for Information Systems and the Decision Sciences Institute. Her research interests include electronic commerce, ethics in computing, C2C commerce, and online trust. Her publications have appeared in *Journal of the Association for Information Systems, Journal of Computer Information Systems, Journal of End User Computing, Information & Management, Journal of Organizational Computing and Electronic Commerce*, as well as in other journals, and *Proceedings* of various Conferences.

Dahui Li is an assistant professor of MIS at University of Minnesota Duluth. His current research areas are business-to-consumer relationships, IT innovation and diffusion, and online communities. His articles have appeared in *International Journal of Electronic Commerce, Journal of the Association for Information Systems, Decision Support Systems, Journal of Computer Information Systems*, and other journals.

Robert MacGregor is an associate professor in the School of Information Systems and Technology at the University of Wollongong in Australia. He is also the former head of discipline in information systems. His research expertise lies in the areas of information technology (IT) and electronic commerce (e-commerce) in small to medium enterprises (SMEs). He has authored a number of journal and conference publications examining the use and adoption of IT in SMEs. Along with Lejla, MacGregor was the recipient of the 2004 Australian Prime Minister's Award for Excellence in Business Community Partnerships (NSW). MacGregor is also the founding editor of the Australasian Journal of Information Systems and was conference chair of the Australian Conference of Information Systems in 1992. In his spare time, MacGregor writes music. His most recent work is the symphony *Alba.*

Ross A. Malaga received his PhD in 1998 from George Mason University. He is currently an associate professor of management and information systems in the School of Business at Montclair State University. His research focuses on search engine optimization, online auctions and electronic commerce. He has published articles in *Communications of the ACM, Decision Support Systems, Journal of Organizational Computing and Electronic Commerce, Electronic Commerce Research,* and the *Journal of Electronic Commerce in Organizations*. Malaga serves on the editorial review board of the *Information Resources Management Journal* and the *Journal of Electronic Commerce in Organizations*.

Penelope Markellou is a computer engineer and researcher in the computer engineering and informatics department at the University of Patras. She obtained her PhD in techniques and systems for knowledge management in the Web (2005) and her MSc in usability models for e-commerce systems and applications (2000) from the above University. Her research interests focus on algorithms, techniques and approaches for the design and development of usable e-applications including e-commerce, e-learning, e-government and business intelligence. She has published several research papers in national and international journals and conferences and is co-author of two books and eight book chapters.

Ioanna Mousourouli is a graduate computer engineer from the computer engineering and informatics department of the University of Patras. Currently is a postgraduate student at computer science. Her research areas are personalization and recommendation techniques in e-business and e-learning systems, information retrieval techniques and Web usage mining techniques in adapting content and structure.

Joseph B. O'Donnell, PhD, CPA, is currently an associate professor of accounting information systems at Canisius College. He holds a PhD and MBA from the State University of New York at Buffalo and an undergraduate degree from the University of Notre Dame. He formerly worked as a systems consultant and auditor for an international accounting firm. He has published articles in the *Journal of Marketing for Higher Education, Review of Business Information Systems, The CPA Journal, Journal of College Teaching and Learning,* along with other journals. His research interests include diffusion of innovation, continuous auditing, e-commerce, and accounting information systems education.

Anthony M. Orme is an assistant professor at Athens State University in Athens, Alabama. His primary research interests are in software engineering (software metrics), distributed systems, and knowledge engineering. He received his PhD in computer science from the University of Alabama in Huntsville.

A.B. Patki obtained his MTech from Indian Institute of Technology (IIT), Kharagpur in 1975. Presently, he is working as Scientist—G with the department of information technology (DIT), Government of India. He has been a referee for IEEE Transactions on Reliability for over twenty years. His research areas include soft computing, software engineering and cyber forensics & security. He has been trained in VLSI Design at Lund University, Sweden and Mentor Graphics, USA. He holds a copyright for FUZOS©- Fuzzy Logic Based Operating Software. His hobbies include Hindustani music, homoeopathy and vedic studies.

Tapasya Patki is a final semester student of BTech (computer science and engineering), in Maharaja Surajmal Institute of Technology, affiliated to Guru Gobind Singh Indraprastha University, New Delhi.

She has an internship experience of over four months at the department of information technology, Government of India, where she specialized in applications of fuzzy logic and rough set techniques. Her areas of interest include software engineering, artificial intelligence and bio-informatics. Presently, she is exploring potentials of soft computing to knowledge management practices and software code obfuscation. She is also a violin soloist and an amateur poet.

Graham Pervan is a professor at Curtin University of Technology in Perth, Western Australia, has over 30 years experience in education, research, and practice in Information Systems and Information Technology (IS/IT). He has published on various issues related to IS/IT management, electronic commerce and decision support systems in journals such as *Journal of Information Technology, Decision Support Systems, Information and Management, Journal of Computer Information Systems, Journal of Group Decision and Negotiation, Journal of Research and Practice in IT,* and *Communications of the AIS* as well as most major conferences. He is the Asia-Pacific regional editor for *the Journal of Information Technology,* the IT management editor for the *Australian Journal of Management,* and president of the Australian Council of Professors and Heads of Information Systems.

Md. Mahbubur Rahim, BSc (civil engineering, BUET), MS (computer science, UPM), PhD (Melbourne) is currently a lecturer at the Clayton School of Information Technology, Monash University, Australia. Rahim has considerable international teaching experience and has published over 20 research articles in leading IS/IT journals including *IT & People, Behaviour & Information Technology, Information & Software Technology, Information & Management,* and *International Journal of Information Management.* His research interests include e-business and IT adoption in organizations. He serves on the review panel for *Journal of IT Cases & Applications Research.*

Cheul Rhee is currently a PhD candidate in the department of management science and systems at University at Buffalo. He holds his bachelor's and master's degrees in agriculture and education from Seoul National University. He has research interests in e-learning, knowledge management, virtual communities, and e-business strategy.

Sanjay Saini is a professor of radiology at Harvard Medical School and serves as the vice chair for finance in the Department of Radiology at the Massachusetts General Hospital. He is a specialist in gastrointestinal radiology. He has degrees from Duke (AB), Tufts (MD) and MIT (MSc) and did his post graduate training in radiology at the Massachusetts General Hospital in Boston.

G. Lawrence Sanders, PhD, is a professor of management science and systems in the School of Management at the State University of New York at Buffalo. He has taught MBA courses in the Peoples Republic of China and Singapore. His current research interests are in the ethics and economics of software piracy, systems success measurement, and systems development. He has published papers in outlets such as *The Journal of Management Information Systems, MIS Quarterly, Information Systems Research, the Journal of Strategic Information Systems, the Journal of Management Systems, Decision Support Systems, Database Programming and Design,* and *Decision Sciences.* He has also published a book on database design and co-edited two other books.

Pradipta Sarker is currently a research associate in the department of business information technology, RMIT University. He has received his PhD from Deakin University, Australia. His has also published in e-commerce related journals.

Surendra Sarnikar is a doctoral student in MIS at the University of Arizona. He has an undergraduate degree in engineering and a master's in management information systems. His research interests are in the area of healthcare data and communication standards, medical information filtering, and medical event reporting systems. He has also presented papers on medical information filtering and information distribution mechanisms at the Americas Conference on Information Systems.

Graeme Shanks is a professor and associate dean of research in the faculty of information technology at Monash University, Australia. His teaching and research interests include information quality, conceptual modelling, identity management, implementation and impact of enterprise systems, and decision support systems. Graeme has published the results of his research in over 100 refereed journal and conference papers. He is a member of several journal editorial boards, a member of IFIP WG8.3 Decision Support Systems, a fellow of the Australian Computer Society and was recently a member of the College of Experts of the Australian Research Council.

Judith C. Simon is a professor of management information systems, director of the Center for Innovative Technology Management, and co-director of the Center for Information Assurance at the University of Memphis. Her bachelors and doctoral degrees were received from Oklahoma State University, and her MBA was earned at West Texas State University. Her research interests include information security management and IT quality. She has written nine textbooks and published numerous articles in academic journals. She also serves as membership chair for the Memphis Chapter of the Society for Information Management.

Spiros Sirmakessis is an assistant professor in the Technological Educational Institution of Messolonghi and the manager of the Internet and Multimedia Technologies Research Unit of the Research Academic Computer Technology Institute. He is also an adjunct assistant professor in the University of Patras, teaching human computer interaction and e-business courses. His research areas include human computer interaction, human factors, e-business strategies, efficient techniques for designing interactive systems and web mining. He is co-author of three books and several research papers published in international journals and conferences.

Jaeki Song is an assistant professor of information systems and quantitative sciences at the Rawls College of Business Administration at Texas Tech University. His research interests include electronic commerce, web design, information systems strategy, and technology adoption. His research appears in *Management Science, Information and Management, IEEE Transactions on Professional Communication, International Journal of Information Management, Information Systems Frontier*, and *International Conference on Information Systems.*

Olav Sorensen is a professor of international business at the Centre for International Studies in Aalborg University in Denmark. He is widely published in prestigious journals like the *Journal of Business* and *Industrial Marketing and Electronic Markets*. Sorensen is also the author and editor of several seminal texts on internationalization, marketing and international business. Sorensen's current research interests encompass small firm internationalization, foreign direct investment, and e-business.

Athanasios Tsakalidis obtained his diploma in mathematics from the University of Thessaloniki, Greece (1973), his diploma in computer science (1981) and his PhD (1983) from the University of Saarland, Saarbuecken, Germany. His is currently a full professor in the computer engineering and informatics department at the University of Patras and the r&d coordinator of the Research Academic Computer Technology Institute (RACTI). His research interests include data structures, graph algorithms, computational geometry, expert systems, medical informatics, databases, multimedia, information retrieval, and bioinformatics. He has published several research papers in national and international journals and conferences and is co-author of the *Handbook of Theoretical Computer Science* and other book chapters.

Paul de Vrieze is a senior researcher at SAP research, Switzerland. Previously, he worked as a postdoctoral research fellow at CSIRO ICT Centre, Australia. He worked as an IT consultant at AT-Computing, The Netherlands. He received his PhD in information systems from Radboud University Nijmegen, The Netherlands in 2006. His main research interests are in user modeling, systems modeling, and semantics integration.

James C. Wetherbe is the Stevenson Chair of Information Technology at the Rawls College of Business Administration at Texas Tech University. He is the author of 21 books and over 200 articles on systems analysis and design, strategic use and management of information systems, information requirements determination, and cycle time reduction. He is quoted often in leading business and information systems journals, and was ranked by *Information Week* as one of the top dozen information technology consultants.

Lai Xu is a senior researcher at SAP research, Switzerland. Previously, she worked as a senior research scientist at CSIRO ICT Centre, Australia. She was a post-doctoral researcher at Organisation and Information Group of the Institute of Information and Computing Sciences of the Utrecht University (2004-2007), the Netherlands and Artificial Intelligence group of the department of computer science of the Free University Amsterdam (2003-2004), the Netherlands respectively. She received her PhD in computerized information systems from Tilburg University, the Netherlands in 2004. Her main research areas are in process integration, multi-party process monitoring, web services and service-oriented applications, development method for product software. Her research has appeared in publications including *The European Journal of Information Systems, ACM SIGecom Exchanges*, numerous IS conferences' proceedings and book chapters.

Kyung Hoon Yang (yang.kyun@uwlax.edu) is currently an assistant professor in the department of information systems at the University of Wisconsin-La Crosse. He received his PhD in management information systems from Purdue University in 1989 and has been a professor at the Chungang University in Korea from 1989 to 2004. His major research interests include knowledge transfer and knowledge based organization. He has published more than 20 articles including *Decision Support Systems, Expert Systems with Applications* and *Omega.*

Index

E

F

G

H

I

K

M

N

O

P

R

S

T

U

V

W

Y